History of the researc

Christmas Eve, 2018, wa ... ny
introduction to an **_ISOLATED_** Worl ... *D*
NOT HAVE EXISTED in the sma... ... the
Department Of The Somme, France.

The grave was marked with a French Military Cross and memorial plaque.

Aviator AMERICAN UNKNOWN Died For France - IN 1943

Photograph:
Christmas Eve - 1991
Willis S. Cole, Jr.

We had visited the private military collection of Mr. Robert Lefevre, a local French military veteran, who had been tending the isolated grave for many years, when he asked my friend, Mr. Bernard Leguillier, to take me to the cemetery and show me the grave. Then, he asked me to identify the American in the grave, so they could fully honor the grave of this American during the upcoming 50th Anniversary of "D-Day", in 1994.

I told Mr. Lefevre, with Bernard translating for me, as we left for the cemetery, that I had been studying Graves Registration in World War One and World War Two for a long time and I was very aware of all the effort they had made to insure isolated war graves, like the one I was being told about, did not exist. However, after visiting the grave, I would do all I could to identify the man in the grave.

Before Bernard and I left the Cartigny cemetery, I had made a very personal promise to the remains in the grave. That I would not stop until his family and everyone involved knew exactly who he was and the full truth of his death. Twenty-seven years later, the promise still has loose ends. This book concerns those loose ends. Perhaps, you might be able to help.

1

(**Note**: 1 February, 2019. To me, questions still exist concerning World War Two combat dead in Europe. The eight aviation crew dead in this book are the first of more than eighteen to be questioned and all are still lacking full closure!)

As we were on our way to the Leguillier Christmas Eve dinner, Bernard told me what he knew of the existence of the grave. There were several rumors and no one seemed to know, which one was right.

It was the remains of a man who had fallen from the sky and landed in a farm pond. The farmer had found what was left of the dead man, after watching birds flocking to the pond and going to see what they were doing there. The man's remains were recovered and moved to the cemetery.

Another story was somewhat matching, in that the American had been running away from a German patrol when he fell into the pond and drowned.

A third story said, the grave contained parts of several men hidden by the medics from a nearby American hospital unit.

Twenty-Seven years later, the real truth of the grave is known. It contains two-thirds of the remains of three American air crewmen who died during the early morning crash of a Top Secret B-24J, Liberator, SN: 42-51**226**, that had been **shot down by "Friendly Fire"** on 10 November, 1944. It had crashed near another small village, named Tincourt-Boucly, located five kilometers from the grave site. And yes, **American medics had been verbally ordered by a young Colonel to bury the remains in a hidden grave**!

This book, is the fifth evolution of the true history of the B-24J crash, "**226**", and the crash of a B-17G, the "*Lady Jeannette*", SN: 42-97904. The B-17G had crashed in the Bois de Hattonville, Department of the Meuse, on the 9th of November, fourteen and a half hours earlier and one hundred and thirty-eight miles to the southeast of the B-24J crash-site.

The first book evolution, written in 1997, was titled "*The Last Flight Of The 'Lady Jeannette!'*", ISBN: 0-9662728-0-3, used hundreds of interviews and thousands of document to prove the "*Lady Jeannette*" had crashed at Tincourt-Boucly. On 9 November, 1944, we held 50th Anniversary Memorial Services at the crash-site and grave. Attended by Russell Gustafson, the surviving Flight Engineer, family members of two of the dead, and a large Honor Guard of "Le Souvenir Françias" with their flag presentation Honors.

The first evolution book is a pure military history book, laying out the travels and research required to identify the remains in the grave. The National Archives, Military History Division, the US Air Force Historical Research Agency and others, all agreed the book laid out all the required proof and each agency agreed with the conclusion before the book was published. Even though a few questions concerning survivors that were seen by villagers still existed and needed more research.

In May, 1998, two relics recovered from the Tincourt-Boucly crash-site indisputably proved the bomber that crashed there was a B-24 and not a B-17. Later in September, with the help of another French friend, Bernard Delsert, we finally

2

found the **true location** of the B-17G, *"Lady Jeannette,"* crash-site hidden in a large woods near Hattonville, 22 miles southeast of Verdun, France, **138 miles southeast of Tincourt-Boucly**!

Proving nearly all the evidence I had previously found and used was false! I immediately removed the first evolution from the market, as I had proven myself, wrong when no one else could! It was a shocking development, finding the truth that so many official documents supporting my original conclusions were either totally falsified or large portions were falsified. Including official aircraft records, unit records and the two **Congressional Medal Of Honor Citations** awarded to the two pilots of the *"Lady Jeannette."*

Another eight years of research followed, including many research trips to France, many archives and interviews with those who were involved before the second evolution was published in 2007. Later followed by the third and fourth evolution, published in 2013. Each contained updates based on newly located evidence. A process that is still ongoing.

The title, of those evolutions was, *"The Best Kept Secret Of World War Two!"* It came from a direct quote by the head Military Historian at the National Archives, College Park, Maryland, USA. During one of my research visits there, I brought him up to date on my research, showing him where historical documents had been altered, either by adding information or removing information and he told me, "He had no doubt that I had discovered, the best kept secret of World War Two!" And, I did it by proving documents that should contain information, did not!

Another ten years has passed with addition evidence being found and then on 28 July, 2018, my friend, Russell Gustafson, Flight Engineer, Top Turret Gunner, the last survivor to bail out and the last survivor of the crash of the *"Lady Jeannette"* completed his "Final Transfer."

Of the thousands of Veterans, I had met and talked to about my research, Russell was the last directly involved survivor. In 2006, we had been told by the surviving wife of one of the officers who had been verbally ordered by a very young Colonel from General Eisenhower's Head Quarters to hide combat dead, aviation aircrew remains, "...that after all this time, no one can be hurt..." Thus, the title of this fifth evolution has been changed to match the truth. When finished, I believe you will understand why General George S. Patton, Jr. had to be prevented from telling the truth, **as he knew the truth**! "He was going to quit the Army, so they had no hold over him and **he was *going to destroy those Bastards who were trying to destroy him*!**"

This evolution tells the story of how General Eisenhower, using **verbal orders only**, in a day by day, year by year time-line, made the crash of the Top-Secret B-24J, "**226**" disappear, in order to protect the Allied Top-Secrets aboard it from German spies known to exist in the area of France where it crashed.

I do agree with the temporary need to hide the crash of "**226.**" If the Germans had discovered what the top secret cargo of that B-24J was capable of doing and had duplicated it, the war could have lasted longer and a large number of additional military and civilian deaths could have occurred before the war ended.

3

I do not agree with what was done later, still based on General Eisenhower's verbal orders, to cover-up what had he had ordered done. Within two months, the combat situation had changed so much, that the **Top Secret Radar and Radio (electronically) Jamming** aircraft were flying daylight missions with the 8th USAAF and no longer flying night missions with the RAF.

However, from the Narrator's point of view and all those who were involved, Patton's death became extremely important. If, what they had done became public knowledge, careers would have been ruined and lower ranked people like the narrator, all the way down to the privates involved, would have faced military prison for what they had done. **However, thanks to General Patton's timely death, the coverup worked exactly as planned!**

The original coverup, concerning the dead, was done before the seven men's "declared Official Remains" were turned over to Graves Registration. Over the years, I had interviewed many WWII Front Line recovery Graves Registration personnel and everyone agreed, none of them would have done what was done.

At a temporary American Cemetery in Belgium, Graves Registration personnel added information to the official burial documents of the three B-24J crew dead, that proved their partial remains were being illegally buried in Belgium. As Army Regulations in place at the time, required their burial to take place in France, at the American Limey Temporary Cemetery. This regulation can be re-researched, if a reader desires.

In order to reduce the number of Unknowns, Army Regulations laid out specific burial locations for recovered dead. For instance, all killed in France, were to be buried in France. All killed in Belgium were to be buried in Belgium and the same in The Netherlands. Combat dead to the east of those countries were to brought back to the country directly west of their location of death. The reason is extremely easy to understand. In the case of an Unknown dead, they only had to search for Missing In Action (MIA) dead who had served in those countries or to the east of those countries, instead of reviewing all the Missing In Action, Individual Deceased Personnel Files (IDPF).

When finished with this book, you will have learned how our highest commanders, military and civilian, were directly responsible for the desecration of the combat dead at the two crash-sites. They also debauched the **Congressional Medal of Honor** by using two falsified medal awards to hide what they had done, in order to protect their own military and civilian careers, in a step that led all the way to President Roosevelt. President Truman signed the applications and awarded on General Order 38, on 16 May, 1945. However, I do not believe, he knew the truth and if he had, he would not have signed!

Why falsify the awards, think about it for a moment. Just how many false **Congressional Medal Of Honor** awards exist and **who would dare question such an award?**

For the first time, you will be presented with a **true, viable motive**, explaining why General George S. Patton, Jr. could not be allowed to live and return to the United States. Where, he planned to expose the truth of what had been

done by those who were attempting to destroy him!

A very young Full Bird Colonel from General Eisenhower's staff was observed by all of the on-site people we interviewed, who had been involved at each location. He had forced Privates to Generals to break a wide range of regulations, using only verbal orders from General Eisenhower! All involved would have their careers and lives destroyed and many would have faced prison time for what they had done, based on those verbal orders.

If, you were anyone of those men and you were told, that it was you or General Patton, <u>what would you have done?</u>

Extensive evidence found during my research, proves that young Colonel existed and he created the events that led to this book, so I have selected him to be recreated in this book as the "Narrator."

The narrator will tell you what he did and why Patton had to die!

The skeleton of what you will read is true, the flesh of the story has been filled in to smooth out the events.

- - - - - - - - - - - - -

A mostly non-fiction military history book by:

Willis S. Cole, Jr. "Sam"
Battery Corporal Willis S. Cole Military Museum
13444 124th Ave NE, Kirkland, WA 98034-5403 U.S.A.
wscjr@ww1.org - ww1.org - (425)823-4445

Dorothy Ringlesbach
AuthorHOUSE Book
ISBN: 1-4208-1582-2

"... Captain James Hudson who was in SI-(Secret Intelligence) and played a big part in the rescue of thirteen US Air Force nurses who crash-landed in the Albanian mountains while Germans occupied the country. With the help of British Intelligence agents and the OSS the nurses were able to escape. Captain Hudson was the commanding officer of SEAVIEW, a cave on the Adriatic coast used during the escape. He also served with the OSS in the Middle East as the photographic censor of the armed forces in that area. But now with his story.

In March of 1944 Hudson was trying to infiltrate from Otranto, Italy into the coast of Albania. Sterling Hayden of the OSS Special Operations and Hollywood's gift to the OSS on a fishing boat, Yankee, piloted him. They took off about sundown and headed east on the Adriatic. It was quite calm and they anticipated an easy voyage, but the sea can be treacherous and quickly became choppy and finally turned into a roaring storm. They lost all their supplies that had been lashed down on the deck and barely made it back to the tiny port of Otranto.

They headed for a very small town looking for food and drink. At 3 AM everything was closed and dark. Finally they found a tavern and noisily awakened the owner and demanded he open up for them. He did and they ate and drank until they were satiated. They maybe had more vino (wine) than necessary, as the rest remains foggy in their minds.

How and why they went their separate ways looking for a friendly house in which to spend what was left of the night remains unclear. How Hayden made out Hudson never asked, but apparently Hudson found a small hovel and fell asleep. The next morning a very large and unhappy lady awakened him. The language barrier kept them from understanding each other, but Hudson soon got the impression that she would be much happier if he would vacate the premises and the sooner the better. Why she did not kill him and how he got to her house only God knows, but he sheepishly made his exit and made it down to the dock where he finished his nap...."

- - - - - - - - - - - - -

An excellent book, it's seven chapters tell stories about the personnel who served in the OSS. When read, you will find excellent foundational proof of how the OSS involved in this book helped the cover-up succeed for so long.

Captain James Hudson "Capt. Jim"
O.S.S. Veteran

(Written For 2nd Book Evolution In 2007)

Willis S. Cole has been doing considerable research on this important incident after we had obtained Victory over the Axis Powers in WWII. Traveling to Europe numerous times and throughout the United States researching the records as only an expert on Graves Registration and military history is qualified to do.

The condensed results of this research is defined in his new book, "*The Best Kept Secret Of World War Two!*" This book not only provides an excellent motive for General Patton to have died, it provides a basis for all the books about the planned death of General Patton in an automobile accident to be most likely false, as Willis provides what was probably the real plan for Patton's death that day.

The book offers proof that General Patton did have information available to him which would have greatly damaged or destroyed the careers of General Eisenhower, General Arnold, General Marshall and Presidents Roosevelt and Truman. Along with the careers of all involved lower ranked participants.

If General Patton had lived to present the proof he held to the American public at time of his death, in the manner which they knew he was going to do so, the families of American War Dead would have demanded an intense investigation which would have led directly to those just mentioned.

This was an excellent motive to kill Patton, in order to prevent the disclosures that would have been detrimental to top world leaders.

The magnitude of "D-Day"and the opportunity for personal aggrandizement or absolute disgrace, were too enormous to be free of manipulation.

I find this to be an enlightened message clearly presented in this book. Having personal experience with General Patton, both with the King of Yugoslavia at Christmas 1942, and in the flesh at Comiso Airdrome in Sicily, the second day of the invasion when he personally kicked me off "his island," Patton has always been a sympathetic character in my memories of WWII. I liked Patton and admired his skills as a Leader and Aggressive General.

We needed him desperately.

Captain Jim Hudson, WWII, OSS Veteran
Hudson Associates, Woman Owned VE Consultants
Patricia W. Hudson, SAVE, Value Engineering
James W. Hudson, CVS, FSAVE, BICSI
7430 Miller Lane, POB 399
Spotsylvania, VA 22551-0399
jhudson399@aol.com   valumanagement-hudson.com   (540)895-5551
Author: *Two Persons For One Job*   -   *The Ship That Won World War II*
    Beyond OSS   -   *In The Name Of The Luftwaffe*
        The Victory Mail Of World War II, V-Mail, The Funny Mail

(Capt. Hudson has since, followed orders and completed his "Final Transfer.")

Then, Sgt. Charles D. Butte, landed in France on "D-Day+1," or the 2nd day of the "D-Day" Invasion of France. He was an Enlisted man, belonging to the 603rd Graves Registration Company.

Upon landing, Sgt. Butte's unit established the first temporary cemetery on Omaha Beach. They conducted the actual burial tasks, while T/Sgt. Wilmer Henderson's platoon of the 606th Graves Registration Company were moving along the beach, the rising bluff and above, recovering combat dead and delivering them to the beach cemetery.

---

http://www.database-memoire.eu/prive/en-us/cemetery-temporary

A good read, that will introduce you to the Graves Registration service in Europe during World War Two. The temporary cemetery was developed by the 603rd GR Company on the 7th of June. It was placed on the beach between Vierville and Saint Laurent on the Normandy landing site called "White Dog." Today, a small memorial in home's front yard, marks the location.

When it was closed on the 10th of June, 457 Americans, a small number of Germans, English, Sailors, and Royal Air Force aviators were buried there. All were moved to another temporary cemetery at St. Lawrence and then to the larger cemetery at Saint-Laurent sur Mer, which was later, selected to become a permanent American "Over There" cemetery.

T/Sgt. Henderson's platoon, of the 603rd Graves Registration Company, had landed at 11:00 on Omaha Beach on "D-Day" and though Eisenhower had announced he wanted the dead recovered at once, a Full Bird Colonel on the beach, told them to stop doing remains recovery and carry cans of machine-gun bullets up the bluff to the fighting men. They were not allowed to conduct any remains recover, until after 18:30 that day. T/Sgt. Henderson did not have a day off until after the war ended. When they were relieved, the 603rd Graves Registration personnel had recovered over 25,000 war related dead. Most histories show no Graves Registration personnel arrived until "D Day +1." Perhaps, on purpose to not take away from Eisenhower's declaration. They were there, just not allowed to do their original duty.

(**NOTE**: "D-Day" - In French, "Débarquement-Day," in English, "Debark-Day," and simply put, "Get Off The Ship Day." Every combat landing had a "D-Day," though it has come to known as the day, 6 June, 1944, that the Allies landed on the beaches of France.)

8

Charles D. Butte "Bud" LTC USA Retired
WWII Graves Registration
(Written For 2nd Book Evolution In 2007)

First, I should introduce myself, Charles D. Butte, LTC USA Ret., I joined the army, as a Private, in February 1943 and retired, as a Lt. Col., on 1 March 1967, I received a direct Commission while in Belgium in 1945. My first unit was the 603rd Quartermaster Graves Registration Company, I was with the unit all through WW II, landing in Normandy the second day, my platoon, the Third, was attached to the 90th Infantry Division, the First Platoon was attached to the Fourth Infantry Division, The Second Platoon was attached to the Ninth Infantry Division, and the Fourth Platoon was attached to the 82nd Airborne Division, with Sgt. Elbert Legg of the Fourth Platoon landing with the Division, via Glider, on D-Day 6 June 1944, and starting the Bloseville Cemetery for the 82nd on 7 June 1944. The Company was assigned to the First US Army during the entire war and attached to the Seventh, Eighteenth, and Fifth Corps at different times during the War in Europe.

We established Ten Temporary US and Enemy Cemeteries during WW II in Europe. We also did battlefield recovery of US, Allied and Enemy dead, operated Division and Corps Collecting Points for US, Allied and Enemy Dead. In addition, during the War and after the war we did isolated burial recoveries. Which was going out locating graves of deceased military, where the military, enemy and civilians had made temporary burials. This included investigating downed aircraft reports and recovering remains from these crashes.

In addition, I was stationed in Italy during 1947-1950, with the American Graves Registration Command. I personally conducted search and Recovery in Sicily and Central Italy. (**Note:** Bud is recognized as the "Official Father of Baseball in Italy" having introduced his Italian workers to the game, forming the first league and creating today's Italian interest in baseball.)

This, investigating downed aircraft reports, seems to be the specialty of Willis S. Cole, Jr., "Sam," in which he has become very efficient, but nothing can be recovered, reported or recorded without the complete cooperation of all evolved.

I have investigated downed aircraft, but never ran into as many obstacles as he seems to have, in his investigation of the particular downed B-24. Relative to this instance, in 1994, I told him that he seemed to be barking up a tree that someone had built in personal obstacles, which of course is against all human feeling, decency and desire to learn the truth regardless of Pride, Self Protection, and downright, I believe the law calls it, Obstruction of Justice.

When hitting one of these obstacles, instead of stopping his research into these aircraft crashes, Sam intensified his research. He has attended Graves Registration Reunions to meet those of us who served in Europe during WWII, to learn of our personal experiences. He has spent weeks at the National Archives, going through Graves Registration Records in search of any other explanation for

the un-accounted-for remains he is still searching for and over the years, Sam has kept me fully informed of his research.

One might say about Sam, is he does not stop when a wall appears. He will not stop, until he is positive, there is not a way over, around or under what others considered a wall and Sam, considered a closed door, and he just needed a key.

When he could find no explanation for remains from the B-24 crash being buried in Belgium, Sam kept searching until he found one of the Graves Registration men, who should have handled the remains once the original recovery team had turned the remains over to their senior hospital just to be certain, his research was correct. For instance, it took Sam over ten years to do it, but he also located the only man still alive, of the three men from the 397th BG(H) who recovered the first remains from the B-24 crash.

Those are the remains that became the remains in the three men's Official Graves. A second hospital's medical recovery team is responsible for hiding the rest of the remains of the dead aircrew, recovered later in the day at the crash-site. Those remains, which the French helped recover, were hidden in an unmarked grave. Thanks to a Frenchman who saw them hide the remains and a Village Priest, those are the remains that are contained in the Unknown American's Grave in France, that started Sam's research in 1991.

Almost all of what Sam has found out, was against every Regulation at the time it was done. And, Sam's conclusion that no real Graves Registration personnel were involved except at the cemetery sites is correct. I have to agree with Sam, for my personal knowledge is, that we would never have permitted what was done at both crash-sites to the remains of the seven men! And, if any of us had found out, what was done, a full investigation would have followed every lead to the men who permitted it to be done. We owed no less to the dead.

All barriers, logjams and personal feelings and beliefs must be put aside in order to obtain the truth.

As a retired Officer myself, I am certain that the Squadron and Group Commanders would never have created the *Congressional Medal Of Honor* applications containing false crash and death information, unless they were verbally ordered to do so by someone very high up in their Chain of Command. And, thanks to Sam's research, I believe, there can no longer be any doubt, but that is exactly what had to have happened.

Just think, what if it were you that were missing and your mother and father had to carry a thought of questionable doubt as to just what happen to you during the War, never a moment of complete rest, always thinking "tomorrow he will show up, having had amnesia all these years."

If General Patton had lived to do what Sam has found General Patton intended to do, I believe that General Patton would have succeeded in exactly what Sam theorizes in this book.

Sam also mentions the *Congressional Medals of Honor* awarded to the two crewmen, do not be alarmed, the first *Congressional Medal of Honor* that was awarded during WW II, a pilot by the name of Kelley, was a farce, President

10

Roosevelt let it be known he wanted a hero, those in the position to do the job picked Kelley and wrote up a big story, however, later it was found to be a farce, Kelly was nowhere near the action stated in the citation. There is nothing sacred, except the dead and we are supposed to cherish and protect their memory.

I appeal you to assist Sam in his quest for truth and honesty.

Charles D. Butte "Bud" LTC., US Army (Retired)
733 Fairhaven Place, North Palm Beach, FL 33408-5216
(LTC Butte has since, followed orders and completed his "Final Transfer.")

For the years the author knew these two men, both helped him in many ways.

Captain Hudson, was a member of the OSS and the first to interview Hanna Rause, Hitler's pilot after the war ended.

He started out, setting up the "**Victory Mail**" system to photograph documents and mail being sent back to the U.S.A. Among the first of the American military to land in Egypt. The documents would be photographed and reduced to a very small size. Then the negative would be returned to the USA, blown back up, printed and delivered to its final destination.

Later, as that need became less important, he entered the Office Of Special Services, (OSS), and served in Italy and the Balkans, helping downed aircrew return to safety. One group, contained nurses whose plane had been shot down.

Then, as the Germans retreated in Italy and the war ended, he was one of the first Americans to enter Germany from that war front, where he later met and debriefed Hanna.

LTC Butte, when I first met him at a Mortuary Affairs reunion, in 1994, was absolutely positive in very strong language, that my research would find nothing. Over the years, he became a good friend and told me, before his "Final Transfer," that he was no longer the best expert on Graves Registration during World War Two and he was going to pass that Honor(?) on to me.

When you are done reading this book, I trust you will have the information, to understand why Bud told me his opinion.

.

26 March 2019 ~ First Book Sold ⒸⓌ

Why We Killed

General Patton!

IN REMEMBRANCE‽

"The Best Kept Secret Of World War Two!"

Willis S. Cole, Jr. "Sam"

Willis S. Cole, Jr. "Sam"

Thanks for being the first.

Battery Corporal Willis S. Cole Military Museum
A Nonprofit 501-(c)-(3) Washington State Corporation
13444 124th Ave. NE, Kirkland, WA, 98034-5403 U.S.A.
(425)823-4445
Email: wscjr@ww1.org – www.ww1.org

A Battery Corporal Willis S. Cole Military Museum Book
Printed in the United States by
Battery Corporal Willis S. Cole Military Museum
13444 124th Ave NE
Kirkland, WA 98034

Why We Killed General Patton
"The Best Kept Secret Of World War Two!"

First Impression - 2019

ISBN: 978-0-9662728-5-7

Printed in the United States
Battery Corporal Willis S. Cole Military Museum
SAMCO Publishing

"Sure, he bears the
'Burden of Wonderment'
while I bear the burden!"

Photograph: Willis S. Cole, Jr.

To the one person that made this book possible

Carol Lorraine Reinbold Cole

Over twenty-seven years' research and counting.

Perhaps the one thing worst than bearing

"The Burden of Wonderment"

is being married to one who does!

. . . .

Mr. Bernard Leguillier
"Sam, we are going to visit a grave."

Graves Registration - World War Two

To those who served and the records they kept!

Mr. Gaëtan Chaulieu
"It was a B-24, not a B-17!"
One among thousands for 54 lonely years!

And special thanks to the, literally,
thousands who contributed in so many ways.

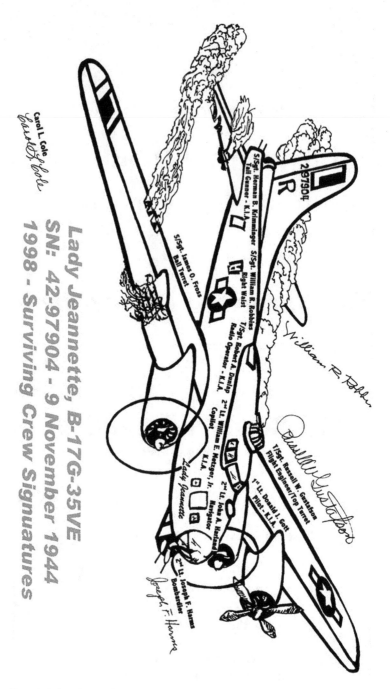

Lady Jeannette, B-17G-35VE
SN: 42-97904 - 9 November 1944
1998 - Surviving Crew Signuatures

Special thanks to the survivors who signed this drawing and spent so much time with me over the years of research and especially for their friendship before completing their "Final Transfers."

Acknowledgments

The author wishes to acknowledge the Modern Military Archivists at the National Archives in Maryland. One of them is directly responsible for the original title of this book: *"The Best Kept Secret Of World War Two!"*

Mr. William Freienmuth, Editor of *"The Sawbuck Gazette,"* for his memories and help with the discovery of the "Friendly-Fire" shoot down of the Top-Secret B-24.

Mr. George Parker, a member of *The Ninth Air Force Association, Inc.* and the *397ᵗʰ Bomb Group Association,* who found the missing key in the haystack that opened a locked door and restarted my stalled research in November 2001.

Mr. Mickey Russell of the *Air Force Historical Research Agency*, who first fought and then accepted the truth about false records, becoming a strong supporter of the truth.

Charles Butte, LTC., US Army Ret., **WWII Graves Registration**, who at first argued about and then accepted the truth of the desecration of American war dead, and helped guide my Graves Registration research.

Captain Jim Hudson, WWII, OSS Veteran, author, and appreciated provider of a window into the OSS operations during WWII.

Mr. Stephen Hutton, author of *"Squadron of Deception - The 36ᵗʰ Bomb Squadron in World War II,"* ISBN: 0-7643-0796-7.

Mr. Bernard Leguillier, a friend in France, who told us about the November morning in 1944, when he found a man's face at a nearby B-17 crash-site. Then, with the help of Mr. Robert Lefevre, Bernard and I visited the grave of the Unknown American Aviator in the Cartigny Cemetery on Christmas Eve, 1991. A grave, that by all American military regulations of World War Two **should not have existed!**

Mr. Claude Obert (Tincourt-Boucly) and Mr. Robert LECLERC (Hattonville) who became the foundation of my research in their villages.

All the American veterans and family members who let me bend their ears and listen to their stories, including the members of the *452ⁿᵈ BG Association* and the *109ᵗʰ Evacuation Hospital Association*.

All the French, who helped find the truth, came to the meetings, the memorial dedications, and memorial services, who continue to Honor those who died while fighting for the *"Liberty of France."*

The French organizations, *Le Souvenir Français, Union National Combatants, Les Amis de Vaquois* and especially the *Commemo-Rangers*, who accepted my challenge on Utah Beach (of "D-Day" fame) at 02:30 hours, 6 June 1994, during the 50ᵗʰ Anniversary of the invasion of Europe, to help me identify the grave. They found the vital information in the Mayor's office at Cartigny, without which there would be no book and the secret would still be a secret!

I am so indebted to those survivors who welcomed me into their homes and who let me into a part of their lives that some had hidden for a long time, as well as the families of those who did not survive or had since died, for telling me about their loved ones and letting me dig through personal papers, photograph albums, and personal letters. They all granted me permission to use whatever I wanted.

Then there are those who are not mentioned above, who have become sources of new research involving other World War One and World War Two events that were brought to my attention during all the years from when this research project began. Some of them are just as intriguing as what you will read in this book.

Avril Williams (Avril Williams Guest House, Tea Rooms, and Military Museum, Auchonvillers, the Somme, France - www.avrilwilliams.com) Who runs a B&B where you feel at home, when researching in France.

If I missed you in the above, you know how much you helped and you know how much I appreciate your help.

Remembering Claude OBERT

In early September, 2012, we visited Nicole and Claude OBERT in Tincourt-Boucly. With us, during the visit, were the daughter, Judith (Grey) Lukensmeyer, granddaughter, Alison (Lukensmeyer) Lohse and grandson, Jeremy Lukensmeyer, of 2nd Lt. Frederick G. Grey. His daughter, Judith , was born two months after his death in France and she had made special arrangement with us to show them where her father and their grandfather had died.

Claude, in his usual way, had made arrangements for us to visit the field and Lt. Grey's family was able to locate relics of the crashed "**226**" and remember their very personal connection to the field.

Claude was very sick and unable to visit the Memorial site he had made possible, nor the crash-site. However, we had an excellent meeting at their home.

Upon leaving the OBERT'S, we visited the Grave at Cartigny, which contains two-thirds of their father's and grand-father's remains. Mixed in forever with the two other crewmen who died with him.

On 10 November, 2012, sixty-eight years to the early morning when he had watched the "**226**'s" final seconds, Claude completed his "Final Transfer" and, as I like to believe, he joined the legions he had worked so hard to remember.

A few years earlier, due to a road enlargement, the original "**226**" memorial location was being destroyed. Claude approached the Department of the Somme and donated a new location at the edge of one of his fields to the French government, so the memorial now has a protected permanent location.

Table Of Contents

Narrator's Preface

I existed, many people saw me involved in what you will read. However, I am what the author has made me and that permits me to tell the whole story until the publishing of this book. Almost everything you will read happened. If not exactly as written, it still happened. Some of this book, such as my origin, is fictional and what happened after the war cannot be proven by the hard evidence available at this writing, to have or have not existed. However, what we left behind, as we protected ourselves after the war does exist. And yes, if you question, you can find references to me and the earliest existence of a person like me in documents before and during WWII. If, you are good enough and the author challenges you to do so, please find exactly who I was and help complete the final truth of this story.

As a man who has certainly completed my "Final Transfer" by now, I can no longer be hurt by the truth!

. . . .

I left the Army in 1964, after 25 years of service. During that entire 25 years, except when I was assigned temporary duty to complete my university degrees and attend the usual staff schools, I was deeply involved in the secret side of our military.

Upon retirement, I moved directly to a Firm and was in charge of their security operations around the world. After my second retirement, I am still a paid consultant to the Firm, concerning internal and international security.

I had not planned to write a book like this; it was forced upon me when I was contacted by people who were supposed to contact me, when certain events took place. One day, out of the blue, I received a telephone call warning me that an unknown historian was researching an event that I had been deeply involved in.

As of that day, he had penetrated through many of the walls I had built into the records to prevent such researchers from finding the truth. He had now succeeded to such a point, that the security notations on the files required the archivists to contact me and give me a heads-up on the researcher and what his research was seeking to prove.

Exactly who I am, is not all that important. How I came to be in such a position of authority to be able to do what was done, is vital to this story. During Chapters One and Two, I will digress to establish my credentials to the point where General Eisenhower and I created, *Why We Killed Patton* "*The Best Kept Secret Of World War Two!*" And yes, they are creative fiction by the author beginning on this page.

I was, for some years, on the staff of General Eisenhower. From the first moment when we became aware of the crash of the top-secret B-24J in France, that forced the creation of what was done, I planned, and I guided the full implementation of all the actions taken. At all times, acting under direct verbal orders and full support of General Eisenhower.

When you have read this book, and if I have met my goal, you will understand how these events led directly to the involvement of three Presidents of the United States. Two of that immediate era and one, who later became President.

In addition, you will come to realize there is a direct trail from the involved events, the crash of the B–17G, the *"Lady Jeannette,"* and the crash of the Top Secret B-24J, "**226**," to the death of General George S. Patton, Jr.

If, what you read in this book had become public knowledge in January, 1946, all the lives of those involved in making what happened, happen, would have been destroyed and world history would be very different today!

Our goals at the time *were fully justified in our minds*. By doing what we did, we may have saved the lives of thousands of Allied air crew, ground soldiers and even more civilian lives in the war zone. All those lives saved, with the only real cost being the ***desecration of seven American War Dead***. And, as you will learn, the sudden and fully motivated death of one American General.

We succeeded for more than six decades!

This book tells the story of how, we did it!

Chapter One
Narrator's Foundation

As another stretcher bearing a dying man was brought into the tent, the nurse was helping a dying German soldier with his "Final Transfer" from life to death. She was comforting the soldier and holding his hand and she listened in case he asked for his mother, wife or girl friend. Then, as she always did when the dying asked for their loved one, she leaned over and whispered in the ear of the dying as she grasped his hand a little tighter, "I'm here, I'm here, right beside you."

Her German was not all that good. However, since she had been forced into the German Army as a nurse, she had learned enough to talk to and help German soldiers die. It had been two years since the war had started in 1914, and the German officers running her hospital still did not trust her. She was French and with her French upbringing and the war, to insure she could never hurt a recovering German soldier, she had been put in charge of the "tent of the dying."

As the stretcher bearers moved the just-arrived dying man from the stretcher to an available bed, he showed no signs of life other than a slight rise and fall of his chest. He and his clothing were very dirty, his right pants leg had been cut away and his right thigh was bandaged with a white covering heavily stained with his blood. After the transfer was made, the two men who appreciated her beauty, even though she was French, approached the nurse and told her the new man's history.

He had been hit by a shell two days before while delivering supplies to Le Sars, which was very close to the active front line. The shell had contained white phosphorus and it had first broken when it hit the wall of the house where the man had taken shelter. Then a fragment of the broken, burning shell hit the man in the right thigh, tearing away much of his muscle and tissue, and badly burning the area at the same time. The local aid station doctor determined the wounded man could not survive. So, he ordered the man's stretcher to be placed with the others who would soon die, allowing the doctor to spend his time with those who might survive.

After two days had passed, the shelling had settled down somewhat and the inflow of wounded slowed enough to permit the dead to be cleared and buried. When those assigned the task of burying the dead picked up his stretcher, he had groaned lightly. They called the doctor at once, who then made the decision to have the dying man evacuated to the German hospital at Riencourt-les-Bapaume, which is located to the south-east of Bapaume, Department of the Pas-de-Calais, France.

In due time, after his arrival at the hospital, the soldier was taken into the operating room and placed on the table to be surveyed by the doctor on duty. That doctor also determined the man could not live and he sent the wounded solider to the "tent of the dying," where the French nurse would see to his needs until he died.

The French nurse had been born in 1893, and raised on a large farm at Vervins, Department of the Aisne, in northern France. She had three brothers, two older and one younger, plus two younger sisters making up the family.

Her father and mother, from a very early age, had expected her to become betrothed to the only son of a close friend. This would in, due time, lead to the merging of their farms and the family wealth would grow.

Though they were good friends, she had never felt of the boy that way and her mother always said, "That was she was the spirited one of the three girls with her own strong mind." The War of 1870 had moved though their region of France and she grew up with many stories of that war. Her father often talked about the nurses who had helped save his life when he was wounded. She had read books about Clara Barton, the first Red Cross nurse, and other brave nurses and she became determined to be a nurse just like those women.

Even though her parents continued to pressure her to marry and raise children to help on the farm, she maintained her desire to be a nurse. Finally, when she graduated from high school with Honors, her parents decided she could attend the nurses' school at St-Quentin, located some distance to the west of Vervins.

She began her studies in the fall of 1911 and graduated at the head of her class in the spring of 1914. She was accepted to the staff of the large hospital in Sedan, with her new position to begin on the 1st of September, 1914.

Instead, the sudden war stepped in to change her life. All of her brothers were French Army Reservists and they were called up as the clouds of war raged. Then the storm broke and the Germans soon reached their farm. A German field hospital took over the farm and house and forced the family to live in two upstairs rooms. Her parents were in one room and the girls shared the other.

Her youngest sister had already married and fretted all the time about her husband who was with the French Army. The sister next to her in age, had told her of the boy she had met in Vervins one shopping day, who lived at Hirson. He was also in the army and she only knew from his last letter, he would soon be in combat.

There were not all that many wounded Germans in the house. But one day after they had arrived, while she was returning from a call of nature, one of the men had suddenly become restless and ripped off his bandage. Without thinking about it, she quickly went to the man and calmed him. And then, the best as she could, she reapplied the bandage.

Unknown to her, the German doctor in charge had just entered the room and seeing her quick reaction to the situation, he realized she was not the average French farm girl. When she had finished and before she could go up the stairs, the doctor approached her and questioned her about what she had done to help the man. The doctor could speak French and she could do nothing, but tell him of her nurse's training and her new position at Sedan.

The hospital left the farm a few days later. It had to maintain its distance from the front line which was moving south and west, as the Germans conquered more of France. Suddenly, the nurse found herself impressed into the German Army and she was forced to leave with the hospital when it left her home. Her father was holding back his anger, as he knew the Germans could easily shoot him. Her mother was crying and tears flowed as a stream down her face.

The options, as they were explained to her family, were very simple. If her family wanted to keep the farm, she would volunteer as a German Army nurse; if she did not volunteer to go, the Germans had several other options for her, none of which involved nursing in a French hospital and they would find others to run the family's farm without the family.

For the next two years, the hospital she had been assigned to was close to Bapaume, in the Somme battle zone of France. An area that had quickly settled into the trench war system with little movement. After the expected British attack started on the 1st of July, 1916, she had been helping even more of those who could not survive, to meet death as easily as they could.

She now had six men in her tent and by the next morning, she and her assistant would help most, if not all of them, make that "Final Transfer." They both worked 12 hours on and 12 hours off, since there were only the two of them to maintain the "tent of the dying."

The man whose hand she had been holding and to whom she had been whispering, began to take shallow breaths and she knew from much experience that soon the growing pressure on her hand would weaken and then he would be gone. She leaned over him and let him hear his mother speaking, as he completed his life and transferred to the "Legions of the Dead."

She pried her hand from his now dead hand and then ran her hand across his forehead to close his eyes for the final time. She reached over and took the cloth from the washing bowl and cleaned his face and hands before placing his arms across his chest and pulling the blanket up over his head.

As she turned to call the orderly to make arrangements for the body to be removed, she thought about how short a time it had taken this one. He has just let his life slide away without much fight, when his wound really did not seem all that bad. She had seen others in the hospital who had fought for their lives and had lived with much worse wounds.

None of the other dying men were conscious. So she moved from one to the other to help as she could. First, she did what nurses had to do, she lifted their blankets and checked to see if they had wet or soiled the cotton rags used as diapers. If necessary, she replaced the soiled with clean and washed the dying man's private areas. Then, with clean water, she washed each man's face and hands and then, she smoothed his blankets.

As she came to the new arrival, she thought it was a shame that such a good-looking man should have to die in such a way. Seeing no ring on his finger she thought, if he speaks he will ask for his mother and not his wife. After checking for bowel and bladder evacuations, she found a clean bandage and went back to him to exchange the bloody bandage on his leg.

He stirred, as she began to work to release the bandage from the wound with it's scabbed and burned flesh. As the bandage came free and she could see the wound under it, she was nearly sick to her stomach. There were many maggots in the wound and suddenly, one fly flew free as it was released from its trapped position under the badly soiled bandage.

This bothered the nurse so badly she called an orderly to attend to him, while she went to see the doctor who had made the decision to send this man to die. When she asked about the maggots, he told her, "The man had been lying in the open for two days. He had been expected to die where he was wounded and as you know, the flies toward the front were numerous as they had so much rotten flesh to feed on." In fact, the doctor told her, "That man was lucky the rats had not gotten to him before the burial men realized he was still alive and was evacuated."

When the nurse asked, if she should clean the wound of maggots, the doctor told her not to waste her time. However, he said, he had heard of men who might have died of gangrene, who were saved by the maggots eating the dying and dead flesh infected by gangrene.

As she walked back to the "tent of the dying," the nurse said to herself, "I hope, he dies soon and before he wakes up. I do not want him to see what had happened to him, with the maggots eating him while he is still alive."

The next morning when she began her twelve-hour day shift there were only two men in the "tent of the dying." One was new, brought in during the night, and all of those, but one from the day before had died. That one man was the man with the maggots in his wound.

As she talked to her assistant, who had been on duty all night, she learned the man had been showing more signs of life. He had groaned some and shifted his body around, but never became conscious. Both agreed that he was really taking his time in accepting his death.

To ease this man's transfer to death and since, the other dying man remained unconscious, she decided she would take the time to clean up the man with the thigh wound as much as she could. Usually they came in dirty, sometimes conscious and scared, however, most of the time they were unconscious until their death. The one thing almost all of them had in common, was the fact they usually died in the same, very dirty condition they were in when they arrived at the "tent of the dying."

After the orderly came back with a bucket of fresh hot water, working as a team, they began to cut the remainder of his clothing away even though it caused the dying man to groan. Then she placed a covering over his uncovered body to preserve his privacy. "Even the dying deserved that much," she told the orderly.

When they had completed that task, the orderly had to leave and she began to wash the man. His hands were somewhat clean from when she had wiped them the day before. However, from the hands up, it took a lot of water and washing to clean the grime from the man. It was very obvious, thanks to the recent attacks by the English, that he had not been able to properly clean himself for some time.

That day, during the rest of her shift, there were no additional men brought to the "tent of the dying." After washing the man, she went to check on the other dying soldier in the tent and she found he had just slipped off on his own. As she always did, she cleaned his hands and face, folded his arms over his chest, pulled the cover over his head and called for the orderly to have the body removed for burial in the cemetery across the stream flowing along the north side of the village.

Now she had just one man to help die and for the next few hours that is what she did. But this one was going to leave, as clean and fresh as she could make him. When she was finished, she again covered him with a light cover. Then she placed the rough blankets over him, sat by his side and just waited - either for his death, or for another to arrive, whom she could help. It really did not matter much to her. She had helped many German soldiers and a few contract German civilians die in her tent. In the most secret area of her mind, each one who died was another who could not hurt her brothers and her sisters' loved ones.

From the very few letters that got through from her family, she had learned that her youngest brother had been missing since the first day of the war. Her older brother had been wounded, captured by the Germans and was now a Prisoner Of War (POW) doing slave labor in Germany. Her older middle brother was somewhere in the French Army, still alive as far as her parents knew.

As her mind wandered, the man began to move a bit and soon he groaned. And as she watched, he moved his lips in an attempt to speak. Knowing he had been without water or food for days, she wet a small cloth and pressed it to his lips and to her surprise, he began to suck at the cloth to get the water into his mouth.

She quickly got a cup of water and lifting his head, she held the cup to his lips and he began to slowly sip the water. As the cup emptied, he stopped sipping and she felt his body go slack. Thinking he had died, she lowered his head to begin her task of preparing him for burial.

As she leaned back, she realized he was still breathing and in fact, his breath seemed deeper and stronger. One thing, she decided, was this man was not going to slip away easily. He was a fighter.

She continued to sit and watch him and again his lips began to move. She realized he was speaking, but very weakly. She leaned over to listen to him ask for his mother, wife, or girlfriend in German, and she always remembered the shock she felt, when he was asking for his mother in perfect French. Before she could assume her roll of the mother to the dying man, he asked for his father. But this time he was speaking in German. Who was this man, she thought?

As he began to stir even more, she again lifted his head. He sipped more water from the cup and he began again to ask for his mother in French. He was obviously semiconscious and not really aware of what he was saying.

Learning over with her mouth close to his ear, she asked the dying soldier in French, "Where are you from?" She did not think he would reply and yet, he answered her question at once, as he whispered in French, "I am from Alsace-Lorraine and I am a Frenchman." The answer ran directly through her mind to her heart. Here was a Frenchman, who just like her, who must have been forced to serve in the German army. The Germans had controlled the Alsace-Lorraine area of France since the War of 1870. And deep in her heart, she knew, when this war was over, Alsace-Lorraine would again be a part of France and this soldier should live to see that day.

She leaned back from him and thought of what she should say to him. Then she leaned over to put her mouth near his ear and she whispered fairly loudly, "You must live, you must live to take me to visit your Alsace-Lorraine."

A few minutes later her assistant came in to relieve her for the night shift. For once, she told her assistant that she would remain with this dying man and her assistant, could have the evening off to have a bit more leisure time to herself.

Occasionally he would stir and ask for his mother; each time he would sip from the cup, but he never regained full consciousness. She decided to remove and replace the bandage on the damaged leg, noticing the maggots had almost completed eating the dying and dead tissue remaining in the large wound in his thigh. For the first time, as a woman, she thought to herself that at least he showed no damage to what made him a man. This thought made her blush and she looked around to make certain no one had seen how looking at him had brought color to her cheeks.

She went into the hospital to fetch antiseptic, some swabs and a fresh bandage, returning to the "tent of the dying" to remove the bandage covering the wound. Then, she began to swab the wound with the antiseptic. As she worked, for the first time in a long time, she felt again that she was a real nurse and not just someone who helped the dying, die.

As she swabbed, the maggots moved away from the antiseptic. Soon she thought, they will have nothing to eat unless he does die. She realized, that she was determined to keep this Frenchman alive and perhaps, one day, ... he would take her to see Alsace-Lorraine.

A few hours later her assistant came in and she told her to keep an eye on the man and to make certain she was there all the time, to give him water if he appeared to want it. He had lived this long after the doctors had said he would die and they must not do anything to help him die unless he gave up on his own.

She left for her shared room in one of the village homes and, as she went to sleep the woman in her again came to the surface. It had been hidden so long, what with all the death and now, she was feeling something deep inside her that she had never really felt before.

The next morning there was another in the "tent of the dying," and during the day, a total of eight men had come and five had gone as the approaching fighting flared. Three with her help, as they called for their mothers. However, as she found time, she returned to check on her German-Frenchman and it seemed to her, his color was getting stronger. He was drinking more and more water each time he stirred. Twice during the day, the main doctor came to see the "dying" man. First, the doctor came by himself and during his second visit he had two other doctors with him. The three doctors had come to the "tent of the dying" to see this man who was not dying, when he should be dead.

Once during the day, she had again cleaned and treated his wound and this time she removed some of the maggots and threw them into the brush near the tent. When the doctors looked at the wound that should have killed this man they remarked about how the maggots had helped save his life. They also agreed, that what had really saved the man's life was the burning of the white phosphorus in the

broken shell case. It had sealed the veins as it burnt him and the simple fact, the shell had failed to tear open the major artery supplying blood to his remaining leg.

The nurse hovered near the doctors as they discussed his situation and she was pleased to hear they were now, not so sure he was going to die. The original doctor told the others, "As the man was so sure to die, I had just sent him to the 'tent of the dying' and I am very surprised to find the wound so clean."

He turned to the nurse and asked her, if she had cleaned the wound? And she told him, "The soldier has lived so long, I decided he should not die as dirty as when he came in. And, since I had extra time yesterday, I cleaned him and the wound." The doctor turned to the others and said, "I say, we leave him here. If he lives, his service is obviously over. If we leave him here, this nurse can continue to look after him and if he is lucky, one day, ... he may live to leave this tent."

They all agreed and as they left, the head doctor told the nurse to continue exactly what she had been doing and to keep him informed twice a day concerning the man's condition. With such a wound, by now he should have died of infection, if not directly due to the wound.

After they left the tent, the nurse went to the soldier's bed and sat down beside him. She took his hand in hers, squeezed it, leaned over and again whispered in his ear, "You must live, you must live to take me to visit your home in Alsace-Lorraine." As she finished, the man stirred a bit and then settled down again.

Now, since the doctors had really left him in her care, she called the orderly to watch the tent as she made her way to the building where their meals were served and for the first time in her life, she used her beauty to obtain something for someone else. She batted her eyelashes, as she asked the cook to prepare a special broth for the man in her tent. He wanted to object to wasting good food on a dying man, but who could refuse this beautiful French nurse, in the German army. Before she left, he had agreed to personally take the broth to her tent, four times a day. Besides, since she had asked so nicely, he would begin to add small pieces of cooked meat that were small enough to be swallowed without choking the sick man.

That night, as her assistant helped the others in the tent to die, she again sat by the soldier's bed and watched over him as he lay there. She did not hold his hand, but occasionally, she did lean over and low enough so she could not be heard by others and whispered into his ear, "You must live, you must live to take me to visit your Alsace-Lorraine!"

The next morning when she went to the tent to begin her shift, her assistant told her, "The man seemed to be regaining consciousness and had taken water and broth, three times during the night."

By noon, there were two others in the tent, both unconscious and with obvious wounds that would soon cause their death. In fact within the hour, they were gone and the nurse was again sitting by the soldier's side and holding his hand.

She was daydreaming, about what Alsace-Lorraine was like, with its hills and forests. Her family's farm consisted of mostly flat fields with woods growing in the shallow valleys and places where the soil did not support crops. When she

suddenly felt his hand returning the pressure and when she looked at his face, his eyes were slowly opening and focusing on her face.

He had been born in 1892, in the townhouse his family owned in St-Avold, in the Lorraine Region of, then Germany. They stayed there when not at their large farm and forest holding near Homburg-Haut, close to the old German border with Alsace-Lorraine.

His father had always thought of himself more as an upstanding German citizen of Alsace-Lorraine, while his mother was very proud of her family being French forever. It often led to some controversy among his family. This wounded soldier was the fourth of four sons and he had a younger sister.

As a fourth son, from his earliest years he had been told, "You will never inherit the estate, but you will be supported in a career of your choosing." It was his parent's hope, that he would choose the field of medicine for his career. With his French mother and his German-leaning father and the long German occupation of Alsace-Lorraine, he grew up speaking both German and French.

The family was well off and each summer they took a vacation to visit other places. His father usually wanted to go to places in Germany and they had toured many of Germany's largest cities. However one year his mother insisted to his father, that they had to go to Paris, as the children must know her Paris.

In Paris, he had met some English boys whose family was also visiting Paris and they were allowed at times, to go off on their own. As his father told him, "It would be good for you to find out how much better you are than those English boys you have met." During that summer he realized, that he had a talent when it came to language and, as the English boys struggled to learn French, he quickly became conversant in English.

It was during that summer, when he became very interested in England and English, that he had decided he would learn proper English, either at a school or from a private tutor. During his final year in high school, his family went to England for the summer. This was thanks to his constant begging his mother to intervene with his father, who was again planning on going to Germany.

Upon their return to the farm from England, he informed his parents that he was going to attend university to become an English Professor. He had checked in St-Avold and the school had told him, if he achieved his planned goal, he could be employed there. Realizing, that forcing their son into some career he did not want might force him away from the family, his parents agreed with his plan.

In the Spring of 1913 he graduated from university and it was a very bad time in his life. His father and brothers had been very busy at the farm and could not attend. Then, while en route to his graduation, his mother and sister were both killed in a train derailment.

Upon his graduation he got the new position and he became an employed English Professor (in France, the title of a high school English teacher) in St-Avold, starting with the beginning of school in the fall of 1913. He lived in the family's townhouse in St-Avold, surrounded by memories of his mother and sister.

At the beginning of the summer vacation in 1914 he left for an extended visit to England with a group of his best English students. As the clouds of war raged across Europe in midsummer, he and his students hurried back to Alsace-Lorraine. His three brothers were called into the German army at once. Two of his brothers had completed their required military training some time ago and his third brother would have completed his training that year. However, thanks to his University Degree, career as an English Professor, and his father's political connections, when his orders to report for duty arrived, he was not ordered to the front. Instead, he was ordered to join the German army supply service to help keep the soldiers at the front supplied with food. And, as he had graduated from a university, he entered the German army as an officer.

During the previous two years he had never been all that close to the front line. It was his job to collect supplies, with others making the risky delivery trips to the front. Once in a while, a French or English airplane would drop some bombs somewhere near him. But never close enough to make the fear of death outride the thrill of watching the airplanes dropping bombs. Several times, he had watched airplanes fall from the sky. Some on fire, with others just falling like a leaf. Once he had seen the plane's pilot, either jump or fall from the spinning, burning airplane and fall to earth streaming fire and smoke behind him.

Then one day, he was told he would have to take the transport forward, as there was no one else to command the soldiers in the transport column.

All he could remember was, he had been standing somewhere in darkness, calling for his mother and father and thinking, they were fading away. Suddenly, he thought he heard an angel telling him he had to live. He had heard her and yet he continued along the road he was on toward the bright light in the distance.

Then, just as he had almost reached the bright light before him, he faintly heard the angel again, calling for him to live. As her voice faded, he turned around and began to retrace his steps into the darkness he had been leaving, to see if he could find his angel.

He realized his eyes were closed and he slowly began to force them open. For some time it was hard for him to focus. As he did, he saw his angel and she was even more beautiful than he had imagined. He had a moment before she turned to look at him and for the rest of his life, my father would describe exactly how my mother, his very own angel, slowly turned and looked into his eyes.

My mother always said, "I was no angel, but as our eyes met, I instantly knew that one day I would visit Alsace-Lorraine with this man."

After a minute she spoke to the man in French, to tell him that she had to let the doctors know that he was awake, however, she would return soon.

The doctor came as soon as he could and seeing the man awake and talking, he told him how lucky he was to be alive, as they all had expected him to have died by now. The doctor then removed the leg dressing and saw that the damaged flesh was beginning to heal. He instructed the nurse to continue what she had been doing. The doctor continued, saying to her, "Nurse, congratulations, you are the

one who really saved this man's life." This caused the nurse to blush. And, this time others observed her reaction.

After the doctor left, my mother told my father how serious his wound really was. She explained to him, that that in due time he should be able to walk, probably with a pronounced limp. She also had to tell him, he was in the "tent of the dying" and, if he wanted, she would ask to have him moved to a recovery tent.

It took less than an instant for my father to tell my mother, "I am staying right where I am until you push me out the door." For a while he remained there and then the English began a new drive. Two weeks after his arrival, even though he wanted to stay, he was evacuated to a German hospital at Cambrai. It was obvious that his service in the German army was over and when he had recovered enough to travel he would be sent home.

Just three days after his arrival at the hospital in Cambrai, he looked up as someone entered the room and it was his angel. Her hospital had come within dangerous range of the English artillery and was ordered to move to Cambrai.

He was sitting up, when my mother pulled a stool over to his bed and they began to talk. He was in a bed that had been given some privacy by curtains separating the beds and as she leaned over to talk in a lowered voice, my father kissed my mother for the first time.

At the end of October, when he was told he would soon be released from the hospital; he began to plan how he could prevent himself from being sent home, away from his angel. He realized, that the German army had no use for him as a soldier, however, with his language ability he could be of great help to them in many ways, such as helping with interpretation between the French and English speaking patients.

There were always problems between the Germans and French and soon he took advantage of a group of badly wounded English soldiers who had been brought to the hospital. The staff was having trouble talking to them and he volunteered to interpret for them. Soon he was being used daily for communications between the Germans, French civilians and the English-speaking POW's.

The doctors realized that he possessed a special linguist talent, and soon the other officers with whom they mixed, stopped by the hospital and sought father's help in their dealing with the local population. One day the local commander asked to talk to him about becoming a civilian contractor for the German army after his medical discharge. This was exactly what Father desired and he rushed as fast as he could limp along, to tell his Angel he would be staying there and not going home.

Both had written home about their new friend and both had received letters from home, discouraging the development of their relationship. Her mother had a son who had just disappeared, and one who had been wounded by the Germans and was now a POW. Her sister's husband had not been heard from for some time and it was the fault of the Germans. Father's youngest brother had first been wounded and then killed by the French and neither family was happy, that their child might marry the enemy. Neither cared that his Alsace-Lorraine was originally a part of France, and that after the war ended it might again be a part of France.

On Christmas Day, 1916, my father proposed to mother and they agreed that their individual families would have to accept them as they were. On New Year's Day, 1917, they were married with the help of the local German commander, who wanted to ensure his valued new civilian contractor would be there when he needed an interpreter.

At first, the apartment they were assigned was bare and lacked much of anything to make it home. Then with father's local connections, furniture was soon found and the home became a place where mother's fellow nurses could visit. When visiting at their home, the nurses did not feel the pressure of being one of the few available German women in a sea of German soldiers, especially in a city where every woman was usually suspected of being in and treated, as if they were members of the world's "oldest profession."

Soon, between the women and father's friends, it was understood that a nurse met at their home was just that. If something developed, that was swell with them, but there was to be no pressure and all were most happy to have some place that was more like home than anyplace else they could go.

Other than occasional waves of patients during the various offensives during 1917, the hospital where mother served had enjoyed a much lower number of men who arrived at the "ward of the dying." During 1917, mother's mood improved greatly, what with her marriage and having to help fewer soldiers to make the transfer to death. Overall, 1917 was a much better first year of marriage than many enjoyed, even when there was no war.

However, great winds of change were blowing, rumors were rampant and soon, many realized that 1918 was not going to be as easy a year for them as 1917 had been. The Americans were now in the war and with what news they received, it seemed the Americans must have a conveyor belt of shipping to be moving so many men to France, so quickly.

As most of their friends were nurses and higher-ranking German officers, they were kept informed of many things the lower ranked Germans never heard. And normally, before they began, the hospital prepared for the various British and German offensives and often they had prepared for enemy attacks before the first shell burst.

It had been decided since the hospital had been in position for so long, they would remain at Cambrai instead of following the front line. They would become a third level hospital, when sending casualties to the rear. At the very front, were the aid stations that tried to preserve life so the wounded could be transported to the second level hospital installation. Those hospitals were as close to the front line as they could be situated, without being within artillery range of the enemy.

At that hospital level, those who could be easily treated received the treatment required and those who required extensive care were stabilized as much as possible, before all were forwarded to the third level of treatment. A hospital that was equipped to handle most cases. At the third level hospitals, those with the worst wounds who still had a chance, were again checked to be stable and forwarded to the fourth level of hospitals where extensive reconstructive surgery

was available, as well as extended recovery facilities. The less wounded were held until they could return to the front and the rest sent to major hospitals further back.

As the Americans began to arrive in France, it was soon obvious to father and mother, that America's new, fresh, and willing manpower outweighed anything the Germans could muster. At the same time the visitors to their apartment often secretly spoke about the end of the war. All because of those damn Americans!

In late August, their hospital was alerted that it would soon be moving south east to Sedan as a new enemy attack was suspected to occur sometime soon in the Cambrai area and the hospital could soon be at risk. Father, quickly visited his friend, the local German commander and informed the commander that he would not be remaining behind, as his wife went to Sedan. The commander told him, he would write a letter of recommendation to his good friend, the local commander of Sedan, to recommend they contract for father's services when he arrived there.

By the second week of September, 1917, both were in Sedan, with mother continuing to be put in charge of the "ward of the dying" and father employed in the same position he had held in Cambrai.

Their apartment was not nearly as nice even though with father's contacts they had been able to bring all their furniture.

In mid-February 1918, a week's leave was granted to mother and father took a week's time off. Using the passes and transportation orders provided by his friend, the local German commander, for the first time the married couple went to visit their homes and families.

First, as it was fairly close, they went to Vervins. It was only a day's visit, but the reception was chilly. Even though he was really French and had been discharged from the German army for some time, father was still serving the Germans who had inflicted great damage on the family.

They were to leave early the next day for St-Avold and during the evening, my grandmother took my mother aside and asked, "How could you do such a thing to the family?" Mother, told her mother that she loved my father, he was truly French, and if they could not adjust when the war ended perhaps life would be much different from what it had been.

Arriving at St-Avold, father and mother were greeted at the rail station by father's father and father's brother, who had also been wounded and also using a cane. However, the greeting was muted and my mother was treated in a polite manner as, if she was a visitor instead of a new member of the family.

During their one day visit to St-Avold, it was no different from their visit to Vervins. Father's father took him aside and asked, "How can you insult the family by marrying an outside French woman?"

He went on to say, "There are now many unmarried and widowed women in our own area of Alsace-Lorraine. Why did you have to marry a woman from France? The French army was responsible for your dead brother, your own wound, your brother's wound and perhaps, before the war was over they might kill another member of this family."

That night and during their travel back to Sedan, mother and father discussed the reception at both families' homes. Before reaching Sedan they decided the war would not last much longer and they would again visit their homes after the war. At that time they would have to make a hard decision about the rest of their lives.

During the months of the great German Somme advance in the spring of 1918, and then after August 8, during the great German Somme retreat, several soldiers a day were being helped by mother and her assistant to die. Some days she was crying when her shift was over, as now she had much more sympathy toward the unknown dying German soldiers. For now she knew, not all of them were there because they were German.

In late September, far off in the distance they could now hear the thunder of artillery. It was a long way away and then, day by day, it began to get closer and closer. At the same time, mother's ward began to receive additional men and the occasional woman who were sent back with hope, but their doctors decided their efforts were better spent with the less wounded.

Toward the end of October, mother realized that a natural function had not occurred as it should have earlier that month. She waited a week before she told my father, that she thought she must be with child. Both were a bit surprised, as they had planned to wait until the war was over. Still, it would soon be over and if the coming month proved she was with child, it would be a wonderful start to the new life they would soon lead.

At the beginning of November the long range artillery began to creep closer and closer to Sedan. The hospital was told there was no place for it to go and they were to continue to operate as long as they could and if necessary, they would surrender in place.

Each night, especially as the artillery began to rain down within Sedan, they discussed their options. When the artillery shells began to fall close to the city, they found a room in their cellar that was well protected, even if a larger shell fell on the building. And, with a candle as the only light, they comforted each other about their future, while listening to the artillery shells land nearby.

With father's connections to the local commander, he was aware before many, that the end was very close and he told my mother what he was going to do. He would wait until the Americans, who seemed the closest, arrived and he would then take the risk meeting the first ones. He thought, in his civilian clothes and with his limp, they would have no reason to suspect him. He would ask the Americans in his best English, about providing his language skills to the American army as he had the German army.

It was not until midday on the 12th of November that a group of soldiers in uniforms, recognized by father as belonging to Americans, appeared and he decided to put his plan into action. They were prepared for trouble, but were obviously not hunting trouble. When they reached a clear area that was large enough so they would not think he might be a threat, he showed himself and stood with both hands on his cane so they could see he was unarmed and not a threat.

As they approached, my father made the statement he had been practicing for the past few days, "Hello, welcome to Sedan." One of the Americans answered, "Hi, Bud, what can we do for you?" Then the American turned and told a man a bit further down the line, "Sarge, I think you had better talk to this guy."

The solider to whom the one had been talking, stepped up and all the men gathered around them, as father told the sergeant that, "I am a person who could interpret between English, French and German without any delays." As father finished, the sergeant told him to stay right here. Then, the sergeant turned and told one of the other men to run back and get the lieutenant up here as fast as he could and the fellow took off running back in the direction they had come from.

Within a couple of minutes the fellow was coming back and with him was a group of four more Americans. One had a silver bar on his shoulder and was obviously the lieutenant the sergeant had sent for.

The sergeant walked a short way toward the oncoming group. They stopped and talked for a couple of minutes and then they came to the original group, that father was still talking to about Sedan and what it was like.

The officer was obviously impressed by father's easy conversation with the others. The men all straightened up somewhat, but did not come to attention as the officer came up to the group. Father, immediately realized they were taking no risk of father setting up their officer for a sniper hidden from view.

The officer began to talk to father about what the sergeant had already told him and father told the officer, "I am a Frenchman and I was forced to join the German army. When I was in the German army, I was in the supply service until I was wounded and then I became a civilian contractor working as an interpreter." He added, "I am married to a French woman, who is a nurse. She was forced to join the German army and she is on duty at the German hospital today."

The American officer then said to father, "Fellow, if it's up to me, you are hired. We need you right now to come along with us and when we meet up with my commander, I am certain he will agree, we need your help. So Bud, you got a job."

Within a day father had gone from working for the Germans to working for the Americans and he quickly learned, the latter were much nicer to work for.

From that day on, my father instructed my mother in English, which she learned very quickly with the help of visiting Americans. For a while mother continued with the German hospital, while they began to move the wounded back to Germany. Then one day, the American Red Cross came into the hospital and she began working for them as the transformation from war to peace began.

They remained in Sedan until the week before Christmas, 1918, then my father informed the Americans he was working for, that with regrets, he must now take his wife and find out where their life after the war would begin. A couple of the Americans, with whom my father had become friends and who were somewhat aware of my parents problems with their families, perhaps in a somewhat joking way, told him, "Hell man, if they kick you out of here come to the good old USA. We don't put up with that crap back home."

The Americans made certain father and mother had ample transportation for their furniture to the farm at Vervins and the driver would not take any payment when they arrived. However when he left, he did not refuse the bottles of the "Produit de Ferme" they insisted he take as a reward.

Christmas, that year of 1918, was not a good one nor was it looked back at over the later years with any fond memories of any kind. One sister's boyfriend had not come back from the war and her future was bleak, as so many young men had been killed. The married sister's husband, who had been wounded and was a POW in Germany, as had one of her brothers, had written they were okay and would be home as soon as they could.

Her badly wounded brother had survived the war and was already at home and helping with the running of the farm. The large farm had suffered no war damage other than being short of the number of people required to run it properly.

As for her youngest brother, who had left for the Army at the beginning of the war and whom they could only track for a short time, he never returned. The army never reported him as killed or wounded. In fact, they never reported on him again. He just did not come home. After WWI, the French did not account for more than 500,000 men who left, but did not come home. (A wonderful French film, titled "Life, But Nothing Else" tells this story very well). For years her mother and father would hope that he was one of those "Lost Ones," who had lost their minds and that his memory of home would return. However, in due time, after many years both parents spoke less of their missing son and both quietly accepted the fact that he was gone and he was never coming home. He had been the youngest child. The youngest boy, the one who would never inherit, but he had been their favorite and they were hoping he would join the government one day and represent their family in the French government. It was a grand dream and it would never be.

Mother and father were leaving Vervins for St-Avold two days after Christmas and on the final day mother was taken aside by her parents for a quiet talk. They told her, that he seemed to be a very nice fellow and their marriage was obviously one of love and now, that she was beginning to show, she should really think of making their permanent home in St-Avold with her husband's family.

At the same time both reassured mother, telling her the farm had not suffered much and with so much land ruined in the battle zone, the farm income would grow and she would receive an allowance for some time. Then her parents told my mother, even though they did not directly approve of the marriage, her dowery would be available when she and her husband made up their minds about their future.

The parting was much nicer than their previous visit and they agreed, as they discussed it on the train, they were off to a new life. Perhaps, that new life would begin at Saint Avold.

At Saint Avold, they were greeted by father's father, the wounded middle bother and his older brother who had returned from the war, a defeated soldier of Germany, to live in the Alsace-Lorraine which had again become a part of France. Both were now married, the older brother to the wife of his best friend who had

39

been killed. She had two children when they married, and between them, they now shared a new life that was to arrive in due time. His middle-brother had one young son and soon, he and his wife planned to have another child.

During the first day at home, father went to the school where he had taught English and he was told, there might be a position during the next school year. However, they had heard that he had married a French woman while he was away. The head of the faculty, informed father that he thought, his new wife could become a problem with the faculty. It was going to be a hard time for some years and father and his new wife must not expect to be well received by all.

On New Year's Day, after a very subdued New Year's Eve, my father's father asked him to come to the library for a smoke, drink and conversation. Knowing that his father had leaned more toward Germany, than France, what they discussed was really no surprise to father, nor to mother when he later told her of the meeting.

His father began by telling my father, even though one son had died, the two oldest boys had returned and it was obvious that he (father) would never directly inherit the farm. However, that did not mean he would be disinherited. With the war over and the wide need for food and with so much country destroyed, the oncoming years should prove very profitable, so his allowance would continue and in due time, he could expect some inheritance.

Speaking frankly, his father stated one major problem, "Your French wife." He continued, telling my father, "She seems like an excellent person and it is obvious to all that you are in love and now, with the child on its way, you must settle somewhere." Then his father dropped the expected bomb, "Your brothers and I have discussed this many times and we believe, since you decided to go your own way in marriage, it would be best if you settled somewhere else, other than Saint Avold. Perhaps, near your wives family farm at Vervins?"

Later that afternoon, father and mother went for a walk around St-Avold and he showed her many places of interest, including his special places when the family was staying in the townhouse in St-Avold. During the walk, where they could not be overheard by others, my father repeated to my mother what his father had said, and he told my mother, "We are people without a home."

Then, my mother guided my father over to a shaded bench out of sight of the passing people, and with tears in her eyes she reminded him, "We were people without a home when we met in the 'tent of the dying' and you were reborn." She continued, "We had created a very nice home in the middle of the war and we will make our own home again." Then she wiped her eyes with her handkerchief, grasped father's hand and with a determined walk, they made their way back to his families townhouse bound to determine their future as soon as possible.

The next morning, when they woke up and looked out the window at what was going to be a very nice day, both began to talk at once. Father stopped talking and told Mother to go ahead, she insisted that he go first, but he in turn, insisted she should start. After an awkward pause, Mother told Father she had dreamed of their

apartment in Sedan when the Americans visited. Even though they had both been in the German Army, not one of the Americans ever held that against them.

Before she could continue, Father nearly choked and then he began to laugh. As he got control of himself, he told mother, "You will not believe this, but I dreamed of the two Americans who told me what I repeated to you, just before we went to Vervins. Remember when the Americans told me, 'Hell man, if they kick you out of here come to the good old USA. We don't put up with that crap back home.' And when I was waking up, all I could think of was how to ask you, if you would agree we should go to America?" Then Mother told Father, "When I was waking up and looking out the window, all I could think of is, how to tell you we should go to America and begin a new life there with our new child."

That morning, as they sat down for breakfast with Grandfather, father told him they were going to immigrate to America, where his credentials should be accepted for teaching English, French, or German. Also Mother's nurses training and war experience would surely permit her to work as a nurse, sometime after their child was old enough, if that was ever required.

I was told, my grandfather took a deep breath, let it out slowly, and told them he had not wanted them to go so far, but if they insisted, he could not stop him. Then he told them, "I will tell the boys and we will discuss your decision and I will inform you of what we think of it, this evening."

When breakfast was over father and mother went to the telegraph office to sent a telegram to her family at Vervins. Telling Mother's family, they had decided their future life, and that they would visit them during the coming week to explain their decision to them.

That night, every one of the family ate dinner in the big dinning room, and for the first time laughter was often heard with everyone smiling. For the first time, mother told father's family all about her family farm at Vervins.

At the end of the meal, my grandfather stood up and told everyone, "To fill their glass." First, he toasted the new marriage and my upcoming birth. Then, he told father and mother, "We have decided to pay for all the expenses of your move to America; you can expect an allowance no less than twice a year and we plan a quarterly transfer of funds, if that is acceptable to you?"

Mother and father were stunned by what they had just heard and before they could say anything, my grandfather continued, "There is only one stipulation to what we propose. You must promise the child will speak German as well as English and when he is old enough to travel, you must come to visit during the summer, all expenses paid." My grandfather continued, "I have friends and you know them, who lost children to America and we refuse to do that. We insist that you come back and the child learns about us and Alsace-Lorraine."

My mother looked at my father with tears running broadly down her cheeks, unable to say anything. Then she saw that my father also had tears running down his face and was wiping them with his handkerchief. As mother watched, he wiped his eyes again, blew his nose loudly, stood up, picked up his glass, and on behalf of his wife, their child and himself, he stated, "We agree, without reservation."

Everyone stood up and lifted their glasses and, clinking them to either side across the table, all took a drink. No sooner was the toast given than my grandfather clinked a knife against his glass and said, "We are gathered here tonight, as much a family as we can be, but three of those who were family are not here, as we would wish. Please drink a toast, to your mother, sister and brother."

Less than a week later, at Vervins, an almost perfectly duplicated scene took place at mother's home. This time it was her family gathered together at the table and it was her family who had accepted the new husband, their child and their plan to immigrate to America.

Her parents told her, she and her husband would be beginning their new life in America with the help of her dowery and that, they would also be sending an allowance as the farm prospered. Then, to do no less than father's family, they insisted that they would share the expense of our visits to France when the child was old enough. However, to offset father's family's demand that the expected child learn German like a German, they told my parents that they also insist, the new child would learn to speak French as well as German and English.

It took some time to obtain the proper papers. To speed the process, father went to the American Headquarters in Verdun, where he presented his record of employment and talked to several Americans, all of whom listened to his story and all told him they would provide all the help they could. This included laying out all the steps that he must take in order to obtain permission to emigrate to America.

With their help, his visit to the American Embassy in Paris was set up and there, my father quickly received assurance, that the mail would soon arrive with all the documentation required for their immigration to the United States.

By April, they had all their required permissions, gave all their collected furniture to mother's sisters and at the end of April they took the train to Cherbourg to board their ship to America. And, by the time they left for Cherbourg, mother said, "I hope the ocean voyage is a smooth one, as I am beginning to think the baby might be wanting to walk to America."

Map of France, showing the major locations. Bapaume, upper left, father was wounded just to the west. First hospital was a few KM south. Cambrai, 2nd hospital location. Vervins, mother's home. Hirson, nearby market town. Sedan, basically where WWI ended and mother's and father's second apartment. Michelin Route Planning France 2014 # 726 1/1 000 000

Chapter Two
100% American

It was a fast, smooth trip and by the beginning of the second week of May they arrived in New York. Two days later, they arrived at the hometown of one of the Americans whom father had known in France. By the end of May, father was accepted as a Professor of German at the local university on the condition he agreed to complete a few specified courses at the university within two years.

With the help of his friend, mother and father were hosted at several other professors' homes and a few of the more prominent citizens' homes. As a result, when I was born on 27 June, 1919, mother and father were very surprised by all the people who came to visit, to see me, and present them with the missing things they had not purchased because they did not know if I was to be a boy or a girl. Much to Father's pride his first child was a boy and my Father's first words to me were spoken in German.

It was at this time, mother and father learned about an old custom in that part of the country of giving gifts for births and weddings that had been used by the presenting family. Passing the good luck of their lives onto the receiver that was contained in the used gift, as the giver had taken the risk of breaking in the gifts and passing on their own good luck within the gifts. Then the giving family purchased new replacement items, that in due time and the proper event would be passed on again with all that loving experience contained within.

My mother did not get to return to nursing for some years, as within a year my first sister arrived and then two years later the twins arrived.

Even before I learned to walk, one day in our home was English. The next day was German and the day after that, French. We grew up having to be able to switch from one to the other and then to listening to questions in all three and instantly having to reply in whatever language mother and father suddenly required.

With father at the university and mother's background as a nurse, we were expected to do well in school. We did have a big advantage, as the requirement to be able to speak the three languages also sharpened our minds while we were very young and we were always at the head of our classes. Twice, I was prevented by my parents from advancing ahead of the other kids I was growing up with when the teachers wanted me to skip a year of school, because I was usually that much ahead of the classes being taught. On each occasion, what seemed at the time like a good idea to me, was explained as one that would rob me of childhood and that I would be grown up all my life and a child for much less time than I realized.

In the late spring of 1924, my mother and father had made arrangements with their families in France to bring their four grandchildren home to visit. Father had made arrangements to leave the day after his classes ended and we took a train to New York, were in France just over a week later, and on a train to Vervins to mother's family's farm.

One somewhat strange thing happened during our visit that year. Both farms had grown as the families purchased land from other families who had lost their inheriting children and the problem of being German/French and real French had faded. During the weeks we were at Vervins, between the time the crops were planted and harvest would begin, father's family came to Vervins and the men and boys of both families were soon sitting by themselves in one of the sheds. The men were drinking the "Produit de Ferme" and without any direct intent the war came to be the subject of the conversation.

It turned out that one of father's and one of mother's surviving brothers had been in the same area at one time or another during the war and at that time, there were many battlefields to be visited. Before they had time to think about it, plans were made for all the men to go on a day trip and show the boys their war.

On our first day trip, we enjoyed a short visit to the Butte de Vauquois where both uncles had served. It had been an old French village on top of a hill when the war started. At the beginning of the war the Germans had come from the north and the French came from the south. For most of the war, until the Americans flowed around the hill in the summer of 1918, the Germans and French fought on that hill. Blowing each other up without gaining any advantage, as they fought each other.

When the war was over there was nothing left of the village and the hill had been torn open by 16 underground mines placed by both the Germans and the French. When we visited, the hill looked like a large loaf of bread that had been cut down the center before it was baked.

One of my father's brothers was telling us about living in the tunnels on the German north side where they had showers, bunk rooms, mess halls, and once in a while, as an officer, he even saw some women in the tunnels. He had been there for some time, when one day the French blew a mine and a large chunk of chalk fell on him resulting in his first wound.

He had no sooner told us the date of the explosion than my mother's brother who had also been wounded during the war started laughing. He was asked, what was so funny and he told the family group of men and boys, that he had helped carry the explosive for that day's mine into the hill when the mine was being set up.

Instantly, while he was still laughing, my French uncle reached across to grasp the hand of my French-German uncle and told him, they should consider themselves even as the German army had really got him a short time later.

Late that evening back at Vervins, as the "Produit de Ferme" came to grips with the men and their memories of the war, father's brother was talking about how the visiting American should take his son to see his war, as such vacation tours were now being conducted throughout the war's zones of devastation.

My father said his wound was one of being in the wrong place at the wrong time and it was their war that told the real story. Before we boys were aware of it, plans were put in place to send the women and girls shopping in Paris while the men and boys went for a long tour of the Great War battles.

It was not all that far from Vervins to Verdun where we stayed in the Hotel Bellevue and took daily tours to see the Verdun battle areas. Of course, we left very early one day when my German-French uncle took us back to the north side of the Butte de Vaquois to visit his German trenches and tunnels and my French uncle took us to visit his trenches and tunnels on the south side.

Though, he was a supply officer and interpreter, my father had not actually fought on the Somme. However, both families did go there one weekend to find the village where he was wounded and the village where mother and father had met. We visited memorials to the British, the Canadians and the Australians, including, a village named Thiepval where the British were constructing a very large arch as a memorial to those with no marked grave.

Visiting the village where he nearly died did not affect my father as much as I thought it would. However, when we arrived at the village where mother's hospital had been located, they asked the rest of us to wait for a while, as they walked to the location of the hospital and then across the bridged stream to the German cemetery tucked into the northern hillside.

When they returned, they showed us where the "tent of the dying" had been located when they met. Then, my mother pointed toward the cemetery and told us how they wanted to visit the men who had died under her care. To let them know, "That the one who had got away, had gotten away with her."

I left France that year with a large collection of books and maps about the Great War. Some were in French and some were in German, including a few original trench maps of the areas where each uncle had fought. That visit brought the Great War into my life and it continues as a passion to this day.

Until 1932, every year we made that visit to France. Each year the men and boys would travel to different areas of the war. Each year I gained more insight into the war and the roads of France and Belgium where the war took place. I became fascinated with war and among the three languages I could read and write, I came to know the intrigue of war. At the time, I was also learning Latin.

In the winter of 1931/32, as the Great Depression settled upon the world, my parents wrote to their families in France, and told them they were going to concentrate on saving the money from the trips to ensure their children had an excellent education. With times so bad, it was unseemly for them to show how much they had when so many of their friends were having money troubles.

As the years passed, I did gain a grade on most of my friends and graduated with Honors when I was not quite 17, in 1936, right in the middle of the Great Depression. Then, thanks to father's connection with the local university to which I had always thought I would attend, I instead found myself in one of the well-known universities in the fall of 1936. Of course the fact that each quarter for some years, my parents had been placing their payments from home in the bank to ensure the kids could go as far as they could, helped grease the path.

I had left home with the names of two professors at the university, given to me by friends of my family who had served with them during the Great War, as it was called at that time. They had all been officers in the "Fighting 69th" Division

and were now, members of the "Old Boys, "Fighting 69th"" Association." This did not mean I would receive special favors, but I might be given a chance to prove myself and do as well as I could.

During the first year my philosophy professor, one of the men to whom I had carried an introduction, asked me to wait after class as he wanted to talk to me. I could not think of anything I had done wrong and I was worried until he began to talk. He did not talk about my class work or anything I had done. Instead he told me about an excellent opportunity for me to go to a meeting with him that night as his guest.

One of the men of their division, who had made a name for himself during the war, was giving a talk before a selected group from the university that night and he thought that I should meet this man, as he could be a help in a future career.

That night, as we walked to the meeting, my professor told me that when we met outside of class, I should call him Mark instead of Professor. In class and in meetings during the day I should call him Professor, but otherwise, he was Mark. I admit, until his death some years later, when I was talking to Mark, I called him Professor much more than I called him Mark. I guess to me, it was a sign of ongoing respect during all those years.

I knew, the moment we arrived at the auditorium and I heard who the speaker was going to be, that I already knew a lot about the man. His name could be found in many of my Great War books, William "Wild Bill" Donovan had been in the "Fighting 69th" Division during "The Great War" and he had been awarded the *Congressional Medal Of Honor*. Even now, his name could often be found in the newspapers as a very well known attorney and a friend of President Roosevelt.

"Wild Bill's" speech was very impressive. The subject was the growing sickness in Germany and his belief, that within a few years the world would again be at war with Germany. And, he thought, it was beginning to look like we would soon have a problem with Japan, due to their ongoing war in China and their long occupation of the Korean peninsula.

After the discussion, when those in attendance retired to the bar in the faculty club, Professor Mark introduced me to someone with whom I would have a lot of interaction over the years to come. The introduction was a bit odd, as Mark introduced me to "Wild Bill" Donovan as the son of someone they would have shot the hell out of during the big one.

He went on to say, that I was a top-notch student and one hell of a linguist, able to instantly translate between English, French and German. My professor also told "Wild Bill" not to try to out talk me in Latin, as you do not want to go there. "Heck" I thought, "could I blame Miss Barnett back in high school who, when she found out my French was much better than hers, insisted I be no less than an equal in Latin?"

"Wild Bill" laughed and told me, that a time was coming very soon when people like me were going to have to do something for their country and just what did I consider myself, French or German or what? I straightened up in my chair,

and in my most serious voice I said, "Sir, I am a 100 percent American, as my parents arrived here in May, 1919, and I was born on the 27th of June."

"Wild Bill" really looked at me for the first time and he said, "Son, let me tell you something, the Navy tells all the sailors when it comes to the birth of their children, "The Navy knows you have to be there for the laying of the keel, but you do not have to be there for the launching." In your case, I think it makes no difference where your keel was laid, you have the right opinion of where you were launched!" Then he called a waitress over and ordered three bourbon and water drinks and when she brought them, he paid, slid one over to me and told me he was pleased to meet me.

I told him I was only 17 and not old enough to drink and he said, "If Mark thinks you belong with the "Fighting 69th," then you can damn well drink with us." It was the first liquor other than "Produit de Ferme" that I had ever partaken of and it was the first of many drinks I would enjoy over the years with men, such as the "Fighting 69th."

As we walked back through the campus that night, Mark asked me what I thought of the "Old Boy?" I told Mark that "Wild Bill's" speech had really been down to earth, and some what scary, also that I had really enjoyed being introduced to Mr. Donovan and being invited to have a drink with him.

Mark told me, that I had been set up just a little bit. He had served in Military Intelligence while in the "Fighting 69th" during the "Big One" and even before I arrived for the new school year, a couple of the men who were friends of our family had contacted him and informed him, that I would be a good one for him to guide in the right direction.

Mark went on to say, that tonight could be a beginning or an end for me. If I thought, what "Wild Bill" had to say was important and we must prepare for it, then Mark told me he was willing to be my mentor and help me do just that. However, if I decided, I wanted to go my own way, he would not ask again. It was up to me and no one would push me any further unless I wanted to be pushed.

We walked side by side for some time with no conversation and my mind was running as fast as the "Midnight Flyer" to California. Yes, I was attending university. Yes, I was taking the required basic courses, but I had to admit to myself, unlike my Father, I had not reached a point where I had internally set a course for the rest of my life. When we reached the place where I had to branch off to my living quarters, I asked Mark if I had to make my mind up immediately or could I think about it overnight?

Mark told me, at this time that was not a problem with him. However, he wanted me to know one thing. In the future, if I started down the road he was offering, I could find myself in a position where I would not have hours to think about a decision. Perhaps, if I was lucky, I would have a few minutes or less and yes, my life could depend upon the decision I had to make very quickly. As Mark walked off, he turned his head a bit over his shoulder and said, "Think about that, the decision you have to make will concern the rest of your life."

It was a long night, I don't think I ever really slept or if I did, my dreams were so vivid they were to me, as if I were awake. At some point, it hit me just what had happened last evening, This afternoon I was a kid, some months into a four-year university program and a few hours later, that kid had reached an intersection in his road of life and he had been given a quick review of what one branch offered. And, I had no real idea of what was up the other path.

Mark had been very open to me and Donovan appeared to be very certain that we were heading for another war. The way Mark had put it, either I could prepare to help the country during the upcoming war or I could just go along with the flow and see what happened. I thought about my interest in the Great War and of my interest in military history.

As I drifted along with these thoughts, I wondered what mother and father would tell me to do. I had heard their story of meeting during the war, marriage and emigration enough times to know that they had looked at their options, separated out the wheat from the chaff, and in the end they took a new path, that to many would seem the hardest, when they moved to a new country to begin a new life, and in my own mind, I was a direct representative of their new life.

Tonight, if Donovan was right, this new life, theirs and mine, was soon going to be challenged, then "*by Golly*," with Mark's help I could prepare to make certain their new life and mine were not torn-apart. Or, as Mark had stated, I could just go along with the flow. I thought, as I tossed and turned and perhaps drifted into and out of disturbed sleep, that perhaps I would help create the history of this new war?

That morning, I arrived at my class with Professor Mark a few minutes early and when he entered the room, I told him, I had made up my mind and I would be pleased for him to become my mentor. He told me, that when he left me last night, he'd known what my decision would be. He continued to tell me he had already stopped by Admissions and changed my class schedule for the next quarter. Then Mark said, "You are going to be very unhappy with me as I doubled your class load and have signed you up for a couple of activities. You are going to have to walk the walk, as well as talk the talk."

He was right. From a kid just going along in University, I suddenly became a driven person with a schedule set for me by someone else. Then, when I had a bit of extra time, I was out running with the track team and debating with the best.

To be honest, for the first time in my life I felt I was really being challenged and after a few months I was enjoying my life more than ever. I found I had time enough to join in after-hours discussions at the places where you could get a 3.2 percent beer as long as you did not act up. Then, I began to take on the extra work of reading everything I could on the world condition, as it deteriorated and Hitler continued to push Europe around.

Unlike many students I did not go home much, but apparently my parents knew what I was doing before I told them. When I did, they told me they were proud of what I was doing for their new country and my own country.

"Time flew," I found myself taking classes that I would never have thought of taking myself, basic electronics, chemistry, bookkeeping and a bit of this and that. Mark later told me, my final goal would be a broad Liberal Arts education with a second major in International Relations.

I got home for two weeks during the supposed summer break of 1937, as Mark had me taking a full load of summer classes. Some were toward my majors, but others seemed to make little sense. For example, the theater where Mark directed me to spend a lot of time learning the art of make-up and character creation. It was sort of odd, as he also insisted, that I was to refuse to take any acting parts. As appearing on stage could lead to my becoming recognized by more students which could put me at risk sometime in the future. "The best way for me to go," Mark told me, "was to be the one fellow in the university whom no one remembers was there!"

The school year of 1937/38 consisted of more of the same and I became even more aware of my ability to absorb information and later present what I had learned to others through presentation and debate.

In early March, 1939, during my third year, Mark told me that a couple of friends were coming to visit and he wanted me to meet them at his home one evening. I was to arrive right at 7:00 p.m. and be prepared to answer some unusual questions. No matter what I was asked, I was to answer the questions to the best of my ability and let the two visitors lead the conversation.

When I arrived, Mark told me his wife, Anita, and the kids, Carol, Joyce and Bill, had gone to stay at her sister's across town that Thursday night so we had the house to ourselves.

Mark introduced me to the two men, whom he referred to as old "Fighting 69th" buddies. They started by asking me about my family's visits to France. Then they asked about my friends as I was growing up and they asked me many questions about the classes I had taken and about the world political situation.

About 10:15, Mark who had been lounging in a chair at one side of his living room, sat up and said, "OK fellows, that's enough. If, you do not know what you want by now, you are not going to get it. It's time for a break and a bourbon and water." That was the second time some of the '"Old Boys" from the "Fighting 69th" and I had a drink together.

Mark set a bottle of good bourbon on the table along with glasses, ice cubes and a pitcher of water. Once the drinks were poured, the conversations immediately turned from their serious questions to their memories of the "Great War." Comparing their war to the war they also seemed to think was coming. All three of those older men listened to my opinions, just as much as they listened to each other. For about two hours, until the wall clock chimed midnight, we sat there as old friends and equals. I did not try to match the men, drink to drink. I politely refused each time they offered to refill my glass. However, when they insisted, I gave in and accepted the drink. We spent the entire time talking about the past and the upcoming war. I have no idea of how much we drank, but I do remember Mark putting a new bottle on the table. I left Mark's home that night feeling like I had

been put in a washing machine, washed, put in a commercial dryer and wrung out. It was not for some time that I found out those two hours were as big a test as the previous discussion.

Some years later when I was visiting Mark, we were sitting at the same table and he brought up the time we had sat there with his two friends. He laughed and asked, if I had any idea of what they were doing besides testing my ability to hold a casual conversation. When I replied I did not, he told me, that they were pouring bourbon into me faster than they were drinking their bourbon, as it was also a test of my drinking capacity. They knew, what was being planned for me and the job would demand someone who could handle his booze.

That brought back to me the memory of the next day, when I saw Professor Mark on campus. He had blood shot eyes and was complaining of a headache and when I asked him what was wrong, all he did was groan and excuse himself.

So I told him, that not only did I vividly remember that night, I also remembered seeing him badly hung-over the next morning when he hardly talked to me. His reply was, "The "Old Boys" had found themselves 'drunk under the table' by some 'young whipper snapper' who had no idea of what he was doing."

The next week, on Thursday morning, Mark told me to come to the house again at 7:00 p.m. as someone wanted to meet me. "Here we go again," I thought to myself as I knocked on his door at exactly 7:00 p.m.

Mark, as he let me in, told me his wife was going to start wondering what he was doing on those Thursday nights if we kept meeting like this and he told her and the kids to go stay with her sister. Then he introduced me to two men I had never seen before and reintroduced me to one of the men for the previous Thursday.

For some time that night they laid out exactly what had happened the week before. Then they told me, when the spring classes ended at the end of May they had a proposal for me. The proposal had to be answered that night, as my only option was to take the proposal or leave it. Then I was told, "If you leave it, you are to forget forever, that you had been offered the opportunity they were going to present to you." From the tune of the man's voice, I suddenly realized, he was extremely serious.

One of the men I had just met began to present their proposal, things were getting hotter in Germany, much faster than they had thought just a sort time before. Hitler was obviously setting up to take Germany to war and the United States had to start preparing, even if Congress continued to be Isolationist.

He went on to say, "Wild Bill" Donovan had been acting as a source of information that he fed directly to his friend, President Roosevelt. He had already traveled to several countries directly at Roosevelt's request and he was due to leave on another trip in the mid-July.

During some of his recent trips Donovan had come to suspect that he was not learning all he should. He realized, often, when he asked a question of someone in France, or Germany, the assigned interpreter would take much longer asking the question than he did in translating the answer back to Donovan.

When he got back from his last trip he had reported to Roosevelt and told some of Roosevelt's staff about his doubts concerning the interpreters they were being assigned. Donovan also said, that he knew he could bring his own interpreter. However, he was certain, if he did, he would not be taken to places where an assigned interpreter could not control the interaction.

After a discussion about what to do, Donovan suddenly said, "I think I have an answer." He told the assembled men about a young kid he had been introduced to by a "Fighting 69th" buddy, at a university where he had given a speech. The kid was a linguist who could easily move back and forth between German, French and English, probably in mid-word if he had to. The kid should be most of the way through school now, and perhaps, he could supply an answer to the problem?

He continued, somebody like that kid was exactly what he needed. No one would suspect that a very young aide, assigned to Donovan to gain some Foreign Service experience, could be doing what that kid would be doing for his country. After a meeting that was controlled by an assigned interpreter, if the young man could be trusted to remember the questions and the answers, it would be a great advantage for Donovan. Especially, if the unassuming aide could be hanging around while they spoke in their language thinking no one would understand what they were saying.

Well, that same afternoon they had called Mark and set up the appointment a week ago to test me to see, if I measured up to what Mark had told them. Well, I had passed their test, my situation was discussed at the highest levels and they had set up this second meeting to make it happen, that is, if I agreed.

"Here," one of them said, "is the situation. You will report to Washington, D.C. one week after classes end next month. There you will be commissioned directly into the United States Army as a 2nd Lieutenant. You will not be required to attend any of the normal military training or officer training. You will then attend three classes which I am not at liberty to tell you what they are until you have agreed to our proposal and signed the official secrecy documents that are required for the job you are going to be assigned."

He continued, "At the successful completion of the three classes, you will be given a complete set of civilian clothes that would fit the position you will hold. Then, no later than late July, you will be in Europe, traveling with Donovan and other official travelers as an aide. You will be assigned a basic support task that would permit you to be within hearing range of the meetings and you will absorb all the conversations held, not only between our people and theirs, but specifically their conversations on the side. If you agree, you will become a member of an Army Intelligence organization. And you can be assured, if you do it right, when this job is completed, your talents will continue to be required until the growing situation is under control, even if it leads to a war."

"Well, that's about it, what do you think," he asked? Mark, who had been sitting to the side remarked, "Remember when I told you one day that proper that you would have a life decision to make in a very short time? Well, son, this is one

of them! This is what I have been helping you train for and I want you to know you are up to the task being offered."

I looked at all the men and pointed out that I was just completing my third year here at the university, asking them, "When, will I be able to complete my degrees?" "Son," the Washington fellow said, "I cannot answer that question because I do not have an answer. However, I will tell you one thing. If you live through this, Uncle Sam will make damn certain you will complete your degrees."

I could see he was serious, and looking around the room at the visitors and then at Mark, I said, "Well, where do I sign?" Much to my surprise one of the Washington fellows reached into a leather case at his feet, laid out a set of papers, and told me to read them and sign beside each "X."

Some minutes later, after I had quickly read the papers and signed them, Mark handed him a Bible and the fellow told me to put my hand on the bible and repeat what he was going to say. When we were finished, I had been sworn to secrecy and for many years I would have been unable to write this story. Now ... the laws concerning that secrecy have changed and what the hell will they do to this old man for telling the truth of what we did?

Mark, as I finished my oath, stood up walked to the kitchen and then returned with a tray, on which sat a full bottle of bourbon, a pitcher of water, glasses and a container of ice cubes. Remembering how I felt after the last meeting, I made certain I drank a bit less than the others who seemed subdued that evening.

After the first couple of drinks, listening to the "Old Boys" telling their war stories, I asked the one fellow, if he could tell me the classes I have to take now? He replied, "I guess it will not hurt. The first one will be an intensive class on lip reading. That way, if you are too far away to hear the words, we will expect you to know exactly what they are talking about." He looked at the other Washington fellow and then turned back toward me and said, "I guess, I might as well tell you the rest. You will have two more classes, one is to prepare you for the international foreign relations bull-crap and the other is a course that will last a few days teaching you how to kill people and how not to talk when the bad people might be trying to force you to talk."

With that sinking in, I gulped, reached for my bourbon and water and found out just what happens when a bourbon and water found its way to a place where it should not be. As I was coughing and trying to catch my breath, with the fellow striking me on the back to help, everyone one of them was laughing and I was not so sure if they were laughing at me or with me.

I did get home to see the family for a very short visit. Then I was on my way to Washington. There I knocked on an unmarked door on the side of an old Great War building, as instructed, and introduced myself through a flap in the door. I was told to enter and found myself in a room with two fellows. One asked me to step on the two footprints painted on the floor, then lean forward and place my hands on the line on the wall, as he ran his hands over my body with a trip into an area where no hands other than my own had been since my mother washed me many years before. I quickly realized, that this is going to be serious business.

52

Within an hour I stood in front of an officer with a coat full of medals and all sorts of decorations, to be sworn into the U.S. Army as a 2nd Lieutenant. Then I was taken to an army base, where I was given all the items that were issued to such a rank. After that I was taken to a store where my escort informed the owner to measure me up for a uniform and have it ready as quickly as possible. He told the owner to tell me the amount of the bill and I nearly died. No one had said anything about this. He did add, that I would be receiving a briefing on being a 2nd Lt.

As we left, he was laughing and told me that I was being given very special treatment and my records were being set up now and any excess payments would be taken from my future pay. From there, he took me to a nondescript building in a nondescript area around Washington and introduced me to the person who was going to give me an advanced and very demanding course on lip reading. Both told me either I met their schedule or I would regret the day I did not.

The last thing on the itinerary that day, was to take me to a nearby hotel. It was a rather low class hotel, where I was checked in and told, this was where I would stay and eat while I was not down the street learning my lessons. And, I had thought I was out of school!

I met their schedule and was told I had finished much faster than they had anticipated. I enjoyed the same result with the foreign relations class. However the kill and/or be killed and shut up class lasted just as long as they said it would.

As a graduation present I guess, I was taken to a large store by someone from foreign relations. Upon his instruction, the sales people set me up with a complete wardrobe of clothes so I would blend right in during the upcoming trip.

The instruction for my phony job, which was in fact a real one, took all of ten minutes and by the middle of July, 1939, I was on my way to Europe.

I was in Europe and somewhat a witness when Hitler started World War Two and I was in Europe, when that part of the war ended in 1945. I did make a few short trips to the United States during that period when I had to deliver several vocal messages that were too secret to be documented in any way, to people very high up in the Chain of Command .

In December, 1939, I returned with one mission to the States and was called into my commander's office where he handed me a small box and a set of travel documents. He told me to get home for two days, have my mother and father place the insignia of a 1st Lieutenant on my shoulders and get back, as I was scheduled to be a liaison officer in England, between the American, British and French Armies.

For nearly two years I served in that position, which grew in responsibility after the "*Phony War*" ended in 1940, and Germany forced the British and French evacuation at Dunkirk. During that period, I came to know the future President of France on a first name basis, which proved to be a big help later in my army and civilian career. With growing responsibilities came growing rank, and I was promoted to Captain in the summer of 1941. On the day the Japanese bombed Pearl Harbor I was notified that I was to report to the central United States Command at once and take on new intelligence responsibilities.

During this period of the war, I was exposed to the intelligence involving the British use of the body of a man (who had killed himself) to save thousands of Allied lives during the invasion of Sicily. The British considered the use of and later, the desecration of the body to be fully justified, as the major military goal was reached. **Which proved, the end did justify the means.** This Top-Secret British project was the subject of the book, "*The Man Who Never Was*," Author: Ewen Montagu, released in 1953, ISBN: 978–1-4088-0921-1, eight years after the war after ended.

Another intelligence coup I had been involved with, was the use of a German, Enigma coding machine the British had recovered from U-559, on 30 October, 1942. Termed ULTRA, this program permitted British Intelligence to read German messages, giving the Allies a major weapon in the defeat of the enemy.

Another instance of the use of dead and even living personnel by the British, was the death of the English actor, Leslie Howard (*Academy Award, "Gone With The Wind,"* 1939). On June 1st, 1943, he was aboard an aircraft in flight between Spain and England, when it was shot down by German fighters. The British had become aware, thanks to the Enigma decoding machine, that the German fighters were going to attack the aircraft. The British could have saved the aircraft by diverting its flight path. However, had they done so, the Germans might realize the British had been able to read the Enigma coded messages concerning the attack, ordering the fighters to shoot down the civilian aircraft, forcing them to change the broken code.

For the *__greater good of the British Empire and the Allies__*, those aboard the aircraft were *__permitted to be killed__*, and that decision saved a large, unknown number of Allied lives during the war. *Again, __the end justified the means!__*

There are several other good examples. However, I would just be *__"Gilding the lily__*," when just a single proven "**desecration' of the dead**" by the British, provides the solid foundation for all the *Institutional Knowledge and Memory* required to justify what we put in place that you will be reading further on.

At the time General Eisenhower became the Supreme Allied Commander, in December, 1943, I was serving in a position that automatically moved me into a staff position providing General Eisenhower with daily updates on the changing intelligence of the various organizations from which I received reports.

During this early period, Ike called me into his office one day concerning an ULTRA question and when I had answered the question, as I was ready to leave, he slid a box across the table and told me, "You're doing a good job son, put these on," and I became a U.S. Army Major.

When the "D-Day" build-up began, I became very busy and began to be responsible for liaison between various American, British and French intelligence units and Ike's HQ. One of these led to the renewal of an old friendship with now Brigadier General Donovan, in command of the Office Of Special Services (OSS). This relationship lasted throughout the war and beyond, even after the OSS was disbanded by President Truman in late 1945. I still wonder, if the reason that President Truman disbanded the OSS, was for the published reasons, or that he

learned about the two **false Congressional Medal Of Honor Applications** that he had signed in May, 1945?

There were, in particular, three occasions after the OSS disbandment when a certain amount of cleaning up had to be undertaken. With ex-OSS men involved, some still in the service and some who were civilians involved with the newly created Central Intelligence Agency, (CIA), were prepared to do what had to be done, in order to insure their own military and civilian careers were not lost because they had done exactly as they had been ordered to do by their highest Commanders during the war.

The OSS had been formed soon after the beginning of the war in 1942, when President Roosevelt asked his good friend "Wild Bill" Donovan to create the new military unit. The OSS quickly became the one unit most involved in secret military operations in countries occupied by the enemy, both in the European and the Pacific theaters of war.

In 1947, President Truman finally realized his mistake in disbanding the OSS, and he created the CIA. Fairly quickly, many of the OSS Veterans of World War Two found themselves absorbed into the CIA.

Early on, when the invasion of Europe ("D-Day") was in planning, a problem that occurred during the African and Sicily Invasions caught Ike's attention. Taking care of the dead was a direct responsibility of the Quarter Master Corps (QMC), Graves Registration (GR). During that time, the control of the handling of American and other Allied dead had not been fully codified and many problems had occurred during the during proper identification of the dead.

Ike called me into his office one day and told me, that the time was soon coming when we would be on the ground in Europe. And, he wanted the Allied dead to be cleared as quickly as possible. He did not give a damn about how many dead Germans our troops saw and walked over. He wanted them to see as few dead Americans as possible.

As it was going to be an Allied invasion and not just an American invasion, Ike wanted someone on his staff who would be fully integrated into the recovery and disposition of the Allied and German dead. With my language ability and direct intelligence background, he had decided I would be the perfect staff member for that assignment. General Eisenhower told me I could complain all I wanted, however, I was going to be fully informed on the subject of the dead. As he put it, if he was asked one question about the dead, he wanted someone behind him to provide an answer, and you are going to be that person, like it or not. Then he said, "This should make you feel better about your new assignment, and he handed me a box containing the Gold Leafs of a Lt. Colonel."

So, during the oncoming months, I began to spend time with the **Q**uarter **M**aster **C**ommand, **G**raves **R**egistration units and the Allied Burial Commands, learning all the rules and regulations concerning the dead.

It was common knowledge to military historians during the Great War, that the French Army's casualty counts, especially the count of the dead, was off by a very large number. I know, included in that large number of unreported dead was

an uncle killed before I was born. As I have written, he left home in France, was in the French army and just, never came home after the war ended.

During one meeting a major decision was made. The only way to ensure that American commanders could not hide the truth of their losses would be for the Americans to put in place an extremely stringent set of regulations that would not permit any opportunity to hide our war dead. Or, so I had thought at that time!

When a military person was alive, they were in the inventory of the US military, such as the Army or Navy. They were assigned a military personal serial number and just like any other military inventory item, they became serial numbered inventory items to be used as required, thus the **GI** for **G**overnment **I**ssue.

Army **M**edical **C**orps personnel were attached to the active inventory item's commander to perform inventory maintenance.   And immediately, after an inventory item was damaged or broken, the physical control of that newly damaged/broken inventory item, became the **responsibility of the AMC personnel.**

When the GI inventory item was slightly damaged, the assigned AMC personnel would quickly repair the item for continued use. If, the damage was more extensive, the attached AMC personnel would submit the damaged inventory item to the next higher AMC repair depot for further repair. Slightly damaged GI inventory remained under the control of the active commander, until it recovered enough to return to active use. If, the GI inventory item had extensive damage requiring long-term repair, its control was turned over to the higher AMC repair depot by the active commander's AMC personnel. With that new physical control of the inventory item, the inventoried item's commander could seek a GI replacement inventory item.

In the case of a fully broken inventory item, the physical inventory control was to be immediately removed from the active commander, who in effect, lost all control over that particular **GI** inventory the moment it ceased to be active, either by accident or by design.

At the moment the **GI** inventory item was *broken beyond repair*, it was to be placed under the *full control of the QMC, GR.* When the **GR** personnel were unable to immediately recover the broken item, the **AMC** personnel attached to the active commander *became fully responsible* for the broken **GI** inventory item.

The unit's attached QM, MC were fully responsible for the broken GI inventory item until the human remains of the inventory item was officially transferred to QMC-GR Control. It is important that the reader remember the above when it comes to the memory of some men, later in this book.

If, a badly damaged GI inventory item could be fully repaired, it would be put on the GI inventory shelf, until it could be reissued to another active inventory commander, seeking replacement GI inventory items. Otherwise, the very badly damaged inventory item moved through higher and higher **AMC** repair depots, until it could function as well as it could be made to function as well as possible and then the GI inventory item was removed from the Army inventory and sent back to its place of original acquisition.

In review, as long as the GI inventory item functioned as designed, it was part of the active commander's inventory. The moment that inventory item became damaged or broken, the inventory item became the responsibility of the QM, Medical Corps personnel, attached to the active combat commander's unit.

Effectively, the moment the GI inventory item ceased to function, or at the moment of death, the "*living* **GI Personnel File**" of that inventory item was closed and a new "**Individual Deceased Personnel File**," or "**IDPF**" was created for the newly broken GI inventory item. The "living GI" Personnel File contained all the information required when the inventory item was functioning. The IDPF contains all the inventory item's information after the inventory item had ceased to function.

A transportation system directly controlled by the QM Corps was set up to move the information required by the QMC-GR Command. When a broken GI inventory item or "human remains" was turned over to GR that had no solid identification, it created a special inventory item control problem. If there were no inventory item serial numbered control tags (Identity Tags or Dog Tags), the inventory item's remains would be assigned a "**X-File**" (X- for Unknown) number at the temporary cemetery where the unidentified GI inventory item would be stored. Then, every effort was made by special Graves Registration investigative teams to find the correct GI inventory item identity of that broken inventory item.

I learned all this, as no nicety was involved in the meetings and field training sessions I attended. And, just about every gruesome way such an inventory item could be broken was discussed. It was possible, that no actual GI inventory item remains would be found if a large explosion occurred in the same location as the inventory item. It had been discovered during the African Campaign that the current inventory control tags would not survive the same conditions that destroyed the GI inventory item. To prevent this situation, as much as possible, tests were conducted in the United States using donated human remains in the various destruction processes the GI inventory items could suffer to determine the best materials for inventory control tags that would survive such destruction processes. Another prime example, of the "**desecration of the dead**" for the greater good.

The chosen material was determined to be a form of stainless steel, to be held onto the inventoried item by a chain created from the same material. Midway through the war, that new material was used to identify all the new GI inventory items. Existing GI inventory items, who had inventory control tags made of a monel metal that was easily destroyed were issued new inventory control tags made from the new stainless material.

As an item of interest, since the new inventory control tags contained an indentation on one rounded end, an ongoing rumor has existed that it was there so the control tag could be jammed into the feeding mechanism of the controlled GI inventory item after it was broken. This rumor has no standing in truth, the notch's sole purpose was to key the blank inventory control tag into the correct position in the embossing machine, which created the GI inventory control information on the ID tag, that was required for each GI inventory control tag.

Another known problem, was when certain destruction levels were reached, the GI inventoried item tended to come apart and the recovery of the broken GI inventory item's pieces had to be conducted in such a way as to insure that all the separated pieces of the GI inventoried item were collected. This was very important in the "*Final Disposition*" of the GI inventory item.

If the original recovery of a torn-apart GI inventory item was not properly conducted, *__missing pieces__* of the GI inventoried item might be found later. Then, instead of being correctly recombined with the correct GI inventory item, the newly found "remains" of a broken GI inventory item could result in a "X-File," or Unknown-File, being created when it should not have been created.

A decision was made, that specific controls had to be put in place to control such situations with the direct purpose of ensuring such situations would be reduced to a minimum. Therefore, **each time such a situation was created it had to be flagged and a special Graves Registration investigation had to be held to correctly resolve the situation. This investigation was under the full control of the QMC-GR Command. The active commander, the broken GI inventory item had served under, was removed from any control of that process.**

The special control put in place, **specified whenever more than a single recovery was required to recover the GI inventory item's remains, all recoveries had to be placed in a secure location.** They were to be **held at that secured location until a specific team of Graves Registration experts could investigate all the circumstances leading to the multiple recovery.** Each investigation was then codified and used to create new instructions that were sent to working GR units and field commanders to help prevent future repeats of the situation in question.

Even, if the originally recovered GI inventory item's remains had already been buried, those remains had to be disinterred to be placed with the additionally recovered GI Inventory Item's remains in the secured location. The multi-recovered remains could not be buried until the investigating QMC-GR team released the remains for burial in one or more official graves, as their findings specified.

During this time, I participated with Graves Registration companies as they trained in England recovering the dead from accidents and returned bombers. One specific incident, that I directly participated in, was at a much higher level than the GR men involved knew, the recovery of the dead at the Slapton Sands incident in late April, early May, 1944.

During an invasion practice, German E-Boats penetrated the shipping and sunk several ships. Among the dead were men with full knowledge of the planned "D-Day" invasion and Ike rushed me to the location to ensure each of their bodies and the invasion plan information they had were specifically accounted for, as it was possible that one of them could have been captured by a German E-Boat.

In the end, we accounted for all the specified GI inventory items. However, I did learn from T/Sgt. Wilmer E. Henderson of the 606th GR Company that was assigned to conduct the recoveries, the difference between a "floater" and a "sinker." A "floater" was an inventory item made nonfunctional by concussion and

a "sinker" was an inventory item made nonfunctional by a penetrating destructive force that rendered the GI inventoried item's natural ability to float, inoperable.

The final days leading to the invasion remain no more than a blur to me. However, General Eisenhower made the decision and after some worry, it became an outstanding military operation. When the time came, Ike made the decision to move his headquarters to the landmass of Europe, beginning at the end of September, 1944.

On the day before the move, I gave Ike an update briefing on the Top-Secret American Air Corps Squadron, that I had been involved with for some months.

On the night of 30/31 March, 1944, the Royal Air Force (RAF) had suffered its largest, single night's loss of the war. The Germans had figured out how the RAF had been confusing the German Radars and with this new knowledge, the Germans arranged to change most of their radar frequencies at once. That night with excellent radar reception and the use of a new method of intercepting the RAF bombers, using night fighters with top mounted machine-gun angled upward. The German pilots attacked from a blind spot under the RAF bombers. It was a bright moonlight night, their approach radar worked well and the RAF bombers could be seen from some distance away, they were very successful!

When the RAF returned to England the next morning on 31 March, 1944, 11.113 percent of the RAF bombers that had left for that night's mission did not return, 794 bombers had left England, 90 did not return.

The loss stunned the RAF and they stopped all missions for a short time. A most interesting circumstance is, that on 31 March, 1944, the first of our (USA) loaned Top-Secret B-17s loaded with new Top-Secret Radar Counter Measure (RCM) electronic equipment were attached to the RAF's 100th Group for testing.

The B-17's mission was to test the effectiveness of the Top-Secret electronic equipment's ability to electronically interfere with the German radars, and radio systems, this was to be done electronically, instead of using a mechanical device as the RAF had been doing. This consisted of dropping tinfoil strips cut to the specific frequency length required to match the German radar's radiating frequency. Dropping enough of this material out of their aircraft, created false returns on the German Radar displays. The British referred to this electronic wave reflecting material as "Window" and we referred to it, as "Chaff."

The first American B-17s, later changed to B-24s, due to their higher weight capacity, used the latest in Top-Secret electronic equipment aboard the aircraft to radiate electronic beams toward the German radars. This would created electronic interference on the German radar displays, which appeared as electronic snow on the displays, greatly reducing the German radar Operator's ability to see the RAF aircraft on their radar display screens.

General Eisenhower was extremely interested in the effect of the airborne Top-Secret electronic radar jamming equipment that we had attached to the RAF at the end of March. It was very quickly evident, the Top-Secret electronic equipment was proving itself, by constantly saving many RAF aircraft and their RAF air crews.

When the success of the Top-Secret equipment became known to Ike, he had informed me that I was to be directly involved with that squadrons operations (first the 803rd BS, then the 36th BS (RCM-Radar Counter Measures) and that I was to provide mission reports to him on the success of the missions of these aircraft,

General Eisenhower was positive, that as long as the secrets of the Top-Secret electronic equipment could be kept from the Germans, it would help lead to an earlier end of the war, while saving tens of thousands of lives. Ike was very concerned, that the Germans might somehow learn of the technology and use it against us. Just as they had now used the British mechanical radar counter-measure knowledge against the British and us, once they had learned the secret. Ike realized, if the Germans learned these new secrets it could lead to a longer war and the death of even more military personnel and civilians on both sides.

When I completed the briefing, General Eisenhower handed me an open box with two Silver Eagles in it and told me, Colonel, go ahead and pin them on, as you might need the wings to get to Heaven if anything goes wrong "Over There."

I had turned 25 just after the invasion. For someone not directly involved in the fighting, without the normally required military training, when I had my bourbon and water that night, I felt very proud of my achievements.

The next day, I was on a separate aircraft on my way to France and the new forward HQ, a short distance northwest of Reims.

A day after Vervins was cleared of Germans, I arrived at my mother's family farm with two well-armed guards accompanying me, to find that all but one of her family had survived the war. The production from their farm had helped feed the Germans and as long as they behaved, they had been reasonably safe.

My mother's sister's husband, who had been wounded and captured by the Germans during what was now called World War One, had been caught when he was helping an American flyer evade the Germans. The Germans had sent the American to a POW camp. My uncle, one of the men who had traveled with us along the previous war's battle zones during my visits to France, had been executed by the Germans. His body was later turned over to the family, as an example to the people of Vervins of what was done to those who aided the enemy.

After Ike's HQ arrived in France, I was also assigned an additional duty of keeping an eye on General Patton, when he was released into the battle. This, I accomplished, with the help of General Hap Gay, who was assigned as Patton's Chief of Staff. Gen. Eisenhower was constantly worried about Patton's tendency to talk, when Ike thought he should shut up. I met with Patton many times while working on various projects for Ike and found, like me, he was a bourbon man.

One night while in Verdun, I spent some hours with Generals Patton, Gay, and Weyland, the XIX Tactical Air Command Commander. We were reviewing plans for a new drive to drive the Germans the rest of the way out of France, which Patton was opening on the 8th of November, 1944. Patton, as he had with many others, told me that, "Weyland was the best damn general in the Air Corps and without Weyland his breakthrough across France could have failed."

On the night of 8 November, 1944, the day General Patton's drive against the German stronghold of Metz opened, I was back at Ike's forward HQ, where I was to stay, as Ike was on a personal inspection tour to the newly captured German city of Aachen.

After following dispatches updating Headquarters on Patton's new attack all day, I spent the evening in the "O" Club. There, I discussed the news with others and we all decided, that Patton might be on the way to end the war earlier than many thought was possible and, if that happened, he would certainly earn the Honors for doing so.

I went to bed, at Gurex, expecting a good nights sleep and if I dreamed, all memory of those dreams disappeared the moment the telephone rang and I answered it to learn the "Crap Had Hit The Fan And The Results Were Never Distributed Evenly."

And, my deep involvement in what happened over the next few days began that morning and has continued to this day.

(**Note**: Now you know, who I am and what you will be reading next is why I was forced to become involved and follow the verbal orders given directly to me by General Eisenhower.)

(**Note**: The author has included many photographs and supporting evidence to prove to you, that the events in the following chapters, did take place!)

United States Army In World War II
The European Theater of Operations
The Supreme Command
by Forrest C. Pogue
CENTER OF MILITARY HISTORY
UNITED STATES ARMY
WASHINGTON, D.C.. 1989
Library Of Congress Catalog Card Number: 53-61717
First Printed 1954-CMH Pub 7-1

Page 277: "In accordance with his policy of keeping a small advance headquarters as near as possible to the army groups, General Eisenhower directed that a camp be built forward of Versailles. This headquarters was opened on 19 September, at Gueux about seven miles north-west of Reims, just off the Laon highway"

"General Eisenhower continued to use this advance site until 17 February, 1945 when the forward echelon of SHAEF moved to Reims."

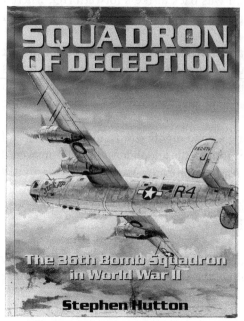

A complete story of the 36th Bomb Squadron service during World War Two in Europe. Contains over 330 rare photographs and illustrations, published for the first time.

Chapter Seven - Includes "**226**" A must read to fully understand why the shoot down of "226" and the coverup took place.

Schiffer Military History
ISBN: 0-7643-0796-7

Chapter 7 Night and Day - I Walk Alone

November, 1944, consists of twelve pages which will fully flush out the story of "**226.**" With permission of the author, Steven Hutton, information from his book was used in this book, with the author, in turn sharing his research.

At the time the book was written, the exact location of the crash had not been located. Plus, they thought "**226**" had been shot down by FLAK. This author personally interviewed the survivors and with additional research, discovered that "**226**" had been shot down by "**Friendly Fire**" and its **Official Aircraft Record states, the aircraft been turned over to the RAF as a fully functional aircraft twenty days after "226"and three crewmen had become small pieces in a field in France.**

Chapter Three
"The <u>Next To Last Flight</u> Of The '*Lady Jeannette*'"
Over Enemy Lines

Early in the damp, cold, fall morning of 9 November, 1944, at the Deopham Green, Station 142, American Eighth Air Force Base, a Flight Engineer/Top Turret Gunner T/Sgt. Russell W. Gustafson was standing on the hard stand, next to the forward escape hatch of the B-17G-35VE, "Flying Fortress," named "*Lady Jeannette.*" He was anxiously waiting for the arrival of the bombardier who had not shown up for the earlier briefing.

The rest of the crew had arrived over an hour ago and except for Gustafson they were waiting in the B-17 for the mission to begin. Hanging on the wing hard-mount close to Gustafson was a 1,000 pound bomb. There was another 1,000 pound bomb on the other wing and eight 500 pound bombs loaded into the bomb bay. All the flight checks had been completed and it was almost time to "start engines." Soon, the bomber would have to begin its taxi to the runway, if it was to meet its scheduled take-off time.

The bomber Gustafson was standing under was the Boeing B-17G-35VE, SN: 42-97904, named "*Lady Jeannette.*" She had been built at the Lockheed plant in Burbank, California, and delivered to the Army Air Corps on 1 April, 1944. After a refitting just more than two months later, she reported for duty with the Eighth Air Force in England, on "D-Day," 6 June, 1944. She was a slick, silver-skinned bomber with the group's large white identification letter **L** inside the black box painted high on her vertical stabilizer.

Just under the box was the bomber's serial number with the 4 removed from the front, so it read 2-97904. A large **+R** was also on the tail painted below the serial number, showed the B-17 belonged to the 729th Bomb Squadron,

T/Sgt. Russell W. Gustafson
Gott Crew: Flight Engineer
          Top Turret Gunner
Jamestown, New York
Photograph: R.W. Gustafson

452nd Bombardment Group (H)
Tail Marking

Graphic: Willis S. Cole, Jr.

729th Bombardment Squadron (H)

Photograph:
USAF/Historical Research
Agency (HRA)

452nd Bombardment Group (H)

Photograph: USAF/HRA

while the Square L showed she belonged to the 452nd Group (H).

A previous crew had named the bomber in late June or early July and her name, *"Lady Jeannette,"* was written in a red script across the nose. It is most likely the name resulted from a previous 452nd Bomb Group bomber, named *"Lady Janet."* A B-17 bearing that name had been destroyed on the ground in Russia in May, 1944, when the Germans followed an overflight mission that had bombed Germany, and landed on Russian airfields.

That night, the Germans bombed the Russian air bases used and destroyed a large number of American bombers. There is some existing proof that the second sign painter miss-spelled *"Janet"* and instead, he had painted *"Jeannette."* Most likely, a misunderstood communication between the painter and the person who told him the name. At that time Jeannette was a well-known name and if you sound out the two names, with the right accent they do sound very similar.

All, but two of the regular Gott crew were on board the *"Lady Jeannette"* for this mission. Crews, from the time they were assembled in the United States during training, would carry the pilot's name throughout their service together. The Command Pilot was 1st Lt. Donald J. Gott (Harmon, Oklahoma) and there was a substitute Copilot, 2nd Lt. William E. Metzger, Jr. (Lima, Ohio) who was on his second mission with the Gott crew, in order to gain experience with a crew that was already combat hardened. Metzger was normally a member of the Green Crew, which was also flying their second combat mission.

Second Lieutenant Gerald W. Collins (Los Angeles, California), the normal Gott crew copilot, would be flying aboard the Green crew's B-17 during this mission, to provide that pilot (Green) and the Green crew with an experienced combat pilot during their early missions.

As he waited, the flight engineer had a lot on his mind. It was part of his job as Flight Engineer(FE)/Top Turret Gunner (TTG), to work with the ground crew chief to insure the bomber they were to fly was ready for the mission. If there was an in-flight equipment problem, the FE/TTG was expected to fix it.

64

2nd Lt. William E. Metzger, Jr.
Congressional Medal Of Honor
GO38 16 May 1945
Copilot: "*Lady Jeannette*"
B-17G-35VE   SN: 42-97904
KIA: 9 November 1944
Buried(?): Woodlawn Cemetery
            Lima, Ohio
Photograph: Jeanne Metzger
            Scholfield

1st Lt. Donald J. Gott
Congressional Medal Of Honor
GO 38 16 May 1945
Pilot: "*Lady Jeannette*"
B17G-35VE   SN: 42-97904
KIA: 9 November 1944
Buried(?): Fairmont Cemetery
            Harmon, Oklahoma
Photograph: Winona Gott Derrick

In flight, as the FE, he had no seat and stood behind the pilots during the mission to provide instrument checks and fuel control. When the B-17 was in enemy territory, he assumed the TTG position and he would be sitting on the bicycle seat in the rotating Sperry top turret. There, his job as TTG, was to provide defensive cover fire against attacking German fighters in the air space above and around the bomber.

This was the Gott crew's third combat mission aboard the "*Lady Jeannette*." They had just been assigned the "*Lady Jeannette*" as their permanent bomber, after their last mission to Ludwigshafen. She was to be the crew's permanent bomber for their remaining eight combat missions.

During their previous missions, the crew had flown in whatever bomber they were ordered to fly. As the FE/TTG states, "It was kind of like working at a bus barn, on a large bus that needed nine men to run it. We went to the office and they told us to take the number ten bus one day and the number three bus the next

day. It was a good sign that we were fast becoming an old crew when we were assigned a permanent bomber."

As Gustafson waited, he thought of home and the letters he and the rest of the crew had been writing, telling their families they were planning on being home in time for Christmas.

He had just eight more missions after this one to reach the required, magic number of 35 combat missions, and at the rate the Squadron was flying, they should easily reach that number by early December and he could be home for Christmas.

The Gott Crew was assigned to the 729th Bombardment Squadron (H), the (H) meaning a heavy bomber such as the B-17 or B-24. The 729th Bomb Squadron was one of four bomber squadrons assigned to the 452nd Bombardment Group (H). The other Group Squadrons were the 728th, the 730th and the 731st Bombardment Squadrons (H). The 452nd Group along with the 96th and 388th

2nd Lt. John A. Harland "Jack" Gott Crew: Navigator Chicago, Illinois

Photograph: Harland Family

Groups made up the 45th Combat Wing of the 3rd Air Division of the Eighth Air Force of the United States of America. The Group was based on Air Station 142, located at Deopham Green, Norfolk, England.

Though the 452nd Bomb Group consisted of four squadrons, it was common practice for only three squadrons to go on a mission, while the fourth squadron, in rotation, "*stood down*" for rest and maintenance. It would take an average of 48 group missions for a crew to fly their required 35 combat missions, if they flew every available mission. It was normal for most crewmen to miss one or more missions due to sickness, training and other squadron duties. To make up for the missed missions, they often became a standby crewman and were assigned as fill-ins for crewmen of other crews who were unable to fly that day's mission.

If, a crew member lost his position on a regular flying crew, he would fly his remaining missions as a fill-in crew member and it could take weeks longer to complete the required number of combat missions so that he could rotate home.

The flying personnel of the squadron were woken up at 02:00 on the morning of 9 November 1944 for the 162nd mission of the group. They grumbled as usual when they got up, washed, shaved well so the oxygen mask would not itch as much, got dressed, went to eat breakfast, and then reported to the Group's briefing room to be briefed for the day's mission.

During their briefing that morning, the 729th Bomb Squadron's crews were told the target of this day's thousand plane mission was the Metz-Thionville region

2nd Lt. Joseph F. Harms
Gott Crew: Fill-In Bombardier
2nd Combat Mission
New York, New York

Photograph: Joseph F. Harms

of France. For the record, it was the second day of General Patton's long planned battle to complete the drive to force the Nazis out of France. The purpose of the mission was to soften-up enemy targets that were hindering the advance of Patton's Third Army. The Secondary Target, in case they were not able to bomb their Primary Target, was to be railroad marshaling yards and German airfields, located close to the city of Saarbrucken, Germany.

The crew Navigator, 2nd Lt. John A. Harland, (Chicago, Illinois) made copious and methodical notes during the crew briefing. Harland listed the altitudes, the headings and the Emergency Landing Field (ELF), that was to be used for emergency landings in Europe during this mission. The mission's flight path was charted on the large wall map, and he used a flimsy (a light paper that was easily destroyed) to list the required information for him to navigate the bomber to the target, even if the rest of the bomber group was missing.

The navigator made special note of the ELF location. It was a recaptured French air base near Péronne, France. The base had been occupied by the German Luftwaffe until the end of August, who left just before that area of France was "Liberated." It was now referred to as Station A-72 and it was the current base of the 397th Bombardment Group (M), a B-26 Group (M - for Medium Bomber), that was part of the Ninth US Air Force. The air base was located about 150 air miles west-northwest of the primary target and 190 air miles from the secondary target.

If the "*Lady Jeannette*" got in trouble after crossing over into Europe, this was the place to land, if possible! The weather for that day's mission over France was reported to be 8/10ths cloud cover.

At the beginning of the briefing the Pilot, 1st Lt. Donald J. Gott had been checking his crew's attendance and he realized the crew's regular bombardier was not at the briefing. 1st Lt. Gott reported this to the squadron operations personnel and upon completion of the briefing, he and the rest of his crew departed for the "*Lady Jeannette*" located on her hard stand.

At the hard stand, the crew installed their machine-gun, crawled into their flight suits and, except for "Gus", climbed into the B-17. They finished their checks and assumed their take-off position in the B-17G. It would soon be time to start the engines and officially begin the mission as the wheels rolled. Below the nose, the

FE/TTG talked to the ground crew-chief, while waiting for the missing man.

Other nearby B-17s were starting their engines when a jeep pulled up to the *"Lady Jeannette."* Second Lt. Joseph F. Harms (New York, New York) the officer sitting in the shot gun seat, got out and hurried over to the men standing under the waiting bomber. The arriving officer told the men he was the replacement bombardier. To complete their bombardier listing on the required flight manifest/loading list. Gustafson asked the replacement bombardier for his name and serial number and entered the information on his flight manifest/loading list. As the officer swung up into the forward hatch, the FE/TTG finished filling in the form on his clipboard. Gustafson removed a copy of the flight manifest for himself, which he stuffed into his flight jacket pocket. After he gave the ground crew chief the manifest clipboard, he swung up through the escape hatch and made his way up through the crawl-way between the pilots to take his standing position behind them. As soon as he was in his position the pilot and copilot prepared to start the engines, to warm them before they began their mission roll. The crew on board the departing *"Lady Jeannette"* consisted of:

T/Sgt. Robert A. Dunlap
Gott Crew: Radio Operator
Miles City, Montana
KIA, 9 November 1944
Buried(?): American WWII
    St-Avold Cemetery, France

Photograph: Bonnie Dunlap
    Owens - Sister

27 Pilot:	Gott, Donald J., 1st Lt.	SN: O-763996
2 CoP:	Metzger, William E., 2nd Lt.	SN: O-558834
19 Nav:	Harland, John A.., 2nd Lt.	SN: O-723355
1 Bomb:	Harms, Joseph F., 2nd Lt.	SN: O-2056698
25 RadOp:	Dunlap, Robert A.., T/Sgt.	SN: 39696406
26 B.T:	Fross, James O., S/Sgt.	SN: 38462533
26 T.T:	Gustafson, Russell W., T/Sgt.	SN: 12139299
22 T.G:	Krimminger, Herman B., S/Sgt.	SN: 34890339
25 R.W:	Robbins, William R., S/Sgt.	SN: 11051000

Within a few minutes, the wheels of the *"Lady Jeannette"* began to roll along the taxi-way to reach the take-off runway. For them, Mission 162 had finally, officially begun and soon the bomber would depart the Deopham Green area for the Group's assembly, before departing for Europe

S/Sgt. William R. Robbins
Gott Crew: Right Waist Gunner
            Crew Photographer
Worcester, Massachusetts

Photograph: William R. Robbins

As the *Lady Jeannette,* B-17G, "Flying Fortress," began her taxi-roll, the maintenance chief walked away, reviewing the Flight Manifest/Loading List he would soon turn over to Flight Operations. Each of the onboard crewmen's combat mission total, his crew position, his name, rank and his serial number was listed on the form. To insure all that information would be available if the B-17, for any reason, did not return from the day's mission.

As the *Lady Jeannette* began its mission, the crew worried about all the things that could go wrong in the next few hours. Especially during take-off and assembly, which could be considered the most dangerous time of any mission. The bomber was weighted down with a full bomb load, full ammunition load, and required fuel load. The loss of one engine at a critical time during take-off, could cause the bomber to crash in explosion and flame with the loss of the entire crew.

Once, the *"Lady Jeannette,"* had completed a successful take-off she still had to circle and climb to the correct altitude to rendezvous with the other bombers of the squadron and group. This late in the year, they were taking off while it was still dark and the air over East Anglia, England would be full of bombers and fighters. While over a thousand airplanes gathered into the formations required to protect the bombers in combat. The Norfolk area of East Anglia was nicknamed *"Little America"* because of all the Americans stationed *"Over There."*

At 05:30 hours, Group-Time, on 9 November, 1944, the 729th lead squadron took off. One of those many bombers thundering safely off the runway, disturbing the early morning sleep of the English people around the air bases, was the *"Lady Jeannette"* and her crew of nine men.

When the last of the Group's bombers had taken off, the 452nd Group had 35 bombers en route, and four PFF B-17s equipped with H2X-AN/APS airborne radars (named: *Mickey*) was used for blind bombing and navigation during poor visibility conditions. The mission's assigned Primary Target was a German defense point located twenty miles north-east of Metz and ten miles east of Thionville.

Referred to as the "A" Squadron in all the Group's 162nd Mission Reports, the 729th Squadron was the lead Squadron in the group formation. The *"Hot Dog"* unit' (as it was called by members of the other squadrons) Lead Navigator, 1st Lt.

Stephen H. Rhea, reported the leading squadron of the 45th Combat Wing had left the ground to begin forming up over the Buncher Beacon, Number 20, located near their base at Deopham Green, England.

The Buncher Beacon was a low powered radio beacon used by the group to assemble the airborne squadrons in flight formations. The bombers would fly a box pattern, using the signal from the beacon as they climbed at a specified climb rate, and as they assembled, they formed into their combat formations.

"Lady Jeannette" climbed slowly and after two and one-half hours, the 452nd Bomb Group completed its formation and left the Deopham Green Buncher Beacon area for the First Wing Assembly Point at Mildenhall at 08:05 hours, at an altitude of 18,000 feet.

During this period of time the crew completed their tasks required before combat, and when told to do so by the bombardier, the right waist gunner, S/Sgt. William R. Robbins (Worcester, Massachusetts) pulled the safety pins from the bombs. Many aircrews' bombardiers would remove the fuse safety pins,

S/Sgt. James O. Fross
Gott Crew: Ball Turret Gunner
McAllen, Texas

Photograph: Fross Family

however on the Gott crew, S/Sgt. Robbins had been given the task. The fuse pins had to be pulled before reaching a high altitude, as the pins might freeze in the fuse if the crew waited too long before pulling the pins. Following his usual practice, Robbins placed a couple of the fuse pins with their tags, in his pocket as a souvenir of the mission. After they got back, he would write the target of the mission on his souvenir fuse safety pin tags.

As altitude was gained, the crew put on their uncomfortable oxygen masks and began breathing using large oxygen tank system placed throughout the bomber. In addition, they had portable oxygen bottles available in case they had to leave their positions at high altitudes.

At 08:36 hours, the 45th Combat Wing joined the other four combat wings, the 4th, the 13th, the 92nd, and the 93rd, to form the 3rd Air Division at the 3rd Air Division's assembly point. Once that was achieved, they flew toward the coast and crossed the English coast at 08:54. Three hours and twenty-four minutes after take-off, while over the English Channel, each gunner fired a short burst to be certain the machine-guns were in working order.

As the bombers continued to climb, they flew into a tail wind at the altitude of 20,500 feet, blowing from 330 degrees at 32 knots. The further east they flew, the more they became part of a large stream of bombers and fighters heading toward targets in Europe.

As they approached the day's mission target, German **FLAK** began to blossom around the formation.

Photograph:
S/Sgt. William R Robbins
Gott's Crew - Waist Gunner

The 452nd Group crossed the "Enemy Coast" (even after Liberation, the European coast was considered the "Enemy Coast") at an altitude of 20,500 feet, at 51-00 degrees north and 02-00 degrees east, which is just north of Calais, France. As they continued along the planned flight route, the cloud cover was eight-tenths of the sky/ground and as they got closer to the "Primary Target," the cloud cover continued to increase to nine-tenths cover.

"Little Friend" P-51
Markings: CVX, Tail No: 2107602

Photograph: S/Sgt William R. Robbins.

The Group reached the bombing altitude of 23,000 feet at 09:13 hours at 50:37 degrees north and 02:50 degrees east as it approached Lille, France. As the bomber stream continued east along the flight route, maintaining their assigned bombing altitude, the tail wind changed from 330 degrees to 303 degrees, blowing at 60 knots (69.04 mph wind speed).

When the 452nd Group closed on the IP, or Initial Point of the bomb run, of the Primary Target, Rethel, France, they noticed the group ahead had turned off the bomb run and started for the Secondary Target; the 452nd followed in turn. The secondary was to be bombed on the decision of the 45th "A" (729th Squadron) Leader. The squadron leader had been informed by radio that the dust raised by the bombs dropped by the preceding groups and the increasing clouds obscured the Primary Target. Therefore, the remaining groups were to select the mission's Secondary Target, the railroad marshaling yards of Saarbrucken, Germany.

When they reached the Secondary Target's IP, the group turned south toward the Secondary Target located about fifty miles south of the IP. (The IP is a landmark easily visible from the air and one which could also be seen on the radar display, aboard the PFF aircraft accompanying the Group.)

The "**Lead Bombardier's**" report states, "...the bomb bay doors were opened three times during the mission. First, the bomb bay doors had been opened

over the Channel, again at 05 degrees east and then again after leveling off after the turn at the IP, en route to the Secondary Target.

The report continued, "At IP it was seen that the run would have to be started PFF, or radar controlled. Strong drift was encountered but *Mickey* Operator got it killed early. *Mickey* checks were coming in good and the dropping angle found by synchronizing short held good. A break developed in clouds and I picked up marshaling yards and began relining rate. **FLAK** came up pretty accurate and did its best to interfere with run. I was knocked off sight (*Norden Bombsight*) by **FLAK** and did not have a chance to pick up Target again before bombs away."

The "*Lady Jeannette*" was flying in the number-four position in the squadron's formation, which was the leading squadron of the group formation. The bombardier had opened the bomb bay doors, once the bomber had leveled onto the bomb run after passing the IP.

The crew was all in position, with "**FLAK** jackets (armored jackets)" on and all wore their helmets. In the nose the bombardier, Harms, was watching the lead bomber. His job was to toggle or release the bombs out of the "*Lady Jeannette*," when the first bombs fell from the bomb bay of the lead bomber. The navigator, Harland, was sitting at his table plotting the flight and assuring himself that the plot was correct.

In the cockpit, the pilot, Gott, was attempting to keep the bomber flying in its formation position as smoothly as possible in the wake of the bombers ahead and the copilot, Metzger, was scanning the dials and helping control the bomber during the bomb run. His hands rested lightly on the controls, just in case the pilot was suddenly put out of action.

Sitting on the bicycle seat of his Sperry turret was the flight engineer/top turret gunner, Gustafson. He was facing toward the nose, scanning the sky for enemy fighters, although after flying 26 combat missions Gustafson knew the major threat to the "*Lady Jeannette*" was from the shells of the German anti-aircraft guns or "*FLAK*," and not from German fighters.

As the front lines shrank during the German's retreat, the Germans were able to concentrate their anti-aircraft artillery around their cities and factory targets. The Germans now had radar fire control for their anti-aircraft batteries. This electronic gun-aiming control enabled the Germans to track the height, speed, and direction of the enemy's flight, allowing them to aim their anti-aircraft cannons so the fired shells would have much higher odds of reaching the correct altitude and position in the sky before exploding.

In the radio compartment, located behind the bomb bay, radio operator T/Sgt. Robert A. Dunlap (Miles City, Montana) was sitting at his crew station working his radios. Behind him, down in the ball turret, all scrunched up behind his guns was the ball turret gunner, S/Sgt. James O. Fross (McAllen, Texas). Fross's turret was rotated so he was looking toward the nose, so he could count the bombs as they dropped from the wings and bomb bay. Once the bomb drop was complete, Fross would tell the bombardier and pilot how many bombs had fallen so that they

could determine that no bombs were hung up in their shackles and the bomb bay doors could be safely closed.

Standing at the right waist machine-gun was the right waist gunner, S/Sgt. William R. Robbins (Worcester, Massachusetts). Not far away was his duffle bag, for Robbins always took everything he had on a combat mission. If Robbins was going to bail out, he was going to have his stuff, should he become a POW.

When the Gott Crew arrived at the 729th Squadron, listed as Crew Inventory item: Crew 33-C (Crew AC-75, PV900CJ/16349CJ-4/4), on 17 August, 1944. All the enlisted men were Corporals and they were given an automatic promotion to Sergeant (Temporary). However, before their first combat mission took place, one of the ten men on the Gott Crew, left waist gunner Sgt. Irving (No Middle Name (NMI)) Hirsch (Chicago, Illinois) was relieved from his assignment. After the rest

A bomber of the 452nd Group, that drifted over the Gott Crew's B-17 at the time of bomb drop. This is a famous Eighth Air Force photograph often used in books and on posters. The pilot had the bombardier close the bomb bay doors and they carried the bombs back to England where the group commander chewed out the pilot for not dropping the bombs on the Gott Crew's B-17.

Note: The name of the over-head bomber has been censored.

Photograph: S/Sgt. William R. Robbins, Gott Crew
Right Waist Gunner, original proof copy

of the Gott Crew had flown its first mission, Hirsch was sent to a "repo-depot"or GI inventory replacement depot. From there, he was shipped to the 15th Air Force in Italy and served as a ball turret gunner aboard B-17s until the end of the war.

The Army Air Corps was somewhat short of qualified gunners at the time and since the enemy fighter threat had been greatly reduced, the arriving crews were stripped of one waist gunner. Another very good reason for this action was the fact, that waist gunners aboard full ten man crew bombers had shot at other bombers in their own formations. If their side of the bomber was on the same side formation then German fighters flew through the formation, the gunner would shoot away and sometimes spray another bomber. Therefore, it was somewhat safer for the rest of the bombers to have just one waist gun position normally manned, the gun position on the side away from the formation. The inside formation waist position did have a machine-gun in the position and the waist gunner could switch from one to the other as required.

Tucked away back behind the tail wheel and under the bomber's tail was the tail gunner, S/Sgt. Herman B. Krimminger (Marshland, North Carolina). Just behind him, along the small crawl-way to the waist, was a small escape hatch that opened just under the right horizontal tail plane. He was responsible for the airspace behind the "*Lady Jeannette,*" Krimminger was scanning the sky for enemy fighters and watching the other bombers following in the formation stream behind the "*Lady Jeannette*."

Though none of the gunners aboard "*Lady Jeannette*'' had ever shot their machine-guns at an attacking German fighter, they were busy scanning the skies just in case. After their first missions, the crew had worked out in their minds, if they were attacked by German fighters, they had a chance with them. They could shoot back at the attacking fighters. However, the possibility of the **FLAK** ahead caused each of them to be uneasy. They had all seen bombers go down, bombers shot down by German **FLAK**! Damaged bombers with few or no parachutes seen to follow the bomber down. They knew they could do nothing about the German **FLAK**, but hope "*Lady Luck*" was on their side during the mission.

As the bombers approached the "Bomb Release Point," three **FLAK** bursts opened up and stained the air in front of the group. From the position of his bomber in the formation, Collins saw that they were right on target and directly in front of the formation's path. The squadron was only four minutes from their bomb drop and Collins mused, "That with '*Lady Luck's*' help he would soon be through it." No sooner had the thought crossed his mind, when another bracket of German anti-aircraft shells burst in front of his B-17.

Aboard the B-17G, "*Lady Jeannette,*" Gustafson's turret was facing the nose when he heard and felt the **FLAK** burst strike the "*Lady Jeannette*" which suddenly jerked and wobbled. She had been hit, and hit hard.

Metzger, who had been flying with his hands lightly on the copilot's controls, mimicking Gott's handling of the control, felt Gott begin to make control movements and he joined in the effort to bring the bucking and swaying B-17 back

under control to maintain formation. As Gott called for him to modify the various settings, Metzger used one hand to follow Gott's control wheel movements.

With the other hand, he quickly began to modify the fuel feed to the left and right wing engines in order to regain equal output on each wing's engines. With Metzger's help, Gott (Collins told the author during an interview, that he thought Gott was the best pilot in the Air Corps) began to regain control of the B-17, and try to maintain her formation position.

In his turret Gustafson quickly looked to his right, and what he saw amazed him. He had seen several bombers return with an engine missing. However, they were only missing the engine and the engine cowling. The engine-mount and the rest of the engine nacelle leading to the wing remained on the wing when the B-17s had landed back at their base.

Gustafson's eyes opened wide in amazement as he realized the number-four engine had disappeared from the right wing. Not only was the number-four engine gone, the engine cowling was gone, the engine mount was gone and the engine nacelle had been torn off all the way back to the leading edge of the wing. This left a gaping hole in the leading edge of the right wing, with what remained of the heavy engine beams, that supported the engine mount, sticking out of the hole.

As Gustafson rotated his top turret to his right, so he could see better, what he saw sent a cold chill down his spine. There was a stream of fire billowing out from beneath the wing and streaking back past the tail. As he concentrated at the position on the wing where the engine used to be, he realized they were lucky as the missing engine's fuel line had to have been bent down below the wing's bottom surface by the explosion and the escaping fuel had then caught fire.

It was obvious to Gustafson that the **FLAK** shell had burst at the very top and front of the number-four engine and the explosion blew the engine, its cowling, its motor-mount its and its nacelle down and off the bomber. It was a clean removal, except for the fire raging below and behind the wing.

The fire was like a huge blow torch and Gustafson quickly realized they had been very lucky. The fuel line must be bent down or the fire from the flowing gasoline would already be melting the wing and setting the fuel in the wing tanks on fire, resulting in the wing breaking off the bomber. This would have forced the "**Lady Jeannette**" into a sudden spin which would have trapped all of them inside the spinning bomber until it crashed.

Gustafson believed the fuel that was burning was far enough below the wing to prevent the fire from melting the wing. Although the fire was very visible and very scary, the fire was manageable for the time being. However, he was also certain the fuel line shut-off valve had to have been torn away with the engine. This meant that they had no way to shut off the gas to the broken fuel line and consequently, without the shut-off valve, they had no way to put out the fire.

As flight engineer, he had to keep the pilots aware of the condition of the bomber and to help as needed. Fighters weren't a problem right now as they were in the **FLAK** concentration zone and German fighters were known to stay away from that zone. The immediate condition of the bomber was more important. He

had to get to the pilots and tell them what he knew about the fire and its immediate threat to the bomber and help them with controlling the damaged bomber.

The "*Lady Jeannette*" was bouncing up and down and straining to remain in formation, as Gustafson started to rotate his turret to the rear so he could step down from the turret. As he prepared to step down, Gott and Metzger worked together to maintain full control of the B-17.

Meanwhile back in the formation, Collins and his pilot were fighting their own control problems, as their bomber was also jerking around from the concussion air waves formed by the **FLAK** explosions and as he watched, he saw "*Lady Jeannette*" begin to come under control. Just then, another bracket of **FLAK** shells arrived, one of which burst right under "*Lady Jeannette's*" left wing just a few feet below the number-two engine.

Gustafson had completed swinging his turret to the home position and had started to step down and out of it. As his right foot touched the deck of the cockpit and began to take his weight, a fragment from the second bursting **FLAK** shell tore through the side of the cockpit and flew through his lower right leg, taking a one inch section of leg bone with it. The fragment continued on and hit the hydraulic tank located behind the copilot on the bulkhead wall, puncturing the tank and releasing the hydraulic fluid.

Gustafson fell down and ended up sitting in agony behind the pilot's seat, still conscious enough to think about his parachute which was stored behind 2nd Lt. Metzger, the copilot. When he reached for it, so he could clip it onto his parachute harness, he realized the parachute was soaked with the fluid from the punctured hydraulic tank.

Back in the rear of the bomber, the first thing Robbins thought of after being shaken by the first explosion and seeing a wall of flame out his gun position's window, was Fross in the ball turret. Fross could be wounded and therefore would need help if he was to survive a crash, as it was hard enough to get out of the ball turret at the best of times. However, first, Robbins had to make certain they could get out and he moved to the hatch door and pulled the emergency release, allowing the door to fall free of the "*Lady Jeannette*." This done, he hurried to the ball turret position to see if Fross had managed to align the ball turret so Fross could open the hatch and get out of the turret through the ball turret access hatch.

Just then the bomber shook from the second burst, and bounced all over and began to go out of control, while starting a dive toward earth. Robbins held onto the ball turret mechanism and listened as the fragments of the **FLAK** shell were crashing and crunching into and through the aluminum of the "*Lady Jeannette*." And soon Robbins would realize, also into and through the flesh of his fellow crew men. Robbins' mind, for a split-second, remembered when a fragment of a fuse cap had broken into the bomber he was aboard, where it dropped into his open duffle bag. Sixty-three years later, another 452nd BG, B-17 flyer, Caesar Benigno, a 729th ECM (Electronic Counter Measures) operator described the sound of FLAK, "As if someone had thrown a handful of gravel at the bomber."

In the radio compartment, just after the engine was blown off the wing, the radio operator Dunlap was alone at his position and probably scared by the noises he was hearing. However he stayed at his position in order to transmit anything the pilot required, running equipment checks to insure it would work.

When the second **FLAK** shell burst, some fragments entered the number-one engine, the outboard engine on the left wing next to the pilot's side of the bomber, and the engine immediately stopped turning. Other fragments entered the number-two engine and broke something that caused it to lose power and start smoking. The **FLAK** fragments probably damaged one or more cylinder heads, which permitted the remaining cylinders to keep the engine running with reduced power output. However, as oil was pumped into the broken engine cylinders, it flowed past the pistons and then struck the exhaust pipes which turned the oil into flowing smoke that marked the passage of the "*Lady Jeannette*" across the sky.

(**Note**: Over the years, pilots have told the author the right outboard engine was number one and others have stated, it was the left outboard engine. The author chose to use, what the surviving aircrew had told him during interviews.)

Some fragments ripped their way through the bomb bay destroying the bomb drop mechanism and tearing through electrical lines causing the intercom and other electrical systems to stop working. The jolts of the two **FLAK** bursts also caused the bombs to jam in their shackles, so all attempts by the bombardier to drop them from his nose position failed.

Another fragment tore its way through the side of the bomber, continuing upward at an angle through the radio compartment's front bulkhead, striking Dunlap in the left thigh and tearing through his desk. As it burst through the desk, it ripped through Dunlap's lower right arm, which was stretched across the desk to his radio controls. The fragment's sharp edges had cut through Dunlap's right arm just above the wrist, nearly severing Dunlap's right hand and wrist from his arm, leaving his right hand and wrist attached to his lower right arm by uncut muscle and tissue.

In the nose of the bomber, some fragments flew past the navigator and the bombardier, cracking and hissing through the air. Holding on to whatever they could, they hoped for the best as the bomber seemed to stumble, catch herself, and then, appeared to be spiraling out of control. They looked first at each other to see if they were okay, then quickly looked back through the side windows. On the right side they saw the continuing flame from the missing number-four engine and on the left they saw the number-one engine had stopped rotating without being feathered and the number-two engine was smoking and struggling.

The B-17G's engines were designed to conserve enough oil when hit, to allow the pilots to "**feather**" the blades. That is, to turn the blades of the propeller so the narrow edges faced forward. This would permit the propeller blade to slice through the air, instead of trying to push its way through the air. When the pilots tried to feather the number-one engine's propeller, it was obvious the prop on the engine could not be feathered and it was creating a lot of drag. As the flowing air

pressed against the three, big paddle-shaped propeller blades of the dead engine.

(**Note:** If they had managed to feather the prop at this time in their last physical flight, this book would not exist.)

Still sitting on the cockpit deck, Gustafson took a good look at his right leg and realized that the shell fragment had torn a great hole in his lower right leg. When he attempted to move his right leg, his right foot just flopped around. He was sitting at an angle, with the damaged foot between the two pilots in the crawl-way to the nose. The pain was serious and Gustafson reached for the nearby first aid kit attached to the cockpit wall. He removed one of the morphine syringes and began the process of trying to inject it into his leg, just as he had been taught. However, the pain was so bad he was barely able to open his flying suit to reach his leg. He was going to need help and he decided to let Metzger know he was wounded and lying on the deck.

S/Sgt: Herman B. Krimminger
Gott Crew: Tail Gunner
KIA: 9 November 1944
Marshville, North Carolina
Buried(?): Arlington National Cemetery

Photograph: Krimminger Family

The Pilots, Gott and Metzger were working together, to bring the *"Lady Jeannette"* under control, after the B-17 had began to rapidly lose altitude and go into a spin. In all the other bombers in sight, crews watched for parachutes from the falling bomber they knew was going to crash, as it moved to the west of the Group's Combat Formation. Throughout the falling *"Lady Jeannette,"* each compartment had its own emergencies!

Collins, seeing his regular crew's bomber first falling away from the group's formation and then appearing to come under control, told his crew to watch for parachutes. As the bomber went out of sight, streaming flame from one side and smoke from the other, no parachutes had been seen by any of the returning mission aircrew. Realizing this might be the last time he saw any of his original crew, Collins told his navigator to record the location, and the A/C was last seen at 49-13 degrees north, 07-00 degrees east, Time: 10:04, Altitude: 23,000 Heading: 208.

The *"Lady Jeannette"* was very badly wounded, leaving the pilots facing a simple situation. They could lose all control and the B-17 would crash, perhaps killing all of them. Or, they could work closely together, which they did, and slowly they were able to make the control corrections that brought the damaged *"Lady Jeannette"* back under their control.

During the follow-up investigation for General Eisenhower, I visited the B-17's Group and directly interviewed several of the pilots who saw the B-17 fall out of formation. None of those experienced pilots thought the *"Lady Jeannette's"* pilots could regain control, and they all believed the B-17 was doomed as it began to leave the formation. These pilots were all experienced, and they agreed that only the extraordinary piloting skills of the two pilots, Gott and Metzger, permitted them to regain control of the spinning B-17, *"Lady Jeannette."*

Over the years I have met with other experienced pilots, Boeing engineers and experienced aircraft field representatives. For many of those years, none of them were able to explain to me how the *"Lady Jeannette"* was brought under control by Gott and Metzger. Just before my second retirement, while representing the Firm during a trip through Seattle, I met a retired Boeing engineer who had helped design the B-17. One evening, over drinks at Francisco's Bar and Restaurant, I told him about the B-17G I had been involved with, explaining that everyone who saw it thought it could not fly, and yet it did.

Using a bar napkin, I laid out all the damage and how the pilots had kept it flying for almost an hour after it was damaged. At the time he told me he would have also thought it had to crash. However, if I would give him my card, he would bring up my B-17 with some other engineers who had worked on the B-17 and he would let me know what they came up with.

A few weeks later I returned to my office to find a message. The fellow had called and that evening I returned his call. The engineer told me they had a couple of good fights over my question - "How could the B-17 continue to fly?" In the end, it was agreed that it should have crashed and only the two pilots' skills, and the fluke of all the combined damage, enabled them to keep it in the air as long as they had managed, before they had crashed.

Looking at the total damage, as he put it, if the number-four engine had not torn off the right wing as it had, the B-17 would have crashed. If the number-three engine had not been able to maintain full emergency power, the B-17 would have crashed. If the bomb bay doors had been closed, the B-17 would have crashed. If the number-two engine, had one more or one less cylinder head damaged by the **FLAK** burst, the B-17 would have crashed. If the number-one engine had been able to be feathered, as it was supposed to have been, the B-17 would have crashed and at the very end, if the tail gunner had not died the way he had, they would have crashed very differently. Most of all, they agreed, without an extraordinary set of pilots who had to have worked well together, the B-17 would have crashed.

When I hung up after our discussion, I thought back to how involved I had been after the crash of the B-17. I was deeply involved in the B17's officially documented end, her actual and undocumented end and her dead crew. That night, while sitting and reviewing my participation over a bourbon and water, I felt a bit better about part of what I had done after the B-17 had crashed.

Back in the sky over western Germany, within a minute of the *"Lady Jeannette's"* first **FLAK** hit, another of the squadron's bombers, "**833**," would close up the formation. Moving into the number-four position, the B-17 was

immediately struck by **FLAK**. One engine lost power and the bomber, "**833**," later crashed in Germany. The crew was captured and carried as Missing In Action, until the International Red Cross reported them as POWs. The German **FLAK** may have been fairly light that day, but one unit's guns were right on heading and altitude. That afternoon, they painted two more stripes around their anti-aircraft gun barrels.

Aboard the "*Lady Jeannette*," each man found himself in great danger as the B-17 began to come into control and level out. Each one's mind handled the danger differently. Gustafson was hurting so much from his wound that day, that for over five decades, he believed he remembered every second the B-17 remained airborne. However, he was unconscious for at least a minute before the "*Lady Jeannette*" crashed. Robbins compressed the rest of the flight into a much shorter time, than it lasted. Telling the researcher at first, that they had bailed out within a half hour of the first **FLAK** burst.

At some point, the B-17 reached a lower altitude and the crew no longer required supplemental oxygen and the men could take off their oxygen masks.

After inspecting his hydraulic fluid soaked parachute, Gustafson realized his parachute would probably not work when needed. He had to get the spare parachute that he knew was in the radio compartment and he could not move. Gustafson tried to call anyone over the intercom, which he was still connected to. Finding the intercom did not work, he unplugged his headset and reached up and tugged on Metzger's left sleeve to get his attention and let him know of the wound.

About that same time, Gott and Metzger realized that Gott was now able to control the damaged bomber well enough by himself to keep it flying. It would be a risk as Gott could always lose it, but Gott had to know the condition of the B-17 and its crew.

Gott and Metzger had tried their intercoms to get a damage and crew check as the second shell burst had hit the bomber, destroying the intercom system. Having no feed back via the intercom, realizing it was dead, and with Gustafson down, someone had to find out the bomber's condition. Metzger told Gott he would go check the bomber and crew and he got out of his seat. Metzger passed by Gustafson who was now trying to open his heavy flight suit to poke the morphine syringe into his upper leg without success. As he passed, Gustafson asked Metzger to get the spare parachute in the radio compartment and bring it back to him.

Up front, Harms realized he could not drop the bombs from the nose, so he started for the bomb bay to drop them manually, when he saw Gustafson, he stopped to help him inject the morphine into his leg.

The bomber was filled with the noise of the two working engines, the whistling winds blowing in and out of the **FLAK** holes, and the open doors and hatches of the bomber. All communications in the bomber had to be done by yelling loudly, as that was the only way the person communicating could be heard.

As Harms was helping Gustafson, Gustafson saw the flares contained in the flare bag on the bomb bay bulkhead behind Lt. Gott suddenly burst into flame. The flares were for the Very Pistol, a pistol used to fire colored flares from the cockpit

to inform the personnel on the ground if the bomber had damage or wounded men on board when they returned to their base after a mission.

Either the **FLAK** or the damaged and overheated electrical system had caused the flares to ignite. Realizing the danger and thinking quickly, Gustafson grabbed the burning flare bag and handed it to Harms who pitched it through the crawl-way between the pilot's seats, toward the front escape hatch. At the hatch, Harland, the navigator, had already pulled the emergency release of the front escape hatch and dropped the hatch. He saw the burning flare bag coming, grabbed the burning bag and threw it out the open hatch and that immediate danger was gone. There were reported aircraft lost, due to the flares catching fire in those aircraft and damaging the aircraft controls so badly they crashed.

In the rear of the bomber, Fross and Robbins had aligned the ball turret and opened the access hatch. As Robbins helped Fross out of the ball turret, he noticed that Fross was very dazed and confused. Jolted by the first **FLAK** shell, Fross was now somewhat concussed and he had wounds in his head. As small metal fragments from the exploding second **FLAK** burst had entered his ball turret. Some had whizzed around and around, and others had struck and penetrated his head. When Fross climbed out of his turret, he still had his cloth flight helmet on and Robbins did not remember seeing any wounds to Fross's head before both men bailed out.

As Robbins was helping Fross out of the ball turret, Krimminger came crawling into the waist from the rear. He too, Robbins noticed, seemed very dazed and he was obviously extremely nervous and agitated. The tail gunner, Krimminger, had been belted into his seat at the very back of the bomber when the first **FLAK** burst tore the engine off. Suddenly, off to his left, he had seen flames blowing back past the tail.

He quickly released his seat belt and was starting toward his escape hatch, when the second **FLAK** burst caused the tail to wildly whip and gyrate, throwing and banging Krimminger around in the small passageway. When he recovered enough to look around, he still saw the flames off to his position's left (the bomber's right, as he was facing toward the rear) and now, he saw the smoke pouring back from the damaged number-two engine on his right. At that moment, adding to his terror, he thought the bomber was going to crash immediately and he had to get out, and get out now, but he decided not to go out his escape hatch due to the fire outside. As Krimminger crawled forward past his escape hatch, he saw Robbins at the ball turret position as he entered the waist compartment to join Robbins and Fross, who was just emerging from the ball turret.

As the pilots regained control of the B-17 and turned her toward the west, the *"Lady Jeannette"* was struggling. It soon became evident to the pilots, they could not hold her in a straight line or maintain a steady altitude. She was barely staying airborne, with the number-three engine delivering full emergency power and the number-two engine's delivering limited power, between the two they were just able to keep her in the air. As she flew, the pilots of the *"Lady Jeannette"* had to

maintain a slight turn to the right and constantly lose, precious, altitude to maintain sufficient air speed, just above the required 120 mph, to prevent stalling out.

The bomber was just able to stay in the air and after attempting to change and balance both engines rotation speeds, the pilots realized changing either engine's output could cause the bomber to stall and fall out of the air. All they could do was to maintain the control they had and they were heading in the right direction, west toward the front line. They now had some time to make their decisions. To make those decisions, they had to know exactly what the damage was and what was the condition of the rest of their crew.

Realizing that they had not seen Dunlap since the **FLAK** bursts, Robbins opened the door into the radio compartment and found it splattered with blood which was flowing from Dunlap's torn right arm. Dunlap was laying on the deck and Robbins could see he was close to passing out from the shock and loss of blood.

Robbins immediately grabbed the medical kit and began binding up Dunlap's wounds. As he worked on Dunlap, the fill-in Copilot, Metzger, and an officer he did not recognize came through the door from the bomb bay.

After hearing Gustafson's request and being told there was a spare parachute in the radio compartment, Metzger had without hesitation, unclipped his own parachute and given it to Gustafson. Both knew it was much easier to walk along the bomb bay catwalk without a parachute than it was with one, and Metzger could get the spare parachute to replace the one he had given away as soon as he reached the radio compartment.

When Harms started to crawl into the cockpit he hit Gustafson's wounded leg and Gustafson let out a scream, and a few very choice, swear words. Taking care to keep from further disturbing Gustafson's leg, Harms made his way into the cockpit and then Harms helped Gustafson get his morphine injected and had worked with him to bandage the flopping leg. As soon as he could, he manually dropped the two bombs hanging under the wings and started into the bomb bay.

On his way through the bomb bay, Metzger tried to kick the jammed bombs out. When he realized he could not kick them out by himself, he continued on into the radio compartment. There he found the waist gunner working on the wounded radio operator. Joining the gunner, they worked together to complete bandaging the wounds as Dunlap lapsed into full unconsciousness.

Then, Harms entered the radio compartment and helped complete taking care of Dunlap. When finished, the three men tucked Dunlap's wounded right arm inside his flight jacket, zipped it up and re-buckled Dunlap's parachute harness and discussed what their options were and what should be done. They realized, they had two options, the first was to throw him out the bomb bay using the emergency rope to act as a static line to open his parachute and trust, Germans on the ground would get him medical help. However, they had all heard of what often happened to landing crewmen and none of them really thought that option would really help Dunlap. They did search for the emergency static line that was supposed to be there, but could not find it. Leaving them with no other option but to continue to

whatever end awaited. So, Metzger and Harms started back forward with Metzger carrying the spare parachute.

Meanwhile, in the cockpit, Gott continued to nurse "*Lady Jeannette*" through the skies of Germany, drawing closer and closer to the front line where they would pass over into friendly Allied occupied territory.

While collecting the spare parachute, Metzger had told the crew in the rear about the flight engineer's broken leg and that he had been injecting himself with morphine as Metzger came to the radio compartment. Harms told them about the burning flares and the punctured hydraulic tank. Metzger advised them to stay calm and he would go back to the cockpit and tell Gott what he had found in the rear.

As Metzger and Harms started back to the cockpit, Dunlap was lying unconscious on the floor of the radio compartment. Robbins was headed to the rear of the bomber to stand by the escape hatch with Fross and Krimminger. Where they watched the fire stream back past the tail as they waited for an order from the cockpit to bail out.

Metzger and Harms stopped in the bomb bay above the open bomb bay doors. Between the two of them, they were able to kick the bombs free. As they kicked, one by one, the bombs dropped out the bomb bay to fall within Germany.

Metzger arrived back in the cockpit and passed Gustafson, who was sitting on the cockpit floor, "Just about out of it," Gustafson had told the researcher over 50 years later, "I was sitting there, out of the loop and just hurting. I'm still not sure if I ever got the morphine in and I do not remember the bombardier helping me with the morphine injection or bandaging my wound." Then when reviewing his part of this book for the researcher, and after reading about Harms coming through the crawl-way, Gustafson told the researcher, on 30 June, 2007, "Now, I remember Harms hitting my leg, my screaming and Harms helping me with my leg."

After Metzger got back into his seat, he and Gott discussed their situation. They were in a bomber with the number-one engine not running and not feathered. The number-two engine was smoking and delivering only partial power and it could stop running at any moment. The number-three engine was the only engine delivering full emergency power and, of course, the number-four engine was gone and the fire continued unabated below the right wing. Gustafson, was out of it, not hearing much of what was going on because of the noise in the cockpit and the pain in his leg being so intense. Dunlap was lying on the radio compartment floor, while three men waited anxiously at the rear escape hatch and in the nose, Harms was standing in the crawl-way to the cockpit and Harland was waiting by the escape hatch, all waiting for the order to bail out.

The non-working number-one engine and its propeller were creating great drag on the left side of the bomber, pulled only by the damaged number-two engine. The right side, with its strong engine and ripped open, gaping engine position completed the picture of a bomber that could barely stay in the air. The bomb bay doors were also open and could not be closed, contributing even more drag to impede the B-17's flight.

Across the skies of Germany and France, the *"Lady Jeannette"* struggled to reach friendly territory. Model interpretation, based on crew survivors and eye witness testimony.

Model & Photograph: Willis S. Cole, Jr.

The bomber had lots of holes and open areas, but it was still flying. Gott and Metzger, after discussing it, decided the bomber would continue to fly as long as the engines kept going and they could maintain enough speed and altitude. Speed and altitude could be their savior and the loss of either could be their death.

They discussed the possibility of the crew bailing out over enemy territory. The crew might land safely and become captives, however Metzger would have pointed out, that Dunlap was unable to bail out and if he didn't get the fastest possible medical attention he would die.

The Copilot, 2nd Lt. William E. Metzger, Jr. had, just before the Green Crew left for England, called a crew meeting and he told the crew, including Waist Gunner, Sgt. Harold E. Burrell (Yuba City, California,), "That he would never bail out if there was a wounded man still on board."

After discussing all the possibilities, Gott and Metzger decided to keep going as long as they could. They would try to get past the front line and into friendly territory. Then, find a location where they might safely crash. This, they agreed, would give Dunlap and Gustafson their best chance of getting the medical care they both needed.

To save altitude loss, the pilots agreed that it was necessary to throw out all the extra weight they could. As the pilots held the controls, Harms went back to the back and told the men in the waist that they were going for friendly territory and to throw out everything they could to lighten the plane. Once they had thrown out what they could, they were to continue to stand by the escape hatch, so they could bail out as quickly as they could in case the bomber started to crash. As he returned to the cockpit, Harms checked Dunlap's condition again.

Harms informed the pilots that the men in the rear were beginning to lighten the aircraft and all three were OK, and ready to bail out.

As *"Lady Jeannette"* traveled to the west, the rear crew threw out what they However, they were unable to jettison the ball turret due to a missing wrench, so its weight continued to help pull the bomber down.

Harms then went forward through the crawl-way to the nose to tell Harland the plan and to help throw out all the excess weight they could from the front of the B-17. Then, he stood in the crawl-way between the pilots to give whatever help he could, while Harland returned to his place next to the forward escape hatch ready to bail out as soon as he was ordered.:

Both Robbins and Harms report **FLAK** bursts near the bomber, as the *"Lady Jeannette"* flew to the west and approached the Moselle River. Soon, the city of Metz was seen off to their north and if she kept flying, they would soon be crossing over to the friendly side of the front line.

Though some **FLAK** bursts continued to spread across the sky, the bomber received no further damage. The **FLAK** soon stopped and they passed over the Moselle River into friendly territory.

Author, after clearing forest floor, discovering all the impression craters and marking them. The torn-off right wing root came to rest in this crater, with the wing tip leaning against the tree to the right. The crash-site is now fenced with a (almost) hog free. The photograph is to the south and the debris trail stretched 400 feet to the north.

Photograph: Willis S. Cole, Jr.

Early September, 1994, with the help of Bernard Delsert (center), the author and his wife, Carol, discovers the true *"Lady Jeannette"* crash-site and the impressions the large pieces left in the forest floor. The pile by the tree is the first collection of relics to be carried home.

A metal cover from the *"Lady Jeannette"* Number Two Engine, recovered by the author from the impact crater in November, 1998.

The engine serial number plate, found in the same crater, is shown on another page.

Photographs: Willis S. Cole, Jr.

Chapter Four
"The <u>Next To Last Flight</u> Of The 'Lady Jeannette'"
Friendly Territory

Laid out in front of them, Gott and Metzger could see the Plain of the Wöevre stretching for some miles until into the distance, it was broken by the rapid rise of the eastern heights of the Meuse River. The ground was fairly flat with large wooded areas and large fields stretching from their position, all the way to the rapidly rising hills in the distance. Even at that distance, they could see open fields on the top of those hills. If, they could maintain their current altitude loss rate, they might reach those fields and slide in for a safe crash-landing.

The major problem facing the pilots, was their inability to gain full control of the "*Lady Jeannette,*" due to the extensive damage. All they could do was to keep her flying in a gentle right turn, while constantly losing some altitude to maintain the air speed required to keep the B-17 from stalling. By that time, they were very aware that any attempt to change the basic flying characteristics established by the two **FLAK** bursts, could lead to a sudden spin, crash and death.

The decision was one that was basically being made for them, as they were forced to continue as they had been and trust at the last minute that they would find an open field where they could safely crash the "*Lady Jeannette.*"

Meanwhile Harland, in the nose by himself, reviewed the proper way to parachute to safety. The major thing to remember was to not pull the "D" Ring of the parachute too early. It was important to wait for the bomber to pass before pulling on the "D" Ring. The "D" Ring pulled the rip cord from the parachute pack, releasing the parachute from the pack. Once the parachute was released, it would quickly fill with air, slowing his falling speed to a point where he would land safely. If, he thought, I pull the "D" Ring too soon, the opening parachute could catch on a part of the bomber, with the caught parachute carrying me to my death as the B-17 crashed. Another thing that could go wrong if he opened the parachute too soon was it could be ripped by something on the passing the B-17, causing the parachute to "*Roman Candle,*" allowing him to fall so fast he would be killed upon contact with the ground.

As Harland was running his checks and checking his parachute, he realized it had been damaged by a **FLAK** fragment. The fragment had torn its way into the parachute pack during the second **FLAK** shell burst and Harland decided that his parachute would probably not operate properly if he had to bail out. So, he reached up through the crawl-way and tugged at Harm's pant leg. When Harms bent down, to see what Harland wanted, Harland told Harms about the dangerously torn parachute pack.

Harms told the pilots about Harland's damaged parachute and **without any hesitation Metzger removed the spare parachute he had earlier retrieved from the radio compartment for his own use** and handed it to Harms. Harms bent

down and handed the parachute to Harland, who quickly removed his damaged parachute, threw it aside and clipped on the good one. ***It was the second parachute Metzger had given away and now he had none for himself, Metzger was now fully committed to staying with "Lady Jeannette" to the end.***

Decades later, Harms was asked about the parachute that was still attached to the radio operator who could not use it. He said, that no one in the B-17 would think of taking the wounded man's parachute from his unconscious body. **Also, we know from Sgt. Burrell, that Metzger's mind set was such that if there had been ten spare parachutes, he would still have ridden the bomber down, as there was a wounded man on board.**

The *"Lady Jeannette's"* **last physical flight** had only a few minutes left. The end was very near. It was time to get the men out, and Gott told Harms and Gustafson to get ready to bail out. Harms leaned down and hollered through the crawl-way to tell Harland to stand by the nose escape hatch and to be ready bail out. Gustafson gathered himself and began to think about how he could get through the crawl-way to the escape hatch in the nose. He decided that it would have to be elbows, butt and good leg. Scuttling like a crab, he would get out through the crawl-way and then out the forward escape hatch. To succeed, he would have to scuttle on his back, so he could lift his flopping right foot in front of him with his right hand, as he scuttled along.

Harms told Gott, he was going to the waist and tell the men there to be ready to jump when Gott ordered him to tell them to bail out. Then he would come back and wait for the actual bail out order, after which he would go back and tell the men to bail out and he would follow them out the rear escape hatch.

In the waist, things were getting desperate. By this time, Krimminger was even more agitated, extremely anxious to bail out. He kept looking out of the escape hatch and telling Robbins and Fross that they were too low, and wanting to know why they hadn't been told to bail out. As Krimminger talked, he continued to fidget with his parachute harness, checking and rechecking his parachute webbing and grasping the "D" ring. Many years later, Robbins told the researcher, he had not realized Krimminger was actually tugging on the "D" ring each time he checked it. It was just a little tug each time, but in the end ... each light tug counted up, unknown to Krimminger or the others in the rear of the B-17G.

S/Sgt. Robbins, the only crewman in the rear of the *"Lady Jeannette"* who had not been wounded, concussed or dazed, tried to calm Krimminger, but with little success. Fross offered little help, as he appeared to be somewhere else most of the time. Robbins told the interviewer, he thought Fross's bell was still ringing from the second **FLAK** burst, even as they left the bomber.

All of a sudden, Krimminger who had continued to fidget, grasped his parachute's "D" ring, and his hand instinctively again tugged lightly at the "D" ring. Robbins said that he remembered it, as it had happened in slow motion, as he and Fross saw Krimminger's parachute pack begin to open. The packed parachute fell from its pack and began to inflate, as the air stream flowing through the B-17 from the open bomb bay doors and the many **FLAK** holes caught the parachute and

began to fill it. The air stream was moving as fast as the plane and almost instantly, the parachute was being pulled out though the open escape hatch.

Robbins realized at once what was happening and much faster than it can be written, the parachute filled with air and was pulled out of the escape hatch by the flowing air. Krimminger also realized what was happening and grabbed at the deploying parachute, but all of them were too slow and in that split-second, the parachute was out the hatch and over the right horizontal stabilizer. As it moved, the shroud lines were beginning to pull Krimminger toward the escape hatch.

As Krimminger began to be pulled toward the hatch, yelling and screaming, both Robbins and Fross grabbed Krimminger in an attempt to keep him inside the B-17, but they could not hold him. The pull of the parachute was too strong and Krimminger was pulled out of their hands and out through the escape hatch.

When Krimminger was pulled out of the hatch, he fell downward and under the horizontal stabilizer, instead of being pulled over the top of it. As Krimminger fell, his parachute shroud lines that were wrapped around the leading edge of the horizontal stabilizer tightened and he was swung upwards by the air stream to slam against the right horizontal tailplane control, pushing it up and forcing the B-17 into a sudden climb. Inside, Robbins and Fross looked on, unable to help Krimminger.

As the B-17 began the sudden, sharp pitched climb, the pilots who had been holding the controls in one position for nearly an hour felt the controls, suddenly slam back toward them. They quickly realized the sudden, unexplained climb would lead to an immediate stall and spin out and they pushed the controls forward and with their combined strength pushing on the controls, they managed to bring the "*Lady Jeannette*" back under partial control.

Knowing they could do nothing for Krimminger, who continued to yell at them. With the beginning of the sudden climb, Robbins pushed Fross part way out of the escape hatch and told Fross to jump. As soon as Fross was out, Robbins started to followed him out, while listening to Krimminger yelling as he fell away.

Harms was making his way through the bomb bay, toward the tail, when the sudden climb of the B-17 pushed him toward the catwalk and open bomb bay doors. He had no choice but to hold onto whatever he could to maintain his balance.

Two kilometers to the south of their flight path, in the field *Lambré Jarin*, at *Louiseville Ferme*, a French farmer was supervising a group of displaced Polish workers in a field. They first heard and then saw the bomber coming from the east. It had flame flowing from one side and smoke pouring from the other to mark its progress and it was a sight the French farmer would never forget.

As the men watched, the B-17 began a sudden climb and at the top of the climb they saw a man fall from the bomber; then the bomber began to dive back toward earth.

In the cockpit, as the pilots pushed forward on the controls, just as quickly as the B-17 had begun to climb, it began to dive toward the ground.

Just before the French saw Fross falling from the "*Lady Jeannette*," Harms had regained his balance on the bomb bay catwalk and began to make his way back to the waist to tell the men to get ready to go bail out. He could see that Dunlap, the

89

Radio Operator, was still on the floor of the radio compartment and when Harms looked through the open rear radio compartment door, he could only see two men and one of them was already most of the way out of the hatch. It was obvious to him the last man was ready to go as soon as the hatch was clear. Suddenly, Harms was being thrown upward as the B-17 began to dive. He was lifted off his feet and had to hold on to whatever he could to keep from being thrown about inside the bomb bay compartment. Suddenly, he was really scared he might be trapped there during the plane's crash.

In the field, the Frenchman saw the falling man's parachute open as the bomber immediately went from climbing to diving toward the ground. Unknown to the pilots and the Frenchman, when the pilots forced the controls forward, that forced the horizontal stabilizer down, causing Krimminger's body to swing down and away from the horizontal stabilizer during the movement from climb to dive.

Then, just as the pilots fought to regain what level flight they had since regaining control after the two **FLAK** strikes and loss of control over Germany, Krimminger's body again forced the horizontal stabilizer upward, forcing the "*Lady Jeannette*" into another unexpected climb.

Harms had regained his balance and had just started back to the cockpit to tell the pilots what he had seen, when he was again pushed down and then nearly floated, as the "*Lady Jeannette*," repeated the sudden climb and dive movement.

The Frenchman could hardly believe what he was seeing as he and his workers watched the bomber start to climb again. And again, at the very top of that second climb, directly to the north of where they were standing in the field, they saw a second man's body came into sight and as the bomber began to dive again, the falling man's parachute opened.

The farmer had seen several crashing aircraft during the war and he considered his farm work more important than going to help the parachuting men. So, the group watched as the bomber, now somewhat lower, flew to the west toward Hattonchatel located on the Heights of the Meuse.

Once the "*Lady Jeannette*" came out of the second climb/dive, Harms regained his balance and went into the cockpit to tell the pilots that he had seen one man was gone and the other two were bailing out before he started back to the cockpit due to the sudden maneuvers. Then, Harms stood between the pilots, at the entry of the crawl-way to help in any way he could. To his left, still slumped on the floor, Gustafson was also waiting for what was to come next.

As he returned to work, the Frenchman thought the first man would land near the village of Haumont-les-Leachatussee and the second would be landing just to the east of the *Hazavant Ferme* compound where there was a large field bordered on both sides by a large woods. Fifty-four years later, he could point out the exact location to the researcher, where he had been standing the day he and his workers watched the B-17. Then, he explained to the researcher his theory of what he saw that day. The Frenchman thought, the B-17 had been so low that the pilot had made the two climbs and dives to get high enough height during each climb, so that one man could safely bail out of the burning B-17.

90

Then, he described what followed. After the bomber had flown out of sight to the west and he was getting the standing men working again, he could hear the noise of the bomber fading away to the west. Then, much to his surprise, he heard the noise getting louder and when he looked out to the north-west toward the large woods there, he saw the flash of a fire, a billowing cloud smoke, followed by a loud whooshing explosion. The sound he heard, as he described to the researcher was not an explosion of bombs, that was a sound he had heard many times, but it not what he heard on this occasion. The sound seemed to him to have been just like the noise he heard when he wanted to burn field waste and he poured essence (gasoline) over the material to be burned, backed up some distance and threw a lit match on the pile. It was the same whoosh of burning essence that he had heard that day.

The farmer and his helpers were working in an open field conducting their daily farm work when the bomber came from the east. To the south of them, was the 109th Evacuation Hospital, which was located in the field across from the American World War One St-Mihiel Cemetery. Numerous personnel from that unit were outside their tents that day and watched the scene unfold in front of them.

The 109th was located on the slightly sloping side of a hill that formed a saucer shape around the south end of the Plain of Woëvre. The hillside was high enough, as the B-17 came from their east with smoke and fire pouring from it as it flew toward the west, the B-17 appeared to be about level with them when it was directly north of their hospitals position.

From their position, the B-17 then appeared to be making a large circle, when it suddenly disappeared into the woods, followed by the flash of a fire and a billow of smoke that lasted only a short time.

Aboard the "*Lady Jeannette*," Gott and Metzger, as they brought the B-17 out of the second unexpected climb within seconds of each other, prepared for another sudden, unexpected maneuver. They held tightly onto the controls, while they again achieved as level flight as the "*Lady Jeannette*" would fly.

This required Gott and Metzger to hold additional, constant pressure on the controls that they had not had to hold before the first unexplained climb. Now they had to constantly push the controls slightly forward, when before they had to maintain a slight pressure to the rear on the controls to maintain their altitude. It was, as if the tail planes had been trimmed in a slightly up position before and now they had to be trimmed in a slightly down position. While at the same time, they had to maintain the same slight, right turn control pressure to stay airborne.

Meanwhile, back at the rear of the "*Lady Jeannette*," S/Sgt. Krimminger, unknown to Gott, Metzger and the remaining men on board, was hanging under the tail with the rushing wind pushing his body up against the horizontal tail plane. However, when the upward pressure of his body was now counteracted by the pilots hold on to the controls in their combined effort to gain as much flying distance as they could before the "*Lady Jeannette*" had to crash.

The people of Haumont-les-Lachausse had hurried out of their homes, as had every French and American who could rush into the open when they heard the noise of the obviously damaged bomber coming from the east. When interviewed

91

by the researcher, fifty-four years later, several of the people of Haumont-les-Lachausse, who were under the B-17's path, remembered being puzzled by the voices of men yelling from the bomber as it flew over their heads toward the west. Then, they saw the first man bail out just to the west of the village. The parachutist landed before anyone could reach him and he had started walking toward their village where there were several tents, home to the men of the American Army who had been in their village for some time. When the Americans met with the man, they took him directly to the tent marked with the Red Crosses and later, the villagers saw the man put in an ambulance and driven away.

By the time Gott and Metzger had the *"Lady Jeannette"* under control again, they were starting to fly over a large forest. Right in front of them, running through the trees at an angle of 45 degrees from southwest to northeast was a large complex of smaller fields named the *les Grands Paquis*, which pointed like a large finger through the woods.

It would have provided an excellent field for a safe crash, if only they could have completed a partial turn to the left and if they were not so high. Now, all it offered was an excellent place for the remaining three crewmen to land if they bailed out at once.

Gott yelled at Gustafson and Harms, telling them to get out. Instantly, Harms dropped down and through the crawl-way to the nose and reached the escape hatch so fast, he beat Harland out of the escape hatch even though Harland had been waiting next to the hatch, ready to bail out.

Harland followed Harms out the hatch and the parachute Metzger had given him, worked perfectly except that his chin was stripped by the shroud lines as they whipped tight. **Until his death, Harland carried a newspaper article in his wallet about his B-17 pilots. He told each of his children when he showed them the article, that they would not be alive if Metzger had not given him the parachute that saved his life.**

The chest parachutes the men were wearing tended to force the bailing out men to roll over when they hit the air stream, so they would be looking up as the bomber passed over them. After Harms cleared the escape hatch and the open bomb bay doors, he found himself looking up at the bottom of the *"Lady Jeannette,"* as she passed over his head.

It happened so fast, Harms could hardly believe what he had seen. There was a man hanging under the tail of the B-17 as it flew by him. Then Harms pulled his "D" ring and when his parachute snapped open, he found himself hanging in the harness facing to the west and watching the B-17 as it flew toward the high hill in the near distance. He could see, the *"Lady Jeannette"* was too low to clear the hill, something had to happen and it had to happen very quickly.

Gustafson heard the order to go and watched as Harms disappeared. Gustafson followed his planned exit strategy to get out of the damaged bomber. He grabbed his lower right pant leg with his right hand and lifted his dangling foot off the deck of the cockpit. Holding his foot in the air, he crabbed along on his left foot, butt, left and right elbows as he crabbed through the crawl-way.

Gustafson later told the researcher, "I will remember them to my dying day, as I worked my way through the crawl-way. I was looking up at the faces of Gott and Metzger and they were very intent. Both men were looking forward and very much in command of the *Lady Jeannette*." Then Gustafson finished crabbing his way through the crawl-way, to the forward Escape Hatch.

Gustafson explained to the researcher, how he had lifted his wounded leg above the escape hatch and shoved the leg with its dangling foot out of the hatch as he slid down and out, to drop away from the *Lady Jeannette*." Gustafson was interviewed many times by the researcher and even though he did not remember opening his parachute, he was certain he had never passed out. It was not until fifty-eight years later that Gustafson finally determined that he had to have passed out. It was only after the researcher had shown him a plot of the last minutes of the *Lady Jeannette's*" flight on a French map, proving the B-17 had to have flown away from him, turned over the village and then flew back past him, before he woke up and watched the *Lady Jeannette*" crash into the woods.

As the last survivor to bail out, Gustafson cleared the fuselage of the *Lady Jeannette*" when she was no more than 3 kilometers from the large hill with the village on its top and the village of Hattonville at its base. To keep from stalling out, the *Lady Jeannette*" had to fly a minimum of 120 miles per hour or two miles per minute. Three kilometers equals 38% of 5 miles, based on the formula, that 8 kilometers are equal to 5 miles.

This indicates, when Gustafson bailed out, the *Lady Jeannette*," the B-17G was no more than 1.9 miles from the south-east edge of the village of Hattonville and the pilots had less than 57 seconds for them to make a command decision and then, to carry out that quick decision's commitment. It was a decision and a commitment that could lead to their death, by diving the B-17 into the ground before they reached the village or living for a while longer and perhaps, finding a place to safely crash-land.

During the past minute, after regaining control after the last sudden climb, both pilots became aware that the flying characteristics of the damaged aircraft they had been flying for almost an hour had suddenly changed. They realized it now appeared they might be able to make a

S/Sgt Krimminger was trapped under the tail when Lt. Harms saw him, as Harms bailed out and the B-17 flew past him.

Model Interpretation: Willis S. Cole, Jr.

Photograph: Willis S. Cole, Jr.

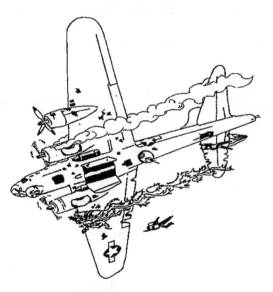

controlled turn to the right, without going into a fatal spin.

By then, they had also realized the two sudden climbs and dives had cost them any hope of clearing the village at the top of the hill in front of them. If only, they could have had an additional two hundred feet of altitude, their B-17 would have been able to fly over the village on the hill and slide in for a safe crash-landing in one of the sloping fields close to the western side of the village.

The trees located in the small village of Hattonchatel, the chateau and church steeple were 475 feet higher than the ground level at Hattonville, located just to the east at the bottom of the steep hill. It was very obvious to Gott and Metzger, by the time the "*Lady Jeannette*" would reach the village on the hill, they would be too low to clear the village.

Just to the left side of the steep hill, they could see a field sloping up a valley leading

T/Sgt. Russell W. Gustafson leaving the "*Lady Jeannette*," the last survivor to bail out of the damaged B-17G. S/Sgt. Krimminger can be seen hanging under the horizontal tail plane. In the cockpit, 1st Lt. Donald J. Gott and 2nd Lt. William E. Metzger, Jr. were making their decision to attempt a right turn or dump her into the field before they reached Hattonville, just 2 km away. In the radio compartment, T/Sgt. Robert A. Dunlap is lying unconscious on the floor.

Drawing: Carol L. Cole

from the lower level to the top of the ridge. It would be the perfect place to slide into a safe crash if only they could turn the B-17 a few degrees to the left. However, Gott and Metzger knew they could not turn the damaged B-17 to the left, they were not high enough to clear the village on the hill and now, they had less than two minutes before they had to land.

They knew the "*Lady Jeannette*" was unable to lose height fast enough to, without losing flight control, to safely crash-land before they reached the village at the foot of the steep hill. Gott and Metzger had to have felt the control of the B-17 change after the last, unexpected sudden climb. They now realized they might be able to turn the B-17 to the right, even though they could not turn it to the left without going into a stall and crashing. Of course, they had no knowledge that Sgt. Krimminger was hanging under the right tail plane, and with the additional drag produced by Krimminger and his parachute, the B-17 had a little more control.

94

Gott and Metzger had to have made a quick and mutual decision. Gott would have stated, and Metzger would have instantly agreed with what had to be done. If they continued as they were going, they could crash into the village at the bottom of the hill or they could crash into the hill behind the village and with the fuel on board, they could start a fire and damage homes and people in both villages.

Neither man was prepared to risk the life of others to save his own, which the last two minutes of their lives were to prove, several times.

Gott and Metzger had to have decided in less than 45 seconds that their only opportunity to safely crash and get Dunlap the medical attention he required would be for them to attempt a right turn. Yet, they were so close to the village if the attempt to turn right did not succeed, the B-17 could crash directly into the village in front of them and neither Gott nor Metzger would permit that to happen.

Metzger would have immediately agreed with Gott, when Gott shouted to him, "*Let's try to turn to the right and if either of us thinks we will not make it, we put her in the ground before we reach the village!*" From the time they had to make that decision, and put it into motion was a few short seconds and in unison they began the turn. *Rather than risk another life on the ground, both Gott and Metzger were proving they were willing to give up their own and Dunlap's lives*.

In front of them in and around the village, at that low altitude they could see people running around in the village. Those people, in the village, realizing that the bomber might fall on them, had begun to run away from where they thought the bomber would crash. Then, as the bomber began its turn and pilots realized they were succeeding, they knew they would clear the village. The village was lost from sight as the "*Lady Jeannette*" flew over. She was well into her turn when she flew over the south-eastern edge of the village to complete the first 90 degrees and continued her turn as she passed over the church and the village hall/school.

As the B-17 continued through the turn, Metzger was looking to his right to see if there was anyplace where they could straighten out and leave the village, flying to the north to reach a safe cash site. As the turn progressed, Metzger and Gott could look to the north and the ground was covered with fruit trees, so they decided to continue the turn. As the "*Lady Jeannette*" completed a 180-degree right turn, she ended up flying parallel to their inbound flight path, just a few hundred feet, further to the north. They had come from the east and now they were flying back to the east. However, "*Lady Jeannette*" was less than 350 feet in the air and less than a minute to live.

Both Gott and Metzger had to have hoped as they started the turn, that they would find an open field to the north. Or, if they safely completed the 180-degree turn, they would be able to select a location in the large field they had just passed over, where three of their crew had bailed out. Then, as they lost the rest of their altitude and made that final right turn, they could slide into a safe crash in the large field just to the east of Hattonville.

As the "*Lady Jeannette*" completed her turn, Metzger looked over to the field on his right and he had to be shocked to see people and vehicles, including an ambulance, streaming out along the field toward the three men who had just bailed

out. The people on the ground were already in the area of the field where the pilots had thought they could safely slide into a crash-landing.

They could not control when they would run out of altitude and now in the last place they might safely land, there were people! **Neither Gott nor Metzger would put those people in that field at risk.** Their only remaining hope was to continue even further to the east and then turn toward the open field.

As they flew further to the east, it became obvious to both men they were blocked from turning into the field for a safe crash-landing to save their lives! As there in the air above the eastern end of the field, still hanging under their parachutes, were the three men who had just bailed out.

If they tried to fly between the men they might snag a parachute or the airstream of the B-17 would affect the men's parachutes and if one of the falling parachutes collapsed, that man could fall to his death. Neither Gott nor Metzger would permit that to happen. *They only had seconds left to live!*

Looking to the east, it was obvious to Gott and Metzger that they did not have the altitude required to fly beyond the eastern edge of the large woods they were now flying over. Right there in front of them, just beyond the woods was a large field that would have made the perfect emergency crash-site, but... they were too low.

Gott and Metzger instantly decided together as they had each time before, that they would not place others at risk to save their own lives. Both were determined to fly far enough past the first man who had bailed out, Harms, to make absolutely certain they would not risk his life and then they would make another 180-degree turn to the right and hope they still had enough altitude left to clear the trees and make it back to the open field.

Harms had watched the "*Lady Jeannette*" fly away, make her turn over the village and then fly back toward him. He watched as the "*Lady Jeannette*" reached a point directly to his north and then the B-17 began another turn to the right. The "*Lady Jeannette*" had just completed more than 90-degrees of its turn, when Harms saw that her lowered right wing began to disappear into the woods.

Harms was at the tree top level as he watched the B-17 begin to settle into the woods. The leaves had fallen from the trees, so he could see for some distance and as he watched, the "*Lady Jeannette*" flew below the tree-tops and began to break up as she came closer to him.

As Harms watched with growing horror, the forward fuselage continued to travel through the woods. Then, just before his feet hit the ground, the broken fuselage nose of the B-17 struck the ground, pivoted, and was heading right at him. Then, the nose finally stopped moving less than 275 feet from where he had just landed. Around the place in the woods where he could see the stopped forward fuselage, the woods were suddenly lit up by a great flash of fire, with a whooshing explosion as the flame mushroomed and the smoke billowed upward.

Harms landed in the field, very close to the edge of the woods and the now burning crash-site. He looked around and saw that he was not that far from people running toward him. As Harms was not absolutely positive, he was within friendly

96

territory he got free of his parachute harness and ran to the edge of the field where the woods angled around the field, intending to hide for a while.

Harms ran into the Hattonville Woods (Bois de Hattonville) and made his way deeper into the woods until he came to a narrow forest road. He stopped there for a while, listening to people yelling in the direction of the crash-site. After a few minutes, he decided he had better move and staying a short distance from the road, he followed it deeper into the woods, moving from tree to tree in case he had to hide. Soon he came to a small intersection in the road with a piled earth berm, a few feet high, that ran along the forest floor. On his side of the berm, there was a very rough road along the berm and a foot path made its way alongside the road.

Off to his right Harms could see shiny airplane parts in the distance and then, he was certain he heard someone talking in English. Deciding that he was within friendly territory, Harms opted to take the path alongside the road and berm, and follow it to the crash-site of the B-17 in the distance.

As Harms reached the path and started to walk toward the crash-site, he began to see the first evidence of the plane's descent into the woods. At first, he saw broken branches that had just fallen to the ground from the tallest trees, as the "*Lady Jeannette*" under control of the pilots, finally ran out of altitude and began to smash her way into the trees as she lowered into the Hattonville Woods.

As Harms was walking along the path toward the crash-site, he could see a broken wing and the tail of the B-17 in the distance, with another wing and the forward fuselage even further away. In addition, he could see a group of men around the broken B-17 and even from where he was, Harms could tell some of them were wearing American uniforms.

As he walked down the path toward a small stream with steep banks, Harms began to notice bright red and white objects lying between the branches and bomber debris in the woods to the left of the path. When Harms managed to get across the slippery clay of the stream banks and started climbing the gentle slope toward the crash-site, he saw even more debris to his left, consisting of bright red and white items among the aircraft pieces torn from the B-17 as it settled into the woods.

About 100 feet beyond the stream, partway up the sloping, wooded hillside, lying in what Harms remembers to be a crater, there was a wing lying at an angle against a tree and behind it was the tail which had broken off the bomber. As Harms began to walk around the wing that had blocked his full view of the rest of the crash-site, two Frenchmen were standing near the wing, watching him walk up the slope toward where they were standing.

Harms remembers arriving at a position where he could see the right tail plane of the broken tail and then he saw the remains of a tattered parachute on top of the tail plane. Instantly, he realized the bright red and white stuff he had been seeing along the debris trail, were the torn-apart remains of the man he had seen hanging under the tail. The last thing Harms remembered for three days was that he had started to scream and swear.

Harland was slowly falling to earth under in his parachute when he watched the crash of the "*Lady Jeannette*." As soon as his parachute let him, he broke free of his harness and ran into the woods. He hid there until through the trees, he saw an American Ambulance turning into the large field. Then Harland made his way along the inside edge of the trees until he reached an angle in the woods, where he found himself crossing a German World War One artillery position to gain access to the field and ambulance.

Gustafson had pulled his "D" ring after he fell free of the escape hatch, and the shock of the parachute opening caused him to pass out for just over a minute. When Gustafson woke up, the "*Lady Jeannette*" was to his left, just above the tree tops of the woods surrounding the field and she was flying away from him. Gustafson watched the "*Lady Jeannette*" begin a right turn, watching as the right wing lowered into the woods. Her exit from Gustafson's view was quickly followed by a flash fire, whooshing explosion and smoke.

Gustafson's feet hit the ground and with his damaged right leg screaming pain, he fell, only to find himself being pulled slowly across the ground by his partially collapsed parachute catching the gentle wind blowing across the field. Gustafson knew he had to dump the air from the parachute, but he also had to hold his right leg high enough, to keep his dangling right-foot clear of the dirt.

He was attempting to maneuver the shroud lines to dump the air out of the parachute, when a Frenchman ran up, grabbed the moving parachute and stopped his movement. The Frenchman collected the parachute as he went to Gustafson and was attempting to talk to him, when an American soldier arrived and asked how he could help. As the shroud lines had tangled around him, Gustafson opened the retaining strap of his favorite hunting knife he had attached to his chute harness. Giving the knife to the soldier, he asked the soldier to cut the shroud lines free from his body.

As he was being freed, Gustafson heard a motor and saw an ambulance driving up to his location. Two men got out, as the ambulance was turned around. The two men who had just arrived were checking his leg when the ambulance driver got out and opened the back door of the ambulance. He got out a stretcher and put it next to Gustafson. Then three men lifted Gustafson up and onto the stretcher. Once he was on the stretcher, the men were putting Gustafson into the ambulance when Harland came walking up to the ambulance. Introducing himself, Harland got into the ambulance after Gustafson's stretcher was placed inside.

The American, who had cut the shroud lines of Gustafson's parachute, handed him the rolled-up parachute as he was being loaded into the ambulance. Gustafson was grasping his parachute across his chest as the driver closed the doors and soon, the ambulance was bouncing across the field. As the ambulance made its first turn onto the larger dirt road leading into Hattonville, Gustafson swore and told Harland, "That SOB kept my knife."

Five decades later, when he was first interviewed by the researcher, at a Memorial for Lt. Gott in Arnett, Oklahoma, Gustafson was still amazed that less than fifteen minutes after he had landed in the field in France, an American

ambulance, with him in it, had arrived at a hospital and the men from the hospital were helping unload his stretcher. And, he was still upset that some SOB had kept his favorite hunting knife at the crash-site.

T/Sgt. Gustafson's stretcher had just been set on the ground at the 109th Evacuation Hospital, when Pfc. (Private First Class) Ted Plant, the fellow who helped unload him from the ambulance, asked if he would mind if they cut out a piece of his parachute as a souvenir. "Sure," said Gustafson, thinking the fellow would cut off a small piece and give the parachute back to him.

Just then, a couple of nurses walked up and asked Gustafson what was wrong. He thought it was rather obvious, but he told them and they looked at his wounded right leg and told a couple of other men to take him to the cast tent. As he was picked up, the nurses began to talk to Harland and that was the last time Gustafson ever heard or saw Harland, until the researcher had contacted him.

In the cast tent, they gave him a shot and that was the last memory T/Sgt. Russell W. Gustafson had of 9 November, 1944.

As they took the flyer away, Fisher from the pharmacy walked by and Plant asked him to use the scissors he always carried on his belt, to help cut the parachute up for souvenirs. It took some time, however, every member of the 109th received a souvenir of the only aircrew treated at their hospital during the war.

S/Sgt. Robbins had watched the B-17 fly away as he floated below his parachute, then he looked down and realized he was going to land inside some woods, next to a large field. He was still in the air as he listened to the noise of the "*Lady Jeannette*" fade into the distance and then, just before he entered the woods, he realized she had to have turned and was getting closer.

As he fell into the woods, Robbins cleared all the large branches and was snagged by some small ones, but no damage was done to him. In the distance, he heard a whooshing explosion and he knew the "*Lady Jeannette*" had crashed.

Robbins was amazed to find himself standing in the woods, with his parachute caught in the trees above him. It was a picture perfect landing in a wood and he didn't even have a scratch from a branch. Even though his flight jacket was smeared with Dunlap's blood, there was none of his own. Robbins landed facing toward the large field and he was very close to the edge of the woods when he heard, and then saw a jeep careening across the field toward the woods. Robbins popped his harness straps and leaving the harness and parachute hanging from the trees, he walked out of the woods to meet the oncoming jeep.

The jeep driver seeing all the blood on his jacket, asked if he was hurt and Robbins told him that he didn't think so. The driver told him to climb into the jeep and they took off across the field. In the distance, Robbins could see smoke rising from the crash-site and thought the driver was taking him there. They headed across the field toward the farm buildings (*Hazavant Ferme*) at the western end of the field. Passing through the farm compound, the driver turned right onto a paved road, and began to drive away from the crash-site. Robbins asked the driver where they were going and the driver replied that he was from the nearby Etain Air Base and they were going there so he could be checked by the medics.

Within a half hour of landing, Robbins was at the Etain Air Base and the medical tent of the XIX Tactical Air Command. A doctor asked Robbins if he was hurt, Robbins told him he was fine and after the doctor did a couple of quick checks, he told the driver to take the airman to the headquarters.

At the XIX TAC Headquarters, Robbins was interviewed by a couple of officers and he told them everything he knew, including the fact that the tail gunner, S/Sgt. Krimminger, was hanging under the tail when Robbins left the B-17. After the debriefing, the driver was told to take him to the flight line as the officers had arranged a flight to take him to Paris, the first step to being returned to flight-duty. As there was always a shortage of flight-crew, they had a priority to get back.

__While Robbins was waiting for the small plane that he had been told would take him to Paris, he walked out to the flight line to see the parked fighters. And he specifically remembers, walking around two P-61 Night Fighters to inspect them as he had never seen one before.__ (**Note**: *Important to remember!*)

By 16:00 hours on 9 November, 1944, Robbins was in Paris. When they had landed, the pilot got him a ride into Paris to a fancy building that was close to Notre Dame. After checking in at the Enlisted Transit Quarters, he was released to walk the streets of Paris.

"There I was," Robbins told the researcher, "walking in Paris with Dunlap's blood still staining my flight jacket. As I was walking, I stopped in front of a famous perfume company's store. I looked at the very low prices for large bottles of fancy perfume and thought of my escape packet still attached to my parachute harness still hanging in the woods. Now," he continued, "I was wishing I had taken the escape packet with its French money as I really wanted to get my wife, Shirley, a bottle of that perfume. But all I had, were a few English coins to rub together in my pocket."

In due time, after seeing famous buildings, boulevards and a tower, Robbins went back to the transit quarters and for Robbins, 9 November, 1944, ended with him lying in a bunk in the enlisted men's transit quarters in Paris, thinking it had been "One, hell of a day!"

A short time after the arrival of Gustafson at the 109th, another ambulance arrived with another survivor from the B-17 lying on a stretcher. Once a nurse had the man walking to the proper treatment tent, Pfc. Ted Plant who had helped take his stretcher out of the ambulance, moved the stretcher to the stack of folded stretchers. That was where they put all the spare stretchers used to replace those an ambulance had to leave. As Plant lifted the stretcher's end up to slide it onto the stack, something fell out. Picking it up Plant realized, he now had two souvenirs of that day. One was a piece of parachute from the flyer with the broken leg and the other was a silk escape map from the second flyer who appeared to be dazed.

S/Sgt. Fross was taken to a treatment tent, and when he was checked for wounds they found he had several small head wounds. However, as Fross was still very much out of it, the doctors suspected Fross's wounds may have caused some concussion and they decided to sedate him for some time.

The 109th Evacuation Hospital Adjutant, Captain William E. Weller, had watched the B-17 crash and he ran to the headquarters tent where he found Colonel Prazak's's jeep and driver, Kenneth Simpson. He jumped into the jeep and told Simpson to take him to the crash-site and step on it.

On the way, they passed several ambulances heading toward the hospital and one of them had to contain Gustafson and Harland.

The road did not go directly to the crash-site. However, at each cross roads they found French people looking toward the crash-site and the French pointed out the road they had to take. At the south end of a small village named Hattonville, located just below the town on the hilltop, they picked up a Frenchman who guided them down a farm road toward the light smoke column in the distance.

Some distance later, along the northern edge of the large woods they came to a road branching off into the large field to their right. They could see American vehicles parked in the distance at the eastern edge of the woods, very close to the light smoke column still raising from the crash-site.

As they arrived, two Frenchmen were helping a person who was obviously a crew member of the crashed B-17, down into and back up the bank of the ditch that ran along the edge of the woods. Weller had Simpson get as close as he could and as the three men cleared the ditch, the guiding Frenchmen jumped out of the back of the jeep. Weller moved to the back seat and indicated the two Frenchmen should place the man they were helping in the front passenger seat. As soon as they did, Weller threw the French his open pack of cigarettes and told Simpson to head back to the hospital and he started talking to the flyer who seemed very upset.

On their way back to the hospital, they had to pass the ambulance that had transported Gustafson and Harland to the hospital, as it hurried back to the crash-site. Fifty-four years later, when interviewed at a 109th reunion, Pfc. Ted Plant, who helped unload the wounded man remembered very clearly how that ambulance driver had insisted he replace the removed stretcher at once, so he could get back to the crashed B-17, and he remembered that driver as being very rude that day.

In the time it took the jeep to get back to the hospital, Weller had talked Harms into trading his leather flight jacket for a magnum bottle of Cognac. As Harms was taken for treatment, he gave Weller the flight jacket. After which, the doctor who treated Harms, ordered his sedation for three days.

(*NOTE*: At the 109th reunions, many of those in attendance remembered that jacket. Weller had it tailored to fit him and during the upcoming winter, he was envied by everyone for being warm while they had less warming coats.)

Six years later, Weller was involved in another crash that the author had researched. He was the Hospital Commander at a Air Force base in California, when a B-29 had a major failure during take-off and crashed. Weller was in his private car, on his way to work, when the crash happened and he drove to the crash-site. There, a badly wounded man was placed on the rear seat and he rushed the man to the hospital for treatment. The man that had bloodied up his car's rear seat

and a atomic bomb had been aboard the B-29. Soon, the air base was renamed, as the Travis Air Force Base, for the General who died there on 5 November, 1950.

By the evening of the 9th of November 1944, all five survivors of the "*Lady Jeannette*" crash were under treatment at the 109th Evacuation Hospital or in Paris. As Harland was barely injured, there is a good chance that he was taken to Tours that same afternoon and put of an evacuation hospital train to Paris. The policy of the 109th Evacuation Hospital was to clear patients up the hospital chain as soon as they could and most patients spent less than 24 hours at the hospital.

When the "*Lady Jeannette's*" right wing began to cut into the Hattonville Woods, the branches of the 75 to 80-foot tall oak trees began to tear at the bomber's surfaces. Just to the left side of the bomber's path, there was a large oak about 100 feet from where the debris began to fall to earth. As the forward speed of the aircraft slowed, the passing air could no longer hold Krimminger's body against the right horizontal tail plane. Still hanging from the parachute shroud lines, Krimminger's body had begun to swing down from the bomber's tail, when one of the large limbs of that oak tree struck the moving, helmeted head of S/Sgt. Krimminger and removed it from his body.

As they entered enemy territory, the Gott crew had been ordered to prepare for the expected combat. Krimminger, put on his **FLAK** helmet. The helmet had hinged metal ear flaps on each side that fit over the earphones contained in his cloth flight helmet.

When later interviewed, S/Sgt. Robbins remembered seeing Krimminger coming from the tail with his helmet on and the chin strap still fastened. Robins remembered having told Krimminger that he should take the helmet off sometime before Krimminger accidently opened his parachute and was then pulled out of the B-17. Because Krimminger had refused to take the helmet off, when the "*Lady Jeannette*" lowered into the woods, Krimminger still had his helmet on. When the oak limb struck his helmeted head so hard, it bent the metal ear flap of the helmet almost double to form a clam shell shape, and broke the flap off of the helmet that was violently removed from Krimminger's now, obviously torn-apart head.

At that point over 400 feet from the location where the first large piece of the B-17, the engine-less right wing fell to earth and came to a rest, S/Sgt. Krimminger's life, instantly ended. After the flap was bent, his body continued to be torn-apart and spread along the debris trail by the limbs of the forest trees for the next 320 feet.

As the cockpit began to be struck by branches, Lt. Metzger put his right arm and hand in front of his face to protect it. The action did no good, as his recovered inventory identity tag would later prove. Both Gott and Metzger died as more branches broke into the cockpit, shattering the windshield and striking their heads hard enough to create multiple fracture of both of their skulls. However, thanks to their cloth flight helmets and their skin, their skulls were held together, even as the forward fuselage continued to lower further into the trees of the Bois de Hattonville (Woods of Hattonville).

At a point about 350 feet along the debris trail, the bomber hit a large tree, that broke into the left wing root hard enough to break free two of the internal control shutters inside the heat transfer box located deep within the wing on the cockpit side of the number-two engine. Another tree struck the right wing and it was torn completely off at the wing roots. As the left wing was torn from the fuselage of the B-17, the non-operating number-one engine broke free and flew for another 60 feet before digging itself deep into the lay of the forest floor.

A number-four engine mount support, one of only two pieces of the B-17 the researcher has found, that can be plotted as being in exactly the same location on the day of the crash, as it was found fifty-nine years after the crash. The right end of the tube above was torn off when the engine was lost over Saarbrucken and the left end was bent and broke when it was jammed into the forest floor.

Photograph: Willis S. Cole, Jr.

The still-operating, partially damaged number-two engine, stayed with the left wing to fall to earth, 120 feet away from where the right wing stopped moving.

As the right wing was torn off, it flipped over and fell to earth to come to a stop, leaning against a tree. The, still-running under emergency power setting, number-three engine ripped from its engine mount and rolled 100 yards to the west of the crash-site before it stopped moving.

As the right wing fell to earth, it jammed a heavy metal tube about four feet into the ground at the bottom of the impact crater it created. The two and one-half inch square tube was part of the blown off number-four engine mount and nacelle. It came from the area where the oil tank fill tube was located. The engine mount tubing had been sticking out in front of the right wing since the first **FLAK** shell had removed the engine, along with most of the engine nacelle, all the way back to the front of the wing. The right wing was the first major item of the broken B-17 to strike the earth along the debris trail and come to a stop of the floor of the Hattonville Woods, creating two impact points in the clay of the forest floor.

The jolt of the wings tearing off caused the tail to break away from the forward fuselage and as it fell away, it carried the rear radio compartment bulkhead and door along with it. This left the forward fuselage, consisting of the open radio compartment, the bomb bay, the cockpit and the nose to continue for another 127 feet before the chin turret machine-guns began to dig two trenches in the clay floor of the Hattonville Woods.

The broken tail fell just beyond the point where the right wing came to rest, pressing into the earth, creating an impression of its form and absolute proof of it's crash-site location that can bee seen to this day. The broken off forward-end of the tail came to rest over the still to be seen hole where the number-one engine had buried itself deep into the earth.

As the forward fuselage continued in the air, the left wing, now flipped over to the right side of the fuselage came to rest leaning against a tree. The limbs of the trees had ripped the wing's fuel cells open and for some distance atomized fuel was spreading over the crash-site. When the rear edge of the left wing jammed into the clay and the forward edge slammed against the tree, the number-two engine that had served so heroically, broke free, rolled about 20 feet, came to rest. The left wing's tire assembly, stored in the number-two engine nacelle during flight, broke free and fell to earth.

Then, the atomized fuel was set alight by some unknown ignition source and it whooshed into a flash fire, which set the tire and engine on fire. Even though the whooshing fuel fire was over in less than two minutes, the tire and engine continued to burn and smoke for some time.

As the broken forward fuselage continued forward, no higher than 10 to 15 feet in the air, the wounded radio operator, T/Sgt. Robert A. Dunlap, rolled out of the broken end of his radio compartment to fall into an area heavily covered with blackberry bushes. ***His complete body*** broke through the bush and landed on the floor of the woods. The forest floor was covered with up to a foot of forest duff, equal to a soft mattress, when Dunlap's body struck the ground. When the flash fire took place, the blackberry bushes protected his body, preventing major fire damage. (**Note**: It is important to remember his fall from the still moving fuselage.)

As the chin turret machine-guns began to dig their trenches in the clay, the nose was already beginning to push the clay forest floor ahead of it and the nose quickly slowed from its forward flight. At a certain point, the pushed up clay in front of the nose became large enough, strong enough, and slippery enough to divert the nose of the forward fuselage almost 90 degrees to the right. It then began to take a westerly course, directly toward the edge of the woods where Harms was just landing. The fuselage finally stopped with its broken end about 9 feet past what remained of the pile of clay it had pushed up.

The nose was just 227 feet away from the western edge of the woods when the forward fuselage stopped moving, ***S/Sgt. Herman B. Krimminger's torn-apart remains were scattered on the ground and in the trees along the debris trail for 400 feet before the point where the right wing came to a stop***. From the first evidence of debris seen by Harms to the tip of the nose, the "*Lady Jeannette*" left a debris trail over 600 feet in length.

(**Note**: Obviously, she did not dive toward the earth and explode twice, as stated in the **Congressional Medal Of Honor Citations**.)

In the branch-damaged cockpit of the "*Lady Jeannette*" still sitting side by side, slumped over in their seats, their heads damaged by the branches that broke into their cockpit, were the dead, ***but complete bodies*** of 1st Lt. Donald J. Gott, Pilot, and 2nd Lt. William E. Metzger, Jr., Copilot.

At the 109th Evacuation Hospital, Dale L. Fish (Saginaw, Minnesota) driving his truck near the WWI cemetery, could hardly believe his eyes as the plane disappeared and the cloud of smoke from its crash expanded. John S. Lindsey (Oneida, New York) watched the bomber crash and John later stated to the researcher and other members of the hospital's reunion association that, "I had never felt so helpless in my life. I knew the bomber was going to crash and I knew men were probably going to die and there was nothing I could do, but watch them die." Dave Wasser (Wichita, Kansas) saw the parachutes opening as the bomber appeared to spiral near a village and then he saw the flash of fire, followed a short time later by the sound of the flash fire, hoping they had all gotten out.

Then, those on duty returned to duty and those who were not, talked to each other for some time about what they had just seen, happening in front of them.

Flight Engineer - Russell W. Gustafson
Fill-in Bombardier - Joseph F. Harms
Holiday Inn in New Jersey, meeting after 52 years and discussing 9 November, 1944. Late in the evening with both men learning more of what happened that day.

Photograph: Willis S. Cole, Jr.

Until this meeting, Gustafson had thought it was Metzger who had helped him with his morphine injection and also throwing out the burning flare bag.

Before that evening ended, they and the author were able to tie up several loose ends. Such as Harms had also helped bandaging the wounded radio operator, Robert A. Dunlap.

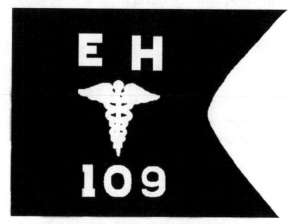

109th Evacuation Hospital

Scanned: Willis S. Cole, Jr.

109th Evacuation Hospital - Lison, France, 1944
History of the 109th Evacuation Hospital
21 June 1943 - 25 December 1945
Howard M. Kitgaard - 13 June, 2001

Scanned: Willis S. Cole, Jr.

9 November, 2000 - Woods Of Hattonville
56ᵗʰ Anniversary of the crash of the *"Lady Jeannette."*

Left to Right:
Jeanne Metzger Scholfield, Sister of 2ⁿᵈ Lt. Metzger, Jr., *"CMOH"*
Art Scherbarth, Captain, Ambulance Company Commander
(Located 4 miles north, his unit was not
involved on 9 November 1944. After the
war Art tracked down the nurse he had met
at the 109ᵗʰ and married her.)
Blanch Scherbarth, Nurse, Lieutenant, 109ᵗʰ Evacuation Hospital

Leaving the forest road onto the berm road/path over which the *"Lady Jeannette"* had flown sixty-six years earlier. On the way to visit the *"Lady Jeannette"* crash site and conduct a Memorial Service. Jeanne's brother, Bill (Lt. Metzger), had died while passing over this road/path on 9 November, 1944, that the tractor will follow to the crash site, located 400 feet away.

At this point, Lt. Harms, the *"Lady Jeannette"* Bombardier who had followed the forest road to this intersection, began to walk down the same path the tractor will be taking to the crash-site.

107

Hattonville - 9 November, 2000
The Air Force Furnished A Color Guard

They stayed with us for two days and three other Memorial Dedications

The "Stars And Stripes" military newspaper sent two representatives.

Two French Military Associations
Le Souvenir Français
Union National Combatants
Provided Honors with their Flag Presentation

The author and French interpreter are to the left of the memorial.

Photograph: Carol L. Cole

Chapter Five
The French - Hattonville

The American Army personnel, about 80 in number, had arrived in the village of Hattonville, Department of the Meuse, on 14 September, 1944, and they would leave on 2 December. For the past two months, they had made themselves at home in Hattonville and since Hattonville was a very small village the villagers knew all the Americans. If not by name or personal relationship, they knew the Americans by sight and often they knew the job the Americans had within the American Army.

The commanders or highest ranking officers were living at the Mayor's home and the other officers were living in the church presbytery. The German lower officers had lived in the presbytery during World War One and then the Americans lower officers had lived there for a while, after they and the French had driven the Boche away from the village. For a short while in 1918, the edge of the village woods, the Bois de Hattonville, 3.1 kilometers away, had become the German front line, before the Boche was driven further from Hattonville.

During the morning of 9 November 1944, the village had heard the thundering of explosions in the distance toward Metz, and at times could see the reflection of the sun off the American bombers that were dropping the bombs. They had heard bombs much closer, many times, and were very pleased the Germans were receiving the bombs today.

Mrs. Elise LECLERC, the wife of Louis LECLERC, was in their home with her young son, Robert, who was playing on the floor. The house was set at a northern angle across the main road from the church. The distant thunder of the bombing had become inaudible, when she began to hear other noises coming from the streets In front of her home.

Checking the clock on the wall, Mrs. LECLERC saw the time was about 10:30, as she went to the door to see what the noise was all about. As she stood in the doorway holding on to Robert's outstretched hand, she could see the Americans were acting like bees whose hive had been disturbed. She walked a short way out into the road, so she could look to the north along the road to where the combination village hall and school was located.

Mrs. LECLERC's home is visible on the left, at the end of the street. The church is off to the left and the top of the hill and the village of Hattonchatel are visible over the roof tops. The B-17 was lower than the hill to the west of Hattonville or it could have overflown Hattonchatel to a possible safe landing.

Photograph: Willis S. Cole, Jr. 2005

Map of Hattonville
The circle represents the church, the presbytery, and fete hall are just to the right of the church. The road to the crash-site is at the bottom center leading to the right. The village town hall/school is just above the intersection by the church and to the left.

Map: Willis S. Cole, Jr.
Guide De La Route
Selection du Reader's
Digest

The Americans had taken over the building, where upstairs they were known to be recording where airplanes were located and the American commander had taken over the Mayor's office for his own use.

Standing with Robert, Mrs. LECLERC could hear exclamations from that location and for the first time since they had arrived in Hattonville, she heard most of the American vehicles running their engines.

Immediately, Mrs. LECLERC realized the Americans knew something she did not know, and with her son in front of her, she turned back into the house closing and locking the door behind her.

It was almost 11:00 when she heard the Americans get really stirred up and she again opened the door to see what they were doing. As she did so, off in the distance toward the Moselle River, she could hear the noise of an aircraft and after five years of war, she knew the noises of airplanes, especially when they were in trouble or were shot down. More than 40 aircraft (including French, British, American and German aircraft) had crashed in the local area.

The engine noises she heard had to belong to a badly damaged aircraft, as it sounded like the airplane's engines were tearing themselves apart. At their home's angle across from the church, she could look down the road that split the town to the north of the church and she could see well into the distance. Mrs. LECLERC realized, some of the Americans at the Fete Hall were also looking down the same street to the east. Taking Robert by the hand, she left the door and went a bit to the north, so she could see better in the direction from where the sound was growing louder, as the plane approached the village.

In the distance, a large airplane came into sight. It was over the woods owned by the village and it was flying right toward the village. There was a bright flame coming from the left side of the airplane and smoke was billowing back from its right side, as it approached her and the village.

The aircraft was getting closer, and she could tell it was one of the large American "Fortress" bombers and that it was very low. Suddenly, Mrs. LECLERC saw an object fall from the aircraft, followed by another, then a parachute opened over the first dot and she knew for certain she was watching men bailing out of the badly damaged fortress. Just after the second man was visible, another appeared and then there were three parachutes at the far end of the *Les Grands Paquis.*

110

But that was not what bothered her. Taking a good look at the damaged bomber, she realized it was certainly coming right at her and the village. At the same time, other French people and many of the Americans who were outside, were suddenly very afraid. The darn thing might crash right on top of them. For all they knew, there was no one left in the bomber to guide it and it was coming right at them. It was time to run and run fast.

Grabbing Robert and grasping him tightly in her arms, Mrs. LECLERC began to sprint down the main road toward the south end of the village. As she ran, she heard the noise of the bomber getting louder and louder and she was expecting to hear it crash and explode. Then, she realized the engine noise was changing pitch. Slowing and looking back over her shoulder, she could see the bomber was beginning to turn and that it was high enough to clear the church, the tallest building in the village.

Mrs. LECLERC stopped running, put Robert down, and still holding on to one of his hands she turned around to watch the bomber, spewing flame and smoke behind it, leaving a trail in the sky. As she watched, the bomber completed a 180-degree turn and headed back toward Germany. However, it was very low and she stood there and watched, as it seemed to start another turn over the village woods. Then it disappeared from sight, with a large fireball and smoke appearing above the woods, along with a whooshing explosion that reached her ears in a short time.

As the noise of the approaching bomber began to broadcast its arrival, two men from the village, Pierre and Claude, were in the south-east corner of the combination of small fields that made up the large open area of *Les Grands Paquis*.

They watched in awe as the B-17 thundered overhead, heading toward Hattonville. Three men left the aircraft with their parachutes opening above them. Pierre and Claude started running toward the parachuting men, but it was a large field complex, nearly a kilometer wide at that point and they had to climb over fences and cross over a soft stream area on their way.

At first, Pierre and Claude ran, then they walked fast as they could, as they observed the bomber fly straight at Hattonville, turn over the village, and then fly back toward them. Pierre, who was in better physical condition, gained on Claude and he was beginning to get close to where the first man was landing, just as the bomber crashed into the woods beyond the man and then, a great fire erupted.

Pierre had to stop to catch his breath for a moment and he was surprised to see the landing man turn and run toward the woods in the opposite direction from where Pierre was approaching.

Pierre caught his breath and was soon where the man had dropped his parachute. Further on, a short distance inside the woods, he could see the crashed bomber. The flash fire he had seen was already out, and making his way down into and out of the ditch along the woods, Pierre ran to the broken nose of the bomber, realizing as he ran, that the bomber had broken into several large pieces. As Pierre approached the nose of the "Avion Fortress," there was an engine lying close to it, with a smokey oil fire still burning around it. A short distance from the engine, near a wing propped against a tree, a tire was still burning and melting the wheel hub.

111

When Pierre arrived at the cockpit, he tried looking into it; however, his view was blocked by the broken tree branches sticking through the broken cockpit windows. He could make out that the pilots were there, but was unable to see them with any clarity. He walked alongside the fuselage to where the tail had broken off and found that he could climb into the broken-open bomber, to get to the cockpit.

The broken open compartment was full of electronic equipment and there was a lot of drying blood on the floor. Pierre started through the doorway at the front and realized he was on a catwalk in what had to be the bomb holding area and just beyond the door, he could see the two pilots still in their seats. Pierre saw no movement and went into the cockpit area to take a closer look at both pilots. He saw that both pilots were dead and slumped over in their seats. Moving further into the cockpit and standing between the two dead pilots, he saw that their heads had been damaged by the branches breaking through the cockpit during the crash.

Pierre saluted the two dead pilots, turned around, and made his way out of the cockpit, bomb bay, and broken radio compartment to climb out. Claude had arrived and saw Pierre go into the fuselage, so he walked toward the broken tail. He heard Pierre climbing down from the broken end, and called for him to come over and see what he had found lying midway between the forward end and the tail some distance away.

To get to Claude, Pierre had to break through the fire-seared bramble bushes that covered the floor of the woods in that area. Pierre could soon see what Claude wanted to show him, as there was a body lying on the ground. The dead man had been slightly damaged by the flash fire. Then in the distance, close to the edge of the woods, they heard French and American voices, as well as American vehicles driving to the edge of the woods.

Pierre and Claude discussed how this man had died and came to the conclusion, he had bailed out so late that he had landed inside the flash-fire and the fire had killed him. Neither realized, the body only had one hand showing outside his coat. Both men then walked to the broken tail. Finding no bodies there, they were walking back to the burning engine, when the first Americans arrived at the crash-site. Two of the arriving men were the ones they referred to as the doctors and two were the men with the gold leafs on their shoulders, who were living and eating at the Mayor's home. They were two of men in charge of all the Americans living in the village, that lived in the Mayor's home.

The Frenchmen showed the Americans how to get into the cockpit to see the two dead pilots and they pointed out the dead man lying in the bramble bushes.

During a later visit, I was told that the time the Americans had been in the village was the best period of medical care the village had ever enjoyed. The local medical care had been better than World War One, when the Germans and the Americans had stayed in the village. Pierre, the first man to see the dead pilots told the researcher, that if you felt bad you went and saw the regular doctors (the enlisted medics) and they would give you some pills which usually worked. If you were hurt or were very sick, they would call one of the gold leaf men, who was known to be a real doctor. He would sew up cuts and gave excellent advice,

seeming to be able to do anything any French doctor might do. All this medical care was available right in the village and a patient did not have to travel any distance to find a French doctor, as they usually had to do.

After the gold leafs were there for a short time, they told the doctors to get into the broken fuselage and get the two pilots' bodies out of their seats. Pierre and Claude assisted them in that job, by helping them move the bodies through the bomb bay and carrying the bodies down to ground level, as the bottom of the broken-off floor was a couple of feet above the pile of dirt the bomber's nose had pushed up as it struck the earth.

Then Pierre and Claude, along with the doctors, carried the two bodies to the western side of the crash-site, where someone had placed a canvas on the ground upon which the pilot's bodies were laid side by side. Once that was done, the Frenchmen took part in breaking down the brambles, so the doctors could retrieve the other body and place it next to the other two.

As they had been inside the bomber, helping remove the two bodies, two of their friends, Michael and Jean-Paul, had walked over to look at the broken tail and wing at the start of the actual crash-site. Looking up the debris trail, they saw a man walking toward them, who was obviously an aviator. They correctly assumed he was one of the bomber's crew who had survived the crash and who was now coming to see what happened.

They looked up and saw the American gold leafs and a couple of other Americans were standing near a fire that had been started at the side of the crash-site, near the dead men's bodies and paying no attention to the approaching man, probably because they had not seen him walking toward the crash-site.

The man crossed the small stream and had almost gotten around the broken wing, when suddenly he began to jump and down, screaming, and swearing at the top of his voice. It was obvious to Michael and Jean-Paul that the American did not have control of himself and they quickly went to the man and each grabbed an upper arm, as they began to help him walk up toward the group of Americans who had now turned and were looking at them.

When Michael and Jean-Paul got to the two gold leafs with the American flyer, one of the gold leafs pointed toward the edge of the woods and they continued to help the man along. None of the Americans accompanied them and, as they were reaching the edge of the woods, an American jeep was approaching. When they reached the field on the other side of the ditch, the jeep stopped right in front of them. A friend, Christian, who had guided the jeep to the crash-site got out of the back and the American officer who was in the jeep moved to the back and pointed for them to help the American flyer into the front seat of the jeep.

As soon as they were done, the American officer gave them an open pack of cigarettes and the jeep immediately left in the direction of the road to the village. As they lit their good American cigarettes, Michael and Jean-Paul crossed back over the ditch with Christian to again survey the crashed American bomber.

As they approached the three dead men's bodies lying on a piece of canvas, and the group of Americans standing alongside, one of the doctors had found another piece of canvas and he was getting ready to put it over the three bodies.

By this time, a large number of nearby villagers had arrived at the crash-site and were standing around watching what the Americans were doing. Many observed the three complete bodies on the canvas before they were covered up.

Three young boys, whom they recognized as coming from the village of Vieville-sous-les-Cotes, located just around the steep hill and back in a valley to the north of Hattonville, came up behind them pushing the bicycles they had ridden to the crash-site. Their village was in a location where no one could see the B-17 in the air before its crash, but could hear what did happen in the distance.

The young boys were Jean-Marie Baltzinger, Géard Gassert and Claude Ligier. They had been at the crash-site for only a few minutes after they watched the man put a canvas over the three dead bodies. One of the Americans was wearing an avion (flying) jacket that, they believed, had to belong to one of the survivors. Especially, since it still had blood on it, the boys were certain he was a crew survivor. As they moved closer to all the Americans, the man in the avion jacket reached in his pocket and gave each of them a stick of gum.

Shortly afterward, one of the gold leaf men who was known to be second in charge of the American unit in the village told all of them, that they had to leave at once. He went on to say the crash-site was going to be guarded for some time and anyone who came close to the crash-site could be shot.

The French boys believed the man and they quickly pushed their bicycles back to the edge of the woods, got them over the ditch and began to ride back home. Along the way, they met new groups of people on their way to the crash-site. They knew all the people and they stopped each group to tell them the Americans would not let them reach the crash-site. Then they talked to the people about what they had seen and heard.

By the time they got home that afternoon, they knew the full details of the approach of the "Avion Fortress" bomber and how it turned over the village of Hattonville, to go back and crash into the woods. They, like all the other French people who had been to the crash-site, thought only three men had died in the crash.

None of the French had seen the torn-apart remains of the fourth man. Those remains and their condition after the crash were only reported by the survivor who walked to the crash-site. Then, two days later, the battalion attached **AMC** personnel who had recovered the torn-apart remains, submitted four (desecrated) remains, and four falsified Medical Form 52b's to Graves Registration personnel at the Limey Temporary Cemetery, concerning the four crewmen's deaths.

That night, at every table in all villages and towns in the immediate area, the main subject was the "Avion Fortress" coming from the east, that was spewing flame and smoke.

114

Chapter 6
563rd SAW BN (RCM)

563rd Signal
Aircraft
Warning Battalion

Drawing: Unit History/USAF/HRA

On 14 September, 1944, the Headquarters of the 563rd SAW BN, or Signal Aircraft Warning Battalion, arrived in the French village of Hattonville, Department of the Meuse. Hattonville is located 19 km to the east of St-Mihiel and 31 km southeast of Verdun. On 2 December, 1944, the Battalion Headquarters departed Hattonville for Cit. Des Charbonnages, which is 6 miles southwest of St-Avold.

The Battalion was under the direct command of General Otto Paul Weyland, XIX Tactical Air Command or XIX TAC, Ninth US Air Force. The XIX TAC was well known for the air support the unit had provided to General George S. Patton's Third Army during its drive across France after the Normandy breakout. General Patton was known to refer to General Weyland (or "Opie" as General Patton called him) "as the best damn General in the Army Air Corps."

The 563rd provided radar and ground observer support to the XIX TAC Command Center, providing the location and identification of aircraft in their Air Defense Zone in that area of France. Each radar battalion's coverage overlapped the battalions to either side, to prevent a gap in radar and ground observer coverage.

Though the 563rd SAW Battalion consisted of nearly a thousand men, the Headquarters Company and the Plotting Center personnel, who were actually in the village of Hattonville, numbered around 80 men most of the time. The other men were in the various Radar and Ground Observer Companies spread from Nancy in the south-east to Luxembourg to the north.

The 563rd Ground Observer Companies were situated along the front line among the ground fighting units. From their front line fox holes, the job of these was to provide visual information back to the plotting center at battalion headquarters, which would then be forwarded to the XIX TAC Control Center.

As I was directly involved with a very limited number of the men of the 563rd, to prevent a large number of names detracting from the events that took place. I will only use the names of those most directly involved in what was done. Four of the men who were deeply involved took the secret of what we did to their grave, they were AMC Medical personnel attached to the Battalion and each stated to the end to anyone who asked, *"I have no memory of any bomber crashing while I was in Hattonville."* If, I did not already know, I would wonder why!

Lt. Col. William L. McBride, was the 563rd SAW Battalion Commander. The Executive Officer was Major Maurice Byrne, Boise, Idaho; Major Yashar A. Venar, Cleveland, Ohio, US Medical Corps, was the assigned Battalion Surgeon and Graves Registration Officer. The senior Medical Corps Medic was Sgt. Frank Boatman, Castro Valley, California. Two others in the Medical Section were Dominic Berardi, Brockway, Pennsylvania, and, Pfc. Otto Zeman, Cleveland, Ohio, the ambulance driver. One of the officers working at the plotting center was Lt. Godfrey A. Welham, Tulsa, Oklahoma and T-5 Alfred Madl, Glendale, Wisconsin, who worked in the Battalion Operations Center.

At about 10:15, 9 November, 1944, an outlying 563rd radar station called in their first plot for a new target that had just appeared some distance to the east of Metz. The radar equipment the unit used at that time could track aircraft up to 80 miles, depending on the height of the aircraft and its size. Radar was basically an electronic device, that radiated a strong radio beam from its rotating antenna along a line of sight. The antenna then received a very faint radio signal reflection from an aircraft within its range. Electronic amplifiers were fed the faint electronic pulse return and amplified it until it could be shown on the radar display screens under the constant observation of radar operators.

Once a moving target was defined, the location of the target, its altitude, its speed and flight direction were all called into the 563rd SAW Battalion Plotting Center. As the inbound aircraft continued to "paint" or show on the radar display, an identity of the target had to be established. Once the path of the target was established, the target information flowed from the actual radar operator to his local

position plotter, to his battalion plotting center and then up the reporting chain to the XIX TAC Control Center.

As the new target was over the German/French border and located well inside the German occupied territory on that date, it would have first been an Unknown or Probable Enemy Target (PTE). Then, as the target continued to paint on the radar and target plots were placed on the plotting board. The involved men in the plotting center realized that the target was on a flight path, with a slight right turn and it appeared t be heading directly toward their headquarters location.

For the next 30 minutes, the target continued to follow the same flight path, however it was constantly losing altitude as it approached the front line from the east.

The Germans were known to fly bombers down the Allied radar beams in an attempt to bomb the radar antennas out of operation. At some point, the pucker power of the direct approach of the Unknown, Probable Enemy Target would force the plotting center duty officer to call the Battalion XO, (Executive Officer), who was also the Battalion's radar expert, the Battalion Duty Officer, and others to inform them, that a possible attack on

The Hattonville combination village hall and school. The 563rd SAW Battalion Plotting Center was located on the upper floor of this building. The photograph was taken from the front of the church, looking to the north-west.

The 563rd personnel in this area were looking up at the bottom of the B-17 when it passed directly over their heads, about 300 feet above them.

All of the 563rd SAW BN HQ unit personnel who were contacted remembered the B-17 flight overhead and subsequent crash. That is, except for the Executive Officer and three attached medics, who were directly involved with the dead at the crash site due to standing Army regulations. For some years and to their death, each claimed to have no memory of the event.

Photograph: Willis S. Cole, Jr. - 2005

their location appeared to be taking place. As this information spread around the notified personnel of the 563rd in Hattonville, the natives noticed the Americans began to act like a bee whose hive was being tampered with.

The XIX TAC Command Center meanwhile, would have realized the situation and begin to vector fighters to intercept the oncoming target, and shoot it down if it was found to be an enemy.

(Note: Oddly, no such records exist today!)

117

At the same time, as the incoming Target's course was being called into the 563rd Plotting Center, the plotting center personnel were also reporting out to their Front Line Ground Observation Posts. Instructing their ground observers about the incoming PET and requesting they watch for the inbound aircraft as they might be able to identify the target via visual observation.

About 10:40, a ground observation post reported they were able to see an aircraft inside the German line that was on fire and smoking. Concentrating on the inbound aircraft, they were soon able to report back that it was a B-17 and it was in big trouble, as German **FLAK** bursts were beginning to zero in on the B-17.

Back at the Hattonville plotting center, the pucker factor began to ease. However, the higher ranking and plotting center officers were aware that the Germans had captured some number of American B-17s and there was still a remote possibility that this could be one of those captured B-17s, crewed by Germans. It was possible the Germans could be using the fire and smoke as a ploy to allow them to pass over Allied controlled territory to conduct a behind-the-line surveillance of Patton's advance, now in its second day of attack.

The message was passed to the unit's Hattonville personnel to stand by, as the now Probably Friendly Target (PFT) continued to fly a path that would have it flying over Hattonville, unless it changed course.

As the damaged B-17 passed over the Moselle River, the radars, and ground observers both called in to say, its altitude was about 5,000 feet and that the B-17 was continuing to lose altitude at a rate of 250 feet per minute. By now, they had established the B-17 was flying at a speed of 120 mph, as it approached France. At the Moselle River, the B-17 was approximately 20 miles from Hattonville and after a quick mathematical calculation by the plotting center officer at Hattonville, he realized the B-17 could be running out of height as it approached Hattonville.

Again, the pucker factor began to climb, and this time as the word passed, the men outside began to start up the engines of their vehicles and look to the east. To the French in the village, the disturbed bees were now acting like their hive had been knocked over.

Major Venar, the Army Medical Corps Surgeon attached to the battalion, had arrived at the plotting center to see what was going on and he found Major Byrne, who was observing the constant reports on the approaching B-17. Venar had already told the Army Medical Corps enlisted personnel, attached to the battalion, Boatman, Berardi, and Zeman to have the ambulance ready to go, as they might be needed. *Major Venar knew, anyone who was on board the inbound bomber, who was wounded or killed (had become damaged or broken GI inventory) would immediately become his direct responsibility if the aircraft landed or crashed in the geographical area the 563rd Battalion Headquarters was responsible for.*

At 10:55, off in the distance, the noise of the approaching aircraft could be heard and Majors Byrne and Venar left the plotting center and went down stairs to stand outside the Mayor's Office/Battalion HQ with Lt. Col. McBride. There, they stood along with some of their men, all looking to the east, in the direction where

they could now hear the engine noise of the approaching B-17. Soon it was seen, it was very low.

Two hundred feet to their east, T-5 Alfred Madl was standing with a group of the battalion men outside the village Fete Hall, that served as the unit's mess hall, where the men were waiting for early lunch to be served.

They were standing on the same east/west village road that Mrs. LECLERC was looking down, as she and her son, Robert, came out of their house to see what was going on.

To the west of the Fete Hall, with connecting walls, is the church presbytery. Living in the second floor, south-east corner room of the

Hattonville Fete Hall

In 1944, the Fete Hall served as the mess hall for the 563rd BN HQ personnel.

Photograph: Willis S. Cole, Jr. - 2005

presbytery, Lt. Godfrey A. Welham was awake and off duty when he began to hear noise coming from the east and he went to the window to see what was causing the growing noise.

About 10:56, the people in Hattonville, who were either standing outside or looking out their eastern windows, saw the flaming and smoking B-17 coming into sight. The French knew it was over a large forest, part of which belonged to Hattonville. Most of the Americans did not realize the large field starting near the south east of the village, lanced like a large finger between the woods they saw in front of them, or the fact the B-17 had come into sight over the very woods owned by the village.

The burning and smoking aircraft, was now less than 3 miles from the village and it was coming at them at a speed of 2 miles per minute. Within seconds, as the B-17 grew in size, everyone saw the first dot appear beneath the bomber that was now, no more than 550 feet in the air. Then another larger dot had appeared and a parachute had just opened above the first dot, when Major Venar yelled at the medics and told them to get out to where those men were going to land. He knew, if any of the parachutists were wounded he would be responsible for him.

Zeman had the engine running and as soon as Boatman and Berardi were in, he put the ambulance in gear and started to move down the main road toward the south end of the village. He knew there was a farm road there that ran out to where the parachuting men were going to land. He knew it well, as there had recently been one of their radar units out there in the field, that he made some trips to when men had to be brought to Hattonville to see Major Venar.

As the medics ambulance began to move, those on the ground watching the incoming B-17 saw a third person fall from the aircraft and by then the man who

119

Front of the Hattonville presbytery
The lower ranked officers lived here. The church is to the right. Lt. Welham was in his upstairs room at the rear (South) on the left (East) side.

Photograph: Willis S. Cole, Jr. - 2005

fell from the bomber was close enough for his arms and legs to be seen when his parachute opened.

As Zeman's ambulance charged down the street, they passed the Leclerc woman with her kid in her arms, running like the devil was after her. At the same time, some French and Americans began to run from the village toward the parachutists, as did some Frenchmen and off-duty Americans who were out in the fields helping the French farmers.

In the village, when the people saw the third man bail out and his parachute opening, more were quickly realizing the B-17 was losing height as she flew at them. To many it seemed it was going to land right on top of them. Some realized they had no way to know if anyone was in control of the aircraft and it was coming at them, personally. This on anyone's scale, has to equal about the highest pucker factor that anyone can feel, without being involved in their own direct, life or death situation. Yes, they were directly involved, but those who stood their ground either felt they had no choice or they realized the bomber was high enough, it would fly over them. Many had begun to run, including Mrs. LECLERC, and others, who either did not feel the threat or were too engrossed in what they saw, stayed, and watched as the "Avion Fortress" came closer to the village.

Up in his room, Lt. Welham saw the bomber come in sight and watched as the men bailed out. Then it dawned on him, if it crashed into the presbytery he was probably going to die, as it was too late to run. So Welham stood his ground and watched as the bomber roared toward him. Down in the street, T-5 Madl thought it was going to be just to the west of where he was, so he stood his ground and watched as the B-17 came so close it began to be lost from sight for split seconds as it was hidden by buildings.

The B-17 had almost reached the first of the buildings of the village when the people in the village saw the plane was starting to turn to the north. Welham watched it disappear right over his head and most people in the village had a perfect view of the final moments of its most westward flight, as the bomber completed the first 90 degrees of its turn just a bit west of the church. As the B-17 got close to beginning its turn flying over the village, the men from the battalion plotting center heard it getting louder and louder. They ran down the steps and away from the light-blocked upper floor of the village school. When they arrived outside, the men looked up to see the flaming and smoking B-17 pass right over their heads.

As the B-17 completed its turn, every villager and most Americans thought or said a quick prayer. Then, if they were not running across the fields or already in a vehicle heading down the road, toward the woods and field where the parachutists would be landing. They were hunting for an open view of the B-17 as it began to fly back to the east just north of its inbound flight path.

For about a minute, long enough to burn the memory into (almost(?)) everyone's mind forever, they watched that flaming, smoking B-17 getting lower and very close to the top of the woods as it flew away from them toward the east.

Then in the distance, they watched, as the right wing lowered and the B-17 began a right turn. As they watched, it was as if the trees were eating the B-17. It appeared to level out a bit and then they could no longer see the B-17. Within split-seconds, a large flash-fire followed by a column of heavy smoke was all they saw. Two minutes later, all they could see were two small columns of smoke rising from the woods. Of the thousands of people watching the events that day, fifty-nine years later, only four would later claim it never

Lt. Welham was in the upper, south-east room of the presbytery, which is under the 2nd chimney from the right. The church is just to the left of the building, which indicates the *"Lady Jeannette"* flew right over the position where this photograph was taken.

Photograph: Willis S. Cole, Jr. - 2005

happened, and *by U. S. Army Regulation, three of them were the attached American Medical Corps personnel directly responsible for the wounded and dead of the "Lady Jeannette!"*

With the head start given to him by Major Venar, Zeman's ambulance had reached the road to the field and had started toward the parachuting men, as the B-17 arrived over the village and started back to the east. As the ambulance was bouncing down the road, at first the B-17 was parallel to them heading west. Then, suddenly, the B-17 was directly north of them and heading back toward the east. Zeman watched as he could, and the three men in the ambulance saw the bomber's final attempt to turn and then its disappearance into the woods. From their location, they could look up the length of the field complex and they were "eyeball" witnesses, as the woods erupted with a flash fire. At the same time, between them and the flash fire, they could see the first of the three parachutes collapse as that man landed. Then, they saw the second parachute collapse over the 2nd man.

Zeman had the "pedal to the metal" and he was pushing the ambulance as fast as it would go, never mind the potholes in the road. Boatman and Berardi were bouncing around and holding on to whatever they could and swearing each time the ambulance bounced out of a pothole.

They were driving up the sloping road to the north side of the large field. When the third parachute began to settle, it did not fully collapse and they realized it was moving with the slight wind and it had to be pulling the man with it. They could also see two men running, who were almost to the parachutist and Zeman kept it rolling.

Zeman reached the turnoff road into the field from the road to the woods, on which they had been traveling, and as he turned onto the new road, they were within 300 feet of the flyer who was being helped by the two men.

The wounded men and his helpers were at the edge of a crossroads of field roads and as they reached the small group, Zeman stopped the ambulance so that Boatman and Berardi could get out to check on the wounded man. Then he turned the ambulance around so they could load the man and he could head directly to the 109th Evacuation Hospital.

As Zeman turned the ambulance around, he saw two men running toward the edge of the woods where two much smaller columns of smoke were still rising above the crash-site woods. Zeman did see two parachutes lying on the ground in the distance, but he did not see anyone near them.

Zeman stopped, jumped out, opened the rear ambulance door to get a stretcher and turned to check on the situation with the parachutist. Boatman was on his knees at the man's side, and he had pulled up the man's right pants leg to view the wound and its bandage. It was obvious the man had a broken leg as the man's foot was just dangling. The flyer swore as Boatman was examining the damage. And, **at the moment Sergeant Boatman arrived to treat the flyer, T/Sgt. Russell W. Gustafson, (GI), was under the official authority of the Army Medical Corps**, and no longer part of the inventory of the 452nd BG (H).

Boatman began to fill out the flyer's Form 52b, as Berardi helped Zeman lay the stretcher along the man's side and the two of them got on their knees, slid their hands and arms under the flyer, as easily as they could. As Boatman attached the Form 52b to the flyer's chest, they lifted the flyer and placed him on the stretcher. As they were putting him into the ambulance, Gustafson told them, both pilots were still in the B-17 and offered them his flight manifest copy, they refused.

As the stretcher was lifted into the ambulance, the American soldier who had arrived first, and helped the flyer by cutting loose the parachute shroud lines from his parachute harness, put the cut-away and rolled-up parachute on the flyer's chest, who thanked him.

With the flyer's stretcher loaded, Boatman told Zeman and Berardi to finish locking down the stretcher for transportation and for Zeman to head to the hospital and get back as soon as he could.

Another person had walked up to the ambulance, while they were loading the flyer. As they turned away from the ambulance, having finished loading the stretcher, he introduced himself as 2nd Lt. Harland, the Navigator of the crashed B-17. The man in the stretcher called out, "Hey, Harland, it's me ,Gus, did you see anyone else?" Harland said, they had been the last ones out and he had seen the

bombardier running toward the woods. So when he landed, he also ran into the woods and did not come out until he had seen the ambulance coming along the road.

Boatman told Zeman to wait a minute, while he created a Form 52b for the 2nd flyer who had chin cuts. (*And 2nd Lt. Harland, (GI), instantly became the responsibility of the Battalion's attached AMC personnel*). Then Boatman told Zeman again, he was to take the two men to the hospital as fast as he could and then, lose no time in returning. Boatman then told Zeman, he and Berardi were going to find the other parachutist and see, if anyone else had survived the crash.

As they started to lope toward the crash-site a kilometer away, Zeman got into the ambulance, started it up and headed back toward the village. He had only gone a short way, when he encountered Majors Byrne and Venar in a jeep coming from the village and he stopped just long enough to report that he had two survivors in the ambulance. One had some cuts on his chin and the other had a compound fracture of his right leg, just above the ankle. Zeman reported, that Sgt. Boatman had told him to get these two to the hospital and return as soon as he could. As soon as Zeman was finished, Major Byrne, who was driving, put the jeep in gear and headed toward the crash-site. Zeman then headed to the 109th Evacuation Hospital, located across the field from the World War One American St-Mihiel Cemetery, about 8 miles away by road. In the back of the ambulance, as they bounced on the dirt road, Gustafson, referring to the American who had handed him his parachute, told Harland, "That Son of a Bitch kept my knife!"

Just as the panting Boatman and Berardi reached the parachute next to the woods and a short distance from the crashed B-17, they heard a jeep coming and they stopped and waited for Majors Byrne and Major Venar to arrive. They told the officers that they had seen some Frenchmen go into the woods toward the B-17, as they had left on foot for the crash-site, from where they had helped the flyer and Zeman had started to the hospital.

Boatman told the Majors, the man from this parachute must have run into the woods and they had not seen him yet. Major Byrne said, "He will find us, so let's get over and see if anyone lived though that," as he looked at the still smoking crash-site in the woods beyond the ditch.

The men scrambled across, and up over the piled up dirt inside the edge of the woods. When the ditch had been dug, the removed earth had been thrown onto the wood's side of the ditch and it was now covered with brambles and young oak trees that snagged at every movement, as well as holes which could hold a large fox or perhaps a badger if such a thing lived in France.

Once clear of the overgrown edge of the woods, the men could clearly see the broken nose of the B-17 through the trees, just 200 feet away from them. The nose had broken off from the tail, which was some distance away to their left. One wing was leaning against a tree very close to the nose and an engine, and a tire were still burning very close to the wing. From that distance, as the four Americans walked toward the crash-site, they could see there were broken branches sticking into the cockpit windows making it impossible to clearly see the pilots. About 150

feet from where the nose was located, at an "L" angle to the north, the tail and another wing were lying on the downward-sloping hillside inside the woods.

As they approached the broken nose of the B-17, they saw two Frenchmen walking up from the direction of the tail. Between the tail, the leaning wing and the forward fuselage was a large bramble area, showing some damage from the flash fire. The two Frenchmen came to meet them and one of them told the Americans, he had gotten into it, pointing to the nose, and that he had found both pilots dead, acting it out as he said it. He then pointed toward a mashed area in the bramble bush and told and indicated to them, that a third man over there was also dead.

The Frenchmen were from the village and all the men either knew each other directly or were familiar from seeing them in the village. As they talked, other Frenchmen were arriving as were a few other men from the battalion headquarters.

Major Byrne started to tell most of the Americans who arrived, to take a good look and then get out. *There were three dead men at the crash-site and the dead had become the official responsibility of all the AMC attached personnel, Major Venar and the medics*. One of the men, who had just arrived, was the Military Police Sergeant of the Battalion. Major Byrne ordered him to collect a few of these men and begin to get a perimeter set up to keep all the French from the crash-site and Byrne ordered the sergeant to make certain the guards were armed.

As Byrne was talking to the security sergeant, Venar told Boatman and Berardi to check on the dead pilots and to use the two Frenchmen to get their bodies out of the B-17 and place the bodies at a location he pointed out to them about 15 feet from the tire, which was still burning.

Boatman and Berardi motioned to the two Frenchmen and pointed to the cockpit and made motions to show that they were going to remove the dead pilots and they wanted the Frenchmen to help them.

When Boatman and Berardi made their way to the cockpit, just as the Frenchman had, they found the pilots slumped over in their seats, obviously dead from the tree branches breaking into the cockpit. Then, Berardi and Boatman had to push the tree branches away from the pilots, so they could free the bodies from the branches and their cockpit seats.

However, they were forced to cut one of the seat belts to free one pilot, as his seat belt buckle had jammed. Once the pilots' bodies were free, Boatman and Berardi had to work together to lift and remove each pilot's body from its seat. Then each body was moved back through the bomb bay's cat walk and out into the broken-open radio compartment floor, with the help of the two Frenchmen, where they laid the bodies on the floor that was already covered with semi-dried blood.

It took the four men about five minutes to remove each one of the bodies from its cockpit seat to the radio compartment floor. Then, with both pilots' bodies on the radio compartment floor, again with help of the two Frenchmen who were the first to arrive at the crash-site, they lowered the bodies, one at a time, out of the broken end of the radio compartment and carried them to the position indicated by Major Venar to place them on the tarp that had been spread out.

124

By the time they had carried the first body to the location Major Venar had specified, a piece of canvas had been laid down and they placed that pilot's body on the canvas and then they went back to retrieve the second pilot's body.

As they were walking to do that, Zeman was at the 109th and telling Pfc. Plant, who had helped unload the stretcher with the flyer on it, to hurry up and give him a replacement stretcher. To Zeman, there was at least one more man at the crash-site who might require an ambulance. However, the 109th man did not know that or apparently in Zeman's mind, did not care. During the researcher's interview fifty-four years later, Pfc. Ted Plant still remembered how he thought that particular ambulance driver had been very obnoxious when he brought the flyer with the compound broken leg to the 109th. "Here I am," he thought, "moving hundreds of wounded men some days and this fellow thinks, he deserves special treatment."

After Boatman, Berardi, and their helpers had placed the second pilot's body next to the first, they went to retrieve the third man's body from the bramble bush area. Venar had been in the bramble area with the third man's body, when they were working to get the other two bodies out of the nose. Venar was removing the dead man's parachute harness and his flight jacket, which still had his dry blood on it. As he removed the dead flyer's flight jacket, noting it was his size, Venar found the airman's right hand was almost cut off, and he had suffered an additional wound to his left thigh.

In the upper left shirt pocket of the dead man, Venar found a basically undamaged wallet. Taking off the light field jacket he had on, Venar put on the dead man's blood-stained flight jacket and went to show Byrne the wallet.

The wallet contained one American $5.00 bill. It was interesting in that it was the dead man's "*Short Snorter*," (a souvenir from their Atlantic crossing) and they would soon know that it had been signed by one of the dead pilots. It also had the signature of several other men, along with the serial number of a B-17. There was a Birth Certificate, an address book, a Social Security Card, a Marksman H.P. Certificate, a money order receipt, a WDAGO - Form 29 and six English Pounds.

When the medics had placed the third man's body next to the other two, Venar told Boatman to check the other two bodies for identity tags. When he opened their flight jackets, Boatman found each men had two ID tags on the chain around their neck. Boatman reported what he found to Venar who wrote down each man's name and serial number in a pocket notebook and told Boatman to leave the ID tags hanging outside their clothing. Then Venar told Byrne that the signature of one of the pilot's was also on the "Short Snorter."

As Boatman was opening the pilots' flight jackets, he found one of the pilots had suffered a badly broken right arm. As he moved the arm, Boatman heard something inside the dead man's shirt and near his arm pit. Looking inside the shirt, he found an identity bracelet with a broken chain, that had the man's name on it. He handed the identity bracelet to Venar, who put it in one of the pockets of the flight jacket he was wearing, along with the other man's wallet.

As they were finding something to cover the bodies, Boatman saw two Frenchmen down by the other wing and the tail, pointing in the direction from

which the B-17 had settled into the woods. Looking in that direction, he saw a man dressed in flight gear walking toward the crash-site. He realized that this airman had to be the man who landed at the edge of the woods and then ran into the woods.

They had found a piece of canvas and were covering the three dead bodies, when all of a sudden, someone was hollering and screaming down by the tail. Looking that way, Boatman saw the two Frenchmen going to the flyer, who was jumping up and down, screaming and swearing at the top of his voice. Boatman looked at Byrne and Venar, and saw that they and the others were also looking in

T/Sgt. Robert A. Dunlap's $5.00 "Short Snorter." North Atlantic Crossing 30 July 1944. Plane (B-7G): 43-488184. Names and partial names visible: Bob Dunlap, Irvin Hirsch, Russell Gustafson, Earl L. Penick, Glenn T. Fuller, Herman B. K(rimminger), JA H(arland) and Bill Robbins. 43-488184 collided with 43-37941 on 1 September 1944 north of Caen, France, with 17 **KIA** and 3 **R**eturned **T**o **D**uty. (The lower left corner is gone through handling over the years. **It was undamaged when received by Dunlap's family in 1945.**) His sister gave it to the author for his help in learning what had really happened to her brother and involving them during the Memorial installations.

(**Note**: In his grave - "**Fractured: all major bones, skull & mandible; distal ends of rt radius & ulna missing.**" **And, the above was in his pocket when he died?** We know his main body had no visible injury, why is so much missing?)

Photograph: Willis S. Cole, Jr.

at the flyer. As they all watched, the two Frenchmen half-carried and half-walked the flyer toward the group next to Boatman.

When the two Frenchmen, who were half carrying the now silent flyer, arrived at the group of Americans, Byrne and Venar were talking. Venar had just told Byrne that he was expecting Zeman back at any moment. So Byrne pointed and told the two Frenchmen to take the flyer to the field, just beyond the woods, where Zeman would see to him when he arrived at the crash-site.

Boatman had been talking to Berardi, as they watched the two Frenchmen lift the man up into the field from the ditch, when a jeep drove up. Within a minute, with the flyer now in the passenger shot gun seat, the jeep was leaving as the three Frenchman made their way back into the woods to the crash site.

About that time, Venar and Byrne were talking about the torn parachute wrapped around the tail plane. For some reason, none of the men of the 563rd has said they saw or heard the man under the tail as the "*Lady Jeannette*" passed over them in the village. So, it appears they were thinking the flyer who used the torn parachute must have fallen to this death after his parachute had been caught by the B-17's tail.

The home of the Mayor of Hattonville at the time of WWII.

Photograph: Willis S. Cole, Jr. - 2003

Boatman told Berardi to follow him and they walked down to the tail to see the parachute for themselves. Boatman was thinking about the man who had seemed to go nuts and was wondering why that had happened. Talking to Berardi about that man's actions, they walked around the wing to where the flyer had gone nuts. The men were now walking back down the path, Boatman had seen the flyer use as he had approached the crash-site along its crash trail.

Meanwhile Zeman, who was rushing back to the crash-site from the 109th, had seen the 109th Evac.'s jeep coming and as it approached, he saw a man in the passenger seat who had on the same flight clothing that the two men he had just taken to the hospital were wearing. The man was wearing a jacket that was still stained with what appeared to be blood and as the jeep rushed by, Zeman correctly thought that he had to be the third man who had bailed out at the crash-site.

Still, he thought that there could be another survivor at the crash-site. The B-17 was obviously under full control, in order to be able to make the two turns. That meant, at least one pilot was on board when they saw it crash. So, he put the "pedal to the metal," reached over and flipped on the siren and he came as close to flying as he could, as the traffic parted and he rushed back to the crash-site.

Boatman and Berardi had followed the path about 60 feet, when looking off to his right where the B-17 had left its debris trail of broken branches, aircraft parts and other stuff, Boatman saw something that appeared to be out of place. Yet, at the same time, it looked like something he was familiar with. Boatman pointed out the right red and white thing and he and Berardi, climbed up on the dirt berm to get a close look at what Boatman had seen.

WW2 Emergency Medical Tag

Every Medic, enlisted, and officer carried these tags. The completed form 52b tag was then attached to the chest of the dead person if possible. Carbon copies helped prepare the necessary reports.

Photograph and Information
http://med-dept.com/emt.php

Instantly, Boatman knew exactly what had made the man go nuts. Boatman was looking at part of the body of a man. It was a piece of a man's body that had to

Form 52b Medical Department (Revised October 25, 1940) 16-15434

An example of the form that Major Venar would have filled in for each of the dead and attached to the bearer's chest.

When the bearer was dead, the form was removed at the cemetery by medical personnel attached to Graves Registration and then forwarded to the Chief Surgeon and then to the Surgeon General's Office.
Photograph and Information
h t t p : / / w w w . m e d -dept.com/emt/php

have been torn-apart by the tree limbs, as the B-17 had smashed through the woods.

(**Note:** *At that point, the Battalion's attached Army Medical Corps personnel, in the persons of Venar, Boatman, Berardi and Zeman had assumed full responsibility, under Army Regulations, for the four dead men's remains <u>Which consisted of three complete bodies and one torn-apart body, spread out along the crashing B-17's debris trail!</u>*)

128

Boatman suddenly felt a bit sick and turning to Berardi, he told Berardi to hurry and go get Majors Venar and Byrne. Berardi took off, running toward the officers to ask them to come down to where Boatman was standing. Within a couple of minutes, the small group was looking at the partial, torn-apart remains of a fourth dead crewman of the B-17.

Venar told Byrne that they needed to start collecting the torn-apart remains right away. Byrne told Venar to come along and they went back up to where the fire was now burning, fairly close to the three bodies now covered by canvas.

On the way, Byrne told Venar, he would make certain the sergeant and his Military Police would keep the site clear of any French, as it was obvious that none of the French had seen the remains of the fourth crewman. Byrne also decided he would also tell the sergeant to also keep any interested Americans away, who he or Venar had not personally authorized.

Boatman and Berardi followed the officers and as Major Byrne was finishing telling the MP Sergeant exactly what he wanted, three young French boys came up to the group, pushing their bicycles. Venar took a pack of gum from his pocket and gave a stick to each boy and the Byrne told them and the other French present, that they all had to leave as the Americans were putting armed guards in place and if any French tried to enter the crash-site before the guards were removed, they might be shot. After taking a good look around the crash-site with wide-open eyes, the boys, chewing their gum, started to push their bikes back to the edge of the woods, where they joined the other Frenchmen leaving the crash-site.

Glancing at his wrist watch, Boatman realized it was only 11:40 and he could hardly believe that so much had happened so quickly. It seemed to him like he had been at the crash-site for hours, instead of 30 minutes.

Venar and Byrne, when Byrne had finished talking with the MP, turned to Boatman and the others and then Venar told Boatman they would have to recover all they could find of the torn-apart man and that his remains should be put next to the other three bodies, but kept separate from them.

Boatman reminded Venar and Byrne that they had not had lunch and it was going to take a lot of time to collect the torn-apart man's remains that were spread out along the debris trail. Venar and Byrne discussed their options and then Venar told the three men they still had time to go to the village to eat lunch before returning to the woods to collect the remains.

Byrne added, that he would tell the MP Sergeant to make certain he ran into town and got a few off duty men, who had already eaten, to replace the current guards, so they could eat and return as soon as possible. Byrne said he would talk it over with McBride and told Venar, he would go see the cooks and have them set arrangements to set up a system to keep the guards and the three medics recovering all the torn-apart man's remains, supplied with hot food and coffee as needed.

Venar agreed with that plan and Byrne called the MP Sergeant over to tell him to get into town at once to get the temporary guards and make certain, he told the Adjutant, Captain Schurke, about what Byrne had been ordered him to do as soon as he got back. In addition, the sergeant was to tell Schurke, that Byrne would

see him, as soon as Byrne got back to town, as Byrne wanted to verify all that Schurke had to do to ensure the men at the crash-site were taken care of.

Venar told the MP Sergeant that he needed to keep one guard about half way down the debris trail, as the remains of a fourth man were scattered along the debris trail. The guard's specific duty was to ensure that any birds and animals were kept away from the dead man's remains spread along the debris trail.

Once everyone felt they understood what was to be done, Venar told Boatman, Berardi and Zeman to have something to eat and get back as soon as possible. Before long, the ambulance was heading across the field, back toward the village. But, before they left, they were to bring him a book of Emergency Medical Form 52b's and five Personal Effects Bags, as he needed to begin to begin recording the death of the men and, he wanted a spare bag, just in case.

When they arrived at the ambulance, Shipment got the requested items and sent Berardi running back to the Majors, as Zeman turned the ambulance around and they prepared to leave for the village and their meal.

Major Venar, using a piece of metal from the B-17 as a support, began to fill out the Form 52b and Personal Effects Bags for each of the dead. He knew the personal information for three, but would have to wait to find the identity of the torn-apart man. One has to wonder how much easier it would have been, if Boatman, Berardi and Zeman had not refused the copy of the Flight Manifest, offered to them by Gustafson, the B-17's flight engineer.

As Major Venar completed the Form 52b's and labeled their Personal Effects Bags, he tied the Medical tag to the Personal Effects Bags for the four dead men. The torn-apart man's identification would have to wait until some form of information proving his existence could be found. Somewhere out there along the debris path, there should be two identity tags, personal clothing laundry marks and any other personal effects the torn-apart man would have on him during a mission.

The medics got to town, went to their billets to wash up and were asked many times what they had seen. All three told the questioners that they did not have time to tell them right now, but would tell them later. However, they did tell those who asked, that four men were killed in the crash.

When the medics got to the mess hall, the first thing Boatman did, was to go talk to the senior cook, as the medics and cooks looked out for each other. Boatman told the cook that they had to leave for the crash-site again, as soon as they had eaten. He added that it was going to be messy work, that would take some time. Boatman asked the cook for a couple of big thermos bottles full of coffee, along with some sugar and cream to be readied, so they could take the coffee with them. The cook assured him it would be no problem, and asked if they wanted any sandwiches. Boatman replied that it was not going to be work that created any hunger, but if they had any cookies or cake they would be happy to have them.

130

Personal Effects Bag, Tubular-shaped Khaki Cotton Bag
    7" in diameter and 8" in height, provided with a drawstring at the top, made from water-repellent cotton to protect contents. The Personal Effects Bag is Stock No. 27-B-250. Bag used to return the small personal items of deceased personnel to the effects processing depot for the personal items to be returned to their LNOK or Legal Next Of Kin.
    The white form stitched to the side of the bag contained locations for the following information: Serial Number, Name, Grade, Rank, Organization, Address, Nearest Relative - Killed In Action, Date, Battle Area, Died of Disease, Hospital, Information, Place of Burial, Point of Coordination, Description of Body, Members Missing, and Signed.

Field Manual, Graves Registration (15 Jan 1945)
    Not issued as of the time frame involved.
    The Emergency Medical Tag, U. S. Army, Form 52b was modified several times during the war. However, all previous editions would be used until their inventory was exhausted.

Photograph and Information Source: http://home.att.net/combatmedic/

    As the medics were eating, McBride, Byrne and Venar were at the Mayor's home (where the three men were staying), eating the lunch prepared for them by the Mayor's wife, whom they were providing with what she needed for their meals and some extra for the family.

When the Mayor, who was eating with them finished and left, the officers talked about the B-17 crash-site and the dead men. Byrne told McBride about assigning the guards and Venar told him about the arrangement to recover the torn-apart man's remains. Venar went on, telling McBride that he was preparing the required paperwork, and if the medics completed the dead man's remains collection that afternoon, he would have Zeman deliver the four dead men to the new Limey Cemetery location. Venar explained, that the Andilly Cemetery had gotten so muddy, Graves Registration had opened a new cemetery at Limey for American burials. However, the Limey cemetery was closer than the Andilly cemetery, where Zeman had taken the body of Pfc. James Rymer, their Forward Observer who had been killed at Gorz by Germany artillery fire on October 15th.

McBride agreed with what Byrne had done so far, and told Byrne to set up the rest of it with Captain Schurke, to ensure the men were found to maintain the guard as long as they had to. It was going to be somewhat hard to maintain such a guard with their limited man power, but Schurke would see it was done.

Over in England, at the Cheddington Air Base, men of the American 36th Bomb SQ (RCM), attached to the 100th Group RAF, who were to fly that night's Top-Secret mission began to stir. First Lt. Joseph Hornsby woke up, as he and his crew were again scheduled for a night mission with the RAF over eastern France. When he was ready, he collected his copilot, Casper, his navigator and Top-Secret electronics controller, Grey, and they went for their mission briefing scheduled for 14:15 that afternoon. When they arrived at the briefing room, they found the rest of their crew and the rest of the scheduled crews waiting for the briefing.

They were part of the 36th Bombardment Squadron (RCM), the RCM standing for Radar Counter Measures. Hornsby's supposed job was the Command Pilot of a B-24 crew. However, Hornsby felt he was more of a bus driver than a command pilot. It seemed, he was a bus driver who required seven other men to make the bus fly, just so all of them could transport Grey to where Grey did what Grey did. Oddly, the same feeling as T/Sgt Gustafson of the "*Lady Jeannette*."

None of them knew exactly what Grey did and they were told it was all Top-Secret and they were not to ask. Secrecy had been beat into them with the main reason being, if they ever captured, they couldn't tell the Germans what they did not know. At the briefing all Hornsby, Casper, and the enlisted men received was a light overview of the night's mission.

Lt. Grey was briefed separately and only he knew, exactly what was going on. It was a strange situation, but it was the situation they had, thought Hornsby.

They were told it was to be an important "**Spoofing Mission**." The only RAF planes flying that night would be RAF Mosquitoes working with the B-24's radar jamming screen to force the German night fighters into the air. After a false start, they were told their take-off time was being changed to, just after midnight. So, they were sent back to their quarters to rest and sleep as they could.

At the Mayor's home in Hattonville, when the officers were finished with their lunch and wine, they thanked the Mayor and his wife for another excellent

meal. Then all three men left the house, got into the jeep and headed to the headquarters, where Schurke's duty mainly consisted of keeping the Headquarters Company running smoothly.

Schurke had just returned from his own lunch with the lower ranked officers in the presbytery, where he shared his memories of the B-17's approach and crash with Welham and the other officers, when McBride, Byrne and Venar arrived. Byrne and Venar discussed the recovery with Schurke and Venar thought the medics might finish up that afternoon. However, if they did not complete the recovery by dusk, the unit would have to maintain a guard at the crash-site overnight and until the remains recovery could be completed tomorrow.

The officers discussed how the need for the extra guards and the medics being busy in the woods would affect the company. Venar said that he would plan on taking "*Sick Call*" by himself, in the morning or if necessary, it could be delayed until afternoon. That way, the medics would be free to take all the time required tomorrow to complete the recovery of the torn-apart man's remains.

With that, each of the men went his own way and Venar went to the dispensary where he saw the ambulance and found the three medics preparing to leave for the woods. They had drawn three buckets, three sets of waterproof gloves, three smaller canvas tarps and four mattress bags from supply. They told Venar, they felt they were ready to return to the crash-site.

Venar told them, if they were not done by dusk, arrangements had been made for guards to be at the crash-site during that night and as long as required tomorrow. Venar also told Boatman, if they did not complete the recovery that day, he would handle tomorrow's "Sick Call" by himself. That way they could get to the woods much earlier tomorrow to complete the recovery.

With that, the three men trooped out to the ambulance and soon they were crossing the ditch into the woods to begin the gruesome task of collecting the torn-apart man's remains. The guard at the crash-site had also just returned after being relieved to eat along with the other three men who were now out at the perimeter that Major Byrne had specified. As the Sergeant of the Guard described what the guards had been assigned to do, he told the three medics, that the guards would keep the fire going, so they would not have to worry about that.

The medics were not in all that much of a hurry to start picking up pieces of the torn-apart man up, so with the guard they first climbed into the broken nose and tail of the B-17. As anyone would, they took their time, searching for their own souvenir of the crash that could be sent home without any problems.

The inside of the forward fuselage had suffered little damage, except they had some trouble getting into the nose compartment. The nose compartment of the forward fuselage had suffered the most damage as the tree branches tried to split it open. They did discover that something had blown up under the cockpit floor (an Oxygen bottle). It had blown the top turret out of its position. However, there was no real fire damage inside the cockpit, the bomb bay or the radio compartment.

They also spent some time in the broken-off tail, taking turns to crawl back to the tail gunner's position and standing at the waist gun positions, thinking about

firing the guns at attacking German fighters. The trees had greatly damaged the ball turret as the B-17 broke its way through the woods. Then, when the tail had fallen down after breaking off the nose, what remained of the ball turret had been pushed all the way up into the waist. After looking at what was left of the pushed-up ball turret, the four men easily agreed none of them would want to be cooped up inside the ball turret or even stuck back where the tail gunner had to sit. "No sir," they agreed, "I like my war much better than that poor bastard's air war." S/Sgt. Robbins, when he was interviewed years later, had told the researcher about his duffel bag remaining in the waist when he bailed out. In the confusion of the moment and when his life was on the line, the last thing Robbins thought of as he bailed out through the hatch was his duffel bag. One of the questions that has remained unanswered over the years, during all the investigations and research, is exactly what happened to that duffel bag and its contents?

One of the boys, when they were interviewed fifty-eight years later by the researcher, remembered seeing something that looked like a green canvas bag sitting next to the three bodies, when the man in the flyer's jacket gave them the gum. If, it was Robbins' duffel bag, no one else has ever accounted for it. I had forgotten all about it and it was only when I started to open the files deep in my head to write this book that I remembered Robbins, during his debriefing interview, talking about his open duffel bag with the hot **FLAK** fuse fragment falling into it during one of their previous missions.

When Boatman and the others were satisfied with their visit to the crashed aircraft, they laid out one of the tarps next to the other three bodies, to place the collected, torn-apart remains of the fourth man on. Then each picked up a bucket, put on the waterproof gloves and with Zeman carrying the other tarp, they walked down to the debris trail to start picking up the man's remains.

Boatman had Zeman take the extra tarp so they could use it to carry the larger pieces of the torn-apart man. When they reached the berm and had spread out across the debris trail to start the recovery, Boatman looked at his watch and saw it was already 14:15. From what he could observe, the debris-trail was spread out though great clumps of brambles, small trees and brush. He thought, "Byrne and Venar have no idea of what we are going to have to do during this recovery in this woods." For the next two hours, the men tried to move in a line along the debris trail as Boatman thought, this is just "one step, this side of hell." It was not so much the bits and pieces of the torn-apart man. He, and the men with him, were used to being sent to the butcher by their parents to get a clump of red meat and bone. In our day, most the men in the army, who did not grow up in a large city had experience either on their family farms or when visiting family farms, helping kill live animals and then preparing the meat for the family table.

As the medics found more and more of the dismembered man's remains and put them in the buckets, they found more and more bits and pieces of the man that still had his flesh and hair on them. Some of those pieces were recognizable to the man picking the piece up and when a very easily identified piece was recovered, the

others were told and they would gather to look at that human bit and think about the poor bastard it had come from.

Such a find sometimes called for a break and a cup of coffee. As the woods were very damp and very cool, and especially as the sun moved to the west and the woods grew darker, it was harder to break their way through the brambles and brush. The brambles and trees grabbed at their bodies as they moved in those areas, and when they had to bend over to pick up a finger or other body part, it could be dangerous as a bramble bush branch stabbed at an eye.

In time the men heard a jeep approaching the woods, and soon McBride, Byrne and Venar were making their way down along the debris trail to where the medics were still fighting the brush, to conduct the best search they could under the conditions in the woods.

McBride asked Boatman how it was going and was told that it was not going well at all. Boatman told the officers, they had only covered about three-quarters of the debris area and he estimated they had collected less than half the man's remains. The problem was that the tree limbs and plane debris falling from the crashing bomber tended to disturb all the leaves, as did the man's remains. Boatman continued by saying it was not an easy job of just looking for what was on top of the carpet created by the leaves that had fallen. They had to look under every disturbed leaf or areas of disturbed leaves to make certain there were none of the man's remains hidden under them.

McBride looked at his watch and told them to keep going for another half hour and then they could call it quits for the night. That would let them get back and clean up in time to get supper and they could finish up in the morning. With that, McBride, Byrne and Venar walked back to the crashed B-17 and then, they did the same thing the enlisted men had done. They got into the broken bomber's tail and nose to see what it looked like and one has to suppose, each left with at least one souvenir. As they walked away, Boatman saw that Venar was still wearing the one man's flight jacket, only now the dried blood had been removed.

The half hour was not over, when Boatman spoke to the other two men. "Let's go, its too damn dark and we are going to have to go over this ground again, tomorrow, if we keep going now." The three officers were standing by the fire, talking to the MP Sergeant, when they got back to the fire and poured the contents of their buckets onto the growing pile of body parts. The sergeant looked at what they were doing, gagged, turned his back and continued to talk to McBride.

McBride was telling the sergeant that the Mayor had been asked him to go hunting for wild boars in these woods and that there were fox and other animals that might come to the debris-trail and the bodies in search of food. The bodies already had a distinct odor, especially the pile of torn-apart remains and McBride was certain the wild animals would be smelling that for some distance, which would bring the animals in search of food.

McBride told the Sergeant of the Guard, he would personally hold the sergeant responsible if he found out any wild animals had gotten to the remains during the night. McBride also told the sergeant, as insurance to keep the animals

away, the fire would be kept going all night and that it should be very bright. At the same time, he wanted two guards walking a post between the fire and the far end of the debris trail, which was more than 600 feet away from the nose.

As they walked, they could pick up wood from the branches the B-17 had knocked down, to use as fuel for the fire. In addition, the guards were to have good flashlights. Between the fire and the walking guards with flashlights, McBride was certain, if the guards did not screw up, the wild animals would keep their distance.

By 17:15, Boatman, Berardi, and Zeman were in the ambulance, heading back to the village to clean up and get supper. As they reached the road along the forest, looking back, Zeman saw the officer's jeep lights come on as they left the crash-site for the village.

After dinner at the Mayor's home, the Mayor and the three officers settled in for the evening and a long discussion of the B-17 arriving at the village and then going back to crash in the village woods. McBride told the Mayor that no French could be allowed at the crash-site until the remains of the dead were removed. The Mayor agreed and said he would make certain, early the next morning, that the men who had cattle near the crash-site or those who might be working near the crash-site were well aware they had to stay away from the woods for a while.

Throughout Hattonville that night, at every French home and gathering of Americans, there was only one topic of conversation. More than one had the same story - "That damn "Flying/Avion Fortress" B-17 was coming right at me and I took off like a bat out of hell. But you should have seen the woman living across from the church. She had her kid in her arms and her skirts were flying, as she passed me, heading south." Most of them were enjoying "Produit de Ferme" at the same time, as it seemed all the farmers worked the fields all summer long and spent all the winter making their own special liquors. One in this area, mostly reserved for the men, was the Mirabelle liquor made from the yellow Mirabelle Plum. It was clear and contained 45 percent alcohol, making it stronger than American bourbon. Some of the men, called it "lighter fluid" and they were not all that far off.

That evening's conversation, in all the villages and army camps along the route the B-17 had flown, was about the B-17 that had flown over their head or within their sight. It had flames past the tail on one side and smoke trailing back to Germany on the other. Damn, it was a hell of a sight as it went by!

At the 109th, as those who saw the B-17 were relieved by those who had not, they were told the story of the B-17 they watched crash and the four men who were brought to the hospital for treatment. By then many of the 109th personnel had their own parachute souvenir. Pfc. Ted Plant also had a silk escape map to go with his handkerchief size piece of the parachute from the flyer with the broken leg.

At supper that night, at the 109th, both the members of the hospital and the walking wounded discussed the B-17's flight across the sky to their north. That night, Pfc. Lindsey told his friends, "... about never feeling so helpless than when I watched that B-17, on fire and smoking, with men bailing out, and knew I could do nothing but watch the men who had to be inside it, die." However, he had his souvenir to go with the memory to help remember them.

136

One of the truck drivers told of coming up the hill by the cemetery and watching the B-17 crash in the distance. Another, who had been off duty that morning, told everyone who would listen, "I was leaning against an apple tree in the orchard across the road and drinking from my bottle of cognac as the B-17 had come into sight and then crashed."

This would be a day that everyone in the unit who saw that B-17, and some who had not, would remember until their dying day. Those four flyers were the only flyers of the 25,267 patients treated at the 109th Evacuation Hospital during the war. And, it had crashed within sight of their hospital location.

Slowly, as the next day's work started early and the explosions of the battle around Metz became even more muted, all the people made their way to bed. Out in the woods, the guards continued to walk along the debris-trail. Once in a while they would shine their flashlights in the direction where they heard noises and would see shiny eyes reflecting back at them. All it took was a yell and the stamping of feet and the eyes would turn away and disappear.

At Ike's HQ, I was sitting in the "O" Club shooting the breeze with some of the other intelligence personnel. Patton's drive was progressing well and the losses of the Air Corps that day had been very acceptable. The good news that night, or so we thought, was the feeling it was beginning to look like the war might end, earlier than we had been hoping.

I was concerned about my family and hoped my grandfather and my uncles had their families at the farm, some distance from St-Avold. I knew exactly what we were capable of doing to towns like St-Avold and I was very worried, that the town house might be a pile of rubble when I was finally able to get there. It would be a loss, but it could be replaced; my grandfather and my extended family in eastern France could not.

It was late on the 9th, over at the Cheddington Air Base in England, when Lt. Hornsby and his crew climbed aboard their B-24J-2-DT, SN: 42-51**226**. The B-24J was identified by a large, black, R4 on each side and a large black L on each vertical rudder. During this "**Spoofing Mission**," the B-24 would be loaded with more than four tons of Top-Secret electronic equipment. This would be used to jam the German radars and radios during the mission, to draw the German night fighters into the air to attack RAF aircraft that were not there.

(**Note**: They had planned to have a name painted on the nose, but it ("I Walk Alone") had not been done before "**226** crashed at Tincourt-Boucly.)

The B-24J, "**226**," was a new bomber, when she had been assigned to the 803rd BS, the predecessor to the 36th in June 1944. The first Top-Secret equipment to be installed, were six MANDREL units installed on 15 July. MANDREL or RC-183 and AN/APT-3 MANDREL was an US development of a British device used to jam the early Freya, Mammut and Wassermann German Radars. As the year progressed, and the 803rd BS became the 36th Bomb Squadron (RCM - **R**adar **C**ounter **M**easures), a partial floor was built into the "**226**" bomb bay, in September,

to create a heated and oxygen provided area where a crew member could work during their missions.

By the end of October 1944, "**226**" had been loaded with additional JACKAL equipment. The AN/ART-7 JACKAL was an electronic device that was used to jam the VHF radio transmission of German vehicles, often referred to as an SCR-522 jammer. Other new equipment consisted of two MANDREL III sets, which was modified IFF and four DINA sets were also installed, along with the necessary antennas, on the outside surfaces of the B-24J. To do their job, the antennas had to be shaped and formed to match the electronic frequency that it was going to broadcast. There were several antennas on each wing and others located in plastic domes on the B-24J's belly. (USAF/HRA - "*Squadron of Deception*")

DINA sets were a development of the original MANDREL sets, featuring a greater frequency range. Its major use was against the German early warning radars, to confuse their radar operators and to delay the German night fighters from getting radar fixes on the RAF bomber streams.

Hornsby did not know exactly where they were going, but Grey did and soon, they were just sitting at their positions waiting for the signal from the control tower to start their take-off.

The minutes ticked over and as midnight approached, and when it became 10 November, 1944, Hornsby, his crew and "**226**" was still setting on their hard stand, waiting to start the mission as Grey had not told them the actual starting time when he joined the rest of the crew at the hard stand.

(**Note**: Found in the engine impact crater in the Bois de Hattonville, on September, 1998, by Bernard Delsert. Unlike the average Missing Aircraft/Aircrew Reports (MACR) for some unknown reason the 452nd did not place the B-17's engine serial numbers or its machine-guns serial numbers in the required locations.

Without those serial numbers in the

"Engine Serial Number Plaque - "*Lady Jeannette*"
Photograph: Willis S. Cole, Jr.

official records, there was no positive proof of the identity of the B-17, that crashed in the Hattonville Woods. And, as you will read later, the engine of a B-24J that crashed 138 miles away, when recovered in 1946 would have exposed what had been done to fool the Salvage Board and the American public.

Taken at recovery location with dirt wiped off.
Note: No damage and no burned on soot.
Photograph: Willis S. Cole, Jr.

That is, until an unaccounted-for Inventory Item's Identity Tag was recovered at the crash-site, proving absolute proof. Of course, **I** would have no idea, why the Commanders of the 452nd failed to properly fill out the "*Lady Jeannette*" MACR. As recovered from the crash-site, near fire area, in May, 2000, by Robert LECLERC and Willis S. Cole, Jr. **Notice no fire damage!** Absolute proof that even the Unites States Government could not dispute, that 1st Lt. Donald J. Gott had died at this location.

The sad truth is, the "*Lady Jeannette*" left a debris trail of more than 600 feet from the time she began to lower into the Hattonville Woods until the location where the tip of the nose stopped moving. This indicates she would have needed the additional height of the trees in the woods, about 80 feet, and another 200 feet or more to cover the distance from where she started to hit the trees to where she would have cleared the trees.

Sadly, if she had that extra altitude, she would have cleared the trees and village of Hattonchatel on top of the ridge and she could have slid safely into the open fields to the west of Hattonchatel. Meaning, she would not have had to turn over Hattonville and most likely, Gott, Metzger, and Dunlap would have survived a slide in crash-landing.

In addition, remember the wrench that could not be found? If that wrench had not been removed by someone who wanted a wrench more than he valued the crew's lives, this book would never have been written. As dropping the 1,200 pound Ball Turret would have lightened the "*Lady Jeannette*" enough, by the time she reached the high ridge west of Hattonville, she would still have been high enough to fly over the village of Hattonchatel on top the ridge. And most likely, the B-17G would have slid into a safe crash-landing in the fields to the west of the village. In that situation, Krimminger may have lived as the additional height would have helped calm his fear of bailing out when the B-17 was too low.)

"For the want of that missing wrench, four lives were certainly lost."

However, they still had a chance even with the ball turret still attached, once they had accomplished the first right turn. However, the last possible safe crash-site location was occupied by unknown people and their parachuting crewmen. They could not try to land and put them at risk.

It is now obvious, that what finally forced the now historic end of the men inside the *"Lady Jeannette,"* were the Americans, the French and a *moving ambulance* the pilots could clearly see in the large field that was the only location of relative safety where the pilots could have safely crashed the bomber and saved their own lives. But, that would have risked lives other than their own and neither Gott nor Metzger would do that and so, they died in the Bois de Hattonville.

If the true story of the deaths of 1st Lt. Donald J. Gott and 2nd Lt. William E. Metzger, Jr. had been told at the time by General Eisenhower and those under his command, the final actions of their last two minutes of life would have deserved the award of the *Congressional Medal Of Honor*. The first part of the Citation describes the action, the lie began when the crash occurred. To be awarded that medal, at that time, an officer had to witness the action in question. At Hattonville, thousands of American military, Enlisted and Officers, watched what took place. Many officers, as high ranked as a Colonel were present and observed the final minutes and seconds of Gott's and Metzger's lives.

However, that recognition of their heroism during their last two minutes of life, would not have protected the future career and plans of General Eisenhower! Nor, protect all those used by me to make what happened, happen.

By midnight, I was in the bunk, dreaming of the war ending soon. Without a thought about the Top Secret "jamming and spoofing" mission, that I knew the British were going to conduct near Verdun.

USAAF/HRA
36th Bombardment Squadron (RCM)
Stephen Hutton

Chapter Seven
Top-Secret B-24J - SN: 42-51226

Hornsby Crew Official Crew Photograph,   USAAF, USAF/HRA
Standing L/R: Sgt. Pete B. Yslava, 2nd Lt. Robert H. Casper, 1st Lt. Joseph R. Hornsby, *2nd Lt. Frederick G. Grey (KIA)*, Sgt. Charles R. Root. Front: *Sgt. Frank A. Bartho (KIA)*, Sgt. Jack K. Chestnut, *Sgt. Raymond G. Mears (KIA)*, Sgt. Joseph P. Danahy (**Note**: Sgt. Root was not on the "**226**" final mission.)

First Lieutenant Joseph R. Hornsby, the pilot of the Top-Secret B-24J, "**226**," was sitting in his seat, safety buckles fastened, while waiting for 2nd Lt. Frederick G. Grey, the navigator, the real mission commander, to give him instructions for the upcoming take-off and flight. They had been sitting in their seats for a while now, after boarding the B-24J just before midnight. It was now 10 November 1944, and all he knew was, they were going on a "**Spoofing Mission**" to eastern France.

On nights when there was not a major RAF raid, the command would sometimes send up a "**Spoofing Mission**" which would lead the Germans to believe

Official Photograph: USAF/HRA

This Hornsby crew photograph shows the crew next to the right waist gun position of the B-24 they were inspecting.

Photograph: Stephen Hutton and Joseph Danahy, Hornsby Crew, radio operator

a major raid was in progress. The Germans would have to respond and send their night fighters up to defend against the attack. Which forced the Germans to use up replacement parts, lubricants, fuel and to tire out the German pilots and ground crews.

To Hornsby, it was all part of an extremely strange set of military circumstances. He was the command pilot of the B-24J. Yet, when they actually flew missions, he was just the bus driver. A bus driver who was being told by one of his passengers, what to do and when he was to do it.

Hornsby did not know where they were going, only Grey knew their destination and exactly what they would be doing. Hornsby did not know all that much about where they were going and nothing about what they were doing. Only Grey knew what they would be doing, how they would be doing it or where they would be doing whatever it was they would be doing - damn!

From experience, Hornsby knew that Grey would have him fly to a certain point, then begin a "lazy eight" orbit pattern between two set points, and only Grey knew where the points were located. At an appointed time, that only Grey knew, he would start or stop what had to be done to complete the crew's mission. Grey might use Danahy, the radio operator, and sometimes he might use Mears, a gunner, to help operate the more than four tons of Top-Secret electronic equipment that was tucked into the bomb bay and various other locations inside the B-24J. All of it was attached to the numerous antennas located under the wings and along the belly of the B-24J. Then, after a time, Gray would give Hornsby a heading back to their base in England.

The "226" radio operator, Danahy, described what he and Mears did, when they were helping Grey. They would be in the bomb bay area and listen to the intercom as Lt. Grey instructed them to turn on and off various toggle switches that controlled the operation of the Top-Secret equipment. During the time, the ongoing mission was operating, Lt. Grey would tell them to turn on switch number two and turn off switch number 5 and so on. Danahy made a strong point about the fact that he had no idea of what he was doing or what the equipment he was switching on and off was doing. Danahy would say that he had figured out that there had to be some tie between the time he turned on and off the switches, but what it was, he did not know. All Danahy knew was that it was part of his job and he did what Grey told him to do. "None of us," Danahy maintained, "other than Grey knew what we

142

were doing." A statement, that the Pilot, 1st Lt. Hornsby, **to his death** supported 100 percent.

"When they arrived at the 36th," Hornsby told the researcher, "the crew was again informed that what they were going to be doing was Top-Secret and they were not to talk to each other or anyone else about what they were doing. They were not to write home about what they were doing and if anyone persisted on asking them what they were doing, they were to turn that person's name over to base security."

Waiting there, sitting in the command pilot's seat while looking out at the dark, Hornsby thought about how he had gotten to this place, at this time. After completing flight and crew training they had just arrived at Westover Air Base in Massachusetts, with orders to continue on the northern route to

Official Photo: USAF/HRA
Consolidated Liberator, B-24J-2-DT, SN: 42-51226. Shot down by American *"Friendly Fire"* from a Radar controlled P-61, Black Widow, Night Fighter, 425th NFS, at 02:00, on 10 November 1944.

Photograph: Stephen Hutton

England, when he received new orders to take the plane and his crew to Langley Air Base, in Virginia, for special training duty before they would depart for England.

Upon arrival at Langley and reporting in, Hornsby was told that Lt. Grey was being detached for temporary duty and while Grey was detached, they would be assigned a different navigator who would be taking the crew up for additional, specific flight training.

During their first briefing, while waiting for Grey to complete his course, the crew was told, what they would be doing was so Top Secret they were never to talk about what they were doing, not even with their fellow crew members.

For the next two weeks, they would arrive at their B-24J and then the training navigator would take over. When ready, the navigator would tell Hornsby and Casper to start the engines, then when and where to taxi. When the B-24J reached the runway, the navigator would tell Hornsby when to begin his take-off roll and exactly what course he should take as the aircraft left the ground.

The navigator would then give Hornsby a course setting and then inform him when he was to turn from that course. After some time on the course, the training navigator would tell Hornsby to turn into what became a 'lazy eight' orbit between two set points, known only to the navigator.

They would fly the orbit pattern for a set time, then the navigator would give Hornsby a heading or two to get them back to the base and the navigator would have Hornsby land the B-24J. During this training period, they would fly one or two training missions each day, one in daylight and one at night.

No one in the crew knew what they were doing or why they were doing it. It was only during the day missions, when they could tell their general location by land marks that they had some idea of where they were. At night, unless a visible ground point was seen, they had no idea where the navigator had taken them.

When Lt. Grey had finished whatever, it was that he had been doing, the crew gathered for a briefing. All Grey would tell them, was that what he had been doing was none of their business. It was Top-Secret and that he would not discuss it with anyone. During that briefing, they were given new orders to go to England and upon arrival in England, they were to join a specific squadron. They were also reminded that they were now involved in a Top-Secret operation and it was to remain that way.

After all that Hornsby thought, "Here I am, sitting in "**226**," waiting for another "bus trip." And, all he needed was for Grey to tell the Command Pilot, what the Command(?) Pilot had to do.

"It's a hell of a war," Hornsby thought, and as he moved around in his seat to settle in all the parachute and safety harness, Grey's voice came over the intercom to tell him to start engines. When the engines were warm and set to go, Grey told him to taxi to the correct runway.

Once they had rolled onto the runway and ran the engines up to test them, Grey then told Hornsby, the "bus driver," to begin the take-off and when airborne, assume a specified compass course. It was approximately 00:30, 10 November 1944, when the B-24J, "**226**," R4 L, began her take-off roll. Once airborne and on the course Grey had specified, Hornsby followed Grey's instructions for the climb rate and when "**226**" reached a certain point Grey told Hornsby and Casper to turn the B-24J onto a new compass course which they knew, would take them to eastern France, just to the west of the "Fire Zone" over the Front Lines.

Along the way, Grey would occasionally call up a slight course correction, as they progressed across the English Channel and over France.

At his navigator's table in the nose of "**226**," Grey was plotting their position in relation to the specified orbit points he had been given during his briefing. The orbit position of the "**Spoofing Screen**" was between 50:17N-05:00E, over south-eastern Belgium, and 49:02N-05:00E, located a short distance south-west of Verdun, France.

The mission would be conducted at an altitude of 20,000 feet, at a speed of 160 miles per hour and Grey would conduct the Top-Secret electronic equipment operation, or "**Spoofing and Jamming German Radars and Radios**," from 02:00 to 04:00 hours.

Once "**226**" reached the northern orbit point, Grey would have Hornsby make the required 91 degrees turn to the south, to bring "**226**" to the west of the southern orbit point where Hornsby would complete a 182-degree turn to the north. This would set up the "lazy-eight orbit" they were to use, while the Top-Secret electronic radar jamming equipment was in use under the direction of Lt. Grey.

During his briefing, Grey would have been given the location of the eastern Air Defense Zones over the eastern Allied line. At both the northern and southern

orbit point, "**226**" would be flying 25 miles to the west of the Free-Fire Zone of each Air Defense Zone. As long as "**226**" remained to the west of the Free-Fire Zone, the friendly Air Defense night-fighters, and anti-aircraft artillery would not attack them. If they drifted into that zone, as what they were doing was Top-Secret, the Air Defense Zone personnel had no idea of whom or what they were, they would be subject to "**Friendly Fire**."

As they approached the northern orbit point from the west, they came within range of the northern most radar units of the 563rd SAW BN, which reported to the XIX TAC Control Center, as well as the 566th SAW BN, radar units located further to the north.

The personnel operating the radars and making command decisions at night were used to seeing radar targets coming from the west and passing to the east, and then coming from the east and passing to the west. They had seen many RAF missions come and go and when those approaching aircraft, flying in a continuous stream one behind the other, appeared at the extreme western coverage of their radars, they would be considered "Probably Friendly," unless they did something to change that identity.

At the XIX TAC Control Center, their main concern were targets over Germany and over their Air Defense Zone. They had control of the day fighters and night fighters within their air defense zone. At night, when they had their night fighters in the air, each night fighter's radar plots, carried a Friendly tag.

Depending on the German activity on the night in question, the XIX TAC would have a varying number of their available night fighters orbiting set positions, while maintaining others for immediate take-off in case several German targets came within range. Among them, were P-61 night fighters, assigned to the 425th Night Fighter Squadron.

There was one thing the controllers were certain of that night. Just two types of targets flew north/south flight paths at night. The first would be Allied night fighters and the second would be German night fighters or bombers. The RAF and their night missions came and went, basically along a west/east route and then back along an east/west path. If the RAF bombing target was within range of the XIX TAC radars, they could watch as the RAF reached their bomb drop point, turned and immediately flew back to the west toward England.

It was getting close to 02:00 in the XIX TAC Control Center when suddenly, the first Probably Friendly target of an RAF night mission that was heading east, made a turn to the south. Both SAW Battalions reported the target turning south.

In Hornsby's B-24J, Lt. Grey was busy verifying their location in relation to the orbit point that they were to enter. However he was not aware that he had a problem. The clouds which covered much of the sky had blocked his view of his last "hard ground" reference point and all Grey could do, was to use direct reckoning, using his estimated wind speeds and known aircraft speed of 160 mph. Unknown to Grey, since his previous "hard ground" reference point before the missed one, "**226**" had into an upper wind, soon to be known as "Jet Stream."

The Jet Stream increased their ground air speed beyond Grey's estimated speed to a point, when Grey instructed Hornsby to make a 91-degree right-turn to begin the north/south orbit, they were already east of the plotted ground position. The "226" had been blown more than 25 miles east of the actual orbit point and "226" was near the border between France, Belgium and Luxembourg. When instructed by Grey, Hornsby made the turn and when "226" completed it, she was beginning the first, southern leg, of that night's mission's "lazy eight" flight-plan.

During a later interview with Hornsby, through a gap in the broken clouds, he saw the moon reflecting off a river, which for 63 years he thought was the Rhine River. *As Hornsby had been informed by his Squadron CO, that "226" had been proven to have been shot down by German FLAK.* In fact, he had seen the moon reflected off the Moselle river and not the Rhine, as he had been told.

At the XIX TAC Command Center, the moment the target was seen to be turning to the south, everyone's attention was alerted. The men watching the movement plots as they were called in on the target, expected the target to complete a 180-degree and start back to the west. Perhaps, it was an RAF bomber that had suffered engine failure and was aborting its mission to return to its base.

As *"Bad Lady Luck"* would have it, very close to the position and altitude where "226" made its required turn to the south, a night fighter from the 425th Night Fighter Squadron was orbiting his set point location. The P-61 Black Widow, was stationed at one of 425th's forward bases, the same Etain Air Base, where the XIX TAC HQ was located. In the very early morning of 10 November 1944, one of those P-61s was being controlled by a XIX TAC night controller, using radar plots from the 563rd and radar control from a unit belonging to the 566th SAW Battalion.

On 10 November, 1944, the 425th NF Headquarters, on some records, was located at the Porsnes Air Base, located about 20 kilometers south-east of Reims, France. However, they had split up their aircraft and sent them to various forward bases, to be under the direct control of the closest TAC controllers for their night flights. Other records show the 425th HQ had moved to Etain on (1)9 November. One might wonder why there are so many (1)s in front of 9s in this book? However, I know exactly why so many documents have gaps and false information.

At least two of the 425th Night Fighter Squadron's, P-61, Black Widow, night fighters were stationed at the Etain Air Base that night. The same location, as the XIX TAC Headquarters on the night of 9 November, though the P-61's do not show up on the XIX TAC's records. Or, other Ninth Air Force records where they should show up as being stationed on that date!

S/Sgt. William R. Robbins, Waist Gunner of the *"Lady Jeannette,"* the B-17 that had crashed at Hattonville on 9 November, had walked around the P-61's at the Etain Air Base, in the early afternoon of 9th, while waiting for his flight to Paris, arranged by XIX TAC HQ. The researcher has also found photographs of a 425th aircraft maintenance man, taken at the advance Etain Base while he was preforming maintenance on a P-61, before the supposed 425th HQ move to Etain took place on (1)9 November, 1944, documented in some records as taking place on the _19th)?

146

(**Note**: It is easy to modify a 9 to 19, I know, for over the years, I have had some experience doing just that.)

Hornsby's "**226**," was the first of the Top-Secret B-24Js from the 36th to head toward eastern France, on 10 November 1944, on a night that the RAF did not have a normal mission scheduled. One would expect that the RAF would notify the Allied Forward Air Defense Zones about scheduled, regular bombing missions. However, the security designation of the aircraft and mission of the 36th BS(RCM) and the 100th Group, RAF, both involved in the "spoofing and jamming" of the German radar and radio systems, was so Top-Secret, all evidence points to the XIX TAC not being forewarned of the "**Mission**" that was going to be carried out that night. In addition, the Top-Secret aircraft were not supposed to fly that far to the east, which would place the aircraft in the Free-Fire Zone of the Forward Air Defense Zone. Another good reason to keep what they were doing from the forward units, is very simple. If the night fighter crews and ground controllers knew what "**226**" and the others like her were doing to the German radars there were odds, a pilot or a controller could become a German POW and "*spill the Top-Secret beans*" to the Germans, who would quickly make arrangements to overcome it.

In the early morning of 10 November, 1944, a 425th NFS, P-61, began a chain of events that were so sweeping, *if those events had become public knowledge after the war in 1946, world history would be very different today*.

Just after Hornsby had begun to turn "**226**" to the south, the XIX TAC night fighter controller vectored one of his night fighters toward the suspicious "Unknown Target." The luck of the draw had placed the night fighter in an orbiting location where it could reach the position of the target very quickly.

At that point, several radars were reporting to the XIX TAC Control Center, in addition to one radar unit, that reported to the radar battalion plotting center of the SAW Battalion located to the north of the 563rd. That plotting center had overlapping radar coverage of southern Luxembourg with the 563rd and 566th. As all the radar units were calling in constant position reports on this target, they suddenly realized the target had made a sudden maneuver in the Free-Fire Zone as it had made a sharp turn to the south, which was very suspicious.

At the XIX TAC Control Center, they realized the target had not made a complete 180 degree turn to return to England. However, it had completed a 90-degree turn to the south and it had begun flying a north/south flight path. The first thought that came to the controller's mind was a German night fighter had flown to the west. Remaining undetected, it had then turned to the east to blend into the RAF bomber stream they hoped to find with their on-board radars. Now the enemy was turning again to reposition itself in a new attempt to find a RAF bomber.

The XIX TAC fighter controllers had been briefed on how the German night fighters had penetrated into the RAF bomber stream at the end of March, when they shot down more than eleven percent of the RAF in one night. It now appeared to the XIX TAC controllers, that the target was turning back into a suspected RAF bomber stream, in an attempt to find a target in the bomber stream.

What the suspected German night fighter crew did not know, was no RAF bombers were coming that night. However, they had now revealed themselves and it was time to "Vector," (or direct) the 425th night fighter to the target, to shoot down the now declared Enemy Target.

At that moment, the Hornsby crew and "**226**," were trapped in a vast web of Secrecy and Top-Secrecy, that prevented the XIX, TAC controllers from doing anything else, but follow SOP (Standard Operating Procedure).

They had what had been a "Probably Friendly" target, complete a maneuver in the Free-Fire Zone that forced its identification to be changed from "Probably Friendly" to "Probable Enemy" and, as they had a night fighter very close, the night fighter crew was vectored to "**226**."

The night fighter's pilot had followed the vector perfectly and very quickly their airborne radar had locked onto the aircraft in the night sky. The aircraft had no lights showing and it was flying in a direction that no identified Allied Target should be flying. Perhaps, the P-61 pilot was inexperienced, perhaps he really did not know his aircraft silhouettes, perhaps it was too dark to see or he approached at a high speed and had an itchy trigger finger. Whatever the reason, that night the American, P-61 Black Widow crew made a split-second decision, and the pilot lined up with the target's right wing engines, laid his sights on the engines and pressed his fire button. Instantly, four Hispano M2 20 millimeter cannons spit a hail of explosive cannon shells, that cut the target's outboard engine into pieces, stopping the engine and propeller. At the same time, the cannon shells had badly damaged the right wing inboard engine, to a point where a fire in the engine nacelle could be seen by the P-61 pilot, lighting up the aircraft target.

In the nose of the target, Sgt. Frank A. Bartho had seen something that caught his attention and he began to hydraulicly rotate his turret so he could bring his guns to bear on the shadow. As he turned, he saw flashes at the front of the shadow and flashes as shells hit the B-24's right wing engines, then the shadow flew out of his sight. Then before Bartho could report what he had seen or rotate his turret back to its neutral position, his intercom, the hydraulic power to his turret, and his indicator lights went out leaving his turret dark and stuck in the position it had been located when the power went out.

The B-24J "**226**," was flying at 20,000 feet, just above the corners of the borders of the countries of Luxembourg, Belgium and France, when suddenly, both Hornsby and Casper saw flashes of light at their number-four engine and it came to a stop. As Casper was looking out his window, he also saw the inboard number-three engine was in trouble, and a fire appeared to be starting inside the nacelle.

In that split second, 2nd Lt. Grey was no longer the bus commander and 1st Lt. Joseph Ross Hornsby became the Command Pilot! And during the next twenty-nine minutes, Command Pilot, 1st Lt. Hornsby, made the command decisions aboard the "**226**." During "**226's**" final minute of flight, others made their own command decision of life or death.

The sudden loss of power on the right side caused "**226**" to begin to slew out of control and Hornsby, with Casper's aid, began to use the fuel and flight

controls to bring "**226**" under control. As they struggled, Casper saw the fire flaring to his right and told Hornsby, that it looked like the number-three engine was getting worse and then the electrical power to the interior of the B-24J faded.

As Hornsby and Casper fought with the now wallowing "**226**." Casper set off the fire extinguisher for the number-three engine and reported the engine was continuing to burn. At that point, Hornsby made the decision to put "**226**" into a shallow dive, in an attempt to blow out the fire in the number-three engine. As he put "**226**" into the dive, Hornsby began a slow turn to the right during the dive, with the intent to head back toward England.

At the same time the night fighter pilot was radioing his controller and stating, he had hit his target. At that time, the SAW BN radar operators began to see another target coming from the west, exactly like the one they had just shot at.

In "**226**," Hornsby yelled for Danahy to send out an emergency SOS and as Danahy turned to the radio to do so, the dial lights faded and the radio went dead, as did all the interior lighting and powered interior equipment inside "**226**."

Suddenly, the night fighter pilot was on the radio calling his controller and the pilot was telling the controller, that the target was on fire and diving and that he had just had a good look at the target and it appeared to be a B-24. Immediately, the controller told the night fighter to break off and the controller gave the pilot a vector back to it's base at Etain.

As "**226**" was diving, Casper attempted to switch the interior power supply over to the emergency power generator, that was located on the number-two engine, which was located on the left wing. All the instrument indicators had a radium coating on their needles that required a UV lamp, powered by the interior power supply, to keep them bright. Without the UV lamp, the instrument indicators quickly began to fade and Casper grabbed his flashlight to help illuminate the instruments, so they could see what the dials indicated. While he was holding the flashlight, Casper tried several times to switch to the interior emergency power and even though the meter showed it was available, the interior power of "**226**" never came back on. Resulting in continued hydraulic power loss to Bartho's nose turret.

One of the aircraft checks that was done every time they flew the aircraft, was to test the emergency power supply. This was accomplished by switching the power supply from the number-three engine generator over to use the power supplied by "**226's**" emergency generator located on the number-two engine. Each time the pilots had conducted an emergency power check, the dial indicator for "**226's**" electrical voltage, showed the number-two engine's generator was operating and supplying the required power to the test-switch. With that indication, they quickly switched the power back to the normal interior electrical supply.

But this was a Top-Secret B-24 full of Top-Secret electronic equipment. At times, the crews were not allowed to go aboard their own bomber because the electronic "**genies**" (electronic equipment maintenance personnel) were installing, servicing or changing Top-Secret electronic equipment.

At this point, it is extremely important to remember that the equipment was so Top-Secret that no one aboard the aircraft, except Lt. Grey, knew what it could

and would do. All the rest of the crew was kept completely uninformed for the sake of that Top-Secrecy. If one or more of them were captured, they could not tell the Germans something they did not know, even if they had been instructed not to tell the Germans whatever it was they might know.

What the Hornsby crew did not know, was something even Lt. Grey, most likely, did not know, was that the "genies" had previously modified "**226**." It had become obvious to the "genies," as more and more Top-Secret equipment, was added to the B-24 that the heavy forklift batteries which had supplied the power to the Top-Secret equipment at first, could no longer carry enough of a charge to maintain the electrical voltage at the currents required by the additional equipment.

This was tossed back and forth by the "genies," until one of them had the bright idea that there might be sufficient electrical power aboard all the B-24Js. Each of them had a back-up generator on the number-two engine, so why not hook it up to the Top-Secret equipment? The first test showed the normal back-up generator on the number-two engine was too small to supply the required voltage and amps. However, the mount for the back-up generator was the same as the larger, normal generator on the number-three engine. So they said to themselves, "Shucks, let's get extra standard power generators and switch them out with the under-powered emergency generators." It worked like a charm during the tests and missions. There was no bleeding off of voltage and amps and the Top-Secret equipment worked at full broadcast power, throughout the longest mission requirement. That is, until one of the aircraft had suffered an unexpected main generator malfunction while the Top- Secret electronic equipment was being used. The variation of power output of the main generator forced the pilots to switch from the normal generator to the back-up generator, which resulted in major damage to the Top-Secret electronic equipment.

The pilots did not know what had happened, other than main power was going in and out. They could fly and keep going, but it was very annoying. So the pilots made the decision to use the back-up generator, as the varying electrical voltage from the main generator might fail at any second.

Flipping over to the back-up power, the voltage meter settled right down for a few seconds and then it began to bounce and the navigator began swearing over the intercom, asking the pilots, "What the hell have you guys done up there? My equipment has all shut down."

As the emergency generator appeared to be even worse than the original main power generator, the pilots switched back to the normal power supply generator and following the navigator's new instructions to abort the mission, they made it back to base with no further trouble.

Again, the "genies" who never put their butts on the line during missions, got together and decided the Top-Secret equipment was far too valuable and too hard to replace. There was one simple step they could take, that would prevent another flying crew from making the same mistake. They opened the electrical panel that both generators fed to and leaving the new, heavy duty generator installed on the number two engine hooked up to the voltage test switch, they removed the

actual bus bar that carried the switched over emergency current to the interior emergency power system.

With that modification, the normal pilot's power checks would show the emergency generator was supplying emergency backup power to the system, when in fact, it was not.

It was just a little cheat and there was only one time during the war, that the actions of the "genies" resulted in something other than saving the Top-Secret equipment. That time, was this time aboard the B-24J-2-DT, SN: 42-51**226**. Down at the XIX TAC control center, the controllers were suddenly looking at something on their plotting boards that did not make any sense. Several radar units were reporting to their 563rd and 566th SAW BN Plotting Centers that the Target that had been hit, had turned and was heading west, while losing altitude.

At the XIX TAC control center, their P-61 pilot, who had just called telling them of a successful hit on the target, was now telling them it was a B-24 and heading west and not east, as a German aircraft would have done. Now in a panic, the XIX TAC radar controller vectored the P-61 pilot back to Etain and then their pucker factor hit its highest possible peak.

Suddenly, at the XIX TAC control center, the lower-ranking officers who were always stuck with the midnight shifts, doubted their order to fire. They had followed SOP to the "tee" and now the target was doing something that no damaged German would have done. It was flying west as fast as it had come, while losing altitude. At the same time, along the same path from the west, the now departing target had come from, more east bound targets were moving toward their Air Defense Zone. This indicated they may have shoot down an RAF bomber stream bomber, with "Friendly-Fire." But, there was no mission scheduled and the P-61 pilot said it was a B-24, yet the Brits did not fly B-24's. They had to have thought, what the hell was going on?

A runner was sent to wake up their next higher ranked officer, who, when he was told of the problem, told the runner to wake up his next higher ranked officer and so on. Within a short time, the control center was filling with officers of the XIX TAC, along with calls from the XIX TAC HQ, questioning the judgement of those young fools who gave the order to fire.

For some minutes, the now visually identified by the pilot which had shot at it, as a Probably Friendly target flew to the west. The target was still visible on the radars reporting to the XIX TAC control center for some time and then it faded, as it lost altitude and flew beyond the radar's range.

Hornsby decided that he was not going to be able to kill the fire in a dive and working in the dark with Casper, they brought "**226**" out of the dive. Then, with Casper using his flashlight, Hornsby started to bring "**226**" to a compass heading that led back toward England.

Suddenly, Casper lost control of his flashlight and its beam flashed into Hornsby's eyes, causing him to lose whatever night vision he had left. As Hornsby and Casper fought the controls of the B-24J, as "**226**" began to wobble and jerk through the air.

As Hornsby and Casper struggled to bring "**226**" under their control, their task was difficult, as the propeller governors were electrically operated and Hornsby and Casper had to maneuver the fuel controls to maintain what control they had, as the engines surged and slowed.

As Hornsby's night vision returned, the number-three engine was dying and the fire in the engine area continued to burn. Now, all they had to get them back to England were the two good engines on the left wing.

When they again had control of the B-24J, Hornsby told Chestnut, the flight engineer/top turret gunner, to go around the bomber and tell the crewmen to prepare to bail out. Danahy heard the instructions Hornsby gave to Chestnut and when Chestnut went to the rear, Danahy followed him. In the waist, Chestnut told the men there to prepare to bail out and then he went to the nose to tell the two men there, Grey and Bartho, about Hornsby's order to prepare to bail out when ordered.

After following Chestnut to the rear, Danahy and Mears helped each other adjust their parachute harnesses. When the men in the back were ready to get out, they stood around the escape hatch, waiting for the order they hoped would come very soon, as the ground was getting close.

Chestnut did not see Bartho, who was manning the front turret that night, but he did see Grey, and told Grey to get ready and to pass it onto Bartho. The interior of the B-24J was basically dark inside, except where the men had a flashlight turned on. After making certain everyone knew to prepare to bail out, Chestnut made his way back past the men in the waist to his position behind the pilots. He told Hornsby that everyone had been notified and then Chestnut checked his own parachute harness and parachute. When he was certain he was ready, he stood by the pilots, waiting the word to go.

Now, the secret actions of those "genies" electronic personnel came home to roost. They probably, never did realize what they had done. In fact, the "genies," most likely, continued to believe their Top-Secret electronic equipment aboard the aircraft was more important than the men flying the aircraft.

This model of the B-24J, had been built by the Consolidated Plant, located at San Diego. It was equipped with Consolidated hydraulic gun turrets at the nose and tail. The turrets provided hydraulically controlled horizontal turret rotation and vertical rotation for the two 50 caliber machine-gun.

Sgt. Frank A. Bartho
Hornsby Crew Gunner
Sauk Rapids, Minnesota
KIA: 10 November 1944
Buried(?): WWII American
 Henri-Chapelle Cemetery,
 Belgium

Photo: His Family.

As a hydraulic controlled turret, each turret required a hydraulic pump driven by the interior electrical power, provided by the number-three engine main generator or the emergency power backup generator on the number-two engine.

Before the electronic equipment "genies" had taken the number-two engine's emergency generator's output away from the B-24's interior, they were still having problems keeping the Top-Secret electronic equipment fully powered, using the very limited amount of extra output from the normal interior system. Originally, the "genies" had the tail and nose gunners shut off their hydraulic pumps when electronic equipment was working, basically rendering their turrets useless, unless an enemy fighter flew right where the guns were pointed. However, even with the turret's hydraulic power units turned off, the normal generator and original emergency generator were still underpowered. Based on that situation, they tried using part of and then, *stole all the backup generator's output in order to safely (?) operate their Top-Secret electronic equipment.* To the Genies, *"their desired end justified the means!"* As their Top-Secret electronic equipment was more important to them, than the men aboard the B-24J. In the end, it cost S/Sgt. Bartho, S/Sgt. Mears and 2nd Lt. Grey their lives!

Now, all these years later, it remains obvious, that in a true emergency, when men's lives depended on the aircraft having emergency interior power, *the US Army Air Corps and the "genies" valued the Top-Secret electronic equipment higher than the crewmen's lives aboard the aircraft!*

As the interior power failed, the nose turret gunner, Bartho, was in the turret with both turret access-hatches closed and the turret rotated from its neutral position. Aged 38, Bartho, was an older fellow, who had volunteered for the military service when he was above draft age. On that mission, for a reason known only to them, Bartho and Mears had switched positions.

When the "Friendly-Fire" blew up the number-four engine and damaged the number-three engine of "**226**," Bartho was in the nose turret and Mears was in the rear. As Bartho's luck would have it, when the "Friendly-Fire" destroyed the far right engine and then the inboard number-three and its generator failed, Bartho's turret was not in its neutral position.

As Hornsby put "**226**" into the dive, the interior power went off as the generator on the number-three engine failed. At that moment, the two gun turrets' hydraulic pump motors had stopped running. Consequently, the two hydraulic gun turrets were stopped in the position they were at, when the interior power failed.

Bartho, in addition to finding his turret jammed at an angle, was held in his seat by his seat belt, as he was being pushed into and then almost thrown out of his seat as "**226**" dived, wobbled and climbed. As soon as he could, he tried and found out he could not move the turret. As his turret's hatch was not properly aligned with the hatch inside "**226**," he could not get out. Both his turret and the interior hatch had to be aligned for Bartho to get out of the nose turret, he realized he was trapped unless he could manually turn the turret!

As the intercom was out Bartho could not communicate his situation to the rest of the crew. He was trapped and even if the manual method of rotating the

turret worked, Bartho could not get out of the turret unless someone was in the nose of "**226**," to open the interior hatch.

When Chestnut had told Grey to get ready to bail out, Grey most likely checked out his own parachute harness and pulled the two levers opening the nose wheel doors for their use as an escape path. After that, he went to tell Bartho who was still in the nose turret, to prepare to bail out. When Grey checked the interior hatch, he would have been surprised to find the turret was not aligned. Mears, who often helped Grey by turning on and off switches on the Top-Secret equipment in the bomb bay, always had the turret pointed forward and frankly, most likely, Grey did not know exactly what to do when it was not right.

It was obvious to Grey. He could not leave the nose to tell the rest of the crew of Bartho's situation. If Bartho managed to line up the turret and Grey was not there to open the interior door and let him out, Bartho could not get out.

The B-24J was constructed in such a way that the pilots had no direct contact with the men in the nose. In a B-17, the pilots could contact the men in the nose using the crawl-way between the cockpit and nose. Aboard "**226**," the men in the nose had no direct contact with the pilots or the men in the rear. Even with all the access doors open, the bomb bay was full of Top-Secret electronic equipment. It was located on a floor that had been installed to permit the equipment to be placed in the bomb bay. Resulting in the installed equipment and other obstructions preventing a direct visual view through the bomb bay. Grey must have realized he had no choice, but to wait for someone to come to the nose and have that person contact the pilots, to tell them that Bartho was stuck in the front turret.

In the cockpit, Hornsby and Casper had no idea of where they were, other than the fact they were probably over France and were heading toward the channel. What Hornsby did know, "The B-24J was a lousy flyer on two engines and even worse, when both working engines were on the same wing. He and Casper, had to hold constant pressure on the rudders to keep "**226**" in a somewhat straight flight toward England, basically sliding though the sky instead of straight flight."

The B-24J was constantly losing altitude and somewhere in front of them was the English Channel. Hornsby realized if he waited too long to have the crew bail out, in the hope "**226**" would clear the Channel and make it to England, he was putting the crew in greater danger. Hornsby knew in his heart that "**226**" would not make it and if they stayed aboard "**226**," he was certain they would all die in the Channel. If he waited much longer, not knowing where they were, they might suddenly find themselves over the Channel and all of them would die in the water in the night. His options were few and all but one was not worth any further risk of his crew's lives.

Watching the altimeter wind down almost to 8,000 feet, Hornsby made his next to last command decision aboard "**226**," by telling Casper and Chestnut to prepare to bail out.

Hornsby had already decided that when "**226**" passed through 8,000 feet, he would tell the men to bail out. Then he would wait until he was sure everyone was out or until "**226**" passed through 4,000 feet before he would go. No one in

154

"**226**" other than Bartho and Grey knew that Bartho was stuck in the turret and Grey was in the nose trying to help Bartho get out of the turret.

By this time, back at the XIX TAC Control center, the Commander, General Weyland was deeply involved. He must have been saying something along the line of, "What a hell of a 24-hour period! First, we had that B-17 crash at Hattonville, and now we have shot down some B-24 that was where it should not have been."

Like it or not, Weyland had to pass the buck up the line and General "Opie" Weyland put in a call to the Ninth Air Force HQ and he told his operator to have their operator get General Vandenberg on the line ASAP.

When Vandenberg came on the line, Weyland told him that he was fairly certain one of his night fighters had shot at a friendly B-24, where such a B-24 should not have been. Weyland based the information he was giving Vandenberg, on the reports he was receiving from his control center. They were now tracking other aircraft that were making the same maneuver to the west, outside of the "Free-Fire Zone" that the B-24 had made while it was inside it. In addition, Weyland continued, other aircraft were now dropping "Chaff" while heading toward Germany. Weyland went on to say to Vandenberg that it now appeared to be one of the raids the RAF ran to bring the German night fighters into the air when they did not have a regular, night bombing mission taking place. Apparently, General Weyland told General Vandenberg, the B-24 that was shot at had entered the "Free-Fire Zone" and, his men had done what they were authorized and had "Standing Orders" to do - they had shot at and hit the "thought to be an enemy," friendly B-24.

Vandenberg told Weyland that he would contact his operations center and have them report any information they might have and both of them should wait a while to see how all of it played out. "Perhaps," Vandenberg said, "if they had shot at a friendly B-24, it might make it back to England. Then we will hear all about it later today."

About 02:27, when they hit 8,000 feet, Hornsby told Casper and Chestnut to get out and on his way, Chestnut was to go to the rear and nose and tell the others to get out. Both men reacted at once, Casper was the first of the crew to get out, using the pilot's escape hatch, located just behind and above the pilots.

Chestnut got to the back and told the men there to get out and then he headed to the front to tell Grey and Bartho to go. As Chestnut headed to the nose, Ysalva and Veliz dropped out at once, almost together, through the escape hatch in the floor of "226." Danahy, who was not really wanting to bail by himself, sat down on the side of the escape hatch and Mears was standing beside him, as Danahy began to slowly lower himself through the hatch.

As the wind began to pull Danahy down Mears yelled, asking Danahy if he had seen Bartho? "Mears and Bartho were best friends," Danahy told the researcher, adding, "I hollered back at Mears and told him, I hadn't seen Bartho. Mears yelled back to me, that he was going forward to find him." Danahy continued, "I did not want to leave and I hollered for Mears to wait as I tried to pull myself back up into the waist. However, the wind was too strong and as I tried to lift myself back into the plane, the wind pulled me out. My last sight of Mears was

of him starting toward the nose in search of his friend, Bartho."

Chestnut had reached the nose and was ready to drop out through the nose door escape path, when he yelled at Grey to bail out. Obviously Chestnut did not see Bartho or wait for Grey to tell him there was a problem with the turret, as Chestnut dropped out past the nose doors within seconds of when Danahy was pulled out the back.

At the same time, up in the cockpit, Hornsby kept the B-24J under control and watched the altitude indicator spin through lower and lower numbers. In the nose, out of Hornsby's sight, the final acts of three of his crewmen's lives were playing out, unseen and later un-talked about, and vastly un-rewarded.

Mears had reached the nose and Grey told him that Bartho was trapped. Both of them had parachutes strapped to them that were perfectly good and they knew, there was an escape path right there as Chestnut had already used it. They knew they had been ordered to bail out, and yet neither left the damaged B-24.

2nd Lt. Frederick G. Grey
Hornsby Crew Navigator
Sioux Rapids, Iowa
KIA: 10 November 1944
Buried(?): Long Tree Cemetery
       Sioux Rapids, Iowa

Photograph:
His Daughter Judy
Lukensmeyer

In the nose turret, Bartho was learning a hard lesson that other men had or would learn; some with very different results than Bartho's experience would be. The turret did have a manual method which would permit the gunner to rotate it back to its neutral position. If a gunner was in the hydraulic operated nose turret and the power failed, he could manually rotate the turret back to its neutral position and if someone was inside the nose to open the inside hatch, the gunner could open his turret's hatch and 'get the hell out of there.'

To operate the manual control, the gunner had to sit on the gunner's seat (in Bartho's situation, in complete darkness) and then he had to bend over to locate a manual crank that was stowed under the seat. When he had retrieved the hand crank, the gunner had to bend back over, find a small hole in the floor at the rear edge of the seat and insert the geared edge of the manual crank down to mate with the turret gear ring which the hydraulic motor gear drove to rotate the turret during normal operation.

Once the gunner had the hand crank's gear in place, he had to release the hydraulic motor's gear to keep it from resisting the turret's rotation. This release permitted the gunner to turn the hand crank and move the turret back to its neutral position. It was a set of movements that is somewhat hard to write about and much harder to accomplish in the tight confines of the Consolidated turret.

The researcher interviewed a couple of other B-24J nose turret gunners, from a unit other than the 36th, to try to figure out why Bartho, Grey, and Mears did not leave the aircraft? Especially, after Hornsby had stayed with "226" more than an adequate time for all the men to have safely bailed out. It was one of those things that intrigued the researcher, me and even Ike, once I had told him there was no apparent known reason for the men who died, to have died.

American Service Memorial
John Lindsey (109th EVH), Art and Blanche Scherbarth (109th EVH)

The Memorial was originally dedicated, at Tincourt-Boucly, France, Department of the Somme, on 10 November, 2000. The Memorial honors the Top Secret B-24J - SN: 42-51226 ("226"), the B-26 - **"Where's It At?"** of the 1st Pathfinder Squadron, attached to the 397th BG(M), the 452nd Bomb Group (H), and the Americans, who served in this area of France during World War One and Two.

The Memorial was rededicated on 10 November, 2007, after it had to be moved from its original location due to road construction. The new location is 1.4 km west of the cross-roads to the north of Tincourt-Boucly, on land donated by Mr. And Mrs. Claude Obert, to the Department of the Somme, in the Buire-Courcelles Commune to insure the Memorial will never have to be moved again.

"Where's It At?" crashed into the woods at the top left edge of this photograph. The Memorial is now located near it's crash-site.

Photograph: Willis S. Cole, Jr. - 10 November, 2000

157

To me, after all these years, and the researcher's interviews with Hornsby, it is obvious that both Grey and Mears, once Mears knew about Bartho being trapped, attempted to get Bartho to correctly position the turret, so they could let him out and they could all could get out of the B-24J before it crashed.

Both of the B-24 nose turret gunners, who were interviewed, were much shorter than Bartho, who was a tall, thin man. Both told the researcher that a short person had a problem bending over in the confines of the turret when they had to reach the crank and to do what had to be done to align the turret manually. They added that in their opinion a person like Bartho was described to be, would not be able to do it.

One of them described a time when his B-24 had been hit by **FLAK** and he had his turret in the neutral position and he still could not get out of the seat because the pilot had made the same attempt to blow out a fire. As the gunner explained it, you had to release your seat belt, open the turret hatch, and get out, and when the plane was making such maneuvers it was basically impossible to do it. Then, even if you were able to force yourself to attempt to open the inside hatch, the odds of the other man in the nose (the navigator) being there to open the inside hatch was low. Each crewman was holding on to whatever they could hold to keep from being tossed around and it was not until the pilot pulled out of the maneuvers that you might get out. Otherwise, you rode the flight out where you were!

We are now certain, that Bartho had rotated the turret to look at the night fighter or the damaged engine, when the dive started and before he could rotate to the neutral position, his electrical and hydraulic power went out. Then, no matter how much he struggled, his height prevented him from getting out of the nose turret.

When Hornsby decided it was time for him to get out, as the altimeter passed through 4,000 feet, Mears and Grey were still attempting to help Bartho get free. As Hornsby left through the pilots' escape hatch, Hornsby had no knowledge the men were in the nose. Command Pilot, 1st Lt. Joseph Hornsby, had made his final command decision aboard "**226**" when he left via his escape hatch.

As Hornsby dropped free and pulled his parachute, the last thing he remembered for a short time, was the sight of the flaming B-24J starting to roll over and dive toward the ground. Then, his parachute harness, which he did not have as tight as it should be, yanked at his body as the parachute snapped open and his parachute chest buckle wacked Hornsby in the chin, rendering him unconscious.

That night, there were two cloud layers over that part of the Somme River valley as many of the citizens and Americans in the area awoke to the noise of the aircraft. At the nearby, A-72, Péronne Air Base, Pfc. Barney Silva, ambulance driver attached to the 599th BS (M - Medium) of the 397th Bomber Group (M), woke up when, in the distance, he heard the noise of an aircraft that had to be in trouble.

As he sat up in his bunk, inside his tent, the sound turned to the scream that he had heard at the movies when an aircraft began to dive to its end.

In many villages around that area of the Somme valley, Driencourt, Buire-Courcelles, Bussu, Hancourt, Courcelles, Estree-en-Chaussee, Estrees-Mons, Bernes, Vraignes-en-Vermandois, Cartigny, Templeux-la-Fosse and Tincourt-

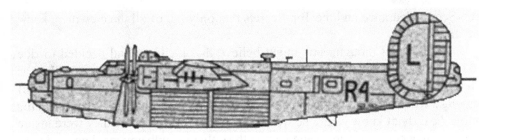

Drawing, B-24J-2-DT, SN: 42-51226
Top-Secret B-24J, 36th BS(RCM) Attached 100th Group RAF
Shot Berardi by: "Friendly-Fire:" 02:00 - 10 November 1944
Crash-site: 02:30 - 1,200 feet north of Tincourt-Boucly, France
3 KIA
2nd Lt. Frederick G. Grey, Navigator
S/Sgt. Frank A. Bartho - Gunner
S/Sgt. Raymond G. Mears - Gunner
The various aerials can be seen under the wing and
below the propellers, as small black half-bubbles.

Drawing: Carol L. Cole

Boucly, families were awakened and were opening their shutters to look in the direction the sound was coming from.

Before Hornsby had left his controls in the cockpit of "**226**," in the nose a major and final individual command decision had been made by two men, 2nd Lt. Grey and S/Sgt. Mears. Both men knew they had been ordered to bail out. Both men knew that Chestnut had already bailed out of the escape hatch that was right there, where either one could drop through it and save his life. And both knew that the pilot would soon be bailing out to save his own life. Both men had to know "**226**" was going to crash soon, and yet they made their own command decision to stay with "**226**" until the very end, in their attempt to save Bartho's life! Grey and Mears were still trying to help Bartho free himself from the nose turret, when'"**226**" began to roll over and begin her final dive to earth.

She was traveling at an estimated speed of 140 mph, when "**226**" rolled and at that moment, even though the open escape path was so close, the two men who could have saved their own lives only seconds before and the man in the nose who was certainly doomed, knew they would ride "**226**" to a mutual end.

One thing bothered me when I first learned of the Top-Secret position Lt. Grey held when the B-24J crashed. I knew, at that time, with his knowledge he was not expected to be captured alive. My knowledge of Top-Secrets kept me a certain distance from the front line and if I had to, for any reason, made my way beyond a certain distance from the front line, I was always accompanied by two sergeants, whose sole purpose was to make certain I was not captured alive by the Germans. Perhaps, Lt. Grey had been informed, he was not to be captured alive because of his

159

Top-Secret clearance and the Top-Secrets that only he, of all the crewmen, knew anything about!

With that thought, one might believe that Lt. Grey had decided to ride "**226**" down, no matter what, to protect the Top-Secrets only knew? Just as Metzger had stayed in the B-17 only 14 and ½ hours earlier to die with, instead of leaving a wounded man behind to die by himself. As Grey had no contact with the pilots, he did not know where he would land and it was possible they were inside of German occupied territory and he was the only one with any real knowledge of the Top-Secret equipment and he had decided to ride her down, with Bartho and now, Mears.

I do not know about Grey's last personal command decision, however there can be no doubt that Sgt. Raymond G. Mears, without hesitation and with full knowledge and will, forfeited his life while attempting to save the life of his friend, Sgt. Frank A. Bartho. Personally, I prefer to believe, that Lt. Frederick G. Grey made the same solemn decision to remain in that failed attempt to save Bartho.

In the village of Tincourt-Boucly, the change from laboring engines to the scream heard by all, sounded like it was right over their heads. One person interviewed, Claude Obert, a young boy at the time, told how his father had just opened the shutters on the north side of their house. He had crowded as close to the window as he could to see what was happening, when he saw a flame falling from the sky. Then, it suddenly exploded and in the flash of that explosion he saw a large bomber for an instant, before it disappeared again. Only to be followed by an even larger flashing explosion when it hit the ground. Its remaining fuel and perhaps bombs, had flashed into an explosion and fire and their house was washed with the sound of the loud explosion. In that instant of time, three men's lives and "**226**" ceased to exist.

As quickly as they could, the father and son dressed and leaving their village farm compound to the street on the south side, they joined the flow of people walking to the cross roads in the center of Tincourt-Boucly, where they could take the road to the north, leading to the crash-site about 400 meters past the last house in the village. That night, the war came directly to their village.

Still hanging in their parachutes, the survivors were slowly falling, through the cool night air, all of them thinking that all the men had survived. They had all seen the flames of the burning bomber reflecting off the higher cloud layer. Then as it began its dive, they saw the growing glow in the lower clouds as "**226**" dived through the lower cloud layer.

The flash of the first explosion in midair, and the immediate flash-fire of the second explosion helped them see the ground, as they began to land. Lt. Casper realized he was above a village and it looked like a factory was directly under him. He tried to maneuver, but the parachutes they wore offered little maneuvering ability and he found himself landing on a roof of the factory. He had landed on one side of a steeply sloping tile roof and with the clatter of broken tile sliding with him, he began sliding down the roof.

Inside the Cartigny sugar factory office, the night watchman, guard and fire-tender, Mr. Chaulieu, had heard the approaching aircraft and looking out a window to the east, he had seen the flames of the diving airplane and the flash of both explosions followed by their sound. Standing there, watching the glow in the distance, he decided, he would go to the crash-site as soon as he was relieved and was closing the window, when suddenly there was a noise of something falling on the roof of the office. He could hear pieces of tile falling from the roof, and he followed the sound of whatever it was, as it slid down and off the roof near the front door to the factory office.

Lt. Casper slid down the roof, and as he began to free fall to the ground, he grabbed at the spouting without success. Suddenly, his fall was slowed by the parachute shroud lines, as the parachute had collapsed and fallen on the other side of the sloping roof. As he began to fall, Casper had taken up the slack and then the shroud lines tightened and pulled at the parachute. The parachute began to be pulled over the top of the roof and its resistance slowed Casper's fall to a point where he found himself standing in front of a door with a lighted glass panel while his parachute continued to slide down off the roof, as he caught it in his arms.

Mr. Chaulieu was still wondering what was sliding down the roof, when someone knocked on the office front door and when he opened it, there was a man standing there with a parachute bundled up in his free arm.

Casper quickly introduced himself as an American and the watchman asked Casper if he would like a cup of coffee, as he invited the American into the factory office. While Casper was drinking strong American coffee (thanks to the factory's owner's shrewd trading with the Americans at the nearby air base, trading lots of sugar in exchange for good American coffee), the brewing, however, was Mr. Chaulieu's own secret. The watchman called the factory manager and told him about the American "Aviateur" at the factory. The factory manager, Mr. Delmotte said he would call the American base at Estree-en-Chaussee to tell them to come pick the man up at the factory office.

Having bailed out very close together, Ysalva and Veliz could see each other's parachutes while still in the air and they yelled at each other as they heard and watched the glowing clouds and flash of their B-24 crashing. They landed very close together in a pasture to the west of the small village of Boucly that is a sub-village of Tincourt. Boucly is located across a small stream to the south of Tincourt, named the Cologne River.

(**Note**: As such, the sub-village's official name on a French map is Tincourt-Boucly. It was not until the researcher located Hornsby and Danahy fifty-four years later that they finally knew exactly where "**226**" had crashed and where they had landed in France.)

As quickly as they could, they got together and as they were not far from the village, they could see lights through open house doors and people moving in the light. They decided to walk to the nearby houses and as they approached the

houses several people came to greet them. The night was still lit by the dimming glow, reflecting off the low clouds, of the dying fire at the crash-site.

Introducing themselves as Americans, the villagers invited them into their homes and the two men went into one home where they were offered coffee and French bread with strawberry jam. When they were settled, one of the villagers, using sign language and a little English, told them he was going to a nearby home that had a telephone and the people there would telephone the American air base at Estree and tell them where the two men were located.

Danahy, in the fading light, found himself on the ground near a pond and a stream, with a dog barking in the distance. As he did not know where he was, he decided to stay there until daylight. He had not been physically hurt, unless one would count the fact that when his parachute snapped open, his harness had tightened over a very private part of his body and he was still suffering major pain in that region. As Danahy waited, he heard something splashing in the stream and as the glow from the crash-site had diminished to a point where it was of no help, Danahy thought it was probably the barking dog coming to find him.

Then Danahy heard the noise maker entering the other side of the pond and unable to think of what else to do, he began to whistle, "Yankee Doodle." He was very surprised, when from the other side of the pond, someone else began to whistle "Yankee Doodle." Much relieved, Danahy watched as Chestnut arrived, after wading across the pond. Neither man knew where they were, but Chestnut told Danahy he had landed by a road and could see the burning crash-site in the distance. So, he had decided to move away from the road, just in case there were any Germans around, and headed down hill and away from the crash-site.

Both men were certain they were some distance from the crash-site. However, when the researcher located where they had been, it turned out they were less than two kilometers away when they landed, with Chestnut landing within one kilometer of the crash-site. From the crew's landing pattern, the researcher was able to determine there was a fairly light wind blowing from the east-south-east to the west-north-west that night. The wind carried each the parachuting men some distance to the west of the B-24's flight path, as she rolled over and crashed. With the first out, landing further to the west than the next four, as he was in the air for a longer time. However, due to the flight direction the last survivor out, Hornsby, still landed the furthest west and the closest survivor to their base in England.

Danahy and Chestnut talked about their options and decided they would go back to the road that Chestnut had seen and follow it to a village. Before long, after crossing the pond and stream and walking up a hillside, they found the road and stood in the middle of it. They were still making up their mind which way when church bells in the villages began to ring and Chestnut saw someone approaching them on a bicycle.

Danahy had taken high school French and he told Chestnut that he would ask the bicycle rider for help. So, Danahy stepped into the road and raised his hands to indicate the rider should stop, as he began to introduce himself in his high school French. He had just realized the rider was a young boy, when the rider

162

began to crank that bike as hard as he could, which surprised Danahy so much, he remembered the boy as one of his major memories of that event in his life.

Danahy said, "That boy's eyes opened as wide as dinner plates, as he twisted the bicycle to miss my outstretched arms and he took off down the road, hell bent for leather." When Danahy was describing this to the researcher, he laughed and said, "I think that boy is still pedaling, he appeared to be that scared."

Disappointed at their failure to communicate, the two men decided to walk down the road in the direction the speeding bicyclist had taken. After a while, they came around a corner in the road and in the distance they could see the dark bulk of a town on the far hillside and a light being held by someone walking in their direction on the same road.

Hornsby, some time earlier, had regained consciousness to find himself still in the air, hanging under his slowly falling parachute. He woke up just in time to observe a streak of fire fall to earth, then he saw the flash of the first explosion, when the fire in the number-three engine reached the B-24's fuel tanks, followed by the much larger flashing and sustained fire, as noise of both explosions washed over him. When he was getting close to the ground, Hornsby realized, he was going to land in an area of fields and brush. His landing, had been made easier by the reflected glow of the continued fire, Hornsby collected his parachute and decided to go to cover, until he was absolutely certain he was in friendly territory. He had been there for some time, when he noticed there was a steady movement of vehicles moving along a nearby road and he decided to try his luck. Hornsby walked to the road where he flagged down the next vehicle coming along the road. It turned out, the first vehicle to come along, was actually driving away from the crash-site. However, when the driver told Hornsby, he was on the way to a nearby air base. Hornsby got into the vehicle and accepted a cigarette and light from the driver as they departed for the nearby base.

By that time, all of those of the Hornsby crew who had survived, was either already at the Péronne Air Base or making their way to the base. None, knew that three of their fellow crewmen were soon to be accounted for, in a very gruesome manner. It was no later than 05:40, in the morning of 10 November 1944.

(Note: Recovered from the "*Lady Jeannette*" crash-site. It was found at an obvious villager's scrap metal and fire location. As they tore the "Fortress" apart, they hauled their share to their own location to complete the scrapping.

Note, the seat belt buckle was never opened. It was around the waist of 1st Lt. Gott, CMOH, or 2nd Lt. Metzger, CMOH, when they died and the belt had to be cut to remove the body away from the seat.)

8th Air Force Association Reunion
452nd Bombardment Group Association
Savannah, Georgia - 1994

Remembrance Table
1st Lt. Donald J. Gott, CMOH
2nd Lt. William E. Metzger, CMOH

Both families had members in attendance and the author invited each family to bring the actual Medal, presented to the families in June, 1945.

For nearly two days, the author and his wife, were responsible for the safety of both medals and knowing the story behind their award made that task easy.

During the dinner, the audience were asked to stand and deliver a "Salute" to the men's memory.

After the dinner, during the dance, everyone in attendance, slowed their dance as they neared the table and often, stopped to honor the men for their bravery.

Several of the French who were helping with the research came to the reunion to help celebrate the lives and honor the sacrifices of 1ts. Lt. Gott, CMOH, and 2nd Lt. Metzger, Jr., CMOH.

Chapter Eight
Barney Silva And The French
Early That Morning!

599th Bomb Sq. (M)

Photograph: *"World War II Combat Squadrons of the USAF - USAF/HRA"*

397th Bombardment Group (M)
Yellow stripe at vertical angle on tail.

Photograph: www.publicenquiry.co.uk/groups/bg397th.html

Pfc. Barney Silva, San Luis Obispo, California, after hearing the drone of the aircraft in the distance, then the scream of its dive, followed by a great boom, had slid back down into his bunk and was trying to sleep when the squadron's intercom speakers came to life with the usual static. He listened to the message, "Pfc. Silva, get your ambulance and report to the dispensary at once. Pfc. Silva, get your ambulance and report to the dispensary at once." "Damn," Silva thought to himself, "I know where I am going now."

Silva sat up, pushed the covers down, swung his legs out onto the cold tent floor, searched around for his clothing, got dressed, went to the head, did what had to be done there and went to get his ambulance.

When Silva arrived at the 599th BS (M) Dispensary, 397th Bomb Group (M), Ninth Air Force, with his ambulance, the Group Night-Duty Medical Doctor, Capt. Judson, and one of the squadron's medics, Sgt. John Pennington, were waiting at the dispensary door. They got into the ambulance and Judson told Silva to head toward the northeast, they were to locate the airplane's crash-site. All three men, were members of the Army Medical Corps, attached to the 599th BS (M).

Once they had left the base and entered onto the French roads, Silva found it very easy to find the crash-site. At every intersection he came to, there were

French people standing outside their homes in their night clothes and they always pointed out the next road he should take to get closer to the crash-site.

Judson told the two men that the headquarters duty officer had told him it was not one of ours, as we had no aircraft flying missions over France at night.

There was an Army Medical Corps Hospital attached to the group, consisting of Section 'A' of the 108th Medical Dispensary. It was a small hospital, with 10 or so beds, a small operating area, one surgeon, a few enlisted medics and one ambulance driver. The squadron doctors were used to provide help to the hospital surgeon when needed and they each had nights, along with their enlisted personnel, when they were the assigned as the group's on-call doctor/emergency team. The on-call doctor, was responsible for taking care of basic medical emergencies during the night. Tonight, as they headed for the crash-site, Captain Judson told the men, *"We have drawn the short straw on this one!"*

As Silva made his way cross-country, they saw several other American vehicles heading in the same direction. When they arrived at the crash-site, it was 03:30 in the morning, just an hour after the unknown airplane had crashed.

Judson told Silva to pull into the field where the aircraft had crashed, and drive right to the large crater they could see in the field. There was a large group of French people, with some Americans, already gathered at the crash-site and as Silva drove into the field, they parted to let the ambulance drive to the edge of the impact crater.

Using the ambulance's head lights and the spot light on the ambulance, all they could really see was a deep hole cut into the field. There were lots of smaller bits and pieces of the airplane spread around the hole and the debris trail continued into the distance for about the length of a football field, in a northwestern direction. It appeared to them that the largest pieces of the unknown plane appeared to be a long distance from the crater. One thing that stuck in Silva's mind over the years, as he told the researcher, "There certainly was nothing that looked like an airplane at the crash-site."

The medic and driver got out of the ambulance with their flashlights and leaving the ambulance lights on, Silva and Pennington began looking at the ground to see what they could find. As they were searching, Captain Judson was talking to some other Americans, who had arrived earlier, to learn more of what happened. They told Judson, they had found some torn-apart human remains between the airplane's bits and pieces when they looked, so Judson went to ask Silva and Pennington what they had found.

As soon as they had started their search, both men had seen small pieces of torn flesh and broken bone, so they picked up a few pieces to show to Judson. Judson told Silva and Pennington to get a prepared set of two sheets and two blankets out of the ambulance and spread them out on the ground in front of the ambulance. Then, Judson told them to put all the recovered crew remains on the top sheet of the set.

As Silva and Pennington began to recover remains again, Judson asked all the Americans with vehicles to point their vehicles toward the crash-site to help

illuminate the crash-site and to leave their lights on, as the extra light would help the searching men recover the remains of the dead. Captain Judson helped them, when he was not talking to new arrivals and seeking the help of the Americans to keep everyone from the site, where the crew's remains might be located. It was an open farm field and the people walking around the crash-site created mud that was hiding remains that might otherwise be recovered.

Most of the French had no transportation and they arrived at the crash-site via the roads and cross-country through the fields, and it was impossible to keep all of them away from the crash-site. After a while, the Americans just guided the incoming French around the crash-site to the grouped crowd in one location.

Many of the French, had been there for some time and most of them were farmers or farm labors and that day's work was fast approaching. Once the Americans began to hinder direct access to the crash-site, some of the French, included Claude Obert and his father, had turned around and went back to their home to get whatever sleep they could or to prepare to do what they had to do that working day.

Silva and Pennington worked without a break, as they first climbed into the deep crater and searched for remains there, before they began walking ever widening circles around the crash crater, recovering human remains and other items that might help identify the dead. Over the following two hours and fifteen minutes, Silva and Pennington collected enough human remains to create a fairly large pile on the sheet/blanket set spread out in front of their ambulance.

During that time, they found a damaged wallet, containing an EM's Class "B" Pass, Social Security Card and Bicycle Permit all made out to Bartho, Frank A. In the wallet, there were also other miscellaneous documents, photographs and souvenir coins, however they did not find any identity tags for Bartho.

They did find two identity tags, belonging to a FREDERICK G. GREY, as well as an Officer's Identity Card # 65-1 made out in Grey's name, along with misc. papers, photographs and 7£/10s/00. Most likely, a wallet was found which contained the listed items, but it was too damaged and bloody to keep and Captain Judson separated out the useable items and disposed of the wallet, as it is not listed.

In addition, they also located a set of Escape Photos and misc. photos and papers, bearing the name Raymond G. Mears. That was all they found to help to identify the man, named Mears.

Several times, starting about 04:30, they heard single aircraft, some distance to the north, apparently heading back toward England. If anyone really thought about those aircraft, as the noise was one heard on many nights, when the RAF night missions brought their flight path into this part of France.

The 397th BG(M) Commander, Col. Richard T. Coiner, Jr., had called his HQ's Duty Officer, when he woke up to the sound of the crashing bomber. At that time, the duty officer told Coiner, the Duty Officer at the Headquarters of the Ninth Air Force had called a few minutes before to alert the base, that the XIX TAC, located near Verdun, had shot at and hit an airplane that turned out to be an Allied plane and it appeared, the damaged plane was flying in their direction.

Col. Coiner, told his Duty Officer to get back to the Ninth Air Force HQ right away and inform them about the nearby crash and for him to get the Duty Doctor out to the crash-site at once. He also told the Duty Officer to get some Military Police, (MP), to the crash-site to guard the downed aircraft to keep the locals away and make certain the MP had a radio that would allow direct communication from the HQ to those at the crash-site.

Coiner, then told the duty officer he was going back to sleep and to contact him at once, if notified of any change in the situation. At 03:45, the Duty Officer called back and told Coiner, the airplane that crashed was an American airplane, because Doctor Judson and the men with him, had found a set of American Identity Tags at the crash site.

Coiner, immediately told the duty officer to call that information into Ninth Air Force HQ and that he would be there in a few minutes. Coiner, knew American aircraft should not be flying over France in the middle of the night, however he also knew, there were some secret outfits that could be doing anything. Col. Coiner got dressed, found the duty jeep and its driver out front of his quarters and by 04:00, Coiner was at his own headquarters, in charge of the situation.

By then, the base had begun to receive calls over the French telephone system, from various locations where Americans from the crashed airplane were waiting to be picked up. Coiner, immediately sent vehicles to each location and then, he called the Ninth Air Force Headquarters to speak to the duty officer, Coiner was surprised to find General Vandenberg was at the Ninth's Headquarters and was going to take his call, personally.

When General Vandenberg came on the line, he asked Coiner if he knew exactly where the crashed airplane was located? As the XIX TAC had reported one of their night fighters had fired on a target about 02:00 and the pilot had stopped the attack, after he realized it was a B-24. Col. Coiner told Vandenberg the crash-site was a few miles east of Péronne, but he could not verify the airplane's model. He could tell him, his doctor, had found American ID Tags at the crash-site, so it appeared to be an American plane. He also told Vandenberg, they would soon know, as survivors were in the process of being picked up to be bought to his headquarters. Vandenberg told Coiner to call him back just as soon as he knew anything. Then Vandenberg thought for a second and told Coiner, he was going to contact the Eight Air Force Headquarters in England, and tell them, he believed they had a plane down near Péronne. Col. Coiner, agreed, that was a good idea and the men hung up. Vandenberg did not tell Coiner that he was certain the plane the XIX TAC had shot down, was probably one of the Top-Secret American B-24's flying Top-Secret night missions with the RAF.

About 04:50, a vehicle pulled up outside the HQ, and after thanking the driver, two enlisted airmen were brought into the HQ. When Coiner began to question them, they refused to tell him anything about the mission they were on and all they would say, were their names, Ysalva and Veliz, and that they were members of the 36th Bomb Squadron and they had been in a B-24. Coiner, was not very happy with their refusal to provide further information, however, he told the men

they would be taken to the mess hall for breakfast and back to the headquarters for further debriefing after they were done.

Col. Coiner picked up the phone, as soon as they were out of his office and called the Ninth Air Force HQ and asked for General Vandenberg, who answered at once. Coiner, told him, two sergeant gunners from the plane had been brought to his headquarters and they refused to say what mission they were on, but they did disclose they were on a B-24 that belonged to the 36th Bomb Squadron.

Vandenberg told Coiner that he was just about to call him as the Eighth Air Force was very upset. And, it was now obvious, the XIX TAC had shot down with their "Friendly-Fire," an American B-24, flying a Top-Secret Mission with the RAF that night. Vandenberg went on to say, the reason he had not gotten back sooner, was that he and the duty officer at the Eighth Air Force had decided that Eisenhower had to be told at once about the "**Friendly Fire**" shoot down of the Top-Secret bomber in France, as there were many German spies still spread around the Somme country side. Vandenberg went on to tell Coiner, in addition to the problem of the "**Friendly Fire**" shoot down, he had been informed by the Eighth Air Force Duty Officer, the incident would definitely involve the possible compromise of Top-Secrets that were aboard that B-24.

Vandenberg told Coiner that he had placed a call to General Eisenhower's headquarters and the duty officer had put him in touch with a colonel, who was the specialist involved with any night flights of US aircraft over Europe. Vandenberg went on to tell Coiner, that the colonel wanted them to get immediate proof of the casualties and the condition of the B-24 and get back to him as soon as possible. And, the colonel had insisted that Coiner was to send enough guards to the crash-site at once to keep the French away until the colonel could contact him directly.

Vandenberg gave Coiner the telephone contact information of the colonel at Eisenhower's forward headquarters. Vandenberg continued to tell Coiner, the colonel had immediately told Vandenberg they were all now involved in a very Top-Secret situation and all those involved, Weyland, Vandenberg, Coiner, and any others were to restrict the knowledge of the B-24's "**Friendly-Fire**" shoot down and it's crash, to as few people as possible. Vandenberg told Coiner that he would personally be held responsible, to insure nothing was removed from the crash-site.

As they were talking, one of Coiner's headquarters personnel handed Coiner a message, which Coiner scanned. Then, Coiner told Vandenberg, the doctor had radioed to tell them, he had found enough identification and torn-apart human remains to know, at least three men had died in the crash. The report also stated, there was nothing left of the aircraft of any size, except for some wheel assembly parts that ended up some distance from the large crater the crash had created. Coiner, told Vandenberg that according to his Doctor Judson, who was at the crash-site, the damage was so extensive they could not tell what type of bomber it was and all the crew remains were just bits and pieces of the three dead crewmen.

(**Note**: What happened to the two aircraft, happened as written to this point, and the reactions of the involved personnel took place. However, starting here, I am providing the flesh to complete the body of the coverup I created. The actions I am laying out, took place. Verified by extensive research, re-research, interviews with involved personnel who remembered seeing me, and actual visits by the researcher to all the locations in France, that I was at during the coverup.)

Vandenberg, told Coiner to get in touch at once, with the colonel at Eisenhower's headquarters and inform him of everything Coiner had just told him. Col. Coiner agreed and the two men hung up.

At Eisenhower's forward headquarters, a short distance north-west of Rheims, I was dreaming of my father's and my visits with my uncles and cousins, when we were seeking out hidden spots of the Great War. When the phone rang, it jerked me out of my dreams into a new reality, one that would affect me the rest of my life. I picked up the telephone and the operator told me, the duty officer had instructed him to transfer this call to me and that it was the Commanding General of the Ninth Air Force, General Vandenberg. I had no idea of why Vandenberg would be calling me this early in the morning and with the curtesey due such an officer, even when he calls in the middle of the night, I told the operator to connect me to General Vandenberg.

General Vandenberg immediately told me that General Weyland of his XIX TAC, stationed at Etain, near Verdun, had called him and it was now obvious, one of their P-61, Black Widow night fighters had shot down a friendly B-24 about 02:00. He went on to say, he had just been contacted by Colonel Coiner of the 397th BG, stationed at the A-72 Air Base near Péronne and that a plane had just crashed at 02:30 to the northeast of their base. Vandenberg told me that Coiner had already sent a doctor and several MP's to the crash-site.

Then, Vandenberg told me, what I had already realized had happened, that he was sure the XIX TAC had shot down one of our Top-Secret B-24's, flying tonight's Top-Secret night mission with the RAF.

Vandenberg did tell me, that he took it on himself to contact the Eighth Air Force about the possible loss of what he thought, was one of their Top-Secret aircraft and the duty officer at the Eighth had told him, they would contact the aircraft's Squadron and the RAF command at once and that he should contact General Eisenhower's headquarters at once. Which, led to his call to me.

I was somewhat stunned, but good training quickly stepped in and I told Vandenberg to get in touch with his Colonel Coiner and I continued with what I wanted done. Including the fact, all further communications on this subject must be by secure phone.

I was also immediately extremely agitated, as I knew there was to be no major RAF mission tonight and I knew, the 36th BS (RCM) and the RAF was scheduled to conduct a "**Spoofing Mission**" near Verdun. It was so Top-Secret that even though it was obvious to me that Vandenberg was aware of what happened, I could not let him know what I knew during this call, that would come later. And,

170

for a second, I hoped, it was an RAF aircraft involved in the mission and not one of our Top-Secret B-24s, but a light came on in my mind and one problem was solved.

This was the only 36th BS aircraft to crash in Europe. Thus, It was the only one that was lost anywhere near a location where we thought the Germans might be able to obtain any knowledge of the crashed B24 and especially, the Top-Secret electronic equipment on board. Now, we had shot down one of them ourselves and it had crashed right in the middle of an area of France, where we knew some French people were sympathetic to the German cause. "Damn!" I thought, "How many German spies had already been to that crash-site?"

Hell, the most likely reason it was shot down, was because of the secrecy of the aircraft and the missions. We did not tell anyone in Europe about their overflights at night, other than alert the Ninth Air Force, that some aircraft would be operating in their area to the west of the "Free Fire Zone. That is how Top-Secret those B-24s and their electronic equipment were, more important in some ways, than the people on the aircraft, who were just GI items required to operate it.

The 36th BS (RCM) was flying with the RAF and the RAF was mostly responsible, at that time, for how they were used. We had run an experiment a while earlier, to check on using them during our own day missions. It had gone well and we were planning to move them back to the 8th USAAF at the first of the year. However, we were not going to allow these Top-Secret electronic systems, that were now saving hundreds of RAF bombers and thousands of RAF crew lives, to somehow leak to the Germans. I was positive that Eisenhower would feel the same way. Within minutes, I was dressed and in my office.

It was not long, before Vandenberg called again on the secure line and told me, that Coiner had called him about the crash and that his doctor had just reported that it was an American airplane and that he had accounted for **three torn-apart dead crew members**. As to the plane, it and its dead crew were destroyed, with nothing very large left of either. Vandenberg told me that he had given my name to Coiner and told Coiner to call me directly, to give me the latest information.

I gave Vandenberg instructions to call Coiner and Weyland and tell them to immediately restrict the number of people involved as much as they could. He was to tell them, it was very secret, and that we could waste no time making certain, it remained that way. And to tell all those involved at the shooting end of this mess, as *far as they were concerned, it was a friendly RAF Mosquito!*

Then, I called the operator and told them to get General Eisenhower on the phone, and that I had to talk to him at once. I knew Ike was on an inspection tour in the Aachen, Germany, area that we had just captured and was not here at his HQ. In addition, I told the operator, I would be at my security scrambled telephone and he was to patch General Eisenhower's return call to that phone.

Within a couple of minutes, the phone rang and the operator said General Eisenhower was on the line. I acknowledged I was ready and he switched over the phone. General Eisenhower spoke first, asking me what had gone wrong now, as he knew I would not wake him up at this time of night, unless it was a big problem.

171

I laid it out to General Eisenhower, just as I knew it. Weyland's XIX TAC had a P-61 Black Widow night fighter airborne and it had shot down one of our Top-Secret B-24's from the 36th Bomb Squadron. The B-24 had crashed a few miles northeast of the Péronne Air Base and that, Vandenberg had been in contact with me about the crash. He had also been in contact with a Colonel Coiner, who was the Commander of the 397th Bomb Group at the Péronne Air Base. And, that Coiner had a doctor at the crash-site, who had accounted for three dead crewmen and reported the B-24 had blown up on contact with the ground and there was not much left, but bits and pieces of the men and the aircraft. I added, the doctor had stated the plane's destruction was so complete, there was no way he could tell what type of plane was, which I injected, could be good news for us.

I told General Eisenhower that I knew the RAF was running a **"Spoofing Mission"** over eastern France, near Verdun and the Top-Secret B-24s from the 36th BS(RCM) would have been involved. Then, I informed Ike, of a major problem at the probable B-24 crash-site. We knew there were many French people in that area, who had sympathy with the German cause. The Germans had occupied the crash-site location for long periods during both wars and in the Péronne area, we knew some French people were still spying for the Germans even after they had been Liberated. I did tell Ike, Weyland was going to use my Mosquito story at his end.

General Eisenhower, listened to all I said and there was silence for a moment. Then he told me to let him think about it for a while and to get back to him when I knew for certain it was one of those B-24s that crashed. General Eisenhower then said, as much to himself as to me, *if it is one of them we have to make this go away!* I told General Eisenhower, I would establish direct contact with the commanders involved and that I would be thinking about a solution to the problem, as I agreed, *we had to make this go away! The sooner, the better!*

Over in England, the Eight Air Force Duty Officer, had called the RAF and the 36th Bomb Squadron about their missions that night and they verified that a **"Spoofing Mission"** was in process at the time of the call. The Eighth Air Force Duty Officer, told the RAF Headquarters Duty Officer about the probable shoot down of an American B-24, by an American night fighter in a Free-Fire Zone, near Verdun, and all the rest he knew about the crash. All the RAF Duty Officer would tell the Eight's Duty Officer, was that they had no report of any losses. However, the aircraft normally practiced complete radio silence while on a mission and they could not be sure until all their aircraft had returned to their bases.

In Germany, after determinating the weather of the night of 9/10 November would be too bad for the RAF to send a bombing mission, the German Night Fighter Groups released almost all the crews from duty that night.

Then, just after 02:00, their long distance radars began to show the interference pattern that the RAF had been able to create for some months. Among the jamming interference patterns on their radars displays, their best operators could see faint targets coming from the east and heading toward Germany. This changed the situation and upon review, the duty officers contacted their commanders with

the growing radar data, that the RAF appeared to be mounting a mission that night, despite the weather.

The alert was sounded to recall all the off-duty pilots and ground crews, and preparations were put in place to get the night fighters into the air to attack the oncoming RAF bomber stream. When the higher ranked officers arrived and reviewed the data collected so far, they decided the RAF was sending a major mission toward Mannheim which was a target that deserved all the air defense they had. As the night passed and the RAF's "**Spoofing Mission**" progressed, more and more groups of German night fighters were airborne. In due time, the Germans had sent six groups of their night fighters airborne to meet the oncoming RAF.

For nearly two hours, the German night fighters searched the air for the targets their commanders had determined would be there, to no avail. Suddenly, at 04:00, their radars cleared and the only targets on the German radars, that were moving, were a very few RAF aircraft on specific missions and a lot of German night fighters. The night's activity had use up a lot of aircraft, lubricants and fuel.

I was sitting at my desk, wondering just how this could be made to go away, when my telephone rang and Colonel Coiner, identified himself and told me he had just interviewed two sergeants, from the crashed plane, and it was a B-24 from the 36th Bomb Squadron. He also told me, the men would not tell him what they were doing and he had sent them for breakfast. However, he had vehicles out picking up other survivors and he was expecting them back anytime and he would keep me fully informed about what they would report. In addition, he repeated what General Vandenberg had told me, there were three dead, torn-apart crewmen accounted for at the crash-site and that the plane had been destroyed.

When he was done with his report, I told him about the secrecy and that he had to keep the number of people involved as low as possible and his men at the crash-site had to keep the French away and especially, keep them from taking souvenirs from the crash-site. With that, I told Coiner to keep me posted of any important new information, especially on the crew and we hung up.

I did not tell Coiner that the men were doing exactly what they had been told to do and if all went right, he shouldn't get anything new from the survivors being brought in, other than being able to account for all the men in the crew.

At the 397th, just after the first two surviving crewmen had been sent for breakfast, other survivors began to arrive. One had landed on the sugar factory at Cartigny and Coiner immediately began to question the 2nd Lt. He told Coiner that he was the copilot of the B-24 that crashed with a crew of nine, and they belonged to the 36th BS. He also refused to tell Coiner what they had been doing that night.

As Coiner was talking to Lt. Casper, the duty officer received a call from the radio center for the group. It was located in some woods, on a hill to the north of the air base, near Doingt, which was far enough away, if the Germans ever used Radio Direction Finders to pinpoint the radio center's location and then bombed that location, only the radio center would be destroyed, with no damage to the base.

Decades later, the researcher was to learn that the French were positive that the radio center was manned by a bunch of Americans who were always drunk.

What the French did not really understand was that the call sign of the 397th Bomb Group was "**Drunkard Control**." Consequently, almost all of local French were confused to the point, that the radio place they visited where all the Americans kept referring to "**Drunkard**" meant either, that all Americans there were drunks, or the base sent their drunks there for punishment.

At the same time as the boy, Alphonse Rabache, and his bicycle were approaching Chestnut and Danahy, the church bells at the various villages in the region had begun to ring. And before the bells stopped ringing, the two men had started walking in the same direction the bicyclist had fled, hoping to find a village. Soon, they saw a man with a lantern walking toward them on the road,

With some worry, Chestnut and Danahy approached the man. Paul Chaulieu, the man with the lantern, began to speak to them and Danahy did the best he could to make himself understood. The man came to them, shook their hands and indicated they should walk along with him. Soon, they were entering the eastern edge of the village of Buire-Courcelles, and the man led them through the gate of a farm compound and into the kitchen of his home. His wife was in the kitchen and she was making fresh coffee to go with the French bread, butter, and strawberry jam on the table. The man indicated they should stay there to enjoy the coffee, bread, butter and jam and he would be right back.

Outside, Paul Chaulieu went to the young boy, Alphonse Rabache, who had seen the men and who, because of the very bad French of Danahy had immediately thought they were German spies as he twisted his bicycle away from them. He then rode his bicycle as fast as he could to his Uncle Paul Chaulieu's farm, where he worked. The boy lived in Tincourt-Boucly and had gone to see the crashed airplane right after the crash. The aircraft had been so destroyed, that none of the French who were at the crash-site while he was there, had any idea what it was, other than an "Avion Fortress." They knew that sometimes the Germans did fly over France at night and that was why Alphonse thought the men he saw might have been German spies, as the man's French accent was so terrible.

After telling Paul Chaulieu about the two men, the boy had hidden himself and his bicycle in the barn while his uncle went to meet the possible spies, get them to his house and then excused himself and went to meet Alphonse in the barn.

Uncle Paul told the boy to ride into Buire-Courcelles, to the home of Mr. Lenain, who was in the "Resistance" and inform Mr. Lenain, his uncle was going to bring the possible spies to his home. Mr. Lenain could speak English, so perhaps he could determine if these men were spies. Again, the boy took off on his bicycle as fast as he could.

Paul Chaulieu went back into the house and sat with the two men for a short time. Then he motioned for them to follow him and he walked with them into the village to the home of Mr. Lenain. Mr. Lenain talked to the men in English and when he was done, both he and Mr. Chaulieu were still very suspicious about these two men claiming to be Americans, who they knew did not fly at night.

After a few minutes, Mr. Lenain told the men he was going to take them to a place where there were Americans and he opened a garage door to show them his

automobile. Danahy told the researcher, "It was a lot like a Model T Ford, except it was not. However, it did have more chrome on it than any car he had seen. Then they had gotten into the car and the Frenchman drove away from the village."

The road was following along a hillside, approaching a village, when suddenly Mr. Lenain pulled the car over to the right side of the road and stopped. On that side of the road there was a hillside farm field and they could see a small woods on top of the hill. The driver told the men to get out, as he opened his door. Chestnut and Danahy whispered to each other as they got out, "That they were very worried why this man had stopped in the middle of nowhere."

As the driver came around the car, they saw that he had a pistol in one hand. He pointed up the hill with the pistol and indicated they should start walking ahead of him, up the hill toward the woods, known as the Bois de Rocogne, located near Doingt. On the way up the hill, Danahy thought fondly of his "45" cal. pistol that, each of the crewmen had been issued to wear during their missions. But, after a few missions, the pistol had become a heavy thing hanging from one side that hindered the men during their missions. So, since they never flew over enemy territory, before long, the pistols remained where his was at that moment, hanging on one end of his bunk back at Cheddington. "If this man was going to shoot them," Danahy told the researcher, he was thinking, "Damn ... I'm dead!"

Both men had thought the Frenchman was taking them up into the woods to shoot them. Then, as they got close to the woods, they saw camouflage netting stretched out inside the tree line and a number of boxy vehicles under the netting. As they got closer, both were relieved to see there were some people watching them climb up the hill and they were Americans. The Frenchman surely would not take them to a place to shoot them where there would be American witnesses.

As they entered the Bois de Rocogne, two men in American uniforms started to talk to them and as they talked, the Frenchman put the pistol back in his belt. These two men he had suspected, he now realized were Americans, just as they said they were. The Americans in the woods, told Chestnut and Danahy, they had seen and heard the crash and were wondering if there had been any survivors?

Once the questions had been asked and answered, the men said they would call their headquarters and see what was to be done. After a couple of minutes, one of the men came out of the trailer full of radio gear and told Chestnut and Danahy, their commander wanted the two men up at the base headquarters just as soon as they could get there.

The problem was, he told Chestnut and Danahy, there were only the two of them on duty and neither could leave until relieved. However, he was certain Mr. Lenain would take them to the base and when he asked the Frenchman if he would do so, he quickly agreed with a broad smile. That moment both Chestnut and Danahy thought, "Now the SOB smiles!"

Before they left, Mr. Lenain knew positively, that the two men were survivors of the ***American "Avion Fortress" B-24*** that cashed at Tincourt-Boucly that morning. When he returned to Buire, he told Mr. Paul Chaulieu, the bomber that crashed was an American B-24 "Avion Fortress" and not an American B-17

"Avion Fortress." In due time, Mr. Chaulieu, told his nephew, Gaëtan Chaulieu, that no matter what anyone else might say, as the Americans you will soon read about were insisting, the crashed "Avion Fortress" was a B-24 and not the B-17 "Avion Fortress" those men insisted it was. For fifty-four years, Gaëtan, a short, stout Frenchman stood alone among thousands, testifying to the truth as he knew it. That is, until one American Memorial Day, when the researcher stood up in a village meeting hall and told the assembled group of Frenchmen, that he could now prove Gaëtan's version of the identity of the "Avion Fortress" was correct and we are all wrong in our belief, that the bomber that crashed north of Tincourt-Boucly was a B-17 "Avion Fortress." **Gaëtan is right, it was a B-24J and not a B-17!**

The French people could recognize American bombers. However, to them all bombers were "Avion Fortresses" no matter what the Americans called them.

The radio station sergeant gave the men instructions on how to get to the base and one direction Danahy remembered 54 years later was the sergeant saying to them, "Take the road to the left, when you get to the intersection with the burned-out Sherman tank." To Danahy, the memory of seeing that burned-out Sherman tank was a real example that there was a real ground war going on down there on the ground, that he had not experienced nor seen from high up in the air.

Located for bear for their missions at the Peronne, A-72, Air Station. Officers of *"Where's It at?"* standing before their tent.

1st Pathfinder Squadron
    Attached to the 397th Bomb Group
(Left to Right)
1st Lt. Raymond H. Bocettcher
1st Lt. Richard P. Britanik
    Soldiers Medal
1st Lt. Joseph M. DuBois
    Soldiers Medal
1st Lt. Hugh W. Robbins - *KIA*
Not Shown:
S/Sgt. Hugh G. Glass - *KIA*
S/Sgt. Mike Flores

Photograph: 1st Lt. Britanik

Back at the 397th Bomb Group Headquarters, Coiner could now account for eight of the nine men that the first two men had told him, were on the B-24. He had just re-read the note that the duty officer had written, saying Captain Judson had just sent a message stating they had collected about 150 pounds of remains and identification for three men. From the bits and pieces they had recovered, Judson was certain they were now recovering the remains of than three men.

At 05:50, another vehicle pulled up to the headquarters and another survivor from the B-24 was brought in to see Coiner. The man had a covering of dried and semi-dried blood on the front of his flying clothes and he was holding a compress against his chin. The survivor told Coiner his name was Hornsby, and Coiner knew at once he could now account for all nine men who made up the crew of the crashed

B-24. When Coiner began to question the Lieutenant, all he would say was his name and he was the pilot of the B-24 that belonged to the 36th Bomb Squadron. He added the fact that he had not seen any of his crew since he had ordered them to bail out.

Col. Coiner told Hornsby that he had some good and bad news. There were already three of his crewmen at the base, two more were in transit, and with him at the base, he could now account for six survivors. The bad news though, was that the group's duty doctor had been at the crash-site for two hours and he had found the identification and the remains of three dead crew members at the crash-site. The man swore, more to himself than anyone else, and asked Coiner who they were. Colonel Coiner told Hornsby, "That his doctor had found Identity Tags for an officer named Grey and two Enlisted men, Mears and Bartho." Hornsby was shocked and showed it. He told Coiner, he could not understand why they had not bailed out. It had been at least four minutes from the time all the men were told to bail out to when he had bailed out and as far as he knew, everyone had bailed out of the B-24. It did not make sense to Hornsby, as everyone had plenty of time to bail out and he had no reason why three of them had not done so. Hornsby asked how the other men were and Coiner told him that he appeared to be the one with the worst wound, as a couple of the others had shroud line marks, but they were fine. Already knowing he would hear no more new information from this man than he had from the others, Coiner told Hornsby, he was sending him over to the hospital to get his chin wound treated.

Hornsby asked Coiner where the other survivors were and Coiner told him they were being assigned quarters away from the rest of the men in his Group, until it was all straightened out. Hornsby agreed that was good and he was ready to go to the hospital.

Danahy later told the researcher, "That he thought they had landed close to the front lines and that the air base they had been taken to was a fighter base." He said, "The people were all walking around with pistols hanging from their waists like a bunch of cowboys." Actually, he saw the air crews of the B-26, Medium Bombers, that the men of the 397th Bomb Group flew. Unlike those aboard the Top-Secret B-24s of the 36th BS (RCM), these men flew missions that put them in a direct threat of crashing within German territory and the possibility, of being captured by the Germans meant they carried their side arms.

As Hornsby walked away, Coiner told the duty officer to get a message to Judson that all the crews were now accounted for. Six had survived the crash and three had died when the B-24 crashed. Col. Coiner then picked up the telephone and called me. It was 06:00 when the secure telephone on my desk rang.

As soon as I got the information, I called General Eisenhower and by the time I hung up, it was 06:20. General Eisenhower had told me to get a solution and get it quick! General Eisenhower continued to, *"Insist that the Top-Secret B-24 crash had to disappear and if necessary, I was to use his name to make it happen."* I told General Eisenhower, as he knew I had some background with what the British had done to protect their Top-Secrets earlier in the war and I reminded

him of the time when the Brits had used the body of a suicide to convince Hitler that our Sicily Invasion was going to Greece and Sardina, instead of Sicily.

General Eisenhower agreed, that had worked, but even though he might be able to help me hide the true fate of the B-24, when our men died (as I knew), all control of the dead was taken out of his hands and automatically went to the Quarter Master Corps. General Eisenhower said, he certainly did not want to get the QMC Graves Registration on his back when it came to our dead and their treatment. I told him, that would become part of my future actions with this problem.

As soon as I got off that call to General Eisenhower, I had the operator get Weyland on the line, to find out the real truth of the shoot down of our Top-Secret B-24 by an American unit under his direct command.

When the operator came on the line, so I could set up that call, he told me that General Vandenberg had called and he wanted me to call back as soon as I could. I told the operator to get Vandenberg on the line as soon as I hung up on my call to Weyland. And then, I asked for the senior operator or officer present. Very quickly I was talking to a 2nd Lt. who knew who I was and I, verbally ordered him to ensure that every telephone call, to or from me, even if I was in transit anywhere, until I told him otherwise, was to be placed on secured telephones, *only!*

In a few minutes, the secure telephone rang and a woman's voice said that General Weyland was available. I asked, if she had been fully briefed by the officer in charge? She said, they had all been informed of the situation and she completed the connection, via a secure telephone, to General Weyland.

As you already know, I knew Weyland, because anyone in my position would know Weyland, as the "Darling" Air Corps General of General Patton. Who referred to Weyland, ... "as the best damn general in the Army Air Corps." I had been involved with many meetings where General Weyland had been present and felt comfortable talking with him.

He obviously knew who I was and why I was calling him, direct from General Eisenhower's headquarters. The second thing Weyland said to me, "Was it had been one hell of a day as they had a B-17 crash yesterday morning, and now, less than 24 hours later, a lieutenant followed the SOP exactly and gave permission to fire on an aircraft that had shown every sign that it was an enemy aircraft."

Weyland told me he had chewed on the damn lieutenant's butt, but the Lieutenant and the 425th Night Fighter's P-61 pilot had both done exactly what they were supposed to do under the SOP. Weyland insisted, if there was any blame, it was on the crew of that aircraft and not his command.

I asked Weyland, if he knew exactly what that aircraft was? He told me that Vandenberg had called him and said, "There were some dead Americans at a crash-site near Péronne. From the first survivors they had found, it was the American B-24 that his night fighter had shot down." Weyland went on to say, "I have no damn idea of what an American B-24 was doing flying at night in a 'Free-Fire Zone.' Especially in a 'Free-Fire Zone' in eastern France and I needed to make certain that General Eisenhower understood that no one in his command had failed to follow SOP. If there was a fault, it belonged to the shot down B-24."

I waited until he was finished and then I told him that the damage was done. However, the B-24 they had shot down was on a Top-Secret mission and that it was filled with Top-Secret electronic equipment. I went on to say, "They had picked out one hell of a friendly aircraft to shoot down and why didn't they shoot down one that was not so secret?" Then I asked him about the B-17 he had mentioned?

Over the next few minutes, Weyland told me about a B-17 that had been hit over Saarbrucken the day before. The B-17 should have crashed at once, as it had one engine blown off, clear back to the wing and another engine had stopped without feathering, leaving only two working engines and one of them was badly damaged. In addition, the B-17 had a fire burning under one wing and smoke flowing from the other, leading all the way from Saarbrucken to where it crashed. According to what he had heard, the pilots had to be outstanding, to have kept it in the air for a couple of minutes, let alone the hour it took to reach friendly territory.

Weyland said he had not seen the B-17 in the air, but it had turned right over the headquarters of the **563rd Signal Aircraft Warning Battalion which was under his command**, and then it crashed in some woods a couple of miles from the village where the headquarters was located.

The battalion commander had reported the arrival and crash of the B-17 to the XIX TAC, and one of the survivors had been brought to his headquarters by one of his medics on the way back, after taking a man to an evacuation hospital.

The survivor had been debriefed and according to his XO, Weyland told me the tail gunner had been trapped under the tail when the survivor had bailed out. Later his SAW Battalion Commander reported that four men had died in the crash. Both pilots and two enlisted men were killed and one of the ***enlisted men had been torn-apart*** along the debris trail as the B-17 crashed. Then Weyland said, "The last he knew, they were still picking up the remains of the torn-apart flyer."

Something clicked in the back of my mind and I told Weyland I would be getting back to him. General Eisenhower had told me he thought he could help hide the B-24 crash, but not it's dead. Perhaps he could also help hide the crash of the B-17? Me, I was starting to figure out what we had to do with the dead!

When Weyland was finished describing what he knew, I told him to get the men in his unit who had talked to the survivor, and get every bit of information they had, and then, tell them that as far as they were concerned, they had never heard of the B-17 crash. Then he was to call the SAW Battalion Commander at once, and find out every detail of the crash of the B-17 and it's dead. And make certain, the SAW Battalion Commander made certain, that he'd gathered all the possible information concerning the torn-apart man. Weyland was also to inform the commander that if they had not recovered all the remains yesterday, they could continue today, but they were to keep all the remains at the crash-site unless they heard from Weyland or someone higher up, to give them, the go-ahead to deliver the dead men's remains to Graves Registration. I asked Weyland where the B-17 had crashed and he told me it had crashed in the woods near the village of Hattonville, about 15 miles south-east of Verdun.

179

I knew most of that area of France, as my father's family lived at St-Avold and we had toured all the Great War battle lines during our family visits. I had more than six hundred Great War books at home, and many of the French and German books had a lot in them about the battles around Verdun.

I knew where Hattonville was located; I had been there, or I should say, I had passed through the village while on a family tour. The rebuilt Chateau of Hattonchatel overlooked the village from its location on top of the high ridge just to the west of Hattonville. I knew, that General Patton's tanks had moved through Hattonville after the battle of St-Mihiel during the Great War and the American 26th Division, on 13 September, 1918, had Liberated Hattonville during that war, with the help of the 39th Division of the French Army on its left flank. One thing was certain, those people would appreciate the Americans in their village, now that they had been "Liberated" by the Americans for the second time in 26 years.

My first thought was, so far the number of units involved with the B-24 crash had been very limited and from what Weyland was saying, his command was the main command involved with both the B-17 crash and the **"Friendly Fire"** shooting- down of the Top-Secret B-24. Then, I thought to tell Weyland, what I had to consider very important, as far as anyone else was concerned. From now on, he was to say, "They had shot down by '**Friendly Fire**,' a friendly RAF Mosquito and were to always refer to the downed aircraft, as a friendly RAF Mosquito, OK?"

As I was about to hang up, I told Weyland to tell his SAW Commander, that this was something very Top-Secret, and he was to insure everyone who was directly involved was told to talk to no one about the B-17 crash. However, I also told Weyland to be very careful about the numbers involved at both units, as the smallest possible number of people with knowledge of the events was the best way to succeed in keeping the involved secrets from being compromised.

At 06:05, at the crash-site at Tincourt-Boucly, Captain Judson was called to the MP jeep with the radio and told the duty officer wanted him. When Judson got to the radio and reported he was present, he was surprised to hear the man on the other end identify himself as Colonel Coiner. Coiner, told Judson he had now accounted for all the survivors and with the three dead men Judson had located at the crash-site, the whole crew was now accounted for.

Judson told Coiner, he had enough remains and identification to create three Burial Packages for the dead men and that he and his men had done enough to recover the dead. They had been there for almost three hours, with little sleep, doing a very hard task, and they needed a break. So Captain Judson asked Coiner's permission to complete their work at the crash-site and take the three Burial Packages he would create to the hospital in St-Quentin. With that done, the Group hospital could send another recovery team to the crash-site as soon as it was full daylight to recover the rest of the dead men's remains and take them to St-Quentin to be combined with the remains Judson had recovered and would be delivering to the St-Quentin hospital, per Medical and Graves Registration Regulations. Since, there was nothing but small bits and pieces of the men, there could be no exact division of the remains and it would be easy to combine both recoveries at the main

hospital after the second recovery, exactly as required by Army Regulations in force at the time.

Basically, Judson explained to Coiner, the human remains now left to be recovered were small enough, the remains were being trampled into the mud they were making, as they searched. If they kept it up, they would be covering up as many remains, as they were finding. Coiner, thought it over for a moment and told Judson to go ahead and follow through with his suggestion and that Judson was to report to him, the moment they arrived back at the group.

Barney Silva told the researcher, that Captain Judson had called him and Pennington back to the ambulance and told them, "I am sick of this and Colonel Coiner had just told me all the B-24's crew are now accounted for." He continued, telling them, "That six of the B-24's crewmen have survived and these three died in the crash, so we are going to stop recovering remains now and take what we have recovered to the St-Quentin hospital."

Though Regulations stated he should create a mass burial Judson did not want their mothers to know how bad their death's were, so Judson told Pennington and Silva to get out two more sets of sheets and blankets and spread them out on the ground, beside the set they had been putting the recovered remains on. When that was done, Judson told the two men to equally divide the remains they had recovered among the three sheet/blanket sets. "That way," Judson said, "we will create three equal Burial Packages of crewmen remains, which is as fair as we can, considering the way the men died." And, their mothers never knew the truth.

As the two men worked at that gruesome task, Capt. Judson prepared the required medical forms for the deceased men. He created three EMT Form MD #52b tags, listing all the information they had on each man. The form would list their recovery as accomplished by the Aid Station, 397th Bomb Group HQ at **Tincourt-Boucly**, France. Each form was signed by Glenn L. Judson, Capt., MC 599th B Sq. With the note, the body had been tagged at 02:30 hrs, 10 November 1944. The time used for the tagging time on the forms was the best estimated time of death of the person involved and not the actual time the tag was created. As this airplane had crashed at 02:30, 10 November 1944, that was the time written down by Judson.

When each tag was complete, he filled out the information required on a Personal Effects Bag for each man and placed any personal effects they had found for that man in the Personal Effects Bag. Then, he tied the Form 52b tag to the neck of the Personal Effects Bag, using the same string to tie on any of man's Identity tags they might have found.

Silva told the researcher, "That he and Pennington had not tried to sort the remains to insure equal, identifiable body parts in each pile. All we did," Silva continued, "was to divide the pieces as evenly as we could. When we had finished dividing all the remains, Judson had handed us the rope that was carried in the ambulance and told us to wrap up the blanket sets as tightly as we could into a bundle and tie each bundle with the rope."

As the men completed tying each bundle, Judson would attach one of the EMT Forms and its Personal Effects Bag to the rope of the bundle. By that time, the men had been at the crash-site for nearly three hours and the dead crewmen's torn-apart remains had dropped in temperature to that of the cool November night.

The fresh set of sheets and blankets of the first two bundles, when the bundles were complete, were dry on the outside when they finished the bundle tying. However as they wrapped the first sheet/blanket set into a tight bundle, the men realized, it was soaked through with the fluids from the remains they had first recovered. The body fluids had not had a chance to dry or congeal from the cold before they were placed on the first sheet/blanket set. **So, when they tied up the previously soaked blanket set, the outside blanket was covered with congealed body fats and fluids.**

Silva got a stretcher out of the ambulance and both Pennington and himself, were both happy when they lifted that last Burial Package onto the stretcher and then lifted the stretcher into the ambulance, where Silva secured it in place for transit to the St-Quentin Hospital.

By 06:30, Silva had the ambulance out of the field and they were on their way to the hospital located at the St-Quentin Air Base. By 07:00, he had pulled into the hospital receiving area, where they had help to remove the stretcher carrying the three small bundles representing the three men's remains. Captain Judson, once the stretcher had been unloaded and a replacement stretcher given to Silva, told the two men to head over to the hospital chow hall for breakfast, saying that he would meet them there, as soon as he had made arrangements for the men's remains.

By 08:30, Silva had dropped Captain Judson at the Group's Headquarters. Then he took Pennington to the Squadron Dispensary, before heading to his usual location on the days the Group was conducting air operations. His ambulance was soon parked next to the Péronne A-72 Air Base Control Tower, and Silva was sitting on a beater chair on the control tower lawn, talking to the other ambulance drivers who assigned there during flight operations.

Silva had not been told to shut up about what he had seen, so when the others asked, he told them about the crash and what he and Pennington had done.

When he got to the end, when he was telling them about the dead men's bundles, he described how bloody and greasy the last one had been and that he could still feel that stuff on his hands, even though he had washed his hands several times since he had held that bundle.

To finish the story, he stuck out his hand and asked the other drivers to shake. Not one of them would shake that hand!

For the rest of the war, as a reward for his coolness when handling the dead, Silva was sent to every crash-site which involved one or more non-functioning inventory items.

Barney Silva

(**Note**: It took the author, 10 years, 10 months and 25 days to locate the only living survivor of the first recovery crew. His information welded together many items of evidence the author had located before they met. Barney proof read and approved what the author has written)

Barney Silva - Receiving Honors - Buire Village Hall

Photographs: Willis S. Cole, Jr. - 2002

Pfc. Barney Silva - (2nd from right)
May - 2002
Attached Ambulance Driver
599th Bomb Sq. (M) - 397th Bomb Group (M)
"Final Transfer" - Completed

(**Note**: Graves Registration Regulations were specific about what was to be done, when two or more deaths occurred and the remains could not be differentiated (individually separated). All such dead were to be buried in a common grave. However, during the war, most of the men recovering the dead, would not want it reported to their parents, that they had died in such away, that their remains could not be separated. Thus, they would divide the remains to give each dead his own grave. Later, after the war and recover continued, many common graves were established.)

183

**Barney and Sophia Silva
At the A-72 tower where he
and his ambulance had spent
a lot of time during missions.**

**Barney and Sophia Silva
At the grave of the Remains he had
left behind at the Top Secret B-24
crash-site.**

Photographs: Willis S. Cole, Jr.

Chapter Nine
Cover-Up - The Plan

As Silva was driving his ambulance to the hospital at St-Quentin, back at General Eisenhower's Headquarters I was deep in thought, as I had heard the same term used at both crash-sites. At each site someone had described the dead as **torn-apart**. That was a coincidence that seemed heaven-sent to me. I now knew about the crash of two American bombers, both in France, within 15 hours of each other and at each crash-site there was at least one person who had been *"torn-apart"* during the bomber's crash.

This was the common thread that could provide the background needed to tie the two crash-sites together. After the war, if some ex-GI's were at a bar and they happened to talk about the B-17 or B-24 that crashed nearby and the fact, that one or more men were torn-apart when they died. It was most likely, during their next drink, this common thread would most likely lead to both admitting they might be wrong about the bomber. *"But they were damn certain some poor bastard was torn-apart when he died!"* The next drink would be to those who died and they would move onto something else.

Soon I was outlining a plan that would enable us to make the crashed Top-Secret B-24 disappear, as Ike desired. I started to lay out my plan on a new pad of paper, and I would insure that every piece of that paper would be burned in my office stove, before I left the room. ***This had to be a non-documented, verbal order only operation, if it was going to happen, and it would have to depend on the power General Eisenhower held and his verbal orders being followed as given, if it were to succeed!***

I put in a call to the Commander of the 397th, Colonel Coiner, and as I waited I was pondering just how tight we could control the two events, the one at Coiner's base and the other at Weyland's SAW Battalion's HQ. As I laid it out, I had two events or two X's in an Algebra problem, the problem was, both X's had a Y factor, the dead. Coiner, had reported his X had three Y factors and Weyland had just told me, his Y factor was four. I noted that $(2X+7Y)-(X+4Y)=X+3Y$, which meant, we had to make one X and four Y's go away, if we were to make the Top-Secret B-24 disappear by swapping out the B-17 crash from Hattonville to Tincourt-Boucly. The B-17 crash-site had four bodies, for a total of seven dead crew. So, it was obvious to me, somehow, three complete bodies had to disappear at the crash-site!

The telephone rang and I was connected to Colonel Coiner. Col. Coiner told me, "He had been expecting my call and that his doctor had just reported in. The doctor was at their next level hospital, at the St-Quentin Air Base, where he had just delivered the three Burial Packages, made up of the partial remains his team had recovered. Coiner then added, he was preparing to send a second remains recovery team from their Group hospital to conduct a second recovery at the crash-

site in the daylight, to insure all the dead men's remains were recovered. Then, when they were done, they would take the additional remains to the St-Quentin hospital, **to be combined or joined with the Burial Packages already delivered to the St-Quentin hospital by his doctor, as the QMC Graves Registration Regulations required**."

The moment Coiner began talking about a second recovery at the crash-site and the regulation that remembering required the combining of the two separate recoveries, *I realized what he was talking about could destroy my plan before I could even tell Eisenhower about it!*

I was only half listening as my mind began to roll into high gear. This was becoming something I could not handle over the telephone. I was going to have to jump in with both feet and dance like the devil, if what I was planning was going to work. I was already north-west of Reims and very close to the Roman road from Reims to St-Quentin. With a good driver, I could be there in less than two hours. When Coiner finished, I asked him how close his base was to the St-Quentin hospital and he told me the base was about 10 miles west of St-Quentin, on the Amiens road.

In reply, I told Coiner to contact the hospital commander at the hospital where his doctor had delivered the Burial Packages and inform him to be prepared for a visit from me by 09:30. Then, I told Coiner, to get me the exact instructions on how I could get to the hospital as I came to St-Quentin from the Reims/Laon road and then from the hospital to his base. If all went well at the hospital, I should be at his base around 10:00. Col. Coiner said he would do that and I hung up and put in a call to Ike to tell him of my plan to make the B-24 crash, disappear.

That morning at the 109th Evacuation Hospital, T/Sgt. Russell Gustafson, Flight Engineer/Top Turret Gunner, slowly woke up, looked around, realized he was in a hospital and discovered he was in a full leg cast. As he looked to one side, he saw a Purple Heart pinned to his pillow and as he straightened his head, a woman came into view. She was dressed in a plain, old Army uniform. But to Gustafson, every woman was a hot tomato and he gave her his biggest smile, the one that always got him the girl. The nurse smiled back, and said he was scheduled to be transported to Tours very soon, where he would be put on a hospital train to Paris. Then she grinned and picked something up that was on the blanket over his chest.

The nurse was holding a small handkerchief size piece of his parachute and Russell remembered telling the man at the ambulance that he could take a souvenir piece of his parachute. But, he had expected there would be a lot more of his parachute left, than this little piece. The nurse pressed the silk parachute fragment into his hand, winked, and thanked him for her souvenir.

Fifty-four years later, the researcher could tell Gustafson what happened to his parachute. As Pfc. Plant had told him, he had helped unload the stretcher and the wounded man had given him permission to cut a piece out. Plant saw Mike Fisher from the pharmacy, walking nearby and as Mike always had a pair of scissors in a holster on his belt, the parachute could be cut up. In about ten minutes, the parachute shroud was a bunch of handkerchief-size pieces to be given to other

PFC Plant's Souvenir Piece Of Wounded Man's Parachute
Given To The Author By PFC Plant At 109th EH Reunion
Signed By The Wounded Man, Russell W. Gustafson - July, 2001

l, as a souvenir. However, Pfc. Plant did make certain the flyer got one of the pieces from his parachute.

Once the nurse left him, the next hospital person Gustafson saw was a guy asking if he needed a bed pan. Then, they started his long journey home.

Perhaps in the same ward, perhaps in two other wards, 2nd Lt. Harms, Bombardier, and S/Sgt. Fross, Ball Turret Gunner, were both still asleep from the sedatives being used to treat their nervous, invisible interior wounds.

As they slept and Gustafson was prepared to move, a major part of my worry was not in France, but with the RAF and the Eighth Air Force, to whom the Top-Secret B-24 actually belonged. If these organizations would not go along, then what Ike wanted done could not be accomplished. And since I could not personally visit them for some time, Ike would have to call them himself and get an immediate agreement from them.

The phone rang and in seconds I was talking to General Eisenhower, who told me to hold on and I heard him tell someone that he had to be alone for a while. In the background noise of the telephone, I heard a door close and then General Eisenhower asked me if I had a solution.

It took some time to explain exactly what I thought we could do. I told General Eisenhower there was a major risk to the career of everyone involved, as it would require us do to use the same methods the British had used to preserve their Top-Secrets when they were at risk. I told General Eisenhower that each time the British had done it, *the desired result had justified the means required to accomplish that result*!

187

First, I told General Eisenhower that all the time he had me involved with the QMC Graves Registration people in England could now turn out to a great benefit. But basically, it all depended on him. **With his commands, all to be given by verbal communications only, he could authorize me to do what had to be done**. If, he personally swore a handful of the involved commanders to the secrecy required, considering what had to be done, I was certain my plan would work. It was obvious to me, most of the important commanders were already personally involved **and, given the secrecy involved, he could use their careers as an additional threat** to gain and maintain their help. I assured him, "If you can get the right commanders here and in England to go along with my plan, **we can make the crash of the B-24 disappear**! However, as soon as possible, I would be required to go to England to insure all the units' official documents there would **support the B-24 flying back to England instead of crashing in France!** Then, with the help of the same people, we could move the physical location of a crashed B-17 that I had just heard about, up to the location of the Top-Secret B-24 crash-site, making that location, the *B-17's official crash-site*."

That way, I explained to General Eisenhower, if the Germans had anyone with possible access to any of the records, they would think a mistake was made by their spies, if any spy reported it was a B-24 that crashed there instead of a B-17. As far as the actual B-17 crash-site was concerned, the unit and personnel involved there and higher up the Ninth Air Force chain of command who might know about the actual crash-site, would never have access to the **official documents that showed the B-17 had crashed elsewhere**.

Before I could go on, General Eisenhower asked me about the dead, as we could not hide the dead that way. I told General Eisenhower that I was certain we could handle it. But I had to cover some of the QMC GR Regulations first, to lay out the ground work. As he knew, the dead were to be transported to the control of the QMC Graves Registration by Army Medical personnel over whom he had little control. To make it work, we had to do what had to be done, before the dead were turned over to Graves Registration. Because, as he also knew, when the remains were turned over to Graves Registration, their Burial Reports would contain the truth about their crash location. However, we still had some control over the data that would be on their Graves Registration Burial Report when the remains were actually turned over to Graves Registration.

What do you mean by that? General Eisenhower asked me, and I gave him the descriptions of the dead I had been given by Col. Coiner and General Weyland. The Top-Secret B-24 crash-site had three dead, who had been *torn-apart up with the B-24* and there was nothing much left of them or the bomber and its Top-Secret equipment at the crash-site. I told General Eisenhower, a partial recovery of those remains had been accomplished and the three Burial Packages containing those partial remains had already been turned over to a Ninth Air Force Base Hospital at St-Quentin. Then, I informed General Eisenhower, the major problem at hand was the very fact those partial remains had already been recovered and turned over to the hospital, creating the greatest threat to the plan I was laying out for him.

With that, I told General Eisenhower about the ***B-17 and it's dead***. Which consisted of three complete bodies and by a strange coincidence, ***another man*** who had been hanging under the B-17's tail when it crashed into a woods, and he ***had been torn-apart*** by the trees during the crash.

General Eisenhower replied, "That's a hell of a way to die. But, exactly, what are you suggesting be done?" I told General Eisenhower. "It is really fairly simple. We can use your position to get the involved Eighth Air Force units in England to modify their records to make the B-24 and its Top-Secret electronic equipment arrive back in England and to move the B-17 crash-site to the B-24 crash-site." I went on to tell General Eisenhower, from what I knew, the B-24 and its equipment had become small pieces of material and dead crewmen. We were lucky it was in such a condition that almost no one knew it was a B-24 that had crashed. That would be a big help at the B-24 crash-site, as we had to make the French people at that crash-site believe it was a B-17 that crashed and not a B-24.

General Eisenhower replied, "So you get that done, what about the dead?" I told him, I was going to have to quickly review other Graves Registration Regulations about the burial of our war dead, in order to be able to give him the foundation on how I was going to make it happen and account for all seven dead.

I told General Eisenhower, as he was already aware, Graves Registration Regulations specify that every American killed in France had to be buried in France. Every American killed in Belgium, had to be buried in Belgium and it was the same for Holland (now the Netherlands). The purpose of that regulation was really very simple. With those specifications, when Graves Registration received or recovered an Unknown, they only had to review the records of units that had served in the country where the remains were known to have died, and not all the units that had served in Europe. I went on, reminding General Eisenhower, thanks to ULTRA, we knew the Germans were fully aware of that regulation and in addition, we knew the Germans were constantly receiving updates on the Graves Registration burial of our military dead. We believed they were obtaining the information from the German POWs and employed locals who were German spies, as we used those people to save our man power, they were used to dig the graves and do most of the physical work at our cemeteries.

Based on that, I had looked up our Air Force loss reports and there had been no American bombers crash in France for the past week and then, yesterday, we had two. If we were to use one crashed bomber to hide the other, we could not bury the dead crew from two different bombers in the only open cemetery in France. If we did bury two different groups of remains, the German Intelligence might realize we were hiding something and that could be worse than doing nothing.

So, General Eisenhower asked me, "What are you going to do about the dead?" I repeated to General Eisenhower that the problem is already in place, due to the second remains recovery required at the B-24 crash-site. That was the biggest problem right now. So, if he verbally ordered me to go ahead, my first step was going to have the St-Quentin Hospital Commander put our careers on the line to preserve the secrecy of the B-24. To do that, I would need his full approval of my

plan as soon as I could get it, if I were to make the B-24 disappear as he wished. I told Ike, "*That such a multiple recovery of American War Dead Remains would automatically force a Graves Registration Investigation that we could not control*. So I had to hurry up to the St-Quentin Hospital and get that commander to send the already recovered remains to Belgium. It would be an illegal burial, according to Graves Registration Regulations. But there had been so many crashes in the Belgium burial zone in the past week, the Germans would have no way to tie any additional bomber crew dead to a crash-site in France. Unless, they got their hands on the Burial Reports as they were prepared and to date, we had never found those records to be at risk."

"Once I had that in hand," I told General Eisenhower, "I had to get with Colonel Coiner, the Base Commander, at the base near the B-24 crash-site and get his help. *As it would also be a career buster and possibly jail for all of us*, Coiner might require a call from him, but I had to get Coiner to help me *hide the additional partial remains of the dead crew* before they were taken to the St-Quentin hospital. That would prevent any further involvement of the St-Quentin hospital personnel and keep the local Graves Registration personnel from starting an investigation."

General Eisenhower remarked that it sounded like it was getting rather complex! I replied that it was just starting to be complicated! One crash-site had three dead and the other had four dead. If we moved the B-17 crash to hide the B-24 crash, we would have a problem with the dead. It was not so much that the B-17 crash-site had four dead and the B-24 had three dead. It was the fact, that the all French witnesses at the B-24 crash-site knew there was nothing but torn-apart bits and pieces of men recovered at that site. However, the commander at the B-17 crash-site had reported they had three complete bodies and were still recovering one dead man's remains, that had been torn-apart and that a lot of the French had seen the complete bodies.

"So Colonel," General Eisenhower asked me, "what is our solution?" "General," I replied, "I know Americans do not hide our war dead and *I am not suggesting we hide the bodies and their deaths.* What I am suggesting is, we use the partial remains already recovered at the B-24 site to account for the death of the three men at that crash-site." I continued, "*General, then we do hide the rest of their remains recovered during the second recovery, it will eliminate the problem of Graves Registration starting an investigation of the dead at that crash-site.*"

"General," I continued, "the hardest part, the biggest problem is, we have only torn-apart men at the B-24 crash-site, and at the B-17 crash-site we have three complete bodies and one torn-apart man. *The only way we can have success, is to use the one man's torn-apart remains at the B-17 crash-site to create all four official graves for the dead at that crash-site*. Then, we will have to hide the complete bodies of the other three dead men. *However, when I am done, they will have official graves and their deaths will be fully accounted for in the Graves Registration records.*"

I went on to tell General Eisenhower, "We can divide the torn-apart man's remains to create all four men's Burial Packages before we turn the remains over

to Graves Registration. If we do it that way, the official Burial Records of Graves Registration of the *dead at both crashes would consist of torn-apart remains!* That common thread would certainly make any possible German search for information, to reach the conclusion that there was one burial of multiple torn-apart remains in France and one actual crash of a B-17 and most likely, it crashed at Tincourt-Boucly. That conclusion for us would indicate the coverup was a success.

General Eisenhower then began a series of questions beginning with, "If, I go ahead and order you to do this, how sure are you that it will work?" All I could tell General Eisenhower was that it was very contained. Basically, it was in the hands of two of General Vandenberg's Commanders, the XIX TAC, under General Weyland and Colonel Coiner, of the 397th Bomb Group. If he could get those men and the ones in England on board, I was very certain it would work. I added, that to be absolutely certain, it might take a personal call from him to them, as well as the Commander of the SAW Battalion under Weyland and to General Doolittle at the Eighth in England. He might need to call the commanders of both of the bomber's units, but General Doolittle should be able to prevent that call. With the guaranteed help of those men, I should be able to closely contain all the information required to ensure the official documents reported the situation as we wanted it reported and not, "as it was."

However, I told General Eisenhower that the first steps had to be based on my position on his staff and I had to get going to the St-Quentin Hospital at once, if I was going to make it work. For my plan to work, I had to keep the men's partial remains from the B-24, now at the St-Quentin Hospital, away from any possible possession by the local Graves Registration personnel. Which I would assure by sending the three men's remains to the Fosse Number One Temporary Cemetery in Belgium for burial. Then, as soon as I had that under control, I would get with Colonel Coiner to ensure the rest of the remains from that crash do not make it to St-Quentin. I emphasized, that I would have the time to do that if I leave for St-Quentin immediately. "Okay," said General Eisenhower, "What about this B-17 crash you mentioned?" I told General Eisenhower, that I had already sent instructions to the local commander, via General Weyland and Weyland was to tell the SAW Commander, if their medics had not completed the recovery of all the torn-apart man's remains at the B-17 crash-site, they were to complete the recovery this morning and then do nothing until Weyland authorized them to do so.

Then, if all goes well, I should be finished at the B-24 crash-site by early afternoon and if I pushed it, I should be able to make it to the SAW location south of Verdun by late tonight or early tomorrow morning. I reminded General Eisenhower that I did have an advantage in having my own maps of France which were much better than our military maps when it came to using the secondary roads to bypass areas where our troop concentration and convoys could slow me up. "Okay," General Eisenhower said, "if I order you to get the hell out of there and go do this, where do we stand? And I do mean, where do you and I stand, today, tomorrow, and for some unknown time to come. You know as well as I do," continued General Eisenhower, "that what you propose is total career ruin if it ever

becomes known. ***Hell, look at what I did to Patton for slapping someone in Sicily and you want me to hide bodies from our own Graves Registration?*** It seems damn dangerous for both of us."

I replied to General Eisenhower, that less than two hours previously, he had told me that B-24's crash had to disappear, because the Top-Secrets on board were so important in saving lives. Well Sir, the only way I can think we might pull that off is to do exactly what I have laid out. Then I told General Eisenhower exactly where I stood. If I could use his name, backed by his position as the Commander of all Allied Forces, and with his telephone backup, I was ninety-nine percent certain I would pull it off and keep it so well hidden, that no one could ever figure it out and if they ever did, I was even more involved than he would be.

I went on to explain, that we were extremely lucky in making it happen, as a very small number of units and a very limited number of Americans had been involved, and those units were separated by enough distance, that the odds of the lower-ranking men involved ever meeting had to be extremely low.

Then, ***with as few calls as possible from him, the higher ranked men would have as much to lose as we would***. I went on to say, that with that containment and the war going on, it would soon be over and mostly forgotten by those involved, as new events demanded their attention.

I assured General Eisenhower, that the desired results would be obtained if the commanders of the Bomb Group and SAW Battalion go along with the plan, and the involved people under them fell into place; especially if the real reason it was being done was fully explained to them. Being Air Corps themselves, the commanders had to know about the loss to the RAF in March, when the Germans figured out how the RAF was confusing their radars. If the men understood that it might happen again, only this time on a far greater scale, as the Germans would be shooting down many more Allied aircraft and their crews, and this time, it would be ***their*** aircraft and crews that would be lost! If they knew and understood that, I thought all of them would want to cooperate.

I concluded, by telling General Eisenhower that I could think of nothing else that would make the B-24 crash go away. "As I see it", I told General Eisenhower, "we have two options. The first is to take our chances at the B-24 crash-site and do nothing, hoping like hell that the Germans would never find out about the crash and what the equipment on that plane was doing to their radars and radios. The second is to do what I am suggesting and take the required steps to keep the Germans from learning about the B-24 crash. At the least, we would confuse the Germans enough that the war might be over before they paid enough attention to any information or relics they might receive from any spies at the B-24 crash-site to make use of any of the Secrets involved."

"Damn it, Colonel," General Eisenhower said, ***"you, of all the people on my Staff, know more than any other, that we cannot take that chance. We have to make that B-24 crash disappear!"***

General Eisenhower continued, "I am very concerned about hiding those dead bodies. Will it be forever, long-term, or short-term?" "General," I replied,

"to be honest at this time, I just don't know and I do not have the time to figure all that out. However, if I do it right, I don't see why we cannot make it good later on. At some opportune time in the future, if you authorize me to do it, we may be able to make it good, that is the only answer I can give you at this time."

"Okay, Colonel," General Dwight D. Eisenhower replied, "you are hereby, directly ordered by me, to go ahead with the plan you have just laid out." General Eisenhower continued, "You get the hell out of there and do what you have to do. Keep me out of it as much as you can and where you can't, get back to me with the information I need and the person I have to contact and I will support what you are doing." Then he told me, *"**If, at some point in the future it becomes necessary, I will take the heat off you**. Just remember this," General Eisenhower continued, "**No one in any unit is to maintain any documentation of what we have done, you got that, Colonel**?" "**Yes, Sir!**"* I replied!

I did add, I would probably be required to find any already documented records and modify them after I am done with what I have to do. I will need to go to England as soon as possible, to directly discuss the situation with those involved there. General Eisenhower listened and then said, "Colonel, you call me if you need my help. You tell me what you need and as long as nothing is put in writing, you will have everything you need. **Now, go get it done!**" Then, he hung up and I began the dance to get it done!

I thought about what General Dwight David Eisenhower, Commander of all Allied Forces in Europe, had just ordered me to do, based on my own plan. *He did so, to protect the Top-Secret information available at the Top-Secret B-24 crash-site.* He did so, knowing one cold hard fact, if the Germans compromised the electronic Top-Secrets on the crashed B-24, *the Germans could use those same secrets against the Allies, leading to the additional loss of tens of thousands of soldiers and civilians on both sides. It was something that he, as the Commander of the Allied Forces, had to prevent, no matter the immediate cost*!

Myself, I was to participate in a verbally ordered coverup of the crash of the Top-Secret B-24 and its Top-Secret electronic equipment. *To succeed, I was to desecrate the remains of seven, Killed in Action, American military aircrew*!

Personally, I had no problem with my plan, nor did the British when they had to do the same thing to protect their Secrets and save Allied and civilian lives. *At this moment in this war, one had to worry about the greater good of all involved, the military in action in Europe and the civilians on either side*. If what I planned succeeded, it would be almost impossible to prove the success of the actions taken.

If I failed and the Germans were successful, instead of hundreds of Allied aircraft being lost before the war ended, it could mean there would be thousands of additional aircraft lost, along with tens of thousands more Allied aircrew lives lost. If the Germans used these Top-Secrets against our own radars and radios on the front line, additional tens of thousands of Allied ground troops could be lost and the end of the war delayed for some time. Resulting in an even greater loss of German soldiers, plus civilians on both

sides. I did not at that time and never did doubt, who would be the victors. However, I do believe with the knowledge of these Top-Secrets, Germany could have delayed the end of the war for some months.

As an aside, less than a year later, when I heard about the Atomic Bomb being used against Japan, I had to wonder about what we had done during that cover-up. If the planned cover-up had not succeeded and the Germans had been able to delay the European War, would President Truman have dropped one of those Atomic Bombs on Berlin, as originally planned? At that point, for the very first time, **I was certain General Eisenhower and I had succeeded in what he had ordered me to do!**

After General Eisenhower hung up, I looked over my notes, stood up, picked up all my paper notes including the remaining unused pad, and put all of them into the burning stove. Then I called the operations officer, and told him that General Eisenhower was sending me off on a special investigation, and that I would be gone for a few days. If he had to get a message to me while I was gone, he could contact me through the Commander of the 397th Bomb Group at the A-72 Péronne Air Base. The base commander is a Colonel Coiner and if he tells me you called, I will get back to you as soon as I can. When I am finished at Péronne and ready to leave the Péronne area, I will call and give you the next contact number or see that someone passes the contact number onto you.

When the operations officer had that, I told him to prepare a set of open travel orders for me with no restrictions, authorizing full support and all that BS and have them ready in 20 minutes. He also needed to call the motor pool, and tell them to assign Sergeant Tiff as my driver and that he was to be assigned to me for a few days. Sgt. Tiff, would also need several days of open trip tickets. He should be told to get his stuff together, along with his "45" and his "Thompson," and be ready to travel for a few days and be in front of my quarters in fifteen minutes.

In addition, I also told the Operations Officer he needed to call Colonel Coiner at A-72 at once and get the instructions that Coiner had promised me, as I needed those instructions by the time I picked up the open orders. I ended with a short apology for the rush, telling him, the General would kick my butt if I was not out of there on time and if the General kicked my butt, he can imagine what I will do to his, and I hung up before he could reply.

(**Note: Tiff did exist!** In the early 2000's, the author received an email from with the address of tiff@-----. The writer, wrote that his father had died and among his possessions, they found a diary. On the diary, was a note that it was not to be opened for a period after his death and that it was an "illegal" diary he had kept of his service in Europe. The communications went on for some time and then, tiff was no longer answering emails and the email address went dead. Tiff never disclosed his father's name and he did not provide all the information at once. Over time, however, as I shared my research with him, he would add some more of what his father had done. For a while the author thought, it was someone attempting a

joke, then too much began to fall into place that proved to the author that Tiff's father had existed.

For instance, in the diary he found his father had been sworn to absolute secrecy and never tell what he had done while helping the Colonel involved in the coverup. The oath, included the threat that he could be executed if he ever talked about it. Now, this may sound strange and impossible. However, during that period and up until they died, the author was constantly in contact with four others involved and each of them carried the secret to their grave. While stating, when they were still alive, "I have no knowledge of any bomber crash while I was at Hattonville." Even when a couple of dozen men from that same Battalion Headquarters remembered the crash and their stories, matched exactly with the hundreds of other witnesses the author talked to about that crash.)

When I walked out the door of my billet with my B-4 bag and galoshes, Tiff was there. Tiff, had the back door open for me and he had a big smile on his face. He was just happy to be getting to get away from the HQ and its BS for a few days.

I told Tiff to close the door and I handed him my bag and galoshes. I told Tiff that I would be riding in front to help navigate, so put the stuff in the trunk and let's hustle as I walked to the front passenger's door, opened it myself and got in. As Tiff got in and started the car, I told him we had to stop by the operations center on our way out, so I could get our orders, and then we were heading to St-Quentin, as fast as he could get us there.

The operations officer had his own heavy load and was not happy with what I had dumped on him, but he had my orders and he had Coiner's instructions.

I handed him a sheet of paper with instructions for General Vandenberg, General Weyland, and Colonel Coiner. When I was on my way, I told him, he was to call Vandenberg, Weyland, and Coiner and tell them I was in transit to the Péronne Air Base and I would be arriving at Hattonville very late that night or very early tomorrow morning and, don't forget to burn the paper.

In addition, he was to tell Vandenberg to call the Commander of the Air Base Hospital at St-Quentin and verify my visit with the commander. After that, Vandenberg was to call the St-Quentin Air Base Commander and inform him, he was to have a liaison plane waiting on the runway, ready to fly to Belgium, when I got there. Vandenberg was also to instruct that commander and his pilot that both of them were to do exactly what I told them.

Weyland was to be told to contact the SAW Commander we had discussed, and tell that commander I expected him to maintain the status quo, and he and his involved officers were to be available at whatever hour I arrived tonight.

The operations officer looked at my notes, and as a parting goodby, he told me I had better have a good reason for this extra BS when I got back or he might just kick my butt, himself. As I left, I thought to myself, "Friend, you have no idea and don't worry, I will have a good lie ready when you see me again."

By 08:55, Tiff had proven how good he was and we pulled up to the hospital at the St-Quentin Air Base. I told Tiff I would not be very long, but he

should have time to find the chow hall if he hurried, to get some fresh coffee in the thermos and then wait for me at this same location. As I got out, I handed Tiff a copy of my orders and told Tiff, "If they give you any crap, show them these." It was obvious that both Vandenberg and Coiner had been in contact with the hospital commander, telling him I was on the way, who I was, and that he had better pay attention to whatever I said. As I was immediately taken to his office and as we introduced ourselves, his staff left the room and closed the door.

I wasted no time in getting to the point, as time was very limited. I asked the commander, if I had been vetted to him by Vandenberg and Coiner and he said that both had called him. He knew I was from General Eisenhower's staff and that I was on a mission ordered by General Eisenhower. I told the hospital commander, that the partial remains of the three dead B-24 crewmen were all the remains his hospital was going to receive. And Colonel Coiner had reported his doctor from the 397th, had brought the remains in with all the information required to forward the remains to Graves Registration for burial. The hospital commander confirmed that the hospital had the remains and they were properly marked, even though they were not complete. For that reason, the regulations stated that he was supposed to hold those partial remains until the second recovery that Dr. Judson had told him about, arrived. Then, he would hold the two sets of recovered remains separately, until Graves Registration came and accepted them as their responsibility.

I agreed that was the regulation. So I informed him, that I was there as a direct representative of General Eisenhower to **verbally order** him to give me the remains he now possessed. So, I could forward the remains to the Fosse Cemetery in Belgium for burial. To make that happen, he was to help me get those remains in transit as soon as we could, as I had to get to the 397th. With that, I told the commander that the best thing for him and any staff who might question what was going on, would be for them to forget they ever had the remains in the first place. If he wished, I would get General Eisenhower on the phone right away, who would personally confirm my orders. I added, that I suspected that might not be the best career choice he would make during this war. I did tell him, that General Eisenhower had decided what was going on had to be done, and it involved Secrecy levels far beyond anything that he, as a hospital commander, was cleared to know.

With that, the commander asked me what I needed for him to make me happy. I asked him where the remains were located and he told me they were in a nearby, cool storage room. I asked him, if he could put them in the trunk of my staff car, as it was parked out front? He gestured, that I should walk with him. As we walked out of the hospital, he was pointing out a nearby building where the remains were stored, when Tiff drove up. I asked the commander to get in the car with me, and Tiff took us to the building, where the commander had a Pfc. place the three bundles in the trunk, after he had put down a couple of blankets to protect the floor.

I thanked the commander for his quick help, and asked for directions to the flight line. As we prepared to leave, I told the commander to make certain the Pfc. who loaded the bundles was told the staff car happened to be going in the right direction and that it would save Graves Registration from making a special trip to

the hospital to pick up these remains. I added, that the main thing was, no one at his hospital, other than himself, was to know the remains went to Belgium. And that, I had only told him about their destination, in case he received a call from the Fosse Cemetery about the remains being delivered there. If they did call, he was to tell them the men's aircraft had been hit over Belgium and General Vandenberg had ordered him to send the remains to Fosse Number One for burial. If they still had a problem, he was to tell the Graves Registration people at Fosse to call General Vandenberg directly and Vandenberg would handle the problem.

If he received no call from Graves Registration, he and his staff were to forget there had been any remains and basically, put it all out of their minds.

I thanked him for his help and said I would personally tell General Eisenhower about his help. With that, I shook his hand, got into the car and Tiff headed to the flight line.

Out of the commander's sight, I had Tiff pull over and I got out and went to the rear and erased the entry on Captain Judson's 52b Forms that showed the name of the village where the B-24 crashed. When I was done, all the tags and Personal Effects Bags stated, were the men's remains were recovered by a Captain Judson from the A-72 Air Station.

When we arrived at the flight line, there was a major waiting with the 1st Lt. pilot, next to a small liaison plane and it was obvious again, that Vandenberg was doing his share. It took no longer than five minutes to transfer the three Burial Packages and to tell the pilot, he was to personally deliver the three bundles to the Fosse Number One Cemetery in Belgium. And, tell them, if there was any problem, they were to call General Vandenberg at once and let him handle the situation.

I told the two men, it was obvious this flight would not exist after the pilot returned and both of them would make certain no documentation would exist that could be traced back to this flight. All they had to remember was, if there was ever any problem, they were to contact General Vandenberg and he would cover their butts. As to what they were doing, it was very important to the war effort and that was all I could tell them. However, in due time and if all went well, General Vandenberg would remember them and reward their effort. Then I said goodbye, they saluted, I saluted, and as Tiff drove us away the pilot was already beginning his taxi toward the runway.

As we left the St-Quentin Air Base, down at Hattonville, Pfc. Zeman was stopping the 563rd ambulance at the edge of the field, next to the crash-site. Zeman, Berardi and Boatman got out of the ambulance, Byrne and Venar got out of the jeep they were in. The four men made their way down into the ditch, up the other side, and walked to the nearby crash-site. A guard standing by the fire near the covered bodies and torn-apart remains, observed their approach with interest.

The three medics were not looking forward to recovering the rest of the torn-apart man's body, but they knew they had no choice and were resigned to the task ahead. They stood looking around the crash-site, as Major Byrne began to talk to the guard, who was the Corporal of the Guard in charge of the crash-site guards. Byrne wanted to know if all had gone well that night? The guard told Byrne that

he had only been on duty since 07:30, which was when he and the others around the perimeter had relieved the night guards. Major Byrne then asked the corporal what information the man he had replaced had passed on to him? The corporal replied that the other guard had told him that not much had happened during the night.

Once in a while they had heard animals in the woods, but by hollering and sweeping the area with their flashlights, along with some foot stomping, the animals had gone away. He did add, the night guard had kept the roving guard along the debris trail as ordered, but had stopped once it became daylight. After that, they had put the perimeter guards back out to the positions they had held yesterday. The corporal continued, and reported he had walked out to the edge of the woods to ensure no French people were heading toward the crash-site. The only French he saw were a half-mile away in the field and none seemed to be interested in coming closer to the crash-site.

Byrne asked Venar if he had any questions? Venar said he did not and turned to the two medics and ambulance driver warming up by the fire and told them to stop standing around, and get to it. They each picked up a bucket, from where they had put them the night before and Zeman also picked up the small canvas tarp, used to carry larger pieces. Then the three men started walking back toward the debris trail to begin the final recovery.

When they were far enough from the two officers, one of them said, what the others had been thinking, "If that SOB would get his own damn self out here picking this stuff up, he would not be so damn snide when ordering us out to collect it." The others nodded or spoke their agreement and then, they split to walk over the area they had covered the day before. Instead of starting where they had stopped the day before, Boatman had decided they should start where they had started yesterday, just in case they could find any additional remains of the man they had previously missed.

It was a much harder job today than it had been the day before, when the adrenalin was flowing after seeing the B-17 fly toward them, turn and then crash into the woods. Then, after they had arrived at the crash-site, they had found the four dead men. Today was different, it was in new light and there was nothing exciting about what they had to do. It had become exactly what it was, a gruesome task that had to be done. Here they were, searching around for torn-apart human remains while forcing their way through dense bramble bushes. At the same time, they had to look under the broken branches and search among the disturbed oak leaves carpeting the floor of the woods, for each piece of the torn-apart man.

The floor of the woods was full of root knobs, moss and clay outbreaks that worked to trap their feet and when one hand was carrying a bucket and the other holding thorn bushes from their face, the occasional slip and fall, that yesterday got a ready laugh from the others, was today a fall that led to all of them swearing at the Majors, still standing up by the fire.

Byrne sent the Corporal of the Guard on a check of the perimeter guards. While Byrne and Venar stood by the fire wondering why in the hell, were Generals Weyland, and Vandenberg so interested in this mess and why were they on a hold,

even if all the remains were recovered? Byrne told Venar, he guessed they would know soon enough because the person causing this situation could not keep the dead at this crash-site very long.

Venar agreed, stating that it was his specific responsibility as an Army Medical Corps Doctor and the Battalion Graves Registration Officer, to recover and turn the dead over to Graves Registration at the Limey Cemetery as soon as he could. He could only delay so long, especially since McBride had reported the dead men to Graves Registration as soon as he had heard about them, only to be told by Graves Registration, they were too busy with the dead from Patton's new drive to come pick up the dead. **And, as regulations specifically stated, in this situation, the 563ʳᵈ SAW Battalion's attached Medical Corps personnel had to handle the recovery and delivery of the dead, themselves**.

Byrne told Venar, he really doubted if Venar was going to have a problem with that, as General Weyland had directly ordered McBride to place the remains delivery on hold. So if Venar got in any trouble, he could dump it right back in McBride's and General Weyland's lap. Venar agreed and told Byrne he could think of no reason for them to hang around as Boatman and the others knew what they had to do and Boatman would make certain it was done right.

Byrne agreed, and the two men decided to walk along the debris trail to where the men were searching for remains, and tell them they were heading back to the village. Venar told Byrne he was going to tell Boatman, that when Boatman himself was satisfied they had collected all the remains they could find, the three men were to come back into the village and inform him the recovery was complete.

After Byrne and Venar had talked to the men, they walked back to the fire where the corporal was standing after completing his round of guards. Byrne talked to the corporal and asked if he had all he needed and the corporal told the officers, the mess hall had made arrangements for a hot coffee run, and a hot lunch was going to be brought out. The only question the corporal had, was if Major Byrne thought the guard would be removed that day? Byrne said it did not look like they would be removed and there would be at least one more night of guarding the crash-site before it was over.

After that, the two officers made their way out to their jeep and headed into the village to find McBride and bring him up to date. When they found McBride, he told them that Weyland and Vandenberg had both called him and that whatever was going on, it was out of his hands. However, he had been told a colonel from Ike's staff, was going to arrive later that night, or early in the morning, who would tell them exactly what was going on. In addition, McBride told them, he had been instructed, that all of them would meet with the colonel, when he arrived. The men agreed it was a strange situation, but to have Weyland and Vandenberg involved and now this Colonel, something big had to be going on.

When we had cleared St-Quentin, and Tiff and I were on our way to the 397ᵗʰ, Tiff was making the best time he could. However, there were a lot of oncoming vehicles of all types and the same going our way. All of them were slowed up by large number of horse drawn wagons moving along the road. In

France, one of the things that never changes, is the right of slow farm vehicles to take as much of the road as they wished. I swear, some of them keep a score of how many other vehicles they can delay behind their farm vehicles.

We were now passing through areas that had been fought over during the Great War, the evidence of the various battles in the Somme area could still be seen in the woods and uncultivated areas along the road. Almost every highway sign had some shells and other explosives piled against it, waiting for the French Deminage, bomb disposal experts, to remove and dispose of them. The shells and other mixed ordinance continue to come to the surface in the fields each year, just as frost heave raises heavy rocks to the surface.

Sgt. Tiff, swore softly, as he quickly swung out into the incoming traffic and we barely got back in front of the horse drawn wagon that had been in front of us, as the oncoming American truck, which did not slow up, whipped past going toward St-Quentin. I decided that it was time to make use of whom we were and told Tiff to turn on the siren and flashing lights. Then if he had to, push the damn wagons to the side and force the trucks off the other side of the road.

A couple of times, I was a bit worried that we were going to hit one or the other, but Tiff knew what he was doing and our speed, flashing lights and sirens soon got the attention of the oncoming traffic as he swung into and out of the oncoming lane. Even if the horse drawn wagons in front of us did not move, the other vehicles on our side began to give way as we approached them from the rear.

It took Tiff less than 20 minutes to reach the 397th, and when we pulled up to the main gate it was obvious the guard was expecting us. The one at the gate hardly looked at me as he pointed to the headquarters as he raised the gate. He saluted and waved us onto the air base.

Col. Coiner came out to meet me as Tiff pulled up, and we went directly to his office, where he offered me the use of his private toilet. After the coffee Tiff had gotten at St-Quentin and the rough road trip, I was ready to use the facility. Then I sat down with Coiner in the privacy of his office, after he had told everyone to take a break and to come back in twenty. The first thing I told Coiner was that I expected by now, he knew I was from Eisenhower's staff and that I was there to seek his help in doing what General Eisenhower wanted done. However, if he had any question about my authority, I could place a call to General Eisenhower at once, who would verify who I was and that what I said had to be done, was to be done.

As I expected, by now Coiner knew he was up to his neck in something beyond his control and he was going to do whatever he was verbally ordered to do. He told me he was ready to brief me on whatever I needed to know and follow through on my orders.

My first request to Coiner was for an update on the second recovery that he had told me, was going to be required. He told me that his hospital commander had sent out an ambulance to the crash-site at about 08:45, with three men who were to conduct the second recovery. Then I asked if he had direct contact with the crash-site and he told me he did via an MP jeep with a radio at the cash site and so far, there had been no problem.

My next question was about the survivors. Coiner, told me that the pilot was in the hospital, where he was treated for a cut to his chin and the others were in a small transit area, where they had little interaction with the men on the base. He went on to say that none of them would tell him anything, other than their personal information, their unit identification and that they had been onboard a B-24. He did tell me that before the pilot had been taken to the hospital and the men to their isolated quarters, he had told them three of their crew members had been accounted for, as killed in the crash. Also, that he had been told, that nothing much over the size of a #10 tin can, was left at the crash-site. (A large commercial size tin can, normally containing food.)

Col. Coiner continued, and told me that when he had asked the pilot and other survivors to go to the crash-site to help identify the dead men, all of them had followed the pilot's lead and refused to go to the crash-site. Coiner, admitted he was becoming very suspicious about the men, but figured out that General Vandenberg must know something he did not.

"Great," I told Coiner, "now I'll be a bit fair with you. As you know, the B-24 had been shot down by a night fighter from the XIX TAC. However, that was not the big problem; the big problem is the B-24, was a Top-Secret B-24, loaded with more than four tons of Top-Secret electronic equipment. Some of that equipment could be something that you know a little about, but most of it was something you had better not know anything about. So, it was that Top-Secret electronic equipment that was the big problem at the B24 crash-site."

I asked Coiner if he knew about the big RAF loss at the end of March and he told me he had some knowledge of it. All he really knew was the RAF had the crap scared out of them that night. He had first heard of it during a dinner party in England, with some RAF bomber people present and he heard them talking about it. Then it was mentioned in one of the briefings he had attended.

That helped me, as I was able to tell him what he had heard probably made light of the loss, in relation to the real event. However, understanding how bad that loss was to the RAF was crucial to understanding what could happen if we failed to handle this situation properly.

"If the Germans," I told Coiner, "learn about the Top-Secret equipment on the crashed B-24 and were able to use that knowledge to create their own systems to use against us, the RAF's losses that night in March would pale in light of what could happen to the RAF and to us, once the Germans started to use it against us." *With that possible result in mind, I informed Coiner, "That General Eisenhower had decided that the B-24 crash must disappear*, to prevent the Germans from being able to use any relics from the crash-site to determine what the B-24 could and was doing."

Then I went to even further length to explain what could happen if we failed. I told Coiner, if the Germans did learn the Top-Secrets of that B-24, we could lose thousands of Allied bombers and their crews, as well as a possible loss of our air superiority for a while. I could see by his expression, that my statement

had the desired effect on Coiner, as his command was a bomber command and it was his bombers and aircrew that would be at risk if we failed.

Coiner thought a second, then he asked me what he had to do? The first thing I told him was that *what we had to do could ruin his career, my career, Vandenberg's career and on up to General Eisenhower's career*. So, it was very important for each of us, who were involved, to **realize how serious it would be if just one man, of all the men involved, ever made public what we had done. Every man's career would be ruined and we might even share some time in jail**. I told Coiner that we will all swim together or drown together. Coiner nodded and told me to go ahead.

I told Coiner, that thanks to his help, along with the help of the St-Quentin hospital commander and General Vandenberg, I had already diverted the dead men's remains his doctor had taken to St-Quentin, to Belgium for burial. "In fact," I told him, "while we were talking, they are on board a liaison plane on their way for burial at the Fosse Cemetery in Belgium." I did tell him, that was not that step that could ruin all of us. That step could be somewhat explained, it was the next step of my plan, that could lead to ruin for all of us, and it would have to take place at the crash-site. After that, **we would all be fully committed**!

Col. Coiner nodded, though I cannot say it was a happy nod, and then I told him the next major regulation we are going to break together. It concerned the additional remains his men were now recovering. I had to explain to Coiner the problem concerning the second remains recovery. If those remains ended up at the St-Quentin hospital, especially now the originally recovered remains had been forwarded, they would automatically trigger a Graves Registration Investigation.

That investigation would reveal what had been done and that would make the job of hiding the crash of the Top-Secret B-24 impossible, let alone what it would do to our careers. At the same time, such an investigation would certainly add to the chances of the Germans learning what we were trying to keep secret from them. He asked me, "Well, what's our next step?" I told him, to get his hospital commander to come meet with us, ASAP (as soon as possible), and then we were going to the crash-site and make certain what we had to do, was done properly.

After that, we talked about the problem of keeping the number of men exposed to the truth as low as possible. Col. Coiner, told me, so far including the MP's he had sent to the crash-site, he probably had fewer than 30 officers and enlisted men who had been to the crash-site or knew much about it.

I looked at my watch and asked if he would contact the crash-site and find out how the second recovery team was getting along with their recovery. Col. Coiner got up, went to the outside door and yelled at someone, whom he talked to for a few seconds and then he came back in. He said he had told them to get the hospital commander here faster than ASAP, and a radio call was being made to the crash-site to check on their progress.

During the next two minutes we discussed the best way to hide the additional remains. I wanted them in a place where they would not be found accidently, but at a location that could be identified, so we could go back and

recover the remains when the flap was over. That way, we would be able to correct what we were about to do, some time in the future. I knew it was probably less than a half truth at the time and I suspect Coiner was thinking the same. But neither of us really wanted to look beyond the short-term need at that particular moment.

There was a knock on the outside door and a sergeant came in to tell Coiner that the men at the crash-site thought they had an hour or so before they would be finished. Col. Coiner thanked him, and asked about the hospital commander? The Sergeant told Coiner, the Surgeon was on his way and should be there in no more than a couple minutes.

As we waited, I told Coiner I thought the best thing to do would be to bring his man into the problem immediately and make him part of the solution. That way, the hospital commander would be as much exposed to any failure of the plan as we were. Then, if the hospital commander insisted, I would put in a call to General Eisenhower and have him talk directly to the hospital commander. As Coiner was telling me he did not think that would be necessary, the hospital commander knocked on the outside door and came in to meet us.

Coiner, and I had stood up as the Surgeon came in; Coiner, introduced me to the Hospital Commander/Surgeon and informed him, that I was from General Eisenhower's staff. Col. Coiner went on to explain to the Surgeon that I was there under the direct order of General Eisenhower to help implement what General Eisenhower wanted done at the crash-site. Col. Coiner told the Surgeon that he had already vetted me with General Vandenberg. Then Coiner told the Surgeon of my offer to call General Eisenhower and the Surgeon quickly said that would not be necessary. If Coiner said it had to be done, he would do what he could do to help us get it done.

We were still standing and I interrupted as soon as I could and said to them, "Gentlemen, time is of the essence here, so let's discuss this further in my car, on the way to the crash-site."

Col. Coiner asked me to give him a second to tell his people where we were going and tell them, if necessary, we can be contacted via the MP radio. Before he walked off, I thought to ask Coiner if he had a camera? Coiner, said he had one in his desk and he opened a drawer, picked up a camera and then he went to see his people, as we followed him out of his office.

(**Note**: The camera's photographs will provide 100% provable evidence!)

Within a couple of minutes, with Coiner in the front seat, Tiff was in gear and heading for the gate. Seeing Coiner in the front seat, the guard raised the gate, pulled to attention, saluted and waved us by about the time the car had already passed him. I was looking at his face as we passed and he may know nothing about the crash, other than it ever happened, but I expect he will remember for a long time, how fast the staff car was going when it passed him, as it departed the base.

By that hour, both Coiner and the Surgeon both knew how to reach the crash-site and with a little instruction from Coiner, Tiff drove and we talked about the situation at the crash-site. As Tiff already knew about the diverted remains, I did not hide that, but I did not discuss what we were going to do once we got to the crash-site. The Surgeon asked Coiner, once, if Coiner was 100 percent in and Coiner told him, that they were now deeply involved and really had no choice. Colonel Coiner went on to tell the Surgeon, from what he did know, if they did not help, their own Group could lose a lot more bombers and crews than they had been losing. I could not add anything to Coiner's concise statement and was watching the countryside pass by as Coiner laid it out to his Surgeon.

I was somewhat familiar with this part of the Somme, enough so, to remember the road we were on, as we headed toward Péronne. But, Coiner had Tiff turn right at a small intersection and soon we came to a small village named Cartigny. As we drove down the sunken road leading toward Cartigny, Coiner pointed out the B-24's crash-site, that was visible across the valley, just beyond what I recognized to be a British WWI cemetery. In Cartigny, we passed a working sugar factory and Coiner told me, that the copilot had landed on the factory office roof and pointed out the door, as we passed.

We left Cartigny on the road to Brusle, a small village spread along the road. So far, I had seen no place where we could hide the dead crewmen's remains that could not reach the hospital at St.-Quentin.

A short distance beyond Brusle, I noticed a freshly plowed field on our right, where there was a angle in the road we were on. I asked Tiff to slow down. Then, I asked him to stop as we came to the end of the plowed field. From what I could see, we appeared to be fairly well screened from the sight of the villagers in the villages around us. From that place, I could see part of the villages, but we were far enough from them that no one in the village would really be able to see much of what happened at this location. In addition, anyone stopped at this location would be able to see anyone approaching from any direction while they were still some distance away. From the change in the fields and the road surface, it appeared to me, that we must be at a separation of the Communes, or local government bodies. And in the distance, to the east of us, I could see the beginning of a small village and the road appeared to make a sharp turn to the north and lead across the valley to a larger village near the crash-site.

With the jog in the road, the demarcation line in the fields and the two small villages in each direction, this location could be pinpointed on a map, making it a possible location to hide the additional crew remains from the ongoing recovery at the B-24 crash-site. It seemed to me, unless we saw a better place, this was the location where what had to be done, could be done with little risk.

I told Tiff to go ahead and as we started to move, I told Coiner and the Surgeon what I was thinking and asked them, to help me watch for a better location. As we left the small village, that had been to our east when we stopped, Coiner told me that two of the survivors had been picked up at a house in the village and that the B-24 had crashed just to the north of the next village. The road we were on was

crossing the bottom of the valley and we were heading to the other side of the valley toward a larger village located on the hillside to the north.

As we cleared the valley, crossed some railroad tracks and began the climb up into the village, I saw the village's name was Tincourt. We drove straight across the intersection in the middle of the village and as we cleared the village to the north, we could see the crash-site of the B-24 in the near distance. The closer we got to the crash-site, the more I could see there was not much left of the B-24 that I could see.

Instantly, I was struck by the large number of people at the crash-site. The closer we got, the number of people I saw really bothered me, as this could be a major flaw in the plan, and it would have to be overcome.

I asked Coiner, if he had told the guards to keep the French away? He told me he had, and he had no explanation for all the people we saw. Just outside the village we came to a major intersection. There was an American MP there and two small roads branched off to the north from the intersection. The guard motioned for us to take the eastern road and we drove up past a small woods and turned left to pull into the field where the B-24 had crashed. The people, mainly women with some Americans and MP's standing near the crash-site, made way for Tiff to park next to an ambulance that was close to the impact crater the B-24 had created.

As our car turned off the road to enter the field, as I later learned, about 1,200 feet north of the village, 1st Lt. Hornsby was waking up from being put under while his chin was sewed up. Just before they took him to have his wound treated, he had been taken to a small ward for five or six patients, where a couple of other men were lying in their beds.

Now, as Hornsby looked around, he realized he was alone. Apparently, while he was asleep, the other men had been removed from their beds. This seemed rather strange, but it was a while before he found out, exactly what had happened. He was lying in his bed, his eyes closed, wondering why Grey, Mears, and Bartho had died, when he heard someone whispering on the other side of the ward door.

As he listened, he could hear whoever was out there, was telling someone else, that the man in that bed was a coward. He was the pilot of the bomber that had crashed during the night and he had been found further to the west than the other survivors. To them, it had to mean the three crewmen had probably died because he, the pilot, had bailed out of the plane before they had been able to get out and the plane had crashed with the men in it.

Hornsby was livid, he told the researcher, 54 years later, "The bastards did not know my B-24 was flying west, because they were certain no American bombers flew at night. Based on that, they thought my plane was part of a mission on its way east, when we crashed." Hornsby went on to say what made him mad, "Was the mission was so Top-Secret I could not defend myself. I had to lie there and take it, knowing they were wrong and unable to say it." As Hornsby recovered in the hospital under suspicion for being a coward, the other survivors were keeping to themselves in the base quarters assigned to them. If anyone asked them what happened, all they said was their bomber had been shot down and crashed nearby.

It was about 10:40 when we arrived at the crash-site and I had no set plan. All I could do was to continue to implement my original plan as best I could, modifying it as required to get it done, and soon there would be no opportunity to turn back, even if I wanted to.

(Note: At this point, I would like to recommend the readers interested in the pure military history underlying this book, read an article published in *"The Journal of Military History,"* Volume 70, No. 1, January 2006.)

"Published quarterly by The George C. Marshall Foundation and the Virginia Military Institute for the Society For Military History."

"Apt Pupil: Dwight Eisenhower and the 1930 Industrial Mobilization Plan" Author: Bob Moore, Page 31

The Author of this paper did an excellent job of covering the foundation of General Eisenhower. Several specific points in this paper covers exactly what General Eisenhower had to have later on, when faced with the situation on hand after finding out that the Top-Secret B-24 had crashed in France.

"The Grave At Cartigny"

10 November, 2000, after the new memorial marker dedication.

At the near front, is the French Miliary Cross with the Le Souvenir Français Roundel, indicating the is maintained by members of that volunteer organization, as it has been for many decades.

The newly dedicated plaque is mounted on the base of the first mistaken identity stone that was installed by the Commemo-Rangers on 10 November, 1944, when the grave was first misidentified by the researcher as containing the missing remains of the four men from the *"Lady Jeannette,"* B-17G-35VE, SN: 42-97904.

The concrete cross, berm and red gravel were installed by Emile Berger in 1961, to replace the wooden cross placed on the gave on 23 November, 1944, at the time of the reburial of the partial remains from the hidden grave site.

Over seven decades, this grave has provided proof of American World War Two personnel **hiding American World War Two Dead**. The grave's history has led to this book and the truth, within.

Photograph: Willis S. Cole, Jr.

"Eisenhower was the primary author of the 1930 IMP, which thus benefitted from many of his talents.[71] Two seem especially important.[72] First was his *amazing memory*. His wife, Mamie, later recalled that he 'knew by heart production man-hours on everything from a bomber to a mess kit.'[73] Another of *Eisenhower's great qualities* was his humility; he was usually *willing to* listen to the ideas of others, including civilians, to **profit from their experience**. ... *Eisenhower was easily dominated by more forceful men and their ideas*.[74] ... He was eclectic, *picking and choosing among ideas he thought best* and then adding his own. Consequently, *Eisenhower's work* was almost always *reflective of a greater store of knowledge* than his own experience would suggest.[75]"

Footnote references in the published article.

"71. Industrial Mobilization Plan, 1930; Eisenhower, *At Ease*, 211."
"72. Industrial Mobilization Plan, 1930."
"73. Dorothy Brandon, *Mamie Doud Eisenhower: A Portrait of a First Lady* (New York: Charles Scribner's Sons, 1954), 171."
"74. For Eisenhower as easily swayed, dominated or indecisive, see Brendon, *Ike*, 59, 110, 114, 133, 138, 155, 156, 160, 163, 168, 175; D'Este, *Patton*, 486-89; Carlo D'Este, *Eisenhower: A Soldier's Life* (New York: Henry Holt and Co., 2002), 423, 424, 596, 602."
"75. Steve Neal, *The Eisenhower's: Reluctant Dynasty* (Garden City, N.Y.: Doubleday and Company, Inc., 1978), 74."

As a reader of this book, based on actual events and people, someone had the juice to get General Eisenhower to do what was done. This person had to have already proven himself to General Eisenhower and both had to know of the British's use of the dead and living *as a means to reach a justified end*.

The quoted paper proves that Eisenhower *was a commander who would use such a person*. *The events prove such a person had to exist!*

The author visiting a semi-fallen in French WWI Dug-Out

Photograph: Willis S. Cole, Jr.

With over 80 trips to Europe and over four years in Europe, over the years the author and friends enjoyed many side trips all along the WWI lines and the WWII battle areas.

Some of the best, are just becoming accessible as more and more of the restricted areas can be visited. Though, sometimes, one must sneak in. The lesson is, whenever a friend "Over There" invites you to an adventure, do not refuse. Because, if you do, you will no longer be offered such an opportunity.

An example is when you have visited and explored a location and the French friend takes a found shell home. Then, when you get there, he invites you to the barn for a "Product the Farm" drink and a shell opening.

There are ways to check, if you have a high explosive, shrapnel, or gas shell. In this situation, it was a shrapnel shell and as the French friend unscrewed the fuse, he told me the difference between French farm women and city women. The farm woman holds a burlap bag out in front the shell to collect the flying shrapnel as the shell empties and the city woman runs out of the barn as fast as she can and which one are you?

Well, he is still here, at ths writing, and the author has the shrapnel to display.

Chapter Ten
Cover-Up - Implementation

When Sergeant Tiff drove the car across the field to the ambulance parked near the crash crater, I was surprised to see a long line of men and boys, stretching down over the hillside from the crater's edge. The line stretched for some distance and I had to instantly ask, "What the hell, are they doing?" Neither of the others had an answer and, as we approached the crash-site, I had told Coiner and the Surgeon that I was not going to get involved unless it was absolutely necessary. If I was asked a question, I would pass it onto them or I would ask one of them to get an answer to any question I might have, because I wanted everyone to think I was just a curious visitor to the crash-site. Both men agreed that would be a good idea.

Before we got out of the car, I told Coiner I wanted to know what the line of people was doing. Their purpose was beginning to sink in, as I saw some of them in the process of leaving the line for, or going back to the line from the left front of the ambulance. I could see three Americans standing there, who must be the recovery team that Coiner and the Surgeon had told me about.

As Coiner and the Surgeon went to talk to the recovery team, I stood to the side and surveyed the site, making a mental estimate of what I was seeing. The largest pieces of the B-24 that I could see were some distance away from the crater, at least the distance of a football field. They looked like the only pieces at the crash-site, which I thought appeared large enough to enable someone to identify the type of airplane that had crashed. Those pieces were so far away, they were near the other road that branched off from the intersection we had crossed, where the guard had us take the eastern branch road instead of the western.

The line of men and boys was rotating counterclockwise to the crater and it looked like the recovery team must have had them start at the ambulance and then rotate around the crash-site looking for aircrew remains. They had to have completed about 345 degrees of their circle movement, as they were now closing in on the ambulance from its western side. At the current rate the line was moving, I thought they should complete the recovery walk around the crash-site in 15 to 20 minutes. So, we had that much time to set in place what had to be done and to order the recovery team to do it.

I had moved to where I could see where the men and boys leaving the line were going before they returned to the line, as Coiner and the Surgeon walked over to me. Col. Coiner indicated we needed to walk some distance from the other people around us. So, we headed to the south of the crash-site to the edge of the small woods, where we took the opportunity to step inside and empty the bladder.

Then, standing side by side and watching the line slowly moving in its circle, I had to admit that Coiner's recovery men had done a good job of instructing the French men and boys helping with the recovery. The men closest to the crater, were moving very slowly and had time to look into the crater for remains, while

those in the far end of the line, about 300 feet from the crater were moving at a slow walk while conducting their shoulder to shoulder search for human remains.

Coiner, filled me in and told me that we would walk up when I was ready, so I could see what the line of people was doing. Coiner went on to say that the sergeant who was in charge of the recovery had realized that it would take them a couple of days working by themselves to recover all the remains, because they had been blown all over the crash-site. That is why they had sought the aid of the French men and boys who had came to the crash-site on their own.

The reason the French were present, was because a large crowd was already there and walking all around the crash-site when the Americans arrived. At that time, the French were picking up bits and pieces of the aircraft and who knew what else as they rummaged around the crash-site.

The medical sergeant, when he had arrived, had talked to the MP who had been there for a while and the MP told the sergeant, there were not enough guards to keep the French away, as they were approaching the crash-site from every direction. They were coming by road and they were walking cross-country from the villages where they lived. Without enough guards, the MP realized he could not keep them away. He had told the medical sergeant, "Who the hell cared if they haul off some scrap metal as a souvenir?" When Coiner told me that, I had to admit to myself that if I was that sergeant, I would have felt exactly the same way.

Because some of the Frenchmen and boys were picking up pieces of the dead or bits of paper and other debris, then walking over to the recovery team to show them what they had found, the recovery team sergeant decided the best way to recover the most remains was to make use of all the Frenchmen and boys. Particularly, since the Frenchmen and boys did not seem to be bothered by the bits and pieces of flesh and bone as much as the Americans were.

One of the Frenchmen, who could speak fairly good English, had become a volunteer interpreter for the Americans. When he was talking to the sergeant, he had told him that the remains of the men killed in the crash reminded him of what was left over after they had butchered a hog, when they prepared what was left of the hog to make sausage.

As he talked, the Frenchman used his right hand to make a cutting motion across his left hand, as if cutting the hand into small pieces and repeated, "Just like making sausage."

With the help of the interpreter, the sergeant had called all the men and boys to the east side of the crash-site. Then, while standing on a jeep, the recovery team leader told the French what he was asking them to do.

Starting at the front of the ambulance, they were to line up shoulder to shoulder to create a straight line out to the edge of the crash area and then the line would slowly pivot counterclockwise around the crash-site and crater. This would require the men in the center of the circle to walk very slowly, as the people at the far end of the line had to move slow enough to be able to search while they walked. This would permit the men closest to the crater the time required to climb down into it and look for remains there before they rejoined the line.

210

The French interpreter told the sergeant that almost every man had been in military service and they would understand how to manage their walking to keep the line straight, as it was a basic marching requirement in the French military.

With that, the sergeant told the men and boys that they were to look for any human remains, even the smallest bits and pieces of the dead men, pieces of clothing, pieces of paper, and any item they thought might help identify the men who had died in the crash.

Then Coiner told me, the sergeant formed the line and they had been walking in the circle for over an hour. When I was ready, I could see what they had recovered, up by the front of the ambulance. With that, I told them, "Let's go there now and then I want to walk down to where the larger debris pieces are located." At the front of the ambulance, I saw a disturbing sight that sticks with one's memory. The recovery men had found an articulated bomb bay door that had not been destroyed and they had the French, who found pieces of flesh and bone, pile them on the door. From the size of the pile, I estimated they had already collected around 300 pounds of remains and it was, just bits and pieces of flesh and bone. To me, it appeared about half of the remains that had been recovered had been exposed to fire and smoke, as they had been singed or burnt. Some remains showing less fire damage, while others that appeared to have been exposed to a strong fire. Perhaps, I thought, they had landed where something else had burned for a while after the crash or were covered with fuel when they were torn-apart and, had been burnt when the fuel exploded.

As we were looking at the collection, a young French boy came running up with something he wanted to show the Americans. He was holding it in his hand, and then he used both hands to hold up what he was showing us. It was the face of a man, one of the dead crewmen's faces. It started at the corner of one side of the mouth, went up the side of the face, around the eye, across the forehead, around the other eye, and back down to the other side of the mouth. The man's eye brows were there, his eye lids were there and his nose was there. It was as if a hunter had used his knife to skin the flesh of the man's face from the man's skull. The boy's name was Bernard Leguillier and he was very proud of his find and the recovery sergeant, through the interpreter, told the boy to put the face on the pile, which he did and then he ran back to rejoin the constantly moving line.

(**Note**: In June, 1991, the author was visiting Bernard and as usual during a first meeting, he asked Bernard, to quickly, without thinking about it, what was his most memorable memory of World War Two? Part of the above paragraph describes it, exactly as Bernard told the author over twenty-seven years ago.)

The man's face became etched into my mind in the short time the boy was holding it out for display, I can see it to this day, if I think about it. Some days later while I was England and visiting the 36th BS, I saw pictures of the men who died and I know the face that I saw that day belonged to the man who had been in the nose, Sgt. Frank A. Bartho. The face the boy had held, was that of an older, narrow

faced man, while the officer who died had a rounder face. And the officer and the other man were much younger than Bartho.

Over in England, General Doolittle was engaged in an earnest discussion with General Eisenhower in France, who had phoned Doolittle. Doolittle had heard of the loss of the Top-Secret B-24 within minutes of the RAF and its Squadron hearing that it may have been shot down, and in one way General Eisenhower was verifying the loss to Doolittle.

Both men agreed the B-24's Top-Secret electronic equipment had to be protected from the Germans. *General Doolittle agreed that hiding the B-24 crash by making it disappear, appeared to be the best plan*. General Eisenhower told General Doolittle that the plan was already being implemented, and continued with what General Doolittle had to do.

It was important that the B-24's Squadron and the RAF did not learn the exact location of the crash-site, at least not before the basic cover-up was completed and the Top-Secret equipment, accounted for, either, by being physically found and recovered, or buried at the crash-site, so no one would have easy access to it. To insure that result, Doolittle was to report to the 36th BS(RCM) Commander and "Bomber" Harris, RAF, that the B-24 had crashed near Abbeville (about 60 miles west of the actual location) and that three men had been killed. In addition, Doolittle could tell the unit that, *"The tail gunner's parachute had been caught on the tail."*

(**Note**: Interesting, that this was reported to the Squadron before any of the surviving crew members returned to the Squadron.)

General Eisenhower told General Doolittle that a major part of the plan was to use the B-17 from the 729th Bomb Squadron, 452nd Bomb Group, that crashed on the 9th in eastern France, to mask the crash-site of the B-24. To do that, Doolittle would have to step in and make certain the official documents pertaining to the 36th's B-24 indicated it had returned to England. And, all the official documents of the 452nd had to show the crash-site of their B-17 was the official version's location they would be given, which was the actual location of the B-24 crash-site. Doolittle told Eisenhower that made excellent sense and he would take steps to make the suggestion happen at once.

Eisenhower told Doolittle that a few days and a few missions should pass before anything was done. Within a few days, the men's minds in those units would be off these losses and on new ones. *Eisenhower added that he had verbally ordered the colonel (who had devised the plan and whom Doolittle had met) to put the plan in place*. Ike continued, telling Doolittle that his colonel had advised him, that the plan was for his colonel to go to England to make certain everything was right. Ike did not add, the reason was to ensure that the respective backsides of himself, Generals Doolittle, Vandenberg, Weyland, and others would be protected.

"My plan," Eisenhower told General Doolittle, "is to send my colonel over there in a few days to meet with you and whomever else it may be necessary to meet

with, and ensure all the files have the correct entries." Eisenhower continued that he was certain Doolittle's men would put it to bed and make it disappear, but the colonel could ensure it all matched in France and England. Doolittle agreed, saying he would wait to do that part of it, but that he had a suggestion that might help get the RAF and 36th Bomb Squadron men's minds off their loss as soon as possible.

Eisenhower asked what that was? Doolittle told him that, though they lost the B-24, that night's mission had been very successful. If Eisenhower agreed, he would draft a Letter of Commendation to the B-24's Squadron and send it through the RAF Air Officer Commanding the 100th Group, the RAF unit the 36th was attached to. "If I do that," Doolittle continued, "I know Air Vice Marshall Addison will attach his own Commendation and forward them to the Squadron. Once the Squadron has the Commendations, the Squadron Commander will follow exactly what your colonel will tell them to do. He would not dare question what he was asked to do, or risk the chance of Addison and me coming down on him like a ton of bricks." "Damn good idea," Eisenhower said to Doolittle, "no commander would want to screw up a good thing." Then Eisenhower told Doolittle to send him a copy of what they get, so he could give it to the colonel cleaning up the loose ends as a disposable information source.

Eisenhower ended by telling Doolittle that he had no doubt as to the fact they were on the same page, line, and word. And, with that mutual agreement, he said goodbye to Doolittle and he killed the connection.

Just north of Tincourt-Boucly, Coiner and I walked on down to see the pieces of the bomber that were the furthest away from the impact crater and Coiner took some pictures of the larger debris. What I saw there was of no help to me in saying it was a B-24, a B-17, or some other plane. I suppose a person who was familiar with the landing gear of the B-24 and B-17 might know the difference, but what was the odds of anyone at this crash-site having that information? I thought the odds were very close to nil!

Colonel Coiner, and I continued to walk around the crash-site perimeter and as we walked, I discussed with him what I thought we had to do. First, we would have to talk to the Surgeon and then we were going to have to convince the recovery team they were going to do what had to be done. It was something they would most likely, not want to do. "Don't forget," I told Coiner, "they have to be sworn to secrecy in some manner." We had to ensure that they never told anyone about what they were going to do. At least, not while they were in the military and when they got out they would probably be so unhappy about what they had done, they would never talk to anyone about it.

Then we discussed the large number of French people at the crash-site and the numbers of Americans who had already had access to the crash-site. We agreed, until all the current people at the site had left, we could not suddenly stop them from picking up a piece of the plane as a souvenir or we would create an effect, exactly opposite of what we wanted, which was to make it seem B-24 hadit was just an ordinary B-17, "Flying Fortress," crash-site in France.

We had not completed our full circle around the site, when the line of Frenchmen and boys completed their circle and the recovery team sergeant got up on the fender of the ambulance and thanked all of them for their help. He told them how much he and the United States appreciated their specific help in this very hard job of recovering the remains of the dead men. When the interpreter finished, the group cheered and began to break up.

As Coiner and I walked toward the ambulance, the recovery team (with the Surgeon advising), tried to pick up the articulated bomb-bay door, stacked with the crewmens' partial remains. It was soon very obvious that it was too heavy and slippery for them to easily lift it into the ambulance. Immediately, several of the Frenchmen volunteered to help and soon the aircraft door and its load were slid into the back of the ambulance and the ambulance door closed.

When that was done. Col. Coiner asked the recovery sergeant to stand by, while Coiner and I pulled the Surgeon to the side and asked his advice on how best to get the three men to do what they had to do.

As we were beginning our discussion at the B-24 crash-site near Tincourt-Boucly, down in the Hattonville Woods, Sergeant Boatman made the decision that he, Berardi, and Zeman had done all they could do. They had completed the first basic search of the debris trail and then walked the debris trail two more times and during the last walk, they found no additional remains. With that decision, the three men walked back to the collection point and placed the rest of the remains they had onto the pile of the torn-apart man's remains.

They removed their gloves and washed their hands, using water from a Lister bag the guards had hung on a nearby tree. They wiped their hands on their pant's legs, pulled out cigarettes and after lighting them with a "dead man's match," they took a well-earned break. A 'dead man's match' was a well-known scenario from the Great War, in or near the front lines, a enemy sniper would first see the glare of the match when it flared into fire, then as the first and second men lit their cigarettes, the sniper was able to locate them and when the third man lit his cigarette, the sniper shot at that third man's head. Safe behind the front line, the three men smoked and talked to the Corporal of the Guard while standing at the nearby fire. They told him they were finished and heading back to the village.

The corporal asked them if they had collected all the man's remains and the men lifted the cover off of the torn-apart man's remains, which were spread across the ground-tarp and studied them while they smoked. After a couple of minutes, Boatman said he did not see any thing that would account for the lower right leg, and both the others soon agreed with him. Damn," Boatman said, "I guess we are going to have to walk the entire debris-trail one more time and concentrate on the tall trees." Boatman thought that the only way they could have missed that leg, was for it to be in the air and not on the ground.

The corporal laughed as the men covered up the remains again and began to walk back toward the debris-trail. "Good luck," he said between chuckles, "I hope, you have fun." The three medics walked the entire length of the debris-trail. They did not see any of the man's remains in the damaged trees. When they arrived

214

back at the fire, Boatman told the corporal that he could now have all the fun. Because, while he was checking the guards, he could look for the flyer's missing lower right leg and if he found it, he should let them know. Now, it was medics' turn to laugh, as they headed out of the woods toward the ambulance in the field.

By the time the 563$^{rd's}$ medics had decided they were missing a leg in the woods near Hattonville, Coiner, the Surgeon and I had decided on the best way to tell the 397$^{th's}$ medics exactly what was expected of them. As I stood to one side, just out of hearing, looking at the crash-site, Coiner and the Surgeon laid out exactly what the men were supposed to do and then ordered the men to do it. When they were done following their orders, the medics were to draw an exact location map to give the Surgeon upon their return to the Group hospital.

(**Note:** No one at the B-17 crash-site has ever accounted for the missing leg, as far as the researcher knows, perhaps, it was taken that night, by one of the very large "Wild Boars" or Red Fox, that inhabit the woods. The researcher has seen both in the woods, while visiting the crash-site.)

The Surgeon told them, he would pass the location map onto Graves Registration, so they could recover the remains the men were to bury at the selected burial site. The men accepted the need for a quick reburial of the messy remains they had just loaded into the back of the ambulance, as a matter of fact. The recovery team leader told Coiner and the Surgeon that they would leave right now and get it done and they would report back to the Surgeon at the base. It was just about 11:00, eight and one half hours after the crash of the Top-Secret B-24. It was just a bit of a lie, as the Surgeon was going to send the map by messenger over to Coiner, who was to give it to me, if I had not left, or forward it to me at my headquarters. What neither Coiner nor the Surgeon knew, was that map was the only documentation that I had created that I did not control and when I got my own hands on it, it would quickly be burnt and disappear.

About the same time at the Fosse Cemetery in Belgium, the Graves Registration personnel were creating the official Report of Burial for each of the newly delivered, first recovered remains of the men. Now, unknown to me, I had managed to create and put in place **absolute proof of the first damning failure to follow Army Regulations!**

The three medics of the recovery-team had no real way of knowing that what they were about to do was as bad as it was. Coiner, the Surgeon and I knew exactly how contrary to regulations it was, as did General Eisenhower and General Vandenberg. However at the same time, I knew it was coming together, exactly as General Eisenhower had ordered me to make it happen.

A short time later, to the southwest of the B-24 crash-site, along the narrow Cologne River in the valley, one of the Frenchmen who had been helping the Americans recover the dead as a member of the long line, was just entering a small wood lining the south bank of the Cologne River. He had to leave the crash-site early, when the line was almost done, as he had to get to his job in the village where

215

Absolute Proof That The Americans Know The Truth Of The True Crash Site Of "226."

Photograph copy kept by the Péronne film developer after he developed photographs shot by an unknown American.

Bernard Leguillier and his brother Claude may be among those in this photograph.

On the bottom of the AAF photograph, is a note that the crater was made by the crash of a B-24, SN: 52-51226.

The commander had a village business develop the film and unknown to him, the man at the business, kept a copy of all the photographs he developed for the Germans and Americans.

Photograph: Bernard Leguillier, from collection given to him by local film developer's family.

he lived, Cartigny. He did not have a vehicle or bicycle, so he had walked cross-country to the crash-site at first light and then helped the Americans recover their torn-apart dead, until he had to leave for his job.

After he had left the crash-site, he had angled downhill to the southwest of the crash-site until he reached the Cologne River and crossed over at a narrow spot. After he had crossed over the Cologne River, he had entered one of the many small woods, lining the river's course.

(**Note**: As he crossed the river, he was very close to the position where Veliz and Ysalva had landed, some hours earlier.)

When he was just a short distance from the southern edge of the woods, he heard a vehicle coming from Boucly. He looked in that direction through the trees and he saw an American ambulance heading toward Cartigny, coming along the road from Tincourt-Boucly.

As he was standing, somewhat hidden beside an oak tree, a short distance to the north of the angle in the road that marked the Cartigny and Tincourt-Boucly Commune's border, he realized the men in the ambulance might be the Americans he had been helping at the crash-site. So, when the ambulance stopped at the edge of a recently plowed field on the south side of the road and the driver got out along with two other Americans, the Frenchman recognized the driver as one of the Americans he had seen at the crash-site. As he watched, one of the men retrieved a shovel that was attached to the ambulance and walked back around the rear of the ambulance until he was out of the Frenchman's sight.

Thinking the men had to follow a call of nature, he continued to stand there for a couple of minutes, when he realized the men must be doing something else. He was not in that much of a hurry, so he stood by the tree and waited to see why they had stopped there.

After some time, the three men came around to the back of the ambulance and opened its back doors. As the Frenchman watched, the men struggled to get something out of the back of the ambulance and then they disappeared around the

back of the ambulance and out of his sight. Now he was curious and decided to wait until they left, just to see what they had been up too. Some time later, the man came around the ambulance, closed the back doors, put the shovel back and got into the ambulance and it drove off toward Cartigny. As soon as the ambulance was out of sight, as it entered the small village of Brusle, the Frenchman made his way up the hillside to the road and field to see what they had been doing.

The side of the plowed field, next to the road, had been well trampled by the American's feet. A few feet into the field, there was a higher area of trampled down, freshly piled dirt, compared to the recently plowed area next to it. Realizing that the men were those whom he had helped and seeing what they had removed from the ambulance, he believed, he knew what was under that trampled down dirt.

He began to kick at the dirt pile and slowly, he opened a hole. As he kicked at the dirt, he had to be careful as the soil under his feet was not solid, it was more like standing on a rubbery surface. Then, after another kick, he began to see what he thought was there. He was looking at the bits and pieces of the human remains he had helped the Americans recover. A couple more kicks proved his theory, and he quickly realized the Americans were doing during this war, exactly what the French Army had been known to do during the last war. ***The Americans were hiding their War Dead***!

The Frenchman kicked the dirt he had removed, back into the open hole, recovering the human remains. Then he headed to work at Cartigny, only this time he walked along the road, through Brusle and on to Cartigny and his waiting job.

When the ambulance left the crash-site, Coiner, the Surgeon and I stood and watched it leave. We agreed that we did not

Unless you knew a B-24 nose wheel, could you tell? Photographs: USAF/HRA, 36th BS(RCM) Official Record

From the photograph and debris features, it appears the crashing B-24 may have struck while almost upside down.
Note: On 22 January 1945, a B-26 from the 1st Pathfinder Group struck the filled in crash-site, bounced over the white electrical pylon that can be seen just above the debris, bounced again by the band of trees, then crashed into the Bois de Buire near the notch seen at the top of the hill. Two of its crew members were killed and the crash did create a lot of additional confusion during the author's later research into the B-24 crash.

Photograph: USAF/HRA 36th BS(RCM) Official Record

want to arrive at its goal until after they had completed their task and left. So we decided we would help the guards clear the crash-site and get the remaining French people to leave. After that, no one else would be permitted within the crash-site area and certainly no more pieces of the plane would be permitted to be taken away as souvenirs.

It took some time to clear the site, as the French from different villages would meet friends, and they had to talk about what they had seen and done. Some compared souvenirs and then, slowly, they began to leave the crash-site, with the gentle urging of the guards.

When the site was mostly clear except for some boys and girls, I asked Coiner to get his camera and take some pictures of the crash crater, which he did. I told him, I would need some copies of what he had shot, and he told me he would have the film developed in Péronne and send me as many copies of the photographs as I wanted, then he asked me how many copies I required? I told him I needed two sets. I would need one set to help set up the false records for the B-24's loss and one set to show General Eisenhower, before I destroyed them. I did tell Coiner that he could keep a set for his own private personal file to protect himself, if necessary in the future, but no others were to be kept as we could not risk the exposure later on. Coiner and the Surgeon agreed and they assured me the photographic negatives would be destroyed. (Colonel Coiner's mistake, using the Péronne photographer to develop them!)

What neither they nor I realized at the time was the fact, **the keys to what we had done had already been cast!** One key was a Frenchman who left the crash-site early, and other would be the result of the Péronne photographer, who would develop the pictures for Coiner. Unknown to anyone, for a long time the film developer had been making secret copies of the prints he developed, first for the Germans and then the Americans, and the developer had kept his own private file of those photographs. Decades later, the private collection was given to a local historian, Bernard Leguillier. Who, as a boy, had picked up a man's face, at the "Avion Fortress, B-17" crash-site and showed it to the Americans before putting the face on the pile of human remains being collected.

10 Nov. 1944 X B-24-J-226)

One of those shadows may have been mine? **Notice, the correct identification of the aircraft that crashed on these official photographs. Yet, it's official Aircraft Record states it never crashed! Correct date and location!** The circle in the bottom of the hole, is part of a radar jammer. Photograph: Air Force Historical Research Agency, 36th BS(RCM) Official Record

As we waited for the French to leave, Coiner, the Surgeon and I

discussed the problem of so many of the French hauling off pieces of the crashed B-24 and its Top-Secret electronic equipment. Our discussion was important, as it concerned the best way we could convince all the French involved here, that it was a B-17 and not a B-24. We were certain most of the people did not know what it was, as all we had heard them say about the crashed bomber was that it was an "Avion Fortress." So, it sounded to us like most of them already thought the plane that had crashed was an American "Avion (Flying) Fortress" or B-17.

The B-24 had crashed in the middle of the night. No one had actually seen it before it crashed and had become a collection of small pieces in and around the field. Because it had disintegrated into small pieces, if I handled the problem correctly, it seemed to me the French could easily be convinced it was a "*Avion Fortress, B-17*." However, the souvenirs were another major problem and how to handle that problem was the answer I had to find, very quickly.

The answer had to be something that would ensure the Germans did not get any of the Top-Secret electronic equipment that would expose the equipment's secrets. So, we had to retrieve any souvenirs of that Top-Secret equipment already taken from the site and yet, as we stood there, we were watching people walking away carrying souvenirs with them. In the distance, up the hillside the crash-site was on, I saw the boy who had handed in the torn-off face heading to the north toward the branch road there and he had a bright yellow oxygen bottle with him, as he and another boy walked to the road. At least, I thought to myself, that could not help the Germans and as I watched them walk away, I realized what I had to do.

Coiner and the Surgeon had wandered over to help the guards ease a few more French away from the crash-site and to ensure the guards had been ordered to keep everyone away from the site and especially, allow no more souvenir hunting by new arrivals, either French or the Americans.

I was left, standing by myself, looking over the crash-site and thinking there was no way I could use people from Coiner's base to do what had to be done. If I did, too many of them would begin to question what the hell was going on. Who ever I decided to use had to be from a unit that would be used to keeping secrets, such as those involved at this and the B-17 crash-site. It was no longer only the secrets of the Top-Secret electronic equipment involved in this cover-up, the cover-up now included the hidden remains of the three dead men at this crash-site. I said to myself, I only knew of one group of people whom I could really trust. I was going to have to get General Eisenhower to authorize me to contact General Donovan of the OSS, as soon as I could.

From my job on Ike's staff, I knew the OSS was no longer sending missions to France and that they had been sending many of their people to the Orient. However there were still some OSS personnel in England, either conducting missions to Norway or waiting on orders. Many of the OSS field personnel I knew, could speak excellent French and they could be the final solution to the rest of the cover-up at this Top-Secret B-24 crash-site.

If Ike went along with my new plan, I could get Donovan on the line right away and get him to send two groups of his French-speaking men to France, by

tomorrow morning. We would need more men at the B-24 crash-site than at Hattonville as here they would have to recover the souvenirs the French had taken. If they thought, the souvenir was even remotely a part of the Top-Secret electronic equipment. During that process, they should be able to convince all the French that the bomber that had crashed here, was an "Avion Fortress, B-17!"

At Hattonville, all they would have to do would be to listen to the local people and Americans to determine if the crash of the B-17 was considered just another airplane crash, and the bodies, that had to be hidden, were not suspected of being hid. I was fairly certain that none of the French who had been at the Hattonville crash-site knew about the torn-apart man. Donovan's OSS men could prove that out in a couple of nights at the local bars. If the French knew about that torn-apart man they would be talking about him, just as I had already heard the French at this crash-site talk about the men who had been torn-apart here.

With that, I knew I had a plan and I had to get to a secure phone to get in touch with Ike, as soon as I could. Then I could get in touch with Donovan, to give him as much time as I could. I was not worried about his help, I had known him for years and I knew he would immediately comprehend the need of what I was going to ask him to do.

I walked over to Coiner and the Surgeon and told them, "Let's get back to the base, I need to get in touch with General Eisenhower over a secure phone, right away." By 11:45, we were on our way and when we came to the plowed field by the road, we saw the trampled earth in the location the men were supposed to bury the remains. As we passed along the road to Cartigny, I saw a man walking toward the village. His shoes and pant-legs were wet and muddy and I wondered, if he was returning from the crash-site after helping collect the dead men's remains.

At 12:00, Coiner and I were at his headquarters and Tiff was dropping the Surgeon off at his hospital to talk to the recovery crew and get the location map they had been told to draw. He was to tell them that it would be best if they forgot what they had done, as it might be some time until Graves Registration would be able to get to the remote grave site. _**As they were certain no one had seen what they had done**_, we did not want some French person overhearing them talking about it and perhaps disturbing the remains before they could be recovered.

I asked Coiner to leave me alone with his secure phone and I put in my call to General Eisenhower. It was obvious that Coiner had given the operator the information that I was to get priority for my calls. General Eisenhower came on the line and asked how it was going? I told him that everything was falling into place. However, we had a problem that would need his special permission to handle and probably his help to make it happen. I told General Eisenhower about the French all referring to the crashed B-24 as an American "Avion Fortress" and I thought we could use that to our advantage.

The biggest problem was the large number of souvenirs the French had hauled off. We needed to retrieve all of it that might give the Germans any information about the Top-Secret equipment if the Germans got their hands on the souvenirs. General Eisenhower asked, "What do you need to do that?" He knew

about my friendship and experience with General Donovan, so I told him straight out what had to be done. I needed to contact Donovan at once and get him to send two groups of his most experienced French speakers over to France. The two missions, would require eight to ten men at the B-24 crash-site and two or three at the B-17 crash-site.

The men at the B-24 crash-site would have to visit every village and home within walking and bicycle range of the B-24 crash-site and tell the people they needed to find out if they had any souvenirs of the "Avion Fortress, B-17" crash. If they did, the men would check to see if the souvenir might possibly be part of the Top-Secret equipment. If, it might be, they were to tell the French people they had to give up the souvenir for the investigation of the "Avion Fortress, B-17's" crash and give them a pack of cigarettes. To make certain, the French would remember the Americans and the "Avion Fortress, B-17" questions, the men were to give each family a pack of cigarettes for their time, even if there was not a souvenir to confiscate. Lucky(?) families with one or more items, could get several packages.

If we did that, I told General Eisenhower, I was certain we could convince all of the French people that it was a B-17, "Flying Fortress" instead of a B-24. Then, if any German heard about the crash and tried to figure out if a B-24 had crashed, the French would make them so confused, the Germans would forget about that crash.

General Eisenhower thought for a moment, and told me to get to Donovan and set it up. If Donovan needed to know that he approved of it, I was to tell General Donovan to call General Eisenhower on his own dime and he would back me up. I laughed and told General Eisenhower that I would do just that. Before he hung up, he told me to tell Colonel Coiner that he greatly appreciated his help and that he would be on Ike's good list and then he hung up.

I immediately put in a call to General Donovan in England and then went to find Coiner, as I waited for the call to go through. I told Coiner that I needed his office until the call I had put through was complete, which should not take too long. Also that when I had talked to General Eisenhower, he had told me to pass on the message to Coiner, that his help was appreciated. Col. Coiner, smiled and said if I needed any more help, just let him know and so, I did.

I told Coiner, "That some '*special mission*' Americans would be arriving late tonight or very early tomorrow morning. All would speak excellent French and they would need his full, local support on the QT. They would be arriving by plane from England as soon as they could be sent and when they arrived Coiner was to have quarters ready for eight to ten men away from his own troops. He was to have whatever number of jeeps and trailers they required, no more than five of each should do, plus all the gas and food rations they wanted. In addition, they were to be given any number of cartons of cigarettes they requested, as well as whatever else was needed." I told Coiner, "That I expected, they would quarter themselves in Tincourt-Boucly and if Coiner had any problems with supply and accounting, he was to get in contact with me."

As Coiner was as involved as I was, I told Coiner that the men's mission was to contact every French home near the crash-site and recover any souvenirs that might be part of the Top-Secret equipment. The cigarettes would be given as a gift during the visits, to insure the people remembered the Americans asking in French for the souvenirs of the "Avion Fortress, B-17" crash. Col. Coiner replied that it was a hell of an idea and he will do everything I asked had for, and he would provide any other help, the men who were coming, would request.

I told Coiner that as soon as the call went though, if all went well, I would be leaving at once, as I had other work to do today. However, the direct participation and his personnel's involvement should be over when the arriving mission team had completed its job.

I went on to tell Coiner, I was certain when the men who were coming left, they would have cleaned up any remaining problems here, such as collecting the souvenirs from the French and convincing them it was a "Avion Fortress, B-17" that had crashed there. However, there were two things he did need to do before it was over. First, I asked if he had a bulldozer on the base and he said his engineers had one. So, I told him that the first thing in the morning, he was to send the bulldozer to the crash-site and have the operator push all the aircraft pieces around the crater into the crater and fill in the crater and then smooth out the field. If possible, he should send someone with the operator, who spoke French well enough to talk with the village Mayor and the field owner. That person was to tell the French, the Americans did not want his field to be unuseable, so we were going to get rid of the "Avion Fortress B-17" pieces and smooth out the large hole the "Avion Fortress, B-17" had made. Col. Coiner, laughed, and said that, was a good idea and it would also let him pull his guards from the crash-site. I added, that the last thing he would have to do, would be to make certain that some trusted person was assigned to destroy every item the incoming team collected, in such a manner that no one would ever know what it was if they found it. In fact, he might want to dig a deep hole somewhere on the base where his personnel would not notice, and after the pieces were destroyed they could be buried deep enough to stay buried.

As Coiner agreed to that, the secure telephone in his office rang and I went in, shut the door and began to talk to General Donovan about what I wanted him to do. Donovan listened to what I laid out and then he told me he had a problem with using his organization that way, unless he was damn certain Eisenhower was on board. **Even though he trusted me, he did not trust Eisenhower that much**. So, he asked me to tell him what I wanted and he would, on his dime, contact Eisenhower himself. The moment General Eisenhower confirmed the plan, General Donovan said he would support my request and in the end, everything happened exactly as I requested.

I told Donovan, that the Base Commander was Colonel Coiner and I had already made arrangements for the incoming team to have quarters at the base tonight, and the transportation and everything else required during their stay, available in the morning.

Off the top of his head, Donovan thought the other mission would arrive at the Etain or Toul Air Base an hour or so later. I told him, I recommended that he send them to the Toul A-90 Air Base, as that was away from the XIX TAC who had shot down our own B-24 with their night fighter and why take any risk with his men's lives. Donovan laughed and thanked me for thinking of the well being of his men. I told him I would call General Vandenberg at once and have arrangements made for three of his men to land at the Toul Air Base, and I would personally tell the SAW Commander that they were coming and he was only responsible for some place for them to stay and furnish their rations.

(**Note**: Another undisputable clue that proved decades later, the three men existed at Hattonville, because I forgot the 563rd SAW Bn Cooks would have to create paperwork to get **replacement rations for what they ate**!)

Donovan knew the Péronne area from his Great War service and later visits to France, but I had to tell him that Hattonville was the village located under Hattonchatel, the location of the Chateau that the American heiress, Miss Simpson, had rebuilt in the St-Mihiel battle area. "Oh sure," Donovan said, "I remember now, she is a nice woman, lost her fiancée during the Great War, big place in a small village on top of a steep hill. So, Colonel, exactly what do you want these men of mine to do there?" I explained all that to him and Donovan told me he would call Eisenhower at once and verify my request and if I was right, it would happen exactly as I had asked. Then Donovan said, one of these days, let's make time to get together for a couple of drinks, then we said wished each other the best, and I hung up the phone only to pick it back up and have the operator put in a direct call for General Vandenberg.

While waiting, I sent a sergeant out to the car to tell Sgt. Tiff to get ready. Then I located Coiner to inform him to contact the operations officer at General Eisenhower's headquarters for me and inform him that I was on my way to the 563rd SAW Battalion Headquarters at Hattonville, south-east of Verdun. In addition, he could tell the operations officer, should he have any messages to pass on to me and he had trouble finding the SAW HQ, he could contact General Weyland and ask the General to put him in touch with the 563rd. Also tell him, if the back roads were as clear as I thought they would be, we should arrive very late tonight or early in the morning. Colonel Coiner went off to do that and I picked up the ringing telephone.

I told General Vandenberg, that I thought the situation was well in hand here at the 397th and that Coiner and the Surgeon had been outstanding in their help. Then I told him about the need for support at the Toul Air Base that night and that I was on the way to the 563rd. I asked him to call Weyland and tell Weyland, that everything was going well and for him to tell the Commander of the 563rd, I was on my way. Vandenberg agreed, and I told him I would be leaving at once.

Colonel Coiner walked me out to the car and asked me about eating. Sgt. Tiff was holding the passenger's door open and I asked Tiff, if we had all we needed to reach our destination. He assured me there were fresh sandwiches, hot

Major General William Donovan
Commanding General - OSS
Photograph: US Army Archives

coffee and other snacks in the back seat, as he added the mess hall cooks had treated him very well and he would not mind coming back again.

As I turned back to Coiner, Coiner came to attention and told me it had been his pleasure to serve, he then saluted and said goodbye. I returned the salute, shook his hand and got into the car. Sgt. Tiff, saluted Coiner, who returned the salute and Coiner stood there, as Tiff hurried around the car, got in, started it and moved off toward the gate. Col. Coiner, waved, turned, and headed toward his headquarters.

This time, as Tiff sped toward the gate, the guard had the gate up and was saluting as we passed him, slewing onto the Amiens-St-Quentin road, heading toward St-Quentin and Hattonville.

Meanwhile, over in England, Donovan prepared to furnish the requested personnel and made arrangements for them to fly to France that night. Donovan had started his operation, subject to Eisenhower's approval. His call to Eisenhower was put through very quickly and Eisenhower came on the line and asked Brigadier General Donovan what he wanted? Brigadier General Donovan told General Eisenhower, that he had just spoken with one of the colonels on his headquarters staff. The colonel had told him to contact General Eisenhower on his own dime, to verify what the colonel had asked him to do. Donovan reminded General Eisenhower, that he and the colonel had been friends for a long time, and *the colonel had asked for some help that could lead to a big problem for him and his organization*. He wanted to know, was if General Eisenhower supported the colonel's request? General Eisenhower answered immediately in support of the operation and ***he also told Brigadier General Donovan that his promotion to Major General would be dated that day***.

Immediately, Major General Donovan told General Eisenhower he would receive his full support for the task at hand. With that, General Eisenhower told Major General Donovan goodbye.

(Note: Coincidence/Evidence?)

Within minutes, Major General Donovan had put his operation in place. His people, first checked to see who was immediately available and of those who could speak the best French. In less than an hour he had located eight men to go to the A-72 Air Base at Péronne and three that were to go to Hattonville. The men were ordered to attend a briefing at 17:00 and told they would be fed immediately after the briefing. In addition, they were to get their personal equipment together, planning for up to a ten-day stay in friendly France, leaving soon after the meeting.

They were also told that they only needed to carry their side arms and upon arrival in France, they would be provided with transportation and all the support they would need. Then, during the briefing, they would be told exactly what they would be doing. And, they could rest easy as there was no danger involved.

Meanwhile, Tiff and I arrived at St-Quentin, I navigated him around the city on the secondary roads, and we took off cross-country toward Rethel. If one knew the roads in France at that time, they consisted of straight roads originally laid down by the Romans and spider webbed roads that were originally the trails people and domestic stock walked along between villages before the need of roads for vehicle transportation. The Roman roads offered a quick way from city to city, but they were often choked with traffic, while the secondary, chicken-tract roads had little traffic and offered an open, if somewhat rougher road. Using the Roman roads one usually had to travel at right angles to get from city to city. However, using the chicken-track or spider web roads, one could drive an almost straight line across the right angle and save a lot of travel time and mileage.

It was my intent to go as fast as we could and cross all the Roman roads to keep us off the roads jammed full of military convoys. As we drove, we ate our sandwiches and drank our coffee on the run. At Rethel, we gassed up at a small American unit and continued toward Verdun. To ensure, we made the best time, I told Tiff to let me know if he was tired and that I would drive while he napped. He agreed that it had been some day so far. However, he would prefer I drive during the daylight while he napped and he would drive at night. That way, I would not put us into a tree or wagon in the dark. It wasn't because he did not trust my driving, Tiff explained, but he was responsible for the car. Laughing, I agreed, and soon I was driving down the French back roads and telling Tiff about my mother's family who actually lived very close to where we were. Tiff, told me he and the other Enlisted personnel at the headquarters had wondered why I could speak French so well. I told him to wait until I take you to St-Avold and then he could listen to my German. Tiff, replied that he had some German relatives in the family tree and he knew a bit of that "Kraut" talk himself.

Down in Hattonville, Lt. Colonel McBride had received his call from General Weyland, only to be followed by another call from General Vandenberg. Vandenberg told McBride that he just wanted him to really understand that what General Weyland had told him, was coming from the very top, including the fact that the colonel who was on his way to McBride's unit was to be obeyed, no matter how strange his verbal orders were. McBride said little, agreed a lot, and soon he

was talking to Byrne and Venar, telling them it was obvious they were soon going to hear about what was going on with the B-17 and it's dead.

Aboard a hospital train as it approached Paris, T/Sgt. Russell Gustafson was told that the train was going to overnight in a rail yard in Paris. He was going to be taken to a hospital overnight. Then, in the morning, he would be back on the train, as it had been decided to evacuate him through Cherbourg to England as soon as they could. "Damn," thought Gustafson, "his first time in Paris and all the Mademoiselles would have to wait for his next trip to Paris." Perhaps on the same train, Lt. Harland would have been told he was going to leave the train at Paris. At the officer's transit quarters in Paris, they would make the arrangements for his return by air to his unit. Harland, well known by the crew, as a *"**Ladies Man**"* quickly thought to himself, "Sure, after I can delay that as long as I can, watch out Paris, here I come." As Harland made his plans, Robbins, who was to spend his second night at the Enlisted Men's Transit Quarters in Paris, was told he would be leaving for England on a transport plane tomorrow. Robbins was happy to get out of there, as there is only so much to be seen in Paris when you have no money. Sure, some of the other fellows had helped him out, but he had seen enough and was ready to head back to England without that perfume for his wife.

Two survivors, who were not making plans for that night, were Harms and Fross who were still sedated at the 109th. However, Fross was scheduled to have his sedative stopped that night, so his situation could be reviewed the next day. Harms was scheduled to be sedated another day before being woken up.

In the Hattonville Woods, the bodies of Gott, Metzger, Dunlap, and the torn-apart remains of Krimminger were being guarded for another night by men from the 563rd, warmed by the fire. Nearby, the broken *"**Lady Jeannette,**"* continued to settle into the clay, creating still existing impressions that can be viewed by visitors today.

Ambulance Driver Pfc. Barney Silva, at the 397th Bomb Group, and most of the other men who had any experience at the crash-site, continued to talk about the plane crash that afternoon and evening. But most men had their own bombers and missions to talk about and very quickly the memory of the crash disappeared from the minds of most of the men who were not personally involved at the crash-site. Soon, it was something that Silva rarely talked about until fifty-six years and fifteen days later, when he received a telephone call from the researcher who knew more about the plane crash than he did.

In England, the eleven chosen OSS men arrived at the briefing room, where three of them were told to get a cup of coffee, as they would be briefed as soon as the larger group had completed their briefing.

In the briefing room, the eight men were told they had been specifically selected, based on two needs. The first was their ability to speak French and the second was based on their ability to do what was needed, and then forget they had done it. The briefer, actually one of the eight who was to be their group leader, told the men they would be aboard a B-24, of the 856th BS that evening to go to France and they would arrive at the A-72 Air Base near Péronne, a couple of hours later.

They would spend the rest of the night at the air base, where they would be set up with transportation, gas, and rations. Then, early in the morning, they were going to a nearby village. They would be there for the next week or so. The purpose of the mission would be, well you already know what they were to do and they did it, extremely well.

As the briefing ended, the briefer told them, *"**You are going to participate in the most Secret Mission the OSS has participated in!**"* There will be no documentation of any kind of this mission and none of you are to document this mission in any way, or tell anyone about the mission, now or in the future. Moreover, the day you come back, you are personally to forget all about the time you were gone and what you had done while you were gone. Do you understand," he asked? *"**Yes, Sir!**"* was their immediate answer.

Each of them wondered, just why the hell was this so secret? Some of them had been ordered to murder people during specific missions and full documentation was kept on their mission, beginning with their briefing before they left for the mission, any reports while they were on the mission and finally, they were fully debriefed for the record when they got back from the mission. There was a complete Mission File for each of those missions and ***now, they were going to kill no one, they were just going to talk to the French and it was so secret, no record was to exist***? At least one of them had to have thought, "There must be some real deep crap going down with this one."

(**Note**: ***However, someone created two OSS files on the two super secret missions with the statement in each file, "Keep no written documentation of this mission." File located in the National Archive, College Park, Maryland.***)

When the first group was finished, the men left for to eat and one of Donovan's trusted men (whom you may read more about, later on), then briefed the other three on their mission. They would get a vehicle, quarters and rations for the night at the Toul Air Base in France. Then, early in the morning, they were to go to Hattonville, north of Toul, where they would be supported as long as required by the 563rd SAW Battalion Headquarters. Their presence would be "***off the record***." Then, they were given, the full "no documentation, no talk, and no memory" talk.

(**Note:** Except 3 sets of rations eaten at the 563rd had to be replaced at the 563rd and documents exist that proves they were!)

As to their mission, they were going to participate in making certain the crash of a B-17 was believed by the French and the involved Americans, to be nothing more than the crash of a B-17. The exact reason why they were going was something they did not need to know. All they needed to know, was the directive for the mission, came from very high up the "food chain."

227

Basically, the job at Hattonville was to ensure the crash of a B-17 and the death of its crew was handled as regulations required. When they arrived at Hattonville, they were to contact the 563rd Commander, a Lt. Colonel McBride, and then to mingle with the French and Americans at the local bars. They were to meet the local people and the Americans in the unit and not let anyone know of their expertise with French. They were to listen to as many conversations of the local people and the Americans as they could, to ensure none of them thought the Americans had done anything at the crash-site they thought should not have been done. If they did anyone in the area, French or American was suspicion that the Americans had done anything wrong at the crash-site, they were to immediately tell the unit commander and tell him exactly what they had heard. After that, it was up to the 563rd SAW Battalion Commander to handle the situation.

Then, they were given a code word to have the commander pass on when they were finished and felt nothing wrong had been done at the crash-site, and were ready to leave. With that and a repeated warning about "*no documentation, no talking, and no memory!*" Then, were released to eat and prepare for their flight.

At the 856th Bomb Sq (H), 492nd Bomber Group, "*Carpet Baggers*," General Donovan's direct call to the squadron commander was put through at once. Major General Donovan told the commander that he was to have a B-24 ready at 21:00, to fly a group of his men to France. The first stop would be at the Péronne A-72 Air Base and then the Toul A-90, Air Base south-east of Verdun. The flight was to show no destination and the pilots were to be told to forget whom they took and where they went that night. The commander said he could make that happen, but they had never sent a mission to Europe during the German occupation when they did not show the flight's destination, and his people would wonder what was going on if that flight left without a destination.

General Donovan told the commander, "That problem can be beat fairly easily. Just put in the correct entry tonight and then wait for that entry in the flight log to be a page down from the top. Then remove the destination entry yourself. "Just remember one thing," Donovan told the commander, "there are people much higher up who are laying out the rules in this game and you do not want to let them know you have screwed this up." With that, the commander told Donovan they were on the same page and the B-24 would be waiting for his men.

The Cartigny village priest, Curé Étienne Serprette was preparing to go to bed, when there was a light knock on his door. Opening his door, he found one of his flock, who seemed somewhat agitated. The man asked the priest if he could talk to him, as he had seen something that morning that was bothering him very much. The priest invited the man in, indicated he was to sit at the table and got a bottle and a couple of glasses. He had found over the years, that a small amount of lubricant could make his job much easier when trying to soothe a troubled parishioner.

Curé Serprette asked the man what was bothering him so much, and the fellow began to tell him about his visit to the "Avion Fortress" crash-site at Tincourt-Boucly, what he had helped do there, and what he had seen in the field on his way back to Cartigny. As he finished, he told Curé Serprette that **it was**

obvious to him that the Americans were hiding their war dead, and that was not right, as these men had died on French soil for the *"Liberty of France."*

Both men sat there for a minute or two, deep in thought and then, the priest told his parishioner that he would think about all they had talked about, and he asked the man to come by tomorrow at 13:00, if he could. The man told the priest, he would be here at that time and then both got up, walked to the door and the priest patted the man on his shoulder as he left. He told his parishioner, "We will see those men are treated right my son, we will see they are treated right."

At 21:00, a false marked, covered 6x6 truck pulled up to the idling B-24. A group of men with hand bags climbed out of its rear and then climbed into the B-24. The B-24's door was closed, the chocks were removed from the wheels and the B-24 began its take-off roll at 21:28 to go to a destination, that for some unexplained reason, would fail to show on the flight log of the unit, 50 years later.

Three hours and forty-nine minutes later, the B-24 returned to the runway, taxied to its hard stand, stopped, the wheels were chocked, the engines were shut down, and the crew left the airplane with its flight destination documented. That is, until some unknown date and time, when the destination, that was written on the official log, somehow disappeared. Resulting, in the official flight log of the unit, no longer recording that flight's destination.

At the very end of the day, Tiff was driving and I was in the passenger seat, as the car approached Hattonville from the north. We had taken a secondary road that runs north/south along the bottom of the long ridge of hills, to the west side of the Plain of Woëvre. We had just left the village of Billy-s/s-les-Cotes and had about two kilometers to go before we reached Hattonville.

Thus ended the first day, 10 November, 1944, of the two-day cover-up I was creating to hide the crash of the Top-Secret B-24J-2-DT, SN: 42-51226, of the 36th Bomb Squadron (RCM), flying Top-Secret night missions while attached to the Top-Secret 100th Group, Royal Air Force.

The B-24J that was to have had the name, *"I Walk Alone,"* painted on its nose before the next mission, along with three of its crew had become small bits and pieces in a farm field in northern France, at 02:30 hours in the morning of 10 November, 1944. A Top-Secret B-24J that was filled with more than four tons of Top-Secret electronic equipment, that had been shot down by **"Friendly Fire"** from a P-61, Black Widow night fighter belonging to the 425th Night Fighter Squadron.

(**Note**: The author, during a research visit to the Air Force Historical Research Agency, located at Maxwell Air Force Base, in Alabama, was viewing the unit records of the **856th BS, (H), 492nd Bomb Group, the "Carpet Baggers."** He had read about the unit and its missions, delivering clandestine OSS members, arms and others into occupied territory.

In those documents, he found a listing of all the flights of all the 856th aircraft during their war. He found the page for that date and there was a flight on the date, with departure and arrival times listed. However, the destination was not over the Channel, it was in Scotland.

At the next 8th Air Force Reunion, the author found there was a 492nd BG Group and he went to their meeting room. There, he asked if anyone knew the man who had signed the mission documents. Surprise, he was there and when the author talked to him, he was told that the man had also visited the Air Force Historical Agency and he had a copy of the documents in question. He was very proud of those documents, as he was the only person who ever made an entry in them. Of course, neither of us had a copy at the reunion, but he promised the author he would review the date in question and get back to him. Both agreed, the length of time between takeoff and landing seemed to be very long for the standard, run to Scotland to stock up with whiskey. He also told the author, that he was positive he was the only one who had made any entries and that he had logged every flight that had landed anywhere other than their base. However, test flights that took off and landed back at their base were not recorded.

A few days later, the man called the author and told him, he had reviewed the complete document for every entry when he got home. And, that he was absolutely positive, the entry on that date had been changed and it was not what he would have written at that time.

We agreed, that we would contact some B-24 pilots and give them the two questionable locations in France, and find out if they thought the time required for that mission would match the recorded time.

Each B-24 pilot agreed, the mission reported time did match the time it would take for a flight from their base to A-27, at Péronne, then a take off and flight to A-90, at Toul, followed by a take off and flight back to their base!)

OSS: Stories that now be told - **Dorothy Ringlesbach**   ISBN: 1-4208-1582-2

Page 61 - "The Carpetbaggers were the vital air arm of the OSS and I like to think of them as a sort of taxi service for the rest of the OSS as they dropped needed supplies, equipment, couriers, agents, and small groups of ground troops (the OGs) to aid the underground in France, Belgium, Holland, and Norway."

Chapter Eleven
Cover-Up - Day Two
Hattonville - Morning

Sergeant Tiff pulled up to the Hattonville combination town hall/school, at 00:03 on the 11th of November 1944. Thanks to a couple of quick naps, I felt very good, but I knew Tiff had to be blown out from the difficulty of crossing so much of France on the secondary road network. Especially as he had done all the driving after sunset. I had driven for some time during the day to let him nap. But, I don't think Tiff slept all that well as I careered along those secondary roads, with their especially sharp turns at the intersections in the villages. Later, when it got dark, Tiff refused to stop to let me drive.

Tiff, got out of the car and went to the lighted office, where he found the Sergeant of the Guard and told him that his passenger was to see the Battalion Commander at once. The sergeant had obviously been told we were coming and he told Tiff to give him a moment to alert the commander, that we had arrived. Then he would guide us to the Mayor's home, where the Battalion's Commander, XO (Executive Officer), and their attached Medical Corps Surgeon, were billeted.

I was still in the front passenger seat when they came out. Tiff, told the Sergeant of the Guard to get in the back. With both men in, Tiff headed in the direction the sergeant had pointed while he told us, the house was about a block down the road on the right. I asked the Sergeant if arrangements had been made for us? He replied that I would be staying with the commander at the Mayor's home and he had a billet prepared for my driver.

As we approached the Mayor's house, I told the sergeant that I wanted my driver to get anything he wanted tonight even if he had to get a cook out of bed. Then the car was to be fully serviced as my driver specified, and it was to be done after taking my driver to his quarters.

As we arrived at the large home the sergeant had pointed out, Tiff pulled the car over to the side of the road and stopped. The sergeant sprung out of his door to open my door and at same time the door of the home opened and a fully uniformed Lieutenant Colonel came down the stairs to greet me. At the same time, Tiff had gotten out, opened the trunk and got my B-4 bag and the pair of galoshes I had him load back at headquarters.

The Lt. Colonel introduced himself as the Battalion Commander and his name was McBride. We shook hands; as I introduced myself and informed McBride that I had given instructions to his Sergeant of the Guard that I wanted followed to the 'tee.' McBride looked at the sergeant who said, "I have it all, Sir, and I will get it done right away."

With that, I told Tiff to bring in my bag and then go enjoy himself, get some sleep and I would see him later. I added, that I was not certain what we would be

doing, but I would not need him for some time in the morning. So, he was not to cut his sleep short to have the car ready to go. Tiff, replied, "Yes, Sir."

McBride opened the door and indicated I should enter first. As I walked into the entry hall and then into a large room, I saw two officers who were standing by a large table in the middle of the room. Both were Majors and I assumed, one was the Executive Officer and the other was the Surgeon. As I was taking off my coat, Sergeant Tiff put my B-4 bag in the entrance hall and after placing the galoshes next to it, he left and shut the door.

I handed my coat to McBride, who hung it up in the entry hall and as McBride was introducing me to Major Byrne, the Battalion XO, and Major Venar, the Battalion Surgeon, I heard Tiff start the car and turn it around. After being introduced to and shaking hands with the two men. I told them, to please sit down as I did the same.

There were glasses and several bottles of whisky on the table, including scotch, rye, and bourbon, as well as a bottle of cognac and a clear bottle, half full of something that looked like water. McBride asked me if I could use a drink? I told him, I would greatly enjoy a bourbon and water, and for them to have whatever they wanted. I watched as McBride took a glass, poured a very healthy shot of Jim Beam in the glass, and then got up and walked to the kitchen where I heard a spigot run for a few seconds. McBride brought the completed drink back to me and I thought, "So much for the water bottle on the table."

Then I remembered the clear liquor my uncles and father used to drink in this area during our travels. It was a local speciality that looks like water and it is made from the Mirabelle Plum. It contained more alcohol than bourbon did and it was normally a drink for the men and was poured over a dessert by the women.

We sat there for a few minutes and exchanged small talk about my trip to Hattonville, the weather that day and Patton's new drive. After the first round of drinks had been finished, McBride refilled mine, the three men poured their own, and I got down to "brass tacks."

I told the men that I had heard a lot about the B-17 in the woods and it's dead, but I wanted them to give me the whole story from scratch. McBride told me that Byrne would be the best one to tell the story, as he had been involved from when their radars had first detected the B-17, to the situation in the woods tonight.

I looked at Byrne and told him to start from when they first saw the B-17 on the radar and tell me everything he knew. Forty-five minutes later, Byrne told me the day guards had been relieved at 18:00 and everything was the same as it was when the Medics had completed the recovery of the torn-apart man's remains about noon. He added that the only problem to warrant concern, was the animals in the woods. The night guards were going to use the same successful method to keep them away from the remains that they had the previous night. However, the job should be easier than the previous night because the guards had been pulled into the actual crash-site and they did not have to walk the debris-trail, as they had the night before in order to protect the dead man's scattered remains.

When he was done, McBride asked me if I wanted another drink? I told him no, I wanted to give them the basic briefing on what was going to be done in the morning, and then we needed to get to bed. I told them that we would have to get an early start in the morning, as I wanted to be at the woods as soon as we could see. The three agreed to make certain that happened and asked if I wanted breakfast first. I told them to tell the Sergeant of the Guard to have the mess hall prepare two fried egg and mustard sandwiches with lots of salt, and a thermos of hot, black coffee ready to be picked up when we left for the woods. As to them, they could either do the same or eat early enough to permit us to arrive at the woods as early as we could. They agreed that sounded good to them. McBride said he would call the Sergeant of the Guard and have him pick the order up and deliver it in time for our planned departure to the crash-site.

When McBride finished, I asked Venar for his and his medics schedule for the morning as I was going to need all of them in the woods as soon as they could be there. Venar said there were no sick men in the unit and that he would change Sick Call hours from morning to afternoon. That sounded good to me and when McBride returned, I asked him to call the Sergeant of Guard again to make certain the Medics were woken up early enough to be ready to go out to the crash-site when we were ready, and he agreed to make certain they were there.

I then asked McBride, "If he was absolutely certain we would not be overheard here in the house?" He assured me we would not and told me the Mayor was very accommodating. At his request, the Mayor and his wife had agreed to spend the night at some relatives until I was gone, so that I could use their room. However, both would be at the house during the day to help as needed and the wife was cooking all their meals. With that assurance, I started to tell the men exactly what they would be doing.

"Gentlemen," I stated, "this is what we have to do in the morning. First, as you must know, something has happened that has gotten General Eisenhower personally involved and I am acting directly on his behalf when I am here. You can consider what I am going to tell you, to be a direct, verbal order from General Eisenhower." They each nodded and I told them that, if any one of them had the least trouble with being told to do something by me, they needed to tell me right now. If necessary, we could go to a secure telephone location right now and I would get General Eisenhower on the line right away to personally order them to do what I was going to tell them they were to do. Now, that got their attention. They looked at each other, looked at each other again and nodded. And Colonel McBride said, "I believe, I speak for all three of us when I tell you that we fully understand and will do what you want."

"Gentlemen," I said, "from this moment on, there can be no backing out, no changing of your mind and for your immediate information, there is none now and there will be no documentation of what we are going to do and you will never talk to anyone about what we will do, not even among yourselves and certainly when the work is complete and we go our separate ways."

233

So I said, "Major Byrne, I will start with you. After we are done with tomorrow's work, you will check every official document and insure there is no record of the crash of the B-17 anywhere. If you find something, either submit an updated copy removing the information, or destroy the document and create a clean version. The purpose is simple you must do it to ensure that no German spy, who might have any access to any of your records, can find out through one of your unit's records that a B-17 crashed here yesterday." Major Byrne said that he would have the adjutant to do that tomorrow. I told the three men that from now on, they were the only officers that would have anything to do with this. Also, I told Byrne that he was to personally censor all outgoing mail, even the officer's mail for the next month to ensure there was no information about the B-17 leaving the unit via the men's mail, officer's, or enlisted.

I went on to tell Byrne, "I did not care what excuse you use with them, but as far as those directly involved and all your other personnel are considered, they are to forget about the crash. All three of you will have to talk to the men who are involved in the recovery and the guard duty at the crash-site about the need to not talk about what they have seen or done. It will be absolutely necessary, Colonel McBride, that you personally talk to each of those directly involved. It is important they fully understand they are to forget there was a bomber crash while they were here in Hattonville. Make damn certain you tell them that they are not even to talk to their best friend or among themselves once this is over.

If asked, they can discuss the fact that the bomber flew over and crashed with the men who had not been at the crash-site. But they are to use the excuse that's all they knew and nothing else. If they were grilled by the others, they are to say they had been relieved by Graves Registration who told them nothing." I went on, "They were to tell the three men that it was important that no one clam-up so tight that rumors would start. But at the same time, the men in the know were to shut up about what they knew."

(**Note**: The author had several advantages during his research. He had spent four years in the Air Force as a Radar Operator and while in Morocco for 13 months, he had been assigned as the temporary Mess Inventory Controller, so he knew how rations used, had to be accounted for to replace them and I never thought about those documents and they showed three issues of rations to personnel, not found in any of the other Battalion documents. The author had also three years in the Army, as a Nike Hercules Missile Fire Control Maintenance Man, repairing the computers and radars for that missile system so he knew all about radar frequencies and antenna lengths.

For some years, he belonged to an organization of Radar Operators and was able to locate other men who were involved in Radar during the days in question, such as Major Byrne. They supplied much of the flesh in this part of the book.)

Then I told them, "Some '*special mission*' men were going to arrive early this morning, and they would be staying with them for a few days. And, the mens'

presence was to be undocumented, so when they left, it was to be like they were never there. Then, I filled them in on the men's mission which was to hang around the local bars and mingle with the villagers and their own men, to see if any of them talked about anything strange at the crash-site. When the men were happy that nothing unusual had been noted by the French or their own men, they would tell McBride and disappear. When they were ready to leave, they would give McBride a code word to pass on to me, which would tell me what they had discovered. The main thing is, you must ensure the three men have access to everyone, including yourselves, if asked.

Now, let's talk about this morning and why it has to be done exactly as I will tell you, it has to be done." I asked the men if they had heard the rumors that the XIX TAC had shot down a friendly plane the night before? Byrne said, that one of his plotting officers had told him, that one of their northern units had observed the target and that the XIX TAC control center had seemed to go nuts as they had overheard some controller saying that his flight had shot at and hit a target that had flown west, instead of east. This morning, when the plotting officer had signed off with his counterpart at the XIX TAC control center, he had been told they had hit a friendly RAF Mosquito the night before.

I told them that the "*flyboys*" did hit something up there last night. They had shot down one of our own Top-Secret aircraft and that the aircraft had crashed near Abbeville, north-west of Paris. I figured, it had to be safe, using Top-Secret aircraft and Abbeville, as it was more than 60 miles from where the B-24 had crashed and that was a long way from Hattonville. I went on to tell them that the Top-Secret aircraft had several tons of Top-Secret electronic equipment on board and *the loss of the Top-Secret aircraft in France, had brought General Eisenhower into the situation. He had decided that the crash had to disappear, as we could not take the risk of the Germans somehow learning any of the Top-Secrets on that aircraft and using them against us.*

Major Byrne spoke up and told me that he was also the Battalion Radar and Electronics Officer and he was certain he was familiar with the aircraft I was talking about and its capability. In fact, their unit had been used at times while it was still in England, as a test platform for such aircraft and their equipment. If we had shot one of them down in France, he was prepared to do whatever it took to hide the crash from the Germans. "Damn," Major Byrne told us, "if the Germans get that stuff, we are going to rue the day it happened. With that knowledge, the bastards would shoot down a hell of a lot more of our aircraft and they could even regain air superiority over the front line for a while. That stuff would play hell with our own radars and leave our ground troops open to air attack." I could tell, from the way Byrne was talking, without really saying anything that might tell the other two men something, they should not know, that Byrne probably knew more about the equipment on the B-24 than I did. I thought to myself, "I have a built-in ally here."

I told the men that Byrne was right and that they were to provide the rest of the required steps to basically complete the plan General Eisenhower had sent me to implement. Then I went into the situation of the difference of the dead at the

other aircraft crash-site and the B-17 in the woods ... and I finished by telling them about how they were going to hide the three complete bodies and they were to use the torn-apart man's remains to create the required four official Burial Packages they needed to turn over to Graves Registration.

Major Venar asked if they could ask questions? "Sure," I replied, "as long as they were about getting the job done." Venar said that he did not want me to think that he was not going to help, but he wanted me to know the terrible position I was putting him into. **First, he had his Hippocratic Oath and now I was telling him he was going to have to break his oath. As a member of the Army Medical Corps, I was also telling him he had to desecrate human remains and also falsify official Graves Registration documents.** "Damn," he exclaimed, "you are really putting, my rear-end into the fire!" Venar then asked, If they were to do what I was telling them to do, especially himself, how the heck was I going to assure them that their careers were not going to be ruined?"

"Well," I told Venar, "you have covered the exact situation you and the rest of us are in. **The choice is, do we do what has to be done for the greater good or do we do, what is the best for ourselves and the dead at the crash-site.** And perhaps, be directly responsible for the death of tens of thousands of Allied lives and even more civilian lives before the end of the war?

As of yesterday, General Eisenhower, General Vandenberg, General Weyland, General Doolittle, myself, and several other unit Commanders, including two Hospital Commanders had all done almost the same thing, I was asking them to do. I could only assure them of one thing. **General Eisenhower had personally told me, if it became necessary in the future, he would take full responsibility for what he had personally, via verbal orders, told all of us to do.**" I went on to tell them, "As far as I was concerned, "*this situation was one where the end would certainly justify the means!*"

I also told them, "The main problem each of us will have to face would be never knowing exactly what the end result was. If, we succeeded in what General Eisenhower was ordering us to do, there would be no way in the future to prove the Germans would or would not have found out about the Top-Secret equipment at the B-24 crash-site. In effect, we were going to have to do what had to be done, without knowing, if what we were doing would really help ensure the Germans would not find out and that, was that."

"Gentlemen," I continued, "there is on one thing I can assure you, the chain of people who are as informed and involved as you will be, is made up of professionals with as much or more to lose than you do. *If anyone involved in this chain might disclose what we have done, they have as much to lose as you. At this time I know every person involved and I can guarantee you, this is a chain without a weak link.*" Then I stood up and told the men, "I suggest you do the same thing I am going to do, after ensuring your Sergeant of the Guard has all the information required. Get a few hours sleep before we have to get up." I went over, picked up my B-4 bag and Venar offered to show me to the bedroom I would be using. Along the way, he pointed out the toilet facilities and asked me how much

236

time I needed to be ready to go. I told him, and he assured me he would see I was woken up in time. I told him to have a good night as I entered the Mayor's personal bedroom to find a very nice room, with the covers turned down and pictures of the family scattered around the room. It took a quick trip out of the room and then I was in the sack and I am certain, snoring within minutes.

Down stairs, McBride and Byrne were rejoined by Venar who told them, when I wanted to be awakened. McBride told Venar he had made arrangements for the Sergeant of the Guard to personally make certain each of them was awake, as none of them wanted to oversleep. McBride added, "After all this is over tomorrow, we can make up for all the sleep we have lost tonight. And, since it will soon be over, all of us will certainly sleep better." With that, he wished Byrne and Venar good night, which they returned, and all three headed to their bedrooms.

At the battalion headquarters, the Sergeant of the Guard was swearing and at the same time telling one of the guards who was in the room, "What the hell, do they think I am, their 'Bloody British Batman?'" When he finished writing down all the notes required, to make certain he got it all done, he was thinking, well, at least the driver seemed to be a nice fellow and he was obviously a bit embarrassed by the colonel's orders for his care. The Sergeant of the Guard did not mind helping such a fellow at all and man, he did look pooped out when he got out of the car after parking it out front. Then he strapped on his ".45'" pistol and pulled out that "Thompson." Wow, some driver's job. At least that part would be easy, as he got the keys to the petrol depot and told the guard he had called in to take the car and fill the car with gas, check the oil, and wipe it down to remove the road dust. The sergeant had pulled an old towel out of a drawer for the guard to use, so it would not scratch the car's paint. When he gave the towel to the guard, along with the keys, he told the guard if he found there was any mud and dirt on the car, take the time to get a bucket of water and make himself proud that he had cleaned up some staff colonel's car.

As the guard left, the sergeant reached down, opened the bottom left drawer, pulled it all the way out and got the French magazine that was at the very back of the drawer. It had been shared by many Sergeants of the Guard on many nights and if all went well, it would be shared until it fell apart or they could find another. He leaned back in his chair, put his feet on the desk and settled in for the short time he had to observe French girls the way they should be observed. He had just started, looking more than reading what he could not read, when a grin arrived with the thought that if he had been caught with a magazine like this back home by the tin star town cop in his hometown, he would have been put in the jug for the "bad boys," just for possessing a book like this one. "Well, to hell with you," he thought, "I'm a grownup now!" After one round of the village to check on the standing guards and to ensure all the American equipment was safe and with one very personal visit to the head, he looked at the time, stuffed the magazine back in its hidden location and closed the drawer. Then he went to wake the medics and surprise them with their required visit to the woods. As he left to do that, he thought to himself, "It was really strange, the way they are treating this crash-site,

237

wonder what the hell is so different about it from the others we have seen?" Sergeant Boatman was really unhappy at being woken up and he told the sergeant what he could do with himself. But the Sergeant of the Guard decided that it had been fun, and then he went to wake Berardi and Zeman. They were not any happier, however, both said they'd be ready and at the ambulance at the time they were ordered to be there.

With the medic demand under control, the sergeant walked down the street to the Mayor's home, entered the unlocked door and using his flashlight, he went up the stairs to knock on the four bedroom doors until each man had assured him he was awake. Then, he went back out into the night and made his way to the village Fete Hall (the village meeting hall, which they were using as a mess hall), where the cooks were already busy setting up for breakfast, preparing the coffee and sandwiches for the guards at the crash-site. After the sergeant had given the cooks the order for the officers, he sat down and enjoyed his coffee, French bread, butter, and strawberry jam. "I may be a simple fellow from a small hick town in south-east Ohio," he thought, "but any time in the future, when I can get real, fresh French bread, French butter, and French strawberry jam, I will walk a mile to enjoy it."

At the Mayor's home, as the men came down stairs the Mayor and his wife arrived and she began to make fresh coffee for them and asked what they wanted for breakfast. McBride told her that this morning was going to be a very busy one and they only had time for a cup of coffee. McBride introduced the Mayor and his wife to the colonel and told them the colonel was there for a quick inspection of the crash-site this morning and as soon as there was more sunlight, they were heading for the crash-site. I replied in French, telling them it would be a "Bon Jour." I knew the Mayor was helping keep his people away from the crash-site and speaking in French, I told him that the guards should be removed from the crash-site in the late afternoon. He was happy to hear that news, as several of the families in the village used the eastern end of the field to rotate their stock for feed and their rotation was now off, so they would be happy to get back to their schedule. At that time, I also told the Mayor that it was the policy of the United States to pay for the damage created by our airplanes that crashed and that McBride would be working with him to determine how much damage had been done in the woods.

Immediately, the Mayor told us that the village would refuse to accept any damage payment. Americans had died for their "Liberty" in their woods and they could never accept payment when our brave men had died there. I thanked him for feeling that way and I asked him to please tell the people in the village that General Eisenhower would personally know of that feeling and appreciate it.

He asked me where I learned my French, as I spoke like a Frenchman and I told him about my mother's home at Vervins and my father's home near St-Avold. I went on to tell him I had been born in the United States, but my keel was launched in France and my parents and grandparents had insisted that I learn to speak French like a native. And, I would tell my parents when I saw them next, that the Mayor of Hattonville had told me they had succeeded. With that, the Mayor slapped me on the back and told me to come back sometime, after the war was over and we

would talk about what happened at Hattonville during World War Two. I have to admit, I did not tell him that day, that I also spoke native German.

With that, I could not help telling him I had been to Hattonville before, as one of my uncles had been in the French 39th Division that had been on the left flank of the 26th American Division that liberated Hattonville in 1918. He told me that I was to bring that uncle with me during my visit and perhaps, we could come during one of their memorial services. I told the Mayor I would certainly try, and I did return to Hattonville a few years later. During that trip, I learned about what happened to the crashed B-17, that I was going to visit within the hour. Before I fully retired, my uncle and I did visit a few times. Fifty-four years later, the researcher was introduced to Ernest LECLERC, the brother-in-law of the woman, Mrs. LECLERC, who had run away from the burning and smoking B-17, with her son, Robert, in her arms. Ernest was able to tell the researcher a lot about the crash-site in the Bois de Hattonville.

The field telephone the battalion wire men had installed at the Mayor's home rang and McBride picked it up and listened. He replied, "Fine, we'll be ready," and he hung up. McBride turned to us and told us, "Let's get out to the jeep, the medics are loading the ambulance with our breakfast and coffee and they will be here right away." With that, I left my bag in the entrance hall, put on my coat, picked up my galoshes and went out the door with the men. I stood by the right front seat of the jeep as I folded the seat forward, so the others could get in the rear. As they say, rank does have its privilege. McBride had told Byrne he was going to drive, so Byrne and Venar had to climb into the back.

Just as McBride started the engine, the ambulance pulled up and stopped to give McBride the right-of-way. McBride pulled onto the road, heading south a short distance to where he turned left onto a small road, located between the village and its cemetery which was a bit further to the south.

The farm road was fairly rough and well churned up with pot holes, mud and littered with lots of manure. The ambulance pulled in behind us, far enough back to keep the thrown-up mud and manure from hitting it, as we made our way toward a large field I could see running north-east with large woods on both sides.

We passed a very muddy area off to the right and McBride yelled over to tell me, one of their radar units had been there until a few days ago. The road then turned to run at an angle to the north-east, as we climbed a small slope to the edge of the woods on the north side of the field. The road turned east to run alongside the woods and I could see that the road continued until it disappeared into the trees in the corner of an angle in the woods that jutted out into the field. A short distance from where the road entered the woods, we came to an intersection and McBride turned right onto another field road and then left onto a road running towards the far end of the field bordered by a large woods.

All I saw were woods in the distance and no sign of the B-17, but Byrne pointed out where one of the enlisted crewmen had landed with a broken leg. Venar chimed in that his ambulance driver had picked up that man and an officer, who had walked up as they loaded the wounded man and took them to the nearby Evacuation

Hospital. As we approached the woods, I saw a large area next to the woods that was very muddy and obviously a number of vehicles had recently been there. We pulled into that area and McBride parked near a fairly deep ditch, with my side next to the ditch. I looked into the woods and realized I could see the nose and wing of the B-17 some distance inside the woods.

As we got out of the jeep, the ambulance pulled up, turned around and backed until its rear doors were a short distance from the ditch. As soon as Venar and Byrne got out, I put the front seat back in position, sat down and pulled my galoshes over my boots. As I was putting on my galoshes, Venar told the medics to get four stretchers, forget the mattress bags and instead, get four sheet/blanket sets out of the ambulance and follow us to the crash-site.

As we walked towards the crashed B-17, I saw a fire next to it and a man with a weapon standing next to the fire. When we arrived, the guard came to attention and saluted and I automatically returned it, while looking at two canvas-covered piles, lying fairly close to the fire. As McBride talked with the Corporal of the Guard about moving the guards back to yesterday's perimeter. I looked around the crash-site and noted that the B-17 had obviously been under the full control of the pilots when it began to lower into the woods.

The slewed nose was more than a hundred feet from the broken tail and the two wings had obviously been broken off. But overall, the B-17 had survived to a point where anyone could look at the four major parts and reassemble them in their mind. Then I saw the name of the B-17, painted in red-script along the damaged nose. It took me a few moments to make the name out, due to the damage the trees had caused as the B-17 broke into the woods. It was broken up by the damage, but I could now see that the B-17 had been named "*Lady Jeannette*."

A short distance from the nose of the B-17, there was an engine lying on the ground that had some melted metal on it and it had apparently burned for some time after the crash. Between the engine and the wing was a melted mass of black and aluminum that had to be one of the wheel assemblies. I do remember, the only places I saw melted metal at the crash-site was on the engine and the melted wheel.

When McBride was done with the Corporal of the Guard and the guard had moved off to relocate the other guards, I asked McBride, Byrne, and Venar to walk around the crash-site with me. When we were some distance from the medics, I told the two men we were looking for the best place to hide the three bodies. It had to be a location that would not be obvious to the French people when they came to visit the crash-site. At the same time, we had to know exactly where the hidden bodies were located as it was our intent, that someone would come back later to recover the hidden bodies, when the flap was over and we had time to correct what we had to do now. It was just a little lie at the time, but it would make the job easier for the three men. We had started out walking around the crash-site in a clockwise circle, as the path in that direction had been opened through the bramble bush thicket by others.

As we walked, Venar pointed out the location in the middle of the high brambles, where the Frenchmen had shown them the body of one of the crewmen,

240

named Dunlap. I had noticed by then, that the XO was wearing a flight jacket that was only issued to aircrews. However, I said nothing about it. Someone might as well be warm and enjoy it, since it was obvious the man who had died in that coat had no further use for it.

As we approached the open end of the broken-off tail, Byrne pointed out the engine that had jammed itself into the ground, to end up with the broken tail above it. I had already seen the ripped silk, when Venar told me that was the parachute of the man who had been hanging under the tail. McBride then told me, he had been told by one of his friends at the XIX TAC, that one of the survivors had told them their tail gunner had been trapped under the B-17's tail when he bailed out. Venar then added, that survivor's report had led them to believe the torn-apart man's remains belonged to the tail gunner. And, they had found enough identity items for the man the day before, to know the man's name was Krimminger. They had also learned that the two dead pilots' names were Gott and Metzger.

There was another wing, lying at an angle just behind the broken-off tail and as we walked around it, Venar pointed out where one of the survivors, an officer, had a mental break down the day before as he walked up to the tail. Then he pointed out the debris-trail, stretching for more than 320 feet, based on his having stepped it out. We stopped there and I said it looked to me like it had to be at least 600 feet from the location where the debris-trail started in the distance to where the nose of the B-17 had stopped. McBride said, "It was a damn shame they did not have a little more altitude, as they had almost completed their turn back to the large field, when the B-17 began to settle into the woods."

I told him from what I had heard so far, those two pilots were very good pilots or their B-17 would have crashed long before they got to these woods. I began to walk back along the other side of the crash-site, but instead of breaking my way through the brambles I walked along a path beside a piled-up earth berm, just to the east of the crashed B–17. As I walked, I was looking for foot prints leading to and from the crash-site. There were a lot of footprints along the debris-trail, but I thought most of them came from the Americans. Along the path I was walking, I found very few foot prints, and when I reached a point where the path went on to the south of the crash-site, I could only see two sets of footprints, one set leading to and the other set away from the cash-site. So it was obvious, few people would come to the crash-site from that direction.

At that point, I excused myself and climbed up and over the forest berm, located just to our left, or east of the path. There I relieved myself, while studying the woods in that area. There were a lot of bramble bush areas and a lot of open areas among the trees. If we were to take the bodies that way to hide them, we would leave a highway of our footprints leading to the hidden grave and back again. All it would take is one visitor to stand on the berm as I had or an interested hunter would see it and they could go directly to the hidden grave. A bit discouraged, I climbed back over the berm and then we continued our walk around the crash-site.

I did notice that the woods on the crash side of the berm was exactly the same as the woods over the berm. As we reached the south side of the crash-site,

241

I saw something in the near distance and I walked over to see what it was. It was a large depression in the woods, about three-quarters full of water. It had no inlet or outlet, so it must be some type of sinkhole. It would make a good hiding place, but again, the tracks we would make would lead directly to what we had done. And, in the summer it was probably dry, so that location was also crossed off my mental list. When we had driven through the fields, I had noticed several small wooded areas that I would now bet were other sink holes that could not be farmed. Any of those places could be used, but with the French so familiar with the area, our tracks to any of them would lead directly to a hidden grave. When we arrived back at the fire, the medics were still standing there, smoking and looking around, waiting to be told what to do.

We had not been gone from the village very long, when a jeep with three men aboard pulled into the south end of Hattonville and made its way to the Village Hall. There the three men found Captain Schurke, the Battalion Adjutant, and told him they had been informed that they were expected to arrive today. Captain Schurke told them he had arranged quarters in a local home for them and the corporal at the desk in the next room would take them to the house when they were ready to go.

The man, who appeared to Captain Schurke to be their leader, had no sign of rank or any unit insignia showing and Schurke asked him if they required anything else right away. The leader told him they would like to be taken to their quarters, shown the mess hall location and after that they would follow their own orders. Captain Schurke called for the corporal and told him to show the men the location of the mess hall on their way to the house, and see to it they were settled in before he returned. As the men followed the corporal out the door, Captain Schurke thought to himself, "It's turning into one hell of a war."

Standing by the fire in the woods, I asked McBride, Byrne and Venar to come off to the side with me, as I wanted to talk to them and get this show on the road. When we stopped, McBride asked me what he needed to do and I told him that to be honest, it would be best if he and Byrne headed back to the village as soon as they could and conduct their normal business, as the rest of us completed our work here in the woods. The less they saw of what we were going to do, the better for them to put off any suggestions of what might have been done. Venar agreed and I told McBride and Byrne I would need them for a while longer, then they could leave the crash-site.

Then I asked Venar, if he had the personal effects that they had found on the dead men. He had what looked like an old Great War gas mask bag with him and he told me he had already filled out the required Medical Form 52b Form and Personal Effects Bag for each man, to turn over to Grave Registration with the remains. He continued, saying he placed any personnel items from the dead, that could be matched up, in their individual Personal Effects Bag.

I asked Venar about their Identity Tags and he told me they had left them on the bodies as Graves Registration regulations required. That is, except for the

torn-apart man; they had found only one of his ID Tags, but with the one ID Tag and some paper ID they found, Venar had enough to identify the remains for burial.

After Venar had finished, I told the three officers, "The way I see it, our first problem is to create the required Burial Packages for the four men and get them to the cemetery this morning." Then I told them, "I had asked the commander at the hospital where the other remains had been turned in, how quickly the remains delivered there could be expected to be buried? The commander had told me it usually took two days from the time the hospital called the local Graves Registration people to when the remains would arrive at the open cemetery near Verdun for burial. And, that was the same cemetery where these remains would be taken to be turned over to Graves Registration. With that knowledge it is obvious, the remains from this crash-site should arrive by noon today and I want these remains to arrive no later than noon. So, Gentlemen, we have a fairly short time to make it happen, what do you think?" Venar said it would take about 45 minutes to take the remains from here to the cemetery and McBride and Byrne agreed.

Then, I threw the bomb to them. I told the three men, from what I had seen, the torn-apart man had been torn-apart in an area where there was no fire. They agreed, that was right. I told them from what I understand, the pilots had not been in the heavy fire area, as they were protected by the cockpit from the fire that had burned outside the cockpit. Venar and Byrne agreed, the pilots' bodies had extremely light fire damage from an oxygen tank explosion below the cockpit. However, to me that was the problem, as their bodies showed no fire damage and their clothing very little fire damage. The only major damage to the bodies, other than the copilot's broken arm were their broken skulls. Venar told me the man in the brambles had been lightly burned, but not all that much. His complete wallet had been found inside his left chest pocket and when his flight-jacket was cleaned off, it did not show any real fire damage. "Ok, Gentlemen," I said, "from what you have just told me, all the French who came to the crash-site saw at least one man's body that had some fire damage and two that had very little." The three agreed and then I went on to tell them about the torn-apart remains at the other crash-site, including the fact several hundred French had seen them and than a hundred and fifty French had helped pick up the remains. And, about half of those remains had been fire and smoke damaged.

The hiding of the three bodies would solve the problem with the complete bodies, but we had a big problem with the torn-apart man's remains at this site, which they had just agreed showed no fire damage. I continued, "The hardest thing we will have to do today, is to do something about that difference. It is extremely important the remains from this site match the basic condition of the remains from the other crash-site." No, I did not go into the specific reason why that had to be done, I just told them, "It had to be done and done quickly."

With that, I asked them to show me the dead and we walked over to the canvas-covered remains. Venar told the three medics standing nearby to remove the covers and for the first time, I had a good look at the men killed at this crash-site.

The cloth helmets of the pilots were covered with dried blood that had made its way through the cloth from the multi-compound fractures of their skulls. Both men's faces were badly messed up and one of them had a badly broken right arm. The third man's shirt showed no fire damage, and I guessed the flight jacket I was seeing had come from his body. His head and the heavy flight pants were showing some slight damage from the fuel fire. Each of their sets of Dog Tags had been pulled free and was hanging outside their clothing.

The pile of remains on the other canvas was actually in much better condition than those I had seen the day before. I could recognize several different body parts. The head had been broken into several pieces, as had his pelvis and hips. There was a bloody 'tee' shirt lying on the stack, wrapped around a small bone. A pair of bloody underwear obviously contained a piece of pelvis. Seeing me looking at the clothing and their contents, Venar told me the small bone in the 'tee' shirt, was the man's left radius bone from his lower left arm and it was a part of his pelvic girdle in his underwear. Venar went on to re-state what he had told me before; with those two identified bones that were found in clothing with the man's laundry mark on them, and the one Identity Tag that had been recovered, along with the personal papers recovered, he could provide an identification for the man's remains. With that information, he was certain the dead man was S/Sgt. Herman B. Krimminger, who according to the information from the XIX TAC, had to be the tail gunner who was trapped under the tail.

I asked the three men to walk over to the far end of the broken-off forward fuselage with me, as I had to make my decision and it was time to make it happen. As we walked to the broken end, I saw two grooves getting deeper in the dirt for some feet, then the dug out area where the nose of the B-17 had to have hit the ground and made the excavation as it moved forward and spun around and stopped moving. It took a second, and then I realized, the two grooves were most likely made by the two machine-guns in the B-17's chin turret digging into the ground before the main nose hit the dirt.

(Note: The researcher found a broken-off length of a ".50" caliber machine-gun barrel and two parachute shroud lines buried at this location in November, 1998.)

When we arrived next to the grooves, I turned to McBride, Byrne, and Venar and told them what I wanted done. The three of them were to go to the medics and tell them exactly they would have to do. Once they had told the men what they had to do, McBride was to ask if they had any questions? If they did not, McBride was to swear them to secrecy and tell them as far as each of them was concerned, if asked by anyone in the future, they would say, "*I have no memory of any bomber crash while I was at Hattonville!*"

Then, they were to call me over and I would tell the men who I was, and lay it on the line that what they were being verbally ordered to do, had to be done and that was that. I told McBride, Byrne, and Venar the same thing I was planning to

244

tell the three enlisted men. If anyone, and I mean anyone refused at this time, I would see they became Privates before the day was out and they would be escorted, under guard, to the front line at once, where they would immediately take on the duties of a replacement Infantry Private. I went on to tell them that there would be no jails, no trials, and very few documents. If I had to, I would see to it, that they would be gone from the unit today and a front line replacement tomorrow!

McBride did not look very happy as he told me I had made my point and when I was finished briefing them, they would go talk to the men. I told them to go ahead and turned back to look much closer at the area where the nose of the B-17 had pushed up the pile of dirt.

I heard McBride, then Byrne, and Venar talking to the three men. I did not try to make out what they were saying to the men, as they were their men, and it was their job to explain what had to be done in such a way the men would do it without question and delay.

As they talked, I realized the area of disturbed, piled-up earth created when the bomber pushed it up, had already been trampled part way down by the people getting into the broken end of the cockpit. It looked like the trampled area in the field where the other remains had already been hidden. And just like there, the rain would soon hide any fresh digging in that area, that was not already disguised by someone tramping down the dirt after the hole had been refilled or just throwing some of the autumn leaves on top of the fresh dirt.

To my eye, there was an area almost eight feet square that could easily be reached in which to dig the hidden grave. If the excavated earth was piled along the inbound skid path and then put back in the hole, once it was trampled down, the French who had been here yesterday would never know that three mens's bodies had been buried there. Some might wonder about the softness of the dirt at first, but surely they would put it down to the earth being pushed up and then trampled down. The best part of it, was the three bodies would be in a place where anyone with instructions could find them. All they had to do was to find the broken front-end of the B-17 and dig just to the east of where it stopped. Even if the fuselage had been removed, the area where it had been could be seen. And, if absolutely necessary, they could get a villager to show them where the nose had been and come back later to recover the remains.

As I completed my new plan in my mind, Lt. Col. McBride called me over to where the six men were standing by the fire. I had to say to myself, as I walked over to the group, the enlisted men did not look happy. When I arrived, McBride told me that they had explained exactly what had to be done, and though the men were not happy to have to do it, they realized the necessity of it and were prepared to go ahead as ordered.

I looked at each man and made certain, I looked directly into their eyes and told them, though no effort of their own, they had found themselves involved in something that was so secret, I could not tell them all of what was going on. But they were involved and would have to do what they were told to do. "As Colonel McBride and Major Byrne have told you", I told them, "I am on the staff of General

245

Eisenhower and the only reason I am here is that General Eisenhower has directly ordered me to carry out his plan to hide the fact, that this B-17 had crashed here in these woods."

At that point, I went in a direction that no one else but these six men would ever hear, or so I thought at the time. "Gentlemen, this will be a surprise for your officers, as much as it will be for you. This B-17 had been captured by the Germans and it had been flown by the Germans to spy over our front lines and Patton's new push. Because, it was so secret, it had been hit by the German's own **FLAK** before it got clear of Germany. I can tell you this much, all the survivors are in custody and General Eisenhower has personally determined that he has to make this crashed B-17 go away. That way, we will be able to interrogate the captured German survivors all we want, to learn about their use of captured planes and any other intelligence we can obtain from the captured spies.

In order to make this crash disappear, General Eisenhower has put me in charge of making certain it is done. To accomplish that purpose, via documentation, we are moving the location of this B-17 crash-site to another B-17 crash-site here in France. The entire crew of that B-17 died in the crash (now, it was just a small lie and it would make their future lives much easier, until the researcher caught up to the long-term survivors) and with what you will be doing at this crash-site today. You will help make certain the Germans believe all their spies had died in that crash. The problem is, at that crash-site all the crewmen had been torn-apart when their B-17 hit the ground, while at this crash-site, the real spy B-17 crash-site, there are three complete bodies and one torn-apart body and, of course, the German survivors."

As they had been told, they had to create all four of the dead's official graves from this crash-site, using the one man's torn-apart remains and then hide the three bodies where I would show them." I concluded by telling them, "If what they had to do today actually bothered them all that much, all they had to do was to remember they were doing it to German Spies, and to also remember, what they are doing could save many American lives."

Now, did any of them have any questions? None of the men did and I decided that McBride, Byrne and Venar had to have already made my point and the less they heard from me, the better.

With that, I told McBride and Byrne they could head back to the village and to tell Sergeant Tiff that I would be ready to leave by about 11:00 hours. In addition, I asked McBride to contact General Weyland or his aide and tell them I expected to be at Etain at about 12:00 hours and I wanted to have a private lunch with General Weyland. I also told McBride, if he found out Weyland could not meet with me at that time, he should send someone out to tell me what time Weyland could see me.

I thanked them for their help and told them, I would talk to them again before I left and they could head back to the village to prepare for the village memorial, as we got on with what had to be done. McBride and Byrne headed for their jeep, to leave for the village.

As they were heading toward Hattonville, up in the Somme at Tincourt-Boucly, the villagers heard the loud noise of a strong vehicle engine. Many were standing at the side of the road watching, as the tractor-trailer hauling the bulldozer maneuvered its way around the tight corner of the intersection in the village to head north toward the crash-site. As the large truck made the left turn, the jeep that was following, made a right turn and headed for the village hall.

No one was there, then one of the village people walked over and asked the American if they were hunting for the Mayor? When the American said he was, the farmer told him to wait there and he would get the Mayor. When the Mayor arrived, the man told the Mayor that a group of Americans who were up at the crash-site had arrived to investigate the cause of the "Avion Fortress, B-17" crash and the Americans would appreciate it if they could stay at the village hall for a while, as they talked to the people who might know something about the crash.

The American told the Mayor, that the men had their own air mattresses, blankets, and supplies. All they needed was for the building to be heated and when they left, they would pay for the time they had stayed in the village hall. As to eating, they were very used to French food and they would be eating at the café while they were there. When they came into town later, they would talk to the café owner to make certain there would be not a problem with the cafe's food supply due to their being in the village.

The man asked the Mayor if he knew who owned the field where the "Avion Fortress, B-17" had crashed. The Mayor pointed to a farm compound across the village square and told the American, Mr. Leguillier owned the farm and that was his home over there. The American asked the Mayor, if Mr. Leguillier would be home and the Mayor said he probably was. The American told the Mayor it was important that they talk to the field owner at the crash-site and asked if the Mayor would go with them to get Mr. Leguillier, (no relation to the boys), and then go to the field with them to discuss the damage to the field.

At that time, in the Hattonville Woods, I was telling Venar to go ahead with what he was doing. I was going out to talk to the Corporal of the Guard and make certain all of the guards were far enough away from the crash-site, so they could not see what we would be doing. As I started out of the woods, I could hear Venar instruct the men to lay out the four sheet/blanket sets around the torn-apart man's remains, but not so close to the fire they could catch on fire, and get ready to divide the torn-apart remains among the four sets. He also told one of them to find a couple of strong branches with a good forked end, like the ones they used to roast meat over a fire back home when they were camping.

As I approached the edge of the woods, the guard saw me coming and he crossed over the ditch to meet me. I realized he was the Corporal of the Guard and as I approached, he asked if there was anything he could do? I told him, "Let's go out into the field," and when we were there, "I asked him how many guards were at the site and where were they located?" He told me, "Besides himself, there were three other men. One was to the east of the berm, on the other side of the crash-site." Then he pointed down to a point about a football field away where I could

247

see a man standing by what looked like a crossover into the woods. He went on to say, "The fourth guard was at the road at the north end of the debris-trail."

I thanked him for his input, asked if he had thermoses of coffee, which he said he did, and then I told him I wanted him to relocate his current guard-posts for a few hours. He was to take the coffee with him and move the man he had shown me standing to the south of us, back into the woods to the path by the berm and then the guard was to go south at least another 500 feet to keep anyone from coming up the path. Next, he was to find the man to the east of the berm and have him move further east to the edge of a road I had seen on a map and have him stop anyone from coming toward the crash-site along or across that road. Then he was to find the man at the north end of the debris-trail and have him move another 500 feet to the north to insure no one came from the north. Then, after he had posted the three men, he was to walk west along the road in the woods at the north end of the debris-trail until he came to the angle in the woods. From there, I wanted him to walk out to the south-west corner of the woods at the angle and take a position there. From that position, and I pointed across the fields to that particular location, he could see anyone coming along the road from the village or walking toward the crash-site across the field and he was to stop anyone except someone from the unit, from getting closer to the crash-site.

I concluded that once he was in position, he was to stay there until I left the site with the men in the ambulance, and then I would stop and give him permission to close the guards back to the actual crash-site perimeter. I gave him the good news that they should be pulled from this duty by dinner time.

I asked if he had it straight? "No problem, Sir," he said and he walked over to where there were a couple of thermos-food cans and some thermoses. He opened a food can, stuffed some sandwiches in his pocket, closed it, grabbed two thermoses and started toward the man by the crossover.

As he walked away, I was feeling very good, not only were we a bit ahead of my mental schedule, but I was wearing one of my oldest uniforms and I had on my galoshes to keep my feet dry and warm. However, the galoshes were making my feet very heavy as the thick clay of the field and the woods stuck to them. "Well, you can't win them all," I thought, and I went to the ambulance, removed the shovel from one side and used the shovel to cut off some of the clay on my galoshes, before starting back into the woods.

Chapter 12
Cover-Up - Hattonville
Day Two - Desecration - Afternoon

When I approached the crash-site, Venar was standing by the burned-out engine, using it as a work bench. Four Medical Form 52b, tagged Personal Effects Bags were lying on some scrap metal, lying among the cylinder heads, and the medics were working on dividing the pile of the torn-apart man's remains. When I arrived, they had just started and I asked Venar about the burned pieces. He reached around the engine and grabbed two limbs I had not seen lying against the engine and asked me, "Which one, do you want?"

At that moment, I have to admit, he had me. I had decided it would not hurt the men to see me digging near the broken rear of the forward fuselage; however, I was not really prepared to help with the actual body parts. It was obvious from Venar's face that he realized I really did not see the humor in what he had offered, and he quickly told me there was a problem other than unburnt body parts. I asked him what he meant. He showed me two sets of Identity Tags. *I looked at them and said that I saw nothing wrong with them. So, Venar explained that if we were going to have men torn-apart and burnt, then we were going to have to have their personal items, such as their Identity Tags, showing the same damage.* I looked at the tags, looked at him, looked over at the fire, and told him that I was damn glad he was here. I went on to tell him that when I was at the other crash-site the day before, all that had been handled by someone else and frankly, I had not thought about the need to make the body parts and personal identity items here, match.

Then, I suppose, in some way, I got back at him. I told him I was going to start digging out the hole where we were going to hide the bodies, and he could keep a check on the men dividing the remains. He laughed, just a little, and as I walked on with my shovel and axe, he took the sticks and walked to the fire and told Boatman to stand up and take one.

I had taken a couple of shovels of dirt and pitched them back to the skid area, when Venar and Boatman had Berardi and Zeman impale two of the torn-apart body parts on the forked sticks. They turned to hold the body parts over the fire, just as I had told them they had to. I could not help myself; I stood there and watched as the fire began to heat the human meat, and the fats and liquids began to sizzle and fall into the fire, which began to turn smokey. The fire flared up, just as the fire had when my father and I had gone hunting some years ago and we cooked rabbits over the fire. Only this time, I was watching human meat and bone began to sear and collect burned-on soot.

As human flesh was searing over an open fire in Hattonville Woods, the jeep with the two Americans, the Tincourt-Boucly Mayor and Mr. Leguillier had arrived at the crash-site to the north of Tincourt-Boucly, where the driver of the large truck was backing the bulldozer down onto the ground. Watching the driver

moving the bulldozer off the truck was a group of eight Americans in four jeeps, which had canvas-covered trailers attached to them. There were also several other American guards standing around the crash-site, keeping the French in a group some distance away from the crater.

The jeep coming from the village drove across the field to where the eight Americans and their jeeps were located. After it was parked and the men got out, the American who had brought the two men, introduced the Mayor and Mr. Leguillier to the group of Americans already there. One of the Americans, who was in the group, began to talk to the Mayor and Mr. Leguillier. He spoke French like a native and he explained to Mr. Leguillier and the Mayor that the Americans did not want to deprive the farmer of this excellent field. So they had brought the bulldozer to push all the "Avion Fortress, B-17" parts into the hole, then fill in the hole and smooth out the field so he could farm it next year.

In addition, the American told the men it was the policy of the Americans to pay for any damage they had caused in France. Therefore they were prepared to settle with Mr. Leguillier right now and pay him for the damage to his field caused by the "Avion Fortress, B-17." Mr. Leguillier immediately told the American, since the Americans were going to fill the hole and smooth out the field, there was no way he could accept any money from the Americans, when these Americans had died in his field while helping France regain her "Liberty."

Both Frenchmen were very pleased that the Americans had offered to pay damages and the Mayor told the two Americans that had accompanied them to the crash-site, that they were welcome to use the village hall, as long as they wanted. The American from the group told the Mayor that if he wished, the Mayor could ride into the village with them and show them the village hall. The Mayor was more than happy to leave the crash-site and soon, he was showing the men their accommodation in the village hall. When they were done at the town hall, the Americans gave the Mayor two cartons of cigarettes and invited him to go to the café, so they could make arrangements to eat there while they were in Tincourt-Boucly. Upon arrival at the café, the first thing they did was to purchase drinks for the Mayor and the other customers, and then they gave each of the customers a pack of American cigarettes. Then the Americans began to talk about the "Avion Fortress, B-17" crash in the field with the café customers.

Within an hour, the men were fully settled in and accepted. The café owner was very happy to get the American rations they had unloaded from one jeep and even happier with the carton of cigarettes the men had given him. He had already thought that he was probably going to have the best business he had enjoyed for years, as long as these Americans were in Tincourt-Boucly.

Down in the Hattonville Woods, when the flesh appeared to be burned and smoked enough, Venar removed his stick from over the fire, followed by Boatman and then they lifted the burnt human remains toward Berardi and Zeman, who used a couple of sticks to push the burned and smoked flesh and bone off the sticks and onto one of the blanket sets. Then they took two more pieces of the torn-apart man and stuck them on the sticks.

Even though I was some distance away, I could hear the sizzle of the fat as the new pieces of human meat and bone were placed over the fire to be burnt and smoked. After a while, I realized what it looked like to those men, knowing I would not do what I was making them do.

I used the shovel to cut some of the yellow clay off my galoshes and then I clomped over and took the stick from Boatman, and said he should go dig for a little while. I had marked the corners of the hidden grave, as well as getting a good start on the hole, and I reminded Boatman to make certain all the removed dirt was placed in the already clear skid area.

When I put the forked end of my stick toward Berardi, he grabbed a couple of small pieces off the pile of remains and stuck them on the prongs of the stick, saying as he did so, "Colonel, now you have fun cooking your hot dogs."

Now, all these years later, I realize that was a bit of very good humor considering the conditions under which I was forcing the men to work and what we were doing. But I'm afraid, I did not laugh, as much as they did.

After a short time, Venar called for Boatman to come over to the fire and Venar went and did a bit of shoveling. I have to say, I had to agree with the rotation; the fire was now hot and greasy and the smoke did not smell very good. It was the same hot, sweetish, sickening odor, I had smelled several times in Normandy and across France. "There could be no mistake," I thought, "we are burning human flesh over this fire."

Venar came back after digging for a short time and told Berardi to take my stick and for Zeman to put the pieces on the sticks. I wanted to thank Venar for that. However, I knew it would not be the right thing for me to do, while the enlisted men were still doing a job, I certainly did not want to do. I followed Venar back over to the engine, where he was removing both identity tags from each of the pilot's Personal Effects Bag.

He placed the four selected ID Tags to one side, where he had a small pile of English coins and a wrist identification bracelet with a broken chain. Venar picked up the bracelet and handed it to me, so I could see the damage the bracelet had suffered when the branch that broke the copilot's right arm struck him, as he threw it up to protect his face. Just the size of the dent in the metal was enough to make me realize how forcefully those branches had broken into the cockpit.

As I was looking at the bracelet, Venar told me they would use the fire to burn and sear the tags, identity bracelet and coins, when they were done with the body parts. After they were put in the fire, they would tie the tags to each man's Personal Effects Bag, which already had the required medical form attached to it. When the men were finished dividing the remains and distributing them among the four blanket sets, they would wrap up the blanket sets into bundles like the bundles I had told them I had seen at St-Quentin. To finish the bundles, they would tie them up with rope, while attaching the tagged Personal Effects Bags to the right Burial Package bundle.

Venar said he thought they were making good time and once that was done, he could send Zeman to the cemetery with the Burial Packages, while they finished hiding the three bodies in the hole we had been digging.

Just a few miles away, at the 109th Evacuation Hospital located near the American St-Mihiel Great War Cemetery, S/Sgt. James O. Fross, Ball Turret Gunner, began to wake up. "Man," he thought, "I have to pee." At the same time as his eyes focused, he realized, he was looking at the inside canvas of a tent with the inside view of a large circle on the top of the tent and the shadow of a cross in the middle. "Well," he thought, "I'm not at Deopham Green, so I must be in a hospital." When he was fully awake, he still had to pee and from the bunk next to him, he heard someone saying in German, "I have to piss."

The first thought that came to Fross's mind was, "Damn, he was in a German hospital and to hell with them, if the German had to piss, so did he." So Fross yelled out in English, "I have to piss."

Within seconds, Fross was happy. First, a man in an American uniform appeared, meaning he was not in a German hospital. And, the man was holding a bed pan as he told Fross he didn't have to holler so loud. When the orderly had positioned the bed pan, Fross let go and asked the fellow why he wasn't he helping the German? "Why," the orderly asked? Fross told him, "The man kept repeating in German that he had to piss." The orderly asked Fross if he could control the bed pan himself so that he could grab one for the POW in the next bunk.

The orderly came right back, held the bed pan up in front of the POW, and asked Fross, if he could ask the POW, if he knew what it was and if he could put the bed pan in position? Fross had learned German as a kid from his grandparents and some German kids in the town where he grew up, and even though his German was rusty, the man understood and told the orderly to please hurry, "I have to piss."

Fross laughed and he told the orderly, "That the German was begging him to hurry." The orderly lifted the POW's blankets, positioned the bed pan and as Fross felt content when his own stream had stopped, he listened to the German's flow until it became silent. At the same time, the Germans told both the men, "Thank you, thank you, I really had to piss!"

The orderly, who was standing between them, asked Fross what the POW had said and Fross told him, "Let's just say, he is more of a friend right now than he is an enemy." The orderly asked Fross if he was done and when Fross said he was, the orderly lifted his blankets, removed the bed pan and told Fross that he had not been bull-shitting when he said he had to piss because he had almost filled the bed pan. Fross laughed, and told the orderly, that at least two men in the hospital really appreciated his work. And he had thought, "Being a ball turret gunner was bad?" However, now that he had mentioned it, he really did have to take a crap and could he get up and go to the can?" The orderly told Fross to hold on a moment and after he had taken care of Fross's bed pan, he came back and asked Fross to ask the POW if he was finished?

As he talked, Fross looked over at the man who was a POW and the fellow looked back at Fross, as Fross asked him if he was done? The POW smiled, and

again told each man how much he had appreciated that piss. That caused Fross to laugh and then he told the orderly what the German had said, and when he was done, all three men were laughing together.

The orderly removed the POW's bed pan and again the POW thanked him in German, which Fross continued to interpret. The orderly took the bed pan away, then came back and asked Fross how he was and that it was good to see him awake. Fross told him he felt fine, but he really needed to take a crap. The orderly told Fross that he would tell the nurse that Fross was awake, that he could interpret for the German POW, and that Fross wanted to take a walk and take a crap. Close by, some place in the 109th Evacuation Hospital location, Lt. Harms was still sedated and would be kept that way for another 24 hours.

At the crash-site, I was digging as I needed to dig to get my mind off what was going on. It seemed so much worse than what I had seen at the other crash-site. There, the three dead men's remains were rather remote, anonymous pieces of meat and bone. Here, these remains reminded me of the chunks of meat and bone that I used to see every day when my mother used to send me to get the families daily meat order at the butcher's shop. Here, lying beside the man's torn-apart remains were the complete bodies of three dead men, who looked like all of us except for the two bodies with the damaged heads, which made this a very different situation.

Working by myself, I had the grave dug down to a foot or more when Venar came over and told me that they were ready to wrap up the remains, and asked if I wanted to check them. As you know, I did not want to do that at all. I would have preferred that Venar had come over and said it was done, but he had not and I had no choice but to go give my approval.

To my eye, they had done a good job. Two of the piles contained burnt and seared flesh and bone and the other two had no sign of a fire. When I took a second look at that first pile, I realized that Venar continued to keep his wits about him, even though he might be having more problems with what we were doing than I did.

That pile had to be the one he was going to identify as Krimminger, because I could see the 'tee' shirt and shorts. If Krimminger's remains had been exposed to fire as he died, the 'tee' shirt and shorts that Venar had used to help identify the remains would have burned. As he had not, they had not, and the small pile that made up his now, illegal, official remains had not been exposed to fire damage.

When he was satisfied the items were sufficiently damaged, Boatman was to put the identity bracelet in Metzger's Personal Effects Bag and split the coins between Gott's and Metzger's Personal Effects Bags. Then he was to tie their burned ID Tags to their Personal Effects Bags and put one of the Form 52b and Personal Effects Bag sets on each of the Burial Package bundles after they had secured them. Boatman told Venar, that he understood all of Venar's instructions and then he walked toward the fire.

As Boatman headed toward the fire, Venar asked me if I could use a cup of coffee? I quickly agreed. Venar told the three that we were walking out to the

ambulance for a smoke and a coffee, and we would bring some coffee and sandwiches back to them.

As Boatman walked to the fire, he selected a piece of metal that had fallen from the B-17 and when he got to the fire, he used the metal to scrape some of the fire's ashes to one side. Then, he prepared to put the stuff into the fire's hot spot and cover it over with still glowing greasy and smoking ash, to create the damage required by Venar.

(**Note**: As he was beginning that task, Boatman created one of the two major keys to the future identification of the crash-site and at the same time, he was creating two new pieces of undisputable evidence of what was done at this crash-site to the dead men's remains.)

As Boatman bent over to scrape the hot fire ash aside with the metal scraper piece in one hand and the items to be put in the fire in the other. He began to lose his balance and he had to put one hand down into the mud to help steady himself. He happened to use the hand which contained the items to be placed in the fire pit.

During that moment, one of the previously undamaged Identity

Top: A burned, seared, and smoke-blackened English Coin found in crash-site, open fire location in May 2000, by Robert LeClerc and the researcher/author.

Bottom: The back of Metzger's ID Tag has not been cleaned. The front had been cleaned for display on his original cross at Limey Cemetery. After 3 ½ years of outside exposure and decades of being handled, the fire and soot damage still exists on the uncleaned back of Metzger's ID Tag.

Photograph: Willis S. Cole, Jr.

Tags of the pilot, slipped unnoticed between Boatman's fingers to be buried in the mud near the edge of the fire. Regaining his balance, Boatman swore, dropped the items to be purposely damaged in the fire and pushed still burning ash over them.

When the undamaged ID Tag of 1st Lt. Donald J. Gott, *Congressional Medal Of Honor*, slipped into the mud that day, it was to provide absolute proof that two *Congressional Medal Of Honor Citations* contained, **known false information**, Venar and I had just arrived at the ambulance for a smoke and a coffee, and we would bring some coffee and sandwiches back to them.

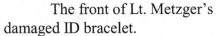

The front of Lt. Metzger's damaged ID bracelet.

The back of Lt. Metzger's damaged ID bracelet.

Note: Though cleaned, you can still see the extreme fire and smoke damage that matches his ID Tag and the damaged coin. It was on the right wrist of Lt. Metzger, seen by dozens to have suffered no fire damage to his body. It was also protected by his shirt and flight jacket, inside a cockpit that had no extreme fire damage. Yet, it suffered extensive fire and searing damage and one must question,

Note: Black searing that survived the bracelet's back and front being cleaned with some type of abrasive. The chain is covered with the same searing. Supposedly, while his body was still in the crushed cockpit. All relics recovered at the crash site, from the cockpit area, show little or no fire damage.

How and by who!

Photographs: Willis S. Cole, Jr.

(**Note:** Though Metzger's identity bracelet should have shown on his Report Of Burial, it was not recorded as it should have been. It was recorded at the Limey Cemetery on an Inventory Of Personal Effects form, dated 9 Nov., 1944. (The best estimated date of death was used on both the Report Of Burial and Inventory Of Personal Effects record, instead of the date the remains and effects were received at the cemetery.) On the form, also dated 11 Nov. 1945, Capt. James T. Passman, 609th GR CO signed the effect's record pertaining to: 1 Gold colored Identification bracelet   No currency ... on 5 July 1945, the bracelet left the Army Effects Bureau at Kansas City for delivery to his parents. On Aug. 14, 1945, his parents noted receiving the bracelet, but stated they had received none of his other effects. The rest of Lt. Metzger's personal effects were shipped to the family on 5 Oct. 1945. Almost eleven months after his death in the Bois de Hattonville.)

As Boatman walked to the fire, he selected a piece of metal that had fallen from the B-17 and when he got to the fire, he used the metal to scrape some of the fire's ashes to one side. Then, he prepared to put the items into the fire's hot spot and cover it up with still glowing greasy and smoking ash, to create the Venar required fire and smoke damage.

While the undamaged items were being damaged, Boatman, Berardi, and Zeman started to tie up the bundles of remains. Two contained remains that had suffered no fire damage. Of those two, one contained non-burned flesh and broken bone, with two identified bones in two scraps of clothing, the other contained a mixture of unburned flesh and broken bones, with parts of a man's skull and jaw. The last two contained, an assortment of purposely burnt and seared human remains. One contained *__no identifiable human remains__*, just burnt and seared flesh and damaged bone. While the other contained the largest amount of identifiable fire and smoke damaged remains and in 1948, the Disinterment Directive for this Burial Package would also specify part of the right leg was missing from the grave.

As they were finishing, creating the four Burial Packages, if all the remains in all four Burial Packages had been laid out on one inspection table, the remains on that table would be observed, to have absolutely no duplication of any human bone! When many duplications should have existed. As all of these men had died under circumstances that would have left many duplications.

But, I was certain, upon arrival at the cemetery, no one would think to question that fact, when these torn-apart flesh and bone remains were received at Graves Registration. *__No one would suspect in any way, that anyone would do to our American war dead, what I had just ordered these men, to do to the remains of the B-17's tail gunner__*.

Venar and I were still out in the field at the ambulance enjoying our break and conversation, when Boatman determined the stuff had to be ready. Besides, he told Berardi and Zeman as he walked to the fire, "He wanted the hell out of this place as soon as he possibly could." Boatman used his metal scraper to clear the ash away and he found the items were obviously burnt, with seared on smoke. The items had a heavy level of baked-on soot from the human fluids that had melted into the fire and had transferred to them.

Obviously the stuff was hot, so Boatman had to get up and find another piece of metal to slide the stuff onto it, so he could remove them from the fire. The fire was hot, the stuff was hot and the metal sheet he was holding heated up quickly, so Boatman backed away from the fire with what he had.

Boatman realized he did not have as much stuff as Venar had given him and he had placed in the fire, but Venar was out there with the colonel and not here, so to hell with Venar. He would do what Venar had told him to do, with what he had.

(**Note**: This created another vital key to provide more indisputable proof of what was done to the dead of the *"Lady Jeannette"* in the Hattonville Woods to some of the dead men's property and Identity Tags.)

Jeanne Metzger Scholfield
Frances Metzger
Fredericks

The day 2nd Lt. Metzger left for Europe, they gave him the Identity bracelet.

Photograph: Metzger Family

As Boatman stood up and walked back to the engine to work with the Personal Effects Bags, the shiny edge of Lt. Gott's undamaged Identity Tag, that had fallen into the mud, was pressed further into the clay by Boatman's shoe. **It came to rest less than two feet from where several of the English coins, which had gone into the fire as undamaged coins, were now as equally damaged as the coins and ID Tags removed by Boatman, except they were buried in the ash**.

Fully fire damaged English coins, which 56 years later would be compared to the undamaged Identity Tag of 1st Lt. Donald J. Gott, *Congressional Medal Of Honor*, to become indisputable proof, that the B-17 did not crash as later specified in both of the men's *Congressional Medal Of Honor applications*!

Boatman arrived at the engine and as the stuff cooled, he picked up the seared and blackened identity bracelet that had been on the copilot's wrist when he died and dropped it into the Personal Effects Bag with Metzger's name on it. Then Boatman selected the two damaged Identity Tags with Metzger's name on them, and slipped them onto the tie string attached to Metzger's Medical Form 52b. Then he tied both to the pull string of Metzger's Personal Effects Bag's and pulled that string tight and tied the ends together. With that done, the accounting of the death of Lt. Metzger in Hattonville Woods, became another illegal step put in place to protect American Secrets.

Boatman then walked over to the "collecting point" and tied the Personal Effects Bag to the now official Burial Package of burnt and seared unidentifiable human remains that Berardi and Zeman had tied up. It was now, the official Burial Package of 2nd Lt. William E. Metzger, Jr. On 23 August, 1948, his official remains were buried at the Woodlawn Cemetery, Lima, Ohio. Before the burial, the cleaned falsely damaged Identity Tag (seen in previous photographs) was removed from his official coffin and given to the family of 2nd Lt. William E. Metzger, Jr., *CMOH*.

Recommended Reading:

XIX Tactical Air Command and ULTRA, **Patton's Force Enhancers In The 1944 Campaign In France,** Major Bradford J."BJ" Shwedo, USAF
The Cadre papers, Air University (AU) Library/AU Press Team - Cadre Paper 10
College Of Aerospace Doctrine, Research And Education - Air University
Maxwell AFB, Alabama, May 2001 http://research.maxwell.af.mil
This paper provides a solid link between Generals Patton and Weyland and how my ULTRA responsibility may have played a major part in my on-going interactions with their ULTRA staffs and the two Generals. Such previous interactions would have immediately provided my authority to carry out General Eisenhower's verbal orders in this situation, when push came to shove.

Boatman walked back to the engine, picked up the remaining burned and seared Gott Identity Tag and slipped it onto Gott's Form 52b sting and tied both to Gott's Personal Effects Bag tie string, which he pulled tight and tied off. As he walked back, Berardi and Zeman were just finished tying up the last bundle and when Boatman attached the Gott Personal Effects Bag to the newly tied bundle, it then became the official Burial Package of 1st Lt. Donald J. Gott, **CMOH**, which in due time, would be buried in the countryside cemetery at Harmon, Oklahoma.

On his final trip, Boatman collected the other two Personal Effects bags with the Form 52b and Identity Tag(s) already on them. He tied Krimminger's Form 52b, Personal Effects Bag, with only one ID tag, onto the tied up bundle containing the two bones wrapped in the dead man's underclothing. And, it became Krimminger's official Burial Package, that was later buried, at his wife's request, at the Arlington National Cemetery. The final Form 52b, Personal Effects Bag, and the attached, undamaged Dunlap ID Tags were attached to the bundle with no fire damaged remains and only a few identifiable remains, for it to become the official Burial Package of T/Sgt. Dunlap, later buried at the American Lorraine Cemetery, at St-Avold, France.

When Boatman was finished, he told Berardi and Zeman they were half way done and had half way to go. Then, all three men turned and looked at the three bodies that were lying uncovered and side by side on the floor of the Hattonville Woods. *No longer identified in any way! Now, just three Unknown American Dead! Thanks to the attached AMC personnel of the 563rd SAW BN, the very men who were supposed to prevent such a thing from happening, who helped to make it happen, and a Colonel from Ike's Staff, that made it happen!*

Venar and I were out at the ambulance, discussing the situation and we had realized that time was rushing by, and it was getting closer to when I had to leave to ensure, I could make it to Etain in time for my private lunch with General Weyland at the XIX TAC. I told Venar I thought the crash-site was in excellent hands and all they had to do now was to finish the hole, put the three men's bodies

258

in the hole, then fill in the hole and after they were finished, trample the dirt down they best they could and scatter some leaves over it to help hide the fresh digging.

I looked at my watch and it was about 09:45, so I needed to get back to the village pretty soon to meet my schedule. I had to clean up, get into my good uniform, finish my business with McBride and Byrne, get Tiff, and make it to the XIX TAC before 12:00. Venar told me the XIX TAC was located at Etain Air Base and it was an easy run up the road, via St-Beloit. When we left Hattonville, he told me, "Just go south to the next village, about a mile to the south and then turn east to St-Beloit. Then, when you reach St-Beloit, you take the left turn and head north. From there it was no more than 30 minutes to Etain."

Venar suggested that we have the men load the completed Burial Packages into the ambulance as soon as possible. Then he would send Zeman to the cemetery with the remains and on his way, Zeman could drop me off at the Mayor's home. Venar added that McBride could get Byrne and my driver to the house (where I would most likely find McBride), in time to allow plenty of time to get to Etain. Again, I thought he was a good man. He talked about what could be done, instead wasting time talking about what couldn't be done, as many men I knew did.

We grabbed the thermoses and sandwich bags and started back to the crash-site. We arrived just as Boatman and the other two had finished loading the completed Burial Packages onto the stretcher, and Berardi and Zeman, were preparing to lift the stretcher, to take it to the ambulance. I thought, it was not that much of a load, as I suspected we had collected no more than 130 pounds of the man's torn-apart remains. But, I had to confess to myself, they looked like the three bundles we had picked up in St-Quentin only a bit smaller in size.

Venar asked Zeman if he needed a cup of coffee before he left? Zeman said, it would be a nice break. Venar told Zeman and Berardi to go ahead and take the stretcher out to the ambulance, load it and then come back for a quick break, as I was going to ride back into the village with Zeman when he left for the cemetery.

As those two walked off with the stretcher, Venar, Boatman and I walked to the partially dug hole and talked about how deep they should dig it. The forest floor clay was hell to dig, as it came out in great, sopping wet clumps and there was already a few inches of water in the newly opened hole.

Venar and I agreed, as the three bodies could be placed on their backs and side by side, the hole could be less deep if necessary. Venar told Boatman that as soon as the other two got back we would take a break, and he would walk out to the ambulance with me and Zeman while Boatman and Berardi began to deepen the hole. Then, bringing the other shovel with him, he would come back and help them with digging the hole and burying the three men's bodies.

I remembered, I had told the Corporal of the Guard that he would be able to pull in the guards when I left. So I told Venar, I would tell the Corporal of the Guard, that it would be another hour or two before they could squeeze in. Venar thought that would be about right and with the other shovel two people digging while one person was cutting tree-roots with the axe. With the three of them working, they would make much better time than one man working alone.

259

When Zeman and Berardi came back and we took a break by the fire, throwing more wood on it, as it was starting to burn down. The additional coffee was good and I really enjoyed the fried egg sandwiches with mustard and extra salt that were to have been my breakfast. As we stood there, I again told the medics how much I appreciated their help. I added, that I knew they have been going through a couple of very rough days and I would be certain to tell McBride, Byrne, and General Eisenhower about their hard work here at the crash-site.

With that, I shook hands with each of them and then, Venar, Boatman, Zeman, and I started toward the ambulance, with Boatman and Zeman carrying the stretcher with the "Burial Packages," as Berardi went over to pick up the shovel and axe and start digging. Boatman and Zeman were not dumb, and they were was soon far enough in front that Venar and I could finish discussing what we had to discuss. I told Venar that I would tell McBride and Byrne to have someone pick him up in an hour or so and that he should make certain the grave was well tamped down and hidden when they were done. I also told Venar I was certain he would have the medics complete any additional clean up required, by burning anything that was of personal nature that they may find around the crash-site. Venar told me, to ensure the medics got back to the village as soon as possible, he would have Zeman return to the woods when he got back from the cemetery.

Venar told me, Zeman should be at the cemetery in time to meet the 11:00 time line, I had set, and he asked me if I realized what time that was? I told him my mind had been on so many things the past two days I only thought I knew what day it was. Venar said the four men's (illegally desecrated and created) official remains were scheduled to be delivered to the cemetery on the hour of the 26th Anniversary of the end of the Great War, I thought, for a moment and told Venar, "Well ... perhaps that will help make up a little of what we have done to them."

When we got to the ambulance, Zeman had already removed the shovel. He gave it to Boatman. As Venar went around the ambulance to get into the driver's seat. I took the shovel from Boatman and used it to shear some of the clumps of clay off my galoshes and handed it back, then I shook Venar's hand for the last time and I got into the ambulance as we said goodbye to each other. As I slammed the door, Venar and Boatman started to trudge back into the woods and Zeman let out the clutch and hit the gas.

I had Zeman stop the ambulance near the angle in the woods and waved to the Corporal of the Guard to get him to come over to the ambulance from where he was standing. I told him that it would be at least one more and perhaps, two more hours, before they could squeeze in. I told him that Major Venar was still in the woods, and that I was going to see Colonel McBride and Major Byrne. And, when one of them came out to pick up Venar, they would release him to have the guards squeeze into the crash-site at that time. The guard pulled to attention and saluted, I returned the salute, turned around and told Zeman to head to the village.

Zeman dropped me off at the Mayor's home and as Zeman turned around to head back south to go to the Limey cemetery, I was sitting on the steps kicking off my clay laden galoshes. As I worked, McBride opened the door and asked me

how it had gone? As I walked up the steps, I was telling him the remains were on their way to the cemetery when the Mayor's wife brushed by us, with a knife in her hand, telling me in French, that she would clean and wash my boots.

It was obvious that McBride, Byrne and Venar were living much higher on the hog than I was at Ike's HQ, and, I thought, good for them.

We walked into the front room and Byrne was at the table with a cup of coffee and asked if I wanted one. I told him, "If you force it on me, I will not refuse," and I sat down at the same time as McBride did, while Byrne got up to get that cup of coffee for me.

When Byrne got back, I told the men the work at the site was not finished, but Venar and the two medics should be done in an hour or so. Actually, I told them the major work was done and on its way, and that Venar had caught a couple of things that I had missed. I told them that Venar was really sharp and they agreed. McBride told me that my appointment with General Weyland was set, my Sergeant Tiff had been shown the fastest route to Etain and that he would be here at 11:00 sharp to pick me up. And, I should be at Etain in plenty of time for my appointment. I looked at my watch and told them I had a few minutes to spare before I headed up stairs to clean up and change. I wanted them to know that I would be telling General Weyland about their help and upon my return to my HQ, I would make certain both General Vandenberg and General Eisenhower knew about their excellent help in solving this situation.

I asked McBride and Byrne if they knew what day it was and they both had it right. McBride told me it was a shame I did not have the time, as the villagers who belonged to *Le Souvenir Français* and *UNC* **(Union National Combatants)** had put together a memorial service that afternoon. Normally, the memorial service would have been held at the village's Great War Memorial at 11:00 sharp. However, today they had agreed to delay it, until as many as possible of the Americans could attend the service. McBride said, that all his off-duty personnel would be required to attend. I had observed *Le Souvenir Français* and the *Union National Combatants* in action during my earlier visits to France and I told the two men, I did wish I could stay. But it was time to get up to my room and get changed.

Byrne said he would run out to the crash-site in an hour and see how Venar was doing and McBride told Byrne there was no reason he couldn't go with him to see how the site looks today. I told the two men that I had talked to Venar about cleaning up and burning any personal stuff they might find before pulling in the guard. And that, I had purposely moved the guards out some distance to make certain they were far enough away from the crash-site that they would have no idea of what we had done. I did suggest they keep the guards at the crash-site until just before the memorial service and then withdraw them. McBride told me not to worry, it would all be taken care of and I should get up to the room, get cleaned up and ready to go. I left them at the table. Then, as I headed up the stairs, the Mayor's wife came in and told me my boots were clean and outside the door. I thanked her with my best French, complimenting her on her looks today. I left a blushing woman quickly making her way to the kitchen! Both McBride and Byrne

were following her with their eyes and then looking at each other, like they could not put that woman and the Mayor's wife in the same body.

Out in the woods, Venar cut the roots the other two men found as they dug. The two medics worked much harder than they would have, had he been sitting to one side. Within a half hour, Venar judged the hole was deep enough and the three men went to move the bodies to what would become a hidden grave.

About that time, I was coming down the stairs to find McBride, Byrne, the Mayor, and his wife sitting at the table. It was obvious I was supposed to stop and talk long enough to enjoy an aperitif with them. Sergeant Tiff was not due for a few minutes and it was the custom, so I sat down in the empty chair and watched as the Mayor took the Mirabelle liquor bottle and poured an extremely large drink for me. He and his wife were sporting large smiles and the Mayor told me, it was "Produit de Ferme." We lifted our glasses clinked around the table, said "Salute" and took a drink. All I can say is, "That if you ever swallow the 'Produit de Ferme' (Mirabelle), you may think you have just taken a drink of lighter fluid and someone has lit your mouth on fire."

I raised my glass again and toasted in French, "The good people of Hattonville, the 'Produce de Ferme', and France." The Mayor's wife let out what was almost a squeal. She clicked her glass to mine and then raising the glass, said "Salut" and downed a large part of her Cognac. That led to the Mayor offering a toast to the Americans for again winning back their "Liberty" and to the "AVIATEUR De Mort" in the Hattonville Woods. We clinked our glasses again. Thank heaven, as that stuff shot down my throat, I heard the car horn, as Tiff pulled up in front.

We all stood up and I said my goodbyes in English and in French. I told the Mayor, "That you are a very lucky man," and walking around the table, I kissed his blushing bride on both cheeks, as I had been taught and said, "Au Revoir." We all shook hands and I left the table, knowing that if I had any more of those "Mirabelle shots," I would fail to make my appointment with General Weyland.

As I was doing that, Tiff knocked, opened the door and enquired if I was ready? Then Tiff picked up my B-4 bag that I had placed in the entry way and walked out the door, picked up my very clean galoshes and went to put them in the open trunk of the car. As I came out, Tiff asked, "Do you want the front or back?" Because I was going to meet a General, I told him, "The back."

He opened the door and as I reached the bottom of the stairs and I got into the car, I was being followed down the stairs by the four who had been at the table. I waved goodbye as Tiff drove off, the last one waving was the Mayor's wife who was standing in the street and holding a white hanky in her waving hand. I looked at my watch and here we were, pulling out of Hattonville exactly 26 years after the Armistice of the Great War and the shooting stopped.

As we were leaving Hattonville, Zeman had arrived at the Limey Cemetery and was turning over to Graves Registration, the four official Burial Packages from the B-17 crash-site in the Hattonville Woods. The Graves Registration men helped unload the stretcher with its load of four Burial Packages. They had carried the

262

stretcher into the processing tent, when a grizzly old sergeant arrived. Immediately, the sergeant began to fill out forms that Zeman recognized from his previous trip to the Andilly Cemetery on the 16th of October, when he had delivered the remains of Pfc. James E. Ryder, a Battalion Ground Observer. Ryder had been killed on the 15th of October, by German artillery fire on the front line, Ryder's remains were brought to the Battalion Medical Dispensary and then taken to Andilly by Zeman. Upon seeing the sergeant again, Zeman knew he was filling out what was to become the finished, Report of Burial, record for each the four men's Burial Packages.

The old sergeant looked at each tag, filled out and signed by Major Venar, and asked Zeman a question or two. Then, as the sergeant continued to fill out his temporary form, other Graves Registration personnel removed the Personal Effects Bag's Medical Form 52b and repeated to the sergeant the information he was asking for. Then, they untied the knots holding the bundle together, and laid out the opened bundle. Then Graves Registration personnel would review the broken inventory item's's remains and then accept full responsibility for the non-functioning inventory from the Battalion's Medical Corps representative, Zeman.

Zeman had noticed on his previous Graves Registration trip that nothing seemed to phase these men. This time, he saw the same reaction and he realized from his own two-day experience, they had to harden themselves or each day's labor would become "A hell on earth!"

The bundles on the stretcher had been laid down, with the pilot's bundle the last one to be opened. As the men were reading out the information for the sergeant to record, he suddenly stopped and told the one man to repeat what he had just said. The man told the sergeant that there was only one Identity Tag attached to the man's Personal Effects Bag. Yet, when the fellow read the Form 52b tag to the sergeant, he had just said the tag stated, two Identity Tags had been recovered.

Now, this was a really big problem, while the GR men had not inspected the torn-apart remains that much, nor did they question what else the filled-in Form 52b and Personal Effect Bag stated, other than to tell the sergeant the remains did show fire damage consistent with the man's personal items. The old sergeant turned to Zeman and asked him, "How the hell, did you lose one of his Identity Tags?" Zeman sputtered and told the sergeant, "He had seen there were two Identity Tags with that man's remains at the crash-site and, as far as he knew, only their Surgeon who had signed the Form 52b had any access to the missing ID Tag." One thing Zeman thought for certain, he was not going to tell that old bastard they had put the stuff in a fire and they may have lost it that way.

(**Note**: Contacted before his death by the researcher, James T. Passman, Colonel, US Army Airborne Retired, a Captain at the time and the Commander of the Limey Temporary Cemetery, told the researcher, that sergeant was an "***Old Army Artillery Sergeant, who had been sent to them after being shell-shocked at the front*** and ***he went by the book.*** Any entry he had made was based on solid evidence or it would not be there.")

Zeman did not know that Boatman had lost the ID Tag in the mud and perhaps Boatman had not realized he had done so. However, Zeman did realize that the missing ID tag must be in the fire or mud at the site. Well, hell, there was no way he was going to end up out in those woods, searching though that mud and the fire for a missing ID Tag. So he told the sergeant again, the only thing he could think of was their Surgeon had kept that one ID Tag for some reason.

The sergeant knew that Captain James T. Passman, his 609th Graves Registration Company Commander would sign the final Report of Burial for this man, after the information from the temporary form had been transferred onto a typed form. He told the ambulance driver, who had brought the remains in with the missing ID tag, that he was going to enter a specific entry on this man's **Report Of Burial** stating, "*One identification tag, other removed by GR Officer, 19TC*."

That added line of type on the official Report of Burial of 1st Lt. Donald J. Gott, would in due time, along with the other keys, force me to write this book more than seventy years later. "So," thought Zeman, "big deal, as long it keeps me out of the mud and away from that crash-site." Besides, there was no reason he had to tell anyone back at the battalion and hell, he had been sworn to secrecy and this would be his own special secret.

When the finalized, **Report Of Burial** forms were signed by Captain Passman, both Lt. Gott's and Lt. Metzger's official "Cause of Death" were listed as: KIA, Burned Plane Crash. Dunlap's "Cause of Death" was listed as: KIA Plane Crash and Krimminger's "Cause of Death" is listed as: KIA Chute caught on plane.

In Hattonville Woods, Venar asked Berardi to grab the tarp the torn-apart remains had been on, take it over and place it in the bottom of the hole. At the same time, Boatman unfolded and locked one of the stretchers that had been left behind by Zeman and laid it close to the man who had been found lying dead in the bramble bushes. When Berardi came back, he and Boatman, with Venar helping, lifted the body up and moved it onto the stretcher. Berardi and Boatman lifted the stretcher and carried it to the completed hole, now to be a hidden grave. With Venar's help, they lifted the body from the stretcher and laid it in the western end of the new grave. They repeated the lift with the body with the badly broken right arm, placing it next to the first body and returned to carry the last body to the grave.

Despite all the care the three men had taken during the digging of the hole and the illegal placement of the first two bodies, the stretcher handles, the stretcher, and each of them were now covered with the very slippery clay.

When the stretcher was in position to place the third body on it, which happened to be the body of the pilot, 1st Lt. Donald Joseph Gott, they again slid the body onto the stretcher without a problem. Berardi, who was at the western end of the stretcher, the end on which the pilot's head was located, stood up when Boatman began to stand up. When Boatman said, "Okay, let's go," both men took the first step to begin the walk toward the common grave. Suddenly, Berardi found his left foot was caught in the suction of the clay and he stumbled. As he stumbled, his foot caught on the tarp that had been under the body and he fell forward, toward the stretcher and the body on it.

As Berardi fell, he was forced to drop the stretcher handles. As his end of the stretcher fell, due to the angle and with the shock of the stretcher handles hitting the ground, the pilot's body slid down and off the stretcher toward Berardi. There was nothing Berardi could do as it happened so fast. He was unable to stop the pilot's body as it slid down the angled stretcher. As his body started to slide, the pilot's damaged head slid between Berardi's legs. The body continued to slide, until the body's shoulders hit Berardi's ankles and shins, with the top of the dead body's head coming to a stop, a short distance from the edge of the fire.

Berardi had nothing to grab onto to regain his balance, as he fell forward onto the stretcher and the pilot's body still partially on the stretcher. As Berardi fell forward, his trapped left foot, forced his left knee onto the pilot's broken head. The pilot's damaged head was held together by his damaged flesh and the flight helmet. As the body slid downward toward Berardi, the helmet microphone cord got entangled in Berardi' left shoe. The cloth helmet was dragged off to the left side of the pilot's head by the pull of the cord.

At the same time, as the pilot's helmet was being pulled to the side, the pilots damaged head was being compressed by Berardi' left knee. With the added pressure of Berardi' knee pressing on the man's skull, the damaged flesh and cloth helmet was no longer able to hold the damaged head together. The right side of Gott's skull began to fall away from the head, taking flesh, hair, and brain tissue with each falling skull fragment. It happened much faster than it can be written.

Berardi managed to stop his fall by placing his hands on the stretcher frames before he fell full length on the pilot's body. With Venar's help, who as quickly as he could, grabbed at Berardi to help stop Berardi' fall. Berardi tried to steady himself as he attempted to swing his weight to be able to stand up. But Berardi' left foot remained trapped under the tarp and fallen stretcher. Venar continued to help Berardi stand upright, as Berardi worked to free his left foot and swing it over the pilot's body, so he could stand by himself. It took about fifteen seconds before Berardi could swing free and by that time, Boatman had lowered his end of the stretcher to the ground. The three men moved away from the stretcher to firmer ground and stood side by side, looking at the stretcher and the body partially laying on it.

As Berardi had maneuvered his foot to get it free, the pilot's microphone cord was freed from his shoe and now the helmet was pulled to the left side of the dead pilot's head. Immediately, they were looking at an oozing hole in the right side of the pilot's head, as some of his bloody skull fragments, covered with flesh, hair, and brain tissue had fell onto the very muddy floor of the woods.

All thee men were speechless for a short time and then Venar used a swear word, the only time the medics would ever hear him swear. With a loud exclamation, Venar said, "SHIT! What, a mess!" Then Venar looked at both men, and told them to forget he had ever said that and he told Berardi that it had not been his fault or Boatman's. It had just happened and he would help them get the body back on a stretcher. "First," he told them, "Let's wash our hands and use a clean stretcher to carry the body." In a few minutes, Berardi had opened another stretcher

and was ready to place it by the body, as Venar lifted the body's feet to allow Boatman to pull the muddy stretcher from under the body. When the body was flat on the ground, its head was fairly close to the fire. The body's remaining hair was starting to burn from the heat of the fire and they could smell it doing so.

Venar told Berardi to get the stretcher in place with the handles far enough from the fire to enable the stretcher to be lifted, once the body was on the stretcher. To Venar's credit, he took the oozing-head end of the body and the three men lifted the body and side-stepped to where they could lower the body onto the stretcher. When that was done, Venar told the men to take a smoke, while he recovered the skull fragments that had fallen free.

As Boatman had done, Venar looked for a couple of pieces of metal from the bomber to use to scoop up the skull fragments. Venar quickly found what he needed and he kneeled down by the skull fragments lying in the mud. Using one piece of metal as a spatula and the other as a tray, he moved the skull fragments, flesh, hair, and brain tissue onto the metal tray and then placed the recovered material on the dead pilot's chest. Venar stood up and looked at the place where the skull fragments had been located, and decided he had done a good job, as all he could see was fluid-stained mud on the floor of the woods.

Just below that fluid-stained surface, a newly buried three inch by one and one-half inch skull fragment was lost in the mud. That skull fragment, covered on one side with flesh and hair and on the other side with brain tissue, came from the skull area that was located just behind and above the dead Lt. Gott's right ear.

The skull fragment was buried, waiting to be found more than five decades later. **Less than a foot to the east, was 1ˢᵗ Lt. Gott's undamaged stainless steel Identity Tag and less than a foot to the west, in the ashes of the still burning fire, were several English Coins**. The English coins had been as undamaged as the Identity Tag, before they had been placed in the fire by Boatman.

(**Note**: Upon delivery of the skull fragment and Identity Tag to the American Army Mortuary Center in Germany, by the researcher and his wife, Carol, on May 26, 1998, David B. Roath, the Army's Germany Mortuary Center's Director, informed them that the skull fragment had been placed inside the earth within a very short time of death. From its condition, based on his experience, the skull fragment had entered the earth with the hair and flesh on the outside and brain tissue on the inside.

In addition, they were positive, the skull fragment had not been exposed to a fire or an explosion! This prognosis was based on the condition of the edges of the fractures that would have been damaged if the bone fragment had been in a fire or explosion.

That item of proof, along with the Burial Records and Disinterment Directives of Lt.'s Gott and Metzger, in addition to their Congressional Medal Of Honor Citations, *provide direct proof, beyond any dispute, the description of their crash and their death by explosive disintegration is false!*)

There were three men who did die, exactly as described in the *Congressional Medal of Honor Citations*! They were aboard the 36th Bomb Squadron (RCM)'s Top-Secret B-24J, "**226**," when it was shot at, crashed, and disintegrated, fourteen and one half hours after the "***Lady Jeannette***" had crashed, *while under full control of the pilots, in the Bois de Hattonville, leaving a debris-trail six hundred feet long, with three complete dead bodies, and one torn-apart dead body*!

Standing by the pilot's remains, now loaded on a new stretcher, Venar told the men he was ready when they were ready. This time, with cleaner hands, clay free handles, and firmer ground the three men made their way to the open hole and there, they slid the pilot's body into the shallow grave to lay next to his copilot. Unrealized by them, a skull fragment had fallen to earth, where it was trampled into the mud, waiting to be found by the Mayor and author over five decades later.

As soon as they had finished, Venar asked one of the men to take the stretcher back and bring the tarp that had been under the bodies for the past day. When Berardi got back with the tarp, Boatman and Venar helped him spread it over the bodies and tuck the edges down along their bodies to keep the fill dirt off them. When they were done, Venar asked the two men for a minute of silence in Honor of the Dead, then Venar repeated the Lord's Prayer.

When he was finished, Venar told the two men to start shoveling the dirt back into the grave. As they began, Venar looked toward the tail and saw the parachute harness lying where he took his new coat off the one dead crewman. He walked to it, picked it up and dragging a torn off shroud line, he carried it up and threw it in the hole, to be covered up, along with the remains. He watched for a while and then he relieved Berardi, who took a short break and relieved Boatman. Using that rotation, the three men had soon shoveled all the dirt they could into and on top of the grave.

When they had completed the shoveling, Venar told both men to use the shovels to help hold their balance while they climbed onto the new mound and tramped it down, as much as they could. As they did, Venar gathered some nearby leaves and when the men were done, he spread them around the fresh, trampled down dirt. Then Venar had the two men search through the fuselage parts for any items that should not be left to the French, who would certainly be crawling all over the aircraft the next day. It didn't take long before all the goods the men felt should be burned were on the fire. As they were completing that task, the men heard and then saw a jeep pull up. Soon McBride and Byrne arrived next to the fire to talk to Venar and just as they arrived at the fire, Zeman's ambulance pulled up and shortly, he joined the group of men at the fire.

McBride first asked Zeman how it had gone at the cemetery. Zeman replied, "Everything was fine, Sir." That is as far as Zeman was going to tell the truth. McBride told the men he wanted a final walk-through of the crash-site, beginning at the start of the debris-trail. They were to look for any remains and items that should not be left at the crash-site, as he was going to pull the guards back to the crash-site and then relieve them to attend the French memorial services.

To the West, at the Paris airport, S/Sgt. Robbins was being told his flight would leave at about 14:00 and he was to be back at the counter at 13:30, ready to board the airplane. With time to kill, he wandered around for a while, found a book, printed in English, lying on an empty bench and made himself at home, to allow the time to pass until he could get back to Deopham Green.

Over at the 109th, just a few miles away from the bodies were hidden in the woods, Fross had been visited by a nurse and then a doctor with a nurse in tow, and they had looked at his head for a while. They seemed to find nothing but some small, partially healed holes and the doctor asked him how he felt? Fross said, he was feeling fine. The doctor then asked Fross if he had been out of bed? Fross told the doctor, "They would not let him get out of bed and he needed to go to the can, BAD!" The doctor laughed and told Fross to go ahead and swing his legs out on the floor and see if he felt anything unusual when he sat up. Fross complied and said he had not felt any different. Then the doctor told him to stand up. When Fross started up, the doctor and nurse stood by him, and though he seemed a bit shaky as he stood, he needed no help. The doctor told Fross to put on the slippers under the bed. Fross put the first slipper on. His body stayed balanced as he shifted legs and raised each foot to slide it into a slipper, and again he needed no help. The doctor, then told Fross to walk a few feet and come back. As he walked, the nurse walked alongside him, however Fross did not need any help to maintain his balance. The doctor asked Fross, if he remembered the **FLAK** shell going off and the fragments entering his turret? Fross told the doctor, "I really didn't remember much after the first **FLAK** burst and seeing the fire streaming past me. All I can really remember, was the sudden panic of seeing that fire and thinking the B-17 was going to crash with me still in the turret.

Then he felt the turret begin to move, and he knew Robbins was going to help him get out. Then, suddenly, the world blew up on him, with the wind pouring into the turret and he could hear the pieces of something, whirling around and around and he had been very scared.

However, he soon felt the ball turret start to move again. As it turned and aligned with the belly of the B-17, he knew with Robbins' help he had a chance. What was really bugging him much more than that, was after he had gotten out of his turret, their tail gunner had opened his parachute inside the B-17 and he had been pulled out of their arms to end up trapped under the tail." Fross continued to tell them, "I had to bail out past the trapped and screaming Krimminger, to save my own life. And all I could do, was leave my friend, Krimminger, the Tail Gunner, to the fate of whatever happened to him. Once I hit the ground, I saw a Red Cross tent a short distance away and I walked to it. There, they had looked at me and sent me here."

The doctor asked Fross if he would feel comfortable helping the hospital staff, interpreting for the German POWs. Due to Patton's new push, they were now getting more wounded POWs than usual and they could really use his help. Fross didn't even think about it, he immediately said, "Sure Doc, I'd be happy to help."

The doctor told the nurse, to have the orderly bring the patient his clothes and they could put him to work with the POWs. As the nurse and doctor began to walk away, Fross told the doctor and nurse, "I really, really have to use the can, could they tell me where it was?" Laughing, the nurse pointed toward one end of the tent and both watched as Fross half walked and half ran in his slippers in the direction she had pointed.

As he was moving away, the doctor told the nurse to make certain everyone knew they were to look for any odd behavior from the man, as he had received a good shock and he still had some **FLAK** fragments in his head.

(**Note:** Many years later, when Fross had begun to progress into Alzheimer's disease, the flight engineer and the researcher visited Fross at home. As the researcher knew what happened that day, he and Fross had a long discussion of everything that happened. A short time later, Fross's wife, Mary, told the researcher that the Veteran's Hospital would not accept the metal fragments found in Fross's head as combat related and they would not help with his care. The researcher submitted his research to the family. The Veteran's Hospital accepted the research and helped with S/Sgt. Fross's care until his death.)

Within a half hour, Fross was pushing a German POW from one ward to another and he found himself in demand to interpret. As he helped, Fross thought to himself, "This is much better than being shot at in a B-17."

As Tiff pulled up to the XIX TAC Headquarters at the Etain Air Base, a captain came out to the car and asked Tiff, before I could get out, if I was in the car? Sgt. Tiff, answered the Captain's question, "Yes, Sir!" As Tiff started to get out to open the back door for me, the captain told him to stay put as he opened the rear car door, introduced himself, and told me he was there to take me to General Weyland. I got out and asked the captain where my driver could eat? He told me loud enough, so Tiff could hear, "The mess hall is a short distance down the street and off to the left." I told Tiff to go eat and be back in an hour, ready to leave.

The captain walked alongside me as we went into the headquarters, guiding me with a slight point of his right index finger. In about a minute, we were standing in front of a closed door on which the captain knocked. He stuck his head inside the door and told General Weyland I was there.

As I walked into the office, General Weyland was on his feet moving toward me, offering his hand and telling me it was good to see me again. We shook hands and he said he had made arrangements for the two of us to dine alone in a room down the hall and did I need to use the latrine, before we ate? I agreed I could wash my hands and we walked down a hall, where he showed me a toilet and told me he would be waiting when I came out. I thought that was rather nice of him.

When I came out, we walked a short distance and entered a medium size room with a table set for two and a side table with food and drinks on it. As Weyland, released the cook who was there, he told me he thought it would be easier

to serve ourselves. That way, we would not have to worry about the extra ears of a server when we talked. I said that sounded like a good idea to me.

We served ourselves, put our plates on the table, selected our drinks and sat down to eat. After we had started, Weyland asked me what the news was and I told him, looking at my watch that about this time the basic problem should be solved and now we would be faced with taking care of any loose ends that might pop up.

Weyland asked me about the 563rd and I told him they had been extremely helpful. Especially the Surgeon, Venar. He was an excellent man with an excellent mind and had helped me a lot. Weyland told me he had met the Surgeon once when visiting McBride and he would remember Venar's help.

I went on to tell him how helpful every one of the men had been and he could be proud of having that unit under his command. Weyland told me he would remember that during the next evaluation period. It was obvious to me that Weyland was waiting for me to volunteer information. However, I had already made up mind not to volunteer anything. I was only going to give an abbreviated response to any direct question he might ask. As far as I was concerned, it was a weakness in his control center and personnel that had caused this mess and now that it was clearing up, I was not going to provide any information that Weyland might use to excuse the un-excusable.

While we were eating, Weyland asked me if General Eisenhower believed the shoot down was purely an accident? Also, did General Eisenhower realize the friendly aircraft had flown into a Free-Fire Zone and then made a maneuver that was considered Unfriendly inside the Free-Fire Zone? I told him that General Eisenhower knew about the overflight and as far as I knew, he realized the shoot down was not the fault of your command. As Weyland did not ask me directly, I did not tell him that I thought his controllers should have held fire for a few minutes, to see what was going on with the suspicious target. It was obvious to me, if they were to understand how they had shot and damaged a friendly, they must appreciate how things could have turned out had they taken the extra time. Just, as they had, when suddenly they saw the other aircraft coming from the west, though some miles to the north and just outside the "Free-Fire Zone" begin the same maneuver. This realization should tell them, that the best decision would have been to hold fire until the suspicious target had been fully and correctly identified before authorizing any shooting.

There were no known Allied bombing targets within immediate range of the target when it turned, and it would have taken that aircraft a minimum of some additional minutes to reach any probable bombing target or to continue its turn to set up an attack on the supposed, incoming bomber stream. And certainly, there were no other aircraft, subject to an immediate attack by the suspected target.

And, they did have their P-61 right there, so they could have waited a few more minutes before shooting. Then, they would have realized it was not a German, even if it was in a Free-Fire Zone. However, that was my personal opinion and I doubted if Ike would ever ask me my opinion on that subject and I kept it to myself. Weyland asked me how it was going in setting this up, so it would never come out?

I told Weyland the same story I had told the men at Hattonville, this chain contained no weak link and I let it go at that.

When we had completed our meal, I asked Weyland if he needed anything else to make this go away? I reminded him that General Eisenhower's direct order included the fact that no units under his command were to have any documentation concerning either bomber. As it had been two days since the B-17 crashed, he needed to get one of his people, perhaps that captain, to check every daily report from his units that might have seen the B-17 before its crash, to ensure no official documents existed, that showed the B-17 crash ever happened. I told Weyland, I expected some of his unit's daily reports had already been forwarded and they had to ensure those records were altered, without letting his units know the records had been changed.

(**Note**: Within a few days, the radar battalion that had controlled the "Free-Fire" shoot down was disbanded and its personnel spread among other radar battalions. I will not claim direct credit for that, but believe my meeting with Weyland may have helped.)

(**Note**: Then 56 years later a record I missed, which the researcher found, proved three men drew rations at the 563rd SAW Battalion Headquarters when they were no accounted for in any other record as being there!)

Weyland assured me, he knew exactly what I meant, as his forward based 10th Photographic Reconnaissance Squadron Commander had reported the B-17 passing to their south and it had been seen by many of their people who had been on the runway looking for a late P-51. I asked Weyland if he could fix the problem or should I fix it? He assured me before he was finished, that the record would show the men were looking for the P-51, and the mention of the B-17 would be gone. I told Weyland that was exactly what was needed to be done and as we were finished and unless he had something else, I was heading back to my headquarters.

Weyland told me, "No ... that's all. I will walk you out to your car and see you off." When we came out into the light, there was the car with Sergeant Tiff leaning against the fender. When he saw me, he sprang over and opened the back door and stood there, waiting for us to arrive. As we approached the car, Tiff came to attention and saluted us, which we returned and then Weyland and I said goodbye to each other, shook hands, and I climbed into the car with Tiff closing the door after me. He snapped to attention again, saluted General Weyland, who returned the salute and Tiff walked around the car, got in, started it and we drove off. As the car began to move, Weyland turned around and headed back to his HQ.

It was now 13:05 as we left the XIX TAC Headquarters and in Hattonville Woods, the crash-site had been cleared to a point where the guards were being pulled in. The officers and medics were all walking out to the field and everyone was very pleased to be leaving this place in the Bois de Hattonville, ***where they had been told to remember, nothing had ever happened***.

For more than six decades some would continue their cover story, *"I have no memory of any bomber crash while I was at Hattonville."* Despite extensive proof of their participation in the events in the Hattonville Woods that is present for the whole world to read, these men continued to refuse to admit the B-17 crashed.

It is odd that the particular people officially responsible for the dead, who were with the dead, refused to admit the dead existed!

Once Tiff and I left the XIX TAC base, I told Tiff to pull over. I got out the back and into the front seat, and told Tiff we were going to have some fun this afternoon as we would be skirting the main east-west roads and doing the chicken-track roads again. "This time," I told Tiff, "you will allow me to drive a large part of it, as I know you have not seen what we will be passing."

We headed toward Verdun and turned right, onto the crown road on the hills along Verdun, where the Great War battle took place. I had Tiff pull over at the first wide spot, where he got into the passenger seat. As I drove, I gave him a running commentary of what we were seeing, as we drove to Fort Vaux for a quick turn around, then on the way back, I showed him the WWI crater where the Germans had executed French Resistance members a few months earlier. We passed Fort Souville and took a quick tour of the Ossuary, with all the bones visible in the grottos in its foundation. Then we drove out to see Fort de Douaumont, the most famous French Fort of the Great War, which the Germans had occupied for some time. After Douaumont, we stopped at the Trench de la Bayonets and Tiff and I walked around the memorial. There we saw the rifles and bayonets sticking out of the ground. As one legend goes, "Under the rifles and bayonets, the French Soldiers still stand, ready to defend their France."

We crossed the River Meuse at Bras-s.-Meuse, then onto le Mort Homme and Cote 304 with its skeletal monument. After that, I took him up the Butte de Vaquois for a quick walk up the south side of the hill. We stood on the French side at the top, to look into the sixteen great craters that blew up there during the four years the Germans and the French fought there about 200 feet from each other. I told Tiff, about one German who was my uncle, and one of the French, who was also an uncle. And how, they had tried every method they could to kill each other, including the mines. Then in September 1918, in two hours, the American 35th Division flowed around the hill, making the four years battle on the hill, moot.

From there, I took him through Varennes-en-Argonne. I showed Tiff the house where King Louis XVI, and Queen Marie Antoinette were taken prisoners before they were beheaded in Paris. Just after we crossed the bridge at the bottom of the hill, I pointed down the first side street to the east, where Senator (soon to be Vice-President), Truman's artillery unit had been during the Meuse-Argonne Battle.

From there, we passed by Cheppy on our way to the Butte de'Montfaucon, to visit the large American Memorial there. Then we stopped at Nantillois to see the building the American 315th Infantry gave the village and the Pennsylvania Fountain Memorial. At *"Madeleine Farm,"* we visited the small German Cemetery. Then we went on to the American Meuse-Argonne Great War cemetery. Which I suppose, I should now be describing, as the World War One, American

Meuse-Argonne World Cemetery. We did not have the time to properly visit the American cemetery located just outside Romagne Gesnes. However, I did point out the grave of Lt. Frank Luke, the ***Congressional Medal Of Honor*** World War One Pilot. Then we headed west to Chatel-Chehery, where I showed Tiff the place where Sergeant Alvin York had earned his ***Congressional Medal Of Honor***. On our way west from there, we saw the hillside where the "***Lost Battalion***" was 'lost.'

Next, we drove through Autry, then through other small villages to Sommepy-Tahure and then on west to the Mont-Blanc American World War One Monument. We stopped for a few minutes to enjoy its fine view over the large, open fields in that part of France, that is so unlike the wooded countryside we had just passed through. At Mont-Blanc, I switched back to letting Tiff drive and I continued to tell him the history of the other memorials we drove by.

Sergeant Tiff told me he was amazed at my knowledge of this area of France and I told him I owed it all to the Great War Veterans in my mother's and father's families, who took us to see their battle fields before the Depression stopped our trips. Tiff said he was very happy that I thought enough of him to take the extra time to show him what he was seeing today. I told Tiff, I was getting as much pleasure as he was, as I was remembering very good times as we traveled along these roads, I last traveled with my relatives.

It took about an hour from there, at Tiff's speed, to reach the headquarters, where I told Tiff to stop by the Operations Center, while I checked to see if I would need him any more today. I told Tiff, he could head to the mess hall or he could sit around for a while. However, if I didn't need him any longer, on his way to the Motor Pool he was to drop my stuff off at the BOQ. He laughed and asked if I was afraid he might steal my uniforms and galoshes? As Tiff and I were greatly different in size, I told him he would not look all that good to the girls if he could not button anything and he had a gap in his coat, shirt and pants, even if he was supposed to be a colonel.

Tiff, laughed and said he would wait right there for a half hour and if I had not given him my status by then, he would come find me. I told Tiff that was great and I got out and walked to operations while Tiff slumped down in the seat and tried to sleep.

I walked into the operations center and found the same duty officer as before, who said he was surprised to see me back so soon and I said to him, "Brother, you have no idea. I'm surprised to be here myself." I asked him for the General's location and if he had heard anything from anyone asking for me or leaving a message. He said that he hadn't ... as far as he was concerned it had been really nice while I was gone and he had almost forgotten about me, before I showed up today like the proverbial bad penny.

"Yuck, yuck," I said, as I went to see what my section had come up with while I had been gone. Patton's new drive was going well. Monty, was going very slow after his Market Garden debacle. It was slow in the Ardennes and the Seventh Army was moving along. Otherwise, it was a normal day during the war.

After, I had decided to go tell Tiff to take the car back. I found him sitting up when I walked to the car and he leaned over and rolled down the passenger side window to hear what I was going to say. I told him to go ahead and check back in but I was expecting some travel to the same areas in the next day or two and would ask for him if I went. Tiff, said he would drop off my bag and boots, and thanks for the interesting time. This, he told me, was the fastest trip he had ever made in France, in more ways than one, and he did enjoy riding with me. We laughed. I waved through the window and headed for my own office, as Tiff pulled out.

Up at Tincourt-Boucly, the villagers were talking to each other about the strange Americans who were staying in the village hall and eating and drinking at the café. All of them spoke excellent French and none of them had the usual marks of rank and units that all the other Americans wore.

Each housewife talked to her neighboring housewife, as did their husbands out in the fields. Already, the village buzz was all about two of the men visiting each house and asking to see any souvenirs they may have from the "Avion Fortress, B-17" crash. The great thing was, for each souvenir they took, they gave the family a full pack of American cigarettes. Even if the family being visited did not have any of the souvenirs of the "Avion Fortress, B-17" the Americans were seeking, they would give the family a pack of cigarettes for each adult as they left.

Across France, where the two bombers had crashed, things began to settle down. That afternoon, the four official Burial Packages that had been delivered to the Limey Cemetery via Zeman's ambulance were buried in their now official graves, 162, 163, 164, and 165.

The "*Lady Jeannette*" had crashed about 18 miles from the Limey Cemetery. Yet it had taken the buried crew remains, two days and four hours to be buried after their death. Meanwhile, the partial remains from the Top-Secret B-24 site had been illegally buried within fourteen hours of their death, more than one hundred and fifty miles from where they died.

I did place my call to General Eisenhower and when he came on the line, I told him the mission appeared to be accomplished, but I was going to have to follow-up at some places. However, I would let him know about that during our next meeting. General Eisenhower asked me about the men involved and I told him I thought we had a very strong chain without a weak link in it. "Great Colonel," he replied, "and if that was all, he had to get going and he would see me as soon as he could, for a full report." I heard the line go dead and I hung up my phone.

About that time in England, Robbins was starting to look for the next leg of transportation on his way back to Deopham Green.

I headed back to my quarters, took a long hot shower, dressed in a clean uniform and went to the "O" Club (Officers Club) to see if anyone was there with whom I could exchange BS until dinner was served.

That night across France, many of the conversations in some small villages were about the "Avion Fortress, B-17" that had crashed nearby. At most of the American camps and bases the crashed "Flying Fortress" came up between drinks

274

of whatever, or as the personnel were eating their meal. Then at most of those places, it began to fade from memory.

There was only one place where the conversation was fairly heated, and that was unusual. General Weyland had received a call from General Patton's Chief of Staff's Aide, inviting Weyland to visit General Patton's quarters that night for dinner and drinks and to join with General Patton and his Chief of Staff, General Hobart R. Gay, in celebrating the 26th Anniversary of the end of the Great War. Gay had been commissioned as a 2nd Lt. on 26 October 1917, and, unlike Patton, Gay had no chance to serve overseas during World War One. So Weyland knew it was going to be Patton's night of memories.

Weyland was younger than the other two and he knew, he would be hearing a lot about General Patton's World War One exploits, such as his tank unit's success during the St-Mihiel Battle and then, how Patton had been shot in the ass during the later Meuse-Argonne Battle. Weyland must have thought to himself, that from what he had heard, Patton might even pull down his pants to show him and Gay where he had been wounded. Then Patton would tell them, that was the real reason some people called him a "half-assed General."

Weyland and Patton were known for "killing a bottle of good bourbon" between them and Patton often referred to Weyland, ... "as the best damn General in the Army Air Corps." That night, General Gay in attendance, Weyland must have expected it to be a good night of listening to each of them reminisce.

During the meal, Patton, Gay, and Weyland discussed the success of the new drive toward Metz and made the usual small talk. After the dinner, they continued to drink and Patton regaled them with his numerous stories of his service in this area during the Great War and his travels afterwards in France, studying and writing about the war. It was getting late and Patton, who referred to Weyland as "Opie." was walking around the room talking about the 26th Anniversary and their being in France again, to get the "French's nuts out of the fire" for the second time.

Then all of a sudden, General Patton walked over to and stood in front of Weyland. Patton leaned over until his face was right in Weyland's face. In a change of voice, from what had been parlor talk to a voice with a tinge of anger, General George S. Patton asked General Otto P. Weyland, "Opie, what the hell is going on in your outfit?"

"Damn it," Patton said to Weyland, "I hear your unit shot down a Top-Secret friendly last night. What makes you think I would not hear about that crash, and the crash of some B-17 at Hattonville?" Patton continued, "Hell "Opie," my tank unit went through Hattonville at the end of the St-Mihiel battle, and you think my other units around your units, are not going to report back to my headquarters?"

General Weyland suddenly felt a chill run down his back and before he could say anything in reply, Patton continued, "Opie," you know damn well that I have big enemies up there. Hell, the only reason I am here, is Ike couldn't pull his own ass out of the fire and he had to call me back here to do it for him. Well "Opie," just so you will know, I have some friends in high places and low places

and I do not understand how you could get involved in this mess without telling me about it as it was going on!"

Weyland said, "George, I was brought into this by the bastards that shot too soon at an unknown aircraft in a free-fire zone. There was nothing I could do about it and after it was done, the shit came down from Ike's staff. General Vandenberg specifically ordered me not to tell anyone about what was going on. There was nothing I could do and I did not know, that you did not know all about it."

"Look, George," Weyland continued, "you have to give me the benefit of the doubt here. I was sworn to secrecy by people who can ruin my career and I don't need this." General George S. Patton looked at his drinking buddy, General O. P. Weyland and said, "Opie, one of these days, you are going to have to get off the damn fence, and either be on my side or the side of that SOB at Reims."

"Right Hap?" Patton asked Chief of Staff, General Gay. Hap answered in the positive and Patton told the two men, "Drink up and let's kill this bottle and get you on your way." Patton reminded "Opie." that he knew a hell of a lot more than those bastards think I do."

As General Weyland left Patton's quarters that night, Weyland knew I was going to be unhappy, General Vandenberg was going to be unhappy and by God, General Eisenhower was going to be very unhappy when he learned of this. Weyland had time to think, as his car headed back to his quarters, and he decided, I had better report this up the line the first thing in the morning.

At the 109th Evacuation, Harms was still sleeping, scheduled to be woken up the next day and Fross was deep in sleep, after a day of helping German POW patients and interpreting for the hospital staff. In Paris, Harland was enjoying another night, wondering at the same time how he could extend this another day?

In his hospital train, sitting on a sidetrack at St-Lo, still on its slow path to the port, Gustafson was sleeping, waking up, and trying to scratch places he could not reach and then drifting back into a troubled sleep.

At the 397th, the survivors of "**226**," were waiting for the next day, talking to no one, not even among themselves, about what had happened. As hard as it is to believe, it was not until fifty-four years later, that any of the crew seriously talked to anyone about the men's death, when the researcher asked about the men who died and what may have led to their death.

They had talked to the son of another squadron member, who was writing a book about the squadron some years before. However, they had never discussed among themselves what had happened during that half hour before they crashed.

It was not until the researcher contacted him again, in May, 2007, that the Pilot, Joseph Hornsby, learned he had been shot down by the "**Friendly Fire**" from a P-61 Black Widow Night Fighter belonging to the 425th Night Fighter Squadron and not German **FLAK**, as he had been told by his squadron commander in 1944.

Meanwhile, in a military cemetery in Belgium, in a field and woods in France and in a military cemetery in France, the desecrated dead waited. Wondering if the truth of what was done to them, would ever be known.

Thus ended 11 November, 1944, the 26th Anniversary of the end of the Great War, and suddenly, the very strong chain of involved men I had forged, contained an uninvited, extremely weak link, as far as I was concerned.

(**Note**: One night in January 2007, before he located me, the researcher was plotting out, known locations and facts about "**226**", such as the known "**226**" crash-site; the pilot verified, plane speed of 160 mph; the 30 minutes between the flashes on their engines, and when "**226**" hit the earth at Tincourt-Boucly. Once he had plotted those facts on a French map, he realized that it was impossible for "**226**" to had been hit by German FLAK, it had to have been "**Friendly Fire?**"

A short time later, the researcher realized, that no one, Hornsby, Danahy, or the families of the men who had survived and later died, had ever mentioned the large bang and gravel sounds of anti-aircraft fire hitting an aircraft. After verifying that fact with Hornsby, the researcher, who was himself a radar operator, and Nike Hercules Fire Control Maintenance Technician at one time, used his knowledge of radar to contact veterans of the WWII SAW Battalions. After a few requests in their reunion association newsletter "***SAWBUCK***," in May, 2007, an article writer and the editor of the newsletter, both remembered the time they had been told about the units to the south, shooting down a friendly Mosquito with a "Black Widow."

Suddenly, a lot fell together. The 566th SAW Battalion had been suddenly disbanded within days of the shoot down and then, there were the P-61 fighters seen at Etain on 9 Nov. 1944 (reported to the researcher, in 1994, by S/Sgt Robbins), when many official records state, none were there. Then checking the weapons carried on a P-61 Black Widow, the flashes on the engines, suddenly fit exactly to what other pilots described, when they shot at aircraft with exploding cannon shells or received such fire themselves. **It was now obvious, that "226" had been shot down by the "*Friendly Cannon Fire*" from a P-61 Black Widow night fighter, instead of German FLAK**. This new information was too late for Danahy, who had completed his "Final Transfer" a few years earlier. In the end, of all the survivors of the Hornsby Crew, only Command Pilot Hornsby, of the Top-Secret B-24, "**226,**" was to know the truth!

The author found some members of the 10th Photographic Reconnaissance Squadron who remembered watching the B-17 pass a few miles to the south of their base and seeing the smoke when it crashed. They had been looking for a P51 on a photographic mission that was late. It had been shot down and not all that many years ago, there was report of its crash site in Germany being discovered.

Certainly, an AAF unit would have recorded another AAF aircraft in distress. However, the 10th did not and no one Fighter Squadron in the XIX TAC has any record that mentions the B-17.)

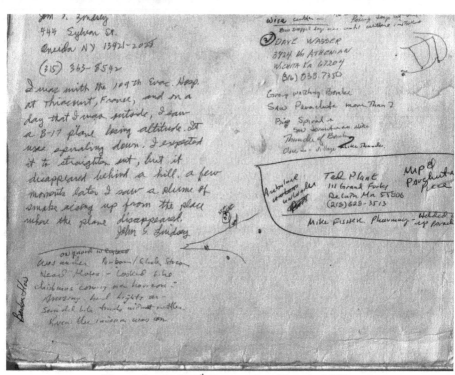

The author's 109th Evacuation Hospital File.

The file's cover contains interaction with members of the 109th Evacuation Hospital Reunion Association. The author and his wife attended several of their reunions before the end came near and "Final Transfers" took command. In an emergency, the file cover acted as the location of notes from John S. Lindsey, verifying his viewing of the crash of a B-17.

Ted Plant, who unloaded two of the flyers, who with the help of Mike Fisher, cut up one of the flyer's parachute for a souvenir for each of the unit members. Ted ended up with two souvenirs that he later presented to the author.

Dave Wasser watched it crash and like Lindsey, he felt hopeless and unable to help the people who might die during the crash.

John Lindsey also added his experience as a guard on "D-Day." The 109th was still in England and stationed under the Airborne/Glider stream heading for Normandy. "Looked like Christmas coming over the horizon. Amazing headlights on (remember, he was, in effect, a ground pounder with no aircraft experience). Sounded like trucks without mufflers, knew the invasion was on.

Getting to know the members of the 109th, opened up so much new information in finding absolute proof that the medal applications had been falsified by someone with the juice to "get it done!"

Scanned by Willis S. Cole, Jr.

Chapter Thirteen
Problems and Cleaning Up
Loose Ends

At the 729th Bombardment Squadron, 452nd Bombardment Group, Deopham Green, England, 2nd Lt. Gerald W. Collins was being shaken awake from a deep sleep and as he woke up, he recognized S/Sgt. Robbins, his crew's waist gunner. Collins knew Robbins had been aboard Gott's B-17 when it crashed in France two days ago. Collins realized Robbins was very distraught and that he wanted to tell Collins about what had happened when the *"Lady Jeannette"* crashed. Collins looked at the clock on the small table next to him and saw it was 01:08, which would make it 12 November, 1944.

The two men talked the rest of the night, after Collins told Robbins, he had heard that Gott, Metzger, Dunlap, and Krimminger had died in the crash. Robbins told Collins that he knew Krimminger had to have died, but he had hoped some of the others would have survived. Robbins told Collins of the fire under the right wing when the first **FLAK** shell tore off their number-four engine and the second **FLAK** shell that had done so much damage to the bomber and the men. Robbins told Collins how scared he had been when he realized the number-one engine had stopped, the number-two was running rough and slow, with smoke pouring from that engine, while the fire under the right wing was blowing all the way past the tail.

During the night, Robbins told Collins how he, Fross, and Krimminger, were certain they were going to crash after the 2nd **FLAK** shell hit the B-17. Robbins admitted, they wanted to get out, but did not go on their own once Gott and Metzger had managed to get the B-17 under control. Even then, Robbins told Collins, if he had not found Dunlap so badly wounded, he was certain they would have left the B-17, while it was still over Germany.

However, when Robbins was helping Dunlap, the copilot had come back, followed by an officer he did not know. Robbins realized that meant Gott was flying the B-17 by himself and Robbins decided they should ride it out until they were told to bail out by Gott. Then, before they had been told to bail out, Krimminger accidently opened his chute and when he was pulled out and the bomber seemed to be stalling, Robbins had told Fross to get out and he followed Fross out. He had landed in some woods and he heard the bomber crash fairly close. Then he was picked up by a man in a jeep and was taken directly to an airbase at Etain, near Verdun. He was debriefed at a headquarters there and they put him on a small plane to Paris, where he spent two nights before getting a flight back to England. Since his arrival in England, he had been in transit to the base. As soon as he got back, he had found Collins to tell him what had happened.

That early morning, Collins described to Robbins what he and the other crews had seen and then thought, as the *"Lady Jeannette"* had staggered, with the blowtorch of flames suddenly appearing at the right wing. Then their B17 had

started what had seemed to all of the observers, to be a final spiral to the ground. Then, just when it seemed impossible to all of them, they saw the B-17 come out of the spin as the pilots regained control. During that early morning, when Collins was telling Robbins what he had seen, and based on what Robbins had just told him, Collins determined he was going to visit the squadron and group commanders and ask that a medal be awarded to both Gott and Metzger for their heroism.

When the mess hall opened, Collins told Robbins they had better go get breakfast as Robbins would have to report in to their squadron commander when the headquarters opened after breakfast. Collins added that he would go with Robbins to meet the squadron commander, and they made arrangements to meet after eating breakfast and go to their headquarters, so Robbins could report and tell his story.

At General Eisenhower's headquarters, I had just arrived at my office when a call came in from General Gay, Patton's chief of staff. Ever since General Gay, with General Eisenhower's help, became Patton's chief of staff, Gay had been reporting to me whenever he felt that Patton might be going to make one of his famous blunders by talking, when he should just shut up. This time, when I heard what Gay told me, I knew at once there was now a good possibility that Patton would become a major problem some time in the future. I thanked General Gay for the head's up and I asked him, if anyone else had heard Weyland's discussion with Patton about the Top-Secret plane? Gay assured me that no one else had heard that statement and he would be certain to let me know if Patton ever referred to the subject again. I told General Gay that I had an appointment that day with General Eisenhower, and I would make certain he knew about Gay's report. I thanked Gay for keeping me up to date and I hung up. "Damn!" I thought, "Sometime in the future this could throw a big monkey wrench in what I had just done." There was no way I could keep this from General Eisenhower. Patton apparently knew a lot about what had gone on. "Christ," I thought, "and here I had been telling everyone that we had a strong chain. Now that Patton's in the chain, being the blowhard he is, ***Patton is an obvious threat to the long-term success of the plan!***"

At their headquarters, S/Sgt. Robbins repeated his story to their Squadron Commander and Squadron XO, while Lt. Collins stood by, providing moral support. Once Robbins was done with his story, the squadron commander told him he was going to be sent to a rest home for a while and when he reported back, they would review his situation.

After Robbins was gone, Lt. Collins told the squadron commander that he had been a witness to Gott and Metzger efforts to save their bomber and crew over Saarbrucken. Collins insisted he wanted to know what he had to do to make certain Gott and Metzger would be given a medal for what they had accomplished. Then Collins asked, his Squadron Commander for a joint meeting with the Group Commander to discuss the awarding of medals to Gott and Metzger.

During that meeting, Lt. Collins told both commanders, they knew that Gott was his normal pilot and they also knew Gott was a hell of a pilot. However, it had to have taken both Gott and Metzger working together, to make it back to France with the damage the B-17 had suffered extensive damage that had been observed

by many other crewmen on the group mission that day. Now they had a witness from inside the B-17 to support the heroism of Gott and Metzger.

The Group Commander told Collins, with Robbins return and with what he had heard, he was now certain that Robbins had been one of five crew survivors and four of the Gott crew had died in the crash. However, there was a major problem with what S/Sgt. Robbins had just told them. The Commander said he had received a message from the Eighth Air Force Headquarters and it stated that their B-17 had crashed east of Abbeville, which was a very long way from Verdun. In addition, he had been told that Gott's B-17 had dived toward earth, exploded once, then exploded again during the crash and the B-17 and it's dead had disintegrated.

With that major different information, the group commander told Collins, he had heard his request and he would keep it in mind until the whole story was known when the other survivors returned. Lt. Collins left the Commander's office feeling unsatisfied and very determined to keep pressure on the Commander to get Gott and Metzger a medal.

When Collins and Robbins arrived at the 729th Headquarters to see their Squadron Commander, Lt. Harms was waking up at the 109th Evacuation Hospital and it was somewhat strange. As he came out of his deep sleep, he was walking up toward the wing and the tail in the crater on a slope in some woods in France, and suddenly he was waking up here in what had to be a hospital, with no idea of how long he had been here.

As Harms moved his body, he felt a pressure between his left arm and his side. When he twisted to move the covers, so he could see what was causing the pressure, he saw something on his pillow and when he could focus on it, he saw it was a Purple Heart Medal. Then, as he lifted his covers, he was very surprised to find a large bottle tucked between his body and left arm.

Harms was looking at the bottle when a woman's voice said, "We're happy to see you waking up Lieutenant, how do you feel?" He thought for second and then Harms told the nurse, he seemed to be okay and he asked her how long he had been there? She told him that the chart showed he arrived on the 9th and this was the 12th. A bit surprised, he asked if he was wounded where he could not see it or feel it? The nurse told him he was not wounded, but they thought he might have been concussed. Then Harms asked the nurse about the bottle and what was in it? The nurse said that one of their officers had put the bottle there. He had instructed the lead nurse that the bottle had better be there when the man came around, and if he wanted, it was to leave the hospital with him. She went on to tell him it was a magnum bottle of Cognac. Now, she had to go and tell the doctor that he was awake. As she left, she told Harms that he could expect the doctor very soon.

With that, she called over an orderly and told him to help the fellow with whatever he needed and make certain the bottle remained with him.

In another ward, S/Sgt. Fross, was pushing a POW in a wheelchair through the ward at the same time two doctors were looking at an X-ray and discussing his case. The flyer had most likely been concussed by the explosion of the German **FLAK** shell and he had several small fragments of the shell metal in his head.

However, the doctor's main job was to get an inventory item's (ours, theirs, or other) damage under control, make certain the inventory item was stable, and then move them up the hospital repair chain for further treatment of their damage.

As they studied the X-ray, the doctors discussed the size and location of the shell fragments in the man's skull. They were small-to-tiny fragments and they were embedded in his skull, but had not penetrated it. They reviewed the treatment he had received after his arrival and saw the treatment of the small **FLAK** wounds included light probing and an attempted magnetic removal. That meant he had received the treatment level he should have received. So, that was it for now and the next higher hospital could make the decision on the shell fragments. What they had to do now, was to consider his current mental situation, concerning the possible concussion, his treating doctor told the other doctor. The man did not seem to be suffering from the shell fragments or concussion. In fact, the patient was acting like there were no head wounds. He seemed to be having no problem functioning and he appeared to be very happy helping the staff with the POWs and interpreting between the staff and POWs.

With that, the two men decided to watch him until the afternoon transport up the line was about ready to leave. Then, since he was "walking wounded," the decision to move him could be made and put in action in minutes, as long as his paper work was ready. By that time, Fross had the POW back in his bunk and was on his way to help another orderly, happy to be helping, and feeling good.

At the Officer's Transit BOQ in Paris, Lt. Harland woke up, thought of the great time he had the night before with what's her name, and he was thinking how he could delay his shipment back to England another day? And, what a great story to tell the boys when he got home. No need to hurry back now that he was in Paris.

Meanwhile, Gustafson was still lying in his bunk on the train. After it had left Paris, traveled slowly for a while and then continued stopping again and again, with some patients being taken off the train and others put in their place. When Gustafson asked the nurse how long he was going to be on the train? She finally told him what no one had really explained to him before. His treatment record stated that his wound had consisted of a **FLAK** fragment badly cutting his leg and cutting out a one inch section of his right leg bone above the right ankle. In fact, he had been very lucky, in that the fragment had been very sharp, it made a clean wound, and it had been very hot, so it sealed most of the blood vessels it had cut. Best of all, it had missed the major blood supplies to his foot. That meant, he would not lose his foot and with proper treatment, he would be able to walk again. But, with the missing bone, he would have a limp for the rest of his life.

The bad news was the nurse told him, it had been determined this type of wound could not be treated at the lower levels of the hospital treatment chain. This meant he was on the train until it reached the Port of Cherbourg, where he would be put on a hospital ship to England. In England, they would take off his cast to review his wound and make the next decision there. However, she added, from what she had seen, he would be on his way back home after some time in the hospital in England. "Damn," thought Gustafson, "well, there was nothing he

could do about it but lay there and wait and hate the itches in places he could not reach." But, being himself, Gustafson thought he might as well make the best of it. So, he flashed that smile at the nurse and asked if she could reach one, special itch that was really bothering him.

Meanwhile, as I had already made arrangements for my private meeting with General Eisenhower, *I knew I had to pass on some news that was not good and would probably continue to be a problem until it could be overcome some time in the future.*

At the Péronne A-72 Air Base, Lt. Hornsby was very happy to be released from the hospital and the "butt holes" who had given him very little service. He was given transport to the quarters where his crew was, and once they had brought him up to date, he was taken to the same quarters where Lt. Casper was staying. Casper told Hornsby that the Commander, a Colonel Coiner, had requested they come to the headquarters and see him as soon as Hornsby was released.

After lunch, they made their way to Coiner's officer and told the sergeant that Colonel Coiner had asked them to report and here they were. Colonel Coiner saw the men at once and told them, with Hornsby out of the hospital he would check on their transportation back to England.

As soon as the men left his office, Coiner put in a call to me and asked what I thought he should do with them. His thought, Coiner said, was he would send them down to Paris to the Le Bourget, A-54C Air Base, where they could get a flight out tomorrow. I asked Coiner, if the men knew exactly where the crash had happened? He told me from what he understood, the copilot did not know and the pilot had mentioned Dreux, where his unit had been last month. Col. Coiner said the only way he could think the pilot had the actual crash location so wrong, was that someone at the hospital had given him the wrong location either on purpose or by forgetfulness. None of the crewmen seemed to have the name of the village.

"That's great," I said to Coiner, "here is what you do. Put them in a truck with a cover on it and let's get them moved around France a bit, until they have no idea of where they crashed. Then, check with General Vandenberg and set up a schedule with him, to get them back no earlier than the 18th." "That way," I continued, "by the time they get back, I will have it under control at their squadron and they will be unable to change what the record will show." Coiner, told me that he had a couple of friends at the Chateau where Rommel had been and he would send them there in the morning and make the arrangements I suggested with Vandenberg. I did realize, that I could have asked Coiner to send them directly to England, either on one of the Courier C-47's that landed at his base every day or on one of his B-26's, but that would put them back too soon and tie a direct line to where they had crashed. "So," I said to myself, "there is no reason to do something stupid like that, right?" And, I agreed with myself, "Right!"

I was just leaving for my meeting with General Eisenhower, when the security phone rang, and the operator said he had a telephone call for me, from a General Weyland. I took the call and listened to Weyland's excuse for telling Patton more than he should. I could understand why he did it, but that was not an

excuse. As far as I was concerned, Weyland should have told that loud mouth that he was unauthorized to tell him anything and that he should contact General Eisenhower and talk to him about it. But Weyland had spilled the beans and now, I expect, in due time I will get an emergency call about cleaning up Weyland's mess before we all slipped and fell on our ass because of his mess.

I had my appointment with General Eisenhower to keep and I went into the operations center to tell the operations officer what my needs would be for the next week - and you know, who it was! It ended the same way, with him not too happy and me telling him I will tell him the whole story later. I guess today, I have to wonder if he is still alive to learn what it was all about?

During my meeting with General Eisenhower, I dropped the bomb about Patton, knowing about Weyland's involvement and that Weyland had told Patton all he knew. Then I told General Eisenhower that I was certain I had done a fairly good job of compartmentalizing Weyland and the rest, and that Patton had enough on his mind right now, so by the time he thought much about it, he should not be fully aware of all we had done. General Eisenhower was unhappy with that, but he realized the worst thing he could do was to take any action against Weyland.

I told General Eisenhower the last two days had gone well, in that the additional remains of the three dead men at that the B-24 crash-site had been successfully hidden, as had the three bodies at the B-17 crash-site. I did tell General Eisenhower about how helpful the three officers had been at the B-17 crash-site, and that the Surgeon, Major Venar, was a damn good man. He had caught a couple of small mistakes that might have led to someone asking questions in the future, and I would recommend him highly for promotion. General Eisenhower told me to give him a list of all the officers involved - just their names, rank and unit - no more, no less. As long as it went well, in due time he would see they received their reward.

Then, I told General Eisenhower, I had helped dig the hidden grave for the three bodies at the B-17 crash-site and there were some really good enlisted men involved. General Eisenhower told me, he felt there would be too much risk in his doing anything direct for the enlisted men. **However, he would ensure the officers and enlisted men involved, were all taken of the hook if it ever became known what we had done. He continued, "You and I, will take the full blame, right Colonel?" "Yes, General," I replied! Now, as I tell the story of what we were all involved in, who is left but me?**

"What's next," General Eisenhower asked? I told him my current plan to take care of any loose ends that might reveal what had already been accomplished so far. Then, I told him, that I thought Colonel Coiner could handle his unit's documents on his own. However, I was afraid that Weyland's man might not get it done. So it was my plan to conduct a surprise paperwork inspection, with General Vandenberg's help, and go review all the official documents for the XIX TAC's and Ninth Air Force's units that might have been involved in any way. That way, I could ensure all the records that might show something about either plane would no longer do so. As I expected I would be done with that by the 16th, then I would then fly to England, taking my own driver with me. I would get a car there and go to the

284

involved group and squadron to ensure their official documents stated what the units had been told to have them state.

I told General Eisenhower that I thought it would take no more than four days in England and I should be back to the headquarters by the 20th or 21st.

We discussed the loose ends a bit more and General Eisenhower told me, "Make it happen and report back to me when you return." He added that he had talked to Arnold, Spaatz, Doolittle, and "Bomber" Harris and he would let them know what I was going to do. So far, he assured me, there has been no permanent documentation trail anywhere other than the minimum required to account for the dead men. He told me that Donovan had to be paid off, but it was going to happen anyhow, in due time. General Eisenhower concluded by telling me, "He felt it was going to work as long as nothing else came up; that is, **if Patton will keep his mouth shut in the future!**"

I could not disagree and I had to tell General Eisenhower, "*Of all the men involved, the only one whom I thought would be a weak link in our chain of involved people, was General Patton,*" and with that we ended the meeting.

My first stop after that was the motor pool and a talk to the OIC (Officer in Charge), and the Motor Pool Sergeant. I asked where Sergeant Tiff was and they told me they could have him here in a few minutes. I told them exactly what I was going to tell Tiff. All the Trip Tickets and any reference to anything that Tiff might have done were to be destroyed and forgotten when we were done, doing what we were doing - and that I wanted the same car and Sergeant Tiff until the 21st.

When Tiff arrived, I told Tiff what I had told them and that he would be with me until the 21st, under the same terms, if that was okay with him. He agreed at once and I told the others to set Tiff up with anything he needed. As I left, I told them, Tiff and I would be leaving early in the morning for the Verdun area and then we would end up in England for a few days. I asked Tiff, if the wrong side of the road thing would be a problem and he told me he had put a lot of miles on in England and had not had any problems before. "Great," I told him, "I will see you in the morning at 08:00," and I left the three of them, with two of them being a bit dumfounded about what was going on.

That afternoon at the 109th, S/Sgt. James O. Fross was told to pick up what he had and was given orders to go to Paris via the afternoon hospital train. At the train terminal in Paris where he would arrive, Fross was instructed to make contact the Army Transportation Office, who would set him up with transportation back to England and the 98th General Hospital for further treatment.

Lt. Harms was talking to a doctor, reviewing how he felt and how his nerves were holding up and wondering, how the hell had that bottle of Cognac arrived in his bed? Apparently, Captain Weller, perhaps a bit unsure about the trade, did not visit him to explain the trade and besides, Weller had already given the flight jacket to a tailor to fit the jacket to him. So there could be no give-backs now. The doctor told Harms, they were going to keep him there for a couple more days, to see if they could make special arrangements for him to leave from a nearby air base, directly for England. Yes, the Cognac did accompany him for later consumption.

Somewhere in France, Gustafson's hospital train was sitting on a siding and T/Sgt. Russell W. Gustafson continued to flirt with the nurses. Asking each of them, with no luck, to scratch places he could not reach himself. One did tell him, she knew of one orderly who would be happy to do that and Russell quickly declined her offer to seek someone else to help with his itch.

Lt. Harland was happy in Paris. He had managed to put them off another day. He did realize he was lucky, as it was November, it was cool, and he was in Paris, where most of the men smelled as bad as he did and the girls were used to it.

At A-72, Colonel Coiner sent a messenger to Lt. Hornsby and Lt. Casper, to tell them he had arranged transport for them. The crew was to be ready at the headquarters at 08:00 in the morning to catch that transport. The messenger told Hornsby, he was going over to the crew's quarters to tell them to be ready and asked if Hornsby wanted him to tell them anything else. "No," Hornsby said, "just tell the men they are to be at the HQ at 08:00 and make certain to bring any stuff they had acquired." That evening at several villages in France, the French still spoke of the "Avion Fortress, B-17" crash. Nowhere was that more pronounced, than in the Tincourt-Boucly area. The Americans staying at the village hall continued to visit the villagers in Tincourt-Boucly and other nearby villages, collecting souvenirs the villagers had removed from the crash-site of the "Avion Fortress, B-17." While continuing to give packages of cigarettes to the people they talked to. Each night they collected in the café, to eat, drink and talk to the French about the "Avion Fortress, B-17" crash and once in a while, buying a round of drinks for all present.

That evening, at Cartigny, where the Americans at Tincourt-Boucly had yet to visit the village, the Village Priest, CURÉ Étienne Sepette, was meeting with the Mayor and the Village Elders to discuss the American aircrew remains that the Americans had hidden within the Commune's border, as he had promised his parishioner he would, during their second meeting.

The conversation was simple - what could they do with the hidden remains? The Priest insisted, they had to be buried in consecrated ground and he would not allow them to remain buried where the Americans had hidden them. The Frenchmen all agreed, the men deserved more than a hidden grave. They had died for the "*Liberty of France*," but what options did they have?

One man thought they should select a delegation to go to the commander at the nearby air base and ask that he correct the hiding of American War Dead. However, they did reach a conclusion that they did not dare to tell the air base commander, that the Americans were hiding their war dead and the Village of Cartigny would not let them do so on Commune ground. One could not make such a demand of those who were dying to ensure the "*Liberation of France*," so they needed another idea.

An elder, who had once visited the nearby Bony American World War One Cemetery, located about 16 kilometers to the north-east of Cartigny, suggested that they send a delegation to that cemetery. The delegation could ask them, if the Cartigny villagers dug up the hidden remains and took them to the cemetery, would the cemetery accept the remains?

That seemed to be a very good suggestion to all in attendance, and they agreed that the Priest and Mayor would make the trip and talk to the cemetery staff about taking the hidden remains of the flyers. With that, they had another drink and retired to their homes.

During the next couple of days a lot happened, but none of it, except for the trip of the Priest and Mayor of Cartigny to the Bony American World War One Cemetery, was that important, at this time. Of course, I did miss that one ration replacement request for the 563rd SAW, didn't I?

S/Sgt. Fross arrived back in England, assigned to the 98th General Hospital on the 14th and on the 16th, Lt. Harland arrived back at the base and was immediately sent to a rest home. Lt. Harms had returned to England, after being taken to a nearby air base by the 109th and put on a small observation plane that flew him directly to England, where he reported to the 98th GH for further observation and then sent to a rest home where he finished the magnum bottle of Cognac.

T/Sgt. Gustafson's hospital train had stopped for the night at the Saint-Lo station and the next day the train arrived at the French Port of Cherbourg. He was transferred to a hospital ship for transport to England and taken to the 98th General Hospital. There they cut the cast off and determined he had to go into immediate traction to hold his leg in place, so new bone could grow to replace the large chunk of bone the **FLAK** fragment had cut from his leg bone. He was put into a new cast at once and sent to the 4114th Hospital Plant, where the new cast was removed and he was put in traction. They told Gustafson, that his traction would last some months. At least, Gustafson thought, when he was put in traction, with all its associated pain, he could scratch some places again that the nurses wouldn't.

By the time I arrived in England with Sergeant Tiff, reported in, got a car assigned and was ready to travel, all the survivors of the B-17 crash had returned to England, to end up in a hospital or at a rest camp.

I had been informed of the situation at the 452nd, so Tiff first took me to the Cheddington Air Base where I met with the 36th BS (RCM) Commander and we discussed the situation at hand. The commander was well aware of General Eisenhower's participation and he told me he had pulled the aircraft's official record and had it in his safe. He had restricted the crash entry in the unit's Daily Log for the day to the minimum amount of information required to account for the dead men. Otherwise, there was nothing in the official documents of his unit that would permit anyone to determine the B-24 had actually crashed in France.

We discussed the best way to handle the actual official Aircraft Record, as it was an official record that could not disappear. We had to make certain it could meet any scrutiny after it was put back in the system. The Aircraft Record, in the future, would have to convince anyone looking at the record, that it had not crashed in France. So, the B-24 had to go away in some other manner.

In the end, we decided the best way to handle the situation was to keep the record in the safe for a while and then make the entry, that the B-24 had been damaged, returned to England, and then we had to really make it go away. The commander told me what I already knew, that the only official report of its crash

was in the RAF Bomber Command Records. And, that entry would not be available to any person in our military or in the US to compare with the official record of the B-24. He suggested that the B-24 could disappear by having its official record show it had been transferred to the RAF, as a repaired and flying aircraft.

That was a good solution and I immediately agreed that he was to hold the record in his safe, and in due time put the record back in his file, showing the B-24 had been repaired and turned over to the RAF as a repaired, flying aircraft, on 29 November 1944. (Individual Aircraft Record Card - Last entry 5/9/45).

Even if someone did look at the RAF records, there would be no record there of the B-24 being turned over to the RAF and since they reported the loss of our B-24, the last official record of the B-24 in RAF would be for the day of the crash. This would leave no way for anyone in the future to tie together the loss of the B-24 and the false turnover of the B-24 to the RAF.

(**Note**: It worked for nearly six decades, until the researcher visited the Air Force Historical Research Agency at Maxwell Air Force Base and thought to look up the official aircraft record and the RAF Mission Report at the same time and compare them. The RAF record was part of a group of RAF historical records that had been turned over to the Air Force Historical Research Agency many years after the war ended and was declassified in the mid-1990's.")

Before I left, we discussed what the commander would do when the crew returned. We agreed that the best thing to do was to ask no questions and to get the men flying again as soon as possible. The commander told me he would interview the men as soon as they returned, and make certain they understood they were to say as little as possible, even among themselves. Something he was certain the men would understand, given the security levels controlling Squadron operations.

At Tincourt-Boucly, the group of Americans hung around for a week to ten days, they had visited many people, and one of the American had made several trips to the air base with a trailer full of junk. There, he stopped at the headquarters to see Colonel Coiner and each time, Colonel Coiner had him deliver the junk to a man who saw it became even smaller junk. When he was done with that, the fellow buried the junk, wondering the whole time, why he had to bury the junk, when it was after all, just junk? After delivering his souvenir junk the American would go to the supply warehouses to draw many cartons of cigarettes, replacement rations, and return to Tincourt-Boucly, to keep searching for "classified relics."

On his last trip to deliver souvenirs, after he had gotten rid of the junk, picked up their rations, a few more cartons of cigarettes and returned to the headquarters to see Coiner. He told Coiner, they had completed their assignment and would be ready to leave in the morning. Colonel Coiner told the "*special mission*" man that he would made arrangements for a C-47 to pick them up at 10:00 in the morning, and it would take them to any location they wanted to go to in England. Meanwhile, he told them that Hornsby and his men were being moved, basically in a circle, around the French countryside near their crash-site.

Down at Hattonville, after their 2nd full day, Donovan's men had listened, bought drinks in four different villages and heard nothing strange about the B-17, "Avion/Flying Fortress" crash. All they heard, were normal conversations about the crash **and the three dead men in the woods**. Even at the 563rd, they found the men had moved on and the few who had been pointed out to them as directly involved would say nothing, other than Graves Registration had taken care of it. With that, they talked to the Commander and informed him he was to contact the person at the number they gave him, and tell him, "It was clean." At the same time, they told McBride they were ready to leave in the morning. The next day they arrived back in England and forgot where they had been and what they had done.

The Hornsby crew had continued to be moved around France and on the morning of the 18th, they were told they were going to the Vallenciennes Air Base in Belgium to go to England. What they did not know, was the base did not exist, nor was the named town located in Belgium. They were also warned, the air base was still under German sniper fire and they were quickly taken to the air base in a covered truck and rushed into an aircraft that would take-off as soon as they were aboard. Actually, they were taken to the Maubeuge A-88C Air Base that was about 50 miles from where their B-24 had crashed - a fairly decent disinformation plan that Coiner and I had put together. It worked well for more than six decades.

That morning, after getting on the C-47 without being fired at by any snipers, the plane took the survivors of the Hornsby Crew to a base in England, where they were picked up by a plane from Cheddington. They arrived back at Cheddington on the 18th, basically eight days after they had left on their mission.

Just after their transport landed, Hornsby and his crew were in the office of their squadron commander, who asked them no questions about the dead men or the crash, as he told them they would begin flying again, at once. There was no time at a rest home for these boys, and they would be flying again within two days. Then, their squadron commander said they were to talk to no one about what had happened in France, nor were they to talk to each other about the crash and the death of their fellow crew members. After the survivors of the Hornsby crew crash left the commander's office, it was decades before the survivors who were still living talked to a few people about their crash. One of those few people was the researcher, who knew much more about that eight days of their lives, than they did.

Just to make certain, the RAF had it straight. I went to see the commander of the 100th Group RAF. The RAF unit to which the 36th was attached, to verify the only information the RAF had, was as limited as possible. And after reading it, I knew no one on their side could ever tie their data back to the actual crash-site in France. As, their best reference point was over 50 miles off.

Of course, I did not tell the RAF that our official American B-24J-2-DT, SN: 42-51**226**, Aircraft Record was going to transfer that B-24 to their control, as an operating aircraft. "Hell!" I figure, "What they did not know, they could never dispute, right?" And, they never did, unless they read this book.

As I felt that part of the situation was well in hand, I went to see General Doolittle and discussed what he knew about the event. I told him how much I

personally wanted to thank him for his help, as General Eisenhower had told me how pleased he was with Doolittle's help, especially the Commendation help.

Doolittle told me I had to discuss the situation with the B-17's squadron and group commanders to make certain I understood all the problems. The commanders knew the B-17 did not have the bombs on board when it crashed and when the men bailed out, the B-17 was no more than 600 feet in the air. General Doolittle went on to explain to me ...there were too many differences between what really happened and what General Eisenhower wanted to happen. It was going to take a visit from me to ensure those commanders were convinced, that it was extremely necessary for them to continue the cover-story. Specifically, the story that their B-17 had blown up in the midair, then dove to earth, exploded again and disintegrated at its crash-site. I had to agree with General Doolittle and I told him, I would be at the 452nd that afternoon and part of tomorrow, and I would get back to him as soon as I had some solution for the problem.

Sergeant Tiff and I arrived at Deopham Green and I was quickly meeting with the Group Commander and the B-17's Squadron Commander. Again, General Eisenhower's interest had prepared the path and the men and I began to discuss the situation at hand.

Both commanders said they had received several different stories about the B-17's crash. One official version stated the B-17 had crashed east of Abbeville and another east of Amiens, that it had dived to the earth, exploding on the way down, then hitting the ground, exploding again and disintegrating with the death of three men. Then, they had later learned four men had died and not three.

Both told me that the normal copilot, a Lt. Collins, who had been flying another B-17 with another crew, had seen the B-17 hit twice by **FLAK**. He and all the rest of the squadron and group crews who saw the B-17 fall out of the formation, thought it was going to crash. Then, when none of them believed it would survive, the B-17 was brought back under control by the pilots and it was last seen, flying toward the west.

The copilot had been visited by the first survivor who made it back, the night he got back. He was the waist gunner, a Sergeant Robbins. The commander looked at a note pad on his desk, and continued that S/Sgt. Robbins returned early on the 12th. Both men had come to the squadron commander's office that morning and Robbins told his story. When Robbins was done and had left, Lt. Collins asked for a joint meet with the group commander and told them he wanted both pilots to be awarded a medal and he had been bugging them every day about the status of their medal applications.

Both said they had major problems existing with Robbins' story, the other survivor's stories and the official versions they had been given. One major problem was that Robbins was positive he had bailed out near Verdun and had been flown out of the Etain Air Base to Paris. Well, that air base was around 130 miles from where the official versions stated the B-17 had crashed.

Plus, S/Sgt. Robbins statements were now backed up by additional statements, from S/Sgt. Fross, the "*Lady Jeannette*" Ball Turret Gunner, who had

been treated at the 109th Evacuation Hospital which was located across the road from the American St-Mihiel Great War Cemetery, south-east of Verdun, France.

And, in support of Robbins' and Fross's statements, they had received word that the fill-in Bombardier, Lt. Harms, and the Flight Engineer, T/Sgt. Gustafson, were now at the 98th General Hospital and each claims to have been treated at the same 109th Evacuation Hospital where the other two had been treated. And, the 109th was located in a field to the east of the St-Mihiel World War One Cemetery, a long distance from the official version's given location. In addition, Lt. Harland, the Navigator, who was now at a rest camp, had been treated at the same hospital and all four men have given a completely different description of the end of their B-17 than what the official version presented to the Group stated.

The group commander referenced his note pad and said, "Colonel, there is just too much evidence pointing to our B-17 crashing a long distance away from the official version crash-site that has been given to us. There is just no evidence at all, that the B-17 crashed the way we had been told it had crashed." I asked him if he had personally interviewed all the men and he told me he had not, as the least wounded, or unwounded ones were at a rest camp and the wounded ones were in a hospital. He added that he had been told the bombardier was going to be held for further observation, perhaps for another week. In addition, he had learned the flight engineer would have his leg in traction here in England for some months and then he would be sent to the States when his condition improved.

With that, I decided to think about it for a while and get in touch with General Eisenhower to get his input. Then I set up another meeting with the two commanders for the next morning. The group commander told me he had made arrangements for me for the night and that I would be his guest. When I was ready, we could leave for his quarters. Before I could say anything, he told me that he had also made arrangements for my driver, who was going to be staying with one of the sergeants on his staff, who would keep my driver entertained that night.

I told the group commander, I had to call General Eisenhower on a secure telephone line in an hour or so, to update him on what I had found. He told me, he and his driver would bring me back to use his office when I was ready and then we departed for commander's quarters.

Upon our arrival at the colonel's quarters where I was to spend the night, he asked me if I could use a drink and I told him I would greatly appreciate a bourbon and water. However, if he would show me my room and give me the toilet location, I would appreciate that drink even more in about five minutes. Laughing, he told me to follow him and he took me to a room next to a bathroom, showed me my B-4 bag, where his driver had placed it and said, "See you in five."

Five minutes later, I was sitting with the colonel enjoying my bourbon and water as we discussed how the Eighth Air Force was actually winning the war.

Fifteen minutes later, over the beginning of a second drink, I looked around, saw no one and asked, if we were where he and I could talk openly?

The commander got up, walked quickly through the quarters, opened and closed a few doors and then he came back to tell me we were the only ones in the

building. With that, I told him, he knew I was going to be calling General Eisenhower in less than an hour and before I did, I needed to know exactly were where, he and his squadron commander stood. Because, if they did not feel they could do, what I was going to tell them they had to do, I would have to recommend to General Eisenhower that both of them be removed from command at once and sent to Greenland. If I had to, I would do whatever it took to prevent them from screwing up a major Top-Secret situation that could affect the end of the war.

Now I have to admit, the commander suddenly sat up straight in his chair and asked, exactly what did I mean by that? I explained to him that what was involved was far above his clearance level. However, I could tell him no matter what he and his squadron commander, and any of the personnel under their command might think, their B-17 had crashed exactly as the official reports they had been sent, stated it had crashed. Unless they could work with that, they would not be working at any air base they would appreciate for the rest of their careers.

Then I dropped the next bomb on them and told the group commander, "He was to talk to his squadron commander on his own and I was not going to be involved in any conversation between them. However, he had better convince his squadron commander that this was going to end one way and one way only. Either both of them were going to end up doing what had to be done or neither of them would be on base by noon tomorrow, was I understood?" He told me, I was. Then I told him, "If necessary, he could accompany me to his office, wait until I had General Eisenhower on the line and I would let General Eisenhower fill him in, if that is what he wanted? *At the same time, he could explain to General Eisenhower how he and his squadron commander felt they could not be involved in following the general's direct verbal orders they were to be given by me.*"

The group commander's face had lost most of its color by that time and he was looking at me like I was the devil seeking his soul. To be honest, in one way I was, just as I had no choice, and neither he nor his squadron commander had any choice, it way my way or the Greenland way.

I gave him a minute and asked what he thought? He said, he needed to talk to his 729th Squadron Commander. I told him to call and get him over here at once, as I needed to make that call to General Eisenhower and I was not going to be delayed, while they made up their minds.

He got up, went to the phone, called his headquarters and told them to find the 729th Squadron CO at once, and get him to the quarters where we were. It was a tense ten minutes until the squadron commander arrived. The group commander stood up, excused himself and the squadron commander, and they went to a room down a hall, where I could hear them in a discussion, but not what was being said.

In a few minutes they came back up the hall and sat down at the table with me, and the group commander told me they were on board and asked what they had to do. He stated that both of them were fully committed to doing exactly what I told them had to be done, exactly the way I told them to do it.

The main problem was the fact that the survivors had completely different stories from the official reports and though most of the group would never read the

official reports, crew survival stories tended to be passed around from squadron to squadron. In due time everyone in the group would know something was different and that would cause rumors. This in the end, could make the ordered goal of moving of the crash-site, a major problem.

I listened to the two men, thinking it was a damn good thing they did not know the real truth of the two crashes and all that it took to put the cover-up in place. If they had, they would really be upset. So, I took the bull by the horns and told them both what I proposed. As I understood it, all the survivors were basically gone from the base for two weeks or so. Both men agreed that was right. At this moment, the only person on the base who really had much information about the crash was the crew's normal copilot, Lt. Collins, the officer that had been pushing them for the pilots to get a medal. Collins had talked to both gunners from the rear, who had survived and their stories supported each other and actually, both commanders thought the pilots did deserve a medal.

I agreed, it sounded to me like the pilots should be submitted for a medal and I asked if they had any particular medal in mind. They said that Lt. Collins had been asking them to submit the pilots for the Silver Star and they had been putting him off until they could speak to all the survivors.

Lt. Harland, the navigator, had come back to the base before being sent to a rest home and the commanders had talked to him about the event. His testimony supported all that was known, but he had never left the nose of the B-17. In fact, his story was such, that it would be hard to put both pilots in for the same medal. From what they knew, the copilot had given away two parachutes and he had died in the crash without a parachute to use, if he had decided to bail out.

The squadron commander then told us that one of 2nd Lt. Metzger's regular crewmen had asked to see him. The crewman, a Sgt. Harold Burrell, "Told him, that Lt. Metzger had called a 'Green Crew' meeting before they left the States. Metzger had told the 'Green Crew' personnel he would never leave the plane if anyone was wounded and could not get out." The squadron commander added, that Metzger apparently died while meeting that promise.

Interesting, I told them, "I will have to take that into consideration in determining the awarding of medals. But first, here is what you will do." I gave the group commander a piece of paper with the true map reference of the Top-Secret B-24 crash-site and the description of the crash that they were to use. I added, "That is the official position and condition of their crashed B-17 and like it or not, they will use that location in all their official reports, especially in their turning over the B-17's Aircraft Record to the Salvage Board, for future salvage."

(**Note**: The Salvage Board was a separate organization from the Army and the Army Air Corps. It's job was to keep track of inventoried equipment that did not come under the direct control of Graves Registration when it no longer functioned. In the case of an airplane crash in England or in Occupied Europe, the Salvage Board and the Eighth and Ninth Air Forces had salvage teams in place that they would send out to the crashed aircraft to search for and recover any equipment

S/Sgt. Harold E. Burrell
Yuba City, California
Metzger's Crew Right Waist Gunner

Photograph: Harold Burrell

that was reusable and needed. They removed those equipment items and sent them to repair depots, where any required repairs were made, and then the items were put back into inventory for further use.

For instance, when a plane slid into a controlled crash, the salvage team would look at the propellers. If the propeller blade next to the ground was bent under, that meant, that engine was not running when the bomber slid to a stop. If all the blades were bent back, the engine was running when its propellers struck the earth and the engine would have been ruined during the crash, so the salvage team did not waste their time checking that engine for re-usable parts.

I knew, that in the Hattonville Woods, the B-17, SN: 42-97904, had broken into four large pieces and that a salvage team might go to its official crash location. The problem with that, was the B-17's actual crash-site did not meet the officially recorded crash location. So, its official record had to state the B-17 had been totally destroyed and its parts, buried and covered over. Therefore, if the Salvage Board did think about sending a salvage team to the given B-17G-35VE official crash-site location, they knew they would find a leveled out farm field. They would be told by the villagers, the "Avion Fortress, B-17" had crashed and it was totally destroyed. That way, the given crash-site condition would now agree with the official records, see pages 448 "*Lady Jeannette*" & 449 "*226*.")

So, I told the two commanders they had to ensure, the official Salvage Board Report stated, the B-17 had disintegrated and the parts had later been pushed into the impact crater and the crash-site leveled out. Therefore, heavy digging equipment would be required to salvage anything at that crash-site.

For their own good I told them, they did not need to know any other information than what I had given them, which was now the official location of their B-17's crash. Then "*BINGO*," the group commander said, "That is odd, the 397[th's] base had been that mission's ELF (Emergency Landing Field)." With that, I felt some relief and I thought, "This will work, as who could argue with the B-17 crashing 5 miles from its ELF?"

I asked both men, "If either one wanted verification of my ability to tell them what to do." Both declared at once, that was not necessary. I told them I would talk it over with the man I report to and I would most likely be back on the

day when their men were scheduled to return. At that time, I would want to talk to each of the survivors, including visiting the man in the hospital. I assured them, when I returned, we would settle this once and for all. Both said, that sounded good, and I suggested they made arrangements to keep the survivors from talking to each other, after we had interviewed them. The Group Commander asked, "If I thought he should arrange it so they all came back on one day, to be available, but kept apart, so they did not know the others had returned." "Now, that is a great idea," I said, as I looked at my watch and told them, "I need to make that call." The squadron commander said he had his jeep outside and would give us a lift, and we left for the group headquarters, so I could make my call.

I put in my call to Ike's office and was told it would be a few minutes, so I went out and talked to the two men about the copilot pushing for a medal. We agreed they would put him off a bit longer, until I could get back, by telling him they were working on it and something was going to happen soon.

Then the phone in the commander's office rang and I hurried in, closing the door behind me and in a few seconds I was talking to General Eisenhower. As usual, he was first off the blocks, asking me how it was going? I told him the B-24 crash had disappeared, but the move of the other was getting a little difficult. He asked what I meant by that? I told him the official version and the survivor's version were not the same, which was causing a problem. General Eisenhower asked me, what I could do about it? I told him we had a week to figure it out. Then, I would have to return to settle it. However, it was coming together as needed and I would fill him in completely as soon as I got back. He agreed, that was fine and he said he would see me then and hung up.

I went back out and told the two commanders they had a guest until morning, when I would head back to France and figure out exactly how we would solve the problem. So, tonight they could show me how the Air Corps spent their evenings, and we headed out to the "O" Club.

The next morning Tiff and I left early and I was nursing what the Eighth Air Force did during their evenings when they had no mission the next day. They had told me that oxygen helped, but I had no access to oxygen and I knew I was not in a hurry to do this again. I did have to admit to myself, many of them acted like this might be their last chance to do what it was they were doing. I can't say, I blamed the poor SOB's, as several of the aircrews' lives had recently become part of my own life's experiences and I now knew up front, exactly what they could face on their next mission, *"in the air, over there."*

Tiff, and I got back to the air base outside Reims, retrieved the car stored at the motor pool and Tiff got us back to the headquarters. When he dropped me off at my quarters, I told him to check the car in and if I needed a driver in the future, I would continue to ask for him until he told me not to. As Tiff got ready to leave, I reminded him that we had been nowhere, he remembered nothing, and that he was to remind the motor pool sergeant to remind the motor pool commander that they had never seen me, they knew nothing about any trip and that it would remain

that way. He laughed and told me, they both seemed to have aged a lot and have become forgetful old men since our last trip.

At that, I laughed, shut the door, picked up my B-4 and headed in. When I checked on my mail I found a note from the operations officer saying he had received a telephone call from a Colonel Coiner, who said, "The team had won," and another message from a Lt. Colonel McBride, which left a message, "It was clean." Otherwise, the operations officer had no need to see me again! I chuckled, thinking the man must still be unhappy with me!

At one small village in the Somme, there was one very serious conversation still being carried on about the "Avion Fortress, B-17" crash. CURÉ Étienne Serpette, (the Village Priest of Cartigny), the Mayor and the Village Elders had met at the presbytery, to discuss the problem created by the Americans hiding American War Dead on their Commune ground.

The Priest and the Mayor reported on their trip to the American Great War Cemetery at Bony and they were not happy with what they had been told. The American supervisor had not returned. However, the French foreman was there and he had told the men they could bring the dead American's remains to the cemetery and they would **bury the remains in a tomb for the Inconnu or Unknown**.

All Frenchmen were well acquainted with French military cemeteries and almost every Frenchman knew that when a French Inconnu Soldier was buried, that meant the remains were put in a mass grave for the Inconnu. The Priest and the Mayor laid out their mutual point of view. As these American men had died for the "*Liberty of France*" and then placed in a hidden grave by the Americans, the least the Commune could do was to **grant those dead Americans the honor of a tomb of their own in the Cartigny Cemetery!**

The others had listened to the story of their trip to the cemetery and it took only five minutes, including the pouring of a new round of drinks, to decide they would wait a little longer. If the Americans did not come and recover the dead men's hidden remains within a short time they would move the hidden remains to the village cemetery on the 23rd and bury the remains next to the French Soldiers who had been killed, while defending the village when the Germans came in 1940.

I met with General Eisenhower as soon as I could and explained that it all seemed to be under control, except for the problems at the B-17's group, where the stories of the survivors were differing from the official reports of the crash of their B-17. None of the three, last-out survivors thought their B-17 had disintegrated.

I also told General Eisenhower that I had made arrangements at both units, and except for the very limited account of the death of their men in the B-24's squadron's Daily Log, including a misleading location of their death, the B-24 was going away in due time. **The B-24's Aircraft Record would show it was damaged, returned to England, repaired and turned over to the RAF, as a flying aircraft on the 29th.** Since the RAF would have no record of receiving the transferred B-24 and the B-24's official record stated it went to the RAF, no one would have a real reason to check and if they did, they would unable to prove it one way or the other.

General Eisenhower said, that the B-24 problem resolution seemed to be going well. But I had to come up with a better plan concerning the B-17, as it seemed to him, that was the only place where the survivors could screw the whole thing up, and that was by sticking to the truth!

So, I told General Eisenhower about my plan to be there when four of the five survivors came back from the hospital or rest camp. And, that it was my intention to visit the fifth man in the hospital, to obtain his version of the crash. Then, before I left in about a week, I expected to fill him in about my plan at the 452nd. "Good," he said, and we got on to the other intelligence information that I maintained for General Eisenhower. When I was done, General Eisenhower told me to keep him fully informed on my plans at the 452nd, as he wanted all the loose ends tied up as soon as possible.

As I got ready to leave, General Eisenhower reached into one of his desk drawers and handed me a documents and told me that General Doolittle had sent him a copy of the Commendations that Doolittle and 100th Group Air Vice Marshall had sent to the 36th Bombardment Squadron to help set up the cover-up of the crash of the B-24. With that, our meeting ended and I was soon back at my desk putting together a plan that would ensure a fix to our problem.

HEADQUARTERS
VII FIGHTER COMMAND
APO 637 AAF STATION F-341
Office of the Commanding Officer

14 November 1944
SUBJECT: Commendation
TO: Commanding Officer, Station 113, U. S. Army
(Attention: Commanding Officer, 6th Bomb Squadron)

1. This Headquarters has received a confidential message D-6717, dated 13 November 944, from the Commanding General of the Eighth Air Force. This message is quoted below.

"Attention Commanding Officer 36th Bomb Squadron RCM, Jamming, screening and diversionary efforts of the 36th Bomb Squadron have contributed greatly to the efforts of the RAF bombing efforts. Mission 9/10 November was one of the most effective in confusing the GAF (German Air Force) and causing them to assemble in great haste to intercept the bomb stream which was not there, and reflects great credit to the Command and the individuals concerned. Signed Doolittle."

2. This Command forwards this message from General Doolittle with great pleasure and wishes to add its own commendation for a job extremely well done.

By Order of Colonel Webster:
Richard N. Ellis
Lt. Col., Air Corps
Chief of Staff

Another Special Congratulations from the Air Officer Commanding RAF 100 Group Air Vice Marshall Addison stated:

> FROM HQ. NO. 100 GROUP
> TO OULTON, NORTH CREAKE, FOULSHAM, GT, MASSINGHAM SWANNINGTON, 36SQDN, CHEDDINGTON
>
> THE RESULTS OF LAST NIGHTS SPOOF OPERATION WERE MOST GRATIFYING. OUR AIM WAS AMPLY ACHIEVED IN THAT THE ENEMY WAS INDUCED TO REACT IN A VERY BIG WAY INDEED FIRST IN THE SPOOFED. THE THREATENED AREA UNTIL HE EVENTUALLY BECAME AWARE HE WAS BEING SPOOFED AFTER THE WINDOWERS HAD RETURNED, AND THEN IN THE RUHR AREA WHEN HE BELIEVED, A REAL RAID WAS TO FOLLOW THE SPOOF. I KNOW HOW DIFFICULT WERE THE CONDITIONS LAST NIGHT, AND HOW THESE WERE AGGRAVATED BY LAST MINUTE CHANGES IN THE PROGRAMME. THE LATTER HOWEVER WERE MADE TO TAKE ADVANTAGE OF THE BEST POSSIBLE WEATHER CONDITIONS ON A BAD NIGHT AS REVEALED BY THE WEATHER REPORTS. I CONGRATULATE ALL CREWS WHO TOOK PART IN THIS DIFFICULT OPERATION. THEIR DETERMINATION ENABLED THE GROUP TO SCORE A VERY DISTINCT SUCCESS. WELL DONE."

Both Documents: USAF/HRA, Maxwell AFB and Stephen Hutton

It was interesting to note, the "Commendations," met the requirement of ***failing to show a loss during the mission*** and provide an excellent final record for that night's mission. Now, it was such a success, ***no commander would risk having those "Commendations" rescinded***, as those Commendations were their tickets to future, higher commands. It was good work and over the years, it worked exactly as I expected, until I got that unexpected warning telephone call.

A few days later, I got a call from the 452nd Group Commander, telling me he had the men scheduled in on a single day and he was set up to keep them from knowing the others were there. He gave me the date and I told him I would be there and that I was beginning to formulate a plan that would solve the problem for all of

us. Then I asked him, if the copilot was still pushing for the medals? He told me the squadron commander had told him, the copilot saw him every other day to see what was going to happen. I told him, they could tell that Lieutenant that something was in the works.

I had been thinking over the events in my mind and what kept coming back to me, was General Doolittle's quick thinking in sending the commendation to the B-24's unit, which had set them up to do what had to be done.

This time I decided, I would get over to the group the day before the men were to report back and set up a way that the squadron and group commanders could interview each one, with me listening in and with the ability to pass questions onto them, so they could ask the men my questions.

I knew that Doolittle's method had obviously cut down the chatter about the B-24 loss and it seemed to me that the same thing could work here. It was obvious the two pilots had gotten that B-17 out of Germany and back into France, when all the others who had seen it or been aboard it, thought it should have crashed just after it had been hit.

The day before the men returned, I arrived at the group and met with the two commanders to discuss what I wanted done during the interviews the next day. The group commander told me he would have a base signal person called in at once, to install a hidden microphone on his desk, so it would pick up their conversation and transmit it to me. He would also have them install a direct phone that I could use when I wanted to pass on a question for him to ask the man being interviewed. I thought to tell the commander to be sure there was a switch on the speaker in the room where I was, so I could shut off the speaker when I called him. Otherwise there might be a back-feed from his office that might give us away.

With that accomplished, I brought up what I thought was the next step we could take. First, I asked the commanders about the normal rotation of the flying crews, and what happened when a man was shot down and made it back. Did they have to continue to fly combat missions or were they treated in some other way?

They told me they might waive the 35 Combat Mission requirement if the man in was question was just a few missions short of his mission quota. However, the normal requirement was for the man to fly as a fill-in to make up the remaining missions when someone was sick or unable to make a mission with his normal crew.

I asked them, since most of the survivors had flown almost the same number of combat missions, what if they were kept apart and each one rotated back to the States without spending any more time at the group? That way, their stories would remain "their" story and the rest of the group personnel would only hear the official reports. Both men thought that would probably work. However, some air crewmen might grumble about that crew receiving special treatment.

My reply was, "That is an easy bridge to cross; let's wait until all the interviews are done tomorrow and then we can reach a final plan on what to do." I did not tell them, that I had already laid out my plan to General Eisenhower, who at first, was very disagreeable about what I had in mind. However, as I laid out all

the benefits, General Eisenhower realized it would do exactly what was required and it would also stop any further rumors before they were created.

When we finished our discussion, I told the group and the squadron commanders to make certain they had Lt. Collins scheduled for an interview, and they told me they had him set up to be interviewed early in the morning.

That night I went to the "O" Club with the two commanders, but I was smart and I limited my intake and enjoyed the view of the men who lived a life, where the next day could be the day they died. Myself, I was still very happy that I was a ground pounder and not a mission flyer. Next morning the interviews began and I only interrupted a few times, to get a question answered on something I needed clarified. The most interesting interviews were those of the Navigator, 2nd Lt. Harland, and the Bombardier, 2nd Lt. Harms who was the only crewman who survived, that actually went to the crash-site.

What I had in mind required an "*Eyewitness Officer*" and it was obvious to me that Lt. Harland could not provide what was required. However, Lt. Harms was a perfect "*Eye Witness*," except for his description of what had happened to him! After Lt. Harms had given his version and the group commander read back the official version, **Lt. Harms became agitated and told the group commander the official version was not true in any way.** With great emphasis, Lt. Harms told the two commanders, "That he had watched the B-17 from the moment his parachute opened until he had seen it enter the woods, where it crashed under full control, coming to rest less than 300 feet from him." He continued, stating, "That he had gone to the crash-site and he had personally seen the B-17 had broken into four large parts. There had been two wings and the tail and forward fuselage lying in the woods and it had left a debris-trail for several hundred feet, as he had walked beside it." **Lt. Harms was very adamant as he restated, "He was absolutely certain of what he had seen, no matter what the official report stated."**

Harms was also adamant, that he did not want to continue flying and he told both commanders about being in a crash in Iceland on his way to England, and it had taken him and his crew two weeks to reach safety. After a short stay in a hospital, they left Iceland in a flight formation of five C-47's and when they arrived in England, one of the C-47's was missing and no one had any idea of what had happened to it. Now, with this crash on his second combat mission, Harms told the commanders, he would fly if forced to fly. But, he felt he might be a danger to the other crewmen as his nerves were shot and he would like to be put before a "Medical Board" to be relieved from "Flying Status," as he believed he was mentally unfit to continue flying combat missions. Harms added, he had been told by the doctors at the 98th General Hospital, where he had gone upon his return from France, that upon return to his group, he should be removed from "Flying Status" by his "Group's Medical Board."

I called the group commander and had him ask Lt. Harms what proof he had that he was right and the official version was wrong. Lt. Harms stated that his medical records would prove that his story had remained unchanged from day one. And the fact was, if anyone visited the B-17's crash-site and walked up the same

path in the woods he had, that person would know that he was right - *and he was, as I had taken that walk myself.* Plus, that person would know beyond doubt that the pilots had control of the B-17 when it crashed. "Sir," Harms told the group commander, "I was there, I saw the whole thing, it did not dive, it did not blow up twice, and it certainly did not disintegrate as your official version states it did!"

When the interviews were over and the men were dispensed around the base, I met with the two commanders and told them, I wanted to go visit the wounded flight engineer in the hospital tomorrow morning. I would need someone to go with me who would do the actual talking while I stood out of sight and listened to the interview.

It was most important, I told them, that I was not seen being involved in what we were going to do. Especially, if what I planned failed, and some other step had to be taken.

The first thing they needed to do was to get Lt. Harms ready to go before the requested medical board. I told them I was certain that Lt. Harms had just laid out the perfect way for us to obtain the pressure we would need to force him to complete what had to be done, to make the situation to go away. However, first we needed to interview the flight engineer, and when I got back from that interview we would know if what I had in mind, might or might not work.

We discussed who would be the best person to go with me to actually talk to the flight engineer. The group commander told me he had one officer who was often involved in their medal application research and that he could be trusted to do what he was told to do.

I asked them to get that officer to their office as soon as they could and meanwhile, I was going to tell them exactly what the officer and I were going to do tomorrow. I told them, from Lt. Collins interview, it was obvious to me that Collins was not going to stop until the two men had been submitted for some higher medal. He had again, during his interview, suggested the *Silver Star*. I told them, I had talked the situation over with General Eisenhower, and I had presented to him, all the information I had. Then, I had suggested to General Eisenhower, that during this visit to the group I could establish a foundation for the award of the *Silver Star* to both men or, as both General Eisenhower and I preferred, they would both be submitted for the *Congressional Medal Of Honor*. That got both men's attention and both quickly agreed, the two pilots deserved the *Congressional Medal Of Honor*. Especially when one knew how they had died while attempting to save the radio operator's life.

I went on to tell the two commanders exactly what their interviewing officer was to discuss with the flight engineer. It would be important to us at the very start of the interview with the flight engineer, that the interviewer base the interview on the official version of the B-17 crash. We had to find out if the flight engineer would be as adamant in his story as the bombardier was with his. I told them, I believed, if we can show the flight engineer the official version of the crashed B-17, and get the flight engineer to agree, then, I thought, we had another lever, that we

301

might need to use on the bombardier to get him to agree to be the *"Eyewitness Officer,"* so the two pilots would receive their **Congressional Medals Of Honor**.

Just before the expected officer knocked on the door, I was telling the commanders to tell the officer he would be conducting the interview, but he was to make certain I would be able to give him any questions I needed the flight engineer to answer. And it was very important that the flight engineer did not realize I was involved with the interview.

With that, the officer was invited in and he was briefed by the group commander about the interview and he was told about the restriction on the flight engineer knowing I was involved.

Once that was done, the group commander called to set up transportation to the 4114th Hospital Plant in the morning. With that scheduled, I told the officer to pick up the transport in the morning and bring the car to the group commander's quarters to pick me up and he was excused for today.

That night, after we had spent the early evening at the "O" Club, we talked for some time in the quarters before we went to bed. Then, as I went to sleep, I was reviewing the progress made, and I felt soon it would all be in place and I could try to forget that I was ever involved in this situation.

The next day, the interview with the flight engineer went well, except for the final details of the crash of the B-17. The flight engineer was certain the B17 had been flying away from him as it disappeared into some woods, right after it appeared to turn to the right. He was positive it had not crashed in a field from what he had seen and he did not remember two large explosions, just the one flash, followed by a whooshing explosion sound. He did know, the B-17's bombs had been kicked out and it could not have been blown apart due to the bombs. However, he had to admit he had given himself a morphine shot after being wounded and that may have affected his memory.

With that, I got the attention of the interviewing officer and he excused himself for a few minutes. We met out in the hallway, where I asked him to put one more question to the flight engineer. If the flight engineer answers to the positive, the was to have the flight engineer sign the prepared statement I had given him on the way to the hospital.

"The key," I told the officer, *"was for him to put the pressure on the man, that unless he agreed and signed the statement, the men may not get the Congressional Medal Of Honor that they were being recommended to receive."*

With that, he went back into the room, pulled up his chair next to T/Sgt. Gustafson's bed and he told Sergeant Gustafson, "That the major reason he was there was they had to have his signature on the prepared statement he had with him. Without his agreement with the crash description given in this statement, he might be directly responsible for Lt. Gott and Lt. Metzger not receiving the **Congressional Medal Of Honor, _as that was the medal the squadron and group commanders were going to recommend they be awarded_**." He then asked T/Sgt. Gustafson, *"Are you so sure of what you have just told me, that you want to be responsible for that failure?"*

302

Just as I thought he would, Gustafson immediately said to the officer, *"Sir, you had not told me they were going to get the Congressional Medal Of Honor. Of course, the morphine may have distorted my memory and I was in great pain from my wound and I am positive that Gott and Metzger both deserve that medal, so where do I sign?"*

The officer, reached into his brief case and handed Gustafson the document, already attached to a clip board. And, told him to sign at the places marked with an "X." Gustafson scanned the document and signed it and the copies. When he handed it back to the officer, Gustafson said he did have one question, "I am alive because Metzger had given me his parachute before getting the spare from the back, and then Metzger had given that parachute to Lt. Harland." Gustafson continued, "Lt. Harland had told me about the second parachute on our way to the hospital in France and I am surprised the document did not mention that Lt. Metzger had given away two parachutes, leaving him without a parachute to use if he did want to get out before the B-17 crashed."

The officer gave T/Sgt. Russell W. Gustafson the prepared answer I had given him. Telling him, since both pilots were being submitted for the same medal, they had decided that it was best to not mention that part of what happened in any of the men's written statements. "You know, Sergeant," he said to Gustafson, "back in Washington, someone who had no real idea of what happened, might not want to award both men the same medal, when one had given away two parachutes." Gustafson, quickly thought about it and told the officer, "That made sense to him."

Within fifteen minutes we were on our way back to the group, and when we arrived the squadron and group commanders and I thanked the officer for his help and released him back to his normal duties. **Of course, I was aware the medal applications would contain false information**. However, I had not thought of the parachute question until the day before, after hearing Harland's testimony. Few would ever know of that difference and none have the juice to override General Eisenhower's approval!

Back at the 452nd, once I was with the commanders, I told the men we were set and all we had to do was complete the rest of the plan. They were to inform 2nd Lt. Collins that he could stop pushing as the two pilots were going to be submitted for the *Congressional Medal of Honor* and they were to tell Lt. Collins he was being rotated back home and with luck, he might arrive in time for Christmas, as we knew he had a wife and new twin daughters.

(**Note**: Collins told the researcher during their conversations, "The memory of his efforts in constantly pushing for the award of medals to Gott and Metzger was one, he was very proud of.")

Then after Collins, they were to do the same for Lt. Harland, S/Sgt. Fross and S/Sgt. Robbins, making certain none of the men would be together again in England. Then, as soon as they were gone from the group, the application for the

medals could be completed and forwarded. The only problem was with Lt. Harms and I was certain he could be handled with the plan I had laid out for him.

From his file, I knew, Lt. Harms had nearly graduated with an accounting degree and he had a pregnant wife back in the States. With that background and the proper use of the medical board, I was fairly certain that Lt. Harms would sign the applications as written. No matter how much he disputed the information on the applications concerning the crash and death of the B-17 crew. *"I Knew Lt. Harms, was no fool and the alternative to signing the applications, as I would ensure it would be presented to him, was something only a fool would do!"*

First, they had to get Lt. Harms started on the way to have him before his medical board to get him off flying status. In addition, Lt. Harms was not to have done to him, as what happened to most officers who requested to be taken off flying status. However, *he was to fully understand that specific option* was available to the group, if it had to be used.

Harms was to be told, the group was not planning on sending him to a replacement depot for assignment as a Front Line Infantry Officer if the medical board decided to take him off flying status. In fact, he was to be informed by the group commander, if the doctors agreed he should be taken off flying status, *and unless there was some unseen glitch*, the group would make use of his accounting education and he would be assigned to the group financial office to become a Group Finance Officer, instead of becoming an instant Infantry Officer.

This time, I had made arrangements for a liaison plane to fly me directly to the 452nd Group from Reims. Once the commanders had agreed to go ahead with my suggestions, I told them they had to talk to their hospital people to make certain, 2nd Lt. Harms Medical Board was scheduled to be held just after he was to sign the applications. I had also told them, I planned to present when Lt. Harms was to sign the two medal applications, as I felt, I had to be there if I wanted to ensure Lt. Harms would sign the two applications *as written!*.

The Group Commander had told me they had a 1st Lt. Irving Math, who was a hell of an application writer. If he continued to be as successful in the future, as he had been to date, the group would end the war with more medals awarded than any other group. "That," I told them, "seemed to me to be the best route for us to follow. So, we will have their man write up the two applications in his own words, except for the actual crash description and a bit that I would furnish to them, and that, *he was to use my furnished comments exactly as I had written them*."

I asked them what they thought of that idea? The group commander told me it would be the best way to do it, as no one in the group would question any application that Lt. Math wrote. In that light, I told them to expect the wording I wanted used for the description of the crash to be there within a couple of days. Then I told them I needed to get out of there before the weather closed in, so would one of them take me to my plane.

(**Note**: The author became a member of the 452nd BG Association in 1994 and met Lt. Math at one of the reunions. One day the author received an email from

Lt. Math, informing the author that he was proud of having written both medal applications, however, he had been forced to put information in the applications, exactly as written. When awarded, both medal Citations were all his, except for the exact crash description and ending that were pre-written and used, as ordered.)

Soon I was in the air and later that day when I had a few minutes alone with General Eisenhower, I told him my plan to use the ***Congressional Medal Of Honor*** seemed to be working perfectly. **Certainly, we agreed, the pilots deserved the medals for what they had done before they crashed and their award would complete the <u>cover-up of the cover-up</u> and tie every loose end together, or so we thought at the time.**

We could be certain, once the applications were heading up the Chain of Command and it became known at the group, no one there would continue to question any differences they might see between the official description of the crash of the B-17 and any rumor they may have heard. ***Then, when the awards were granted, we could be certain that everyone's memory, who were involved with any part of this, would match the applications***. Because any one of them who even thought of questioning the award of the ***Congressional Medals Of Honor*** would then be accused of attempting to destroy the meaning of the medals.

(**Note**: The author has been so accused, many times. Even though all the author has wanted is the truth be known and the hidden remains, recovered. Both Awardees ended their lives in a manner that would have earned them the same medals, if only the truth was followed and the applications forwarded. However, that would not have allowed the coverup of what General Eisenhower had verbally ordered to be carried out and those who followed his orders, including himself. Instead of righting the wrongs later, Ike buried it for many decades!)

General Eisenhower agreed it was what the two men had done before they died that was important for the ***Congressional Medal Of Honor*** to be awarded. In the long-run, the way they really died or the way the applications stated they died, did not matter all that much. General Dwight D. Eisenhower said, ***what did matter, was the fact they died in much more than an attempt to save the life of one man. They had died while <u>unknowingly</u> participating in the possible savings of tens of thousands of our military dead and other tens of thousands of civilian lives. That alone, justified the use of their death and what had to be done to hide the crash of the Top-Secret B-24.*** General Eisenhower continued, "In one way, the medals will also honor the three men who died in the crash of the B-24." I had not thought of that before and I told General Eisenhower that I had to agree with him. By using information from both crash-sites, in the way the information was going to be used, all seven men were being honored. Only, the world would never know about it and if all continued to go well, in the end ... only he and I would know. For more than seven decades, that understanding between General Eisenhower and myself remained just that. But now, you also know.

Early in mid-December 1944, I received a call from the group commander and he told me the survivors, except the flight engineer and S/Sgt. Fross, who were at hospitals, were en route to the States and that the bombardier's medical board was set up, to be held right after he signed the two applications. He told me that Lt. Harms had been told of the probable results of his Medical Board and he had been given a personal tour of the group finance center by the group commander, to ensure Harms would fully understand the importance of the finding of his Medical Board.

The group commander wanted to know, if I still wanted to be there when Lt. Harms was going to be ordered to sign the applications as the required *"Eye-Witness Officer."* I told the commander, "From what I have learned about Lt. Harms, that is the place I have to be, when Lt. Harms has to make his decision to stick to the truth as he knows it, or to bend like a reed in a current he has no control over. To be most honest," I told the group commander, "I have to be that current in that room or I don't believe Lt. Harms will bend!"

In ending, we set an appointment for the signing and I told him I would be there that morning. If the weather was good enough, I would arrive by plane and come back the same day. A couple of days later, 2nd Lt. Joseph Francis Harms arrived at the 452nd Group Headquarters to report to the group commander. Almost immediately, he found himself in the group commander's office, and present, beside his group commander and his squadron commander, there was a young bird Colonel whom he had never seen before and, would never see again.

The group commander told Lt. Harms that he was to be the *"Eye Witness Officer"* required for the group to submit applications for the *Congressional Medal Of Honor* for 1st Lt. Donald Joseph Gott and 2nd Lt. William Edward Metzger, Jr.

The commander pointed out to Lt. Harms, the two applications lying on his desk, and told Lt. Harms to sign on the line above his name on all copies of both applications. Lt. Harms leaned over and read the applications prepared by Lt. Math. He took time to read both applications throughly and then, as he stood at attention, facing the group commander, Lt. Harms told him outright and very positively, *"In all honestly Sir, I cannot sign the applications as they are written!"*

Lt. Harms told the group commander that everything before the description of the crash and the death of the men on the B-17 was correct. However, the crash and death description were so wrong, he could not with any honestly do as told and sign the applications.

Before the group commander could say anything to Lt. Harms, I stepped up beside the group commander. I looked directly into Lt. Harms eyes and very directly, I said to him, "Son, if you know what is good for you, you will sign these applications right now, exactly as they are written! Then, you will salute, turn around, and leave the room! Otherwise, none of us in this room will be responsible for what will happen to you in the very near future!"

I have to admit, I put great emphasis upon the ... **"If you know what is good for you, you will sign these applications** ... and ... **will be responsible for what will happen to you in the very near future!** " Lt. Harms looked at me, then

at his two commanders, then back at me again. With that, 2nd Lt. Joseph F. Harms leaned over, signed the applications, saluted, turned, and marched out of the room.

When Lt. Harms leaned over to sign the applications, he told the researcher over five decades later when he was interviewed, that he was thinking to himself, *"Damn it, don't be a fool! Think! When a full bird colonel you have never seen before tells you to sign something in that tone of voice and detail, you sign and shut up. That colonel knows something I do not know, and I was certain, he was talking about my Medical Board."*

After he had signed the applications and saluted and was on his way out, I said to the departing Lt. Harms, "Good luck with your Medical Board."

As Harms marched out of the group commander's door, and I mean marched out the door, I was thinking that he was marching out of my life forever, and now, as you and I know, I was so wrong.

(**Note**: Over six decades later, the researcher used my exact words to Lt. Harms that day, and copies of a few pages of Lt. Harms medical records to prove he had discovered exactly what we had done!)

After Harms had marched out, the squadron commander closed the door and with that, I turned to the two commanders and told them, "Gentlemen, please sign the applications above your name," which both did. Then, I dropped the whole load of bombs on them and told them, **"They had just committed about the worse thing they could do as commanding officers**. They had just signed two, now very official applications for the *Congressional Medal Of Honor*, our country's highest military medal. **Yet, both of them were absolutely aware at the time they signed the two official applications, that both applications contained false information** concerning the crash and death of the two men being submitted for the awards. "From now on," I told them, "if I were you, I would think of and remember all of the rest of the men who will sign and forward these official applications. Each of them will also know the truth of the falsehoods contained in the applications and each will place themselves at the same risk the two of you have just taken, when they sign the applications, attach their own recommendations and forward the two medal applications."

Gentlemen, it is important that you remember one thing, **"If the truth of what you have just done ever becomes public information, your careers will be ruined. Just as all the rest of the signers will have their careers ruined**. So, gentlemen, you are in good company and there is one thing more to remember. *Second Lieutenant Harms, of all of us, is the only person who stood for the real truth, until we forced him to lie, when signing the applications. Harms will be the only one of us with the official records required to prove what we have done.* Especially, if what we have done ever becomes public."

I continued, telling them that, "Lt. Harms has just presented us with all the ammunition required to ensure his medical board will declare him unfit to fly and remove him from flying status. Based on Lt. Harms own "*false memories*" of the

actual crash of the B-17 in question, who will believe him in the future, when there are two ***Congressional Medals Of Honor Citations* that directly dispute what he might say? After all, he has signed those applications!**"

I told the group commander, he was to ensure the Medical Board officers did exactly as they had been instructed to do. Resulting in the fact, that Harms will be removed from "***Flying Status***" and transferred from his squadron to the Group Headquarters Company, to become a Group Financial Officer.

I also told them, "They should then keep Harms at the Group, until his regular crew completed its required mission number and if he was doing a good job, he should be promoted to 1st Lieutenant and then shipped back to the US with good recommendations and reviews for reassignment as a financial officer. It is very necessary for all of us to remember that Lt. Harms has the evidence to prove what we have done. However, once he signed the two medal applications, Harms will also realize that he is as involved in what we have done, as we are and he will not bring this to public attention on his own." Which Lt. Harms never did, ***on his own!***

It was only after the researcher went to New Jersey to personally interview him more than fifty-two years later that Lt. Harms admitted to the researcher that he had signed the two applications under duress. ***However, Harms did tell the researcher about a very young Bird Colonel he had never seen before, who directly implied a threat against him if he did not sign the applications***. Joe Harms told the researcher, "I was not a damn fool then and I am not a damn fool now. I did what I was told, when I was told to do it and that's the truth. I did not want to end up a statistic at the front line when I had a pregnant wife at home."

The group commander agreed that he would remind the medical board about what they were to do. He would ensure they would not jeopardize the medal applications by making anything out of what he remembered. Just the facts that Harms did not correctly remember what happened at the crash-site, and he had suffered a mental break down is sufficient reason to set aside his flight status and assign him to group financial officer duties.

In late February, 1945, 1st Lt. Harms left the 452nd Group for the States, his wife, Elsie, and their brand new daughter, Janet Lynn, who had been born on the 22nd of February. He stayed in the Army as a F0 until 1947 and became a Captain.

Sgt. Fross remembered spending additional time at a hospital in England after he officially left the group, and he remembered interpreting for POWs at the hospital before he boarded a ship to the United States on Christmas Day, 1944.

Christmas Day, 1944, while disembarking from his ship in the Boston Harbor, S/Sgt. Robbins ran into Lt. Collins. Both of them had been on the same ship from England to Boston without knowing the other was aboard. Robbins and Collins discussed the fact they had not seen each other since the morning Robbins had gotten back to the squadron. When they were done, Robbins told Collins about losing all his money gambling on the way back, and he asked Collins to lend him some money so he could get home. Robbins lived close to Boston, in Worcester, but he did not have a dime to his name to get home. He wanted to get home to his wife, Shirley, (whom he had married at the Rapid City Air Base on the 29th of May,

1944), before Christmas was over. Collins had attended their wedding and there was no way he would not lend Robbins that requested money.

So, Collins lent Robbins the money and several weeks later, when Collins' mail caught up with him, Collins was surprised to find a check from Robbins to repay the loan. That Christmas Day was the last time the two would see each other. However, fifty-two years later, both Collins and Robbins would tell the researcher their stories and tie the two men together again, if not in person, at least in the true history of World War Two the researcher had recently uncovered.

Lt. Harland arrived home in Chicago shortly after Christmas, while T/Sgt. Gustafson remained in traction at the 4114th, until late February, when he was air-transported to the States. Then he spent an additional year in a military hospital before being discharged. Gustafson returned to civilian life with a permanent limp, his life long souvenir of the crash of the *"Lady Jeannette."*

I left the 452nd Group for France, the same day that Lt. Harms signed both *Congressional Medal Of Honor* applications, knowing in my heart that the applications were going to be approved as written. **Every signing officer up the Chain of Command would know his ass was on the line if those applications failed**. All were told the truth up front, and every one of them had a legitimate excuse not to sign the official applications as submitted. Yet, every one of them signed! I was certain each would attach his own reason why the medals should be awarded, including General Dwight D. Eisenhower, Commanding!

It had been planned, once the official applications were forwarded up the Chain of Command from Eisenhower's HQ, each additional signer would be fully, verbally informed about the false information. General Eisenhower owed his command to General Marshall, who owed his position to President Roosevelt and General Eisenhower would not set up either of them to be blind-sided, if and when the truth of the false documentation in the official applications they had all signed, ever became public knowledge.

Each was fully, verbally informed about the official need for the false entries before they signed. Each of them would know the medals had to be approved to ensure that none of them would ever begin to have happen to them what had been done to General Patton for slapping a soldier.

Of course, that may have been the purpose of the quick trip I made to the US to be home with my family for Christmas, 1944, after visiting Washington, D.C.

On General Order 38, 16 May, 1945, 1st Lt. Donald J. Gott and 2nd Lt. William E. Metzger, Jr., were awarded the *Congressional Medal Of Honor*. Both awards were presented to the men's surviving parents on Sunday, 17 June, 1945, at dual ceremonies conducted near their homes. The word that the medals had been awarded arrived at General Eisenhower's headquarters, and was received with great relief by both General Eisenhower and myself. The war was over in Europe and the only thing everyone was interested in was getting home. *At that time, what we had done to ensure so many lives would not be put at risk could still be fully justified - if not to the world, at least within our own minds!* Now we could put what we had done out of our minds forever. Or, so I had hoped.

Major General R. B. Williams attaches 1ˢᵗ Lt. Donald J. Gott's *Congressional Medal Of Honor* around the neck of his mother, Mrs. Mary Lucy Gott, observed closely by Lt. Gott's father, Joseph Eugene Gott and Lt. Gott's older Brother, Otto James Gott on left. The Award Ceremony was held in the Fargo, Oklahoma, high school gym, where Donald had been a basketball star. 17 June 1945

Photograph: US Army - Gott Family

Along with the rest, I had put out of my mind one simple fact. That fact was, the weakest link in our chain was one of the men who had not signed his name to those official documents, and **they could provide him with the weapon he needed to swat us out of the sky any time he decided to do so.**

Between the time the *Congressional Medals Of Honor* had been awarded and their presentation to the families, General Patton had been visiting the United States. **During this trip, Patton was cheered by hundreds of thousands of Americans**, and in every paper, he read glowing articles about the award of the *Congressional Medal Of Honor* to two pilots that he knew *did not die the manner the Medal Citations stated they did*! *And, he knew the Citations were FALSE!*

At that time, General Patton realized that the highest commanders over him, including his President, had done something much worse than when he slapped a soldier. Yet, none of them had suffered in any way for desecrating our American War Dead. It began to fester in the back of General Patton's mind, only to come to a full boil some months later.

Me, I hadn't signed the applications. However, I was the one who had engineered them and my fingerprints were all over the awards!

GOTT, DONALD J. (AIR MISSION)
Rank and organization:
First Lieutenant, U.S. Army Air Corps, 729ᵗʰ Bomber Squadron (H), 452ⁿᵈ Bombardment Group (H)
Place and date: Saarbrucken, Germany, 9 November, 1944
Entered service at: Arnett, Oklahoma
Born: 3 June, 1923
G.O. No: 38, 1 May, 1945

Citation: On a bombing run upon the marshaling yards at Saarbrucken, a B-17 aircraft piloted by 1st Lt. Gott was seriously damaged by antiaircraft fire. Three of the aircraft's engines were damaged beyond control and on fire; dangerous flames from the No. 4 engine were leaping back as far as the tail assembly. Flares in the

cockpit were ignited and a fire raged therein, which was further increased by free-flowing fluid from damaged hydraulic lines. The interphone system was rendered useless. In addition to these serious mechanical difficulties the engineer was wounded in the leg and the radio operator's arm was severed below the elbow. Suffering from intense pain, despite the application of a tourniquet, the radio operator fell unconscious. Faced with the imminent explosion of his aircraft, and death to his entire crew, mere seconds before bombs away on the Target, 1st. Lt. Gott and his Copilot conferred. Something had to be done immediately to save the life of the wounded radio operator. The lack of a static line and the thought that his unconscious body striking the ground in unknown territory would not bring immediate medical attention forced a quick decision. 1st Lt. Gott and his Copilot decided to fly the flaming aircraft to friendly territory and then attempt to crash land. Bombs were released on Target and the crippled aircraft proceeded alone to Allied-controlled territory. When that had been reached, 1st Lt. Gott had the Copilot personally inform all crew members to bail out.

The Copilot chose to remain with 1st Lt. Gott in order to assist in landing the bomber. With only one normally functioning engine, and with the danger of explosion much greater, the aircraft banked into an open field, and when it was at an altitude of 100 feet it exploded, crashed, exploded again and then disintegrated. All 3 crew members were instantly killed, 1st Lt. Gott's loyalty to his crew, his determination to accomplish the task set forth to him, and his _**deed knowingly performing what may have been his last service to his country**_ was an example of valor at is highest.

(Highlights, The Author)

METZGER, WILLIAM E., Jr. (AIR MISSION)
Rank and organization:

Second Lieutenant, U.S. Army Air Corps, 729th Bomber Squadron (H), 452nd Bombardment Group (H)
Place and date: Saarbrucken, Germany, 9 November, 1944
Entered service at: Lima, Ohio
Born: 9 February, 1922, Lima, Ohio
G.O. No.: 38, 16 May, 1945

Major General F. L. Anderson presents the *Congressional Medal Of Honor*, awarded posthumously to 2nd Lt. William E. Metzger, Jr., to his mother, Mrs. Ethel V. Metzger, observed by Mr. William E. Metzger, Sr. In Lima, Ohio on 17 June, 1945.

Photograph: US Army - Metzger Family

311

Citation: On a bombing upon the marshaling yards at Saarbrucken, Germany, on 9 November, 1944, a B-17 aircraft on which 2nd Lt. Metzger was serving as Copilot was seriously damaged by antiaircraft fire. Three of the aircraft's engines were damaged beyond control and on fire; dangerous flames from the No. 4 engine were leaping back as far as the tail assembly. Flares in the cockpit were ignited and a fire roared therein which was further increased by free-flowing fluid from damaged hydraulic lines. The interphone system was rendered useless. In addition to these serious mechanical difficulties the engineer was wounded in the leg and the radio operator's arm was severed below the elbow. Suffering from intense pain, despite the application of a tourniquet, the radio operator fell unconscious. Faced with the imminent explosion of his aircraft and death to his entire crew, mere seconds before bombs away on the Target, 2nd Lt. Metzger and his pilot conferred. Something had to be done immediately to save the life of the wounded radio operator. The lack of a static line and the thought that his unconscious body striking the ground in unknown territory would not bring immediate medical attention forced a quick decision. 2nd Lt. Metzger chose to remain with the pilot for the crash-landing in order to assist him in this emergency. **With only one normally functioning engine and with the danger of explosion much greater, the aircraft banked into an open field, and when it was at an altitude of 100 feet it exploded, crashed, exploded again, and then disintegrated.** All 3 crew members were instantly killed. 2nd Lt. Metzger's loyalty to his crew, his determination to accomplish the task set forth to him, and his *deed knowingly performing what may have been his last service* to his country was an example of valor at its highest.

(Highlights, The Author)

As I read the citations, I remember well the reason for the ending of both medal citations. Yes, it was both men's last "*deed knowingly performing what may have been his last service*." We know that is true, as both men also *performed, unknowingly, one more important deed for their nation* and those involved. Both men's remains were desecrated and hidden by the very military they served, at the direct verbal order of their highest Commander and these medals were a partial repayment of their sacrifice and all to ensure the action of the involved men would never be questioned.

As you now know, the medal awards have been questioned and the fact the Citations contain a false description of their crash and death can no longer be disputed! The purpose is not to question the medals for heroism, but to question the situation and condition of their death.

"*The Copilot chose to remain with 1st Lt. Gott in order to assist in landing the bomber. With only one normally functioning engine, and with the danger of explosion much greater, the aircraft banked into an open field, and when it was at an altitude of 100 feet it exploded, crashed, exploded again and then disintegrated. All 3 crew members were instantly killed, 1st Lt. Gott's loyalty to his crew, his determination to accomplish the task set forth to him, and his*

312

deed knowingly performing what may have been his last service to his country was an example of valor at is highest"

The final paragraph of the applications was exactly as I had sent it to the commander of the 452nd Bombardment Group (H), to be written into each of the applications during Lt. Irwin Math's write-up. To that point it was all Math's original work and with my added words, the men's **_last hidden service_** to their country was also documented within the citations.

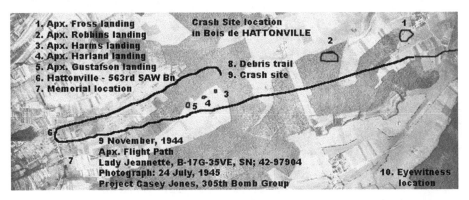

1. Apx. Fross landing
2. Apx. Robbins landing
3. Apx. Harms landing
4. Apx. Harland landing
5. Apx. Gustafson landing
6. Hattonville - 563rd SAW Bn
7. Memorial location

Crash Site location
in Bois de HATTONVILLE

8. Debris trail
9. Crash site

9 November, 1944
Apx. Flight Path
Lady Jeannette, B-17G-35VE, SN; 42-97904
Photograph: 24 July, 1945
Project Casey Jones, 305th Bomb Group

10. Eyewitness location

Official USAAF Photograph taken by the 305th Bomb Group during *Project Casey Jones, the Official Bombing Results Survey* on 24 July, 1945, with an overlay of the last few minutes of flight of the "*Lady Jeannette*," showing the landing position of the surviving crew and a French eyewitness's location.

Photograph: US National Archives - Overlay: Willis S. Cole, Jr.

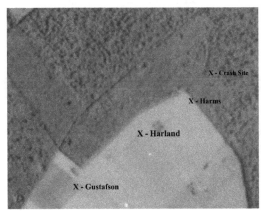

X - Crash Site

X - Harms

X - Harland

X - Gustafson

An enlarged section of the above Project Casey Jones aerial photograph. Just to the right of the center angle in the woods, the curving swath cut in the Hattonville Woods by the crashing B-17G stands out. With a full blow up of the photograph, the right wing and tail assembly shows up as dots. The forward fuselage and left wing are hidden by the summer foliage.

11:00 a.m., 9 November, 2000, 56th Anniversary of the crash of the *Lady Jeannette*" in Hattonville Woods. The United States Air Force Honor Guard presenting Colors along with the Le Souvenir Français, and the Union National Combatants. With the U.S. Air Force Senior Honor Guard, Master Sergeant Symons placing floral arrangements during the Memorial Dedication.

Mr. Robert LECLERC, Memorial Guardian standing at right of the photograph. Seated next to him, just out of the picture is Jeanne Metzger Schofield, the sister of the Copilot, 2nd Lt. William E. Metzger, Jr. *CMOH*.

Two reporters from the Stars and Strips military news paper were present and documented the dedication.

Photograph: Carol L. Cole

(**Note**: It is a sad truth that the names of the enlisted men, T/Sgt. Dunlap and S/Sgt. Krimminger, whose death and remains' desecration contributed to the success of the cover-up are unlisted. Krimminger is not even referred to in the Citations and his remains were the most mistreated during and after the crash of the *Lady Jeannette*," B-17G-35VE, SN: 42-97904, on 9 November, 1944.)

9 November, 2004, 11:00, Hattonville Woods, Hattonville, France. The exact 60th Anniversary of the crash of the *"Lady Jeannette"* into the woods. With the broken off nose and the dead Pilots, 1st Lt. Donald J. Gott, ***Congressional Medal Of Honor*** and 2nd Lt. William E. Metzger, Jr., ***Congressional Medal Of Honor*** coming to rest at this location.

T/Sgt. Russell W. Gustafson, Flight Engineer/Top Turret Gunner, standing about where he would have been normally standing during a mission, right behind where the dead pilots came to rest still in their cockpit seats with both of the head suffering multiple fractures from tree limbs breaking into the B-17's cockpit as it lowered into the Hattonville Woods.

The hidden grave of the two pilots and their radio operator who died with them is/was the length of the bomb bay and radio compartment behind where Russell is standing.

Sixty years and one hour before this photograph was taken, T/Sgt. Gustafson was lying in the large field, located about 215 feet behind the photographer. A closer look at his right leg in this photograph, will show his right leg, just above the ankle, is still crooked from the FLAK burst that had taken a piece of bone out of that leg.

The crash site is now a fenced memorial park, that can be visited. Contact the family Leclerc, in the house to the north of the closed wood working shop next to the *"Lady Jeannette"* Memorial at the south end of Hattonville. If they are home, they will assist you.

Photograph: Willis S. Cole, Jr.

If you want to feel real WWII Aviation History, this the place to do it!

The author on his third trip to the "*Lady Jeannette*" crash site in the Bois de Hattonville, in November, 1998. Finding the impact craters full of water and the wild boars wallowing in them, a drain was put in to dry them out. The author took this photograph from the south of the two craters. It shows the two impact craters from the right wing coming to rest, leaning against the trees to the left. Lt. Harms walked up on the left side of the wing, then saw the torn parachute on the tail to the right of this photograph and began his nervous break-down.

Excellent quality, left hand, leather glove found in the cockpit area at the crash-site of the "*Lady Jeannette*" by the author. Fire and crash damage killed the pilots where this was found at the crash site? Who can believe the Citations? Photographs: Willis S. Cole, Jr.

Chapter Fourteen
Patton's Exit

The history of Patton's exit, or "Final Transfer," from the world of the living, has been documented by numerous authors and researchers. All those authors and researchers agree that Patton was in an automobile accident in Germany on Sunday 9 December, 1945. Then two very different theories started to dominate each of those authors and researchers.

Some pure military history researchers and writers specify, that the car accident was just that, a car accident. A conclusion the author agrees with, *it was an unplanned accident that prevented the planned death of General Patton, later that afternoon in a farm field in Germany, while hunting Pheasants*.

General Patton did die some days later after a period of improving health as an infection invaded his body, **according to the "Official Story," due to injuries** he had suffered in the wreck. Within two days the infection overwhelmed Patton and at the young age of 61, he died and the secret was preserved forever, or so we thought.

Due to the underwhelming damage to both the vehicles involved, other researchers and authors, both military and mystery writers have taken the stance that Patton's death was no accident. It was in fact, a plan that was rather poorly executed, or an excellent plan to kill General Patton that was also, very well executed. Either way, most claim their personally accepted plan to kill General Patton created the accident. Most importantly, in those previous writings, the researchers and authors have only provided, suspect motives. Which, when deeply researched have no underlying, solid foundation of fact that would provide a reasonable and valid motive which would have led to the attempt on Patton's life, as they claim it was carried out.

Many books have been printed and movies have been produced, showing both themes leading to Patton's death on 21 December, 1945, and his later burial at the American Luxembourg World War Two Cemetery on Christmas Day, 1945. Patton was buried without a thorough autopsy being performed, leading to continuing doubt about the exact cause of his death to this day.

All of the books and movies to date, fail in two significant ways to lay out exactly what did happen to General Patton, during a quickly arranged pheasant hunt by his Chief of Staff, General Gay. Adding to the mystery, if one wishes to believe it is a mystery, is the fact that Patton was scheduled to depart for the United States on 10 December, 1945, in order to spend Christmas with his wife at their home in Massachusetts. The day the accident took place on 9 December, 1945, *was the last day that General Patton would be under the complete physical control of the U.S. Army in Europe*! On the 10th, he would have boarded a Navy ship.

During dinner on the evening of 8 December, 1945, General Patton told his Chief of Staff, General Gay that his mind was made up and he was going to follow through with the plan he had told General Gay about in October. General Patton

had told General Gay, upon his removal as the Commander of the Third Army, that he had decided to quit the Army and not retire from the Army. General Patton told General Gay that, if he retired from the Army, he would be left open to pressure by the Army and the government, made up of the very people who were striving to destroy his career.

However, by quitting the Army outright by resigning, that step would free him from any restraint by those bastards. Basically, General Patton, told General Gay, *his quitting the Army, would free him to tell the truth and he could not be bound by anyone to do less.*

There is extensive public information concerning General Patton's feeling about Russia and its intent after the war ended, and how he felt it should not be allowed to happen. His removal from the Command of the Third Army, (the Army of Occupation of Germany), and his assignment to the Command of the Fifteenth Army, referred to as the "*Paper Army,*" where there were no more than 2,000 personnel, was considered by General Patton to be the final straw, and another *direct slap from General Eisenhower*. In Patton's mind, that was the same bastard who had used Patton to save his nuts, when the bastard failed to break free from Normandy or provide the winning solution for the Battle of the Bulge on his own.

Once the bastard felt, he did not need him, he had again cut Patton's throat. There can be little question about the personal feelings of General Patton when it comes to General Eisenhower and those who supported him. As you have read, there are many amazing circumstances in this story or at the least, what many will call normal circumstances - such as General Donovan's official date of appointment to Major General being the same day that official OSS records stored at the National Archives, in Maryland, prove Donovan's OSS Organization had two very mysterious missions to France, that began on 10 November, 1944. The two OSS Missions were so Top-Secret that there is no supporting documentation within their official mission files. Each of the two mission files contains one document and that one-half sheet document states, *"Keep no written documentation of this mission."*

(Note: There are no documents under that cover sheet! It was when the author showed this file to the Head Military Historian at the National Archives, along with his other evidence, that the Head Historian told the author, "*You have discovered the best kept secret of World War Two!*"

At 21:28 on 10 November, 1944, a B-24 departed from the Harrington Air Station 179, Northamptonshire. The B-24 belonged to the 856th BS(H), 492nd BG(H), which was referred to as "*The Carpetbaggers*" for being the specified unit that dropped agents and resistance supplies into German occupied territory. The origin of the unit could be traced back to General Donovan, OSS Commander, who had recognized the need for such a unit to support his Top-Secret OSS Missions.

The researcher found a person who was responsible for logging every flight for the Squadron during the war and after the files were unclassified, he obtained a copy of the Flight Log he had filled out. He was positive he had logged every

flight and each had a destination listed, unless it was a test flight that took off and landed at the air station without landing elsewhere. He was surprised to find a flight that had departed Harrington at 21:28 on 10 November, 1944 with no destination listed. It was gone three hours and 49 minutes, the time required to fly to France, make two landings to discharge Top-Secret OSS teams near each of the two crash-sites and return to Harrington Air Station at 01:17 on the 11th. Combined with the two undocumented OSS Missions, the three do provide additional, very strange circumstances of war, or additional, reasonable proof of something so Top-Secret, that it became *Why We Killed Patton! "The Best Kept Secret Of World War Two!"*

Among the "cannot-be-true doubters," will be many who will say the "*Fog of War*" is responsible for the mix up of the two crash-sites. Of course to them, all of it is nothing but meaningless circumstance. The Cartigny Priest must have been lying when he wrote his statement concerning the creation of a grave in November, 1944. What possible reason would the Priest have to do that? Another, was a B-24 was given to the RAF, when it was actually pieces in a "*Foggy*" hole in France. Because, to the "cannot-be-true doubter," if any evidence begins to fit together, that evidence has to be a circumstance or a lie by someone, instead of positive proof.

There was a absolute motive created in November, December, 1944, and you have been reading about that motive. These were not circumstantial events, they were organized events. *They tied distance events together to accomplish a planned and what we believed to be an extremely well - justified, end.* However, you will hear otherwise by those who will never admit what we did, was done for the greater good and it succeeded for more than six decades.

These same people will find an excuse for every connected circumstance, and declare it supplies no new evidence that can be believed. So, to that end, in this chapter I am not placing any direct accusation against anyone. For, if what I am writing about did happen, one only has to follow the extremely reasonable events to an obvious, reasonable and well justified end for those involved.

<u>With this in mind, all I will say is that the best possible outcome for those involved with me and the worst possible outcome for General George S. Patton, did take place in December, 1945</u>.

General Patton, as you have read, was the weakest link in the chain of people from the lowest ranked personnel connected all the way to the highest ranked. A chain of directly involved personnel, that in the end, led all the way to the President of the United States. A chain of people, who became involved in what General Dwight D. Eisenhower and I created during November, December, 1944.

Following: You will be reading part of a paper by:

Allen, Robert S. "Patton's Secret: 'I am Going to Resign. Quit Outright, not Resign.'" Army 21 (June 1971): pp. 29-33

(Note: Robert S. Allen's, paper, as found on the following Internet site, has been partially quoted by me, in the following pages. The Internet site's address is: www.pattonhq.com/textfiles/resign.html
It is a web site maintained in direct support of General Patton's history.)

(**Note**: Researcher - Errors in the posted paper have been included, as found in the paper.)

["Robert S. Allen, a cavalry officer with service in the Regular Army, National Guard, and Army Reserve, was General Patton's chief of combat intelligence. He was promoted to colonel on General Patton's recommendation and was twice personally decorated by him. He originated the book, ***Washington Merry-Go-Round*** (1931), and the subsequent daily column of the same name, and wrote ***Lucky Forward***, a best-seller history of the Third Army, commanded by Patton. Colonel Allen was co-author of the daily syndicated column, "Inside Washington."] - [paper review]

"Before he was fatally injured in an auto crash, General George S. Patton had decided to dramatically resign from the Army with a ***characteristically spectacular statement*** that he was taking this unusual step, "***to be free to live my own way of life***." (Highlights, Author)

"As a 61-year old West Pointer with more than 30 years of active service, including command of his country's first tank force in World War I, Patton was eligible to retire as a four-star general. ***As a retired officer, he would have continued to be subject to military discipline and control***." (Highlights, Author)

"***Independently wealthy***, ***Patton was in a position to give vent to his outraged hurt and frustration*** with such a gesture. So, with ***typical spirited forcefulness***, he was determined to resign rather than retire." (Highlights, mine.)

"Bringing this poignant story to light at this time, after a quarter of a century, is impelled by a recent rumor that there was something sinister about Patton's fatal accident. These accounts vary, in minor ways, but all are similar in two key respects: ***They are devoid of details or particulars regarding the nature and purpose of the reputed mystery***; at the same time, the inference is pronounced that in soe manner ***Patton was the victim of some dastardly plot to kill him***." (Highlights, Author)

"The stories are wholly untrue, ***They are entirely without foundation or a scintilla of evidence*** in the emphatic opinion of those closest and dearest to Patton. These include his late wife who was with him throughout the 12 days he fought a losing struggle for life; his long-time chief of staff and close-friend, Lt. General Hobart R. Ga, who was with him at file time f the accident; Patton's two surviving children, Brig. General George S. Patton, Jr., Assistant Commandant of the Armor School, and Ruth Ellen Totten, widow of an artillery brigadier. Also, Horace L. Woodring, driver of Patton's car, and Robert Thompson, driver of the truck into which Patton's sedan crashed." (Highlights, Author)

"***Just where, how, and why the rumor got started is as baffling as the tale itself.*** Inquires about the source invariably bring vague and ambiguous high-level answers, ***but there is an ironic relationship between the fatal accident and Patton's secret decision to throw up his commission by dramatically resigning***." (Highlight, Author, I agree one hundred percent.)

*"**Had he not made up his mind to quit with a reverberating blast of indignation, it is unlikely the trip on which the auto accident occurred would have taken place**. So, the tragic event came to pass as an indirect consequence of his anguished determination to end his glory studded military career by **demonstratively resigning rather than routinely retiring**."* (Highlights, Author)

(**Note**: I agree, if General Patton had been properly subdued, and shown those who were beating him down that he was defeated, then he would probably have lived. If he had promised to remain silent, remain under their direct military control by retiring, instead of resigning, he would have returned home, without the planned (by his Chief of Staff, General Gay) hunting trip occurring, with its totally unplanned and unexpected automobile accident. The much discussed automobile accident took General Patton out of the direct control of those who had planned a very different end to that hunting trip and placed him in the control of uninvolved hospital doctors. They, for some time, had General Patton on the road to, at the least a partial-recovery and perhaps, a full recovery in due time. However, we had for many years, a President who was somewhat disabled. And ex-General Patton, if he had recovered sufficiently could have used any remaining disability to improve his situation and plan of attack on those who had worked so hard to destroy him.)

"In June, 1945, Patton had returned to the United States for a series of victory celebrations arranged by the Pentagon. *Everywhere be was jubilantly hailed by vast and idolizing throngs*." (Highlights, Author)

"*In Boston, more than 750,000 people jammed the 20-mile parade route roaringly cheering him very foot of the way*. Comparable crowds welcomed him in Los Angles, his home town Denver, and other cities *He was the hero of the hour and be loved every minute of it."* (Highlights, Author)

"A speaker in Denver *effusively hailed Patton as one of the greatest generals of all time*." (Highlights, Author)

(**Note**: Four months later, due to the direct actions of some of those who had signed the official applications previously discussed, General Patton's reputation had been beat down as far and as fast as they could. However, they still realized at that particular moment in history, General Patton was the one most likely to succeed outside the Army in obtaining a high political office. Especially, if General Patton returned to the United States and quit the Army by resigning, instead of retiring. This, I believe you might agree, was something they could not allow to happen if they were to protect their own careers and reputations from a man who knew the truth and had stressed to General Gay, he was prepared to tell that truth!)

"To him the whole debasing affair confirmed strongly a suspicion that had long been brewing in his mind that *malicious and envious forces in and out of the Army were determinedly bent on destroying him and discrediting his matchless record as a battle commander*." (Highlights, Author)

"The more he agonized over it, the more he became convinced that his curt dismissal as Third Army commander was not only ***completely unwarranted and gratuitously unfair, but in tolerable manifestation of the covert conspiracy against him***." (Highlights, Author)

"He determined to put with such insufferable indignities no longer. He began to think how best ***he could strike back and assert himself fully and freely***." (Highlights, Author)

"But all the while ***Patton continued to fume inwardly*** over what had befallen him, and to <u>mull over incessantly what his next step should be.</u>

These ***inflamed thoughts and the consuming anger that prompted them never left him***." (Highlights, Author)

(**Note:** The following paragraphs are a bit out of sequence from their position in the paper. Those used above have skipped areas that do not add or subtract from the underlying thread of this important paper, which I do wish to strongly point out, was written by a Patton staff insider. ***From my point of view, when reading this document, I came to believe it serves more as a cover for those involved and for what was done, than a defense of General Patton.***)

"As the days passed, Patton became increasingly tense and restless. He took long drives by himself, and at times nervously paced the floor of his office. At dinner, he said little and went to his quarters early. He smoked more cigars than usual. It was obvious he was undergoing deep and gnawing turmoil."

"***Early in December, he informed Gay, he intended to spend Christmas with Mrs. Patton*** at their home in Hamilton, Massachusetts, near Boston."

"Admiral Hewitt has invited me to accompany him to the U.S. on his flagship, the Augusta," Patton said, "I'll fly to London on Monday and join him there. ***When I get home, I am going through with my plan to resign from the Army***." (Highlights, Author)

(Remember that General Patton is talking to General Gay, his loyal(?) Chief of Staff.)

"***I'm going to do it with a statement that will be remembered for a long time***. If it doesn't make big headlines, I'll be surprised. ***As, I told you, I am determined to be free to live my own way of life, and I'm going to make that unforgettably clear***." (Highlights, Author)

(**Note**: Remember, in October General Patton had been talking to General Hobart R. Gay and told General Gay of what he was planning to do later. Such a statement by General Patton, his mentor, could not go unreported. Especially, if the loyal (?) Patton staffer would be continuing his own military career, long after Patton could do what he had just threatened to do. Within a day, I knew what General Patton had said, and so did General Eisenhower. Perhaps, I heard it from General Gay, perhaps someone else. Perhaps, a plan began to evolve and was put in place, perhaps, not!)

""Finally one night at dinner, *he said to General Gay,* "*I have given this a great deal of thought. I am going to resign from the Army. Quit outright, not retire. That's the only way I can be free to live my own way of life. That's the only way I can and will live from now on. For the years that are left to me, I am determined to be free to live as I want and to say what I want to. This has occupied my mind almost completely the last two months and I am fully convinced this is the only honorable and proper course to take.*""
(Highlights, Author)

(**Note**: The time line here is very important. General Patton was talking to General Gay and according to this writer's own time line, General Patton had told General Gay he would be leaving for England on Monday, which would have been 10 December, 1945. Immediately, General Gay made the following suggestion for the following day, Sunday, 9 December, 1945, *the only day available before General Patton planned to leave the tight control of those above him and make his way to Boston, via a Navy ship over which they had no control!* To then arrive in Boston and quit the Army, and do exactly what General Patton, well known for speaking his mind and meeting his promises, had stated he would do!)

That statement by General Patton, made directly to General Gay on 8 December, 1945, may have been the statement that sealed his fate and ended his life on 21 December, 1945.)
"*Gay, who had become profoundly concerned about the inner torment and agonizing Patton had been going through for weeks, anxiously cast about for something to divert* and calm him. *Suddenly an idea struck Gay. Striving hard to be nonchalant*, he said to the general ..."   (Highlights, Author)

(**Note**: Was Gay, who had just heard from General Patton, that he was going home for Christmas in two days, profoundly concerned about Patton or *about what he had just hear Patton was going to do?* Why would Gay have to "*Strive hard to be nonchalant?*" Was he just asking General Patton to go hunting the next day or was *he hiding what he had been told he had to do, if and when General Patton set a hard date to go home and suddenly, an in-place plan had to be activated!*
Think about it? Would you be profoundly concerned and striving hard to be nonchalant, if you had to immediately put into place a plan that had been explained to you by a young bird colonel from Eisenhower's staff? Plus, all of it was based on "*verbal orders only*" and your ass was going to be hung out to dry, if you failed to set up the right exit for Patton?)

"*The stories are wholly untrue, They are entirely without foundation or a scintilla of evidence in the emphatic opinion of those closest and dearest to Patton*, Colonel Robert S. Allen, 1969." (Highlights, Author)

323

(**Note**: Please remember, the writing in "quotation marks " are from a direct paper created by Colonel Allen, a self-described insider on General Patton's staff. My comments, within the confines of the review of the paper, are all in (brackets) and consist of my providing exactly, what the paper stated could not possibly exist!)

The challenge is to provide: A reasonable set of events leading to a viable motive why General George S. Patton could not be allowed to return to the United States and quit the United States Army, by people with the power to stop him!
What if Patton had accomplished his goal of quitting the Army as he planned, and if he had left behind any control of his actions by the US Army? From the moment General Patton met with his Admiral friend in England, and especially from the moment General Patton stepped aboard a Navy ship, to the day he resigned from the Army in the US, General George S. Patton would have been removed from the direct control of those involved.

Even if you are a doubter and a deep believer in normal circumstances, by this time in this book, you must be reaching a point where even you must question the last circumstance. Perhaps *you will begin to realize, that what I am presenting is exactly what Colonel Allen stated in his paper in 1969 could not possibly exist!*
A specific motive, by the people who could make it happen, for General Patton to accidently die during the last day of his full physical control by the United States Army in Europe, Commanded by General Eisenhower.
The researcher has not been able to locate a copy of the applications for the *Congressional Medal Of Honor* for Lt. Gott and Lt. Metzger, Jr. The researcher has tried every archive, where archive historians and research specialists state a copy of the two applications for the *Congressional Medal Of Honor* should be on file. Therefore, he has been unable to trace the actual signers, up the entire Chain of Command to General Marshal and to President Roosevelt and the final signatory, President Harry Truman.

I do know that General Donovan's OSS was placed under investigation by President Roosevelt just before he died, and that President Truman, when he received that report, began the process that ended the OSS in late 1945, about the same time, as the unfortunate, to some, death of General Patton.

I do know that a man claiming to have been once been an OSS agent has written that he was offered $10,000 (a lot of money in the 1940s), to kill General Patton. However, *one has to ask, why would Donovan pay such a person, when he had ex-OSS men available, who were deeply involved in the first cover-up, men with the skills and experience required, who would do the job for nothing just to protect their own careers and reputations*?

If one really understands the public reception that General Patton had received in June,1945,during his visit and tour of the United States. It had to be obvious to anyone with any future aspirations for an extended military career or political office that General Patton would be a hard opponent to beat on the election trail if he had lived, told the truth and ran for President in 1948.

It had to be obvious to those at the top of the chain, if General Patton did quit the Army, as their weakest link, ex-General Patton would be free to stand on the political stump and use the standard he had to bear of his punishment for slapping a soldier and telling the truth against them. Ex-General George S. Patton would eat them alive, just by exposing the truth as he knew it to be.

Every one of us, once Patton told the truth, would feel the wrath of Congress and as the public became outraged by the truth, each and every one of us would have been ferreted out. If we were not prosecuted, at the least our careers would be ruined, and for most, we would become outcasts in our own families. This did provide each and ***every one of us, with a genuine motive to kill Patton!***

Even though Patton knew of the crash-site cover-up at the time, in the end, he would have been cheered for doing so, to save Allied and American lives. However, we who hid what we had done with the falsified medal applications and our immediate failure to recover the desecrated war dead remains would have lost our careers, and individually may have faced long prison terms for our actions after the fact. ***That to me, is a sufficient, provable motive to explain why General Patton did not return to the United States in December,1945!***

Picture this - ex-General George S. Patton, with his Army uniform and all its medals and honors dressing a mannequin standing next to him, tells the crowd of 200,000 and the national radio broadcast system, the truth as he knows it.

Telling them, that today he is going to tell them the truth, the real truth about why he is standing there in front of them wearing civilian clothing, when by all rights, he should be wearing this Army uniform (standing beside him on a manikin) that he had worn with pride during the more than 30 years he had served in the US Army to protect the country he so dearly loved. He could have continued with, "I know this audience is an audience of mothers, fathers, wives, husbands, brothers and sisters, of men and women who served with the military forces of the United States during the recent war. I know out there in this audience listening to me at this very moment, are those who had a loved one that served, who left home and who to this day, has never come home. There are others who stand in silent mourning for a loved one who has never been accounted for. I know there are others in this audience who lost loved ones under heroic conditions, who to this day have never received the medals for their heroism their loved one so justly deserved. I know in this audience, there are those of you who remember the award of the ***Congressional Medal Of Honor*** to the two heroic pilots of the "***Lady Jeannette,***" Lieutenants Gott and Metzger, last May. The Medals were awarded to the two men for their heroism in early November, 1944.

At this point in time, all I can ask of you, is for you to remember what was done to me by the news media and General Eisenhower, supported by the highest military and civilian commanders of our country, for my slapping a soldier. Then last October, when I was relieved from my command of the Third Army for telling the truth about my feelings regarding what the Russians are and will be doing in Europe, in the years to come.

For telling that truth, I was relieved from my highest command and shuffled into a dead end command. That blow to my reputation for honesty and truth forced me to make the decision I did. Instead of doing what those over me, who had so dishonored my service, were certain I would do, I took the only honorable path left for me. I took the major step of resigning from the Army, so that I can stand here in front of you and tell you the absolute truth about what those men have done.

They, with full knowledge of what they were doing, desecrated the remains of seven of our American War Dead. Then, instead of correcting what they had done for a justified reason, they left the desecrated dead hidden in the soil of Europe and debauched our highest Military Medal by using it to cover-up what they had done!

In fact, the most damning evidence I can offer to you is the **Citation** of the *Congressional Medal Of Honor* awarded to each of those men. *The descriptions given in the Citations of their bomber's crash and their deaths are false.* The descriptions, however, are an exact description of the crash and death of three men killed in the illegally covered-up crash of their Top-Secret B-24, while flying a Top-Secret night mission with the Royal Air Force.

Now before I go any further, I do want you to understand, I fully agreed with the absolute need to hide the crash of that Top-Secret B-24, at the time it crashed. That B-24 contained a large amount of our most Top-Secret electronic equipment. If the Top-Secrets contained in that B-24 had fallen into the hands of the Germans during the war, they could have used that knowledge against us, resulting in a large number of additional deaths in our Allied military, as well as an untold number of additional civilian deaths before the war in Europe ended.

I, as a major military commander, fully understood at that specific point in time, the need to desecrate the remains of seven of our war dead, with the specific purpose of saving tens of thousands of lives. What I do not understand, nor can I condone today, is the later use of the *Congressional Medal Of Honor* to hide what General Eisenhower had personally ordered to be done, for no other reason than to prevent any stain to his career and the careers of all those who participated in these acts; and yes, in one way, my own career.

However, when the secrecy was no longer required, instead of standing up and admitting to the world what they had done, to this day they continue to attempt to destroy the messenger of their illegal actions.

To prevent their own punishment for their actions, as directed under Army Regulations. They falsified official records, lied to you, the American public, and abused the *Congressional Medal Of Honor* to hide the truth of what was done. Illegal actions, Ladies and Gentlemen, that are much worse than my slapping a soldier. Whom, I still believe, needed discipline more than he needed sympathy.

At this time, I must ask the question, how many of our Missing In Action personnel are missing because their commanders decided they had some reason to hide the dead men's remains? How many commanders have created cover-ups to hide what they had done, by falsifying official records? How many have gone to

326

the extreme of debauching something as precious as our belief in such medals as the ***Congressional Medal Of Honor***, just to protect their personal careers?

I know at least one who has done that, and my honor and duty demanded that I quit the Army and tell you the truth about that man. And, those who support him in this desecration of our combat dead and debauching of our military medals.

My friends, I have prepared full documentation in support of the claims I have placed before you tonight and they are available to the media, the Army and the President. It is my heart held hope, that our government will ensure those who have desecrated our war dead and our military medals, be punished in an equal manner to my punishment for slapping a soldier who failed under fire.

Today, as I stand here before you, you know I personally apologized to that soldier and his Division and today, I again apologize directly to you. My worst sins may be for doing what I believed was necessary for the good of America. One was when I slapped that soldier, because I deeply believed that is what he really needed at the time. Another was speaking what I believe is the truth about the Russians.

Yes, my friends, yes I have sinned and I was severally punished. Today, I stand here before you demanding equal justice for these desecrated American combat dead, and for their families, whose sons' remains were desecrated by their commanders. Each and every one of these men must be removed from their positions and the men responsible must be prosecuted to the fullest extent of Army regulations and United States Law.

In ending, Ladies and Gentlemen, I beg your forgiveness and ask you to remember that I quit the Army to help protect you against the evil these men have put in place, using our combat dead, their families, and our highest military medal to selfishly protect their careers. I promise you, I will continue to protect this country from men like these men and the Russians, who as I have said many times, wish to control the world.

(**Note: Think deeply about it!** Suppose you were one of the signatories of those two ***Medal Of Honor Applications,*** one of the Generals who helped do what was done or, if you were one of the OSS men involved. Ask yourself, what would you have done to prevent Patton from making such a speech?)

What General Gay said to General Patton on 8 December, 1945, "***You haven't done any hunting for quite a while. How about going tomorrow***? They tell me the countryside is overrun with pheasants. ***With the men away during the war, the birds became very plentiful***. You could stand a little relaxation before you go home." (Highlights, Author)

Please remember, that the statement was reported by an insider, who for some reason believed General Gay had to "***Strive hard to be nonchalant***." Why? Apparently General Patton was not suffering that badly from his inner torment and was not agonizing, as he was willing to go hunting the day before he was to leave his last Army Command!

"It was a lucky try, **Patton perked up instantly and evinced keen interest**."

"You've got something there, Hap," he exclaimed, "Doing a little bird-shooting would be good. You're right. I haven't been out much of late, and *before I leave* I ought to see how good that gun is and whether my hunting eye is as sharp as it used to be. Yes, let's do that. *You arrange to have the car* and guns on hand early tomorrow and we'll see how many birds we can bag." (Highlights, mine.)

At this point, I will no longer be mixing "quotes" from Col. Allen's paper and my comments. So I will no longer use (brackets) to differentiate between the report and my own writings.

The rest is basically, history.

Suddenly, many top commanders, world heroes all, were facing ruin; as did every involved lower ranked person who had anything to do with what had been done - especially if that "big mouthed bastard" went back to the States and did exactly what he was threatening to do! Patton was known to do just that; speak his mind and then back it up, with action!

What were those who had been involved to do? If, they attempted to help Truman, Patton had their ass. If they tried to shut Patton up in the States, Patton would have the stump, the access and the required power to put their ass's exactly where Patton would want to put them, when he sought the righteous revenge that in one way made sense, even to them.

Thanks to General Gay, the involved men had two months warning to plan and put in place what might have to be done. It is important to remember, out in those very same fields, recent German soldiers would be hunting for the same pheasants. Many of the recent German soldiers would have returned home too late to make up for the crop loss while they were being detained after the war ended, and pheasants would be an excellent source of a meal for their families.

Wouldn't it have been a shame, if on his last day in Germany, some Werewolf German, who were Germans who performed terrorists acts after the war ended, shot and killed General Patton while he was pheasant hunting?

That would serve two excellent purposes. First, the chain's "weak link," would be go away and secondly, they would now have "carte blanche" to hunt down and destroy the German Werewolves, who were still killing American soldiers.

All they had to do was to make certain General Patton was in the right place at the right time and the specially selected OSS men were also in the right place. OSS men, who were part of the group of men directly involved at the crash-sites and who would, with a German rifle and bullet, solve the only real threat to the *"The Best Kept Secret Of World War Two!"*

Major General Donovan was one of the very few to hear what had to be done and he certainly had no love for General Patton, who had once told OSS men to leave his office. Perhaps, someone with direct power over the right men and who

328

knew what had to be done, contacted two men to inform them they were going to have their careers ruined and possibly go to jail, after Patton returned home to tell the truth and the public learned they were involved in what was done. Then the public and Patton would demand they received proper punishment.

When finished laying out the problem, the power player asked his carefully selected two, one question. "We cannot let that happen, right?" Their answer was as direct, "Whom do we contact, to get there and when does it have to be done?"

Now, I will not say that I was involved. What I will tell all of you, *is the end often justifies the means required to reach that end!*

It had been in the works for some time, however General Gay had previously, been unable to find the right time to get General Patton out in the field, pheasant hunting. However, when it suddenly became obvious to General Gay that the next day was the last day Patton would be in Europe, he had no choice. What had to be done, had to be done tomorrow! So General Gay, "*strived to remain nonchalant*" and, as soon as General Patton agreed, Gay made a call reporting that General Patton was going to be pheasant hunting in the specified field the next morning, as requested.

Then, some truck driver who was not paying attention, turned in front of another distracted driver, and pure circumstance stepped in to destroy that day's plan of action, **when Patton was accidently injured in a real accident**!

However, many have died of such an injury and if needed, the assets were still in place. There was no rush as long as Patton was in Europe, the assets would remain active, staying in place near the hospital where Patton was a patient. They could be easily activated if Patton began to improve, and was to be taken to Boston by people they could not control. With luck, if General Patton died on his own, the mission was accomplished by pure accident and the assets could go home.

So people waited and wondered if nature would do by accident what had been planned as the murder of one of the most famous American generals by some Nazi bastard, who would have somehow be dead when located.

Then, the unexpected and unwanted news was made public; General Patton was improving as his wife traveled from Boston to be by his side, having set off as soon as she had been told of his accident. By the time she arrived, General Patton had improved greatly. One day, while visiting her husband with General Gay, General Patton's wife specifically asked the doctors, in front of General Gay, if General Patton could be flown home to Boston? She was told it was looking very good and the doctors would immediately prepare his transport to a Boston hospital.

Some might have felt sorry that Mrs. Patton was the one who forced the activation and implementation of Plan B. Most did not care. So, the already in-place assets were activated, to complete the assigned project as soon as possible.

That night, two men dressed as hospital staff and carrying cleaning equipment and supplies entered an unguarded, locked door to the hospital. A few minutes later, one distracted the nurse who was specifically tasked with watching General Patton. Then, General Patton moved in his drugged sleep, as a hand gently

lifted the cover over his foot and another hand quickly injected a substance between his middle toes.

When that man had finished his cleaning chore, he walked past the nurse, who was again sitting and observing General Patton. Then, the two men made their way back through the locked door and away from the hospital. Within hours, both were on an Army plane heading away from their temporary assignment in Europe. Heading back to where they had received their personal telephone call from the one with direct power over them.

At least one of the authors of military fiction has written, basically the same exit for Patton as I have. However, that writer could not present a viable, believable, original motive for Patton's murder. Perhaps that writer was writing from personal experience and perhaps, he was there the night Patton became infected. However, he may have also participated in a very limited way in the events of November '44, and 1945, and it was very important that he created a false motive without a real base in fact, if his original goal was to lay a false trail.

The next day the newspapers were full of the news that General Patton had taken a turn for the worse during the night. Soon, they were reporting that General Patton had an uncontrolled infection, caused by his injuries from the automobile accident, and his prognosis was not good.

Two days later, the same newspapers that would have headlined ex-General Patton's quest for the Presidency across their front pages, and would have helped tear down those who had now ensured General Patton would never return to the United States, headlined their newspapers with the news of General Patton's unfortunate, but to us, timely death.

As General Patton had a broken neck and his wife was present before he took the turn for the worse due to an infection, who could question the source of the infection? Obviously, the infection had to have been a result of his injuries!

At once, General George S. Patton's death was declared to have resulted from his injuries received in the (totally accidental) automobile accident. Then General Patton was buried without a complete autopsy, with full military honors on Christmas Day, 1945, in the American Luxembourg World War Two Cemetery - the same Christmas Day that General Patton had been planning to be celebrating at home, finally free to tell the truth about those bastards who were attempting to destroy his reputation.

As his body was prepared for burial, the small hole between his middle toes was not seen and for more than sixty years, what had been the official story of General Patton's death has remained unchanged.

Of course, as you know ... under the command of the right people, *with a specified end in mind, the means can be found to create the specified end.*

(**Author's Note:** At this point, it is necessary for me to insure the reader understands one major point of this book, let's call it, **"stating my case."**

The obvious fact is, that General Patton died and that he ***died before he could return to the United States***.)

Another obvious fact is, that until you read this book, no one has ever revealed a motive for General Patton's death that was based on any solid foundation of evidence. This book, for the first time reveals a solid motive that you, the reader, can re-research for yourself, if you desire. You can visit all the locations listed. You can stand in a woods in France and know on the 9th of November, 1944, four men died there and the evidence is there to see.

As to the method of death of General Patton. I have heard and read all sorts of theories concerning his death. Rubber bullets, a nut or bolt and yes, one I have somewhat repeated in this book. However, I firmly believe the accident was just that. If, I had the power to hire a truck driver to do what was done, then that truck driver would be dead within days in another accident, doubt it, research his life, he lived a long time and to the end he declared, "It was an accident!"

If you think just a little about what it would have taken to set up such an accident, how many such setups in movies need to be retaken several times? A train blocked the track and would have had to have been controlled to have each vehicle reach the accident point at the second required. How many spotters and controllers would it have taken to arrange that. It was a very active road and the truck sitting on the road for the time to put it all together, would have had a massive back up and all told, there would be dozens of unnecessary witnesses to something supposed to be so secret, no one would doubt the cause of General Patton's death.

How he died exactly, will remain speculation for ever. The fact, that he had absolute evidence that would destroy a lot of people's lives and the ability to make it happen, is true and fully laid out in this book. The truth is, that General Patton could not be allowed to return to the United States and do what he stated he was going to do!

General Patton - never to return and never, as he planned, to destroy those who were attempting to destroy him.

Photograph: US Army Archives

331

General Patton's Grave at the American Luxembourg National Cemetery

Photograph: Willis S. Cole, Jr. - June, 2018

Chapter Fifteen
Clean and Forget!
Tincourt-Boucly

(**Note:** The following is what the Author would like to believe happened, so it may have or may not have happened. Only a fully supported, deep *"Search and Recovery"* of the *"Lady Jeannette"* crash-site in the Bois de Hattonville can provide the answer to the question, where are the remains of the three complete bodies?)

In February, 2001, the Defense Agency now titled " The Defense POW/MIA Accounting Agency," **based on the evidence presented in this book**, had a full "**Search and Recovery**" scheduled and then, because of "**politics,**" the "<u>Search and Recovery</u>" was cancelled. The author was told by a person fairly high up in the organization, that they did not want the American public to know the truth that the remains of two **Congressional Medal Of Honor Awardees** and a crewman who died with them, are not in their "**Official Graves!**"

As of this writing, that has been prevented by the French and American governments. With the French government refusing the required permit to dig below the grass root level at the crash-site, the author has been warned, if anyone is found digging at the site, they may go to prison for some time and knowing French prisons, the law is followed.

In early spring, three years after those December days in 1945, when I thought I had finished tying all the loose ends together, I was reminded I had not left it all behind.

At the time I was working on my doctorate thesis and it was a quarter that I had no set schedule to worry about, as long as my thesis was finished on time. Even though I had been reading about and was fully informed on what was going around the world concerning our war dead, I certainly had not expected to become directly involved in any way.

That morning I picked up the telephone, expecting a call from my lady friend. However, it was from someone else. I would know that voice anywhere! He told me the Limey storage area, where there were some items I might be interested in, was being deactivated and it was time those items were taken care of, once and for all. I asked him what it was that he wanted me to do? He told me to make my excuses at the school and get ready to leave for Germany at once.

I was to contact him at a number he gave me, the moment I arrived in Germany. He said a set of high priority orders were en route to me, via special delivery and when I walked back into the house on my return I was to burn them. Then the familiar voice said, "Talk to you over here, colonel," and he hung up. "Damn!" I said to myself as I got out my B-4 bag and I began to pack.

As I packed, I thought about some of the Graves Registration information I had learned in England. One of the things I had been told was about a conference concerning our war dead in 1943. The conference had at least one goal. However, it ended without a hard decision and the decision's buck was passed on, to a time to be determined after the war had ended.

As often happens, when two or more people are involved in a committee, the solid decision set out to be gained is pushed aside by the people on the committee, and in effect, they pass the buck to others. In this situation, the committee did not make a decision to create or not create overseas cemeteries after the war. Instead, they decided to have the decision made by people who would not know they were participating in one of the strangest elections ever held and one that would never be held again. Once, the long-term costs had been realized!

A few years after the war ended, each **L**egal **N**ext **O**f **K**in, who had lost a loved one overseas with a recovered and identified remains, was sent a document that was basically a ballot for an election, though they did not know it.

On the ballot, the LNOK could select one of several options. They could request their loved one be brought back to the United States and buried in a private cemetery of their choice or at one of the national cemeteries around the United States. Another option available to the LNOK, was to have the remains of their loved one sent to a foreign country for burial in a cemetery of their selection. The final option was to request their deceased be buried in the overseas American cemetery of their choice. This, in one real situation, allowed the Philippine wife of an American aviator killed in Europe in a B-17 crash, to have her husband buried at the American Manila Cemetery in the Phillipines.

What the LNOK, who submitted the forms, did not know was the committee in 1943 had set a level that had to be met, if there were to be any permanent World War Two Cemeteries created overseas. The committee had selected the arbitrary level of 60/40. If more than 60 percent of those submitting Burial Location Forms, selected burial in the United States, then all of the dead would be returned to the United States for burial and no overseas cemeteries would be created.

(**Note:** Such a decision would never be left to the LNOK again. As time has proven, overseas cemeteries are very expensive to maintain, when viewed in a decades and centuries time frame. It is now much easier and economical to return the dead at once and have "Final Disposition" take place at the earliest possible moment. "***Final Disposition***" is an actual term used in WWII burial records.)

When the LNOK forms (ballots) were returned and recorded, and the number of Unknowns added in, more than 40 percent of the replies requested an overseas burial. With that, the committee's decision was made for them, the United States would create a limited number of American World War Two Cemeteries around the world, in addition to our existing WWI cemeteries.

With the return of the completed forms, the election was over and final plans were put in place to care for those with known graves or who were in a grave marked Unknown. The first step was to disinter all the dead, even if they were already interred at a temporary cemetery that had been selected to become a permanent cemetery. During the process of disinterment and re-burial, the original grave was opened under the scrutiny of a licensed mortician. The number of morticians at each cemetery varied. During the disinterment process, they worked in side by side teams, with each team consisting of a trained mortician and his helpers. As each new set of graves was opened, the grave's contents were removed and placed on inspection tables to be processed by a team mortician.

Given the work involved, the sideways movement of a large number of men would create a very messy work environment, so the SOP (Standard Operating Procedure) for grave opening was for the excavating personnel to open the set number of graves in one row. Then, as those graves were processed, another set of graves was opened in the next row, and so on. The row by row movement would be followed until the last row was reached, then the teams would sidestep, more of a "U" step, over to the next set of opened graves in the same row and began to work back down the rows to where they had started at the first row.

With this method of opening the graves at the Limey Cemetery, a different mortician was involved with opening and inspecting of the contents of each grave from the B-17 crash-site. When the graves of the four dead crewmen from the *"Lady Jeannette"* were opened, there was no way for the individual mortician involved to realize that there was something very wrong with what he was seeing. The fact was, they would be working with over ten thousand dead in that one cemetery and who would be looking for the one or four sets of remains that had been desecrated, *as we Americans would not do that!*

Once the contents of the grave were placed on the processing table, the mortician who was working under the requirements of a *"Disinterment Directive"* for those specific remains in that particular grave, would review the contents of the grave to ensure the remains in the grave matched the official record for that grave. During the process, they would create an inventory of the contents in the grave and confirm the identity of the dead, using the original *"Report of Burial,"* along with any other identification evidence the morticians found within the grave, such as one of the dead's Identity Tags.

(**Note**; one was always to be with the remains. If the burial of an identified person had been made without an identity tag, a sealed burial bottle would be located with the body with the identification information contained on the Report of Burial at the time of original burial.)

At some existing temporary cemeteries such as the St-Avold Cemetery, which had been selected to become a permanent cemetery, those remains that had been selected to be buried at the permanent St-Avold Cemetery were disinterred and put through the re-identification process before being placed in a *"Transit Box"*

(temporary casket). Which was stored until the permanent cemetery could be laid out and prepared for re-burial of those who were to stay there forever.

The remains that had been selected to be moved elsewhere were placed in transit boxes and sent to their selected permanent overseas cemetery or to the Antwerp Re-Casketing Point. At Antwerp, the remains selected to be returned to the States, were reprocessed for safety and then inserted into the transportation chain to be transported to the selected burial location in the United States.

At that point in my musing, I was pulled back into the room where I was packing, as someone knocked on the door. When I answered, there was a captain standing there with a sealed envelope. He asked for some identification and I showed him my Army identification card. Then, he handed the envelope to me, at the same time telling me, his contact number was on the top sheet, and when I was ready to act, I was to give him a call. I asked the captain to come in, sit down and wait a minute. I went into the bathroom, opened the sealed envelope and pulled out the contents. As the captain had just told me, there was a cover letter, and under it were the orders I had been told to expect. I noted they were dated yesterday, so they were already valid and I could begin what I had been told to do.

I returned to the front room and told the captain to get some coffee at the nearby coffee shop and that I would be leaving with him in about 30 minutes. I wrote my roommate a note, telling her that I could be gone for up to a month, but I hoped much less. My absence would be concerned with special orders I had just received and I would explain it to her when I returned. I included the captain's name and contact number, with a specific note that she had better be delivering our baby if she had to call him. As she was not pregnant, I thought that would explain it to her and I concluded, asking her to please make an excuse to the university for me and pay any of my bills that might arrive and that I ... but you do not need that!

I finished my packing and was closing the drawers, when the captain rang the doorbell again. Carrying my B-4 bag, I opened the door, stepped outside, locked the door and dropped my keys through the mail slot in the door. The captain took my B-4 bag and I followed him down the stairs and to his car. As we got to the car, I told the captain I preferred the front seat and he opened the door for me and closed it after I had gotten in. He walked around to the trunk, opened it, put in my B-4 bag and got into the car, asking me where I wanted to go?

I told him to get me to the nearby air base operations center as quick as he could. When we arrived, he got my B-4 from the trunk, opened my door for me and as I got out, he asked if I would require him any longer? I told him to go ahead and take off. However, if he got a call for any reason from my roommate, (I gave him the slip of paper with her name and work contact number on it), he was to do whatever was necessary to answer her questions or provide whatever help she might require. He pulled to attention, replied, "Yes, Sir, I will do that," and he popped a really snappy salute. I was not in uniform, so he did not have to do that. So, I returned his salute as snappy as I could, even if I was not supposed to when I was in civies (slang for civilian clothing). I picked up the B-4 bag, turned and headed into the flight operations center.

I went into the base operations center, where a sergeant asked me what he could do for me? I told him to get the highest ranking person in the place as fast as he could. Obviously this sergeant knew someone who thought they were important when he saw them, and in a minute I was talking to a Lieutenant Colonel.

He asked me how fast was I prepared to go? He had some slow birds and one real fast one with two seats in it. He said he had a hot pilot to go with the fast one, who loved to show people how fast he could go. I told, the Colonel to get his man in here and get his plane ready, and I would need to be outfitted for the flight. He asked me how far toward Europe did I want him to take me? I told him, to the closest base with a plane with the range to take me directly to Germany.

He said he knew where that would most likely be, and he would call there before we left to make certain they would have a plane available when I arrived. I told him to make the call, and if necessary, I was to be the only passenger on the plane heading across the pond. He was also to pass on whatever information he needed from my orders to ensure that was fully understood. He told me he would make the call right away and he should know within five minutes if that was the best plan. I walked over to a coffee set up, asked the sergeant if it was okay for me to get a cup? He said, "Sure" and offered me the choice of some cookies and sandwiches in the closed drawer under the coffee urn.

As promised, the Colonel was back in five or less and told me I had two options. They had a scheduled bomber passing through about the time I would arrive or they had a DC-4 passing through a few hours later, which would be more comfortable. However, the second option would require a three-hour delay and a somewhat longer flight time, as the bomber could be diverted to Germany after one refueling stop in Iceland and the DC-4 was scheduled to England and could not be diverted. Then, in England, I would have to get another flight to Germany. I asked the colonel if he had told the person at that base that my orders gave me the power to divert the DC-4 to Germany if I wished? He said he had not, as he wanted to check with me first.

I told him he had made a damn good choice and for him to call the base right back and tell them to make arrangements for that bomber to take me to Germany. At the same time, he was to make certain the bomber was to have full priority on all needs to prepare for the hop. I told him to inform the base operations there what time he thought we would arrive. To make certain, the bomber was set up to take off as soon as I arrived and that the base would give his pilot priority for a turn around to return to this base.

The colonel told me he would do that at once, and then he thanked me for remembering his pilot and plane. Usually pilots doing such ferry work could expect to be put behind everyone else when they landed.

Just as the Colonel returned to tell me it was all set, a kid who looked like he should still be in short pants arrived. He was wearing a flight suit and was introduced to me as the pilot I had asked for. He was a Captain although I did not see any evidence that he was shaving. However the colonel saw my look and when the Captain went to check on the weather at the base the colonel had just given him,

the Colonel turned to me and said, you could hardly believe he was an "Ace" and had shot down two ME-262's while flying fast and fancy in his P-51Mustang!

I had to admit I was surprised, and the colonel told me I would remember this trip east a long time because he was going to tell the pilot I would be very happy to have a record set on our way to Westover. Then he asked me to follow him and he would get me a set of loaner flight gear.

Well, it was a two-seater, but it was a P-51 to the Captain and it was a trip I definitely would remember, because on the way he asked me if he could test it a bit? By the time I got him to stop, he was laughing and I was making use of one of the waxed paper bags, the Base Operations Colonel had been smart enough to stick into one of the pockets of the flight suit.

When we pulled up to the flight line position the pilot had been given by the Westover tower when we landed, I saw a B-17G, all shiny and bright, sitting by itself with a fuel truck pulling away and men removing rolling stairs from the engines. Standing around the B-17, were several men in flight clothing, and they were looking at our plane as the Captain came to a stop next to the B-17. It was obvious they knew I was coming and they were ready to go.

I climbed out when a ground crewman opened the cockpit and I turned and thanked the pilot for the quick trip and for all the fun as he tested the plane and I handed him the now full, waxed bag. I could tell the smile on his face was more in mirth than serious. I told him to tell the colonel, I would have to return the flight clothes when I came back, as I did not have time to search for replacements before I left. We shook hands and then he told me that if I wanted a flight back when I got back to Westover, contact the colonel and let him know, I wanted a return flight.

As I walked to the B-17, the fuel truck which had stopped, rolled around both planes and came to a stop along the side of the two-seater, to "fill her up." At the same time, the men who had been working on the B-17G were asking Speedy, the pilot what he needed? He told them to take my B-4 to the B-17 and fill him up.

When I approached the B-17, a captain walked over and introduced himself as the pilot and said he expected I was the passenger he had been told to get to Germany as soon as possible. I told him I was, and he said I had the choice of a seat in the radio compartment or a squat and lie in the nose.

I told him, that I thought I would prefer the comfort of the nose. He laughed and told me, to enjoy the view. He called over two 1st lieutenants, and introduced them as the bombardier and navigator. They told me, to follow them and get comfortable as we would be leaving in a few minutes. The captain told me he had already filed his flight plan and would make the final entries over the radio with the control tower as we taxied to the runway.

I managed to get up through the nose hatch, after watching the bombardier do it, with the help of the navigator who pushed where and when he had to. He followed me up, then the captain came up through the hatch and looked down through the hatch and he told me the fellow following, was the copilot. When the copilot swung up through the hatch, I recognized him as one of the 2nd lieutenants I had seen making a fool of himself a few years before, in the "O" Club at the 452nd.

He did not recognize me and I did not let him know I recognized him, but I did note that he was also wearing captains bars. It was good to know that at least one of those fellows had made it through.

As I turned to find my best squat and lie position, I was thinking maybe he was one of the ones whose lives we may have saved in November 1944. Then I ruined my own thought when I realized - **we may not have made any difference**!

When the pilot and copilot started the engines and tested them, my mind drifted to France and November, 1944. As the B-17 began to move, I thought, "I'm on my way men, to make it good!" When we took off, I was thinking of the dead men's remains I had last seen in 1944, "When I come home after this final cleaning up, you too will be heading home or to your new home in the earth of Europe."

We landed at Iceland some hours later and filled the tanks with fuel. The captain told me they were ready to take me all the way to the air base in Germany, where they were going to drop me off. Realizing they had to be as tired as I was, I was remembering the story Lt. Harms had told during his interview with the Group and Squadron Commanders, when he talked about his B-17 sliding onto the glacier in Iceland and having to walk out two weeks later. With my lesson learned, I told the pilot to forget the original orders to get me to Germany as soon as possible. I was changing that order from getting to Germany as soon as possible to, as soon as reasonable. Now, we will overnight in Iceland and head for Germany in the morning when we were all nice and fresh.

Then, I told the captain, to see that his enlisted men were taken care of and meanwhile I would see that we were. Within the hour, I was sitting with the officers in the "O" Club, listening to their stories of flying over Europe and the Pacific during the war, when they asked me if I had any good stories? Yeah, I told them, I was in the right places at the right time to learn all the BS where the action did not take place and none of my stories were worth listening too.

Well, they were flyers - they looked at me once, then one of them began to talk about the time their B-17 had drifted over another B-17 just before bomb-drop and the pilot had refused to drop his bombs. When they got back, the 452nd "ass-hole" of a commander ... then the storyteller quickly looked at me and asked me to pardon him for his language, he then continued his story to say that the group commander had told his pilot the next time they would drop the damn bombs on the B-17 below. That way, his and their bombs would have landed in Germany and that was their job. After that day, his pilot was a son-of-a-gun, concerning any formation drift. As you have guessed, he was the one I recognized, and as the others laughed, I also laughed with them. But I did not tell that officer, that the commander he was talking about was actually one of the good ones.

We arrived in Germany the next day and I phoned the man who had called me and we set up an appointment. When I got to the meeting point, he told me he had made arrangements on the side, that I did not need to know about, for three transit boxes from the Fosse Cemetery and four from the Limey Cemetery to be pulled out of at transfer points along their transit route. He went on to tell me he had contacted a person whom I had worked with, in '44 and '45, now fairly high in

the newly formed CIA (Central Intelligence Agency), and two of them were on their way to help me.

They would arrive later this afternoon and after getting our transportation, we could head out early tomorrow morning. He continued by saying, "It was time we cleaned up and forgot as we had promised ourselves in December '44."

I told him we would get it done and asked who were our contact points at the two locations he had told me about? He gave me an envelope and said it contained all the information and funds we might need. With that, he reminded me, "We were to make certain absolutely no documentation would remain when we were finished the job, just like in '44."

With that, he asked me, "Colonel, do you have any questions?" I told him I did not. We shook hands and agreed that I would not see him when we were done, but I would call his office and leave the message, "clean and forget," so he would know the mission was accomplished.

That night, I met up with the two men I had worked with, in '44, without having actually seen them at that time. I realized, I might have worked with them again in '45, again, without seeing them. This time, they would know me and I would know them. We went into town, found a small bar and went to a table in the rear where there were no doors, no windows or people. Over a drink, and with low voices, we discussed what we had to do.

I told them I had the orders and transportation requests we would need to get a car tomorrow morning and my suggestion was to head toward Paris early in the morning to our first job location, do what we had to do there and then head toward Verdun to accomplish the rest of the assignment. They agreed and asked about shovels and such. I told them we would purchase all the gear we needed at outside stores, so the gear could never be traced to us and we would discard the gear when we were done. With that, they had no more questions and since the night was still young, we paid our bill and went down the avenue to a highly recommended bar/dance hall, and then took a taxi back to the base before midnight.

The next morning, they knocked on my door as I finished packing and I told them I would be out in a minute. We caught a ride to the motor pool with a Pfc. who had dropped off an officer, and we left 20 minutes later, in a car with four cans of spare gas in the trunk and strapped to the side of the car. Then we went by the mess hall and with a quick show of my orders, we left there after breakfast with several thermos bottles of coffee, sandwiches, and some "C Ration" boxes.

The roads were all cleared, mostly repaired and somewhat back to normal. However, there was still a lot of damage everywhere, with temporary housing units built out of the materials left when the bombers visited during the war. There were many destroyed or damaged building, and in some places, we could see damage dating back to the German bombers of 1939/40.

We drove most of that day and it was very hard to make good time. In the late afternoon we pulled into Lille, found a hotel where our car could be locked up, and enjoyed the evening before we began our verbally ordered clean-up tasks.

In the morning, just south of Lille, we passed the huge cones of the mining waste around Mons and Lens, then we passed through Arras and Bapaume, to arrive in Péronne about 13:00. Being that late, I decided we would just case the location where the first job was located, to see if anything had changed. Then we would spend the night in Péronne and head out in the morning to find and recover the remains that I had ordered hidden in the field, in November '44.

We found the village of Cartigny, and the road Coiner, the surgeon and I had taken those few years before. We slowed up as we neared the field where the hidden remains were located and found the field had been planted in sugar beets, which were still fairly small plants.

Speeding up, we went on to the next village, Tincourt-Boucly, turned to the right and headed back to Péronne to find a local service station. At first the Frenchman did not seem very interested in selling us gasoline, or essence as they call it, but he soon changed his mind when I showed him a package of American cigarettes. As I paid him, I thought it was sure nice of the general to see the envelope I had received, had contained a supply of German Marks along with Belgium and French Francs.

After I had paid, the other two told me they had been advised to get a draw of funds and if I ran low, all I had to do was ask them. Our next stop was at a local store to get boots, rubber gloves, water proof tarps, some rope and three shovels. Once they were loaded in the trunk we went back to the hotel, locked up the car in the garage at the back of the hotel, and walked around the large town of Péronne to see the sights and work up a hunger for dinner.

The next morning, after a leisurely breakfast we got the car and left for the field. When we arrived, some farmers were moving a herd of cattle across and down the road to another field, so, we drove past the burial site and went on to visit the British World War One British Cemetery at Tincourt-Boucly. I did not tell the men I knew what had created the low place in the field across the way, but I did tell them that the empty spaces they saw between the English graves had been filled with American dead until 1924/25, when we moved them to the Bony American Cemetery, located about nine miles to the east of this cemetery.

They complimented me, on my knowing the history of that cemetery. I told them my father and uncles had been in the "Big One" and I had spent several summers with them some years ago, visiting most of the battle areas and a lot of cemeteries like this one.

As we were leaving the cemetery, a farmer who had been standing by his horses resting under the trees across from the cemetery entrance, heard us speaking English and he walked over to ask us in fairly good English, if we were Americans?

I told him in French that we were and that we were just visiting the area to stop by this cemetery and see where the Americans had been buried after the "Great War." He asked if we knew about the American "Avion Fortress, B-17" that had crashed in the field across the valley? He pointed at the shallow saucer left in the field where the "Avion Fortress" had crashed. I told him we did not know about that, and we listened to his story of being woken up by the crashing bomber. Then,

341

later that morning, he had helped pick up the dead, which he said was like the meat of the hog, when they cut it up for sausage. As he talked about cutting the hog, his right hand made a cutting motion over his left hand.

I asked him what had happened to the "Avion Fortress, B-17" as it looked as if no plane had crashed there? He told us the Americans had come with a big earth mover the day after the crash, and had pushed all the pieces into the hole and smoothed it over. However, he continued, the Germans had come to Tincourt-Boucly, two summers ago in 1946, and they had a steam powered shovel on a truck. They had dug down into the earth, removed all they could find of the pieces of the "Avion Fortress" the Americans had buried in '44 and filled the hole back up. He said that he had watched them do the digging and the Germans had found one engine buried 5 meters down.

That was extremely interesting to me, as I knew the B-24 had not been reported as lost and it was the B-17 that had been reported as crashing here. The Germans in 1946, in order to be able to know how to salvage a buried airplane here, had to have been instructed by the American Salvage Board as to the location of the crashed B-17, including the fact that the B-17 had been destroyed, the pieces had been buried, and they would need a steam shovel to unearth the pieces for salvage. *Now I knew at least that part of my November '44 plan had succeeded.*

When we drove out of Tincourt-Boucly to the hidden burial site, the cattle were in the field and we could not see anyone who might observe what we were going to do. We pulled over and stopped at the corner of the field where the remains had been buried.

I told the other two I was a worker just like they were and we put on the boots as fast as we could and got into the field to dig up the remains. I had already told the men what we were going to be doing, when we had spent the night at Lille. I did not tell them how the remains had gotten there or why we were going to recover them. I just told the men that we were going to be digging up a missed WWII grave.

To keep the farmer happy, we dug down and around each sugar beet plant and lifted it and a good chunk of dirt to the side, before digging down to get the remains. The digging was easy and I was certain we were in the right location, but we were finding nothing. Then, one of the men reached down into the dirt on his shovel and asked me if this was what we were searching for? It looked like part of a bone to me and then looking closely, we all began to see tiny slivers and bits of bone mixed into the earth.

We dug a bit more and it was soon obvious that the remains that had been here were no longer here. There was nothing we could do about it and the longer we stayed exposed in the open, the less sense it made to keep looking and letting the French realize we were searching for something in the field.

I started to fill the hole back up and the others quickly followed my lead. I threw the sliver of bone we had found back into the hole and covered it up. While I shoveled, I had to wonder, where did you guys wander off to and how did you manage to do it?

One thing, that sticks in my mind to this day, was how hot and humid it had become that day, for so early in the year. It was the start, of what the French call a "farmer's spring." And every farmer would be out preparing his fields and planting the year's spring crops.

We trampled down the dug-up dirt, dug places for the plants we had removed and after tramping them back into the dirt, we sat on the car running board and cut the dirt off our boots with the shovels. When we had gotten the boots a bit clean and put our shoes back on, we placed the boots on a tarp in the trunk along with the dirty shovels, got into the car and drove down the road toward Cartigny. Just as we approached Cartigny, I remembered the Frenchman I had seen in '44.

I told the fellow who was driving, to go straight at the intersection in Cartigny. And, as we were passing the sugar factory office where the copilot had landed and were heading toward the Amiens-St-Quentin road, I told them his story of sliding down the roof to end up standing in front of the office door.

As we left the village of Cartigny, had we turned right at the next road and went about a block to the village cemetery for a quick visit, this book would probably have never been written.

Unknown to us, if we had visited the cemetery and gone to the first grave, on the left, just past the service area. next to the French Soldiers' graves, we would have found a small wooden cross with a plaque stating that it was the grave of an American Aviator Inconnu or Unknown, who had died in a nearby aircraft crash.

Down by the church, inside the presbytery, CURÉ Étienne Serpette had his windows open and was preparing his Sunday sermon. As we drove away from Cartigny, he heard the sound of our American car and instantly, he was reminded of when the Americans had arrived at Cartigny after the war, searching for isolated Americans killed during the war.

When he and the Mayor had sort of lied to them, as they told the Americans, they knew of no American war dead buried **_around_** Cartigny. They were telling the truth to the Americans. They knew, there was no American combat dead buried **_around_** Cartigny.

The American Unknown Aviators, who had been buried in a hidden grave by their own people, were now safely buried **_in_** the village cemetery. He had made certain of that.

On the 23rd of November 1944, the Priest had collected the "American hidden remains" and placed them in a grave in the village cemetery. Then he wrote a legal statement for the record about the grave that was placed in the village archives. This document was to be found at a much later date, on 8 June, 1994, by the French **_Commemo-Rangers_** and a certified copy was given to the researcher to help with his research.

Interpretation

American Unknown
Cartigny Cemetery,
Military Tombs
1939-1944

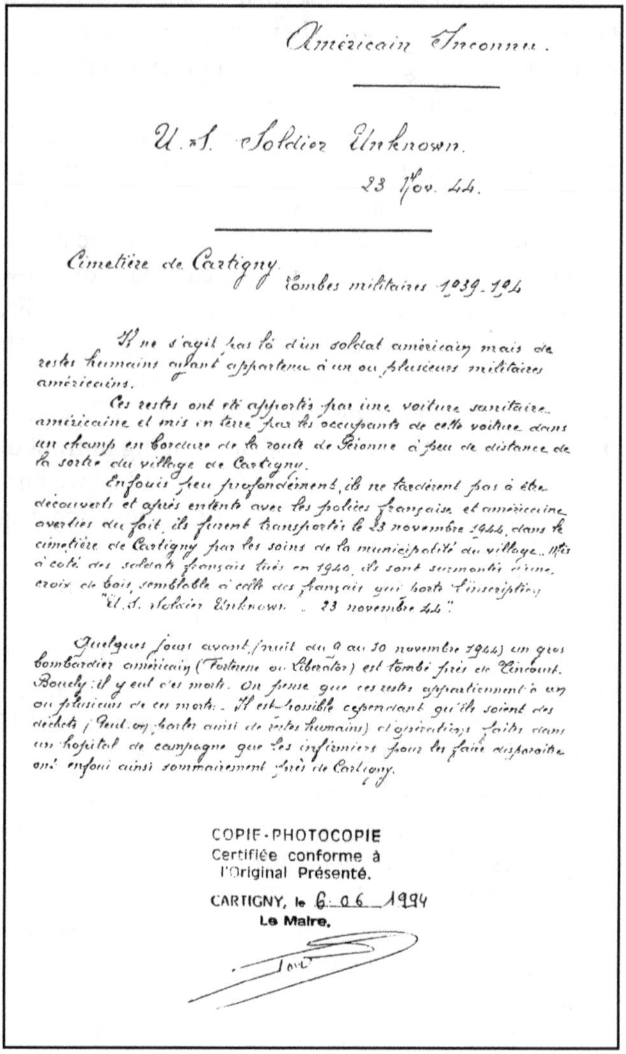

Américain Inconnu.

U. S. Soldier Unknown.

23 Nov. 44.

Cimetière de Cartigny

Tombes militaires 1939-194

Il ne s'agit pas là d'un soldat américain mais de restes humains ayant appartenu à un ou plusieurs militaires américains.

Ces restes ont été apportés par une voiture sanitaire américaine et mis en terre par les occupants de cette voiture dans un champ en bordure de la route de Péronne à peu de distance de la sortie du village de Cartigny.

Enfouis peu profondément, ils ne tardèrent pas à être découverts et après entente avec les polices française et américaine averties du fait, ils furent transportés le 23 novembre 1944, dans le cimetière de Cartigny par les soins de la municipalité du village. Mis à coté des soldats français tués en 1940, ils sont surmontés d'une croix de bois, semblable à celle des français qui porte l'inscription "U. S. Soldier Unknown. 23 novembre 44".

Quelques jours avant (nuit du 9 au 10 novembre 1944) un gros bombardier américain (Forteresse ou Liberator) est tombé près de Tincourt-Boucly: il y eut des morts. On pense que ces restes appartiennent à un ou plusieurs de ces morts. Il est possible cependant qu'ils soient des déchets (peut-on parler ainsi de restes humains) d'opérations faites dans un hopital de campagne que les infirmiers pour les faire disparaitre ont enfoui ainsi sommairement près de Cartigny.

COPIE-PHOTOCOPIE
Certifiée conforme à
l'Original Présenté.
CARTIGNY, le 6.06.1994
Le Maire.

It is not an American Soldier but only human remains that came from one or several American Soldiers.

These remains were brought by a U.S. Military Car and buried by the people who were in this car in a field along the road to Péronne, at a very small distance from Cartigny.

As the remains were not buried very deep in the ground, they were soon discovered and after agreement between the French Police and American Army was reached, the remains were taken to the cemetery in Cartigny on November 23, 1944. They were placed near the French Soldiers killed in 1944 and on the top stands a wooden cross, just like the French one, bearing the inscription:

U.S. Soldier
Unknown
23 November 1944.

A few days before all this took place (night between 9th and 10th November, 1944) a large American bomber (Fortress or Liberator) crashed near Tincourt-Boucly: People were killed. It is thought that these remains belong to one or several of the people killed. However, these human remains could be parts of human bodies that could have undergone operations in a campaign hospital and that the head Nurse would have buried near Cartigny to hide them.

Copie-Photocopie
Certiflée conforme à
l'Irginal Présenté
Cartigny, le 6-06-1944
Le Maire   (Interpretation, Alain Leguillier - 1994, son of Claude Leguillier
                 the younger brother of Bernard Leguillier, both were at the
                 "**226**" crash site on 10 November, 1944.)

(**Note**: Neither the French Police nor the Americans were involved. If, the Americans had been involved, the grave would not exist. It is just a cover story.)

Aviateur AMERICAIN
INCONNU
MORT POUR LA FRANCE - EN - 1943

Photograph: Willis S. Cole, Jr.

In 1961, Mr. Emile Berger, a member of *Le Souvenir Français*, requested and received a French military cross and metal military plaque to replace the wooden cross that was put on the grave on 23 November, 1944. By that time, they knew the grave should not exist, so they changed the date to 1943.

On 9 November, 1994, the grave was wrongly marked with the names of the four men killed aboard the *"Lady Jeannette."*

On 10 November, 2000, the correct information was matched to the grave with the installation of the new Memorial Plaque to the three KIA crewmen of the Top-Secret B-24, in a ceremony attended by a United States Air Force Honor Guard, French Honor Flags, and others who attended all four memorial dedications.

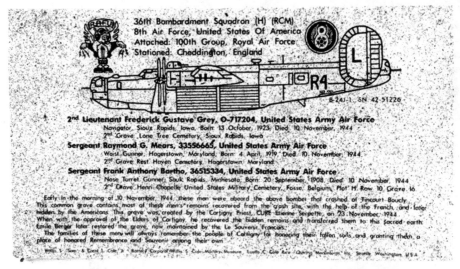

The Tomb Plaque that, after 1961, marked the grave of the Unknown American Airman in the Cartigny Cemetery. The village had the wrong date put on the plaque, so that anyone asking questions could be told the Germans e then bury the remains and they had no responsibility.

Photograph: Willis S. Cole, Jr.

Monument Plaque, Cartigny, Department of the Somme, France, memorializing the two-thirds of the remains of the three men killed in the crash of the Top Secret B-24J, SN: 42-51226, 3 KIA, 10 November, 1944.

The remains in this grave consist of the partial remains recovered during the second remains recovery operation at the crash-site, that were later hidden by the American Medical personnel legally responsible to recover the remains and deliver them to Graves Registration for "official burial," instead they illegally placed the remains in a hidden grave in the Cartigny Commune.

As we left Cartigny, we followed the road to the main road that went from the air base to Péronne. I told the driver to turn left as we came to the intersection, where we turned onto the Amiens-St-Quentin road, heading east toward St-Quentin. As the driver started to make his way onto the road, I thought back to Tiff, swearing

346

at the French wagon drivers as he tried to pass. Perhaps one of them was driving a wagon on the road today and we would never know it.

We spent the night in St-Quentin. At the bar that night, I asked the other two if they would mind if we visited my mother's family farm tomorrow? I would like to stop and see the relatives, as it had been two years since I had seen them. Both agreed they had no reason to hurry and it sounded like a good chance to learn a bit more about France. I did tell them that one of my uncles, had been shot during the war for aiding an American evader.

The next morning I began to teach the other two about the straight and spider web chicken-track roads of France. We started off on the straight, old Roman road from St-Quentin to Guise. Then, we switched off onto the spider web roads at Origny Ste-Benoite, then through several small villages to catch the north-south Roman road from Guise to Laon. We jogged south a short distance to Le-Herie-la-Vieville and got back on the web roads, heading to Sains-Richaumont, Lemé Volpaix, and then to Vervins and the family farm.

All four of my grandparents were now dead. However, my mother's brother, his wife, their children, and mother's now widowed youngest, sister and her children, were happy to see us. It was good to see my nieces and nephews again, some who were now married, with children of their own. They insisted we spend the night, so they could fetch mother's still unwed middle sister from Vervins. That day and evening, as both of the men with me also spoke excellent French, we talked about old times, old wars and possible new wars.

When my uncle brought up the fact that Patton's dying sure screwed it up, as no one was now getting the Russians out of Germany and back to Russia, the three of us listened and with the usual French way of saying "Oui," which sounds like "Wee or Wah," we gave basic agreement once in a while as the speaker was talking. They would never know, my part of insuring Patton did not survive.

As soon as he stopped for a breath, I quickly brought up my executed uncle's work in the French Resistance and we went out to the barn to see the hidden room where evading flyers had stayed, even when there were Germans billeted in the house. Just like the first war, my uncle told us, "They made us stay in one upstairs room for each family and they took the rest of the house." However, from his experience, he thought the Great War Germans were the nicest. But he had not been there, so he only had the women's point of view. Then he made a statement about the visiting Germans, which I had heard before. Telling us, one visiting German is a friend, two visiting Germans are a card game, three visiting Germans are a forward detachment and when you get groups of four or more, they tend to stay and it is hard to make them go back home.

We all laughed and poured another of the "Produit de Ferme" in memory of he uncle the Germans had executed for his Resistance work.

At least one thing had passed from father to son, as my uncle soon insisted that we follow him down into the cellar and see his private collection. The lighting was very dim and he picked up a flashlight and moved the light along the brick line just inside the first arch that showed us at one time the cellar had been bricked up

at the first arch. Then he pointed the flashlight to the area under the stairs where there was a pile of stacked bricks, a couple of sacks of concrete, a number of buckets of sand and a wooden concrete box and trowel. My uncle told us those bricks had saved the family jewels and "Produit de Ferme" during three wars and they were kept ready to serve again. At this point I think I am safe in telling you, as my uncle is now dead, my cousins have never removed those emergency supplies. However, every few years, they do use the old concrete for other purpose and replace it with a fresh supply, just in case the wall is needed again.

The next morning we had a late start and took the major road from Vervins to Rethel, which had been used during the war as an IP Point for daylight bombing missions. Then, as we agreed we were not in that much of a hurry, we went through Vouziers and just east of Vouziers, we branched off the main roads

and took to the secondary roads that would take us through the American World War One Meuse-Argonne Battle Zone.

We stopped for lunch and a couple of beers at St. Juvin. Then, just beyond St. Juvin, we stopped at

Butte de Vauquois - French magazine showing the French preparing a mine under the German trenches.

Scanned From: ***LE PAYS DE FRANCE***
9 September, 1916
Collection: Willis S. Cole, Jr.

Scanned by: Willis S. Cole, Jr.

the American 1st Division WWI Memorial at an isolated road intersection. There, we turned onto the chicken-track back roads through Sommerance to the back entrance to the village of Romagen-Gesnes. The American WWI Meuse-Argonne Cemetery is located just to the east of the village and this time, instead of hurrying through as Tiff and I had in '44, we stopped at the visitor center and then took over an hour to visit the chapel on the hill across from the visiting center and the graves on the northern slope of the hill.

We, chicken-tracked out of the back gate of the cemetery to Cunel and took the intersection toward Nantillois, stopping at the German WWI Cemetery set back

in the woods from the road, next to the "Madeleine Ferme" that had been a German hospital during WWI. Passing through Nantillois, we stopped for a few minutes to see the building the 315th Infantry had donated to the village as a memorial to their unit and the Pennsylvania fountain and memorial. Then we made our way to the Butte de Montfaucon and toured the ruins of the Kaiser's lookout and the ruined church on top of the Butte. After we climbed the spiral stairs in the very tall American Memorial, we viewed the Meuse-Argonne Battlefield using the plaques that point out areas of interest.

I pointed out the Butte de Vauquois in the distance, with its ripped-open top and told the other two that would be our next stop. We got in the car to head for Vauquois and as we drove away from the Butte de Montfaucon, I was wondering if Tiff would ever get back over here to visit these places again.

We stopped in Varennes-en-Argonne at the café next to the bridge and the small river, to enjoy another beer. As we drank, I pointed out the house up on the hill where Louis the Sixteenth and Marie Antoinette had spent the night without crossing the stream and where they had been captured the next morning, to be taken back to Paris and lose their heads to the mob.

As we left, we jogged down a side street to where I could point out the location where President Truman's artillery unit had been during the battle. I told them, Truman had been considered the best swearer in the American Army during World War One. I concluded by telling them I had met an officer who had served with Truman and he had told me, when Harry swore, both the mules and the men would move.

A short time later, we pulled into the village of Vauquois on the southern, or French side of the Butte de Vaquois, a small village replacing the large village that had been on top of the hill when World War One started and the Germans came to visit and stayed for a few years.

We took the foot path to the top of the hill and the men could hardly believe what they were looking at as the craters across the top of the hill came into view. When we reached the top of the hill, we were standing at the southern side or French side, of the line of 16 interlocking craters, next to the French memorial. I told the men how the uncle we had just visited had carried some of the explosive into the Butte to make one of these craters and how one of my father's brothers had also been involved, except he was on the receiving end. We walked down into the craters and followed the rim between two craters and realizing how deep they were. We were soon on the other side, where extensive remains of German trenches and entrances into underground tunnels could be seen. I explained to them, the Germans tended to leave their troops in the same location for a long time and the Germans worked hard to improve their trenches and living conditions.

Both, the French and the British tended to move their troops around and did not let them dig extensive trenches with tunnels under them. They did not wanted their troops to spend enough time in one place to lose their will to fight. They wanted to prevent them from becoming too friendly with the Germans, as the two

warring parties might reach an agreement, whereby they would live close together and try not disturb each other unless forced to do so.

Every time the French or British commands found that was the case, they would force the troops to make trench raids and constantly snipe at the Germans, so the Germans would get mad and fight back. Then, I told them, that my parent's families, with sons on both sides came to know each other very well, and during our visits to France, the men would take me and my boy cousins with them on their long tour of their "La Grande Guerre" or "Great War" battle lines.

From Vauquois, we made our way to Verdun and checked into the Hotel Bellevue. That night, we met several World War One Veterans, some French, some Americans, even a couple of Germans sitting in the bar discussing their war. At two other tables, there were younger men discussing their recent war, my war, in the Verdun area.

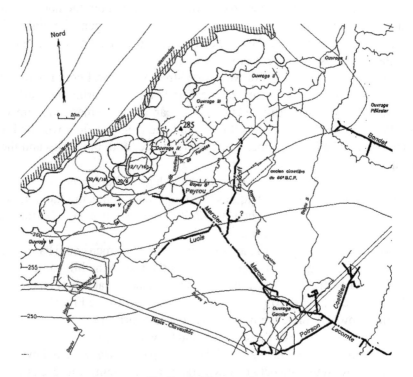

Butte de Vauquois
Drawing Showing Trenches, Tunnels & Craters

Drawing: G. Jacquinet, November, 2006
Scanned from the *"Les Amis de Vaquois*
et desa région, No: 55, Jan. 2007

By: Willis S. Cole, Jr. Member: C963, Since: 1992

Chapter Sixteen
Clean and Forget!
Hattonville

The next morning we made our scouting run to Hattonville and the crash-site. When we stopped at the Mayor's home, his wife instantly remembered me as that very nice American who had visited their house in November '44. While we were at the door, she called to a young boy walking in the street to run and tell her husband to hurry home.

Robert LECLERC, no longer a small boy in his mother's arms running from a B-17 flying toward the village, took off to do what the Mayor's wife had asked him. The Mayor's wife insisted that we come into the house and within a minute we were sitting at the table with the wife hovering over us, and pouring a glass of the "Produit de Ferme" Mirabelle.

I took a very slow and light first drink and watched with pleasure as the other two were realizing they had just swallowed "*lighter fluid*," and I watched the discovery flow across their faces. One choked, sputtered and asked me in English, "What the hell is this?" Answering him in French, I told him, "That it was the pride of the farmer and his charming wife and that he had just proven to them, this bottle was from a very good year."

The Mayor's wife, tittered, blushed and headed for the kitchen to find a snack for the visiting Americans. As she moved around in the kitchen, the front door opened and the Mayor came into the room and recognizing me, came right over to shake my hand as we stood up to greet him.

I introduced the other two and the Mayor insisted we sit back down and he sat down, poured his own Mirabelle and raised his glass to clink with ours and with a "Salute," we drank a toast to ourselves and then one to the "Demort of the War."

During the next hour we reminisced about my previous visit and the Americans who had been in the village during the war. Then we talked about the "Avion Fortress, B-17" that was spewing smoke and fire. The Mayor and his wife told us how they had at first run away from the "Avion Fortress" and then they had watched as it crashed into their woods.

I asked him if the Americans had ever come and recovered the B-17? He told me the Americans had not come to their woods. But in the summer of '46, the Germans had come and picked up all the airplanes, tanks, trucks and other junk that had been destroyed during the war.

He had not directly said they had recovered the B-17, so I pressed him a bit more and asked if the Germans had any problem getting the B-17 out of the woods. The Mayor looked around the room as if someone might be spying on him. Then his eyes met mine and holding the gaze, he put his right index finger in front of his lips to show me what he was going to say should not be passed on. The Mayor of Hattonville told me, since no one appeared to want the B-17 in the Bois De

"Hattonville, they had stolen it in the winter of 1946/47 and sold it for scrap metal. He was so serious, while I was about to laugh in relief! He had just finished providing the final proof that we had been totally successful in November '44, when we moved the crashed B-17's location from here to Tincourt-Boucly.

If the Germans had not tried to salvage the B-17 in 1946, as part of their surrender terms and the French felt they had stolen it to sell for scrap, I could tell the general for certain, our crash-site cover-up in November '44 had been a success.

I told the Mayor we would be interesting in seeing the crash-site, as I wanted to show the others how close the B-17 had come to making a safe landing. The Mayor said he would go to the crash-site with us, but we could not use the road through the field. Early in the year, the field and the road was so wet a tractor had a hard time using that road, however, he would take us there via a National Forest Road that was well paved and useable all year round.

He asked if we had boots, as the crash-site would be muddy and the clay would stick to our feet in clumps. I told him we had brought boots in the car and he said as soon, as he got his boots we would leave for the crash-site.

We left the Mayor's home and headed south toward Vigneulles-lès-Hattonchâtel, and there we turned to the east toward St-Beloit-en Woëvre. At the eastern edge of Vigneulles, we passed the American 1st Division World War One Memorial and headed toward the large woods in the distance. The road ran through the woods; a short distance inside, we came to an intersection with two small roads running into the woods on either side of the main road.

We turned left, heading north, and passed through an unlocked gate and drove for a couple of kilometers into the woods. As we drove through the woods following the Mayor's instruction, I saw several German artillery-positions from the Great War. Then we came to an intersection and turned left, went west for a short way and then made a sharp turn to the north. We followed the road for some distance, until we came to a clearing in the woods, where the road we were on intersected with another road which ran on an east/west axis.

The Mayor told me the road we had come to, was the same road that ran from the village toward the crash-site. Here inside the National Forest, the road was kept up. But once it reached their woods, the road was very poorly maintained. We turned left, west, toward the village and drove about 300 meters, to where two culverts bridged the ditches alongside the road. Off to the left, I saw the end of a berm and a path like the one I had stood on in November '44. Then I realized I was at the road in the woods I had come to when walking along the debris-trail of the B-17 on that first visit to the crash site. We got out of the car and put on our boots and with the Mayor leading, we started down the path along the berm to the south of the road. As soon as I was on the path, I was positive, I was also walking in the footprints of Lt. Harms, the Bombardier, who could still be swearing to anyone who would listen, that his B-17 did not disintegrate.

(**Note**: I knew that Lt. Harms had a copy of his medical file and now, seventy-five years later, the time has come when those medical records will prove

Lt. Harms had always told the truth. And the truth is, we were the ones, along with two ***Congressional Medals Of Honor Citations***, who have lied all these years. But, as the wife of LTC McBride told the researcher and his wife in 2006, "After all these years no one can be hurt..." the author decided, ***with the "Final-Transfer" of the last known person to be involved, it was time to rewrite his previous evolution and properly name the new book, Why We Killed General Patton!***)

Each and every one of us had lied. Starting with me, his squadron and group commanders and all the others. All the way to the President of the United States, who had signed the applications concerning the crash of the B-17, 2nd Lt. Harms had been aboard and the death of the two pilots and their crewmen, of all of us, only Harms had stood for the truth at the time, and we had forced him to lie.

However, that moment of truth would be seven decades on from when I was walking through the woods with the Mayor, and at that time the first thing I saw was all the limbs and fresh stumps in the woods. I asked the Mayor about them and he told me the village culled the forest every 50 to 55 years when they removed the big trees to open the woods for the growth of the smaller trees.

He went on to say that in the winter of 1946/47, it was time to cull the trees and when they went out to the woods, there was the broken B-17, just as it had stopped the day it had crashed. After holding a meeting, the Mayor and the Village Elders decided the Americans did not want the B-17, or they would have taken it during the summer of '46, when they took the rest of the scrap metal in the area, including a B-17 that crashed 3 km to the north.   As the B-17 in their woods was left, the villagers scraped the B-17 and sold the scrap to make some pocket money.

Each of the families in the village, who helped tear the B-17 apart, selected a location in the woods to put their pieces of the B-17 and then, as a family they had attacked the big sections of the B-17 with axes, metal saws, sledge hammers and anything else they had, to reduce it to pieces that could be handled.

To get rid of the rubber and other material on the scrap metal, they put that scrap and all the burnable stuff in a pile near each family's collection point and set it on fire. When the fire was over, the insulation was burnt off the wires and the rubber hoses were gone, leaving only scrap metal to be sold. The Mayor did say, one man had taken the small wheel at the tail and made a wheel barrow out of it and another had taken some skin off the wings, to use as a roof on his hog sheds.

We had stopped walking as the Mayor was talking and as we started walking again, we were at a point where the berm and road turned at a slight angle to the west, and the Mayor pointed out several trees around us. He told us to take a close look at the tree tops and we could see where the B-17 had broken the limbs on the trees as it settled into the woods.

After we had walked another hundred feet or so toward the crash-site, the Mayor pointed out to the west to show us where they had found an engine 100 meters from the bomber, which I knew was the number-three engine that had been running at full power when it broke free from the right wing and rolled into the woods. As he talked, I turned around and looked back and realized the angled

corner in the berm was the place near the beginning of the debris trail where the medics had found the first torn-apart remains of the B-17's Tail Gunner, S/Sgt. Krimminger, which they had told me, were parts of his skull and jaw.

After we had crossed over the small creek the bombardier had talked about, we walked up the slight slope toward the place where the wing and tail had been in November, 1944. The Mayor stopped and told us we were standing at the place where two of his friends had helped a screaming flyer, and close by, the Mayor pointed out the impact craters in the ground that showed us where a wing, the tail and an engine had been. That is, until they were torn-apart for scrap metal by the French. I could see the floor of the woods and the bramble bushes had not recovered from when the trees were cut and the B-17 had been torn-apart and it was a lot easier getting around the crash-site.

(**Note**: Are you a doubter? Just get on a plane, go to France and go to Hattonville and the Bois de Hattonville and there, you will find those impressions are still there, inside a fenced off area to help preserve the *"Lady Jeannette"* crash-site. Once, one sees those impressions and stands beside the location where the forward fuselage came to a halt, the site comes alive again in your mind. You are standing where two men who were awarded our highest military medal came to rest as their final life's light, extinguished)

As we continued up the slope, the Mayor pointed out where the dead man had been found in the bushes and, where the cockpit had been when a friend of his had found the two pilots slumped over, and dead in their seats.

You could still see where the edge of one wing had pressed down into the clay, when it came to a stop leaning against a tree and where the tire and engine had burned. The Mayor was showing the others where the bodies had been placed, while I was studying the dirt where the end of the broken fuselage would have been located. It had not healed from all the activity during the crash and the salvage by the French. We could still see where the nose had plowed the earth, but there was no evidence of the pushed up pile of dirt where it had pivoted and come to a stop. The was no question of where it went, we knew.

The men with me provided the Mayor with a great audience, as he described how the B-17 had flown over the woods and then turned over their village after three men had bailed out, to land in the big field we could see though the woods. The B-17 ended up crashing back into the woods it had flown over.

He told them how much it meant to the village to have the Americans in their village during the war, and they were very sad that three men had died here for the "Liberty of France." Especially after the pilots had saved the village by keeping their "Avion Fortress" from crashing into their village as it flew overhead.

Listening to the Mayor, I knew another part of the plan had worked. The French had never found out that a fourth man had died during the crash. Then we walked out to the edge of the woods, next to the large field. On the way, it seemed

to me I could see the ambulance with the four Burial Packages in the back, waiting for me to say goodbye to Major Venar.

The Mayor pointed out to the others where the three men had landed in the field, and that the one who had landed by the angle in the woods in the distance had a broken leg. That man had been helped by one of the Mayor's friends, before the ambulance from the village had taken him and another American flyer away.

Then he remembered to tell us about the man who had landed just across the ditch from where we were standing, and who later had walked up to the wing and tail where he began to jump up and down, screaming and swearing. Two of the Mayor's friends had helped the man, at the place he had shown us. The Mayor went on to describe how the two Frenchmen had helped the man walk by supporting his shoulders, as they walked him to the Americans who were standing where the tire had burned, close to the dead men's bodies. The Americans had told the two Frenchmen to help the man to the edge of the woods. Then, as they got him across the ditch, right here where we were standing, an American jeep arrived and another friend, who had been guiding the jeep got out and the flyer was put into the jeep and then it drove off toward the village.

A short time later, all the French were made to leave the crash-site for a couple of days before the guards were taken away. After that, the Americans appeared to have lost all interest in the crashed B-17 and on 2 December, 1944, the Americans left the village. Since then, the Mayor said, nothing exciting had happened in the village, except the tearing apart of the B-17 for scrap and most likely, unless there was another war, nothing exciting would happen in Hattonville for a long time.

As we walked back out to the car, I felt like asking the Mayor if they had found the missing leg, then realized he was supposed to know nothing about that leg. With the Mayor's help, we managed to turn the car around, using the bridges for the paths along the berm. Then we headed back to the Mayor's home and had a couple of more drinks as his wife offered us cookies and small cakes. After an hour we left with a long goodbye, and invitations to come back and stay longer. As we left to drive back to Verdun, the Mayor's wife was down in the street again, waving her handkerchief. I do not know what it was because we all spoke excellent French, but the Mayor's wife seemed to have taken a liking to me. My two companions were looking at me with an odd look on their faces, and then back at her as we passed the church, heading north.

The Mayor had been a great help. He did not know it, but he had shown us a safe way into the woods and a place to park, where we could conduct our cleanup, load the items into the trunk, and leave the woods without anyone knowing we had gone back to the crash-site or what we had done. In addition, the hour that we had been at the site in the woods, would be about the same time we would be there tomorrow. It was obvious there were no Frenchmen in the big field this morning and most likely, there would be none there the following day when we came back to clean up, what I had left behind in '44. During the rest of the day, after we got back to Verdun, I gave my two companions a guided tour along the hills above

Verdun, where the great forts that helped stop the German advance in 1916 were located. I took them to the large shell crater where the Germans had killed a large number of World War Two French Resistance Fighters the day before the Americans arrived, and to visit the destroyed forts and the Ossuary, where the basement vaults contain the bones that represent the lives of so many men killed during World War One.

From there I took them to see the rifle barrels with the mounted bayonets at the Tranchees des Baïonnettes. There had been French troops in the trench when large shells arrived on either side of the trench. The ground was so wet and sloppy, it had closed up on the troops and they were not found until one of their officers, while searching for his lost platoon, found the rifle barrels and bayonets sticking out of the ground in 1921.

There are several stories about how the men came to be buried. Some say, the Germans had buried the dead in the trench, leaving the rifles and bayonets in their firing steps to mark the dead. However, I do not believe a group of Germans, who were fighting in that area, would leave a zigzag line of bayonets sticking out of the dirt for them to run into at night or when they were running for shelter to save their own lives.

Me, I prefer to believe those French Soldiers are standing there in their trench, waiting through Eternity with their bayoneted rifles at the ready, always poised to charge out of their trench in order to save France.

That evening in Verdun, at the Hotel Bellevue, we made our plans for the morning and then we again spent the night in the bar listening to the old Veterans talking about their adventures during the real war, their war. It brought back memories of when I was here in the same hotel with my father, grandfathers, uncles, and cousins, not all that long ago.

The next morning, we arrived in the Hattonville Woods about 09:30, put our boots on, picked up some of our gear, walked down the path, past the place where the tail gunner had died, and then to, the location where we had hidden the broken inventory items, in '44.

Until now, the plan here at the crash-site had worked perfectly, even when the French were scrapping out the "Avion Fortress." If and when we completed the rest of the cleanup with no problem, I could tell General Dwight D. Eisenhower that he no longer had to worry about the American war dead we had desecrated. Of course, I would never use the same words with Ike that I used in my own mind.

Almost all of the French had no reason to dig for scrap metal at the crash-site, as all the B-17 was basically laying on the surface or above the impact craters the big parts had created - especially where the earth was all trampled from people getting into and out of the forward, broken fuselage of the B-17 when it crashed, and then again, when they were tearing it apart. What I did not know at that time, was the uncle of the boy who had found the Mayor the day before, Ernest LECLERC, had helped his brother, Louis (Robert's father), and their father to collect their share of the B-17, in the Bois de Hattonville.

When the site was basically clear of scrap, Ernest and his father had gone back to the site for one last time, to search for more scrap metal to sell. His father had told Ernest there might be some buried scrap metal where the nose of the "Avion Fortress" had jammed into the dirt and they ought to dig down to see if they could find any buried metal to sell.

They starting digging and about half a meter down, they had found something other than metal. First, they had found some rotten canvas and then, under the canvas they had found bones and rotted flesh. Ernest's father told Ernest, the French were known to have hidden some French dead during his war. Now, it looks like *the Americans have hidden some American dead during this war*. So, they had put the dirt back over what they had found, and Ernest never told anyone about what they had found for fifty-four years.

(**Note:** In September 1998, during their first research visit to the Hattonville area the author and his wife, Carol, were helped by Mr. Bernard Delsert. He helped them find the truth crash-site and interpreted for them during several visits to France. When they were introduced to Mr. Ernest LECLERC, the brother of Robert LECLERC's father, Ernest told his visitors about his last trip to the crash site with his father during a search for scrap metal and finding buried dead.)

Just fourteen months later, after Ernest and his father had put the dirt back in the hole they had dug, we were in the woods, digging in the same place. When we had dug down about a half meter, we found the rotting canvas and under it, we started to uncover the remains of the three men. Then, based on what we had begun to smell and see, I suddenly understood the exact specifications for the location of new American temporary cemeteries I had learned years from my Graves Registration training.

The specifications stated, a sloping surface with good drainage is required if the remains are to properly decompose. The soils must permit fluids to drain away and permit air and fumes to make their way through the porous soils to and from the decomposing remains. Under the correct conditions in a properly selected cemetery, the human body will decompose in 18 months with the fluids draining away and all that will be left in the grave will be, basically clean bones.

In a clay area, where the water table can be within inches of the surface during the winter and only a couple of feet lower in the summer, the fluids cannot flow away very and the clay and water greatly retard the decomposition process and it can take years to take place instead of months.

That is exactly what we had found as we removed the dirt covering the three remains. The burial sight that I selected in November, 1944, and helped to dig out, was basically a bath tub with very poor drainage. Now, as we dug, water was running into the area we had just dug out and mixing with what was already there. It was quickly becoming a yellowish/brownish, thick soup-like mixture of partially decomposed flesh, body decomposition fluids, clay, and water.

The odor was even worse than the odor when I had been driven through the Falaise Gap area in '44, where we had killed many Germans and their horses. I still remember the time I was talking to T/Sgt. Wilmer Henderson, of the 606th Graves Registration Company, at a check point on a road near Falaise. I had met him twice before in England during two of my Graves Registration training trips. We were both at Slapton Sands situation, when he taught me the difference between a *"Sinker"* and a *"Floater."* When we met again near Falaise, Henderson had told me, "He thought the dead horses smelled worse than the dead Germans." Me, I'm not so sure.

Soon, we had backed away from the opened, hidden grave and were quickly lighting cigarettes to help mask the odor flooding out of the hole. We searched for the upwind side and then, we looked at each other and we all agreed, we were not expecting this! Particularly after what we had found in the dirt while we were digging for the remains in the field near Péronne.

In unison, we dropped the shovels and hurried toward the edge of the woods. The wind was not blowing that way and we were standing back in the woods, so we could look out and not be seen from the field, as we discussed the new situation.

We agreed, that we still have to do the job, however, we were not equipped to do what had to be done today. So, we decided, we would throw the dirt we had removed, back into the hole and tramp it down just in case some Frenchman came to the site while we were gone. Then we would head back to Verdun and find a store where we could get what we needed to do the job tomorrow.

We took turns refilling the hole we had dug, with the digger's face buried in a sweater thrown around his lower face, as he threw some dirt back into the hole and then had to retreat. When the hole was refilled, we hid the shovels under some branches and hurried down to the small creek to rinse our hands and faces, before heading to the car, to get the clothes and tools we would need tomorrow.

In Verdun, we all took a quick shower and called room service to wash our clothes. Then we headed to the downtown stores to see what we could find. We had decided the tarps we had would not work, as no matter what we did, we were going to get stuff with the bones that could leak into the trunk. We had to seal whatever container we used, so the liquids and odors could not get out into the car.

We found several stores with war surplus and each of us picked out and fitted a gas mask. We located some rubberized, waterproof, surplus laundry bags, and bought twenty of them to be safe, as we expected to have to double bag each remains and then double bag, the double bag containing the remains we would be recovering from that stinking hole.

Among the surplus materials for sale, we found some one-piece work fatigues and other fatigues that had been seal-treated to be used in case of a gas attack. Now those, I felt, were something we would really need. We got six pairs of each, just in case we had to spend two days, instead of the planned one extra day recovering the remains. And we bought two stacks of towels that showed a lot of wear, but that wouldn't hurt considering what we were going to use them for.

One of the fellows found several rolls of extra wide electrical tape and we bought six of them. We looked around until we found some really heavy rubber gloves that would reach to our elbows and got three sets for each of us. Once we had them on, we could use the rubber tape to seal the gloves tops tight to keep any of that stuff out of the gloves.

As the other two were loading our recent purchases, I went searching for what it was going to take to retrieve the men's bones from that hole. On my way to another store across the street, I saw a perfume store and I tried several perfumes, until I found one that was strong enough to mask the odor that might get through the gas masks, but not enough to make me sick. I bought two expensive bottles, on Ike!

At the hardware store, I found several garden tools that might help. But nothing that I thought was what was really needed, until I found two hay forks with four strong prongs. The hay forks would let us search for bones, while standing as far from the hole as we could. The others came in and asked me if I had gotten the perfume for my wife? I told them I was not married, and that I would be perfuming them in the woods tomorrow. As we were laughing, my eyes were wandering around the shelving and hooks. Then I saw the real solution to our problem.

Stacked up high, out of sight, where someone would have to ask for them, were a group of replacement French fry baskets. Some of them looked very strong, most likely meant to be used in a restaurant. I asked the French salesman to get a ladder and show us the heaviest baskets they had in stock and soon we left the store with two hay forks and two heavy French fry baskets.

Once we had put those purchases in the car and locked it, we walked around central Verdun and up the long flight of stairs, to the large World War One Memorial in the center of the town. When we got back to the car, I realized we still had time to make one more visit before dinner at the Hotel Bellevue. I took the men to visit the tunnels under the Citadel. Verdun was once surrounded by a large wall and the Citadel was the area where the military lived in buildings on the hill and the inside of the hill was crisscrossed with tunnels where the French took cover during the first war and the tunnels had been used again, by the French, Germans and Americans during the last war.

We had to pay a guide a few Francs, and then he took us to visit the tunnels and point out the room where the French World War One Unknown Soldier had been selected, for burial under the Arc de Triumph in Paris. The guide told us about the Americans who were here during both wars and that he, personally, was very happy to thank their Liberators for what we had done.

The next morning we arrived back at the crash-site with no one seeing us and we made a few trips to carry all we had back into the woods to the hidden grave location. The odor was still present. However, it could be put up with, as what we were smelling were the fluids that had splashed out of the hole, when we were throwing the dirt back yesterday.

We took off our boots while sitting on a nearby fallen log and put on the one-piece surplus fatigues. Then we put the gas-treated fatigues on over them. Next, we put our boots back on, tightly taping the tops with the rubber tape. Then

we recovered the stinking shovels from under the branches and put them next to the dig location. Finally, as one man held a hay fork and the other held a French Fry basket, we slid the forks through the wire of the basket and matched up the two handles. I securely taped each basket handle to the hay fork handle to form two large scoops we could use to recover the remains, while leaving the fluids and small bits of tissue in the hole.

Once we decided we were all ready, we walked a short distance to be upwind, smoked a cigarette, drank a cup of the coffee from the thermos the hotel had prepared for us and a couple of us took the opportunity and used a tree, as a target to get rid of already excess, used coffee.

When we were done, we began to fit our gas masks. They had to be tightly fitted unless we wanted to have the odor leaking in. Then I got a bottle of perfume from the jacket I had hung on a nearby tree. I told them, since we did not know exactly how much of the odor the masks would keep out, I was going to put a spot of the perfume inside my own gas mask. That way, as we dug and fished for the remains, I could smell the perfume and think about how happy my girl would be, when I get home with the other bottle.

Both men remembered my remark about perfuming them in the woods while we were getting the hayforks and baskets, and both agreed they would now like to be perfumed by me.

With that done and our masks on, we began, what quickly became the most gruesome task I have ever done. It was much worse than burning human flesh and bone. Some time later, I read reports about the Graves Registration men recovering remains from the low-lying Pacific Islands where the water table was very close to the surface. Graves Registration used outside personnel as much as they could, and each day after work, the men were issued new clothes, along with all the cigarettes they wanted to help mask the odor. After work, they could shower as often as they wanted and they were given a ration of one bottle of bourbon after each day's work. Few people know of those people in the Pacific and in Europe, doing the same thing we were doing, when the bodies had not been buried under the right conditions. I have never met any of those people, but there might be a few still alive who will read this and I want them to know ... "I know exactly what you poor bastards did and if any of you ever meet me, the drinks, as many as you want, are on me!"

It was slow going. We had no semi-dry clay, as the fluids in the hole had mixed with the semi-dry clay when it was thrown back in the hole yesterday and now we had clay that was almost Jell-O, that we had to dig out of the hole again, before we reached the hidden remains.

Finally, one of the other two had a good idea and he took one of the scoop baskets and was using it to pull mixed earth out of the hole. We were all putting what we took out, onto the same place we had yesterday, leaving us three sides to work with. But, no matter how we did it, clumps would fall back into the hole and the fluid would splash out of the hole and onto us.

The masks and the perfume, while we had them on worked as we fished, and with the three of us working at it, before long we began to reach the remains of

the men. We could talk with the masks on and we had to decide how to keep what we recovered separate, at least as much as we could. With that in mind, we decided the remains located at the east side of the hole would go to the north side of the hole, the remains in the middle would be placed on the west side of the hole and those on the western side would go on the south side of the hole.

Soon, we got to a point where each scoop of a basket returned with bones and attached rotten flesh. Once we had decided exactly where the remains were to be separated, it did make our task easier. When a basket holder found the basket weighed more than he could easily raise, the other basket holder would help. Soon we were proud, how we could recover a fairly large section of bone and rotten flesh and move the baskets together like a large chop stick set to put that part of the man's remains on his side.

After an hour, we had recovered a lot of the remains and discussed taking a break. However, we agreed we did not want to take the masks off, even though the perfume was beginning to fail. The smell I was getting inside the mask was not one my lady friend would want to put on.

So, we stayed at it and after a half hour, we agreed that we had gotten all of the remains we were going to get out of the hole. At that time, the hole was filled with mixed clay, water and other fluids to a point about six inches below the top of the hole. It consisted of a mixture that looked more like thick pancake mix, than anything I could think of.

Still wearing the masks, we walked down to the small stream. We found the low spot where we had rinsed yesterday and today, we used some of the surplus towels we had brought along with us, to help wash each other off, as best we could. After we were done and had walked up to our supply dump, we decided to take the gas masks off and see what would happen. "Damn, we stunk!" There is no other word for it. "We stunk!" We had splashed enough of that stuff on our clothing, so that even after we had we washed it off the gloves and boots, we still stunk!

Within two minutes we were pealing off those fatigues and standing on one of the tarps we had laid out upwind of the hole. We put the used clothing and gloves in one of the rubberized bags and then, we ran back down to the stream to use some fresh towels to wipe ourselves off again. When we went back to the stash, three grown men in their underwear, with goose bumps all over them, swearing and bitching, I told the other two it could be worse. They asked me, how the hell it could get any worse? I told them, "We could see the ghosts of the four dead men standing just over there and laughing at the living, who thought they had it so bad."

That helped calm our mood a bit and we put on the second set of work fatigues and gas sealed fatigues, replaced the boots, taped the tops and then went to take a break and to have a smoke, a coffee and a relief. Then, we doubled up two of the rubberized bags, to create bag-sets. We created three bag-sets and agreed who would have to take off his new gloves to tape the bags tight. I can assure you it was not I, as rank does have some privilege, even though the others were higher paid civilians, in their current "*Spook Work*" careers.

We put the gas masks back on with a reinforced perfumed spot, and while one held the bag-sets, the other two picked up the pieces on one side and placed them in the bag-sets. When we first started, as we picked up the pieces, we would hold them over the hole and shake them, only to jump back when some fairly large masses of rotten flesh came free and fell into the hole with force enough to splash us with the fluids from the hole. Then, realizing we might be losing too much of each remains, we stopped doing that.

It does not take much imagination on the reader's part to understand the three of us were driven to get this done as soon as possible, and we did. When each bag-set contained all the remains we had recovered on that side of the hole we moved the bag-set back away from the hole and I made a mental note of what we had found to help verify the identity of the remains in that bag-set. The middle set of remains had a severely broken right arm and another had no ends at the end of a set of lower arm bones. We did find a right hand, which mostly fell apart as it was put into the correct bag-set. With two bags-sets containing remains with obvious wounds, the third with a broken skull was easy to identify.

When all the bones were in the bag-sets, two of us took the scoops and went to the edge of the hole and for another ten minutes, we attempted to find additional remains. We did find some small bones and the rotten flesh we had dropped, which we could not know who they belonged too. So, they were put in the closest bag-set to the person who found them.

We had taken turns to do the final search and when we were done, each of us took a shovel and as fast as we could we threw the dirt, if you could call it that, back into the hole. We did try to cut down the splashing as much as possible. We filled the hole up much faster than we had dug it out and within fifteen minutes, we had reached a point where we were forced to use the earth in the higher areas around the hole to even out the entire area.

When we were finished, I tested stepping on the filled hole to tramp it down and I quickly realized if I did that, I would be standing in a three-foot deep hole with jellied clay leaking into my clothes and boots. So I told the other two to use the hay forks and baskets to smooth out our work as much as they could and we would take leaves from over the berm and redistribute them over the fresh, liquid mud to hide it from any Frenchman who might come to the site before our worked area would fully blend in with the surrounding forest floor.

Before I could say it, one of them said he would give a hundred bucks to be a bird sitting on a branch, if any Frenchman came here before the mud solidified. The Frenchman would suddenly find himself sinking into a surface of fluid, putrid mud and wondering where the hell had that come from and when he made his way to his village his wife would make him sleep with the cattle for the next month.

We laughed with him, as we knew ... he was probably right. Then, we headed over the berm to gather an arm full of rotten, last fall's leaves to sprinkle around the mud. After a couple of trips to get more leaves, we completed the task. It seemed to me as if all the evidence that the nose of the B-17 had pushed up a pile of dirt before it spun around, was gone. The mud had even flowed down the two

trenches the machine-gun had dug out and filled them, leaving the whole area very smooth, as the researcher found the area fifty-four years later.

When the leaves were spread out, from the point where I knew the B-17's nose had hit and where the broken end had stopped, the ground almost looked as if nothing had ever happened there.

Soon I was holding up a stinking pitchfork and basket, one at the time, as one of the men used his pocket knife to cut the tape. When he was finished cutting the tapes, he walked a few feet from where we were standing and threw the knife as far as he could. At the same time, "He was telling us there was no way he wanted that damn thing in his pocket again."

With the hole refilled, we went and washed our gloves and boots again and then we went to the supply dump again, where we took off our gas masks and gloves and had another cigarette and coffee. When we were done, we put the gas masks back on and two of us put our gloves back on. The third man grabbed a roll of tape and some clean towels and we went to the closest bag-set.

While one gloved man held up the end of each double bag-set of remains, the other gloved man pulled the drawstrings tight and tied loose loops around the bags. Then, he wiped the closed end as dry as he could with one of the towels. The third man, after the others had folded the top over, wrapped the tops with as much tape as it took to seal the bag-set. While he was doing that, the man who was free got a third rubberized bag and when he was ready, all three of us helped slide the new bag backward over the already closed bags and then, that bag's top was closed. It was turned over as quickly as possible and more tape was used to seal it, as tightly as possible. I had the man with the tape put one strip of tape on the bag with the broken arm, who was the copilot, Lt. Metzger, and two on the bag containing the complete skeleton with the broken skull, who was the pilot, Lt. Gott. The third bag remained unmarked and it contained all of what we believed to be the human remains of the radio operator, T/Sgt. Dunlap.

It took nearly twenty minutes for us to complete that task and when it was done, the gas masks were removed and we went to the stream to rinse. When we got back, using two men for each bag-set, the bag-sets were taken to the stream, and on the other side, and they were wiped clean with a fresh towel. We repeated the process two more times and then we went back to clean up our cleanup area.

We used one of the rubberized laundry bags to carry all the wet and dirty towels out to the car and then we carried the three bag-sets out of the woods and put them next to the car. We spent the next half hour carrying all the rest of our stuff from the crash-site and put it close to the car.

At the car, we bagged each of the three bag-sets inside a dry fourth bag and taped the top tightly and duplicated the stripe markings. Then we used rope to tie the final bag-sets into a fairly tight bundle. When we were finished creating the three bundles of remains, we placed the bundles on a tarp in the trunk. As we did that, I was thinking of the three tightly tied bundles, one with caked blood and grease on the outside, that a Pfc. had loaded in the trunk of another car I had been riding in, one driven by Sgt. Tiff.

We had stopped by the stream and rinsed the tools as good as we could, but they still stank! So, we double wrapped them in the remaining tarps and bags and wrapped the tarps and bags with more tape, before putting them in the trunk along with the three bundles of the actual human remains of 1st Lt. Gott, **CMOH**. 2nd Lt. Metzger, Jr., **CMOH**, and T/Sgt. Dunlap.

When all that was done, we pulled off our boots, took off the gas-treated fatigues and the inner fatigues and stuffed them and our gloves and boots in another rubberized bag. Then, three nearly naked men and very cold men, walked back into the woods to the stream where we attempted to wash and wipe off, all we could, of the fluids that had penetrated our clothing. Then we went back to the car, put on our own clothes, consigned the boots to the towel and fatigue bag, pulled its draw string tight and used the tape to seal the odor in. With that in the trunk, we were free to turn the car around and get the hell out of that woods. I can assure you, over the thousands of years that wood has been there, we had to be three of the happiest humans that ever left it behind.

We rolled the windows down as soon as we got in the car and headed for the main road with the heater running at full output. On the main road, we began to put some distance between us and that crash-site. We went toward Verdun, but we still had to hide our tools and stuff some place and I thought, I remembered a good place to do that. So, at the small cross roads of Haudiomont, we turned north to drive along the side of the hills the Germans had climbed to attack the French during World War One. We passed through Châtillion-s/s-les-Côte and took the side road leading toward Moulainville and "Great War" trench systems.

We were driving up the hillside on a small chicken track road through the torn-up earth of the Battle of Verdun that was criss-crossed by German and French Trenches, when just beyond Moulainville, we found a very small road running into the scabby woods on the west side of the chicken-track road. It was marked with a sign, showing a skull and an explosion, and the words De Mort, meaning "Do not enter - you may be killed. The road showed some use and therefore I was really not very worried about our disturbing any World War One shells that would hurt us.

I jumped out, walked some distance down the side road, found a place where we could turn the car around, and went back and told them to bring the car down the side road. When they arrived, we turned the car around and sat there for fifteen minutes drinking coffee, smoking and looking at all the over-lapping shell holes in the wood around us. Off to one side, there was a trench and I walked over to it, telling the other two to keep a close eye for anyone who might be around.

I figured it had to be a French trench, as the hole I had found about 50 feet down the trench, was on the north side of the trench, where a German shell could not fall into it. I went back to the car, got a flashlight and told the two, I thought, we have our hidie-hole and walked back to shine the flashlight down into the hole. It was exactly what I thought it was, a dugout in the side of the trench. The tunnel led down about fifteen feet to the floor of the dug out, with a set of rotten steps leading down into the hole.

Just to be safe, I went back to the car to get one of the men to watch me as I went down the stairs. At the bottom, I found a room about ten feet square with some rotting wood bunks on one side and a rotten table laying on the floor where it had finally fallen apart. I walked back to the entrance, thinking it was perfect.

As I climbed out, I checked the supports on either side and the top. Reaching the conclusion we could ditch all the stuff down in this dugout, keeping one shovel to use to break down the entrance as we backed out. Then we could get rid of the shovel out on our way to Verdun in a trench or a shell hole.

We got back to the car and the other fellow told us, he had seen crows, heard something other than us off to one side, but determined it was not human. He was certain we were alone in the woods. Then while one hauled the stuff from the car and I was dumping it down into the dugout, the third person kept watch. Within fifteen minutes, we were using the last shovel that still stank, to break down the opening's overhead and side supports.

It took us longer to break down the dugout entrance, than it did to find the dugout and put the stuff in it. But I was pleased when we were done. The stuff in the bottom of the dug out could not be seen as it was to one side of the tunnel entrance. Once the entrance had been broken in, someone would have to skinny into a very narrow hole and slide to the bottom, before they could find our stash of hidden grave opening stuff.

Besides, we would be on our way to St-Avold, about 60 miles away, in the morning and in less than a month, the odds of the stinking stuff in the hole being tied to three French-speaking Americans, who had stayed at the Hotel Bellevue, would be zero. I told the two, as we pulled onto the chicken-track road, they could come back in 20 years and get the stuff if they wanted it. "Sure, we'll put that on our calendar," one of the men exclaimed! The quick reply made all of us laugh. About a mile up the road we pulled over, the driver got out and opened the trunk and took out the shovel. Then, he walked a short distance into the woods and threw the shovel into a shell crater full of water that had to be 10 yards across and who knows how deep. The shovel sank out of sight, he came back, and we headed up the chicken-track road, passing the road to Fort Moulainville. At the road's intersection with the Verdun-Etain road, we turned south toward Verdun.

Back at the hotel, we took a long shower and called the hotel laundry woman up to take our clothes away and give them a good wash. I suppose, that night she talked to her husband about how bad some Americans smell.

That night, out in the locked garage of Hotel Bellevue, the three bundles were in the car's trunk and we spent our last night there, talking to the old Veterans. Before long, they were telling of their visit to their War's trenches where they had served and fought, or that is, they had gotten as close to their tench as they could, due to so many "No Access, De Mort" signs. Then, they looked around, put their index fingers to their lips, leaned over and told us they did not pay a lot of attention to those signs as they had to visit the "phantoms (ghosts) of their friends" who had died in the trenches. Since they did not die then, when they could have, they did not

fear death all these years later. I asked if any of them had served near Fort Moulainville? They said, they were further west, in the real fighting.

My dream that night, was about the Hattonville Woods and the ***last flight*** of the "***Lady Jeannette***." **It was a flight made only in the minds of we men who planned and carried out**, *Why We Killed Patton - "The Best Kept Secret Of World War Two!"* I have to admit, as does the researcher, we fooled a lot of people for 54 years, including him for some years with our "***in the minds of men only, last flight of the "Lady Jeannette***" from the Hattonville Woods to Tincourt-Boucly. My dream was not about what I had done. My dream was about the four ghosts of the men killed aboard the "***Lady Jeannette***." They were sitting on the log, where we had changed our fatigues and they were wondering why they still were hanging around at the crash-site? The living men they had watched digging that day were interesting. They did recognize one of the men, as the same man who ordered the desecration of their bodies after they had died.

Now that he and the two others had dug up three of their physical remains and left the crash-site with the remains. The men sat there for a while pondering what to do and soon, their usual visitors of the ghosts of the Germans, French, Americans and many others, who had died near the crash-site during all the wars of the past centuries arrived and a discussion began. All of the visitors were tied to the general location, because their bodies were still in the ground where they had been buried and never moved. However, they had to agree, the new boys from the new war, no longer had a good reason to stay and guard what was no longer in the woods to be guarded.

Gott, Metzger, Dunlap, and Krimminger had been hanging around me for the past two days, as we worked to remove the three hidden remains. They still remembered the day I had three of their bodies hidden and another divided, thanks to General Eisenhower.

They had an advantage that I did not, in that they could see me, they could hear me ,and they could put themselves into my mind. The four phantoms (ghosts) in the Hattonville Woods had been very interested in why an American had done to them, what he had done. For the past two days, they spent some time searching my mind for a good reason. At times, during the two days when we were working at the hidden grave, my mind did wonder about what I had put in place and the whole thing replayed in the back of my mind. Now they knew and now they realized, they were not the only ones in the same situation.

Up near Péronne, there had to be three more American ghosts sitting near their own crash-site, wondering what to do?

As the four Americans told the assembled group what they had learned, all the men from the wars before agreed they did not have to stay. They still had the "***Lady Jeannette***," their B-17. The French had physically taken her away, just as the men today had taken their worldly remains away. However, the ghost of the "***Lady Jeannette***," their B-17 was sitting there before them. It had flown into the Hattonville Woods and by damn, it could taxi out of the Hattonville Woods and take

them to the Tincourt-Boucly crash-site, where they could find the other Americans, who had to be waiting there.

The four men looked at each other, stood up, looked at their "*Lady Jeannette*" and said together, "*Let's do it!*" Their ghostly friends formed a line to the bomber and as the four men walked to board the "*Lady Jeannette*," each shook the hand of the others and soon, Hattonville Woods was again filled with the roar of a sick number-two and a full powered number-three engine.

As the "*Lady Jeannette*" taxied to the open field, its wings and fuselage passed through the solid trees and right over the open ditch. On the other side, its silvery, ghostly shape gained speed and about where T/Sgt. Gustafson had landed, "*Lady Jeannette*" had again taken to the skies of France.

In the village of Hattonville, as the "*Lady Jeannette*" again thundered over the church and turned toward the Somme, not one person woke up or began to run. Some though, did have a troubled sleep and would tell their family and friends that morning, it was as if they were watching that "Avion Fortress" fly over the church again, but this time it flew away and did not crash.

Sitting on the bank of the easterly road, just north of Tincourt-Boucly, Grey, Mears, and Bartho were talking to all their friends. Some of them came each night, from the cemetery across the valley. Among their fellow ghosts were two additional American flyers. 1st Lt. Hugh W. Robbins, a navigator, and S/Sgt. William G. Glass, a radio operator, had both died two months after the B-24 men had died. When their crashing B-26, from the 1st Pathfinder Squadron, attached to the 397th BG (M), "*Where's it At?*" had skipped off the earth at the B-24 crash-site, rose into the air, flew across the road into another field, bounced into the air again and then it crashed into the Buire Woods, three-quarters of a mile to the west. All the rest of the ghosts present, came from the woods and from the fields around the field where these three Americans had died. Three would rise each night from the same field across the road and one of them always complained, that the damned "Boche" had torn-apart what was left of him, when they dug in the field to take away what was left of these "Bloke's airy-plane."

The ghostly gathering here each night was much larger and diverse than at Hattonville, for this was an area of France known as the "*Cock Pit of War*." Wars have been fought here, from almost the time wars had begun. There were Huns, Romans, Spanish, Norse, and so many more. So much so, if you find the war fought here, you could talk to a veteran of that war at this gathering of phantom warriors.

Looking out over the heads of the warriors, the three flyers looked at their B-24, "**226**." Or, what was now the ghost of their B-24. Poor old "**226**" it had been so destroyed, its ghost could not collect enough of itself to ever allow it to fly again. All "**226**" could do, was to sit there, like they were sitting on the bank and wonder if they would be here forever. While "*Where's It At?*" waited alone at it's Buire Woods crash-site for it's two dead crewmen to return.

A few days before, something had drawn the "**226**" three men's ghosts to the cemetery across the valley where so many of their friends mortal remains were at rest. When they arrived, they had seen one of the Americans who had been at

367

their crash-site, when their remains were collected for the second time. He was talking to a Frenchman, who had also helped pick up their bits and pieces. A couple of times a year, the French man would come to the crash-site and think of them and they had to appreciate being remembered.

That night, as usual, the men of many war's past, visited the new war men and talked about their situation. Their remains had been there, then some were taken away, then more. At first, most of their remains had been much closer, before being moved to a cemetery five kilometers away. However, the flyers were still held at this place, their place of death. Perhaps, it was because so much of them was still there in the earth, just small bits and pieces that had been missed during the collection and then buried with "**226**." Still, they felt they had to be here by the unflyable B-24J, "**226**" for some unknown reason, along with the men of *"Where's it At?"*

Suddenly, off to the south-east, they heard a sound they had not heard for more than three years; it was another plane and it really sounded sick. The roar grew in volume and every eye looked that way until one ghost, an Australian "Outback" Soldier with an eagle eye, spotted the metal shining in the moon light, way off in the distance. Soon, every eye was following the ghostly B-17 "Flying Fortress," that was flying toward them, from the south-east.

In the villages around its flight path, villagers might roll over, wake, listen for a few seconds and then settle down to go back to sleep. In the village of Tincourt-Boucly, a few people were dreaming of a night not all that long ago, but none woke up to watch this bomber flying toward their village.

The B-17 circled the assembled men once, and then it smoothly landed in the field, to come to a stop just in front of unflyable "**226**" and all the assembled ghosts trooped down to the newly landed "Avion/Flying Fortress." Four men got out and shook all the offered hands and introduced themselves and began to talk to Grey, Mears, Bartho, Robbins, and Glass.

They told the men they had just found out, this was where the "**226**" might be. The *"Lady Jeannette"* and *"Where's It At?"* could fly and if the five men wanted to come join them, all of them could leave this place and fly for the rest of time and what the heck, perhaps "**226's**" engines cannot run, but she could glide, if we were to rig up a tow rope to the *"Lady Jeannette"* and *"Where's It At?"*

The assembled old war's dead from all the old wars cheered and told the five to go. Their tie here was so little now and they could come and visit any time. With that, the five looked at each other and said together, *"Let's do it!"*

While Robbins and Glass went to get *"Where's it At?"*, from the past warriors came a collection of ghostly ropes the dead had died with along with bow strings, rope belts, harnesses, and soon the skills of those of old wars had braided a tow rope for "**226**" and the Yanks tied one end to the tow rope to the tail wheels of *"Lady Jeannette"* and *"Where's It At?"* Then, they tied the towing end to the nose gear of "**226**," which forever, will not be *"Walking Alone."*

As the nine men's ghosts prepared to board *"Lady Jeannette," "Where's It At?"* and "**226**," the assembled gathering of warriors who had helped them, lined

up. Then the fliers shook every hand of the multitude before they got into their Boeing "Flying Fortress," B-17G-35VE, SN: 42-47904," named *"Lady Jeannette,"* the Consolidated B-24J-2-DT SN: 42-51226, **"226,"** and the Martin B-26G-1-MA, SN: 43-34201, *"Where's it At?"*

As the assembled ghosts moved aside, with their engines roaring, *"Lady Jeannette,"* and *"Where's It At?"* were pulling **"226,"** as all three took to the air and circled above the cheering crowd of their long dead, fellow war dead. As they gained height, the assembled ghosts of war watched the two bombers circle and climb into the night's sky, while the rumbling sound of thunder was heard.

In the distance, coming from the west, they saw huge formations of American aircraft, much larger than the largest formation of the past war. The ghostly planes were manned by the ghosts of their dead crews, though some flew with no one at the controls. As the formations began to pass overhead, the group of the ghosts of the wars at Tincourt-Boucly, watched their three bombers blend into the formation and then the *"Lady Jeannette,"* *"Where's It At?"* and the towed **"226"** were lost to sight for a few seconds, until the same "Digger" pointed toward the sky far above their upturned heads. And there, among those at the head of the formation of the flying ghosts, flew *"Lady Jeannette,"* *"Where's It At?"* and **"226."**

Throughout the Somme, farmers and city folk awoke to the thunder of the storm as it passed over them, as the flash of the lightening glowed against the bombers they could not see. All the living listened to the crashing of the thunder and saw the lighting as it flashed and died, and many remembered those skies full of planes and men, thundering to obtain their "Liberty."

As I began to wake from my dream-filled night, I heard nine voices ever so lightly in my mind. I listened as they told me, "When you are in France and the evenings sky fills with clouds rushing over the countryside from the Channel, take the time to watch and listen. If you are lucky and if you believe just a little in ghosts, watch the lighting flash and listen to the thunder roar. There among the clouds, you may see the *"Lady Jeannette,"* *"Where's it At?"* and "226" in their place. There among the leaders of the mighty formations that fly over France in the sky, from where they fell to their death. The ghosts of those planes and men aboard them fly to protect France, just as those below the concrete and soil of the Memorial at the Tranchees des Baïonnettes stand ready to charge, when the orders come." As I fully awoke, I heard them say, "Come some day and visit our places in France and think about who we were and the bombers we flew. For though we still fly, we are also there for those who remember us, as we were and what we have become."

While on a exploration of the Battle of The Somme, 1916, battle area, we made a great find.

Right behind my friend, you can see a shallow hole and note, he is standing in a deeper hole,

WHY?

In the shallow hole, just below plow depth, we had found eight British Stokes Mortar shells. Damn, great find, but one of the most unsafe weapons one can find from WWI, as the explosive contained ingredients that settled out and a light blow could set it off.

Unsafe for the farmer as, due to freeze and thaw, such items tend to work themselves to the surface.

Solution?

Treat them gentle and dig a deeper hole to re-bury them and trust, when they again come back up close enough to be hit by a plow, they have lost their explosive power.

Chapter Seventeen
Clean and Forget!
St-Avold

That morning, I made an early call from the Hotel Bellevue to one of my contact numbers, and I left the coded message that would let the correct person know we were arriving today. A few minutes later, we were on the road to Metz and St-Avold and less than two hours later we pulled up to the gate of the specified farm compound. A man came to the gate, to whom I gave the special code and the gate was opened to the next step of "Clean and Forget."

As we pulled in, the gate was closed behind us and two men came walking out of the house to join the man who had opened the gate. I did not know any of them, but the two men with me got out and shook hands and then they introduced me as the SOB who had made it all happen in '44 and '45. At first that pissed me off and then I realized, I was the SOB who put these men in a position in '44 and '45, that forced them back here in the in the early spring of 1948 to complete the required cleanup.

They invited us into the house, where we were offered coffee or cold beer and we all took the beer. The fellow, who appeared to be the leader, told us they had a covered 6x6 out in the barn that contained four "***Transit Boxes***" or as I prefer to call them, four temporary caskets.

They did not tell us how they came to be in possession of the 6x6 or the transit boxes, but the temporary caskets contained the official remains from the aircrew dead that had been buried at the Limey cemetery on 11 November, 1944.

In turn, I told them, in the trunk of our car we had three bundles of the real remains of the men who are supposed to be in three of the caskets on their 6x6.

With that, another set of beers was pulled out of the iced thermos chests they had and they asked what we were to do? I told them, and when I was done, we agreed we did not have the clothing and stuff we were going to need and that my team and I would run into St-Avold and get what we needed.

I told them that I had relatives who had a town house in St-Avold and when we were there, I was going to stop by to see if any of them were at the townhouse. If any were there, I knew they would be staying in the old, converted carriage house, as the large house was still waiting for complete repair of the damage from the **"friendly"** American bomb that had blown out one outside-wall, while creating major damage to the house.

Before we left, with the other team's help we removed the three bundles from our trunk and put them on a bench inside another locked area of the barn. To insure no far animal, mice, or rats could reach them.

When we arrived at the St-Avold town house, none of my family was there, so I stuck a note on the carriage house door. The note said we were in the area and

would see them at the farm tomorrow or early the next day. Then we searched for a store with surplus army goods.

Later, when we pulled back up to the gate of the farm, it was opened and we went in to spend the night. Not all that much of a beer man, I pulled out the safely-wrapped bottle of Jim Beam that I had gotten in Germany, from my B-4 bag and put it on the table. Lucky for me, most of them were beer or Cognac men, and in the morning I still had over half a bottle to wrap up and put back in my B-4 bag.

In the morning, I was asked what the plan would be? I said the first thing we had to do was to make absolutely certain no one could see what we were going to do inside the compound. Then, I assured the other three men that they did not want to do what we were going to do inside a closed barn. To get started we need to pull the 6x6 out of the barn in into the barn yard, remove the caskets and then make good what had been done, in '44.

When we were gathered outside in the open compound, I told my two men to walk around the compound and made certain no one could look in and see what we were doing. There was enough room inside the compound, even if someone came to the gate and peeked through the openings there, they would not be able to see what we were doing, though they might be able to smell it.

Within a few minutes, my men were back and assured me no one would see us. Just to be certain, I told one of the men to go to the highest, hidden location he could find and keep an eye out in both directions to let us know if anyone coming along the main road appeared to be coming to the farm.

This time, I only planned to wear a gas mask and supervise the others, as rank does have its privilege. The day before in St-Avold, we had purchased gas masks for five, two sets of fatigues for four, along with long gloves and galoshes. We opened the trunk and passed out the fatigues, boots, gloves and gas masks. The three we had met gave me an odd look when I handed them the gas masks. I told them to take them and that they would be damn happy to have them.

It took a few minutes for the men to don the protective gear and fit their gas masks. Then I told them to put the gas masks to the side, until we needed them. With that done, I told the other team leader to unlock the barn doors. I had the men move the three bundles out of the barn and set them to one side. The 6x6 was pulled out of the barn, the 6x6's tail gate was lowered and the canvas closing off the back of the 6x6 box was pushed to one side. Then, the four, caskets inside the 6x6 were taken out, one at a time and I thought, what I had made happen was coming to a final conclusion.

I had the caskets placed in a row, so we could walk around each casket and then I looked at each ID Tag marker on the caskets to see the name of the remains the casket was supposed to contain. You have already seen both sides of one of the ID tags attached to the temporary coffin of William E. Metzger, Jr.

At that time, I told all of them to prepare to don their gas masks and then, starting with my own gas mask, I put some of the perfume from the bottle I had in my pocket, inside each gas mask. The man, who had been with me in the woods, told his friends they would really appreciate the perfume, very soon. When I was

done with that and we all had our gas masks on, we opened the four caskets to see what was inside, placing the lids to one side.

Each of the caskets contained a small collection of dried decomposed flesh, that looks a lot like dried cottage cheese and bones, most were broken and split bones that had scattered around the bottom of the caskets as they were moved. Realizing the gas masks were not going to be required at this time, I took mine off and put it aside, while telling the men to do the same, but we would need them soon.

I decided the easiest thing to do, would require lifting up the temporary caskets of Gott, Metzger and Dunlap and then tilting them, so the bones inside would fall to one end. Then the men could place that casket over Krimminger's open casket and if they lifted, turned it over very slowly and tilted it just right, the casket could be turned over and all the bones inside would fall into the casket.

The first one was a learner and within a few minutes, we had all of the decomposed flesh and skeletal remains of S/Sgt. Krimminger we could collect, placed in his official Transit Box and I resealed the top. Finally, all the torn-apart remains of S/Sgt. Krimminger, that had been recovered by Boatman, Berardi, and Zeman, of the 563rd SAW Battalion, at the crash-site of the "*Lady Jeannette*" in the Bois de Hattonville on the 9th and 10th of November 1944, then fully desecrated on the 11th were reunited. Next, we had three empty caskets to fill, with the most likely, real remains of the men shown to be in those caskets. "It's time," I told the four men, as I picked up my gas mask, "to put your gas mask on and clear it. You do not want to do what you will be doing if your mask leaks, trust me on that."

Once we were all ready, I went to the first open casket, found its identity tag was for Metzger and I told the men to pick up the bundle with the one stripe on it and bring it to the side of the casket.

My team mate knew what had to be done, so I let him tell his friends just what they were to do. First, they had to untie the rope around the outside bag while making certain, the bottom of the bag was down. Then they had to cut the tape that sealed the bag, using the surplus meat knife I had bought at St-Avold. After that, they had to cut the draw string and remove the outside bag. We agreed the best way to do that would be for two of them to lift and hold the top of the inside bag in the air, as the other two men pulled the outside bag down and off the inside bags, like removing a sock.

When the first outside-bag was removed, the same plan was carried out with the next bag and this time, when the outside bag was pulled off, a small amount of fluid flowed out of it onto the surface of the compound floor. I smelled a familiar odor masked with perfume and my man said nothing, but the other three wanted to know what the hell that odor was. We had told them the night before what was in the bundles. All I said was, "They should be very happy they had the gas masks and the perfume to cut the strength of the odor."

Now we had to work with the last two bags. This time instead of removing the outside bag I instructed my man to slice the outer bag's rubber tape and cut the pull cord, which would allow the inner bag to be opened. The two men holding the bags swore and held on, as the odor crawled over us. It was a sweet, sickening

odor, that had been trapped inside the bag for twenty-four hours and it had really ripened. The gas mask and perfume helped, but it was still a smell that no one could ever forget, as it managed to sneak into the masks and mix with the perfume.

When the outside bag was fully opened, my man skinned it down a short distance before he cut the inside bag's tape and tie cord. The two men who were holding the bags had to work with him to transfer their hold from the inside bag to the outside bag, as my man cut the tape and pull rope of the inside bag. You could actually see the odor from that bag escaping into the air, where thankfully, a light breeze was now blowing most of the odor away from us.

After he had opened the inside bag, my man pulled up the outside bag, so both openings were together. With that done, I told the four men, they had to lift the bag-set over the open casket and then lift it and dump out the contents of the bag-set into the casket.

To do that, the two men holding the top of the bag-set had to keep the tops as high as they could, and move with the other two as they moved the bottom of the bag-set over the casket.

Once the men had the bag-set over the casket, I told them how to dump the contents and they needed to be very careful or they would be very unhappy with what could fall out of the bag-set onto them.

I backed up a way and told the four men what they had to do to make the transfer with the least possible spillage. To do that, the two men holding the top of the bag-set had to continue to keep the tops as high as they could and then, when I told them to, they had to fold over the tops of the bag-set three or four inches and then slowly lower the bottom end of the bag-set into the casket. As I was telling the men what to do, I realized we had a problem that needed to be fixed before the contents of the bag-set was placed in the casket.

The bag-set was sitting on the bottom of the casket, so my man was free and I asked him to grab a bulk of timber by the barn door. As he got the timber, I told the third man to lift the end of the casket nearest to me, so my man could put the wood block under it.

When the wood block was in place, the casket was tilted and I told the two men holding the bag-set top to remember to hold the bag-set upright, while the other two were to go behind, next to the two men holding the top of the bag-set and grab the bottom corners of the bag-set. Now, as a team, the bottom men were to slowly pull the bottom of the bag-set up the tilted casket bottom and at the same time, the top men were to slowly lower the bag-set top into the casket. Then, just as they reached the position the contents of the bag-set began to flow out of the opened top, they were to release the folded over bag-set top and quickly move back to avoid being splashed if the contents came out of the bag-set too quickly. Then, when the bag-set top opened and the contents began to flow into the casket, the two bottom men were to slowly pull the bag-set up and away, to allow the bag to fully drain the contents of the bag-set into the casket.

I asked the four men if they felt they fully understood what they were to do together as a team and each of them assured me, they were ready to proceed.

Well then, I told them, "Let's do it!" I told the men to assume their positions and let's get started. Once the men were in position, we began the dance and as the bag-set top men slowly lowered the bag-set top down into the casket, the bottom corner men slowly moved the bag-set bottom up the incline of the casket bottom and the bag-top men began to lower their end.

The first bag-set with it's contents of remains did not go as smoothly as it could have. With the top men really worried about being splashed, they released their end early and moved back. However, the bottom men realized what they were doing and did not pull their end any further, until what had started to flow out of the bag, had slowed to a point where, they could lift their end up, to allow all the contents in the bag to slide into the casket. At that moment, against the contrast of the casket, the odor could actually be seen, as it swirled and left in the wind.

None of us really wanted to look at the mass of bone, rotten flesh, and semifluid gunk as it came out of the bag a second longer than necessary. I told the two bottom-bag men still holding the empty bag-set at the raised end of the casket, to stuff the empty-bag-set into one of the removed empty bags, and to do it slowly to keep from spreading the mess. The two top-bag men made up for their earlier problem by grabbing one of the empty, cleaner bags and placing it over the center of the tilted casket end, so the two bottom-bag men could slide the newly emptied bag-set into the empty bag and fold it over, in order to seal in the odor of the empty bag-set. Within seconds, the bags were clear of the casket and placed some distance from the caskets.

Then I had picked up the casket top, dropped it into place and snapped the fasteners tight. Second Lieutenant William E. Metzger, Jr.'s, most likely, real remains were now sealed in his official Transit Box.

I motioned for all of us to walk a short way upwind and I took off my gas mask, and told the men they had done a great job and we only had to do it two more times. I asked them if they wanted to get this over with or take a break and make it last longer. About that time, the wind shifted a bit and suddenly we were all putting on our gas masks as fast as we could. Once they were on, we all laughed as much as you can inside one of those damn things and we agreed to do it now.

Within fifteen minutes, the other two transit boxes were sealed. Within thirty minutes, all four transit boxes had been placed in the back of the 6x6, the 6x6 was back in the barn and a nice fire was burning all the evidence, except for what had to be buried. I called up to the watchman and told him to come on down and with a little shovel work, using a shovel from the 6x6, some manure was placed on the small spill areas and with the blowing smoke, the last whiffs of the hanging odor left the compound and we were discussing the next step to be taken.

It was obvious to me, that the team we were working with thought they had completed their task. However, I had just realized the casketed remains we had just prepared could not be immediately transferred to their assigned, next *"Final Disposition"* location.

The original "transfer caskets" had contained fully decayed human remains, in a very dry condition and we had just dumped a lot of liquid, still decaying

remains into the three caskets. It was now obvious the remains in each casket had to be dried out before transportation to their next location. **This was a problem that had to be handled now, before we left St-avold for our final contact point.**

When we were done with cleaning everything up, we decided that we would all remain at the farm for another night and split up in the morning to finish our task. That evening, all the rest of the rations were used for dinner, the beer was finished, and my remaining bourbon bottle was tossed onto the bottle pile in a small room near the barn, along with the numerous beer bottles. The ice was long gone, but the beer drinkers had become used to warm beer during the war.

That evening, their leader and I, sat to one side and discussed this new emergency. We decided, that in the morning he would head into his office while my team was on its way to the family farm. Then, we would work with him to overcome this new situation.

The next morning when the other team came out of the farm house, the first out, their leader, was wearing a Class-A uniform with captain bars on the shoulder and the next two came out in suit and work clothes. Then I knew, we had really been a mixed lot in 1944/45. The captain had told me, the previous evening, that he was on a very special one-month duty call-up, having left the "Firm" two weeks ago for this special assignment.

As both groups prepared to leave the farm, the captain told me he would hold the four transit boxes in the locked barn until we had a resolution. The compound would be guarded, so they would be safe at this location until they could be reinserted into the production line and no one would ever know they had been missing. The captain then asked me for the telephone number of the family farm, so I could be contacted to make arrangements for our next meeting.

I dug into my wallet and found my uncle's number at the farm, and soon we were waving goodbye to the men in the 6x6 as they took the main road running into St-Avold, and I chicken-tracked off to the family farm to the east of St-Avold.

When we pulled up to the family farm compound, my uncle and a couple of my cousins came out of a shed to see who was there, and were very surprised to see me. We got out and I introduced my uncle and cousins to my team and asked if they had room for the three of us for a couple of nights so we could see the local sights before we needed to head back to Germany.

My uncle told me he was really surprised to see me, as the last he had heard, I was going to a fancy university in the United States. I told him we were a family that liked to jump around and actually, I was only here for a week or two on a special duty assignment and then I would be back at school.

We had a good family reunion and a big meal that night. During dinner, the telephone rang and after answering the telephone, my uncle said it was for me. Only one person knew where I was and had this number. Obviously, the captain was going to help get this problem solved, as quickly as possible.

I picked up the telephone and said, "Tell me about it, captain." The captain was a bit surprised about how blunt I was and before he could reply, I told him only one person knew I was at this number, so I did not have to guess who it was.

376

"Okay," he laughed, and asked me if I could meet him at the headquarters building at the St-Avold Cemetery tomorrow, as he had found there was also a paper work problem that I needed to know about. I asked him, if 10:00 would work and he agreed that was a good time and I told the captain I would see him in the morning and hung up.

I arrived with my team, on time, and we went inside the headquarters building where he had told me he would be and I asked a corporal where I could find the captain? He pointed to a door, and inside I found my captain. He told us to come on in and for the last man in to close the door. He pointed to a chair next to his desk and asked me to sit down. As I sat down, he told me that I also needed to be informed on the additional problem he had found. Then, he slid a form over to me and told me to look it over. At the top of the form was the title "*Disinterment Directive*" and then I saw the name of the tail gunner, Krimminger. Looking down the form, I saw the date his official grave had been disinterred just a short time ago, a list of the contents of the grave and that a 1st Lt. James B. Johns, Infantry, 337 QM SV BN had signed the form. I looked at the captain and told him that I had never seen one of these forms. However, from what I could see, it looked to me as if there was nothing wrong with the form.

He pointed to the line listing the **Condition of Remains** and asked me to reread it. The line stated, "**Advanced state of decomposition; disarticulated**." I looked back at the captain and asked, "So?" He pulled out another form in the file marked with a paper clip and asked me to read it. When I was done, all I could say was that S/Sgt. Krimminger's remains were to be buried at the Arlington Cemetery.

Again, I answered him with the question, "So?" The captain explained to me exactly what the problem was, when he opened another file and showed me the same form from the official burial records of T/Sgt. Dunlap. With the **Condition of Remains**, stating "**Fractured: all major bones, skull and mandible**." Then, I realized, thanks to us, there are many more remains in Dunlap's Transit Box."

The captain continued, telling us that Dunlap's remains were going to be buried here at St-Avold, and his transit box would be used to store his remains until his *"Final Disposition."* Which, would likely take over a year to be re-buried, taking into consideration the rate the remains at the St-Avold temporary cemetery were being disinterred. And the fact, that the new cemetery was still being laid out and it would be some time before it would be ready to accept new burials. Dunlap's remains were going to be under the full control of the QMC-GR during that period of time and what would happen if someone would reopen his transit box to re-confirm his identity and find what is now in the transit box?

The captain told us the problem existed with both mens' remains. Both Krimminger and Dunlap now had all, or almost all of their remains in their transit boxes and their *Disinterment Directives* did not show that information. This was of particular concern since Krimminger's remains and those of the two pilots were going to the States, and all three had to go through the recasketing point in Antwerp.

I knew at Antwerp, their remains would be removed from their transit boxes and one thing was certain, the condition of their current transit boxes would raise

many question that would have to be answered before the three mens' remains went through the acid baths at Antwerp, to ensure all the bones were clean of any tissue and any possible diseases on the bones would be neutralized.

(**Note**: The author has no absolute proof of this however, due to the disinterment of another casket, buried at the Springfield, Illinois, National Cemetery, he has personal experience with casketed World War Two remains. That casket contained, basically complete, non-cleaned, decomposition remains. Leading him to the opinion, remains recovered in the World War One Battle Zone were treated differently than those found elsewhere.)

He then told me, he had solved the problem with the current transit boxes. Three new transit boxes were being picked up today and taken to the compound. There, the current transit boxes would be placed in a locked building with good air circulation to dry the current contents. Their lids would be removed, and as soon as the contents were dry, he would move the contents to the new transit boxes, and put the boxes back into the moving production line and no one would realize what had happened.

Then, when the transit boxes were opened, the duty morticians might question the identity of the remains, based on the "*Condition of Remains*" from the cemetery *Disinterment Directive*. But, they would go ahead and process the remains through the acid baths and then the remains would be close enough to the "*Condition of Remains*" entry on the "*Disinterment Directive*," for them to be recasketed and sent home to be buried.

However, when Krimminger's transit box was opened and his remains put through the acid baths, we could expect the mortician to question the current "Condition of Remains" entry. Remember, the captain reminded me, we had dumped a lot of additional bones into Krimminger's transit box, then, we added a lot to Dunlap's transit box. So, now there were enough additional remains in both of their transit boxes for someone to really question why so many bones could so easily be identified at Antwerp or St-Avold, when they could not be identified at the Limey Cemetery and were not listed in the "*Condition of Remains*" on the two men's "*Disinterment Directives*."

The biggest advantage we had, the captain told us, was the fact there were many morticians and mortician assistants working with the remains at St-Avold and Antwerp. Due to their number, when the men's transit boxes went through the system, the odds of one man opening any two of the transit boxes were basically zero. Since no one man would see both men's remains at the same time, no one would become suspicious because of the difference on the one, somewhat odd form, in the set of paperwork for the remains they were working with. However, he was fairly certain, someone would question the large number of the now identifiable bones in the coffins, that were not listed on the men's "*Disinterment Directives*."

With that simple answer to what was such a large problem, I picked up the "*Disinterment Directive*" form for T/Sgt. Krimminger and asked the captain what

the form needed to have on it to remove any suspicion? He started to tell me and I told him to hold on for a minute. Then I asked him if this was the only copy of the form with this information on it or were there other copies somewhere else? He told me that as far as this particular mans' remains were concerned, this is the only copy that will be directly involved during the transfer of the remains.

I picked up the form and went to a nearby typewriter. Where I sat down and rummaged in a drawer next to the typewriter to look for an eraser, in case I needed it. I found one and I was ready to make my first test. I rolled a sheet of blank paper into the typewriter and typed some 'gobbledygook' and compared what I had typed to the type on the form he had given me. To me, it was close enough and I asked the captain what he felt of the match. He agreed it was a close match.

So, I asked him again, what else should be on the form and to please, write down it down on a piece of paper, so I would have it right on the form.

The captain wrote out the wording he wanted and gave it to me. I rolled Krimminger's form into the typewriter, released the paper control levers and moved the form until it was as aligned as I could get it. I reapplied the paper controls and I typed a semicolon at the end of the typed line in the "*Condition of Remains*" box, so the word disarticulated was followed by a semicolon, and now the form showed the word [disarticulated;]. As the last word on the first line, followed by a colon.

It looked good to me, so I operated the carriage return to move the form up one line and to type the next line, starting below the first word on the top line, "Advanced." My problem was, the "A" in the top line was low and I had to move the form to drop the 'a' at the start of this line, after which I had to move the form again to realign it. I completed the line by adding "all major bones fractured and/or missing except" to the form. With that line typed in, I used the carriage return to raise the form another line and moved the alignment to type, "lt radium & pelvic girdle." With the beginning, "l'" aligned under the new second line "all" on the form. However, the top of the "l" overstruck the lowered "a" of the line of type above it and this line continued to be a bit out of alignment. When I was done, I knew the two lines were a bit out of alignment. But you had to look close to notice the addition and how many people would suspect someone had been tampering with a very important official Form and then actually check the form for such tampering?

When I reviewed my work, it seemed to me, even if I would notice what could be tampering, (the lowed "A" and "a"), it could be blamed on a typewriter, with a repaired "A" key, which resulted in the lowered letters.

However, if you really looked close, you would see, none of the other "a" key letters in the top line or other lines on the form **were lowered**.

The captain had told me, that the Graves Registration personnel were handling tens of thousands of dead and working as fast as they could. When I was done, I rolled the form a bit higher and no one would look at this one form, among thousands of similar forms and believe it had been tampered with. I asked the captain what he thought? He looked at the form and told me it was good enough for him. The worst they would think, he said, was the person typing the original form

had messed up some how and the form had moved a little, as he typed.

I pulled the form out of the typewriter and handed it to the captain and then I asked him if he wanted me to type the same kind of additional information on Dunlap's Disinterment Directive form. He looked at it and said, the key thing was, no one would ever see the two forms side by side and no one would ever realize thatsomeone had added what was required to stop any inquiries after the original forms had been created.

At that point, the captain looked at the form again and then at me and said he was sorry for bringing us in as he could have done what I had just done. And that, he would type in all the additional information that was now required to be on T/Sgt. Dunlap's form himself. Then, we all shook hands and we left for the farm.

(Note: I had thought, we had now succeeded in this cover-up step of what we had done. Then, the researcher

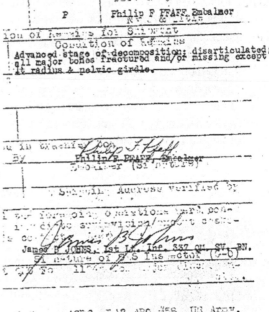

Disinterment Directive
Krimminger, H .B., SN: 34890339
Date of Death: 9 Nov 1944
Date Disinterred: 20 Apr 1948
Remains prepared and placed in Transit Box, Date: 22 Apr 1944 by
Philip F. Pfaff Embalmer
James B. Johns, 1st Lt. Inf. 337 QM SVN
Note: Added : on first line and crooked 2nd and 3rd line, adding remains to the previously prepared official document.

Scan of original copy: Willis S. Cole, Jr.

provided all the information he had, to help me with writing this chapter, and he stated, it is now very obvious that Dunlap's form had been tampered with, as he finally realized, that Krimminger's form had also been tampered with.)

When the captain did sit down to add the information to Dunlap's form, he had to have used a different typewriter then the one I used. His addition, even though it was much smoother and the out-of-line second line was much closer to being correct, the additions were very noticeable due to the typewriter having a

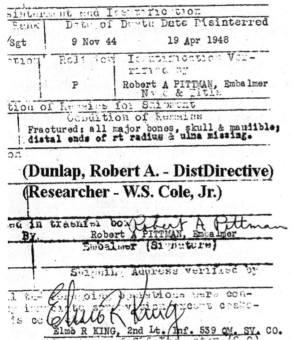

Rank	Date of Death	Date Disinterred
Sgt	9 Nov 44	19 Apr 1948

Religion: P — Identification Verifying By: Robert A PITTMAN, Embalmer

Condition of Remains: Fractured: all major bones, skull & mandible; distal ends of rt radius & ulna missing.

(Dunlap, Robert A. - DistDirective)
(Researcher - W.S. Cole, Jr.)

Robert A PITTMAN, Embalmer (Signature)

Elmo R KING, 2nd Lt. Inf. 539 QM. SV. CO.

Disinterment Directive
Dunlap, Robert A., SN: 3969640
Date of Death: 9 Nov 1944
Date Disinterred: 19 Apr 1948
Remains prepared and placed in Transit Box
Date: 22 Apr 1948 by Robert A. Pitman,
                                    Embalmer
Elmo R. King, 2nd Lt. Inf. 539 QM SV CO
Note: Added: ; on first line and darker second line with additional note to make the remains in the coffin match the known information about Dunlap's death mean nothing, now the proof of wound is missing!

Scan of original copy: Willis S. Cole, Jr.

much newer ribbon. It starts with the addition of the "dible;" at the end of the first line. Apparently, he had tried to erase the period after mandible to add the semicolon and when he did it, he ended up erasing all the way back to the 'n.' Then, when he managed to realign the form as good as he could, he had to add the 'dible' and the semicolon. That is where he made his mistake. He thought the line alignment could be a bit better and he had released the form to do a better job and the evidence after all these years show, he actually made it worse as far as line alignment goes. As you can see, the beginning of the second line is below the first line and the end is beginning to touch it. Still, our work fooled almost everyone all these years.

Fifty-eight years and nine months later, the fellow I had been warned about, that I mentioned at the front of this book, who in the end became my helpful researcher, sent me a copy of Krimminger's Disinterment Directive form and along with it, he sent a small plastic scale. In the accompanying letter he asked me to measure the distance between the word "except" on the second line and the "disarticulated" above it and the same with the "all," under "advanced?" Hell, even at my old age and bad eyes, when I took a close look at what I had thought was so good all those years ago, it was obviously not that good.

Sixty-two years and seven months after the event, he caught the second tampering after agreeing to help me reconstruct exactly what I had done, using all the information and documents he had found during his research. Well, I can see

381

why he was so surprised. It was enough that one Graves Registration form had been tampered with; who would ever suspect two had been tampered with, to make the remains listed show the damage caused by the wounds the two men had suffered, when it had not been there before and was not listed on the Reports of Burial?

Well, back to France. After leaving St-Avold, we went back to the farm and enjoyed another homecoming evening. We said goodbye to all my relatives at the farm the next morning and for once, we stuck to the main roads heading back to the west to Metz, then north through Luxembourg and into Belgium. As we made our way toward the Fosse Cemetery and found our contact point, not far from the Fosse Number One Cemetery, it was almost the same set up, a large farm compound, although not as isolated.

We were greeted by a team of two and both of my men knew these men. Again, I was introduced as the SOB who had made it all happen. The big difference with this meeting was that all we could do was to tell the men the remains at the first site were no longer there. We did not know where the remains had gone, so they could put the three transit boxes they had pulled out, back into the flow as soon as they could. When I saw the transit boxes, I wondered if their families would ever know their official and final caskets did not contain all the remains they should have? Well, it had to be done and I had done it, when verbally ordered to do so.

The two men asked us if we wanted a beer or a cup of coffee. So we got out, used the toilet outside the house, had a beer and were back on the road, heading toward Germany less than 45 minutes after we had arrived at the farm compound.

Late that afternoon, we pulled up to the operations center at the air base in Germany, where I had arrived. I got out and waited for the driver to open the trunk, got my B-4 bag and remembered what had been there for a couple of days and as the B-4 cleared the trunk, I said a quick prayer for those dead. Then, I shook hands with both men and told them, I hoped, I would never see them again. We laughed and I went to the operations center to begin my way back to school.

(**Note:** Some years later, as time passed and we realized another problem had begun to surface, we actually formed our own, "*Old Boys Club!*")

I was told that a B-17 was leaving for Westover early the next morning. That sounded good to me, so I asked the operations officer to get me on that flight and to send a message to the colonel at home to give him the estimated time of our arrival at Westover, and ask him to have "*Speedy*" waiting for me.

With that, I asked the operations officer where I could find a phone to use in privacy and he pointed to an empty office and told me to close the door.

I opened my wallet, found the contact number and told the operator to put me through to that number. In less than a minute, he said, "They are on the line Sir," and I heard the click, as he opened in the connection. A voice I did not recognize came on the line and I left my message, "Clean and Forget" and said I was on a B-17 to Westover in the morning.

He asked if I could be contacted and I told him I would be at the BOQ tonight. I also gave him the telephone number, of the telephone I was using, and added that I could be contacted at that number in the morning after 07:30, for a half hour, before my flight left for the States at 08:10.

That night, I had a good night's sleep and was at the operations center in the morning wearing my borrowed flying gear, waiting in that office and drinking a cup of coffee when the telephone rang.

I answered, identified myself, and the familiar voice asked me if this was the end of the whole thing? I did not think, it would do any good to tell him about the missing remains from the B-24 site, as they had obviously disappeared some time ago and were apparently, out of sight and out of mind, hopefully forever.

So I told the general I was positive he could forget all about it. The general told me, "Colonel, I hope to hell, you are right, we do not need any more weak link problems." The general then told me to stop by and visit him sometime in the future and he ended by saying, "By the way General, I think you will like your next two assignments after you finish at the university." With that, I heard a click on the line and I put the handset back on its cradle.

Looking out the office window, I saw the operations officer raise his right hand and twirl his index finger in a circle, indicating they were about to start the engines on my B-17. So, I picked up my B-4 bag, with its well-padded bottle of fancy perfume and started out to the flight line to the B-17 I was to leave on.

On the way to the B-17, my mind ran over the last sentence out of Ike's mouth. Two assignments and he had called me **_General_**, instead of the usual colonel. I was feeling very good when I arrived at the B-17, to find the same crew and B-17, now on their way back to the States.

I returned the ground crew's salutes, signed the flight manifest and managed to pull myself up into the forward hatch without help. When we taxied up to the flight line at Westover, I saw "*Speedy*" sitting in a jeep next to the two-seater I had arrived in on my way, "*Over There!*" As I lowered myself down from the hatch, "*Speedy*" walked over, saluted, and asked, "If I wanted to get the hell out of here, but use a toilet first, I could ride with him to file his flight plan. As we got ready to leave, "*Speedy*" told me I had to have a lot of juice, with only two crews from where I started to where I was returning. "What the hell," I thought, as I told, Speedy, "Sure I do, so let's ride and fly this baby home."

When we pulled up to the flight line where we started, the remaining waxed bag in my pocket was still there. As I really started that trip getting into that two-seater plane, I will end with getting out of it.

Now you know, along with General Eisenhower, I am responsible for what has to have been "**_The Best Kept Secret of World War Two!_**" And, I am telling you from my heart, it would be a very different world today, if what I helped make happen during November and December '44, had become public knowledge in early January, 1946! **_"And that is why, we killed Patton!"_**

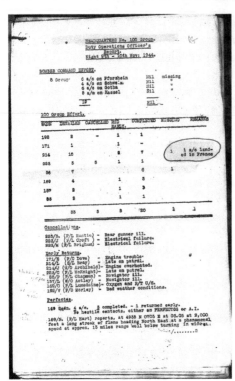

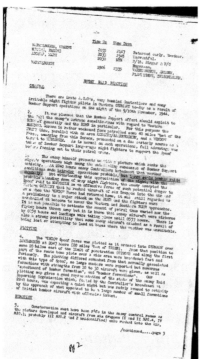

The British Official report to Enemy Raid Reaction for the night of 9th - 10th Nov. 1944.

Copy of the Nightly Report for the night of 9th - 10th Nov: 1944

Notice, it reports the truth, instead of the untruth of the Official USAAF 8th Air Force for that night.

1 a/c ("**226**") landed in France

"There are irate A.C.C.'s, very humbled Controllers and may irritable night fighter pilots in Western Germany to-day as a result of Bomber Support Operations on the night of 1/10th November, 1944.

"For this purpose the MANDREL Screen in rather weakened form ("**226's**" loss weakened the result) patrolled some 40 miles West of the FRONT LINE..."

"226" was blown far enough to the east, to appear to be an enemy, instead of a Friendly.

Coincidence?

General Eisenhower

General Patton

One of these two men would live to be President and one would not.

One thing is obvious, General Patton had a great secret that he felt would destroy those who had worked to destroy him! His mistake was confiding to General Gay that he was going to quit the Army and expose that secret to the American public!

General Gay was involved, just as all of the other Commanders who allowed Eisenhower's <u>verbal orders only to put their careers at risk!</u>

<u>Patton could not be allowed to do what he was going to do and immediate action was put into place to stop it!</u>

His death began on the last day the Army would have physical control of his future!

Photograph: US Army Archives

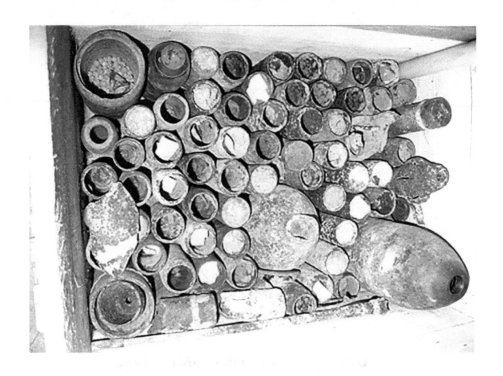

"*Those were the days my friends, we thought they would never end*" and then P.C. stopped it all.

On a trip back through Brussels International Airport, the plane was loading and the author and his wife were almost aboard, when the author was pulled out of the line and disappeared for some time.

The plane closure was late and his wife was wondering if she would see him again, when he was escorted into the plane and the door closed.

Then, she learned the truth, remember the suitcase full of "*Lady Jeannette*," well it was all about that. As soon as I told them, we were researching the loss of the "*Lady Jeannette*," they agreed none of it was a problem and I spent the next 45 minutes telling them the story of the research and what the relics were, if I knew.

(**Note**: The case in the photograph, first went to France by United Airlines (donated shipping) with ten Memorial Plaques to be installed on the Memorials we were putting in place and then, it came back by ship full of scrap metal. It make two more trips by ship, finally coming back with over 600 pounds of "*Lady Jeannette*."

During each ongoing visit to the crash site, it was obvious the French were going to the site, digging up relics and never filling the holes. So, it was agreed with the village, that we would remove all the relics we could find, to prevent such holes, as they were dangerous to older people who visited the site.)

Chapter Eighteen
"Our 'Trojan Horse'"

Life was sweet for some years after we had cleaned up in France. I had connections in the right places and we had lots of enemies in a lot of places. For a while before his death, General Donovan, now Ambassador Donovan, and I continued to play games around the world.

Of course, when General Eisenhower became President, I had a direct line into the ear of the man in charge, and once in a while, projects that Donovan and I were involved in would pop out of his mouth; "Falling Dominos" is one that comes to mind. Then the world began to change. The youth, unlike my day when everyone seemed to want to better the world, became mostly interested in destroying the world without any ideas put forth to replace what they would destroy.

People soon forgot that what was going on in south-east Asia began because the goal was to stop an advance of Communism, that appeared to be on its way to an unstoppable victory in that part of the world. Then, just like Korea, the politicians soon began over-riding what was best for the military and in the end, with strategy torn-apart by people who had no idea of what was really at risk, many still believe to this day, we lost that war. Funny, how so many forget the original goal was to stop the flow of Communism, and even though so many here are happy we lost that war. When in fact, we did win that war in the long-term.

We paid a large price for our hidden victory; that country suffered, and continues to do so today, as many think a war lost, is better than a war won. They forget the millions of Vietnamese and Cambodians who died after the Americans declared victory and retreated. Yet, today that supposed lost victory is undergoing a change within that will lead them to becoming one of the major emerging countries of the world. They are not accomplishing this growth because the Communists won, it is because, after all these years they would rather have what we offered, than what the Communists forced upon them at the end of that war. Right after, we had declared victory, fled, and left them to what we knew was certainly going to happen.

So, as I wrote at the beginning, I saw where that war was going and I decided, I no longer wanted to be part of what I saw was coming. So, I pulled the plug on my military career and migrated into the "Firm."

One does have to wonder what will happen in the world today, as politicians of the same mental state refuse to learn from history, declare victory and retreats. We must also realize, it is best to allow them to fight among themselves in large areas of the world instead of picking a side. As both sides will continue to attack the United States in anyway they can, and their nose is now inside the tent!

This did not mean that I lost contact with the small group of OSS men with whom I had created *"The Best Kept Secret Of World War Two!"* As one does age, one begins to look back and reflect on the things one has done. Our small group was extremely proud of how we had preserved those who we had to preserve. At

the same time, each of our own careers advanced thanks to the "golden hands" that appeared once in a while from above. For instance, when a new contract was won without a bid, or there was a lot of work for "Firms" such as ours, who were somehow, almost always involved in unrest in foreign countries, intrigue and war.

Then in 1968, something began to become obvious to me. The one "golden hand," who from the beginning had told me he would make sure nothing would happen to us for what we had been ordered to do, would soon make his own "Final Transfer." I knew, that all of President Eisenhower's promises to me were verbal promises with no actual documentation of those promises existing. It was now clear to me, that after Ike died our small group of very involved people could hang as a group or individually, if what we had done came to light.

I had no choice but to call each of the men and tell them about my fears, and the truth, that soon we could depend on no one else but ourselves to protect everyone involved in our group.

One of our members, who was a wine maker, artist, a great story teller, and *a pheasant hunter*, volunteered that he had an excellent location in mind, where I could gather the group together. There we could discuss what we had to do to overcome the risks that the death of President Eisenhower could possibly expose us to, if the truth of what we had done ever became public information.

During the first retreat of our new "*Old Boys Club*," at the country house he had provided, we discussed the world's problems and how we would solve them, if left alone. However, what we really had to discuss, was what we had to do to continue to protect our own backsides, as all our "golden hands" were either dead or would soon be dead. It was obvious to our small group, that thanks to what we had done for those "golden hands," they were all safe now. The truth might somewhat tarnish their *golden reputations*," but they all had large resumes of success and their time had now passed.

However, our time was still here and if the truth came out in any way, that truth would still destroy all of us. We had been the tools that made what they wanted to happen, happen and we had done a spectacular job of making it happen. However, we had only done what they wanted, because they had ordered us to do it. Soon, not one of them would still be here to tell other people that they, not we, were responsible for everything that had been done. Even the death of Patton actually laid in their "golden hands" and not ours. But, the real truth was, when one of the "golden hands" told us to do something for the good of all involved, if we had not done it, someone else would have and very quickly that same person would have **seen to it,** *that we were no longer around to tell the truth!* As you know, I was around then and we members in our "*Old Boys Club*," thanks to our compliance to verbal orders only, were still around for many years after Ike's death.

On our last evening together during the group conference, after a bourbon and water for me and the preferred drink of each of the others, the discussion turned to what had to happen to all of us if the truth of what we had done was going to be fully protected against the remote chance of our actions ever became known to the public at large.

As the person whom I suppose could be called the "ring leader," I explained all the steps I had taken to ensure official records that should exist, did not exist. I also explained that almost all of the official records that I had to leave in the system contained no real truth of what we had done, certainly nothing that could easily be traced back to us.

Nearly twenty-five years had passed since it all began and no one had even started to guess what went on, but times were changing. Now, instead of almost all the books being written about the war, being supportive of the war, many authors were beginning to question a lot of the events that happened. I reminded the men, that the story of the British use of a dead man's body to ensure victory had already been available for over twenty years in the book, *"The Man Who Never Was"*. I asked them, how could we know that no author was now working on exactly what we had done at either crash-site or the other two events after the war? No one could ever convict the "golden hand" men whose careers we had ensured, but lots of people would be happy to let us burn for what had happened to Patton.

We sat by the fire that night and determined that we would meet again in two months and by the time that meeting ended we had to know the steps we had to take. Steps that had to be taken, not to protect Donovan, Eisenhower, Arnold, Marshall, or Truman, but to protect ourselves, our families, and our careers.

The goal was that each of us would ponder our situation and when we met in two months, each of us would produce our plan for the group. Then, as a group, we would select the best plan that would enable us to continue our lives. While at the same time, removing any threat of some outsider stumbling over some piece of missed evidence that would in any way lead to us becoming connected to what we had done.

Two months later, telling the wife I was on a phony business trip, I met with the group and we began discussing exactly what had to be done. Quickly we came to the conclusion that we could best protect ourselves by sending any researcher or author off in the wrong direction by using a "Trojan Horse!"

---

http://Encarta.msn

Tor-jan horse
noun
Definition:
1. **hollow horse concealing Greeks**: in Greek mythology, a hollow wooden horse that hid Greek soldiers, left at the gate of Troy. The Trojans were convinced it was a gift to Athena and dragged it inside.
2. **concealed stratagem**: somebody or something that is meant to disrupt, undermine, subvert, or destroy an enemy or rival, especially somebody or something that operates while concealed within an organization.

All of us agreed that the best "Trojan Horse" we could use, would send researchers and authors down a path leading them to the conclusion that Patton's

very accidental car crash was actually a planned and executed attack on Patton's life. Once it was agreed that a "Trojan Horse" was the best way to send the research and author hounds down the wrong scent trail, the rest of our time together was spent on discussing the fine details of what had to be done to make it work.

It was obvious to us, that we had to do much more than start dropping hints about what had happened to Patton. We had to find a way to do it that would make any pursuing research and author hounds fully commit to the false trail being laid, instead of the light hint of an actual trail they may have previously located.

Just like the raccoon hounds, where I grew up, would leave the fairly fresh trail of the raccoon they were pursuing, if they came to a spot where the fresher trail of a fox had just crossed the racoon's older trail, to chase the fox. We needed to do the same to make certain our "collective butts" were protected.

The problem, most of us told the others, was how our own personal careers could be deeply affected, if we had to be the one laying the new scent trail. We broke up that evening, with a good general plan in the works. What we did not have that night, was an actual plan that could be put in place.

Over a last drink, we all promised the others we would sleep on it, and tomorrow after breakfast we would meet again and one way or the other, we would reach a final decision that would enable our intended plan to be put into action.

After breakfast the next morning, we gathered in the library and the fellow who had arranged the location asked all of us to just be quiet for a moment, as he felt he now had the solution to our quandary. He said, "It was obvious that someone who had the correct background would have to be the person who put our agreed plan into action. It had to be someone who had as much to risk as any one of us. Certainly, it had to be someone that all of us could trust with our lives." As soon as he made that statement, there was a group agreement of what he had just said and just as quickly, each of us looked at each other to wonder who that person had to be. Each of us had our own lives and problems, and this could lead to that selected person being believed or ridiculed as the plan proceeded.

Yes, I thought for a moment, I should be the one at risk. Then instantly, I realized that of all the men in the group, my career during the time in question could be fairly easily researched, if the researchers and author hounds were given that head-start to my identity. The moment I started to place the required "Trojan Horse," my background would be researched, and it would probably lead into, instead of away from what we had actually done.

I could see each of the men had the same thoughts running through their mind, when our host again spoke his thoughts. He told us, "Of all of us, only my background during and after the war is such, that all the researchers and authors in the world could back-track my trail and all they will end up with, was that I had served in the OSS. I may have participated in missions of risk and since then, I am exactly what I am, an artist, a story teller and a hunter. In addition, I am the only one of us, who has a life that can be fully exposed, without risk to my current career." Then he added, "Hell, I have nowhere to go with following this plan, other than to become someone who was known to have, ***"lived a life eventful enough for***

a dozen novels." The rest of you have a lot more to lose." He continued, "Me, I have nothing to lose, and I have a lot to gain. Damn, they may even make a movie about what I will tell them I was involved in."

Immediately, I personally had to agree with his plan. He may, or may not have been personally involved in the actual events I had put in place. Perhaps, he was only an "**expert rifle shot facilitator!**" If, the original plan had been completed. I did know, it was basically impossible for anyone to track down his OSS history and then tie his OSS history into one of the events, the rest of us had been involved in.

What can I say, is his statements broke the dam free and the flow of ideas in support of our previous rough plan began to flow like the drinks we were soon enjoying so early that day, so many years ago. First, it was agreed that it had to start, more as a rumor and not a fact. The word had to go out that someone who had been involved with the OSS was beginning to reveal to his close friends about how he may have been involved in the execution of General Patton. *In order to prevent General Patton from doing something that important people did not want done*. For the next two days, we schemed and planned and laid out a plan that has worked so well, that I thought that I would die knowing that the truth of what we had done would never become public. The plan, at first complicated, began to be cut down to the simplest possible implementation of the plan. As we all knew from our own experience, the simplest plan was the best plan and the hardest to unravel.

We all agreed that some kind of documentation would have to exist, in due time, if the plan was to work. It could not be official documentation in any way. We finally greed, the best documentation would be in some diary format, that could slowly be referenced to interested researchers and authors by the man who had volunteered to take on the burden of the load. It was agreed, we could not share in any way, except for providing our on-going help in ensuring the planning and implementation of the "Trojan Horse's" exposure was as flawless as possible.

We also agreed during that meeting, that the "Trojan Horse" would have to give up someone who had been fairly high up the command chain, in order, to help create the false trail. I knew that one friend of mine, who had died over a decade earlier, would be pleased and proud at the opportunity to become that false trail's subject. Among the "golden hands" who had helped us over the years was my very good friend, General/Ambassador "Wild Bill" Donovan. I knew that "Wild Bill" would be looking down at those who should know better and chuckling and laughing like hell. When the "Trojan Horse" used his name to divert anyone who might have previously picked up a bit of a trail before the "Trojan Horse" began to lay his false scents. Including the involvement of "Wild Bill" in the plot to kill General Patton, that so many, so quickly followed for decades to come.

"Wild Bill" had been vilified by one of the very "golden hands" men whose hide he had helped save. In the end, they decided he was an unnecessary addition to their future goals and it was not until, General Eisenhower became President that Donovan's damaged career was resurrected. "Wild Bill' would have loved what we

did in his name, and boy, did the military history researchers and author hounds eat it up and use it, in their papers and books.

Soon after that *"old boy's"* meeting, there were people who were questioning Patton's death and some were even raising the possibility that his accident had been a planned attempt on his life.

Along the way, we did have a bit of fun as we made some of the "Trojan Horse's" claims so ludicrous that anyone who was a real researcher or author should have realized something did not smell right. And, if the "Trojan Horse" was telling stories like that one, the rest could hardly be believed. But the hounds were in full bay and they smelt the blood of those whom they would declare executed Patton in that simple accident. They paid no notice, that it was the "Trojan Horse" and his tales that were creating that smell of blood.

Then, there was the creation of the diary, we agreed was needed to support the "Trojan Horse's" history and what he was supposed to have done. If one man could do a lot, a group of the right men could put together a manuscript of diaries (recopied, of course, by the "Trojan Horse" to make them even more real), that made what he stated was the truth - totally believable, if you were bound to believe them. It was odd, no one ever questioned the "Trojan Horse" keeping of a diary, when no one who did what we did over the years would keep such proof of what we had done. **And if, one had and we learned about it, he would have joined Patton and we all knew it!**

It was so simple, as later reported in one author's write-up, the "Trojan Horse" had parachuted in front of General Patton's Army in order to stop Patton's drive to the east. Sure, the Germans accepted the parachuting man, believed him, and put him out on the road holding up his hand in a German salute, demanding as Patton's jeep approached, that Patton had to stop his forward advance.

Why would those with the "golden hands" send someone in front of Patton's Army to stop his advance, when all they had to do was use their "golden hands" to turn off the tap to Patton's fuel supply and let the military historians and authors, as they still do, fight over whether or not the fuel supply should have been shut off? Such events, certainly would never have empowered Patton to destroy the bastards who were destroying him. All they could have been, they have become, discussions at military schools about Patton's drive across France.

If Patton had intended to use such drivel to attempt to destroy those who where successfully destroying him after he had resigned from the Army, he would have been allowed to live, to successfully destroy himself.

The following years were more fun than we could have believed possible. By March 1969, when Ike died, the rumor was already beginning to make its way around the circles. Within two years the "Trojan Horse" was becoming so effective, that the paper to defend Patton, referred to earlier in this book, was written and **the world was told that what we had done was impossible to have been done**. That one, was worth several rounds of drinks at our next gathering!

Things were soon starting to happen, just as our plan laid it out. However, there remained one thing that had to happen to make it work as well as it could. The

"Trojan Horse" had to have credibility. And what better credence could the "Trojan Horse" have, than for some friends in the "Firm" to invite the "Trojan Horse" to tell his story at one of their very own functions.

Then the researchers and authors who really do little or no real research, other than reading other researcher's papers and author's books, would really begin writing even more articles and books, just as we had planned. Patton had been killed, Patton was going to start wars, Patton was going to expose those who had managed to get rich in Europe, running around and stealing while others were dying. The destruction of Patton had been started by the "golden hands" long before the invasion of Normandy. The simple fact is, if Patton had not been brought back into the war, as Patton himself coarsely put it, "to pull Ike's nuts out of the fire," Patton would have lived to return to the United States.

Simply put, Patton would never have had obtained the information that he did have, that would have destroyed "***those bastards who were attempting to destroy him***," if Ike had not realized that Patton was a hell of a fighter and he was required, if the war in Europe was to end as soon as possible. At the same time, Ike's action, ensured that Patton could not be allowed to leave to return to the United States and follow through with what Patton stated he was going to do.

Over the years, the stories of Patton's execution grew greater and more grandiose and our "Trojan Horse" greatly enjoyed to the very end, becoming exactly what he had set out to become. Taking those, who might have found the real truth and getting them to bark along the false trail, that he had laid. A trail that to this very day was a scent trail, that led to a place and a mind set, that was never less true than it was on the day Patton's car was in an accidental collision; a collision that could have been easily prevented, that disrupted plans already put into place for Patton to die later that day in a very believable way.

Then, when it suddenly became apparent that General George S Patton, Jr. could make it back to the United States, ***Patton died!***

- - - - - - - - - - - - - - - - - - - -

Over time, our small "***Old Boys Club***" would continue to meet and as time passed, it began to become smaller and smaller. Then in 1999, our "Trojan Horse" died, and to the very end he led them to the places we wanted them to go. To this day, his diaries to which we all contributed our bit, continue to lead them down the false trails we had laid.

Now as I write this, I am the last survivor of that group, and as I wrote early on, "What can they do to an old man like me?" They have no proof and Lord knows, those researchers and authors are, for many years to come, going to be reading each other's papers and books and then create even more theories of how and why Patton was killed by that accident.

The telephone rang some time ago and a new person entered my life. A person who knew even more, at times, than I did about what I made happen over the years. Now, you know it too. Enjoy, as what you have read is exactly what someone in the position I held, would have planned and done!

This is the finish of my day by day narration of what was done. However, the researcher, as he had done for so many years, will continue to search for the rest of the truth of what we did and how we did it.

Copy - Official Aircraft Record - Obtained from US Air Force Historical Research Agency, Maxwell AFB

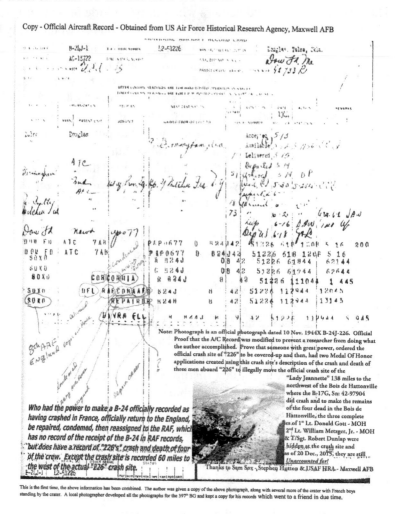

Note: Photograph is an official photograph dated 10 Nov. 1944X B-24J-226. Official Proof that the A/C Record was modified to prevent a researcher from doing what the author accomplished. Prove that someone with great power, ordered the official crash site of "226" to be covered-up and then, had two Medal Of Honor applications created using this crash site's description of the crash and death of three men aboard "226" to illegally move the official crash site of the "Lady Jeannette" 138 miles to the northwest of the Bois de Hattonville where the B-17G, Sn: 42-97904 did crash and to make the remains of the four dead in the Bois de Hattonville, the three complete es of 1ˢᵗ Lt. Donald Gott - MOH 2ⁿᵈ Lt. William Metzger, Jr. - MOH & T/Sgt. Robert Dunlap were hidden at the crash site and as of 20 Dec., 2015, they are still Unaccounted for!

Who had the power to make a B-24 officially recorded as having crashed in France, officially return to the England, be repaired, condemned, then reassigned to the RAF, which has no record of the receipt of the B-24 in RAF records, but does have a record of "226's" crash and death of four of the crew. Except the crash site is recorded 60 miles to the west of the actual "226" crash site.

Thanks to Sam Sox , Stephen Hutton & USAF HRA.- Maxwell AFB

This is the first time, the above information has been combined. The author was given a copy of the above photograph, along with several more of the crater with French boys standing by the crater. A local photographer developed all the photographs for the 397ᵗʰ BG and kept a copy for his records which went to a friend in due time.

The questioning reader can find the above Aircraft Record at the USAF Historical Research Agency at Maxwell AFB. Small pieces of "**226**," Lt. Lukensmeyer, Sgt. Barto, and Sgt. Mears are documented in the photograph of the true end of "**226**." Yet, it is this end that was used in the two Congressional Medal Of Honor as the method of death of the two Awardees. Which one is correct, the falsified Official Aircraft Document or the ID Tag and skull fragment found 138 miles to the southeast of this crash-site?

NARRATOR'S EPILOGUE

What you have just read provides the truth as I know it. With the help of the researcher, I have attempted to tie it all together in this book. However, there is one event, that is based on less than a one-hundred percent foundation. That concerns the exact location of the complete bodies, last seen by outside observers at the "*Lady Jeannette*" crash-site, on 9 November, 1944.

As I have written, the attached AMC Medical personnel of the 563rd SAW Battalion were, by Army regulation, the men directly responsible for recovering and transporting the wounded to the 109th Evac. Hospital and the remains of the four dead men found at the B-17 crash-site, to the Limey Cemetery. The other officer most directly involved in person was the Battalion Executive Officer.

On 7 December, 2003, while conducting research at the Air Force Historical Research Agency at Maxwell Air Force Base, the researcher located the name and current address of the Executive Officer of the 563rd SAW BN. He had written and submitted the Battalion History, with no mention of the B-17 to the National Archives and the AFHRA, in 1993. When he found that history, the researcher was positive, all his questions concerning the dead at Hattonville would be immediately answered, as soon as he contacted the XO.

When the researcher contacted the XO from his hotel room in Montgomery, the XO immediately stated, "*I have no memory of any bomber crashing at Hattonville while I was there*." Then he told the researcher, that all the officers and almost all of the men of the unit were dead. However, if the researcher would call him back after the New Year, he might be able to find the names and location of the few 563rd SAW BN HQ personnel who were still alive.

In January, 2004, the XO gave the researcher three names, all of whom turned out to have been part of the attached Battalion Medical detachments, these were the very men who had the direct responsibility by Army regulations to treat the wounded and to recover the dead at the crash-site of the "*Lady Jeannette*." When the researcher contacted each man, to his surprise, each man immediately made the same statement to the researcher, "*I have no memory of any bomber crash at Hattonville while I was there*."

It was amazing; four men contacted and each made exactly the same statement as if they were reading from a prepared script. Instead of finding the truth, the researcher found stonewalling by the only men who knew the real truth of what happened to the un-accounted-for dead in the Hattonville Woods. Instead of going away as they may have wished, their answers provided the researcher with even more proof of a conspiracy among those involved, to hide the truth of the crash-site and the desecration of the dead.

Their replies led to even deeper research and later this military history novel instead of the pure military history book that could have been written, if one of those four men had told the truth of their actions in Hattonville Woods before he

completed his "Final Transfer." Instead, what ever the Colonel threatened them with had worked and they carried their secret to their grave. Thankfully, Tiff recorded the truth of his participation in his diary, that was **only to be opened after his death**.

Of course, if the secret had been exposed, **as Patton had intended**, it would have become international news. As the United States Government would have to admit to the world, that the United States with over 20,000 World War Two personnel still carried as **Missing In Action** in Europe, had hidden the identified remains of American military combat dead. One has to know, those who had hidden the dead would be prosecuted to the fullest extent of the law.

Few know, that the United States had conducted no new "*Searches*" for those MIA personnel, since 31 December, 1951, when all funding for such "**Searches**" had been discontinued. Until recently, only conducting "**Recoveries**" when forced to do so. To this day, they still claim the credit when MIA remains are found by the people of Europe. At times, the Europeans almost had to force the Untied States to recover their MIA remains, few get proper credit and some, due to prior treatment, will not report the location of a remains, once found.

Thankfully, due to recent media coverage of a private organization locating MIA remains, the Defense Department POW/MIA Accounting Agency has selected some and not other such organization to work with.

(**Note**: An example exists of the French having to wait for over eighteen months before they conducted a "**Recovery**" at a known remains site after receiving a request from the French. Then, it took seven years before the remains were "Officially Identified" though the remains had been found with both ID tags, matching aircraft serial number and matching machine gun serial numbers.)

In ending, if the reader still questions the facts in this book, they may want to think about the author's first direct contact with the 563rd SAW BN - XO, who was at Hattonville on the 9th, 10th and 11th of November, 1944, Maurice Byrne and his wife at their home in Boise, Idaho, in August, 2006.

When departing, the XO's wife clearly stated to the author and his wife, *"**I know all about those bodies in the woods and after all this time it cannot hurt anyone. They should be found and returned to their loved ones**."*

Obviously, the XO's actions in the Hattonville Woods had bothered him so much after the war, at some time he had un-burdened himself and told, at least one person the truth, of what he had helped do, his wife.

It was the hope of the author, that the description of what they had to have done to the one man's torn-apart remains and the complete bodies of the three other dead men, as well as the statement by the XO's wife, would have led to one of the four men to tell us the truth before this book was published. Obviously, none of them would admit to the truth and in the end, carried the truth to their grave.

AUTHOR'S EPILOGUE

For more than twenty-seven years, I have been deeply immersed in the research leading to this book. For years, I struggled with how to convert what I was learning into a readable format. Often, something I found in 1994, did not fit until late summer, 1998. Then something found in 2000 would fit both what I found in 1994, and early 2007, to a point, where it all made sense in my own mind. **For instance, the 10 years, 10 months, and 25 days it took before I found Barney Silva.** With such time periods between the original of a possibility and proof that it occurred, how would the general reader wrap their mind around such a jumble of facts?

I had no idea how I was going to put all of it into a true military history book in a form that would allow the reader to understand all the ramifications of what all my research proves happened.

Then, one day I received an e-mail from an OSS Veteran whom I respected, who knew of my research. He suggested that I should put the research into a military historical novel. Such a step would free me to create the ties required to cross over the gaps left by the falsified official documents I had located and other missing direct links. In addition, it would permit me to explain exactly what had to be done to desecrate the remains of the American War Dead at both crash-sites in the words and actions of those who participated in *Killing Patton*.

The controlling factor, the person telling the story, had to be someone who had to exist, either as one man or no more than three. At least, that was my original view. Then, as the book progressed, I was forced to think of all the things that had to be done so quickly to make what was done the success it was for so many years and I realized, two or three men could not make such decisions in the time required.

Each would have their own personal situation and career to think about and then, they would have to agree on a plan that would also convince General Eisenhower to place his career on the line. The more the Narrator tied it together, the more I realized, someone like the Narrator had to have existed and he had to have General Eisenhower's full trust.

It was not until I was working on the Chapter tying in the 563rd SAW BN that I found proof the Top-Secret B-24 was a victim of American **"Friendly Fire"** and not German **FLAK** as the official records state and the pilot believed for more than 62 years. That shoot down led to the OSS Missions to France falling into place and then it led to the direct involvement of people leading all the way to the President. Forming, a chain of directly involved men and events which provides an obvious motive for General Patton not to return to the U.S.A. in December, 1945.

All of this had to lead to one man, who laid out a plan that could succeed. A plan that would convince General Eisenhower, it would meet his demand, that the crash-site of the Top-Secret B-24J and its Top-Secret electronic equipment disappear from France, immediately!

He had to be an extraordinary person with a broad range of on-hand experience, including the now proven desecration of the dead and permitted killing of the innocent by the English to preserve their Top-Secrets. This would provide the knowledge required *Institutional Knowledge and Institutional Memory* required to protect our own Top-Secrets.

Such an individual had to have a deep foundation in the Allied ULTRA program and our Top-Secret electronic equipment, along with a deep working knowledge of the Army Medical Corps, QMC Graves Registration, and all the regulations that controlled the Graves Registration personnel.

This person, who has been reported at each location had to have all this background to become who he was, in order to be able to do what he did for General Eisenhower. I have a strong suspect, but not the required evidence. Thus, I created the Narrator.

With his help, I can present all the years of the research supporting the events you have just read about in this book in a direct and reasonable time line. Instead of a jumbled time line over twenty-seven years of finding new facts, that continued to change my own previous beliefs.

Including the fact, *that I had to first prove myself very wrong, before I could begin to prove myself very right! And doing it without hard documents and hard facts, often using information that should have existed, but was never placed in the official documents files concerning the true history of World War Two!*

Historical

The first two chapters of this book were obvious fiction. The chapter concerning **Patton's Exit** is based on extensive documentation and the probability that the newly disclosed information in this book provided Patton with the ability to destroy the careers of many people. Some of those people were very famous, with established careers and plans for their own political futures! *At least one of these men now had a viable motive, the people available and the power to ensure Patton did not return to the United States to follow through with his plan to destroy them!*

The chapters about the **Final Cleanup**, are semi-fictional, based on extensive evidence that provides a 50/50 percent chance the hidden remains were removed from the Hattonville crash-site. After spending more than 700 hours at the crash-site, many of them searching for the remains based on the eye-witness testimony of Ernst LECLERC and the tampered with Disinterment Directives.

For example, the researcher/author made another visit to the crash-site in early March 2007 to verify the new, possible burial location as legally permitted. Prevented by French Law from conducting a proper underground search, the author dug small test holes and metal probed the suspected hidden burial site. No hard proof was found either way and the suspected site is still a suspect site. A suspected hidden burial site of three American WWII aircrew combat dead. It will remain so, until a legal and proper "Search and Recovery" takes place.

The dead men's remains, based on US Army Regulations, were under the direct control and responsibility of the attached Battalion Medical Personnel until their remains were properly turned over to Graves Registration!

Until the French Government authorizes a true archeological crash-site search or the *Defense POW/MIA Accounting Agency* conducts a true "*Search and Recovery*" based on all official documents located to date. There is a 100 percent base of proof the hidden, basically complete, bodies seen at the crash-site by dozens of witnessing French people and *proven by their Disinterment Directives* to have not have been in their official graves, **are still hidden in the soil of France**.

It is the hope of the author, the families of the men killed in the crash, and all those deeply involved with the publication of this book that the American public will become aware of the fact that the American Army and Army Air Corps in Europe, did hide the remains of American war dead during World War Two and a public outcry will finally force those in our government responsible for our military dead, to conduct an extensive and complete, French government approved, "*Search*" and perhaps, *Recovery* at the real crash-site of the "*Lady Jeannette*."

The four dead men of the "*Lady Jeannette*," especially, the three dead whose remains may still be in the Hattonville Woods deserve a real "*Search and possible Recovery*" from the government that ordered the **proven desecration of their remains** at their real place of death during World War Two.

2nd Lt. William E. Metzger, Jr. -   **1st Lt. Donald J. Gott**
"Lady Jeannette"   *"Lady Jeannette"*
Pilot   Copilot

T/Sgt. Robert A. Dunlap - S/Sgt. Herman B. Krimminger
"Lady Jeannette" RO   *"Lady Jeannette"* TG

      The sad truth is, after more than twenty seven years, the author is at a loss, why those who were directly responsible by military regulations for the four men Killed In Action in the Hattonville Woods, maintained their false statement until their "Final Transfer."

In April, 1948, the official Report of Burial and the official Disinterment Directive of each of the KIA men, show they had disintegrated when they died. Now, more than 74 years later, it has been proven the French and Americans at the crash-site witnessed three complete bodies. And, the Americans, one torn-apart.

It is important for the reader and skeptic to understand one thing about the dead in northern France. Due to the chalk rock underlying northern France, there are no insects or animals in northern France that eat bones to get vital minerals. Therefore, human bones can last hundreds of years, as the ossuaries in the local cemeteries across northern France will prove to an interested visitor.

Here, at the very end of this book, the author believes it is necessary to lay out one more scenario that could possible account for the condition of the human remains found in the four men's graves in 1948, now somewhat supported by the three men's refusal to disclose their true actions during those 48 hours.

That possible scenario is, one the researcher/author found so unbelievable and so discomforting, it was never used during any of the interviews and discussions concerning what may have happened to the three dead men's remains.

Perhaps the four men were so ashamed of participating in such a scenario, they would rather die with the truth, than reveal the truth while alive or the threat of disclosure was so severe, they and Tiff were scared to tell the truth while alive.

To succeed, the cover-up dead at the B-17 crash-site had to match the condition of death of the men killed aboard the Top-Secret B-24. There are only two scenarios that could have met that set goal, only one has been covered in this book, to this point.

It is remotely possible, the four men's graves when disinterred in April, 1948, did contain all their physical remains. For that to be true, there is only one other scenario available. Each of the three men's complete remains would have had to be deliberately desecrated before burial, by the involved Americans in such a manner, their remains upon receipt at the Limey Temporary Cemetery would basically match the description of the B-24 dead.

That scenario would have required the **attached Army Medical Corps personnel of the 563rd SAW Battalion to basically destroy both pilot's bodies and the radio operator's body by beating and tearing apart the bodies** so completely that all duplication of any identifiable bones were destroyed, which seems impossible!

As the copilot's grave contained no identifiable bones in 1948 and both pilot's basically complete, bodies were seen at the crash-site, what else besides hiding or worse desecration could account for what has happened?

Perhaps the pilot's complete bodies were mostly destroyed by the 563rd SAW Battalion's attached medical personnel. Then both shattered, crushed, and torn-apart bodies would still have had to be placed on the hot fire to be partially cremated. This had to happen in order to have the Graves Registration personnel at the Limey Temporary Cemetery list the "Cause of Death" to be recorded as it was and to account for each grave's contents in 1948.

The radio operator's 1948 Disinterment Directive states, Condition of Remains: Fractured: All major bones, skull & mandible; distal ends of rt radius & ulna missing. For such a result, it would have required his eye witnessed, complete body to have been beaten into unidentifiable pieces with tools like sledge hammers and axes. Dunlap's remains would have had to have arrived at the Limey cemetery in such a condition, that three years later the remains left in his grave, resulted in the recorded inventory listed on the Disinterment Directive.

(**Note:** If Dunlap's remains had so much destruction and so much was missing, why would they list the exact wound's bone loss that Dunlap suffered. **How, would they have known at the crash site and cemetery to list what they listed?**)

Yet, his billfold and its contents that were on his body at the time of his death, arrived at his home, basically undamaged except for some light outside smoke damage. You have seen his "**Short Snorter.**" **How could that have happened?**

Second Lt. Metzger was sitting less than three feet from Lt. Gott, when the B-17 began to enter the woods. Later, in 1948, Lt. Gott had the most identifiable bones in his grave and Lt. Metzger had no identifiable bones in his grave. **How can that be?** When Gott's "lost - then found" ID Tag and his skull fragment, both found at the crash-site in May 2000, showed no damage from fire or explosion and the ID Tag listed in the cemetery records did. *How can that be?*

The best evidence against this scenario, and in support of the events as written in the book, is the fact, there was no recorded duplication of any human bone found in the Official Graves of the four men. It remains obvious, that in 1948, if the contents of all four graves were recovered and placed on one inspection table, that common inventory would have accounted for one dead. Not two, not three and certainly, not four. **How can that be?** As none of the men had died in a way that would have totally destroyed their major bones and joints, there should have some duplicated bones on the inspection table! **How can that be?**

This does indicate the medics followed the scenario in the book and the complete bodies were hidden. However, the second scenario does provide a somewhat reasonable motive, for the four men to not want their true heritage known.

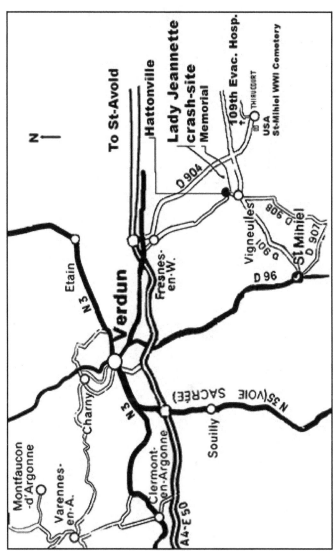

In ending, unless the remains were recovered as written in this book or desecrated as speculated above, the current situation indicates the remains of two of our **Congressional Medal Of Honor** Awardees and the radio operator died with them are still basically "*un-accounted-for!*"

If so, most likely, they are still in the Hattonville Woods or in a location, that as of this writing, no living witnesses exist to provide that answer.

"Lady Jeannette" Crash-Site
Southeast Of Verdun
Hattonville, Department of the Meuse

The final statement of this military history novel, I have to believe, should belong to Mrs. Maurice Byrne, who like Lt. Joe Harms, just told the truth.

"I know all about those bodies in the woods and after all this time it cannot hurt anyone they should be found and returned to their loved ones."

Willis S. Cole, Jr. "Sam"
wscjr@ww1.org

403

Map -Research Area In Northeast France.

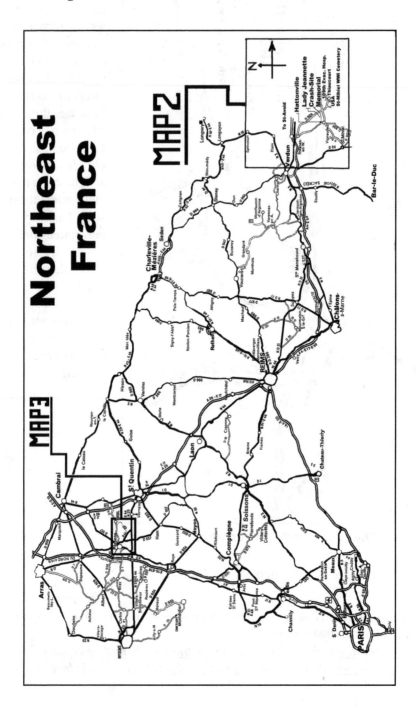

Map - Top Secret "226" Crash-Site
And The Nearby B-26 Crash-Site
The Memorial Is Near The B-26 Crash-Site

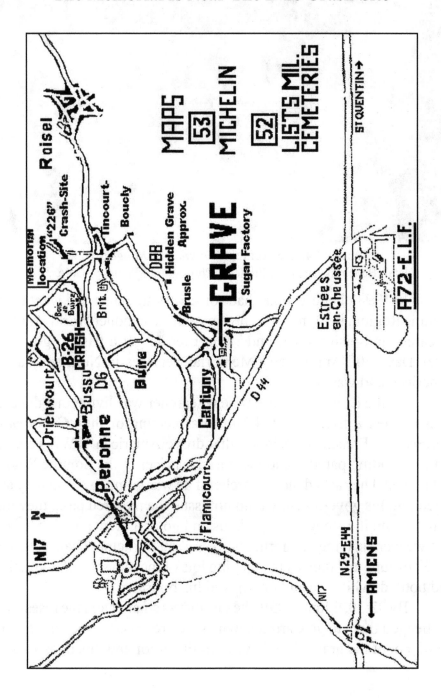

5 June, 1994, late evening - *Commemo-Rangers* Dine
Utah Beach, Normandy, France   Photograph: Willis S. Cole, Jr.

In 1994, the researcher had some very free time and went to the Somme Region, in France, for three months to conduct World War One research, and visit with friends. He tried to get a pass to go to the "Day-Day" 50th Anniversary Memorial Services in Normandy as an American and was refused."

As the date came closer, the researcher was living in a donated house, when a friend invited him to a meeting of the "*Commemo-Rangers*," a French Association that drove American WWII vehicles while attending parades and memorial services in the Somme Region of France. They asked the researcher if he was going to Normandy and when told his government would not issue the required pass, they told him, "Damn it, if they won't, join us and go as a Frenchman. Short to say, we were staying at a farm compound on the actual Utah Beach on the 5th of June and they were enjoying lots of the two special wines they had bottled, while the author enjoyed his bourbon.

By 02:30, 6 June, 1999, the group was smaller and the researcher challenged them to go Cartigny, when they returned home, and get the proof about the grave. You have seen the proof and this book exists.

2012
Visiting The Crash-Sites Of The
"Lady Jeannette" And "226"
Tincourt-Boucly and Hattonville

Any trip to France, is a great time to visit two of the most important locations of American Aviation's involvement during World War Two. The true crash-site of the "Top Secret," "226," at Tincourt-Boucly and the true crash-site of the dual ***Congressional Medal Of Honor*** B-17G, SN: 42-97904, the *"Lady Jeannette,"* of the 729th Bombardment Squadron (H), 452nd Bombardment Group (H), 8th US AAForce.

Landing at Paris, when you leave the airport, you can either go north or south. If, you go north, you will reach the "Grave at Cartigny" and the "226" crash-site within a couple of hours. If, you go south toward Paris, you will quickly take a "Ring Road" to the east to bypass Paris and then, you face a few hours of driving before you arrive at Hattonville. Either way, you will have to circle around to reach the other site to return to the airport.

Going north, the first stop would be at Cartigny, The Department of the Somme and your G.P.S. will take you right there. The village is off the main roads leading to Peronne. It is east of the old north/south road. As you enter, Cartigny, the first road your left will take you to the cemetery. Which is on the right (south) side of the road. When you enter the cemetery, the grave is the first on the left.

When you leave the cemetery, enter Tincourt-Boucly into your G.P.S., that will tell you to turn around, go back to the road you came in on, and turn left. Then continue on that road to the crossroads and go straight across. Just before the crossroads, you will pass the old sugar factory where Casper landed on the roof.

2nd Lt. Frederick Gustaf Grey
Killed In Action: 10 November, 1944
Navigator: B-24J SN: 42-51226
36th Bombardment Squadron (RCM)
Attached: 100th Group RAF
Photograph: Judith Lukensmeyer

Jeremy William Lukensmeyer, Grandson
Christopher Lohse, Son-in-Law
Alison Sue (Lukensmeyer) Lohse, Granddaughter
Judith Ann (Grey) Lukensmeyer, Daughter
Born: 16 January, 1945
Photograph: Willis S. Cole, Jr.

You will continue cross an intersection, go through a small village and then, you may recognize where the Communes split and on the right at that location, the remains were hidden. Continue on through Boucly and through Tincourt-Boucly, keep heading north. You will come to a main road and the "**226**" crash-site is located between the two splitting off roads to the east, about a thousand feet north of the main road. If, you take the road to the right and drive up it, you will see a slight impression in the field to your left. Do not go into the field, if it is crop without finding the farmer and seeking his permission. Normally, if the crop is not too high, you will be given permission. In the field, one can always find additional pieces of "**226**" and your bit might even be a piece of that Top Secret Electronic Equipment, or a piece of a crewman.

Tincourt-Boucly Crash Site of B-24J SN: 42-51226
10 November, 1944
Judith (Grey) Lukensmeyer visiting the crash site
September, 2012, with her son, daughter and son-in-law.

The new memorial location is at the left end of the woods at the left side of this photograph.　　Photograph: Willis S. Cole, Jr.

The B-26, "***Where's It AT?***" bounced off this same field and again just before the small woods, to crash into the Bois de Buire near the tall trees at the left of the woods in the background. During the crash, two men were killed. The Navigator, 1st Lt. Hugh W. Robbins and the Radio Operator, S/Sgt. William G. Glass, were killed.

The B-26 was a part of the 1st Pathfinder Sq. Provisional. Their job was to mark bombing targets for the following bomber groups. That day, 22 January, 1945, after successfully marking their target, an engine was damaged during their mission. In a blinding snowstorm, the pilot was unable to line up the runway and after circling several times, the engine cut-out over Tincourt-Boucly, leading to the bounce, bounce and crash.

The two Pilots, 1st Lt. Joseph M. DuBois and 1st Lt. Richard P. Britanik were later awarded the Soldiers Medal for their efforts in recovering the two men's bodies from the burning aircraft.

Jeremy William Lukensmeyer   Photograph: Willis S. Cole, Jr.
Alison Sue (Lukensmeyer) Lohse
Christopher Lohse
Judith Ann (Grey) Lukensmeyer
Crystal - Interpreter
Claude OBERT
Nicole OBERT

Claude and Nicole saved the memorial when it was going to be destroyed when its original location was replaced by a larger traffic intersection. Then, they donated a particle of one of their farm fields near the B-26 crash site to the French government to insure the memorial's existence could never be challenged again.

Claude was a young boy, when during one November night in 1943, his family awoke to the noise of an approaching aircraft that was obviously in trouble. His father was still opening a north window in their home, when Claude saw a large airplane plunging to earth. Suddenly, it exploded, hit the ground and then exploded again.

Claude completed his "Final Transfer" on 10 November, 2012, 68 years to the day that he watched "226" crash.

The combined "Grave At Cartigny" The Somme Department, France.

     This grave contains approximately two-thirds of the collected remains of the three men, 2nd Lt. Frederick G. Grey, Navigator; Sgt. Frank A. Bartho, Nose Turret Gunner; and Sgt. Raymond G. Mears, Tail Turret Gunner, recovered at the crash site of "226." Their remains were later placed in an unmarked grave by the American Medical Personnel, from the Peronne A-72 Air Base, 397th Bomber Group, who had just recovered their remains. Two weeks later, the French decided the Americans were hiding their war dead and moved the men's remains to their village cemetery.

After visiting the grave, the "**226**" crash-site, the Memorial and walking to the B-26 crash-site. You can leave by turning right on the road you came on and it will take you to the eastern side of Peronne. A major town in the Somme Battle Zone of World War One and one can spend a few days, day tripping out to different battle areas, including two American World War One Cemeteries in the area.

You can actually follow the routes in this book to go to the crash site of the *"Lady Jeannette"* or trust your G.P.S. The author wishes to warn anyone conducting a visit like this, that you will pass so many places you would like to visit, you may become a WWI and WWII "NUT" like him with over 70 trips to Europe and over 4 years there.

To locate Hattonville on GoogleEarth, enter Hattonville, 55210 Vigneulles-Les-Hattonchatel as your search location, enlarge and find the memorial and road.

When you arrive in Hattonville, the memorial is located at the southern edge of the village, on the eastern side of the road. It is on property owned by and maintained by the Robert LECLERC family.

When you are ready to visit the crash site, take the unpaved road leading to the east and keep left at any intersections. Soon, you will find yourself traveling on the west side of the large field complex the *"Lady Jeannette"* flew over while approaching Hattonville and then turning back toward Germany.

Continue on the road into the oncoming woods and you will know when to stop, when you come to the end of the improved road. The path to the crash site is on the south side, along the raised berm.

As you walk into the crash site, just off to your left, over the berm to start with, the first debris fell to earth and at the first bend, Sgt. Kirmminger's head struck limbs of a large tree, that is no longer there. As you reach the fenced area, the attempted curve back to the large field becomes obvious, as the *"Lady Jeannette"* came back over the berm to break apart and fall to earth within the fenced area.

At the crash site, you will find a fenced area to keep the wild boars from rooting in the clay impressions left by the *"Lady Jeannette"* as she laid in the woods for two years after the crash, until she was scrapped out by the villagers. Please make certain the gate is closed when you leave and if you see a hole, repair it, please!

Please feel free to throw any limbs that have fallen into the fenced area, over the fence and do be careful of soft spots in the forest floor.

The first impressions is that of the left wing, the next is the obvious impression left by the tail. The third is where an engine dug its way into the clay. The fourth is where the forward fuselage came to rest and the fifth, is just a line where a wing came to rest against a tree, after an engine and wheel assembly broke free.

1st Lt. Donald J. Gott And 2nd Lt. William E. Metzger, Jr.

Congressional Medal Of Honor Citations

"...With one normally functioning engine and with the danger of explosion much greater, the aircraft banked into an open field and when it was at an altitude of 100 feet it exploded, crashed, exploded again and then disintegrated. All three crew members were instantly killed..."

As you have read, in late May, 2000, a recorded "as unaccounted for Identity Tag" belonging to 1st Lt. Gott was located at the Hattonville crash-site, a fragment of a skull was also located at the crash site. That skull fragment was later identified by mtDNA, as being part of the skull of Lt. Gott.

With those finds, no one can further question the correct crash site of the *" Lady Jeannette" and the location of death of the four, not three, crew members who died on 9 November, 1944, in the Bois de Hattonville, Department of the Meuse, France.*

The model on page 395 uses parts of a plastic B-17 model kit, to create an accurate size layout of the crash site. Hard evidence of each of the large parts of the B-17 is still evident as impressions in the clay of the woods.

Anyone who wishes to question what you have read in this book, please visit the exact location in Europe where these heroes died. Just begin at the Memorial in Hattonville and take the road to crash site in the Woods of Hattonville.

As you walk along the access path to the crash site, think of the fourth crew member, whose death is not mentioned in the Citations. His remains were spread along the crash path as the B-17 settled into the woods and he was torn apart. Which is along the berm to the east of the access path.

There, you can see for yourself, that the *"Lady Jeannette"* did not crash as stated in the two Congressional Medal Of Honor Citations. There you can see for yourself, the exact position where the two pilot's bodies were found inside the cockpit of the crashed B-17 by the first Frenchmen to arrive at the crash site. And, not far away, you can find the approximate location where the radio operator's complete body was also found.

As you leave, due to the restricted turn around space, you can either back a ways to the large turn around or use the space at the end of the road. If, you decide to do that, an outside guide to insure you do not go off the road, is good.

South

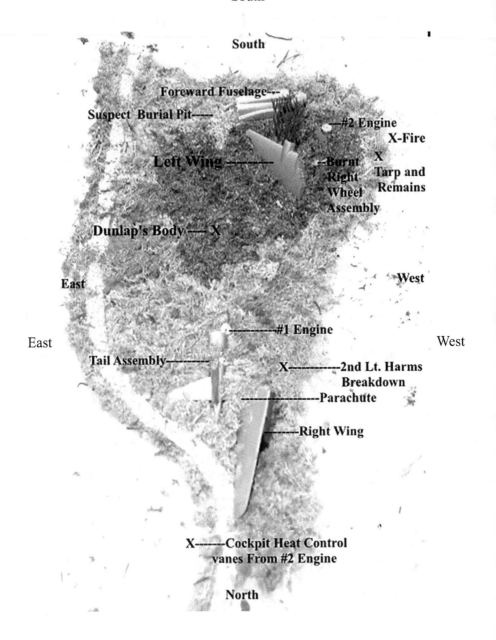

South

Foreward Fuselage---

Suspect Burial Pit----

---#2 Engine

X-Fire

Left Wing --------

--Burnt   X

Right   Tarp and

Wheel   Remains

Assembly

Dunlap's Body —— X

East

West

East

West

---------#1 Engine

Tail Assembly---------

X-----------2nd Lt. Harms

Breakdown

-----------------Parachute

-------Right Wing

X-------Cockpit Heat Control
vanes From #2 Engine

North

North

Model: Willis S. Cole, Jr.

"THE MEN OF THE "Lady Jeannette"

Having read hundreds of books about military subjects, it has always seemed to the author, that a reader had little opportunity to know much about the actual people involved, especially their families. The following pages are about the nine men aboard the *"Lady Jeannette"* on 9 November, 1944. And, an original Gott crew member who watched her plunge to earth, or so he thought on 9 November, 1944.

Gerald W. Collins

23 October, 1919 - "Final Transfer Complete"
Born: Canon City, Colorado
Serial Number: O-0771314
2nd Lieutenant, Co-pilot United States Army
Air Force Original 'Gott Crew' Co-pilot

Gerry was born to **Hazel A. Builderback Collins** and **Harold Collins**. One of three boys, his brothers being Harold Collins, Jr. and Don Curtis Collins.

By the time Gerry was 10 years old, his father was gone out of their lives and they were living in Los Angeles. The boys were all in school and they sold papers every night after school to help with the family budget.

All the boys made it through high school, with Gerry playing football as a member of the Belmont High School team, while still selling papers at night. He did have a long-term girl

Photograph: Gerald W. Collins

friend and she later became his wife.

After graduation, Gerry was able to find employment with the California Public Utilities Commission, to use his words, "As a flunky."

In June of 1941, Beverly Grace Bergstrum and Gerald. W. Collins, were joined in marriage. In mid-1942, Gerry's brother, Harold, left for the new Air Cadet program and pilot training. After completing his training and receiving his commission, he served in the Pacific Combat area as a B-25 Pilot.

Both Don and Gerry put in for the Cadet Program and were accepted into the service program in January 1943.

Upon completing their required ground training, they reported for primary and basic flight training at Oxnard, California. Upon completion, Don went on to fighter training and Gerry reported to Marfa, Texas, to report for his multi-engine heavier aircraft training.

415

In due time, both completed their training and became commissioned pilots. Don went on to fly P-38 fighters out of England and later, in France. During February, 1944, Beverly became pregnant and at his graduation from multi-engine school, on March 12, 1944, Gerald W. Collins became a proud 2nd Lieutenant.

Gerry then reported to Rapid City, South Dakota, to become the Co-pilot on the Gott crew as they prepared for overseas duty.

After 9 November, 1944, and the loss of his operating crew, Gerry would normally have had to complete his full thirty-five missions before leaving the 452nd Bomb Group. ***However, for some reason unknown to Joe, he was suddenly relieved from the requirement to complete thirty-five combat missions and was presented with orders to report to the USA***, arriving at the Boston depot on the same day as S/Sgt. Robbins, 27 December, 1944. (***Note: Why, now you know!***)

Gerry did remember, it was odd that he never saw any of the other surviving Gott Crew members again after that one morning when Robbins came to his barracks, and his accidental meeting with Robbins when they met upon their return in Boston.

November, 1944, was a good and bad month for Gerry, as he also received word, that he was the father of identical twin boys, Ronald and Donald.

Upon his return to the States, he was first assigned to the Air Transportation Service at Long Beach, California. Later on, he was transferred to Bakersfield, serving there, until he was discharged in August, 1945. He was the first of the original crew survivors to be discharged.

Gerry went back to his work for the California Public Utilities Commission for a while and soon, he got a job with the Chamber of Commerce in Los Angles, where he worked until 1955, when he was transferred east to the National Chamber of Commerce office in Washington, D.C. Gerry was exceptional at this type of work and later, he took over the position of the President of the National Defense Transport Association, where he served until his retirement.

Gerry's wife, Beverly completed her "Final Transfer." The twin boys married two girls who were best friends in high school and both now have families of their own to tell them about what their Grandpa did during WWII.

Russell Gustafson and I stayed with Gerry at his home in Bethesda, Maryland, one night in June, 1997, and we enjoyed a nice visit with him. It is always enjoyable to get two old friends together like this and see what pops up in their minds. What one forgot, the other one remembers.

One interesting thing, was Gerry telling Russell how much he enjoyed Russell teaching him Chess, even describing where they sat while playing. Russell, he had forgotten all about that. Bring back his statement, that they were a crew who did not interact like many, each going their own way after a mission, until the next mission.

416

Robert Alexander Dunlap

26 October, 1924 - - 9 November, 1944
Serial Number: 39696406 Technical Sergeant,
Radio Operator, US Army Air Force
Killed In Action
        Bois de Hattonville, Hattonville
        Department of the Meuse, France
        9 November, 1944
        "Lady Jeannette,"
        B-17G-35VE, SN: 42-97904
        452nd Bombardment Group (H),
        729th Bombardment Squadron (H)
Mission: Saarbrucken, Germany Buried:
Official Grave: Plot C, Row 23, Grave 19
        Lorraine American Military
        Cemetery, St. Avold, France

Photograph: Bob's sister
Bonnie Owen

        Alexander Dunlap, his father, was born at Sheffield, Montana, on 29 April, 1888, he died at Miles City, Montana, on 2 May, 1953.   **Martha Scmitt Dunlap**, his mother, born at Eureka, South Dakota, on 4 February, 1898, she died on December 30, 1967.

        Bob, as he was called, grew up and attended school in Miles City, where he graduated from Custer County High School.

During his youth, his rough and tumble outdoor activities fetched him a broken arm when he fell off a horse at his grandmother's ranch and a brain concussion when a bicycle wheel broke during a hard ride.

        He greatly enjoyed riding his bicycle, spending many hours discovering the town of Miles City and the surrounding area with his best friends, Ray Glover and Keith Johnson.

        Ray told me, "We were typical kids, an inseparable trio, growing up in Miles City. We started first grade together and graduated in 1942. It was typical depression times and you had to make your own fun. We might have snuck a few smokes, but we never got into serious trouble."

        Keith lived across the alley until his family moved. He remembers playing marbles with Bob and Ray and later going hunting with Bob and his dad.

        All the boy's dads worked for the Milwaukee Railroad, Bob's dad was a conductor, Keith's dad was a foreman on the repair crew, while Ray's dad was an engineer, driving the trains.

        "Alex, Bob's dad was a fine gentleman," Ray told me. During Ray's first job as a brakeman on the railroad, a job he had taken right out of high school, he often worked for Alex. Ray later went into the Navy and saw action aboard a 110 foot sub-chaser in the Pacific. His ship was sunk during the first typhoon at

Photograph:
Willis S. Cole, Jr.

Okinawa. His brother, who was on another ship there, came to his aid and gave Ray, "A duffle bag of clothes and a fist full of money," as all of Ray's things, except for the clothes on his back, went down with the ship."

Ray worked with Alex, on the railroad, a lot after he returned from the war and Alex often talked of Bob. Ray told me, "I remember Alex telling me, that he had gone up to the Great Falls Army Air Force Base, where he had been presented with Bob's medals." He was proud of Bob and missed him a lot.

Ray Glover remembers his bicycle well. Our dads bought us Ranger bicycles made by Meade Bicycles. Manufactured in Chicago, they were the best bicycle at that time, mine cost around $40.00 and Bob's dad, Alex, got him one that cost $50.00. That was a lot of money during the Depression to spend on a bicycle.

Later, when we got to high school, we went our different ways, I was interested in sports and Bob never did show much interest in sports.

Keith Johnson remembers the last time he saw Bob. Keith also attended the radio school at Rapid City for a time and he heard that Bob was there, so he went to visit him. Bob was working the night shift and was sleeping in a barracks that was kept dark during the day when Keith woke him up. Keith told the author, how surprised he was to see how much weight and height Bob had gained, since entering the military.

Keith later got into the Aviation Cadet after completing his flight training, he was commissioned and became a World War Two pilot on C-47's and later flew C-46's throughout the Pacific.

After high school, Bob took to 'riding the rods' (being a BUM, riding the trains and searching for work) for a while. Later, he later stayed with his older sister, Io Dunlap Hendron, who was living in Bakersfield, California.

Bob enlisted in the Army Air Force at Bakersfield, on March 19, 1943, hoping to be a pilot. However, like so many others, that did not happen and instead, he attended radio school at Rapid City, South Dakota.

Unlike many who were in the service, Bob's radio school was fairly close to home and he was able to go home on leave for Christmas, 1943, and several other times, before he left for England.

Bonnie Dunlap Owens, Bob's youngest sister remembers, "He enjoyed being outdoors, one well remembered trip, that he told me about was a fishing trip to Yellowstone National Park with Dad and our brother-in-law." "Bob," Bonnie said, "was especially close to his older sister, Io, and his father, Alex. He also had a girl friend, Virginia, and on his last furlough home, he gave her a cashmere sweater."

T/Sgt. Robert A. Dunlap - Radio Operator
W.I.A. at Target - Unconscious In Radio Compartment - Fell From Broken Fuselage Into Fire Area

9 Nov., 1944
K.I.A.
Hattonville, France.

Lady Jeannette
B-17G-35VE
Sn: 42-97904

**Lightly Burned Billfold
Returned To Family
Shows He Was Not
All That Badly Burnt**

Disinterment Directive: 22 Apr., 1948
Condition of Remains: "Fractured: all major bones,
skull & mandible; distal ends of rt radius & ulna
missing." How Identified: Two Identification Tags
Report Of Burial, 9 Nov, 1944, shows date of
death with acutal burial 11 Nov., 1944, based
on Inventory Of Personal Effects (Signed by
interviewed Capt., (Retired Col.) James T. Passman,
now deceased) *D.D. signed by: W.R. Bailey*

T/Sgt. Robert A. Dunlap
Listed Missing Remains
T/Sgt. Robert A. Dunlap
Listed Identified Remains
Unidentified Remains
Fractured All Major Bones

Note: All Remains Disarticulated/Crushed

Drawing: Willis S. Cole, Jr.   His wound was just above his wrist and the hand
area is among the first to decompose, yet the above is marked?

James Olin Fross

16 March, 1925 --- "Final Transfer Completed:
Born: Davenport, Iowa
Buried: Roselawn Cemetery, McAllen, Texas
Serial Number: 38462533
Staff Sergeant, Ball Turret Gunner
United States Army Air Force
Wounded In Action *"Lady Jeannette"*
> 9 Nov, 1944 B-17G-35VE, SN: 42-97904 452nd Bombardment Group (H)
> 729th Bombardment Squadron (H)

Mission: Saarbrucken, Germany

Jim was the son of **Glen Charles Fross** and **Cecille Ling Fross**. The Fross family lived at 808 B.C. Ave., McAllen, Texas, when Jim entered the service on 14 June, 1943. He was 5 ft. 2 in., weighting 121 pounds at the time. He spent 2 years, 4 months, 16 days on active duty, separating on November 1, 1945.

Jim had one sister, Jacquelin Fross Hamilton, who was married to Martin (Marty) Hamilton, the parents of a niece, Elizabeth Dawn, and nephew, Joe Martin Clair, Jim's brother, was in the Navy during the war and was later killed in a truck accident in West Texas, while driving for Mayflower Van Lines. Clair's wife, Norma survives him, along with his children, Derrell, Dorothy and Valerie. Clair's son, Jeffrey, died in a vehicular accident.

Jim's mother, Cecille, died in 1982 and his father died in 1992, at 97 years of age. His

Photograph: Fross Family

father was a veteran of World War One, and active in the local V.F.W. chapter until his death, a member of the last man's club.

The family had settled in McAllen, after Jim's father had visited McAllen during one of his sales trips for the Home Comfort Stove Company.

Jim received his draft notice, just one week after graduating from the McAllen High School. Upon returning from the service, Jim attended the Pan American Junior College, in Edinburg, then he joined the family as owners of a large dairy farm. They were also in the orchard care business.

When the family dairy and orchard care operations were later sold, Jim purchased a Phillips 66 service station and operated it for several years. Jim then became a licensed meat inspector for the State of Texas Department of Health.

He retired from the State of Texas in 1987. Shortly thereafter, he was diagnosed with Parkinson's Disease, and later diagnosed with Alzheimer's Disease. It was during medical tests to determine this problem that metal fragments were found in his head. Jim had apparently forgotten all about his FLAK wounds from the day of

the crash. After I had provided Mary, with the proof that Jim had received FLAK wounds that day, Jim was accepted for VA hospital services.

Jim married Mary June Alderman, on July 17, 1955. They had three children. Their oldest son, James Olin Fross II, disappeared one evening from South Padre Island on the Gulf Coast. His car was found there with his personal items, it appeared he went for a swim and was swept out to sea. Their daughter, Kimberly, their son Michael, and Mary now live in San Antonio, Texas. Michael works in hotel management and he is surely his father's son, with mom's sprite personality showing through as well.

Jim loved to build airplane models - he was very proud of all his B-17 models. He also worked at a coin collection, pieces of which were still being found in his belongings after his death. Jim was very active in his church, the First United Methodist Church, of McAllen, where he served many years as a Sunday School Superintendent. He was also a youth sponsor, accompanying the young people's groups on trips far and wide. He was a fine example to these young people and his friendships with some of them endured to his death.

Jim was stuck with one of the ususal nick names for ball turret gunners, he was called 'Shorty' by the crew. Jim did not talk much about his time in the service, and after his death, Mary was quite surprised to find a box with various papers, such as his Caterpillar Club Certificate and the telegrams stating he was missing and returned to action. He also kept his monthly flight records and other papers of interest to a historian: 8:10 Hr. + 5:15 + 12:3 = 25:55 = Overseas.

Jim's personal notebook contained the following flight log:
Logged Time:
Aug 27 - Berlin (Recall)Keil
6:30 Sep. 2 Frankfort (Recall) (Weath)
8:15 Sep. 9 - Dusseldorf
7:00 Sep. 13 - Ludwigshafen
3:40 Sep. 17 - Arnheim-Holland
5:30 Sep. 19 - Weisbaden
7:30 Sep. 21 - Ludwigshafen
7:30 Sep. 25 - Ludwigshafen (Col. No.5)
7:15 Sep. 27 - Mainz6:30 Sep. 28 - Merseburg (Feather #4)
8:40 Sep. 30 - Bielefeld7:15 Oct. 2 - Kassel
8:00 Oct. 3 - Nurnberg8:15 Oct. 5 - Minster
6:30 Oct. 6 - Berlin
8:30 Oct. 7 - Merseburg

8:45 Oct. 12 - Bremen
3:00 Oct. 14 - Cologne (No Bombs)
6:10 Oct. 15 - Heligoland
7:45 Oct. 18 - Kassel
9:25 Oct. 25 - Hamburg
I 7:45 Oct. 26 - Hanover
8:00 Oct. 30 - Merseburg (Recall)
6:10 Nov. 2 - Merseburg
8:00 Nov. 4 - Neukirchen
6:50 Nov. 5 - Ludwigshafen
8:15 Nov. 9 - Saarbrucken
Est:6:30 No. 4 shot off & #1 & #2
Total: 176.15 running away. Para-   Combat
Flight chute over France   Hours.
Pilot, Co-pilot, Tail, Radio, went down with plane.
Home on 14th to base.

Jim's last Individual Flight Record showed a total of 280:20 hours flight time during his service time.

Jim, actually, never returned to the 452nd Base! He was kept in a hospital until shipping out for the USA, on Christmas Day, 1944. He did see Gustafson again, when he and the author visited the family in McAllen, Texas. He did see the waist gunner, Sgt. Irving Hirsh, who had been removed from their crew upon arrival in England, when Irving visited him at his base in Texas before the war ended.

His Honorable Discharge, filed with Hidalgo County on November 20, 1945, gives the information that he received $212.90 in separation pay and that he was eligible for the following Battle and Campaign ribbons: Northern France GO33WD45 Rhineland GO40WD45 Decorations and Citations: EAME Ribbon Purple Heart, GO56-10Nov44, Hq 109th Ev Hos; Air Medal, 3OLC; GO701-25Sep44 OLCGO756-5Oct44; Hq 3 AD OLCGO874-22Oct44. 3BD

Mary told me, she was working as a car hop at a drive-in when she met Jim. He came in for lunch one Day and left a whole nickel tip. He came back again and again, even though she told him, "You are a cheap tipper."

I'll leave Jim's life with a photograph and a statement form Mary:
"My, he was some handsome, darling due then!"

Photograph: Fross Family

(**Author:** Psychic income is very important in my life, especially when I receive a letter from someone like Mary who wrote to me, "I cannot tell you how much it meant to Jim and to me to have you travel all that way to visit with Jim--I do hope you were able to learn some concrete things, and the trip was somewhat beneficial to you. I know Jim enjoyed it greatly, although he was not overly demonstrative, we can attribute that to his illness. I will say he seemed to remember more than I thought he would, and it was fun for me to watch him blossom that Day, even for a moment. Again, how can we thank you enough for your attention. Our prayers are for the very best for you, and yours, you are a very special man." Jim and I sat at an outside table and as I knew so much about the mission, we talked as if the mission had taken place a short time earlier, instead over fifty years before.)

Donald Joseph Gott

3 June, 1923 ---- 9 November, 1944
Born: Family Farm, Harmon, Oklahoma
Serial Number: O-763996
1st Lieutenant, Pilot, United States Army Air
    Force
Killed In Action, Bois de Hattonville,
    Hattonville
    Department of the Meuse, France
9 November, 1944,
    "Lady Jeannette,"
    B-17G-35VE, SN: 42-97904
    452nd Bombardment Group (H)
    729th Bombardment Squadron (H)
Mission: Saarbrucken, Germany
Buried: Official Grave: Fairmont Cemetery
    Harmon, Ellis County, Oklahoma

The author has visited the farm where Donald Gott was born to Joseph Eugene Gott and Mary Lucy Hanlon Gott. The house is now deserted and weather-beaten, as the years are taking their toll. Vandals have destroyed much, including the room where Donald's coffin was displayed with much honor, where now strips of wall paper, familiar from that photograph, hang from the wall.

The address, when it was a viable home, full of growing children and hardworking ranchers, was Route 1, Box 26, Arnett, Oklahoma, located just south and a bit east of where the Oklahoma Panhandle juts out to the west. It isn't a big house and the house is located on what has to be called, 'hard scrabble land.'

As we, myself, Carol, and Donald's cousin, Winona Derrick drove north from Harmon, a little crossroads village with a few buildings, most which were empty, the more the area around us reminded me of Eastern Washington.

It is flat and windblown, and an image of Carol's grandfather jumped into my mind. Carol's "Grandpa Smith," was in my thoughts, he was over 90-years-old when he died. He still lived on the original family homestead, a place of canyons and trees with every bit of farmable ground fought for and well earned, but still hard scrabble. Grandpa Smith once told me, that his grandson, Carol's brother, Bill, would have a hard time making it during the depression. "Bill is a large crop grower," according to Grandpa Smith, "he only grows wheat and barley, so he isn't a real farmer." In effect, to Grandpa Smith, Bill is a grain manufacturer. "Grandpa Smith told me, during the bad times of the Depression, the farmers on the good ground had to depend on dry land cropping with little rain. While Grandpa was able to grow everything a family needed on his broken ground with water here and there. He even had some excess to sell in town to get some ready cash for what he couldn't grow or make himself. He would haul his vegetables, pigs and chickens into Spokane, Washington, and sell them in the neighborhoods for hard cash.

The evening we got to Arnett, Winona Derrick, the Gott's grand-daughter, had shown us many pictures of the family and Donald. I was struck by the face of Mr. Gott. Here was a man, for whom life did not come easy. He had met life head on, Depression and all. And, he suffered the greatest crop loss of all, his youngest son did not return from the war. I'm certain, that grandma and grandpa Smith and grandma and grandpa Gott could have sat down on the front porch swing and talked for a long time about what it took to carry a family through the bad times. The other fellows might be better off in good times, but the hard scrabble farmer knew how to survive in the bad times, as well as the good times.

On 9 November, 1944, Donald J. Gott knew, that he could not desert the fight, he had to bear up, even in the bad times. It was ingrained. Don had two older sisters and an older brother. They were determined to keep Don, away from as much of the load of farm work as they could.

Don was the 'apple of everyone's eye,' the one they all sacrificed for, the one who was to be the real family success later in life.

The Gott family, that Donald was born into, were devout Catholics and they drove to Shattuck, Oklahoma, 25 miles away, to attend St. Joseph Catholic Church. Donald is especially remembered, for his faith and straight-forward living. The family was fair, but strict and Donald never took on the vices of smoke or drink. He was known for his scholarship and honesty.

His first schooling was in the proverbial, one-room school at Kennebec Country School, where Don graduated from 8th grade. Though Arnett was closer, the Gott children attended high school at Fargo, a 16 ½ mile straight shot north. As one drives up the road to Fargo, you are struck by the abrupt change of ground, from hard scrabble, blowing loose sand range land, to large, well groomed, and well cropped farm fields.

Otto, Don's five year-older brother, drove the school bus and was ever so proud of Donald. Donald blossomed in school getting excellent grades, enjoying baseball and basketball and became Valedictorian of his class. The family worked the harvests in the summer, doing custom harvesting and Donald pitched in helping

the family business as he could. However, some jobs like pulling broomcorn, convinced him he liked school better.

He was said, to have a good sense of humor. I met several class mates when the author visited Arnett, they told him that Don was a good friend, liked by all, and surely missed. When Raymond Schneider and his bride, Lucille were married in 1935, cousin Donald presented them with a rolling pin.

As a boy of twelve, he was most likely a reader of the 1930's "funny paper's Katzenjammer Kids." In the comic strip, Ma Katzenjammer always displayed the rolling pin to bring her family into line. Donald must have had this gift in mind, as a weapon in his delight to tease cousin Raymond. Mrs. Schneider used the precious gift from Donald for over fifty years always thinking of him every time she used it.

After graduation, Don chose to attend a technical school at Enid, Oklahoma. At that time, recruiters from companies all over the country were looking for young people to fill positions being vacated by drafted men and openings created by a need to expand to meet war demands.

Leaving behind his girl friend, Earline Mann (Barton), Don rode a bus across the country to take a war production position with the U.S. Aluminum Company in Bridgeport, Connecticut. On the way across the wide country, his mind must have thrilled as he watched the many aircraft speeding across the country as the bus crawled along.

About this time, Don's brother and his brother's wife moved to California and sister Hazel soon followed, all were to participate in the good times of war production in California with long working hours and good wages. Otto Gott ended up living in Washington State.

As with Russell Gustafson and Herman Krimminger, the thought of being a pilot was a driving force and Don soon signed up for the Cadet Program, on 21 September, 1942. He left Bridgeport for active duty as an Aviation Cadet on 22 March, 1943. It would be over a year before Don prepared his Crew 33-c (Crew AC-72, FV900CJ/16349CJ-4/4) to depart the USA., via the northern route to join the 452nd Bombardment Group (H) on 17 August, 1944. On the way, he attended pre-flight school in Santa Ana, California. Going on, in June, 1943, to Primary Flight Training at Glendale, Arizona. Followed by basic pilot training at Gardner Field, California. Then, he went onto advanced twin-engine flight training school at Stockton Field, California.

On 6 January, 1944, Donald J. Gott became an officer, when he was authorized to pin on his gold 2nd Lieutenant bars. He completed his four-engine B-17 transition training at Hobbs Field, New Mexico. On 24 March 1944, his graduation ceremony was attended by his parents.

Donald had been told by his cousin, Loren Schneider, that he could use Loren's 1940 Ford, whenever he wished, when he came home to visit. However, before Donald went home on his final furlough, Don asked his mother to contact Loren, who was now serving in the Pacific. To ask specific permission for Donald to drive Loren's car. **Donald had become a "by-the-book" flyer and that included,**

seeking official permission from his cousin, before Don would use Loren's car during his final leave at home.

It was a fun furlough, he and Earline dated in style, however Donald was uneasy about his future. He had a premonition and when he left, **he gave his sister a two-dollar bill on which he stated**, he did not expect to return. While home, Don saw a friend waiting at the bus stop and stopped to talk to him until his bus came. The friend, Kenneth Sherrill, another Air Corps man was heading for Europe. When Don's (official) remains were returned, Kenneth honored Donald, as one of the pallbearers who carried Don's casket to the grave.

Donald returned to his home one last time.

Photograph: Winona Derrick

426

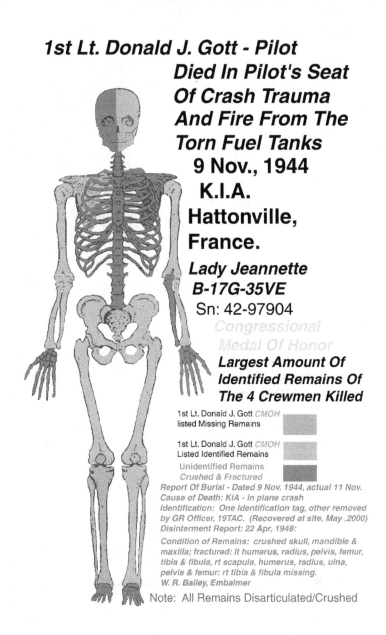

1st Lt. Donald J. Gott - Pilot
Died In Pilot's Seat
Of Crash Trauma
And Fire From The
Torn Fuel Tanks
9 Nov., 1944
K.I.A.
Hattonville,
France.

Lady Jeannette
B-17G-35VE
Sn: 42-97904

Congressional
Medal Of Honor

Largest Amount Of
Identified Remains Of
The 4 Crewmen Killed

1st Lt. Donald J. Gott *CMOH*
listed Missing Remains

1st Lt. Donald J. Gott *CMOH*
Listed Identified Remains

Unidentified Remains
Crushed & Fractured

Report Of Burial - Dated 9 Nov. 1944, actual 11 Nov.
Cause of Death: KIA - In plane crash
Identification: One Identification tag, other removed
by GR Officer, 19TAC. (Recovered at site, May ,2000)
Disinterment Report: 22 Apr, 1948:

Condition of Remains: crushed skull, mandible &
maxilla; fractured: lt humerus, radius, pelvis, femur,
tibia & fibula, rt scapula, humerus, radius, ulna,
pelvis & femur: rt tibia & fibula missing.
W. R. Bailey, Embalmer

Note: All Remains Disarticulated/Crushed

One must question one simple fact. Sitting two feet apart in the
same cockpit, Gott has the most identified remains and Metzger
had none? Plus, the simple fact, of all the identified bones in all
four graves, there is no duplication of any human bone! *When*
there should be four of each!

Drawing: Willis S. Cole, Jr.

427

Russell William Gustafson

11 August, 1922 - Completed "Final Transfer"
Born: Jamestown, New York
Serial Number: 12139299
Technical Sergeant, Flight Engineer/Gunner
    United States Army Air Force
Wounded In Action 9 November, 1944
    "Lady Jeannette"
    B-17G-35VE, SN: 42-97904
    452nd Bombardment Group (H)
    729th Bombardment Squadron (H)
Mission: Saarbrucken, Germany

T/Sgt. Russell W. Gustafson Verdun Battle Area, on road to Fort Vaux. Sign also points to WWI French grave.

Photograph: Willis S. Cole, Jr.

Russell, a proud second generation American Swede, was born to **William Axel Gustafson** and **Edith Gustafson**, Jamestown, New York.

Growing up in the 1930s, Russell found airplanes to be very fascinating and a subject of great adventure to Russell. After graduating from Jamestown High School in 1941, he attended the Elmira Aviation Ground School, to become an aircraft engineer.

During a weekend trip home he heard the news of Pearl Harbor. The news immediately altered his life's direction, as he now knew what his future held. He completed the semester at Elmira, obtaining the "A" part of the "A&E" course, returned home and started the process of enlisting in the Army Air Corps Cadet Program. Russell completed his enlistment process by 29 August, 1942, but he was not called to active duty until 26 February, 1943.

Russell completed the cadet program primary flight training, but "washed out" and, as many of the "washed out" men were, he was soon assigned to become a B-17 flight engineer, attending school at Amarillo, Texas. From there, Russell went through the pipeline to gunnery school at Las Vegas. Upon completion of gunnery school, he was assigned to a combat crew and entered transition training, as the Flight Engineer, Top Turret Gunner on 2nd Lt. Donald J. Gott's crew.

After bailing out, just in time to see the bomber crash right in front of him, Russell spent the next thirteen months in Army hospitals letting his leg grow back together. They placed him in traction for months, so that the missing inch of bone could grow back. However, as he got older, he began to have knee problems, which can be traced directly back to a poor setting of the damaged bone in his wounded right leg, leading to a knee replacement that never functioned well. Russell said, "How, and why I survived that fatal Day, has often been in my thoughts."

Finally, on 20 December, 1945, Russell was discharged with a medical disability. He then entered the Fairleigh Dickinson College, in New Jersey. Russell graduated in 1950, with a B.S. in Business Administration. After college, Russell

went to work for the Marlin Rockwell Corporation Division, a large manufacturer of ball bearings. The company was later purchased by TRW, Inc., Bearing Division. Starting in the New York area, Russell moved to work in the Boston area, in 1959. In 1976, the firm asked Russell to transfer to Oklahoma City. Over the years, Russell a "Babe Magnet" has acquired two wives and six children.

(**Note**: During many travels together, the author noticed, that within minutes of Russell entering a room, every woman there had turned and looked him over. One night after asking what he had, Russell told the author, "Sam, some of us have it and some of it do not and you, **DO NOT!")**

His first wife was Joanne Campbell and they had two children named, Lee Marie and Michael.

His second wife was Phyllis Williams and the four children were: Robin Ann, Amy Elizabeth, Kerry Ann and Erick William.

In 1985, Russell retired from TRW, Inc. and remained in Oklahoma City, for some years, then he later moved to Rockport, Mass. As his health declined his daughters moved him back to Oklahoma, where he died on 28 July, 2018.

At the Savannah 452nd Bomb Group's reunion, in late 1994, Russell met up with their right waist gunner, Bill Robbins, for the first time since they boarded the *"Lady Jeannette"* the day of the crash. Learning Robbins job, Russell figured they had been around each other several times, as he sold bearing to that company for

years and they must have just missed meeting back then. During the 1994, Memorial Day weekend, the author flew down to Dallas, met Russell drive to McAllen, Texas, to spend some time with their ball turret gunner, Fross.

Since, I personally met Russell for the first time, at the Gott memorial in August, 1994, Russell has been a steadfast supporter of my research and we have spent much time together in the U.S.A. and France.

Russell's life was greatly changed by one man, a man who really knew few of the crewmen aboard the *"L a d y Jeannette,"* 2nd Lt. William E. Metzger, Jr., *Congressional Medal of Honor Awardee*. Who, without a second thought gave his parachutes and his life, to others, so they could live. One of those parachutes carried Russell safely to earth and today, six Gustafson children can directly trace their being back to that day in the air over France, when Bill Metzger had no greater love for a crew member, than to give his life to save their father

Russell W. Gustafson, 27 August, 1994

Visiting the "Official Grave" of 1st Lt. Donald J. Gott,.

Photograph: Willis S. Cole, Jr.

Joseph Francis Harms

12 February, 1922 - "Completed "Final Transfer"
Born: Brooklyn, New York
Serial Number: O-2056698
2nd Lieutenant, Bombardier
    United States Army Air Force
Wounded In Action 9 November, 1944
    "Lady Jeannette"
    B-17G-35VE, SN: 42-97904
    452 Bombardment Group (H)
    729th Bombardment Squadron (H)
Mission: Saarbrucken, Germany

Photograph: Joseph Harms

The son of Ernest Edward Harms and Mary Justina Rigney Harms. Joe was the eldest of the three children, his brother was named Gerard Vincent and his sister, Regina Delores.

Joe's father was a foreman for the Western Union Telegraph company.

Joe participated on the school debating team and played an instrument in the orchestra, while in high school. He enjoyed building model airplanes and was very much, a flying enthusiast.

Upon graduation from St. Michael's High School, Joe immediately entered St. John's University. He was in his senior year, finishing his accounting major, when he signed up for the Aviation Cadet Program with the assurance that he would be allowed to graduate before being called up to service.

Joe went ahead and signed up for his final semester and purchased his books. Just as soon, as he had bought his books and was ready for class, he got his call to leave at once. In January 1943, Joe entered the Cadet program.

The next month, he married his high school sweetheart, Elsie Gray, on 19 February, 1943.

Though he had requested navigator school, Joe was assigned to pilot training. As I have heard in several cases, his instructor was one who felt uneasy with students in control and he telegraphed his feeling to his students, resulting in washouts, Joe being one.

Unlike many, who were sent to engineer/mechanic school as enlisted men, Joe was sent to Bombardier school. He had completed his aerial gunnery school at

Harlingen, Texas, and his Bombardier training at San Angelo, Texas, on 20 May, 1944, he was commissioned a 2nd Lieutenant.

When Joe left for Europe, Elsie was pregnant with their first child. Back in the States, she delivered their daughter, Janet Lynne Harms, on 22 February, 1945. A second child was born on 7 November, 1950, Karen Jean Harms.

After training with his original crew, the 'McCollum Crew,' they left for Europe and their exciting visit to a glacier in Iceland.

When the crew finally arrived in England they were assigned to the 452nd Bomb Group (H) per Par 15 S) #287, HQ 70 Repl Dep, dtd 13 Oct '44, and having rptd th this sta 16 Oct '44, are asgned to orgns indicated and will report to respective CO there for dy, per SO 285, HQ 45 Bomb Group. 2nd 729 Bomb Sq, 452nd Gp, Crew 28-B (Cr78, APO 16403 BJ 78) 2 Lt. C. J. McCollum 2nd Lt. Frederick W. Hardin 2nd Lt. Steven A. Mem 2nd Lt. Joseph F. Harms, SSgt. Richard Weemes, Cpl. Marley R. Conger, Cpl. Edward L. Polick, Cpl. Oscar B. Lane. Interestingly, the other crew assigned on the same orders to the same squadron is Crew 20-C (Cr178, APO 16500 AF178). The 'Green Crew' on which 2 Lt. William E. Metzger, Jr. was the copilot. Though they arrived at the Group on the same orders, Joe had never met Lt. Metzger before they worked together to save the plane and one died, not know the name of the other.

After signing, as the required "Officer Eye Witness, for the two falsified Congressional Medal Of Honor applications to proceed, his Medical Board removed him from flight status, and he was assigned as a 452nd BG Financial Officer, he then received a promotion to 1st Lieutenant and returned home in February, 1945.

Upon returning to the United States Joe completed the Army Finance Officer School at Fort Benjamin Harrison and was shipped to the Pacific for a year's duty at Clark Air Force Base in the Phillippines. While there, he enlisted for a second tour of duty and was promoted to Captain.

Upon returning to the States, Joe and his family were stationed at Greensboro, North Carolina.

When Joe was discharged in May, 1947, he left the military as a Captain and established a sales business, becoming a manufacture's representative, taking on various lines of plumbing and heating goods.

He lived in New Milford, New Jersey, and upon retirement he continued to put in time calling on accounts and maintaining his collecting of coins, creating an extensive coin collection.

His two daughters married and presented to Joe, with four grand-children. Jean Lynne Harms Witte and her husband, Richard Witte, have given him two grand-children. Richard, a West Point Graduate, is now in civilian life. William lives and works in the Washington, D.C. area. He and his wife, Karen Jean Harms-Wood have two children, Christine, married to Mark Ianello, and Brooke Wood.

(**Note:** Joe was the last survivor of the crew I located and he provided the input required to know what happened in much of the bomber before its crash. He was

able to tell the author what happened in the nose of the bomber, his action in the cockpit helping Russell, the flare fire, in the radio room helping Robbins and Metzger to wrap up Dunlap's wounds, the kicking out of the bombs, the men in the rear leaving and his own departure. From him, I was able to figure out the exact order of bailing out.)

John A. Harland

Unknown ---- Completed "Final Transfer" June 3, 1994, four weeks before the author located him.
Serial Number: O-723355
2nd Lieutenant, Navigator
    United States Army Air Force
Wounded In Action 9 November, 1944
    "Lady Jeannette"
    B-17G-35VE,SN:42-97904
    452nd Bombardment Group (H)
    729th Bombardment Squadron
Mission: Saarbrucken, Germany

The first "Lady Jeannette" survivor I found, was Lt. Harland. And, I know the least about Lt. Harland.

He grew up in Chicago, I believe, in what is called the north side. Apparently the Depression was hard on his family and he left high school early and started working in order to help the family through the tough times.

He was the son of Mrs. Miller, for which I have two names, Ada or Ida. Mrs. Gott's letter of January 28, 1945 is written to Mrs. Ada Miller, while the Army letter sent to Ida Krimminger, on 8 May, 1945, lists Lt. Harland's mother's name as Ida M. Miller, which has to be the correct name, the one I will use when referring to Lt. Harland's mother.

I have no information about his father. Lt. Harland was born and lived his life in Chicago, Illinois, except while he was away for his military service.

Lt. Harland was always known as Jack to his family. He joined the Aviation Cadet Program and took courses on a college campus in Ohio. When he completed his on-campus courses, he went through the training schools to qualify as a Navigator and he received his 2nd Lieutenant's commission.

432

Upon completion of his schools, he joined the 'Gott Crew' for final training before deploying overseas.

During his time in the service, John was called "Jack" and "Jhonnie" by those who knew him.

After his discharge, John attended De Paul University, before taking a job at a major Chicago newspaper, working in the roll paper department. When he retired, he was the union steward and in charge of roll stock at the newspapers two printing plat locations.

John maintained his reserve status for some years, during which he was promoted to Captain. He was married and had six children, four of whom live in the same block where they grew up. Kathy Greinier, Dianne Kowar, Elizabeth (Liz) Harland, Scott Harland, Debby Harland, and Judy Galloway.

The children maintained a tight family relationship, often visiting each other and taking care of the children of the siblings. John had purchased and lived in a fairly large apartment house, so his children could always have a place to live near him.

He died on 3 June, 1994, just a month before I located his family and he was buried exactly fifty years after the "*Lady Jeannette*" arrived in England, on "**D-DAY**," 1944.

The author would have liked to have talked to Harland and learn everything that happened to him aboard the bomber. However, it was not to be. If the author had been able to talk to him, it may have cut a lot of time from the research to find the others by several years.

(**Note**: Older people will remember those times, back in the mid-1990's when one collected "Milage" for travel by making telephone calls. The author and his wife, used those miles for all their travels in 1994, including two trips to France. The result of many hours, using the telephone to track people down and verify research.)

Herman Bruce Krimminger

29 August, 1923 - 9 November, 1944
Marshville, North Carolina
Serial Number: 34890339
Staff Sergeant, Tail Gunner
    United States Army Air Force
Killed In Action: Bois de Hattonville, Hattonville, Dept. of the Meuse, France
    "Lady Jeannette"
    B-17G-35VE, SN: 42-97904
    452nd Bombardment Group (H)
    729th Bombardment Squadron (H)
Mission: Saarbrucken, Germany
Buried: Arlington National Cemetery
        Plot 12, Grave: 1720 2

Photograph: Krimminger Family

Herman was a tried and true North Carolina boy. Described to the author, as a slow mover and talker, a typical southern boy of the time.

He was born and raised around Marshville, just a bit east of Monroe, North Carolina. Herman was the first of three children born to Bessie Autrey Krimminger and Hugh Clifford Krimminger.

Hugh had served in World War One, where he was gassed during the Meuse-Argonne campaign. He died early in life, from ongoing complications of being gassed during the "Great War." Hugh died in 1930, three months before their second son, Hugh Carson Krimminger was born. Leaving Bessie with two young sons, Herman Hugh, and Elizabeth, their daughter, to support alone, as the Depression raged around their home and lives.

When Herman left for service in the Army, his mother, sister and brother were living at Rt. 1, Box 128, Marshville N.C.

Herman's four year's younger sister, Mary Elizabeth, was married to Otis Riggins. Otis served in the Army as a crew member on 155 mm 'Long Tom' artillery during World War Two. A week after the 'D-Day' invasion, Otis arrived in France, where he served with Patton's Third Army. His unit was participating in the attack on the Metz-Thionville German defense zone, the 452nd 's primary target, the Day Herman was killed. To his credit, Otis had a confirmed kill of a German Panther tank with the 155 mm cannon and a confirmed kill of a BF-109E

German fighter with a .50 caliber anti-aircraft machine gun. It sounds like Otis, was one of those backwoods boys, who could shoot the 'eye out of a squirrel.' "You don't want to spoil the meat, when supper depends on what you shoot," "The author was told by his uncles, Gerald and Charles King. Both were also backwoods boys, however, they lived in the hills of southeast Ohio.

Herman's brother, Hugh Carson, deceased, married Betty Jo Rowell and they had two sons, Michael Hugh Krimminger and in addition they adopted a son, Darren Neil Krimminger.

Michiel is married to Deborah Phillips and they have two girls, Lauren and Kristen, the family lives in the Washington, DC, area.

Darren, who attended our reunion in Savannah, is married to Ginger Louise Martin. Ginger and Darren have two children, Amber Michelle and Haley Nicole. Darren was an enthusiastic helper in my research. When I flew back to North Carolina to visit with him and his family, he drove me to the homes of Cecil and Frances, Metzger's sister to have a meeting with them.

Hugh Carson Krimminger
Bessie Autrey Krimminger
Mary Elizabeth Krimminger
Photograph: Ida Krimminger

(**Note**: Ida Krimminger was an amazing woman. Herman had immediately signed her to be the beneficiary of his GI Insurance policy when they married. Ida, who worked at the Walter Reed hospital at the time of Herman's death, refused the $10,000 and forwarded it to Herman's family in North Carolina.

In 1947, as Herman's LNOK, she could determine where his remains would be buried. She contacted Herman's family and discussed the situation with his mother, Bessie. Between them, they agreed, he deserved burial in the Arlington National Cemetery.

She did remarry, a man who became a very good and respected lawyer in San Francisco. She worked to better the city and has the social building on a city park, named after her.)

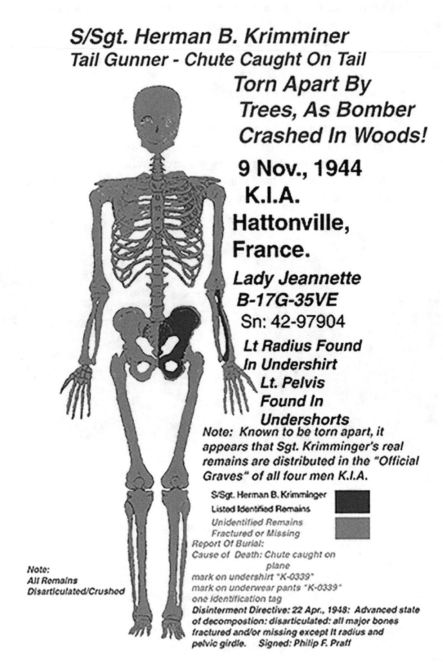

S/Sgt. Herman B. Krimminer
Tail Gunner - Chute Caught On Tail

Torn Apart By Trees, As Bomber Crashed In Woods!

9 Nov., 1944 K.I.A. Hattonville, France.

Lady Jeannette B-17G-35VE Sn: 42-97904

Lt Radius Found In Undershirt Lt. Pelvis Found In Undershorts

Note: Known to be torn apart, it appears that Sgt. Krimminger's real remains are distributed in the "Official Graves" of all four men K.I.A.

S/Sgt. Herman B. Krimminger
Listed Identified Remains

Unidentified Remains
Fractured or Missing

Report Of Burial:
Cause of Death: Chute caught on plane

Note: All Remains Disarticulated/Crushed

mark on undershirt "K-0339"
mark on underwear pants "K-0339"
one identification tag
Disinterment Directive: 22 Apr., 1948: Advanced state of decompostion: disarticulated: all major bones fractured and/or missing except lt radius and pelvic girdle. Signed: Philip F. Pratt

Drawing: Willis S. Cole, Jr.

William Edward Metzger, Jr.

February 9, 1922 ---- 9 November, 1944
Born: Lima, Ohio
SN: O-558834
2nd Lieutenant, Co-pilot
United States Army Air Force
Killed In Action: Bois de Hattonville, Hattonville, Dept. Of the Meuse, France
"Congressional Medal of Honor"
       "Lady Jeannette"
       B-17G-35VE, SN:42-97904
       452nd Bombardment Group (H)
       729th Bombardment Squadron (H)
Mission: Saarbrucken, Germany
Buried: Official Grave:
       Woodlawn Cemetery, Lima, Ohio

    Born to a coal merchant, in Lima, Ohio, Bill was the son of William E. Metzger, Sr. and Ethel Badeau Metzger.

    He had two sisters, Jeanne and Frances. As with most families, times were hard for the Metzger family during the Depression years. Ed, with his own business, was at least employed and people had to have coal to heat their houses at that time. However, collecting the bills was a major problem, with so many unemployed people at the time.

    To earn spending money, Bill distributed a weekly magazine of the time. As with many of his fellow crew members, Bill was very interested in airplanes as a youth. So much so, that he and his sister Frances used to ride their bicycles out to the local airport to observe the planes flying. Frances remembers her first airplane flight well, for Bill had saved his route money and used it to purchase the flight. Her last flight with Bill, was when he took them flying just before leaving for England.

    The early years of Bill's life, he shared with his parent's Presbyterian church. However, the loss of a very good friend at a young age, left Bill feeling the need for a more active church. He then began attending the Church of Nazarene, where he became a very active member. For the rest of his life, he became very involved in his church. So much so, that he was contemplating becoming a minister and entering the ministry.

During his school years, Bill became interested in playing the harmonica and he became very good. Later letters to his parents from people who had met him often mentioned Bill's skill and how much the men in the barracks enjoyed listening to his playing the harmonica.

Bill graduated from the Lima Central High School, in 1940, and quickly obtained employment at the Lima Electric Motor Company.

Before Bill left for England, both of his sisters were married and their husbands were in the service.

Jeanne married George W. Scholfield, who worked for the Nickle Plate, Norfolk and Western and Southern Railroad after the war, maintaining inventory. Jeanne became a school teacher. They lived in Ohio for many years, until they were transferred to Roanoke, Virginia.

George was sent his Draft Notice to report for duty on 28 March, 1942. He and Jeanne were married on 1 February, 1942, and on the 28th of March, George left for basic training at Camp Hulen, Palacious, Texas, located on the gulf coast. Upon completion of basic training he was assigned to the 693rd Airborne Anti-Aircraft Battalion stationed at Fort Bliss, Texas.

The author knows Fort Bliss very well, his daughter, Rebecca Lynn Cole Willsey first visited life there on 27 June, 1962, thanks to Nancy Carol Gibson Cole, my first wife. At the time, I was in technical school training to become a Nike Missile Fire Control Maintenance Man in the United States Army.

By the way, Nancy Carol Gibson Cole and Carol Lorraine Reinbold Cole, the author's second wife, are very good friends. When my second wife, Carol, won two free trips to the Rose Bowl football game in 1991 (while I was in France learning about the grave), she took, Nancy, my first wife, with her to the game!

George Scholfield left with his unit aboard a troop ship transport to arrive at Port Lyautey, Morocco, for the invasion of Africa. The 693rd was first assigned as anti-aircraft protection for two bridges, a railroad and a road bridge near Port Lyautey. Their weapon was a single .50 Caliber machine gun on a tripod and George, now a Corporal, was the lead gunner.

Their method of transportation was aboard C-47 aircraft, thus the airborne designation. Their main duty was the defense of air bases. They would be loaded aboard a C-47 and transferred to forward air bases to provide aerial defense against raiding German aircraft.

George's outfit participated in the invasion of Sicily, arriving for their second "D-Day" on another ship. They left Sicily, via a short boat trip across the narrow straight to Italy. For some time, the unit provided aerial defense for trains transporting war material to the front. They had mounted 20 mm anti-aircraft guns on one end of rail gondolas with a covered shelter at the other. Every time a train left for the front, two or more of these specially equipped gondola cars were mixed in with the regular railroad cars. George had to admit, that he did not ride the gondola Ack-Ack cars very often, as his commander said, "...he couldn't afford to lose any Sergeants." So, he sent the Lieutenants to command the gondola cars and kept the Sergeants back at the unit base.

George told the author, when they discussed his service, "That he had seen a whole lot of the world during those years of service. And, all for free."

Jeanne and George were the proud parents of 3 children and the Metzger family roots continue to grow: Stephen Wayne, Children: Stephanie Masellis, Daughter: Christina Wilkerson, Phyllis Lynn, Married: Frank Prado, Children: Magan, married William Rodman, Krista, married Colin Davidson, Thomas Eugene Married: Ginger Seagal, Children: Tess Seagal.

Frances married Cecil Carr Fredericks, who was in the 13th Airborne Glider Division during the war. Luckily, Cecil's unit was in reserve most of the time.

After the war Cecil worked for Westinghouse selling electronic gear to the Air Force for military aircraft. They lived in England, for some time. Raising a family of four children: Deborah Lou Fredericks Coate, Married: Wendel B. Coate "Bud," Children: Lisa, Dian Sue Fredericks Rubiera, Married: William J. Rubiera, Children: Cecilia Marie Alexander, Betsy Ann Fredericks Intellini, Children: Lynely Intellini, Kristen Intellini, Lauren A. Intellini, Laura Jane Fredericks Creer, Married: Rosco Bradford Creer, Children: Rebecca Morgan Creer, Lauren Alexandra Creer.

On 5 October, 1942, Bill Metzger left his job at Lima Electric Motor and enlisted in Toledo, Ohio, and began his service at Camp Perry, Ohio. Later, he served with an ordinance battalion at Camp Young, California.

In March, 1943, a dream accomplished, he was accepted into Aviation Cadet Program. He entered the pipeline, serving at Santa Ana, Twenty-Nine Palms and Lancaster, California.

He took his multi-engine, flight training, while stationed at Douglas, Arizona. Obtaining his wings and becoming a flight officer. Further training followed at Kingman, Arizona, followed by his transfer to Rapid City, South Dakota where he received his commission as 2nd Lieutenant on 21 August, 1944.

Assigned to the 2nd Lt. Green Crew, they completed final crew training as Crew 20-C(Cr178,APO16500,AF178) before departing for overseas combat service, via the northern route. In England, they were assigned to the 729th Squadron, 452nd Bombardment Group (H).

The original crew consisted of: 2nd Lt. Walter R. Green, Pilot, 2nd Lt. William E. Metzger, Jr. K.I.A., 2nd Lt. Elmer E. Gerard, 2nd Lt. Donald E. Roberts, Cpl. Harold E. Burrell "Tex," Cpl. Robert J. Falsey, Cpl. Edward T. Gorman, Cpl. Walter Jankowski, Cpl. Paul F. Tickerhoof, Cpl. Albert E. Wyant, K.I.A.

Harold "Tex" Burrell told the author about the 'Green Crew' meeting held the day before they began the trip to England. It was during this meeting, that the Co-pilot, 2nd Lt. William E. Metzger, Jr., told his assembled crew members, *"I will never leave an aircraft with a wounded crew member on board."*

When reviewing the families records, letters and pictures of Bill's life, the author found the following high school composition, few of us who have thought so much about how we should be living our lives, when we were that young. Bill Metzger did! In this school report, Bill laid out a way of life, that he followed through to the last second of his life. He gave up two parachutes, so that others

might live. Bill Metzger lived his life, as he believed life should be lived and he ended his life, with a "wounded crewman on board his B-17."

A LITTLE PHILOSOPHY Wilhelm Metzger (A play on the German course he was taking at the same time.) The fact that a man knows what is right does not mean that he will do what is right. Often you will see men who have had good training and whose minds are active do things which they know are harmful to themselves or to others.

Once in a while you meet a person who tells you that he has a right to do what he wants to do without any regards to what others may think or say. Such a person is very likely to be left to go his own way; he will have few or no friends. If you want to live a rich and full life, you need to think of others as well as yourself. Knowledge cannot be stolen from you; it cannot be bought or sold. You may be poor, and the sheriff may come to your house and sell your furniture at auction, or drive away your cow or take your lamb, and leave you homeless and penniless; but he cannot lay the hand of the law upon the jewelry of your mind.

How shall I live? How shall I make the most of my life and put it to the best use? How shall I become a man and do a man's work? This and not politics or trade or war or pleasure is the question. The primary consideration is not how shall one get a living, but how shall he live; for if he lives rightly, whatever is needful he shall easily find. Do not let envy tempt you to do things for which you are not fitted.

Be yourself. Long words get into the minds of men; short words get into their heart. When we wish to talk of the things that lie at the roots of life--birth and death, youth and age, joy and pain--we use the short words that have come down to us through the stream of time. They are words that touch and move us. The only way we have to set out our ideas is by our words. If we wish to make those ideas clear, we shall do well to learn the right use of the short words in our tongue.

Long words may be all right when we want men to know; but when we want them to act, short words are the ones to use. Keep in mind the fact that we act when we feel, not when we know. Tell me what you do in your off time, and I can tell you what sort of person you are.

The way in which a man spends his leisure is a good index to his character and his habits of thinking. The man who really lives, in the best sense of the word, tries all the time to broaden his interests in a wholesome way. He sets apart a time for reading good books, so that he may learn to commune with the great masters of prose and poetry; he develops a sport or a hobby--something to which he can turn his mind and his thoughts in his off time.

A philosophy of life to which a young man of Lima, Ohio, was true to the last. One wonders just what this man would have accomplished, if he had lived to return home and follow his dreams?

The author has read letters that the family received after his death. No matter where Bill went, he attended and was active in his church. People who knew Bill for only a short time, wrote his mother after reading of his death to tell her of the difference he had made in their life in that short time.

He waved goodbye to his mother from the end of the train and for the rest of her life she looked for him, each time a train passed.

On 11 May, 1954, 2nd Lt. Metzger's father died, just 9 days after T/Sgt. Dunlap's father, Alexander Dunlap died in Miles City, Montana. Lt. Metzger's mother lived for another 13 years.

The Copilot, sitting 24 inches from the Pilot had no identified bones, while the Pilot had the most. How does this make sense, as the cockpit suffered only light fire damage and of course, the damage from the limbs breaking through the windshields.

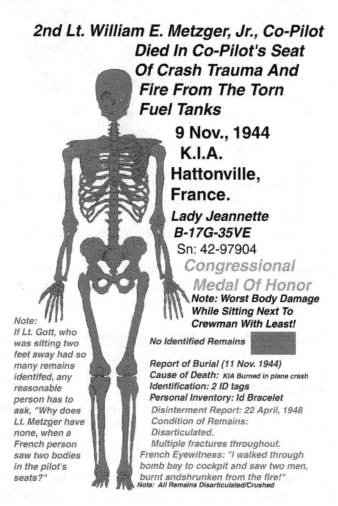

**2nd Lt. William E. Metzger, Jr., Co-Pilot
Died In Co-Pilot's Seat
Of Crash Trauma And
Fire From The Torn
Fuel Tanks**

**9 Nov., 1944
K.I.A.
Hattonville,
France.**

**Lady Jeannette
B-17G-35VE**
Sn: 42-97904

*Congressional
Medal Of Honor*

**Note: Worst Body Damage
While Sitting Next To
Crewman With Least!**

No Identified Remains

Report of Burial (11 Nov. 1944)
Cause of Death: KIA Burned in plane crash
Identification: 2 ID tags
Personal Inventory: Id Bracelet
Disinterment Report: 22 April, 1948
Condition of Remains:
Disarticulated.
Multiple fractures throughout.
French Eyewitness: "I walked through bomb bay to cockpit and saw two men, burnt and shrunken from the fire!"
Note: All Remains Disarticulated/Crushed

Note:
If Lt. Gott, who was sitting two feet away had so many remains identifed, any reasonable person has to ask, "Why does Lt. Metzger have none, when a French person saw two bodies in the pilot's seats?"

Drawing: Willis S. Cole, Jr.

William Russell Robbins

May 6, 1920 - Completed "Final Transfer"
Born: Worcester, Mass
SN: 11051000
Staff Sergeant, Right Waist Gunner United States Army Air Force
Only survivor, not wounded - 9 November, *"Lady Jeannette,"*
    B-17G-35VE, Sn: 42-97904
    452nd Bombardment Group (H)   729th Bombardment Squadron (H)
Mission: Saarbrucken, Germany

Bill was one of those people who makes you think, if the war had not come along when it did, he would not have ventured more than 40 miles from home for many years.

William and Shirley Robbins
452nd BG Reunion - 1994
Photograph: Willis S. Cole, Jr.

William R. Robbins was born to Helen Josephine Robbins and Charles Russell Robbins, who were married in 1919.

He was hardly ever late to school, as he grew up next door to the school.

Bill has one brother, Howard Frederick Robbins.

His father was a World War One veteran, a member of the 104th Infantry, 26th Division. While serving in France he had been gassed. Later, he would become a Commander of his Veteran's of Foreign Wars Post.

Bill graduated from South High School in Worcester and after the service, upon his return to Worcester, he went back to work for the company he had worked for before his miliary service. As he worked, he took night courses to obtain an Associate Electrical Degree.

Bill, the second oldest member of our group, enlisted in the Army on 20 April, 1942, he took his basic training and was shipped to a Military Police outfit at Fort Dix, New Jersey. There he took a physical and a mental battery that qualified him for the Air Cadet Program.

Upon acceptance, he was sent to San Antonio for classroom training and upon completion, he was transferred to primary training at Cimmeron Field, in Oklahoma. Having completed primary training, he began basic flight training and was washed out after ten hours.

He was transferred to gunnery school at Wichita Falls, Texas, then to Scott Field, Illinois and then on to Rapid City, South Dakota, to join the Gott crew for final combat crew training.

Bill had left behind his high school sweetheart, Shirley, and they decided

442

to get married before he left for overseas. So Shirley joined Bill in Rapid City and on 29 May, 1944, they were married.

After a short time at home, when he returned from England, he and Shirley went to Florida for his rest leave and then, they went to the Laredo Army Air Force Base in Texas.

Where, Bill was a gunnery instructor until he was eligible for discharge on 15 October, 1945, with 3 years, 20 days service.

Upon return home, Bill returned to work at Coghlins, Inc., electrical distributor, where he continued to work for a total of 52 years before his retirement in 1986. Beginning in the shipping department, Bill retired after 52 years, ending up as an outside salesman.

Shirley and Bill were the parents of two children, were grandparents of five and great-grandparents of one. William R. Robbins, Jr., Children: Tracey Ann Robbins, Todd Andrew Robbins, Tami Marie Robbins Dumphy, Married: Kevin Dumphy, Wendy E. Robbins Bosse, Children: Derek Matthew Lambert, Lisa Marie Lambert Blodget, Married: Scott Blodget, Children: Derek Joshua Blodget.

Shirley and Bill lived an enjoyable retirement in Worcester. They attended several 452nd Bomb Group Association reunions.

(**NOTE**: Shirley died in 2007 and the last time the author talked to Bill. He told the author, "I'm just waiting around and passing time to join Shirley." As noted above, Bill and Shirley have rejoined and are a team again as of 14 March, 2010.)

S/Sgt. Robbins and Fross, watched as S/Sgt. Krimminger was pulled out of their B-17 due to his opening his parachute inside the bomber. As he went out the door, S/Sgt. Robbins, remembered seeing that Krimminger was still wearing his buckled-on FLAK Helmet as he was pulled out of the hatch..

The author found the flap a couple hundred of feet along the debris trail left by the crashing bomber.

This certainly supports the fact, that his body was torn-apart over the distance of the debris trail.

Photograph: Willis S. Cole Jr.

With friends like these two, one can always find adventure. The fellow on the left is now retired, after a career of being a "Deminer." One who picks up explosive devices and neutralizes them.

The fellow on the right is a explosive expert who blows up building and all sorts of stuff and loves it.

Local, temporary bomb dump, hidden in the fields of the Somme. The fellow on the right, helped the author prove to the French, that the Americans were in their hometown of Driencourt during the Great War.

The one of the left, his brother, has been the key to many of the author's adventures in France.

Memorial Day, 1994, the author visiting the American Romagne-Gesnes WWI Cemetery. Placing flags on the grave of Pvt. Alfred Leach, Washington State. If, there is time, the author and his wife never passes a military cemetery "Over There,' ours, French or German. Each needs Remembrance!

On a good day, one might find something interesting. Such as a length of track from one of the first 50 tanks to go into combat.

When digging it out, the author was telling his friends, that he hoped no one flew over, as we were digging it out, as they might think we were digging a grave to hide a body.

Photographs: Willis S. Cole, Jr.

You may wonder, why there are no names in some photographs. Some of what you have seen is illegal at times and a name, might cause trouble for an excellent friend.

Comparing The Official Remains Of The Crewmen Of The *"Lady Jeannette"*

On page 446, you will be able to compare the contents of all four mens' individual graves and on page 447, you will find a combined remains drawing that proves there is no duplication of any human bones, even if the contents of all four graves were placed on the same table.

Absolute evidence that the two **Congressional Medal Of Honor Citations** contained absolutely false information concerning the death of the two Awardees and the true condition of their bodies at their true crash site!

It is the hope of the Author, that each reader will believe in the research, talk it over with their friends and everyone contact their Congressional Representatives and Senators and demand that they force the Defense POW/MIA Accounting Agency to conduct the full "Search and Recovery" these American Heroes deserve.

Willis S. Cole, Jr.

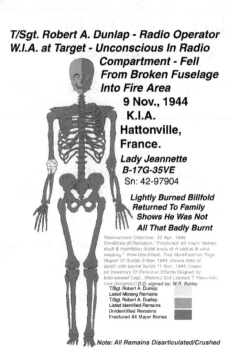

T/Sgt. Robert A. Dunlap - Radio Operator
W.I.A. at Target - Unconscious In Radio
Compartment - Fell
From Broken Fuselage
Into Fire Area
9 Nov., 1944
K.I.A.
Hattonville,
France.

Lady Jeannette
B-17G-35VE
Sn: 42-97904

Lightly Burned Billfold
Returned To Family
Shows He Was Not
All That Badly Burnt

Disinterment Directive: 22 Apr., 1948
Condition of Remains: "Fractured: all major bones,
skull & mandible; distal ends of rt radius & ulna
missing." How Identified: Two Identification Tags
Report Of Burial, 9 Nov. 1944, shows date of
death with actual burial 11 Nov., 1944, based
on Inventory Of Personal Effects (Signed by
interviewed Capt., (Retired Col.) James T. Passman,
now deceased) D.D. signed by: W.R. Bailey

T/Sgt. Robert A. Dunlap
Listed Missing Remains
T/Sgt. Robert A. Dunlap
Listed Identified Remains
Unidentified Remains
Fractured All Major Bones

Note: All Remains Disarticulated/Crushed

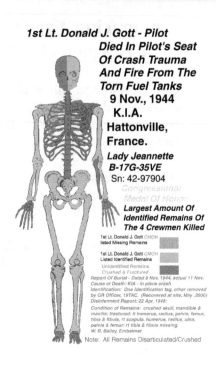

1st Lt. Donald J. Gott - Pilot
Died In Pilot's Seat
Of Crash Trauma
And Fire From The
Torn Fuel Tanks
9 Nov., 1944
K.I.A.
Hattonville,
France.

Lady Jeannette
B-17G-35VE
Sn: 42-97904

Congressional
Medal Of Honor

Largest Amount Of
Identified Remains Of
The 4 Crewmen Killed

1st Lt. Donald J. Gott CMOH
listed Missing Remains

1st Lt. Donald J. Gott CMOH
Listed Identified Remains

Unidentified Remains

Crushed & Fractured

Report Of Burial - Dated 9 Nov. 1944, actual 11 Nov.
Cause of Death: KIA - in plane crash
Identification: One Identification tag, other removed
by GR Officer, 19TAC. (Recovered at site, May .2000)
Disinterment Report: 22 Apr. 1948:
Condition of Remains: crushed skull, mandible &
maxilla; fractured: lt humerus, radius, pelvis, femur,
tibia & fibula, rt scapula, humerus, radius, ulna,
pelvis & femur; rt tibia & fibula missing.
W. R. Bailey, Embalmer

Note: All Remains Disarticulated/Crushed

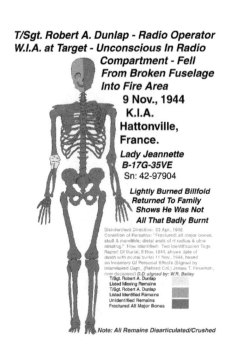

T/Sgt. Robert A. Dunlap - Radio Operator
W.I.A. at Target - Unconscious In Radio
Compartment - Fell
From Broken Fuselage
Into Fire Area
9 Nov., 1944
K.I.A.
Hattonville,
France.

Lady Jeannette
B-17G-35VE
Sn: 42-97904

Lightly Burned Billfold
Returned To Family
Shows He Was Not
All That Badly Burnt

Disinterment Directive: 22 Apr., 1948
Condition of Remains: "Fractured: all major bones,
skull & mandible; distal ends of rt radius & ulna
missing." How Identified: Two Identification Tags
Report Of Burial, 9 Nov. 1944, shows date of
death with actual burial 11 Nov., 1944, based
on Inventory Of Personal Effects (Signed by
interviewed Capt., (Retired Col.) James T. Passman,
now deceased) D.D. signed by: W.R. Bailey

T/Sgt. Robert A. Dunlap
Listed Missing Remains
T/Sgt. Robert A. Dunlap
Listed Identified Remains
Unidentified Remains
Fractured All Major Bones

Note: All Remains Disarticulated/Crushed

2nd Lt. William E. Metzger, Jr., Co-Pilot
Died In Co-Pilot's Seat
Of Crash Trauma And
Fire From The Torn
Fuel Tanks
9 Nov., 1944
K.I.A.
Hattonville,
France.

Lady Jeannette
B-17G-35VE
Sn: 42-97904

Congressional
Medal Of Honor

Note: Worst Body Damage
While Sitting Next To
Crewman With Least!

No Identified Remains

Report of Burial (11 Nov. 1944)
Cause of Death: KIA Burned in plane crash
Identification: 2 ID tags
Personal Inventory: Id Bracelet
Disinterment Report: 22 April, 1948
Condition of Remains:
Disarticulated.
Multiple fractures throughout.
French Eyewitness: "I walked through
bomb bay to cockpit and saw two men,
burnt and shrunken from the fire!"
Note: All Remains Disarticulated/Crushed

Note:
If Lt. Gott, who
was sitting two
feet away had so
many remains
identifed, any
reasonable
person has to
ask, "Why does
Lt. Metzger have
none, when a
French person
saw two bodies
in the pilot's
seats?"

Drawing: Willis S. Cole, Jr.

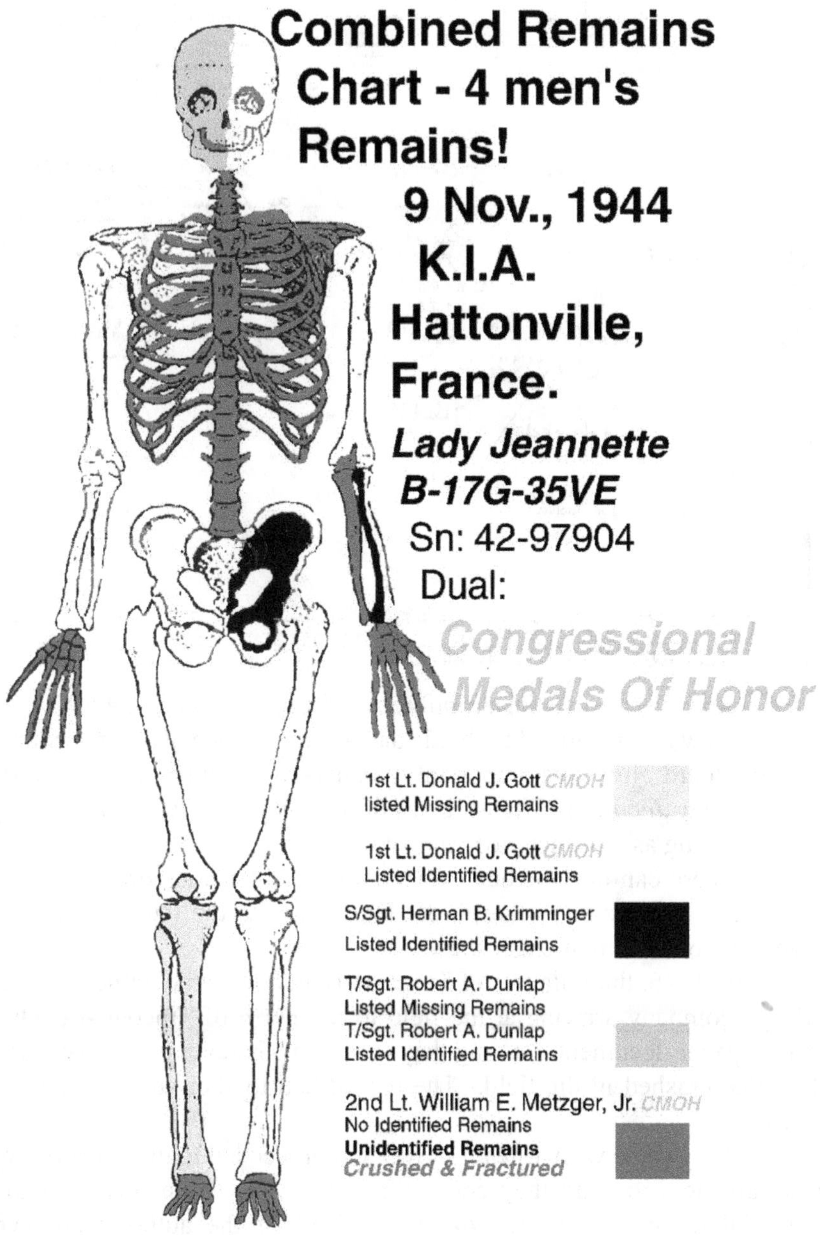

Combined Remains Chart - 4 men's Remains!
9 Nov., 1944 K.I.A. Hattonville, France.

Lady Jeannette
B-17G-35VE
Sn: 42-97904
Dual:

Congressional Medals Of Honor

1st Lt. Donald J. Gott CMOH
listed Missing Remains

1st Lt. Donald J. Gott CMOH
Listed Identified Remains

S/Sgt. Herman B. Krimminger
Listed Identified Remains

T/Sgt. Robert A. Dunlap
Listed Missing Remains
T/Sgt. Robert A. Dunlap
Listed Identified Remains

2nd Lt. William E. Metzger, Jr. CMOH
No Identified Remains
Unidentified Remains
Crushed & Fractured

Drawing: Willis S. Cole, Jr.

	TYPE MODEL SERIES B-17G-35		AAF SER AL NUMBER 42-97904		MANUFACTURER ENG LOCATION Vega, Burbank, Calif.		
	CONTRACT NUMBER AC-35321	FOREIGN SERIAL NUMBER		FINAL DESTINATION IN U S *Dow Field Me.*	
	ALLOCATION PLOT & PRIORITY NUMBER			PROJECT OR LEND LEASE REQUISITION NUMBER *9272511.*	

LOCATION	ORGANIZATION	RECIPIENT	NEXT DESTINATION	CRATED OR FLY AWAY	CONDITION	DATE 1944	ACTION	REMARKS
STATION	ORGAND PARENT UNIT	SUB UNIT	GAINED FROM OR LOST TO		SERIAL NUMBER	MO DA	ON RO	
Burbank	Vega				Accepted	4-1		
			Sresults Mod Center.		Available	3-31		
			"		Delivered	4-1		
			"		Departed	4-3		
			"	18	Arrived	4-		
				6"		4s		
	Mod GTC	Sqds R	Y Kearney		avail (c) 5-29	52363 Cal		
Kearney	"	"	"	23	Arrived 5-31		Opr	
	"	"			arrived 5-31		2nd af at ar	
Dow Fd	haved	"	Bangor Apd 865		departed 6-4		Oxx	
					Dep as 6-6		Oxx	
80X0			A B17G	08 42	97904	6 644	6 944	
80X0			G B17G	08 42	97904	61344	61544	
80X0		CONSALBD	R B17G	8	42 97904	111844	1 245	
80X0	CONSALBD		R B17G		42 97904	111844	1 245	
anxn		CONSALBD	9 B17G	M	9 42 97904	111844	1 245	

Condemmed → Battle Damage
Salvage

Poor original document on microfilm.

Above is the official aircraft record for the B-17G, SN: 42-97904. It states, the aircraft was condemned for battle damage and turned over for accounting to the Salvage Board. It is most important to understand that the official aircraft record for the "*Lady Jeannette*" states it was officially turned over to the Salvage Board for accounting as a condemned aircraft.

There can only be one explanation for the actual aircraft, SN: 42-97904 being torn apart by the villagers of Hattonville, as the required aircraft salvage never took place at that crash site.

In 1946, the villagers of Tincourt-Boucly became witnesses to a German salvage company arriving at the field to the north of Tincourt-Boucly with the official paper documents, stating they could do whatever necessary to recover the B-17 that crashed in the field. The record had to show the wreckage had been buried.

They came with a steam shovel and proceeded to dig a deep hole and take away all the wreckage they could find. In 1994, while preparing to install a memorial to the "*Lady Jeannette*" a friend of the author who owns heavy equipment went to crash site and found, where an engine had been removed from a depth of 15 feet.

Thus, the "*Lady Jeannette*" was officially salvaged and the Top Secret "226" officially disappeared.

448

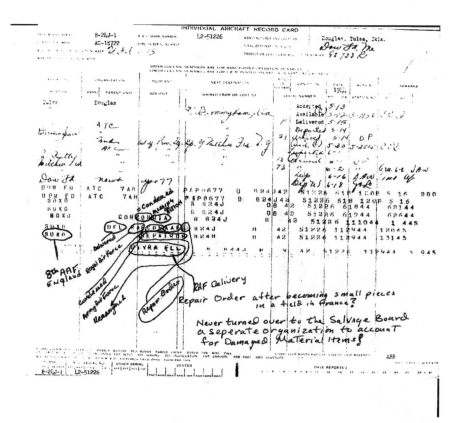

To the left, is an officially identified photograph of an aircraft that crashed near Tincourt-Boucly. Please note the identification! (10 Nov. 1944X B-24J-226) Above is the official aircraft record for the B-24J, SN: 42-51226, which

(10 Nov. 1944X B-24J-226)

states "**226**" was first Condemned and listed as Missing In Action. Then, it shows it was reassigned to the RAF after being repaired.

However, the official RAF mission documents, states "**226**" was shot down on the 10th of November, near Abbeville, France, with three K.I.A. Over 60 miles west of Tincourt-Boucly.

Notice, there is no record of "**226's**" loss being reported to the Official Salvage Board for proper accounting of a condemned aircraft!

2nd Lt. William E. Metzger, Jr., CMOH, ID Tag

Removed at the time of his Official Burial and given to the family.
One side was cleaned and showed little damage, the reverse side shows extreme
fire and smoke damage

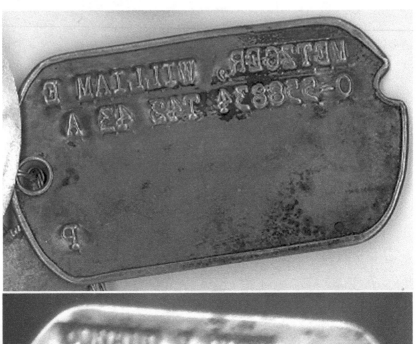

1st Lt. Donald J. Gott, CMOH, ID Tag

Taken at point of location, near the fire location at the true "*Lady
Jeannette*" crash site. **Note**: It was wiped clean of clay and it shows no
fire damage, **what-so-ever!**

Personal Relic Comparison

The shoulders of two B-17 pilots sitting in their cockpit seats are about the distance apart as the length of this book.

1st Lt. Donald J. Gott, CMOH, and 2nd Lt. William E. Metzger, Jr., CMOH

The two pilot's arms were so close, yet 1st Lt. Gott, CMOH, *__has the most identified bones__* in his "Official Coffin." While 2nd Lt. Metzger, Jr. CMOH, sitting close to him, *__has no identified bones__* in his "Official Coffin."

The ID tag belonging to 1st Lt. Gott, in May, 2000,, that forced all the government bodies, even DPAA, to accept the crash-site located in 1998, by the author, was in fact, the crash-site of the *"Lady Jeannette"* and that the B-17G did not crash as stated in both Congressional Medal Of Honor Citations.

How did Lt. Metzger suffer total body destruction and his person effects suffer so much damage, when Lt. Gott has been proved to have suffered no damage, other than his broken skull.

However, both gave the same death description, burned in plane crash. This would have been taken directly from the medical tag for both me and yet the true evidence proves neither died that way.

Metzger's sister, Jeanne and Francis gave him this bracelet, the day he left for war. This is the back and notice the physical damage, plus fire damage,
Photographs: Willis S. Cole, Jr.

451

"Searching For '203'"
The recovery of Missing-In-Action World War Two Combat Dead From American National Cemeteries!

Little did the German above realize, the photographs he sent to American Graves Registration in 1946, taken at the crash site of a B-17 he guarded had for two weeks in 1943. Would take 76 years before it would lead to the true identification of the four dead crewmen found inside the wreckage.

Willis S. Cole, Jr. "Sam"

"Searching For '203'"

Author: Willis S. Cole, Jr.

After more than 15 years research, a new book concerning the mis-identification of, as many as 18, World War Two Combat Dead is moving toward completion in 2019.

The book exposes the **failure of the United States Defense POW/MIA Accounting Agency's (DPAA) to act**, after being provided **absolute proof in 2008**, of the mis-identification of four combat aircrew dead, **who died inside their B-17F**. at the true crash-site of "*203*," as four combat aircrew who died 2 hours early and 260 miles to the east of the true "*203*" crash-site. **That crashing "Fortress" "20,' went down with one crewman bailing out and falling to his death, leaving three crewmen still inside the B-17F when it crashed**.

All official reports of the mission on 6 September, 1944, of the 388th Bombardment Group (H), including return aircrew testimony place the first B-17F' crash, 35 miles west of Strasbourg in eastern France. The official reports also state, a seventh bomber was seen going down in the area where the true "*203*" took place. However, the Defense POW/MIA Accounting Agency continue to refuse to recognized that officially reported loss and they still carry the four dead as MIA.

The official German reports concerning the dead at true "**203**" crash-site, state they recovered four unknown dead from inside of the crashed bomber! Another report states, the pilot, 1st Lt. Mohr, was killed during the crash and three crewmen were captured. However, they delivered the four Unknown dead to a cemetery for burial as American Unknowns!

The author believes this was done because of the condition of the remains, though the bomber crashed as one piece, the fuel tanks split and the fuel flowed toward the cockpit, extremely burning the three men in the cockpit. When removing the dead, they found the pilot's ID Tag, so they knew a man by that name was dead. However, they had no way to tie it to any of the three remains, thus they were delivered as Unknown dead. The ball turret gunner was crushed into the earth in his ball turret, he was known to be dead before the crash and his body was somewhat crushed. His body was removed as a complete body, with clothing that were good enough for the cemetery workers to remove from the body for reuse.

While the cemetery workers were stealing the clothes from one of the Unknown dead, an American ID Tag fell to the floor. They had no way of knowing it had been left in the flight clothing by a man who had fallen to his death the day before, who had worn those heavy flight, outer clothes on a previous mission. He man the ID Tag really belonged too, had bailed out and fallen to his death and nearby, the Germans found three dead inside the crashed B-17F, "**201**," he had fallen from.

The French, with no idea of American Graves Registration Regulations, decided the dead man must be that man and they buried the Unknown remains under the false identification.

When non-combat, behind the lines, Graves Registration men arrived at the cemetery, they also mis-identified the Unknown remains as the man who had bailed out of his crashing bomber, 270 miles to the east of the cemetery.

The error continued after the recovery, as the GR people only asked for records for the mis-identified remains and the three others reported as Missing In Action from his B-17F, SN: 42-30201. Due to the condition of the other three remains, they depended on the first false identification and determined two of the others had to be certain MIA crewmen and the fourth, well, he had to be the fourth MIA crewman.

Later during "Final Disposition" in 1947/48. Almost all the war experienced GR men were gone and the new GR men, tasked with disinterring all the American War Dead, re-identifying them, and forwarding the remains for their "Final Disposition. Had one major task in mind, get it done regardless of obvious regulation failure in the proper identification concerning the eight dead involved.

In a small village, Luvigny, in eastern France, the people looked up to see an American "Fortress" shot down by a German fighter, which also was shot down. As they watched, one man bailed out and landed in a walled garden behind a village. He was obviously falling very fast under a collapsed parachute.

Another man landed in a field close to the south of the village and the Germans quickly captured him and took him to the garden, where he identified the man to the Germans as a fellow crewman.

The crashing "Fortress" crashed on the side of mountain to the south of the village. There was a lot of noise, fire and smoke and the Germans quickly guarded the crash-site and later removed three dead from inside the crashed "Fortress" and buried all four in the village cemetery.

After the war, no Americans ever came the village to recover the dead, nor did the Germans remove the bomber's pieces from the hillside, as the treaty ending the war specified, they had to do.

In due time, realizing the Germans were not coming to retrieve the relics, as they had at several other nearby crash-sites, the villagers (like the villagers at Hattonville) tore apart the relics and sold it for scrap metal.

Fourteen years after the war ended, a French researcher realized there was still an unidentified crash site, using false documents that he created, without telling the Americans, convinced the Germans that it had to be a captured B-17 flown by a German crew. So, the German Graves Registration Service went to the Luvigny cemetery, disinterred the four Unknown (unrecognized) American dead and moved them to the German WWII Cemetery at Andilly, France, as identified German war dead. The author researched the identity and was told, there were several MIA German dead in that area, so they picked four names and buried the Unknown dead, as those, now accounted for dead.

Absolutely True!

The author was told some time ago, by someone fairly high up in the organization, that is now the <u>Defense POW/MIA Accounting Agency</u>, that they did not want to have to admit such errors exist!

Why? Because other families who lost Loved Ones might demand a reopening of their situations.

To correct this mistake, the United States Defense Department POW/MIA Accounting Agency will have to disinter four graves. Two are at the Normandy Cemetery and two are in National Cemeteries in the United States. Plus, it will required, disinterring four graves from a German National Cemetery!

They know, it is the right thing to do. Especially, now they can no longer hide their failure to properly handle the situation when the original misidentification of the four Mohr crew dead took place.

However it appears, they will do anything to continue to hide their failure to properly follow through when first provided absolute proof of the misidentification by the author in 2008.

To correct the situation, they will have to re-inter all eight of the disinterred remains in the graves to be re-selected by the families of the eight dead. Granting full Military Honors and most likely, having to pay the full travel expenses of the families to attend the correction re-burials.

However, they may attempt to demand total secrecy to prevent the American public from knowing such mistakes were made when identifying World War Two dead.

They have done so before, by demanding the Gott family keep the burial of the recently discovered additional remains of 1st Lt. Gott, CMOH, at the Hattonville crash-site, <u>a secret from some</u>.

Their only demand of the Gott family was, they were not to inform the author or any of the crash survivors of the crash, as the publicity would be bad for their organization. Yes, the families did not inform those unwanted people!

However, you can help make it happen, verify and then contact your elected representatives to force the DPAA to act. Please remember, it could have been someone from your family!

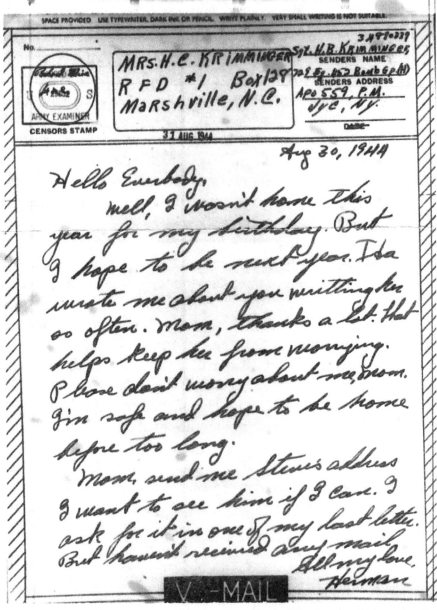

Many readers have never seen a "Victory-Mail" letter. Written by the sender "Over There." It was photographed and reduced to a very small size and then carried by plane to the States, where they were blown up and sent to the addressee. Written by Herman Krimminger and sent home and though he wished, he did not return home alive. ***"Killed In Action."***
Aboard the "***Lady Jeannette***" on 9 November, 1944.

"Thanks to the Krimminger family for the opportunity to review their "keep sake" and photograph as I wanted. Photograph: Willis S. Cole, Jr.

Reader Challenge!

The story line information contained in this book can be fully re-researched by any reader. In fact, if you have doubt, I want you to correct me, if you can!

If, you disbelieve what you have read and have decided to challenge this book based on your own research and finding evidence that I am wrong, please contact me and present the conflicting evidence you have found.

You must provide the sources of your evidence, so I can re-research your evidence and disagree or agree with your presentation.

You must provide the origination of your evidence, such as your path of tracing the evidence from the original location where you found it, back to the document origination of that evidence. Any foot note references from other publications must be provided with a complete information path tracing that footnote back to the original documentation. Many authors fail to follow footnote references back through various publications, leading to false conclusions based upon poorly researched publications.

A prime example is an author who relies on other author's books, who uses footnoted evidence that they have not verified. For instance, readers of my books have contacted me over the years, demanding that I change the name of the B-17, you will read about in this book. They quote book footnote after book footnote, all of which leads back to Roger Freeman's book, "The Mighty Eighth." When I contacted, Mr. Freeman (now deceased) with absolute proof that he had used the wrong name in his books, he refused to change the name in any future publications. Stating, "If, he admitted to such a mistake, readers would begin to question his research."

Unlike myself, who welcomes your properly presented evidence and if you are correct, I will make any required change to my books and give you full credit in future publications.

Please feel free to dispute my conclusions, <u>with foundational evidence, that I can re-research</u>!

There are no footnotes in this book. The author did not depend on footnotes for most content in this book and where footnotes are involved, they are shown. He found foundation documents, which can be found by any true re-researcher searching to prove or disprove the truth contained in this book.

The entire contents of this book and cover, typesetting, photograph positioning, and layout is the work of the author. The only part of this book, not completed by the author is the actual printing and distribution.

Willis S. Cole, Jr. "Sam"
wscjr@ww1.org

2nd *Lt. William E. Metzger, Jr. - A Creed to live by!*

A LITTLE PHILOSOPHY Wilhelm Metzger (A play on the German course he was taking at the same time.) The fact that a man knows what is right does not mean that he will do what is right. Often you will see men who have had good training and whose minds are active do things which they know are harmful to themselves or to others.

Once in a while you meet a person who tells you that he has a right to do what he wants to do without any regards to what others may think or say. Such a person is very likely to be left to go his own way; he will have few or no friends. If you want to live a rich and full life, you need to think of others as well as yourself. Knowledge cannot be stolen from you; it cannot be bought or sold. You may be poor, and the sheriff may come to your house and sell your furniture at auction, or drive away your cow or take your lamb, and leave you homeless and penniless; but he cannot lay the hand of the law upon the jewelry of your mind.

How shall I live? How shall I make the most of my life and put it to the best use? How shall I become a man and do a man's work? This and not politics or trade or war or pleasure is the question. The primary consideration is not how shall one get a living, but how shall he live; for if he lives rightly, whatever is needful he shall easily find. Do not let envy tempt you to do things for which you are not fitted.

Be yourself. Long words get into the minds of men; short words get into their heart. When we wish to talk of the things that lie at the roots of life--birth and death, youth and age, joy and pain--we use the short words that have come down to us through the stream of time. They are words that touch and move us. The only way we have to set out our ideas is by our words. If we wish to make those ideas clear, we shall do well to learn the right use of the short words in our tongue.

Long words may be all right when we want men to know; but when we want them to act, short words are the ones to use. Keep in mind the fact that we act when we feel, not when we know. Tell me what you do in your off time, and I can tell you what sort of person you are.

The way in which a man spends his leisure is a good index to his character and his habits of thinking. The man who really lives, in the best sense of the word, tries all the time to broaden his interests in a wholesome way. He sets apart a time for reading good books, so that he may learn to commune with the great masters of prose and poetry; he develops a sport or a hobby--something to which he can turn his mind and his thoughts in his off time.

2nd Lt. William E. Metzger, Jr., CMOH   ***A man who lived and died as he believed!***

- - - - - - - - - - - - - - - - - - -

Placed on this page, so it can be cut out and used to guide other lives!

CPSIA information can be obtained
at www.ICGtesting.com
Printed in the USA
FFHW011555180319
51096629-56527FF